INTRODUCTION

This is really an exciting time for us: edition 10 of Edinburgh for Under Fives will see in 20 years of the publication: some of the 'under fives' who helped their mothers research the early editions may now have children of their own – and as parents and carers ourselves, we would like to thank all the researchers who have given their time over the years to make this book what it is today.

We've used this anniversary as an opportunity to re-style the guidebook – after all, you want to have a change of look once your teenage years are over! So, the guide now functions in two parts.
Part One offers ideas and suggestions for days out, places to visit, restaurants and cafes which welcome families with small children, and also a new Chapter – Accessible Edinburgh and Beyond – which approaches venues and activities from the viewpoint of disabled access and support. We've also included some helpful names and addresses.
Part Two functions more like a directory: we've listed classes for children and for parents, childcare information, healthcare information, support groups, and services geared towards young children, families or parents/carers.

The words – and pictures – in EFUF are from parents and carers; so, you might find remarks that official guidebooks won't include, and if the chapter pictures don't always seem to be in perfect focus, that's because they're our pictures of our children – and not everyone likes to stay still, even for the shortest time. It's things like this that sets Edinburgh for Under Fives apart, and these are the type of things about the book that we will never change.

We've expanded the remit of the book – we cover much more than just Edinburgh, now. There's information on venues from Aviemore to Berwick, so there really is an abundance of ideas: hopefully, you will find all the inspiration you need for your under five to enjoy and make the most of our wonderful city of Edinburgh – and places far beyond.

If you have been somewhere you like and it is not included, or indeed somewhere which has disappointed you, please let us know as your comments and input are invaluable. This book is produced by people like you – mothers, fathers, and carers of small children, so we are genuinely interested in your comments.

By purchasing this guidebook you are helping us support the National Childbirth Trust, and the training of NCT antenatal teachers for the local area and also SNIP, the Special Needs Information Point, based at The Sick Kids, Edinburgh: any profit generated after printing costs and expenses, will be donated to these causes.

On behalf of the committee and all the researchers of edition 10, enjoy Edinburgh for Under Fives!

Kaye McAlpine, Editor

To keep ahead of any changes to venues in and around Edinburgh, why not check on the website www.efuf.co.uk, where we will flag up changes, additions, closures etc, that we find out about during the guide's 2 year validity. Check under 'Edition 10 Updates'.

CONTENTS

CONTENTS

NOTES

PART ONE

Where Shall We Go Today?

INTRODUCTION

There are dozens of different types of venue where you can enjoy a really great day out with under fives – in Edinburgh and throughout Scotland. In this section we have listed the different types types of venue, firstly in general alphabetical order, and then in the 'in town', 'close to home' and 'further afield' categories. This means we can include many great attractions that we simply could not do in previous editions' formats. We have concentrated on those places that most children should enjoy and which could be visited comfortably by parents with young babies – and we have tried to ensure that our entries will appeal to different age groups and interests.

While children are welcome at all these venues, parents should be considerate to other visitors. And because every child is different, please be aware not every venue might be ideal; the content of some may offer little interest or stimulation to a toddler, but could catch the attention of a four year old, or are great for visiting with a baby; others, by the physical structure of the buildings (dark rooms and corridors, narrow turnpike stairs etc) may concern rather than excite your particular child.

Many of the historic places to visit are managed by Historic Scotland (HS), Tel: 668 8600 or the National Trust for Scotland (NTS), Tel: 243 9300.

Contact them for further information on membership and discounts. Please note that the National Trust for Scotland does not permit pushchairs or backpacks into some of its stately homes for safety reasons regarding your children and their property – babies in a papoose are permitted.

No matter what your preference is – indoor or outdoor, active or more reflective – there are some considerations which concern every parent: will my child be able to access most or all of the venue; are there suitable toilets and nappy changing areas; and if we want to eat, is the venue geared up for catering for children in the 21st Century? We've tried to answer these points too!

As ever, the same rules always apply: when travelling with young children, try to account for every eventuality. With your first child, you might find yourself a little adrift with the different age transitions, but rest assured, if you go with the old adage, 'if something can go wrong, it will', you'll get most bases covered. So, lightweight waterproofs are always worthwhile; put anything spillable or burstable in a sealable pocket or in a plastic bag; and always take a change of clothes. In the nice weather always remember the sunscreen and a sunhat: a child's skin is delicate and must be protected from the sun's UV rays.

Information, leaflets etc. on Edinburgh and Scotland can be obtained from:

Edinburgh Information Centre
3 Princes Street (above Princes Mall)
Tel: 0845 22 55 12

Opening times:
Nov-Mar, Mon-Sat 9.00-17.00, Sun 10.00-17.00.
Apr & Oct, Mon-Sat 9.00-18.00,
Sun 10.00-18.00.
May, June & Sep, Mon-Sat 9.00-19.00,
Sun 10.00-19.00.
Jul & Aug, Mon-Sat 9.00-20.00, Sun 10.00-20.00.

Libraries are also a good source of local information.

For travel information, see:

First Bus
Tel: 08708 72 72 71
(Mon-Fri 7.00-19.00, Sat 10.00-14.00)
Web: www.firstgroup.com choose the appropriate area

Lothian Buses
Tel: 555 6363
Web: www.lothianbuses.co.uk

Traveline Scotland
Tel: 0870 608 2 608
(Sun-Sat 7.00-22.00)
Web: www.travelinescotland.com or phone

NADICS
Web: www.nadics.org.uk
Run by the Scottish Executive, the NADICS (National Driver Information and Control System) site provides up-to-date information on roadworks, delays etc, and can help when planning a journey.

So, where do you want to go today?

ART GALLERIES

Children of any age can be fascinated by paintings and sculpture and Edinburgh offers a wide variety of opportunities to expose the young enquiring mind to art. Holding young children up to see properly and giving constant reminders not to touch can be tiring but well worth the effort. Sometimes a gallery may just be a different place to go with a baby and meet friends.

There are also some great examples of art in the environment throughout Edinburgh – the best central location is probably Princes St Gardens – and here you can look and touch!

In the City

There are four National Galleries of Scotland, all of which have the same opening times, telephone number and website. You can travel free between the four National Galleries using the visitor bus, which leaves the galleries every 45 mins. Please note that if you're visiting the Gallery of Modern Art, the bus leaves from the Dean Gallery, on the opposite side of Belford Rd.

The Dean Gallery

73 Belford Road EH4 3DS
Tel: 624 6200
Tel: 332 2266 (recorded information)
Email: enquiries@nationalgalleries.org
Web: www.nationalgalleries.org

Opening times: Sun-Sat 10.00-17.00.
Extended hours during Festival.
Closed 25, 26 Dec and 1 Jan.
Admission: free – occasional charges for special exhibitions

If you arrive by car, and park in the car park, the rear of the building is facing you. Here you will find the access for disabled visitors – you can also use this for access with prams. The lift provides access to all levels of the building. The imposing grade A listed building has been transformed by architects, with great features for the under 5s such as a see through floor and porthole type windows to fire the imagination. Good pushchair access.

The gallery has a lovely setting, with an expanse of grass lawn to the front. Here you'll find several installations – ideal for youngsters to explore on a warm day.

The Dean Gallery is dedicated to 20th century art – including Dada and Surrealist collections. Highpoints

on our visits are Paolozzi's Vulcan (the 2 room-high iron man) and the reconstruction of the artist's London studio, which is full to the gunwales with a wonderful collection of items.

Shop sells a range of gifts, cards, books etc.

Lift to brightly tiled toilets in basement where nappies can be changed. Café Newton is situated on the ground floor. Open 10.00-16.30. Serves light meals, plus coffees, juices, pastries and cakes – see Eating Out.

National Gallery of Scotland

The Mound EH2 2EL
Tel: 624 6200
Tel: 332 2266 (recorded information)
Email: enquiries@nationalgalleries.org
Web: www.nationalgalleries.org

Opening times: Mon-Sun 10.00-17.00; Thu 10.00-19.00. Closed 25, 26 Dec. Open 1 Jan 12.00-17.00. Extended hours during the Festival.
Admission: free – occasional charges for special exhibitions

Good pushchair access to most of the building via lift at the rear and ramp down into the Scottish wing. Stairs only to Early Northern and Italian Art room A1

Any bus to Princes Street will take you to the gallery.

An outstanding collection of paintings, drawings and prints by the world's greatest artists including Velázquez, El Greco, Rembrandt, Vermeer, Turner, Constable, Monet and Van Gogh. Also holds the national collection of Scottish Art.

Welcomes parties of nursery-aged children, though prior to bringing groups, please phone the Education Department to discuss requirements, Tel: 624 6410.

There are nappy changing facilities in the toilet for the disabled.

The Weston Link

The Weston Link, which runs underground between the National Gallery of Scotland and The Royal Scottish Academy, contains a cloakroom, toilets (pull-down nappy-change units in toilets for the disabled), a café, and a fully licensed restaurant. If you access the Link from Princes Street Gardens West, there's the choice of the revolving door (always an attraction for under fives), or use the push-button access that provides access for disabled visitors and parents with pushchairs.

The café is open during gallery hours, but the restaurant is open 10.00-23.00 (10.00-22.00 on Sat). The shop is spacious and offers a range of literature, jewellery, gifts, stationery and tableware, as well as a children's section.

Scottish National Gallery of Modern Art
Tel: 624 6200
Tel: 332 2266 (recorded information)
Email: enquiries@nationalgalleries.org
Web: www.nationalgalleries.org

Opening times: Mon-Sun 10.00-17.00. Closed 25, 26 Dec, open 1 Jan 12.00-17.00. Extended hours during Festival. Admission: free – occasional charges for special exhibitions.

Bus: LRT 13. Can be accessed from the Water of Leith, lovely walk from Stockbridge through Dean village. Gallery car park is free.

Ramped entrance and pushchair access to all floors via the lift to the right of the main entrance hall. Further lift in room 21 for access to top mezzanine floor.
Scotland's finest collection of 20th century paintings, sculpture and graphic art. Includes works by Picasso, Matisse, Moore, Hockney, Davie, Campbell and Wiszniewski.
The front garden has been landscaped with an award winning design by Charles Jencks, with steep, curved banks and ponds. This is fun for children to walk on but due caution is necessary as the banks are very steep in places: you can get Edinburgh's most artistic grass stains on your rear! Walled sculpture garden to the rear. Welcomes parties of nursery-aged children. Phone the Gallery's Education Department at the number above.
Nappy changing facilities in toilets near café.
Café is open 10.00-16.30, and can be extremely busy at lunchtimes (lunches served 12.00-14.30), but there are tables outside – nice when it's warm – and a garden for children to play in: see Eating Out North.

Scottish National Portrait Gallery
1 Queen Street EH2 1JD
Tel: 624 6200
Tel: 332 2266 (recorded information)
Email: enquiries@nationalgalleries.org
Web: www.nationalgalleries.org

Opening times: Mon-Sun 10.00-17.00; Thu 10.00-19.00. Closed 25,26 Dec. Open 1 Jan 12.00-17.00.
Admission: free – occasional charges for special exhibitions.

Ramped entrance to the right of the main door (West entrance), otherwise a few steps up into building via the front door. Pushchair access to all floors via the lift to the left-hand side of the main entrance hall. You may find that the gilded frieze and the large murals in the entrance hall result in an extended stay there!

Portraits in all media of people who have played a significant role in Scottish history from the 16th century to the present day, including Mary Queen of Scots, Robert Burns and Sean Connery among others. Also houses the National Photograph Collection with regular photography exhibitions. Welcomes parties of nursery-aged children. Phone the Gallery/Education Department at the number above.
Ground floor café (open 10.00-16.30) serving everything from home baking to salads and hot lunches. High chairs provided. Nappy change (M&F).

OTHER GALLERIES

The City Art Centre
2 Market Street EH1 1DE
Tel: 529 3993

Opening times: Mon-Sat 10.00-17.00; Sunday opening for special exhibitions
Admission: free, except for special exhibitions

As well as hosting Edinburgh's collection of Scottish art, the centre hosts temporary exhibitions, often with a very broad appeal. Some exhibitions are aimed at children with workshops for under 5s. Access to all floors by lift and escalator. Toilets for the disabled on the ground floor have nappy change facilities. Pleasant café adjacent to the centre.

Fruitmarket Gallery
45 Market Street EH1 1DF
Tel: 226 8182
Email: info@fruitmarket.co.uk
Web: www.fruitmarket.co.uk

Opening times: Mon-Sat 11.00-18.00; Sun 12.00-17.00. Extended opening hours during Edinburgh International Festival. Admission: free

Contemporary art gallery showcasing the work of international artists and emerging talent. Pram and wheelchair accessible, with lift to upper floor. Ground floor café (highchairs), contemporary culture bookshop and toilet for disabled visitors. No nappy-change station.

BEACHES

In The city

Cramond Beach and Esplanade

A broad paved footpath runs for 2 miles from Cramond through Silverknowes to Granton Point West Shore Rd. An attractive area for promenading with the pram, roller-skating or for learning to ride a bike. Plenty of seats and shelters. Superb views across to Fife on clear days. Suitable for picnics on the Grassy Banks at Silverknowes where there is parking along Marine Drive – but look out for dog mess. You can also walk up to Lauriston Castle from Silverknowes.

Tide charts are available for reference in summer. Ice cream vans, pipe bands and entertainment over some summer weekends. The beach itself is sandy at Cramond and stony elsewhere. It can be oily and there are often pollution warnings about collecting shellfish. The beach is gently sloped but the tide can come in fast and maroon you on a sandbank – be prepared to paddle!

Portobello Beach and Promenade

The paved promenade runs for 1 3/4 miles from Seafield Rd to Esplanade Terrace in Joppa. The west end of the beach is reached from Bath St (Lothian Buses 2/12, 15, 26, 42/46; First Bus 129). Here you will find an indoor amusement arcade with some children's rides, including a carousel, as well as the usual take away snacks. There is a car park in Bridge Street. The quieter end of the beach is reached from Brunstane Rd, where you can park. The beach is sandy, the City Council cleans it regularly, but as on all beaches, vigilance is required and sandals are advisable for children. There are toilets at regular intervals along the promenade and information boards, including an electronic display outside the Portobello Swim Centre, which advises on water quality (summer months only). Playgrounds can be found along the promenade at Straiton Place and at Tower Bank. See Playgrounds and Playarks. At the time of writing a new public garden is being developed at the foot of John Street.

CLOSE TO HOME

Beaches in East Lothian

East Lothian has many good beaches along its shores and all of them are worth exploring. Our particular favourites, and those especially good for pre-school children, are listed here.

Aberlady

Drive through Aberlady on the A198 towards North Berwick. There is a car park on the left, and a wooden bridge provides access to the RSPB reserve. From here it is quite a long walk through the reserve, but well worth the adventure as the beach is beautiful and usually quite empty. Not very suitable for pushchairs, best to take a backpack or sling.

Gullane

Easy-to-find beach 40 minutes from Edinburgh. From A1, take A198 towards North Berwick. In the village, follow sign to the left into a paying car park (Easter-Sep). Pleasant beach with grassy area in front. Play area with toilets nearby.

North Berwick

Take the A198 from the A1. The town has a one way system, but the beaches and car parks are all signed. There are beaches to the east and west of the harbour and Seabird Centre. The beach to the east is long and sandy, with plenty of rock-pools and easy parking along the adjacent road. There is a paddling pool which refills naturally when the tide comes in, and when the tide is out makes a good swimming and boat sailing environment for youngsters (and their carers!). Award-winning family toilets nearby.

Seacliff Beach

East of North Berwick on A198

Private beach. You'll need correct money for unmanned barrier – 2x£1 coins per car. Beautiful bay, rock pools, tiny harbour, island and lovely view of Bass Rock. Car park. Toilets.

Tyninghame

Take the A199 out of Haddington and turn on A198 towards North Berwick. After passing Tyninghame village there is an unmarked turn off to the right, through an avenue of trees, leading to a small car park. From there a track leads down to the beach, and also off through the trees for various woodland walks. Not ideal for pushchairs, so take sling or backpack. The beach is very rockpooly, and can be quite exposed, and is much loved by our youngsters. No toilets. There is a cafe with gift shop and toilet in nearby Tyninghame village.

Yellowcraig Beach

Drive through Dirleton and turn left just before you leave the village.

Paying car park (Easter-Sep). Beautiful beach and nature trail through the woods. Difficult with a pushchair, take a sling or backpack. There is a new climbing frame play park next to the car park. It is themed on a pirate ship, and has separate areas for toddlers and chipped bark on the ground.

FURTHER AFIELD
Beaches in Fife

Fife is wonderful for the bucket-and-spade brigade. Great sandy beaches include:

Aberdour

There are two lovely beaches – the Silver Sands (café, toilets and a car park) and the Black Sands (limited parking, no amenities, but really nice all the same, and it's a winner of the Seaside award from Tidy Britain Group.

Kinghorn beach
(Pettycur Bay)

Safe, sandy bay with two ice-cream shops /cafés on the front. Recent winner of seaside award from Tidy Britain Group. Fife Council Environmental Health Department gave it a good/excellent rating for its water quality.

St Andrews
East and West Sands Beaches

Two lovely large sandy beaches. Clean – and the water status is checked regularly. West Sands continues to hold a Blue Flag award.

Tentsmuir
(near Leuchars)

2 miles from the B945. Follow signs to Tentsmuir Forest and Beach.

A huge sandy beach and forest with extensive walks and cycleways. There is a car park (entrance £1), picnic and barbecue area with toilets, a play area, and an information board. The car park kiosk sells a small selection of snacks.

Elie Harbour Beach

Large, sandy, blue-flag beach with a café at the harbour, and also a pub (The Ship Inn), which has a beer garden, BBQs every Sunday May-Aug and overlooks the beach where the local team play cricket on Sundays. Elie Watersports (Tel: 01333 330962) at the harbour hire out pedaloes, inflatable rides, canoes, dinghies, windsurfers, etc.

BOATS, CANALS AND RIVERS

IN THE CITY

The Royal Yacht Britannia
Ocean Terminal
Tel: 555 5566
Email: enquiries@tryb.co.uk

Opening times: Apr-Sep 9.30-16.30 daily.
Oct-Mar 10.00-15.30 daily
Admission: adult £9; child £5; family £25. Under 5s free

The Royal Yacht Britannia was relocated to Ocean Terminal in October 2001. Tickets can be bought at Britannia, although advance booking is recommended in August. Parking available in Ocean Terminal. By bus: LRT 11, 22 or part of the Majestic Tour, an open-top bus tour. For over 40 years the Royal Yacht Britannia served the royal family, travelling over 1 million miles to become the most famous ship in the world. The visitor centre provides an insight into her history. It includes a royal picture gallery and a reconstruction of the original wheelhouse.

On board ship the 5 main decks are accessed by lift. A children's version of the audio tour is most suitable for 7-11 year olds – under 5s are unlikely to enjoy the slower, detailed audio tour but there is plenty to see and talk about on a parent-guided tour. Close supervision of children is required throughout as the environment/ location is inevitably not entirely child-safe.

The visitor centre and tour of Britannia is fully accessible to single pushchairs and prams. Toilets both on shore and on board. Nappy changing in toilet for the disabled. Shop with range of souvenirs.

See also Shopping - Ocean Terminal

CLOSE TO HOME

Edinburgh Canal Centre
27 Baird Road, Ratho
Midlothian EH28 8RA
Tel: 333 1320
Email: info@bridgeinn.com
Web: www.bridgeinn.com

Opening times: daily, all year round.

Follow 'Edinburgh Canal Centre' signs from Newbridge Interchange. By bus, take no 65 Waverley Travel bus from St Andrew's Sq

Although the canal boats only offer group cruises – with the exception of the Santa Cruises - the Centre is pleasant place for a meal and a wander around. The tow-path makes for a good walk with pushchairs though there are obvious water safety issues for those with tearaway toddlers.

There are a variety of ducks and swans for children to look at as well as a rather old but functioning parent-powered carousel.

Toilets with very good nappy changing facilities (nappies and wipes provided) available in the Bridge Inn. Santa visits from his magical island during the festive season – see Annual Events.

The Bridge Inn offers meals (££-£££), and offers a children's menu – high chairs available. The Pop Inn (£-££) serves a selection of snacks and meals. See Eating Out. Boats can be hired for children's parties.

Linlithgow Union Canal Society
The Basin, Manse Road, Linlithgow
Tel: 01506 671215
Email: info@lucs.org.uk
Web: www.lucs.org.uk

Getting there: signposted from A803, sharp right turn at first railway bridge, then up and over canal bridge. The Basin is on the right.

Opening times: Easter-1st weekend Oct: Sat & Sun 14.00-17.00. Also Jul & Aug weekdays, 14.00-17.00

Trips over the Avon Aqueduct on St Magdalene (40 seater canal boat) 14.00-16.30.

Charges: adult £6.00; concession/student or child £3.00; family ticket (2 adults and 2 children) £15.00.

The price includes tea or coffee and biscuits.

Trips on Victoria (12 seater canal boat). Depart every half-hour from 14.00. Last trip 16.30. 20 minute trip.

Charges: adult £2.50; concession or child £1.50.

Boat trips on the Union Canal. There is also a museum with audio-visual presentation (perhaps more for interested parents than under 5s). The tearoom serves drinks and home-baking. The area is accessible to pushchairs and also wheelchairs. There are toilets, but there are no nappy changing facilities. It's an enjoyable outing for under 5s.

When Santa visits the Basin at Christmas, (usually on the 2 weekends prior to Christmas) there are barge trips and a gift for children (with accompanying adults going free) contact the Society for more details.

Looking towards the town from the Canal Society, there's an old doocot with tended gardens in front of it – nice for a sit down or a picnic. If you walk further along the canal path to the West, you can cut off the path. Go up and over the canal bridge, then walk down the first roadway lined with houses on your left. This will take you into the large Rosemount Park – perfect for a run around! Keep away from the canal end – there's no fencing. There are no toilets here, but you're about 10-15 minutes walk from Linlithgow High Street and those at the Vennel – although plans are afoot to replace current block with a free-standing superloo.

Boat Trips to Inchcolm Island
Seafari
Tel: 331 5000 24 hour (sailings enquiry service)

You can take trips from Newhaven Harbour in the city.

Charges: please phone for 2006's rates. Under 5s free

Cruises at various times through the day. Phone for current sailing times.

Cruise under the Forth Rail Bridge to Inchcolm Island, seeing wildlife, seabirds and seals on the way. Boat seats 225. Snack bar and fully -stocked licensed bar on board. Sailing time 45 minutes each way, with 1 1/2 hr ashore to explore the 12th century abbey, sandy beach and wartime gun emplacements. Beware of dangerous drops in the ruins and on the hill. Picnic area and visitors centre. Toilets on boat and island.

FURTHER AFIELD
Falkirk
Falkirk Wheel
Lime Road
Tamfourhill
Falkirk FK1 4RS
Tel: 01324 619888
Tel: 08700 500 208 (booking line)
Web: www.thefalkirkwheel.co.uk

Getting there: from Edinburgh take the M9 W for Stirling. Follow brown tourist signs for The Falkirk Wheel but beware if travelling to the Falkirk Wheel from another attraction in Falkirk - few direction signs in the town itself!

Opening times: open 7 days. Apr-Nov visitor centre opens 9.00. First boat leaves 09.30. Boats every 30 mins until 17.00. Shorter hours Nov-Mar.
Charges: boat trips; adult £8; concession £6.50; child 3-15 yrs £4.50. Under 3s free. Tickets can be booked by phone on the booking line number.
Admission to visitor centre is free. Pushchairs are not allowed on the boat, nor is there a secure place to leave them in the visitor centre. On our visit some pushchairs had been left outside visitor centre beside boat but the advice is leave pushchairs in the car if possible

The Falkirk Wheel is the world's first and only rotating boat lift. Built as part of the Millennium Link, the canal restoration project that reunited the historic link between Edinburgh and Glasgow. The trip on the Falkirk Wheel is made on a pleasure cruiser that departs from in front of the visitor centre. Once on board small children should sit where they can get a good view over the side of the boat as it moves upwards on the lift. At the top of the lift the boat crosses a short aqueduct before passing through a tunnel that is partially illuminated. The boat then turns round and goes back the way it came. The round trip takes about 1 hour. On a hot day the boat's glass roof can make the trip a bit uncomfortable.
In the visitor centre there are several interactive displays. Younger children may need the help of an adult to work these properly. Remote control boats and playpark. Picnic tables. Also a pleasant café (with high chairs) that sells sandwiches, kids' boxes, home baking etc, and a gift shop. Nappy changing facility in the disabled toilet. Breastfeeding, naturally, is welcome, although no private area available.

Fife

Anstruther Pleasure Trips to the Isle Of May
Tel: 01333 310103 (24 information line)
Web: www.isleofmayferry.com

The May Princess sails from Anstruther Harbour once a day. The crossing takes 45 mins. including a cruise round the island to see the colony of grey seals basking on the rocks. On most trips you can land and spend 2-3 hours ashore exploring. In the summer you are met by a Scottish

Natural Heritage Warden who explains about the abundant wildlife including Puffins, Kittiwakes, Guillemots, Razorbills, Terns and Shags. The boat has hot drinks and light refreshments but it is advisable to take your own too. There are marked routes, which allow you to visit all parts of the island, a small information centre with toilets, the remains of a 12th century monastery and the first lighthouse ever built in Scotland. We managed fine with a 4 year old and a 1 year old in a back carrier and it is safe if you keep to the paths, although supervision of young children is necessary. The Puffins were amazing! Sailing times vary depending on tides. Tickets can be purchased from the Kiosk in Anstruther Harbour 1 hour before sailing or pre-booked up to one week in advance.

CASTLES & PALACES

Despite changes in legislation regarding access to buildings, you should remember that in the case of historic buildings, some areas of castles, palaces and even houses and museums may be hard to access, due to the age of the building and the nature of the architecture. Slings/papooses are recommended for very young children.
We've a wealth of castles and palaces on our doorsteps: there are castles straight out of fairy tales to those stark, eerie hulks that are straight out of nightmares, and all points in between.

IN THE CITY

Craigmillar Castle (HS)
Craigmillar Castle Road
Tel: 661 445
Web: www.historic-scotland.gov.uk
Getting there: 2 1/2 miles SE of Edinburgh off the A7. Lothian Buses 14, 24, 30, 32, 33, 38, 49 have routes that go near here.

Opening times: Apr-1st Oct: Mon-Sun 9.30-18.30. Oct-Mar: Sat-Wed 9.30-16.30; closed Thu & Fri.

Admission: adult £3.00; concession £2.25; child £1.20. Under 5s free.

Handsome castle, dating from the 14th century. Its fortifications are pretty impressive – it certainly has the air of what a castle 'should be' like, especially from the Under 5 viewpoint. It was once a favourite residence of Mary, Queen of Scots. There are attractive gardens at either side of the castle and it is possible to hold a children's birthday party on the green.

Young children need to be closely supervised inside, as there are dark staircases, uneven floors and sharp drops from low open windows. Pushchairs and wheelchairs are restricted to ground floor level only. There's a nappy changing station in the toilet for the disabled. No private breastfeeding area. Friendly custodian. Shop and visitor centre, serving tea and coffee.

Edinburgh Castle (HS)
Tel: 225 9846
Web: www.historic-scotland.gov.uk

Opening times: daily, 25 Mar-30 Sept, 9.30-18.00; 1 Oct-31 Mar 9.30-17.00. Last tickets sold 45 mins before closing. Closed Christmas Day and Boxing Day. Limited opening hours on 1 and 2 Jan – phone for details.
Car and coach parking, max 2 hours. Cars £3.00, coaches £6.00
Car parking not available June-October due to Edinburgh Military Tattoo.
Admission: adult £9.80; child £3.50 (children under 16 must be accompanied by an adult); concession £7.50. Under 5s free.

If you choose a clear day to visit, you can enjoy stunning views over Edinburgh and across to Fife from the Castle Esplanade. You can also see the soldiers on guard outside this famous castle. Within the castle walls are various historic attractions such St Margaret's Chapel, the Honours of Scotland, the Stone of Destiny and the famous cannon Mons Meg, now back out on the battlements.
There are also tableaux of Napoleonic prisoners and sailors who sailed with John Paul Jones in the prison vaults. And, of course, there's also the One O'clock Gun and a related exhibition.
Guided tours and CD-ROM audio tours available.
However, there isn't an awful lot to take younger children's interest – there are also some steep cobbled paths that are not ideal for toddlers or pushchairs. Over 3s might enjoy a short visit – or they might be happy with a walk round the esplanade!

There are 2 cafés –

The Queen Anne Café
££-£££, waiter service, licensed lunch served 12.00-15.00.
Afternoon teas served after 15.00.
Situated in Crown Square.

Emphasis on Scottish produce and recipes. Coffees and lighter snacks available all day. Organic baby food available free of charge.

Redcoat Café
£-££, self-service
Next to the One O'clock Gun.

Range of main meals and carvery items. Offer an 'Edinburgh Castle' lunch box, as well as children's hot meals. Organic baby food available - £1/jar.

The castle has toilet facilities, a feeding and changing room, and also toilets for the disabled. A courtesy vehicle for disabled visitors is also available – this will take you right to the top of the castle.

The Castle also houses the National War Memorial. Visitors going only to this can enter free, ask at the ticket office. Obviously, this right should not be abused.

Lauriston Castle
2a Cramond Road South EH4 5QD
Tel: 336 2060

Opening times: April-October Sat-Thu 11.00-13.00 and 14.00-17.00. Nov-Mar Sat/Sun 11.00-16.00.
Grounds opening times: 9.00-dusk.

Admission: adult £4.50; £3 concession/ children over 6. Appointments required for groups.
Access to the grounds: free

Bus no. 41 from The Mound/George St. There is parking, if you take your car.

The earliest part of this elegant little castle was built in the 1590s, and it's been extended over the centuries and now looks more like a lavish Edwardian house. Its interior has remained unchanged since 1926. It has a secret room – as any respectable castle has – and a notable collection of Blue John ware. Guided tours only, lasting about 40 mins and not really suitable for young children as once inside the castle you cannot leave until the tour is finished.

There are pleasant walks, suitable with a pushchair, in the peaceful and extensively wooded grounds with fine views over the Forth estuary to Fife. They are particularly lovely in the spring when the daffodils are out and the pond is full of tadpoles. Activities are frequently organised in the house and gardens to coincide with school holidays. Ball games can be played anywhere except the croquet lawns on the North side of the house. There is a picnic area with tables and arrangements can be made for large parties – apply to the steward. Toilet facilities (F) have a bench, which is convenient for nappy changing. There is also a toilet for the disabled.

Palace of Holyroodhouse, Holyrood Abbey and the Queen's Gallery
Foot of Royal Mile (Canongate)
Tel: 524 1120

Opening times: Apr-Oct, Mon-Sun 9.30-17.00 (last admission).
Nov-Mar, Mon-Sun 9.30-15.30 (last admission).

The Palace is closed when The Queen or Her Commissioner is in residence, usually in late May and late June/early July. It is also occasionally closed at other times, sometimes at short notice.

Admission: adult £8.50; child (5-16 inc) £4.50; over 60 & students £7.00; family (2A & 3C under 17) £21.50. Under 5s free.

The Palace is The Queen's official residence in Scotland and all state and historic apartments are open to the public. Audio tour equipment is provided for all visitors, including a special 'family' edition. In addition to the Palace, the ruins of Holyrood Abbey, dating back to the 11th Century, can also be visited. There is a limited amount of interest for under 5s. In the Palace pushchair access is limited to the ground floor.

The Queen's Gallery
Opening times as for the Palace

Admission: adult £5.00, child (5-16 inc) £3.00, over 60 & students £4.00. family (2A & 3C under 17) £21.50. Under 5s free.

Situated in the Mews area of the Palace, The Queen's Gallery contains exhibitions from the Royal Collection. Most exhibitions may not interest under 5s.

Toilets are available in the Royal Mews where changing and feeding facilities for babies are available. From late spring and throughout the summer further seating is provided around the forecourt and in the Mews. There is also a café and gift shop. Staff are helpful.

CLOSE TO HOME

East Lothian

Dirleton Castle and Gardens (HS)
Tel: 01620 850330
Web: www.historic-scotland.gov.uk

Getting there: in Dirleton, 3m W of North Berwick. Take A1 then A198 coast road towards North Berwick.

Opening times: open all year – phone for current seasonal variations
Admission: adult £3.30; child £1.30; reduced £2.50. Under 5s free.

Fantastic castle built in the 12th century, great for exploring by young and old alike, but do take extra care with little ones. Famous gardens include an Arts and Crafts herbaceous border – the longest one in the world according to the Guinness Book of Records. Car park & picnic area.

Next to the car park there is a small play park. This has 2 bucket swings, roundabout, slide etc and picnic table.

Make a day of it: See also Yellowcraig Beach in Beaches

West Lothian

Linlithgow Palace (HS)
Tel: 01506 842896

In Linlithgow: by car, leave M9 at J3 and go West along the A803. It is best to park your car and walk up to the palace.

First buses serve Linlithgow. There are also regular trains.

Opening times: Mon-Sat all year 9.30-18.30 (16.30 in winter). Sun: Summer 9.30-18.30, Winter 14.00-16.30
Admission; adult £4.00; child £1.60; concession £3.00. Under 5s free.

Built as a pleasure palace by various Stuart monarchs, Linlithgow was acknowledged as one of the most beautiful palaces in Europe. Now roofless and partially ruined. It is full of nooks and crannies, turnpike staircases and the like, which make it unsuitable for pushchairs. Probably best visited with tiny babies in a papoose or with older children; there's certainly a lot to fire the imagination of little princes and princesses. There are information boards in key rooms in various languages. There's a huge fireplace in the Great Hall – stand inside and look up!

Look out for a skittles slab, the Presence Chamber with its unique floor patterning and the charmingly named 'vomitorium'

(make a day of it: see above in Boats, Canals and Rivers, plus Eating Out)

FURTHER AFIELD

The Borders

Floors Castle
Near Kelso
Roxburghshire
Tel: 01573 223 333

Getting there: 1 hour drive time from Edinburgh. Well signposted from Kelso

Opening times: 25 Mar-30th Oct 10.00- 16.30 pm. Last admissions are at 16.00 Dogs are welcome in the castle grounds.

Admission: A £6.00; C (5-16) £3.25. Conc £5.00. Family £18. Under fives free.

Beautiful castle, built in 1721, and set in stunning grounds. This was the castle used in the film 'Greystoke', and is the largest inhabited castle in Scotland. State rooms with priceless works of art open to public. Woodland and river walks. Children's quiz in castle. Toilets, nappy-changing facilities. Gift shop.

Restaurant:
Self service, licensed,
Open 10.00-16.00
Offers a selection of light snacks and full meals.

Coffee Shop:
Open 10.00-16.30, all year round.
There is also a garden centre within the castle grounds, complete with a children's playground. The Coffee Shop is situated to the west of the Castle, next to the Garden Centre and the beautiful Walled Garden next to the Children's Playground.

Hermitage Castle (HS)
Tel: 01387 376222
Web: www.historic-scotland.gov.uk

Getting there: 51/2 miles NE of Newcastleton, take the B6399, and watch out for the signs.
Opening times: summer only (Apr-Sep), 9.30-18.30.

Admission: adult £2.50; child £1.00; concession £1.90. Under 5s free.

A looming, eerie fortress set deep in the Borders and scene of many dark deeds – it is said that one of its first owners, William de Soules, was boiled alive in his own cauldron! Open in the summer only – and even then it might be wise to throw the wellies in the back of the car! If you have a child who's into battles and castles, this is a great example. From the outside, it's just about everything you'd want from a castle. Inside there's a covered well, a view down into the prison pit and good views out into the bleak countryside. It can be viewed externally in the 'closed' season. The terrain around is uneven and banked, so perhaps best viewed with active children rather than toddlers or babies – this also stands for the interior. There's a ruined chapel and graveyard if you turn left once you have crossed the access bridge rather than right towards the castle. There's a giant's grave outwith the chapel's walls; he was called the Cout o Kielder and owned magic chainmail – ideal story-fodder for children! When at the Hermitage or the chapel, watch out for the river. Picnic area.

Smailholm Tower (HS)
Tel: 01573 460365
Web: www.historic-scotland.gov.uk

Getting there: near Smailholm village, 6m W of Kelso on the B6937, then turn on to the B6404.

Opening times: all summer (Apr-Sep) 9.30-18.30 and weekends in winter (Oct-Mar) 9.30-16.00.
Admission: adult £2.50; child £1.00; concession £1.90. Under 5s free.

Smailholm Tower sits high on a rocky outcrop with a safety rail for safer viewing of the outlying land. It is a typical example of the 'bastles' that once stood all around the country. Inside there is an exhibition of tapestries and costume dolls. Open all summer and at the weekends in the winter. If you visit Kelso, it might be worth the detour just for the look. No toilets.

Dumfries and Galloway

Threave Castle (HS)
Tel: 07711 223 101
Web: www.historic-scotland.gov.uk

Getting there: 3m W of Castle Douglas on the A75.

Opening times: summer only (Apr-Sep), 9.30-18.30.
Admission: adult £3.00; child; £1.25; concession £2.25
Under 5s free.

This is one straight out of days of old when knights were bold. The castle itself stands on an island in the River Dee.

To access it, you ring a bell and a steward will come to ferry you over: boat jetty is 1/2 mile walk from car park. There are toilets and toilets for the disabled in the car park - none on the island. There is a picnic area on the island. The last boat leaves the island at 18.00. Not suitable for prams due to the boat ride.

Fife

Aberdour Castle (HS)
Tel: 01383 860519
Web: www.historic-scotland.gov.uk
Getting there: Aberdour lies about 5 miles east of the Forth Bridges on the A921. Stagecoach buses to Kirkcaldy stop at Aberdour. Most trains to Kirkcaldy stop at Aberdour station (for train info, tel: 01592 416060). Castle is next to Aberdour railway station, and near a bus stop.

Opening times: summer (Apr-Sep) daily 9.30-18.30. Winter: 9.30-16.30 closed Thu and Fri.
Admission: adult £3.00; child £1.20; concession £2.25. Under 5s free (Friends of HS free).

Built in the 13th Century, this partially ruinous step-gabled castle is brilliant for children – especially those interested in knights and castles. The winding stairs are fascinating for older toddlers and children, but are obviously no use for a pushchair! The interior is furnished and accessible.

Tearoom
£-££, high chair (1).
Open during summer and weekends in winter. The shop has reasonably priced themed toys for children's role play (knights' helmets etc).
Make a day of it: we incorporated this visit with a trip to one of the 2 beautiful Aberdour beaches (see above) and had a wonderful day out.

Falkland Palace (NTS)
Falkland
Cupar
Tel: 01337 857397
Web: www.nts.org.uk
Getting there: A912, 10 miles from M90. Take J8, 11 miles N of Kirkcaldy. On National Cycle Route 1. Stagecoach bus stops in High Street.

Opening times – palace: 1 Mar – 31 Oct Mon-Sat 10.00-18.00, last admission 17.00, Sun 13.00-17.30, last admission 16.30

Admission – palace and garden; adult £10; child/concession £7; family (2 A and up to 6 C) £25, and (1 A and up to 6 C) £20. Under 5s free. NTS members free.
Garden only: Adult £5; child/concession £3.50; family (2 A and up to 6 C) £7 and (1 A and up to 6 C) £10. Under 5s free. NTS members free.
Scots Guards and members of the Scots Guards Association, wearing badges, free.

A palace straight out of a fairy tale, built by Stewart monarchs as a country residence/-hunting lodge. Pleasant gardens, with viewing access to the oldest 'royal tennis' court in Britain – built in 1539 and still in use. Partly roofed, the palace itself would have less than minimal interest for under 5s. Fully furnished rooms from all eras of the palace's use – best to give it a bye unless you are interested in the historic aspects (and have a baby in a papoose or sling). Young persons guide to palace on sale at reception. Often have weekends with guides in historic costume (check with property for details). Plenty to see in Falkland village also.

Perth & Kinross

Lochleven Castle (HS)
Tel: 07778 040483
www.historic-scotland.gov.uk
Getting there: situated on an island in Loch Leven, reached by ferry from Kinross, off the M90.
Opening times: daily, Apr-Sept 9.30-17.15 (last outward sailing)
Admission charges: adult £3.50; child £1.30; concession £2.50. Under 5s free. (HS members free). Ferry included in admission price.

Plenty of room on the island for some exploration around the ruins – but watch out, the midgies can be murderous! This castle imprisoned Mary, Queen of Scots, before her dramatic escape in 1568. The ferry journey to and from the island could make this a great pocket-sized adventure. Not really suitable for babies or young toddlers, more for adventurous/active under 5s.

Scone Palace
Perth PH2 6BD
Tel: 01738 552300
Email: visits@scone-palace.co.uk
Web: www.scone-palace.co.uk
Getting there: 3 miles North of Perth on A93, on the Braemar Road.

Opening times – Palace: I Apr-31 Oct, 9.30-17.30
Grounds 9.30-17.45. Winter hours (1 Nov-31 Mar): Friday 10.00-16.00.
Admission: adult £6.95; child 5-16 yrs £4.00; concession £5.95. Under 5s free.
Admission to grounds only: adult £3.50; child 5-16yrs £2.20; concession £3.00.

Ancient crowning place of the Kings of Scotland. Impressive stately home, with plenty of interesting items inside and out – such as the Moot Hill, where the Kings of Scotland were crowned (last coronation, Charles II). The grounds may be of more interest to small children. They are well kept and extensive (over 100 acres). Picnic area, ball games allowed. Adventure playground with children's playhut, swings etc. There's also the Murray Star Maze. Gift shop.
Palace hosts special events: check website for current event.

Servants' Hall Coffee Shop
£, high chairs.

Old Kitchen Restaurant
£-££, high chairs.
Open in July and August. Caters for booked lunches as well as daily visitors.

Stirling

Stirling Castle (HS)
Stirling FK8 1EJ
Tel: 01706 450000
Web: www.historic-scotland.gov.uk
Getting there: At the top of the Old Town, thoroughly signposted.

Opening times: Apr-Sept 9.30-18.00, Oct-Mar 9.30-17.00.
Admission: adult £7.50; OAP/ concession £5.50; child £2.00. Under 5s free.
Parking at Castle Esplanade £2/car for 2 hrs (disabled badge holders free).

One of Scotland's most impressive castles and superb for energetic toddlers and adults, even on rainy days.
Audio-visual exhibits in the kitchens and palace, interactive displays, gargoyles on the walls and odd, secluded corners where there are probably ghosties! Take care if you decide to walk around castle walls. Cannons for pretend play, grassy gardens and stunning views, shop and restaurant. The restored Great Hall is swagged with heavy drapes, has a stunning beamed roof, but for young children, its

main attraction is as a running space. However, the military museum holds little to interest young children and is up some narrow stairs. If possible, take a good look at the map you get with your ticket before setting out from the ticket office so you can be clear about the best route to take with under 5s because the space is large and the signposts are informative but not descriptive.

Unicorn Café:
£-££, highchairs, breastfeeding welcome, seats c. 120.

Café offering a range of sandwiches, soup, salads, baked potatoes. Kids' boxes available.
Castle has various toilets here and there, with various facilities, but there's a good one hidden away within the Great Hall, complete with a nappy-change unit.

If you are going home from Stirling by the 'low road' (the A905) through Fallin, Throsk etc, look out for the signs to the Pineapple before you get to Airth. Follow the narrow road and park up in the small car park. Through the gateway in the wall, you'll enter what was a large orchard and set in the midst is The Pineapple – a 45ft (14m) high building built in the shape of, you've guessed it, a pineapple. Built in 1761, it is now uner the Landmark Trust, so you can't get inside, but it makes a quirky quick stop-off point.

The Pineapple
(NTS maintain gardens, building leased to the Landmark Trust).
7m E of Stirling, off A905, then off B9124. 1m W of Airth.
Open all year, daily: 9.30-sunset. No toilets.

CERAMIC CENTRES

IN THE CITY

The Ceramic Experience
Ocean Drive
Britannia Quay EH6 6JB
Contact: Jenny Garner
Tel: 554 4455
Email: Edinburgh@theceramicexperience.com
Web: www.theceramicexperience.com
Opening times: daily 10.00-17.30.

Ceramic painting studio for families, where babies and children's footprints can be put onto anything from tiles to teapots. Clay imprints can also be produced in a variety of finishes.

There is a café and soft play area. Seating for 100 and plenty of room to run around. Nappy changing facilities available for use by male and female carers.

Free parking available. Premises accessible for pushchairs, with ramps and wide doors. Adults can choose to paint as well or can just relax while children play in the ball pool.

Doodles Ceramics Work Shop
29 Marchmont Crescent EH9 1HQ
Contact: Holly Peters
Tel: 229 1399
Email: painting@doodlesscotland.co.uk
Web: www.doodlesscotland.co.uk
Opening times: Tue-Thu 11.00-21.00, Fri, Sat 10.00-18.00, Sun 12.00-18.00.

An opportunity for children to make ceramic gifts for parents, grandparents etc, decorated with food safe paint. Friendly, helpful staff are available for hands-on advice. If your child finishes their project ahead of time, there are books and toys to amuse them. Free juice for children/tea and coffee for adults. Baby hand and foot prints are a speciality.

Toilet facilities. No nappy-changing room, but there is space for changing. There is no place to breastfeed in private. Premises accessible by single and double pushchairs.

FURTHER AFIELD

Fife

Ceramic Experience
17b Elgin Street Industrial Estate
Dunfermline KY12 7SN
Tel: 01383 840640
Opening hours: 10.00-17.00. Last admission 16.30. Facilities include café, soft play, ball pool.

Perthshire – Crieff

Ceramic Experience
Bennybeg
Muthill Road
Crieff PH7 4HN
Tel: 01764 655788
Opening hours: phone for current opening hours. Facilities include Soft Play, café, ball pool.

CINEMAS

There's a good range of cinemas in Edinburgh, from the independently owned Dominion where the manager greets you in the foyer, or the more 'arty' Cameo and Filmhouse, to the sprawling megaplexes, which seem to be showing every film released in the past six months: take your pick. You never quite know how your child will take to their first cinema outing. Remember that the sound volume can be overwhelming, as can the dark. However, there are the chairs, big and plush to little ones, the décor, such as the planetoid carpet of Vue at Ocean Terminal and the lure of ice cream! Some cinemas have children's film clubs – check out your local one for details.

IN TOWN

Cameo Cinema
38 Home Street
Tel: 228 4141 (box office)
Tel: 228 2800 (24 hour info line)
Web: www.picturehouses.co.uk
Getting there: by Lothian Bus 1,0, 11, 15, 15A, 16, 17, 23,

24, 27, 34, 35, 45. If you're travelling by car, parking is poor. Try parking at Chalmers St and walking down to Tollcross, or park at Castle Ter or Semple St and walk up.

Admission: adult £4.20 Mon-Fri before 18.00, £5.90, after 18.00. Concs: £3.50 before 18.00, £4.20 after 18.00. Monday is cheap day (barring Bank holidays), all tickets £4.00. Wed first screening £1 to concession card holders. Friends cardholder schemes £25.00 per year available offering discounted tickets at all times.

Babies and children of all ages admitted at parents' discretion and subject to normal film certification. Ice cream, popcorn and a wide range of confectionery on sale in the foyer. Children allowed in the bar up until 20.00. There is a permanent nappy changing station located in the cinema.

The Cameo holds a Saturday morning Kids Club with supervised fun and activities followed by a screening. An adult must accompany all children attending the club. Unaccompanied adults will not be admitted.

The Big Scream

The Cameo offers screenings exclusively for parents/carers of young children. Screenings take place on Thursdays at 10.30. Entry is only valid for a carer, plus one other adult. They must be must be accompanied by a baby of 12 months or under. Price: £3.50 (£2.50 concession). A pre-screening complementary tea or coffee is included in the price. Pushchair parking, bottle warming and nappy changing facilities are all provided.

To be updated specifically on Big Scream events please email: cameo.marketing@picturehouses.co.uk.
NB The Cameo may be changing ownership within the next 12 months, so services on offer may change.

Dominion

18 Newbattle Terrace EH10 4RT
Tel: 447 4771
Tel: 447 2660/8450 (information line)
Tel: 447 4771 (credit card booking)

Getting there: By Lothian Bus 5, 11, 15, 15A, 16, 17, 2. By car – parking in nearby streets.
Prices vary as to screenings and times – concessions available on every screening.

As visited by Maisie the Cat! A lovely, old style, privately owned cinema. Shows current releases – children's access determined by rating. Babies in arms are welcome

and best seated close to an exit. Breastfeeding is welcomed. Refreshments and ice cream in sale in the foyer. Comfortable bar/café in basement, selling coffees, alcoholic drinks and chocolate cake to die for! Toilets for disabled patrons on ground floor have nappy changing facilities. Other toilets at basement level.

Filmhouse

88 Lothian Road
Tel: 228 2688

Getting there: from Princes St, take Lothian Bus 1, 2, 10, 11, 15, 15A, 16, 17, 24, 34. Parking – try Castle St, behind the Usher Hall.
Admission: before 16.00 A £4.00; Concessions £2.50. Fri Bargain Matinees A£3.50/ C£1.70. 17.00-19.00 A £5.20; Concessions £3.70. 19.00+ A £5.80; Concessions £4.80.

Art house films and independent cinema releases. Children must be 3 years+ to be admitted to cinema, although younger children are allowed in the café between 10.00 and 20.00 only, which sells snacks, meals with vegetarian options, beers coffee etc. Full facilities for disabled patrons. Nappy changing facilities. Breastfeeding welcomed in café. Bottle warming, nappy changing and pushchair parking available.

For Crying Out Loud

The Filmhouse's scheme for carers/parents with young children. Screenings are on Mondays at 10.30. Up to two carers, who must be accompanied by a child of 12mths or under. Price is £3.00 (£2.00 concession).

Odeon Cinemas

118 Lothian Road   EH3 8BG
Tel: 0871 22 44 007 (booking line)

Getting there: from Princes St , take a Lothian Bus 10, 11, 15, 16 and 17. Parking – not plentiful: a choice of on-street, 'pay and display' or the car park behind the cinema in Semple Street.

Fairly new cinema with four screens. Not particularly targeting children though they do show mainstream children's films. Easy pushchair access and lifts. Nappy changing facilities. Comfy chairs in retail area or on concourse to screens for breastfeeding.

Westside Plaza

120 Westerhailes Road   EH14 2SW
Tel: 0870 50 50 007 (24 hr booking and information line)
Getting there: located to the West of the city. By Lothian

Bus 3, 3A, 18, 20, 30, 32, 33. By car; off the A71 Calder Rd (Bankhead Roundabout) or the A70 Lanark Rd.

Eight-cinema complex. Next to Wester Hailes station. Easy parking and access is all on one level. Ice-cream, popcorn etc. Nappy-changing facilities. Family tickets available.

Under 18 mths free if sitting on parent's knee.

NB. Odeon Cinema's 'Movie Mob' Children's Club does not currently operate in either Edinburgh Cinemas.

UCI Cinema

Fort Kinnaird EH15 3RD
Tel: 669 0777
Tel: 08700 10 20 30 (information and booking line)
Web: www.uci.co.uk

Getting there: by Lothian Bus 30. By car from the East, follow the A1, the take the turning for Fort Kinnaird. From the West, follow the City by-pass (A720) to the A1 and head for Edinburgh. Fort Kinnaird is the first slip road after joining the A1.

Admission: Adult £4.95 (£3.95 before 17.00); child (under 15s) £3.95; concessions £3.95.

Twelve cinema complex. No babies in arms. No smoking in cinemas. Quite popular with parents for child-orientated films. If you have a younger under 5, you might find that the seats fold up even when they're sitting on them – though this might be viewed as an added bonus to the film! Ice cream is on sale in the foyer as well as the usual popcorn, tortillas and dips, hot and cold drinks etc. Child-sized portions available. No nappy changing facilities.

Kids Club

Runs every Sat and Sunday and every day during school holidays. Shows recent releases. Costs around £1.95/child – parent/carer gets in free. No unaccompanied adults. Films are U or PG – check screening before setting off.

UGC Fountainpark (CINEWORLD)

Fountainpark
130/3 Dundee Street EH11 1AF
0871 200 2000 (advance bookings)
Tel: 0870 902 0417 (24 hr information and credit card booking)

Getting there: by Lothian Bus 1, 22, 30, 34, 35. By car: access car park via Western Approach Rd (travelling W), or via Dundee St.

Admission: adult £4.90 before 17.00 Mon-Fri, £5.80 after 17.00; child (aged 15 and under)/ concession £3.60; family

ticket £9 (4 tickets – at least 2 C). Also, 'early bird' price of £3.40 for showings before noon. UGC Unlimited card gives you unlimited screenings for around £9.99/month. Yearly passes also available.

Large cinema complex located in a purpose built leisure park in a central location. Underground car park; fee refunded on exit with voucher supplied by cinema or other outlets. Cinema offers booster seats for children. Parties hosted in a special 'party' room. Phone for further information and booking.

Vue Cinemas

Vue Cinema

Ocean Terminal
Tel: 553 0700
Web: www.myvue.com

Getting there: by Lothian Bus 1, 11, 22, 34, 35, 36. By car: follow the signs to Britannia, parking free in Ocean Terminal car parks.

Admission: Adult £5.80 (£4.80 before 17.00); child £3.50; concessions £3.50; family ticket £15.80 – call cinema for details. Tuesdays £3.50 – any film, any time.

12-screen cinema located on the top floor of Ocean Terminal shopping centre which can be easily accessed by escalators and lifts. Toilets, including nappy changing facilities and parents' rooms, are located nearby in the main shopping centre.

Kids Film Club

Cinema shows a film suitable for children of about an hour long at 10:00 on Saturday and Sunday as well as weekdays in the holidays. Tickets are £2 for a child but accompanying adults go free. (check the film showing – not all are ideal for under 5s).

The popcorn, nachos etc are sold on the opposite side of the foyer to the ticket sales, and although the ice cream and pick'n'mix vending is on the same side, it is set back from the ticket sales area, so if you're trying to negotiate your way to the screen without a tantrum over sweeties it can just about be done.

Vue Cinema

Omni Centre
Greenside Place EH1 3AA
Tel: 08712 240 240 (booking line)
Web: www.myvue.com

Getting there: by Lothian Bus 1, 5, 7, 11, 14, 16, 19, 21, 22,

25, 34, 49, By car: Parking behind complex, in side streets or NCP St James. None of these options are free.

Admission: before 17.00 Mon-Thu Adult £5.00; Child or Concession £3.60 Family ticket (2A &2C) £14.40. After 17.00 and Thu-Sun Adult £6.00; Child/Concession £3.80; Family ticket (2A & 2C £15.20).

12-screen cinema complex, centrally located. Accessible by escalator and lift. Toilets with nappy changing facilities. Good views down on to the traffic (and some fantastic giraffes!) from the huge glass-fronted façade. Snacks on sale above ticket sales, so you can get to the screens without passing by, if you take the stairs!

COUNTRY HOUSES & STATELY HOMES

While a visit to a country house may not be no. 1 on the list of things to do with young children, please bear in mind that many stately homes now have many facilities to attract families. The interior of the houses may hold no interest for an under 5, but the estates are usually a different matter.

CLOSE TO HOME

Midlothian

Arniston House
Gorebridge
Tel: 01875 830 515
Web: www.arniston-house.co.uk
Getting there: approx 40 mins from central Edinburgh, from A7 turn right on to B6372, signposted as Penicuik and Temple, turn right after about a mile.

Opening times: Apr-June, Tue and Wed (guided tours at 14.00 and 15.30); July-mid Sep, Mon-Fri and Sun. Guided tours 14.00 and 15.30.
Admission – house: adult £5, child £2 concession £4. Under 5s free.
Admission – grounds: free.

Large private house, which has lovely, well maintained grounds for walks. Access for pushchairs. Toilets. No nappy-changing facility. Toilet with disabled access.
Arniston House is lovely, but while the guided tour may be of interest to parents, there's little to interest children

under 5. The tour involves a fair amount of stairs – not suitable for a pushchair, but if you have, say, a baby in a papoose, the tour is worthwhile.

West Lothian

Hopetoun House
South Queensferry
West Lothian EH30 9SL
Tel: 331 2451
Fax: 319 1885
Web: www.hopetounhouse.com
Getting there: 12 miles from Edinburgh, join the A904 from the A90 via the slip road. Take the left turning. Approximately half a mile along this road turn right into South Queensferry. Directly under the road bridge there is a sign to Hopetoun House. Follow the road through residential housing.

Opening times: daily end Mar- end Sep from 10.00. Last admission 16.30.
House and grounds admission: adults £7.00; child £4.00; family ticket (2A and up to 4 C) £20.00. Under 5s free.
Grounds only: reduced prices available: adults £5.50; child £2.00; family £9.00.

The House is described as 'Scotland's finest stately home' and approaching it via the sweeping drive, the house certainly creates quite an impact. Inside, there is a magnificent art collection throughout the impressive rooms – and very pleasant guides who will explain interesting features such as serving bells to under 5s. The gardens are extensive, with plenty of room for exploring, watch out for ha-has though (ditches cut into the ground to keep animals in fields without spoiling the view with fences – there's one to the left of the main drive). There is a picnic area, nature trails and a deer enclosure. The restaurant was very child friendly when we visited, and there was live music. Toilets with nappy-changing surface.
Hopetoun host various events throughout the year: go online, or see Annual Events for those most suited to children under 5.

FURTHER AFIELD

Berwickshire

Paxton House
Berwick upon Tweed TD15 1SZ
Tel: 01289 386291
Email: info@paxtonhouse.com
Web: www.paxtonhouse.com

WHERE SHALL WE GO TODAY? – COUNTRY HOUSES

Getting there: 54 miles from Edinburgh. Signposted 3 miles from the A1 Berwick upon Tweed bypass on B6461.
Trains to Berwick hourly am then bus no. 32 from Berwick daily except Sun.

Opening times: daily from 1 Apr-31 Oct, 10.00-17.00 Gardens open 10.00-sunset.
Admission to house and gardens: adult £6.00; child £3.00; family ticket £16.00.
Admission to gardens only: adult £3.00; child £1.50; family ticket £8.00.

The house is in the 18th century Palladian style, with interiors by Robert Adam. It houses the largest collection of Chippendale furniture in Scotland. Guided tour only – with 'Teddy Bear' trail for children. Lift to 1st floor only. Not suitable for toddlers or pushchairs.
There are 80 acres of woodland, parkland and gardens. Nature detective trails for children, lasting approx. 1/2 hour (costs 50p incl. crayon and sheet), and 1 mile of riverside walks accessible by pushchair if dry. Ponies and Highland cattle. Adventure playground, croquet (small charge) and red squirrel hide. There's usually a teddy bears' picnic in July for children, hosted by Paxton Ted, the house's children's mascot.

Café:
£, highchairs (2), licensed.
Serves home-cooked light meals/snacks. Secluded area for breastfeeding. Toilets. Nappy-changing facility (M&F). Gift shop.
Various annual activities and events – phone for details. Winner of various awards.

The Borders

Traquair House
Innerleithen
Tel: 01896 830323
Email: enquiries@traquair.co.uk
Web:www.traquair.co.uk
Getting there: on the B709. First bus service no. 62 from Edinburgh.

Opening times: Easter-31 May, Sep 12.00-17.00: Jun, Jul, Aug 10.30-17.00. Oct 11.00-16.00. Opening times may vary slightly. Please phone for current information.
Admission: adult £5.80; child £3.25; family ticket £16.80. under 5s free.

Oldest inhabited fortified house in Scotland, set in picturesque grounds. Look out for the gates that were locked in 1745 – and are not to be opened until a Stewart returns to the throne. No pushchairs inside as there are many stairs to negotiate, including the secret priest's stairs. Excellent maze in which you can lose your children for some time and pleasant children's play area. Shop selling 'pocket-money' trinkets for children.
Café:
£-££, highchairs (2)
Serves children's lunch-boxes. Nappy-changing facilities

Fife

Hill of Tarvit (NTS)
Tel: 01334 653127
Web: www.nts.org.uk
Getting there: the mansion house is on A916 nr Cupar. Well-signposted from A91 and A92.

Opening times: House: Good Fri – 30th Sept and 1st weekend in Oct, daily 13.00 – 17.00.
Grounds: open all year
Admission to gardens: free.
Admission to house: adult £8.00, child/concession £5.00, Family (2 A and up to 6 C) £20.00 (1 A and up to 6 C) £16.00. NTS members free. Under 5s free.

House has large collection of furniture, paintings and porcelain with lots for the family to see. Free activity sheets for children available at reception. Children should be supervised in house. Large gardens with lots of space for children to run around plus
a steep walk up the hill to the monument. Picnic tables in garden.

Tearoom and shop:
£-££, high chair (1)
Opens 12:00-17:00 (last orders 16:30). Pleasant tearoom selling light lunches and home baking, where staff are friendly and accommodating. . Nappy disposal unit, but no changing area.

FARMS, ZOOS and ANIMAL PARKS

There are numerous farm and animal parks in Scotland. We've listed many of them here, North and South, East and West.
All offer something different, be it rare or non-native breeds, adventure playgrounds, train rides or playparks.

IN TOWN

Edinburgh Zoo
Corstorphine Road
Tel: 334 9171
Web: www.edinburghzoo.org.uk

Getting there: by Lothian Bus 12, 26, 31 and airport bus all go past the Zoo. By car: follow the signs. Ample car parking at zoo.

Opening times: Apr-Sep Mon-Sun 9.00-18.00; Oct, Mar Mon-Sun 9.00-17.00; Nov-Feb Mon-Sun 9.00-16.30.
Admission: adult £9; child £6; family tickets from £28. Disabled visitors £6 (1 carers free). Under 3s free. Discounts for groups booked in advance, min 10. Car park £2. Pushchairs may be hired at entrance.

If you are a regular visitor it is worth considering membership, annual or life. This entitles holders to unlimited entry to Edinburgh Zoo and the Highland Wildlife Park, nr Aviemore, free parking and the use of the Member's House

A great day out for families. Set in over 80 acres of leafy hillside, the zoo has over 1000 animals, though no elephants or camels or giraffes at the time of writing. Constantly upgrading and improving enclosures, the Zoo aims to provide a more natural and stimulating environment for all the animals. It is also home of the world's largest penguin enclosure, complete with underwater viewing and video surveillance of nesting sites. The famous penguin parade takes place at 14:15 from Mar-Oct and 12:40 from Nov-Mar.

Even if it's raining, there is lots to see; for example in the primate and reptile houses and in the 'Magic Rainforest', a covered habitat for tiny monkeys. At various times throughout the day the animals are fed, which is always exciting for children. There are also informative talks and animal demonstrations showing natural behaviour throughout the day in the summer months with keepers on hand to answer any questions.

There are a number of play areas throughout the zoo: the Ark, just opposite the red ruffed lemur enclosure has a rope bridge, slide and stepping stones.

Near the chimpanzee outdoor enclosure, there's a frame which helps children 'ape' the chimps – it has a slide,

fireman's pole, hanging bridge and climbing bars. Nearby is a smaller play area especially for children under 5 years, with a small slide and easy climbing frame.

At the top of the hill, near the hilltop safari drop-off point, is a large play area suitable for children of all ages from 3 – 14. There's a new colourful activity climbing frame right in front of the penguins on the Penguin Lawn.

During Easter and Summer holidays there are activities to interest older children, eg brass rubbing and animal handling sessions (min age 3). The Darwin Centre is a tortoise shaped maze and covered picnic area. Several other picnic sites, self-service restaurants and numerous kiosks, ice cream, confectionery, soft drinks, are situated throughout the Zoo. Most kiosks are closed outside of the summer months. There are two gift shops selling toys, gifts and books with an animal theme.

Access is generally good for pushchairs although the push to the top of the Zoo should be taken in easy stages. The hilltop safari, which is free though they ask for a voluntary donation, takes you to the top of the hill, allowing you to take the easy route downhill. There is a Members' entrance from the car park which can save some pushing as it is higher than the main entrance. Wrap up warm in the winter.

There are several toilets throughout the area as well as in restaurants. Nappy changing facilities available.

PLACES TO EAT

The Den

Summer only, Mon-Sun 10.30-17.45.

££, high chairs, breastfeeding welcome, bottles heated, nappy changing surface, seats 200, licensed, children's menu.

Self-service snack bar. Range of light meals and snacks. Sell children's snack boxes. May be used for picnics.

Stripes

Summer: Mon-Sun 10.30-17.45.
Winter: Mon-Sun 10.30-in line with Zoo closure.

££, high chairs (4), bottles heated, nappy changing surface, seats 120, licensed, children's menu.

Large self-service restaurant serving a variety of hot meals, such as fish and chips, Cumberland sausages etc, and snacks all day. Sell children's snack boxes.

If you go in either of these cafes later in the afternoon during high season, they're not always particularly tidy or clean – that includes the loos.

Mansion House

Mon-Sun 10.00-17.00. Winter closing in line with Zoo closure.

££, High chairs (3), parties hosted, licensed,

Light meals and full luncheon facilities; tables can be reserved by phone. It's recommended that you phone in advance to check that the Mansion house is open on the day you're visiting. Nappy changing (M&F). See also Birthdays and Celebrations.

Upstairs there is a coffee lounge where members can enjoy light sandwich-type lunches. Children's menu available. Great views over the Zoo to the Pentland Hills.

There are six kiosks dotted around the zoo, where you can buy ice cream, sweets, drinks and fruit. Some also sell batteries, sun protection cream, insect repellent and rain ponchos.

The zoo also has three picnic areas: they are situated at the hilltop, in front of the Mansion House, and on the terrace which overlooks the maze. There's also the 'grillin' and chillin' concession outside the Maze Terrace, which serves burgers.

Gorgie City Farm
51 Gorgie Road
Tel: 337 4202
Email: gorgiefarm@compuserve.com

Getting there: Lothian bus 3, 3A, 25, 33. By car, farm lies on Gorgie Rd, which is a busy thoroughfare. There is limited free parking, though you can also park reasonably near in adjoining roads.

Opening times: Mon-Sun 9.30-16.30 (16.00 in winter). Closed Christmas Day and New Year's Day.

Admission: free - donation box. Guided tours can be arranged in advance for a modest charge: contact the Education Officer (Tel: 623 7031) or the Farm for details.

Especially suitable for visits by small children, this community farm is on a one-hectare site, which used to be the main refuse collection point for the city, not far from the city centre. There is a wide range of animals including sheep, goats, a Jersey cow, Shetland ponies, pigs, ducks, hens, bantams and pheasants. Also a large organic vegetable garden, a herb garden, a wildlife garden and an Education Centre. In the Pet Lodge visitors can see a range of pets - rabbits, guinea pigs, finches, budgerigars, hamsters, fish and tortoises kept in good conditions. There is a small children's play area with adjacent picnic area and a tractor to climb on. The animals (and staff!) are friendly and provide an ideal opportunity for children to see farm animals at close range in a suitable environment. Special events and activities are organised at different times. All areas are accessible for pushchairs. Farm has toilets for the disabled and nappy changing facilities.

There is a café attached to the farm called Jemima's Pantry, which hosts birthday parties. See Birthdays and Celebrations.

CLOSE TO HOME

East Lothian

East Links Family Park and Narrow Gauge Railway

Tel: 01368 863607
Mob: 0777 571 3646
Email: grant@eastlinks.fsnet.co.uk
Web: www.eastlinks.fsnet.co.uk

Getting there: 1/2 mile off A1 at Thistly Cross roundabout, next to West Barns Village and John Muir Country Park.

Opening times: 10.00-17.00, until 18.00 during school summer holidays.

Admission: adult £6.50; children over 2years & concessions £5.50; family.

(2+2) £22. Group discounts available.

Entrance fee allows unlimited use of facilities during day.

Set in 20 acres of farmland this has everything for a fantastic day out for all the family, particularly the under 5s. All the activities are located close to the main entrance and include a giant sand-filled pirate ship with sand diggers, pedal tractors and roller racers, soft play, bouncy castle and trampolines; giant children's rabbit warren, flying fox, go-carts, milk can skittles, horseshoe pitching and a 2 acre woodland maze etc etc. More attractions are planned for the coming years.

A lovely narrow gauge railway train takes you on a safari round the whole site, through the animal enclosures, who eagerly await the feed thrown to them by the passengers.

There are lots of farm animals for the children to see, including a field of llamas. There are also lots of small animals such as rabbits and chipmunks.

Pony rides cost £1 when available.

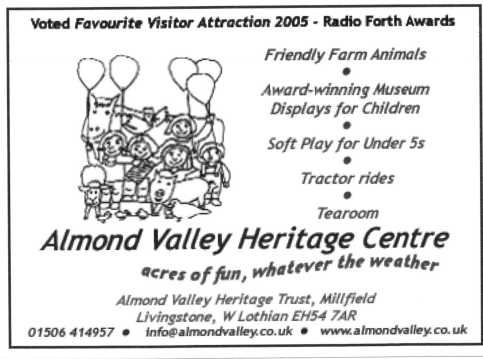

The Picnic Barn provides a under cover area to enjoy your picnic. Schools groups, Birthday Parties and Children's clubs can all book tables in this area for their lunches also.

A well appointed Tea-room can provide healthy lunches for children and parents. Birthday parties can be hosted in the picnic
barn and are welcome to bring their own picnic or the tea-room can provide the catering.

Other facilities include ample car parking, a shop, and toilets including nappy change facilities.

Fort East Links is being built for the 2006 season.

NB Bring this copy of Edinburgh for Under Fives on your visit and you'll receive a free bag of feed for the animals.

West Lothian

Almond Valley Heritage Centre
Millfield
Livingston
Tel: 01506 414957
Email: info@almondvalley.co.uk
Web: www.almondvalley.co.uk
Getting there: by car: Almond Valley is well signposted from junction 3 of the M8 with brown 'Almond Valley Heritage Centre' signs. After J3 follow the A899 towards Livingston, turn off at the A705 and follow this road to the Mill roundabout, then take the first left onto the B7015 and Almond Valley is on the first turning to the right.

By train and bus: for up to date information on train and bus times call the West Lothian travel line on 01506 775288.

Opening times: all year, 10.00-17.00, except 25th/26th Dec &1st/2nd Jan.

Admission: Adult £3.00; children aged 3 -16 and senior citizens £2.00; family ticket (2A & 4C) £10.00. Under 3s free.

An award winning museum, farm and discovery centre where all the family can spend the day together exploring and having fun. The 18th century mill and farm buildings are home to a range of farm animals, such as lambs and chicks in the spring, and milking displays. There is plenty of space to play safely indoors and out. Under 5s can enjoy a play tractor course and indoor soft play area while over 5s can let off some steam in the adventure zone. Train and tractor rides are available at the weekends and most days during July and August. Most weekends and school holidays there are crafts, experiments and activities in the discovery centre. Inside the museum there are levers to

pull and tunnels to explore while discovering the secrets of West Lothian's past. There is also a programme of special events throughout the year such as Spooky Happenings for Halloween and Santa's Winter Wonderland especially for Christmas.

Other facilities: gift shop, picnic tables, tea room with high chairs, good nappy changing facilities. Children's parties available and group bookings welcome.

FURTHER AFIELD

Angus

Brechin Castle Centre
Brechin
Angus DD9 6SG.
Tel: 01356 626813
Email: enquiries@brechincastlecentre.co.uk
Web: www.brechincastlecentre.co.uk

Getting there: off the A90, mid-way between Dundee and Aberdeen.

Opening times: Summer Mon-Sat 9.00-18.00, Sun 10.00-18.00; Winter.

Mon-Sat 9.00-17.00 Sun 10.00-17.00.

Admission: A £2.00; C / OAP: £1.00; Family (2 adults, 2 children or 1A + 3C): £5.00; Season ticket: £20.00.

Large complex with various points of interest: the main ones on our visit were the model farm and the play park. The model farm has range of animals, including horses, sheep, goats, rabbit, guinea pigs etc. There are also displays of vintage farm equipment (lots of big wheels and old tractors!).

The recently installed Dragon's Lair playpark has imaginative equipment which provides lots of opportunity for climbing and sliding.

There is also a miniature railway which runs, weather permitting, in the summer 12.00-16.00, plus a large ornamental lake.

There is also a garden centre , which is of nominal or minimal interest for the under 5s and a shop area, which sells a range of children's books, as well as some clothing (nice wellies!), foods, and kitchenware.

Coffee Shop
£-££, high chairs (4), baby food and bottles warmed, seats 240

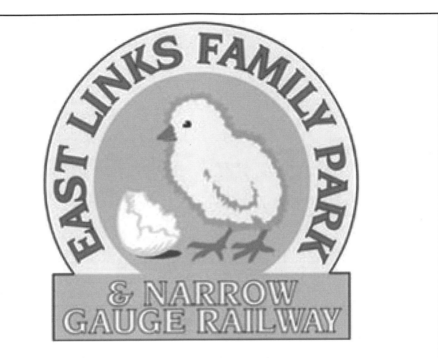

Enjoy a fun-filled family day out

* Train Safari
* Soft Play
* Pedal Tractors
* Toboggan Run
* Horshoe Pitching
* Kids' Rabbit Warren
* Milk Can Skittles

* Farm Animals
* Bouncy Castle
* Roller Racers
* Go-Karting
* Giant Maze
* Fish Nursery
* Trampolines

Near Dunbar
Tel: 01368 863607
or visit
www.eastlinks.co.uk

Proud to support Edinburgh for Under Fives & the NCT

Large, airy coffee shop selling a range of snacks and hot food – the portions were huge when we were there, so it might be worth bearing that in mind.
Nappy changing (M&F)

The Borders

Jedforest Deer and Farm Park
Tel: 01835 840364
Website: www.aboutscotland.com/jedburgh
Getting there: follow A68 south, 5 miles from Jedburgh, signposted on main road, turn off right and travel mile to 1st farm you come to.
Opening times: Easter-Aug 10.00-17.30; Sep-Oct 11.00-16.30.
Admission: adult £4; child £2.50; family ticket £12. Under 5s free.

Farm includes deer such as white Red deer, red deer and muntjacs, plus many rare varieties of most farm animals, such as Soay sheep, Belted Galloway cattle and Tamworth pigs. There is a 'clapping' area where children can touch and sometimes help to bottle feed animals. Walks in wooded area following colour-coded signs lasting 1/2 -1 1/2 hrs.

Large and small adventure playgrounds. Ranger Activities available according to season: mini-beast hunts, tree safari, pond dipping, crafts.
Falconry Scotland is also based in the farm park.
Barbecues for hire, picnic area, cafe with high chair and shop.

Café:
£-££, high chair , no smoking, 1/2 portions available for children, seats 40 inside, more outside.
The café is self-service and provides sandwiches, soup and cakes. Breastfeeding friendly. M&F nappy changing facilities, child friendly, play areas include indoor tractors. Prams and pushchairs can be parked inside the premises. All facilities on ground floor. Children's parties hosted, includes owl treasure hunt.
See also Birthdays and Celebrations.

Fife

Fife Animal Park
Tel: 01337 831830
Getting there: by Auchtermuchty, on B937 half a mile S of A91 Milnathort to St Andrews road.

Opening times: Apr-May, daily 10:00-18:00; Jun- end of Aug daily 10:00-19:00; Sep – Mar, daily, 10.00 – 16.00.
Admission: Adult £3.50; child £3.00; conc. £3.00; Family £11.00.

Over 150 animals. See ostrich eggs, rabbits and newly hatched chicks. Exhibition and information area, as well as 2 play areas, trampolines and an outdoor trail. All facilities fully accessible with pushchairs, and play areas fully enclosed. Small animal room where you can handle animals.
Restaurant with high chairs and children's menu. Free parking.

Kathellan
Kelty
Fife
KY4 0JR
Tel: 871 226 2218
Web: www.kathellan.co.uk
Getting there: follow the M90 and take the turn off at Junction 4. Take a left hand turn once at the top of the junction, Kathellan is located to the left hand side of the road.

Opening times: Mon-Fri 10.00-17.00, Sat 9.30-18.00, Sun 11.00-18.00.

Kathellan combines a fine food shop, a bookshop and a farm park amongst other things. The Farm Park is home to a range of rabbits and chickens as well as a wide range of rare breeds, including sheep and goats; there are also Shetland ponies and a family herd of the extremely rare Eriskay ponies. All the animals are extremely inquisitive and the fact that a bag of feed per person is included in the small entrance fee to the farm means your child will see every breed close up (Take heed of the notices and don't feed the pigs); 5p of each ticket goes to the Rare Breeds Survival Trust.
Shop sells a good range of marinades, spices, preserves etc., and has a well-stocked deli counter. Also sells toys, quality gifts and books.
There is a small adventure playground, with balances and hanging hoops as well as swings. Bark-based.

Kathellan Restaurant
Opening times: Mon-Fri 10.00-17.00, Sat 9.30-18.00, Sun 9.30-18.00.
£-££, seats a wide range of food, from coffees to breakfasts (9.00-11.30), lunches and dinners. Food is freshly prepared and there's a good range of options, including vegetarian.

Children are provided with a huge colour-in menu sheet to keep them busy. Nappy changing (M&F).

The Scottish Deer Centre
Tel: 01337 810391
Getting there: On A91, 4 miles before Cupar. Cupar lies on the A91. Stagecoach operates buses from Edinburgh, St Andrew's Square bus terminus to Cupar and past the Deer Centre.

Opening times:
Park: Apr-Oct 10.00-18.00; Oct-Apr 10.00-17.00.
Shop: Apr-Oct 10.00-17.30; Oct-Apr 10.00-16.30
Admission: adult £5.10; child £3.55; concession £4.10. Various family tickets also available.

There's a deer farm walk to meet the deer, nature trail, picnic area, aerial walkway. Etc. There are also falconry displays three times a day, and trailer rides in summer. Covered all-weather adventure barn. Superb outdoor adventure playground. Restaurant, coffee shop and shops.

Vane Farm Nature Reserve
By Loch Leven
Tel: 01577 862355

On B9097, S of shore of Lochleven, 1 mile E of M90, J5
Centre open daily 10 :00- 17:00. Closed 25,26 Dec, 1,2 Jan. Reserve open at all times.

Admission: adult £3; Concession £2; child 50p. Family (2A & 6C) £6. Under 5s free. RSPB members free. Free entry to visitor centre, observation area and shop
NB. No dogs allowed on RSBP reserves.

RSPB reserve with bright and cheerful observation area/visitor centre with binoculars and telescopes set up, display touch and sound boxes for children, shop and toilets (M/F nappy changing). Two nature trails: one climbing through birch woodland to the top of Vane Hill and one a grassy wetland walk, so not suitable for pushchairs and – stout footwear is essential! The wetland trail is on a reasonably robust path suitable for toddlers upwards. There are 3 hides – the Gilman hide is a large wooden hut with great colourful wooden birds for children to look at and feel and worth the walk along the trail – good for a rainy day. Nest boxes have been put up to encourage birds to nest. The geese that overwinter on Loch Leven can be observed from a hide. There are other hides for serious birdwatchers. View of loch and picnic area.

The reserve has 10 'explorer rucksacks' to loan, containing all kinds of examination devices, such as bug boxes, binoculars, tape measures, magnifying glasses and blindfolds so you can identify things by feel!
Café:
£-££, highchairs (2)
Situated in observation area. has children's books for reading, and the friendly staff and volunteers serve warming fare such as soup and baked potatoes, as well as rolls and afternoon teas. Limited children's menu.

Vane Farm hosts the Scottish Wildlife & Countryside Fair in September. Free car parking at this fair.
Hot and cold snacks – no dogs as it's on RSPB land.

Perthshire

Auchingarrich Wildlife Centre
Comrie, Perthshire
Tel: 01764 679 469

Getting there: easy to find. Take M9 past Stirling to A9. From A9, take A822 towards Crieff, then 2nd turn off on to B827, then follow signs to Wildlife Centre.
Opening times: daily, 10.00-dusk. Coffee shop closes at 17.00.
Admission: adult £5.00; child £4.00; under 3s free; family £18.00.

Wildlife centre set in the beautiful Perthshire hills. There's a fantastic range of animals to be seen, from Highland cattle to meerkats and maras! All the main attractions are under cover and linked by tarmac pathways. There are some areas specifically for under 5s, where they can meet and touch friendly animals. There's also an indoor playbarn with picnic tables, which has a separate area for under 5s – ideal for rainy days. Outdoor playpark comes complete with sandpit, buckets and spades. The Pine Lodge coffee shop serves snacks.

Stirling

Blairdrummond Safari Park & Adventure Park
Blairdrummond
By Stirling   FK9 4UR
Tel: 01786 841456
Getting there: leave M9 at J10 and take A84 for about 3 miles.

Opening times: Apr-Oct 10.00-17.30. Last admission 16.30.

Admission: adult £9.50; OAP/child £5.50. Under 3s free. Prices include most attractions.

Exciting day out with lots to do. Drive through park to see wild animals – lions, tigers, elephants, rhinos etc. Drive takes about 1/2hr and may be uncomfortable on a hot day with the windows closed. Farm/domestic animals – pigs, goats, llamas – in field through which you can walk and touch animals. Facilities for washing hands afterwards are provided. The performing sea lion show is very entertaining. Also a bird of prey show.

Elevated walkway for viewing bears below.

Large adventure playground is suitable for toddlers and older children. Includes 'pirate ship' for climbing and sand area with buckets and spades. Also larger climbing areas for older children. Face painting (extra charge). Amusement park (extra charges) featuring dragon ride, dodgems, bouncy castle etc. Also 5-seater pedal boats and 'flying fox' (no extra charge).

Restaurant with good range of food, high chairs. Tables inside and outdoors. Tables for your own picnics and DIY barbecue area. Private area available for breastfeeding. M&F nappy changing. Park closes 3rd Oct each year.

Inverness

Highland Wildlife Park
Kincraig, Kingussie
Inverness-shire PH21 INL
Tel: 01540 651270
Web: www.highlandwildlifepark.org

Opening times: Apr-May, Sep-Oct 10.00-18.00 (last entry 16.00); June-Aug 10.00-19.00 (last entry 17.00); Nov-Mar 10.00-16.00 (last entry 14.00). Phone ahead if weather is inclement.

Admission: A £8.50; C & students £6.00; Senior Citizens £7.50; family ticket available.

If you're up North, take a trip to the Highland Wildlife Park. You can view animals there that you won't see anywhere else in Scotland, such as Przewalski horses, wolves, European elk and bison. There are also smaller animals, such as beavers, otters, polecats etc.

Café
£-££. Serves a range of snacks and hot food.

HISTORIC PLACES

IN TOWN

Greyfriars Tolbooth and Highland Kirk
Greyfriars Place, Top of Candlemaker Row
Tel: 225 1900
Tel: 226 5429 (Visitors Officer)

Sun services 11.00, Gaelic service 12.30. Kirkyard open 8.00-22.00 daily.

Kirk visitor centre open Easter-Oct Mon-Fri 10.30-16.30,Sat 8.00-16.00 (Due to re-open for visitors Easter 2004).

Edinburgh's first reformed church completed in 1620 – first used on Christmas Day of that year. The kirk provides the only weekly Gaelic service in the South East of Scotland.

Fine 17th century funeral monuments in kirkyard, along with mausoleums and the Martyrs' Memorial, which is dedicated to some 18000 Covenanters who died for their faith.

However, now it's a secluded and peaceful stop in the city centre, much used for picnics at lunchtime as there are sandwich bars in the vicinity. While there are no park benches in the kirkyard at present, the city council is considering installing some.

A statue dedicated to Greyfriars Bobby is situated opposite the kirk gates, at the junction of Candlemaker Row and George IV Bridge. The story of the faithful dog is always popular – and to prove it's true, both Bobby and his master are buried in the churchyard.

Information, souvenirs and audio-visual programme available in kirk visitor centre. Greyfriars also offers visits for groups of nursery age children. Tel: 226 5429 to arrange a visit – the visitor officer will ensure that one of the staff on duty is a story-teller for the young.

John Knox House & Scottish Storytelling Centre

The Netherbow
43 High Street
Tel: 557 5724
Opening hours: phone for current opening hours.
Admission: adult £3.00; child £1.00; concession £2.00.

John Knox House re-opened in late 2005, the first part of the major refurbishment of the Netherbow. While Knox's house doesn't really hold much of interest for under 5s, they might like the actual look of the building, with its plaques and motto stones. Once reopened, the Netherbow, should boast new facilities.

St Giles' Cathedral
High Street
Tel: 225 9442 (visitor services manager)
Web: www.stgilescathedral.org.uk

Opening times: Summer (May-Sep) Mon–Fri 9.00-19.00pm, Sat 9.00-17.00, Sun 13.00-17.00. Winter (Oct-Apr): Mon-Sat 9.00-17.00, Sun 13.00-17.00
NB at any time access may be restricted without notice
Services: Mon-Sat at mid-day, Sun 8.00, 10.00, 11.30 and 20.00
Musical recital at 18.00 on Sun.
Admission: suggested donation of £1 per adult visitor.

A landmark on the Royal Mile. There's over 1000 years of history in St Giles' – John Knox was minister there, there have been riots, executions and demonstrations all around it (and some inside it!), but under 5s may be more interested in the coloured stained glass windows. Free tours and lunchtime concerts. There's a souvenir shop, to mark your visit, and a café, The Lower Aisle, can be accessed on its Southern side – see Eating Out.

FURTHER AFIELD

The Borders

Jedburgh Abbey (HS)
Tel: 01835 863925
Web: www.historic-scotland.gov.uk
Getting there: take the A68 from Edinburgh. Jedburgh is an historic town, set in the heart of the Borders.
Opening times: 25 Mar-30 Sep Mon-Sun 9.30-18.30 (last entry 18.00); 1 Oct-end March Mon-Sun 9.30-16.30 (last entry 16.00). Closed 25, 26 Dec and 1, 2 Jan.
Admission: adult £4.00; child £1.60; concession £3.00. Under 5s free.
Impressive building, founded in 1138. Visitor centre which houses many priceless artefacts found during excavations at the site. Cloister and herb garden. There is also an interactive area.

Car park. Toilets. Shop. Reasonable access with pushchair. Picnic area.

Melrose

This town can be lovely spot to break off a longer journey, or for a day trip. The town nestles below the Eildon Hills – fairy hills or the resting place of King Arthur and his Knights, if you believe the tales. Ideal for a gentle stroll along the streets – though the town sits on a rise. Plenty signed parking areas. Cafés, baker shops etc. Some rather nice ice cream shops too! Public toilets nr the Abbey.
Take the A7 or A68 from Edinburgh. First Bus services cover this – no. 62 is an hourly service from 8.25-19.25 Mon-Sat, very irregular on Sundays. National Cycle Route 1.

Melrose Abbey (HS)
Tel: 01896 822562
Opening times: 25 Mar-30 Sep Mon-Sun 9.30-18.30 (last entry 18.00); 1 Oct-end March Mon-Sun 9.30-16.30 (last entry 16.00). Closed 25, 26 Dec and 1, 2 Jan.

Admission: adult £4.00; child £1.60; concession £3.00. Under 5s free.

Majestic ruins with plenty of intricate carving to admire. Robert the Bruce's heart is allegedly buried in the Abbey grounds – a recent plaque marks the spot. you can see them along an ajoining path, rather than going in, if you prefer, as there is little really to interest under 5s.

Priorwood Garden and Dried Flower Shop (NTS)
Tel: 01896 822 493
Located near the Abbey.
Opening times: 1 Apr-24 Dec. Times vary with season. Phone for current opening info.
Admission: A £3.00, C/concession £2, Under 5s free. Family ticket available.

Specialist garden, where the flowers grown are all ideal for drying. You can enjoy a walk through the orchard – and take a picnic here in the summer. Gift shop sells large range of NTS merchandise as well as dried flower gifts.

If you leave Melrose and head out towards Dryburgh Abbey on the B6404, then the B6356, then you'll see a sign for the Wallace's statue – but keep your eyes peeled. Park in the little car park and walk along the pathway. Keep walking, you turn a corner and you come across a huge statue of William Wallace (dressed in Greco-Roman finery!), staring out across the landscape toward the border with England. Certainly not worth the trip in itself, but if you're passing the area anyway, it's an odd thing that children remember seeing.

MUSEUMS

IN TOWN

Museum of Childhood
42 High Street
Royal Mile EH1 1TQ
Tel: 529 4142
Opening times: Mon-Sat 10.00-17.00, Sun 12.00-17.00 during July and August.
Admission: free.

The first museum of its kind devoted, to the history of childhood. A wonderful collection of trains, boats, planes, dolls, teddy bears and many, many more playthings of the past are displayed in 5 galleries. Hands-on exhibits and activities have recently been added to give children more things to do in the museum. Gallery 1 has a few coin-operated working models including a nickelodeon. Gallery 2 has a rocking horse and hands-on puppets, trains and optical toys for children to use. Gallery 3 has dolls and teddy bears on display with feely boxes, games, a doll's house and family activity sheet. Gallery 4 has board games, a reading corner and a Lego wall for children to use. Gallery 5 has several period room sets with sound effects and a dressing up box. The museum also has different temporary exhibitions running throughout the year.
It is encouraging to see some of the displays at low level, suitable for viewing by small children. In spite of the recent additions mentioned small children may get bored. The museum is partly suitable for pushchairs but there are many steps and it can become very congested. It is requested that pushchairs are left downstairs at the owner's own risk. There is a lift between galleries 1, 2 and 3, ramps to gallery 3; public toilets are in gallery 4. There is a good shop at the entrance, which sells 'old fashioned' small toys/gifts; wooden, tin, paper, posters etc. There are There are nappy changing facilities in the toilets for the disabled, access with a uniformed attendant by the lift to the basement.

Newhaven Heritage Museum
24 Pier Place EH6 4LP
Tel: 551 4165
Getting there: by Lothian Bus10,11 and 16 from Princes St, 7 from The Bridges and 32/32a on the Outer Circle.

Opening times: Mon-Sun 12.00-16.45 (last admission 16.30). Admission: free

A small museum, which tells the story of Newhaven through reconstructed sets of fishwives and fishermen, displays of objects and photographs, written and spoken accounts. Both children and adults can dress up as fisherfolk. There are wooden cutouts of a fisherman and fishwife to stick through your head and look at yourself in the mirror opposite.
The museum also has two 'feely' boxes, one with a 'palm' used by sailmakers and one with a buoy. There is also a tray of shells which can be handled. Small shop selling sea related items, some at pocket-money prices. Friendly staff.
There are no toilets and no public ones nearby, although there are catering facilities nearby. Brewsters, a few minutes walk has a soft play area.

The People's Story
Canongate Tolbooth
163 Canongate EH8 8BN
Tel: 529 4057
Opening times: Mon-Sat 10.00-17.00; Sun 14.00-17.00 during Festival.
Admission: free

A fascinating museum tracing the lives, work and pastimes of the city's ordinary people from late 1700s to present day. The displays include a series of reconstructions – a fishwife, a joiner up a ladder, a servant cleaning a grate, prisoners in a cell, a tearoom and a washhouse. These are all enhanced by smells and sounds as well as photographs and displays of everyday objects which under 5s can appreciate, though on the whole it will be better appreciated by older children.
A 22-min video complements the story line. A lift allows pushchair access to 1st floor. The next level is just a few steps further up but the video room is reached by a spiral stone staircase. Pushchairs may be left at front desk. Counter selling postcards, pencils, badges, toys etc. Roomy toilets for the disabled may be used for nappy changing, where there is a fold-down nappy- changing table, a bin for putting nappies in and also a nappy vending machine.

Royal Museum
Chambers Street
Tel: 247 4422
Web: www.nms.ac.uk/royal

Opening times: Mon-Sat 10.00 - 17.00; Sun 12.00 - 17.00. Late opening Tue (to 20.00). Closed Dec 25 (as is MoS).

Admission: free (there is a charge for special exhibitions). Membership of NMS is available, which offers a variety of benefits, such as free entry to charging exhibitions etc. The price is £20/adult, £28/couple, £34/family.
Children's tours are on Saturdays and Sundays at 14.30 with different topics each day.

This is definitely much more than a rainy-day option! A fabulous museum with plenty to interest and amuse under 5s. This vast, awe inspiring Victorian building houses international collections of Decorative Arts, Science and Industry, Archaeology and the Natural World. In children's terms this means: loads of fantastic stuffed animals, old fashioned toys, mummies and lots more. In the main foyer, there's the Millennium Clock, which chimes at 11.00 (not Sunday), 12.00 14.00 and 16.00 daily. The display of figures and music is fascinating to watch, for young and old alike.

There are various temporary exhibitions throughout the year. There are also two fish ponds which are always our first port of call.
The main entrance involves a flight of steps but these can be avoided using the Tower entrance to the Museum of Scotland next door.
Everywhere has pushchair access with lifts to all floors.
Toilets and nappy changing facilities (in the toilets for the disabled) are available on the ground floor. There is a dedicated parent and baby room beside the female toilets, which is clean and spacious and has chairs for breastfeeding mothers.
The museum shop has a colourful children's section.
NMS members receive a 10% discount.

Café Delos
£-££
Located in the entrance hall serves drinks, cakes and substantial snacks (10.00-16.00 Mon, Wed-Sun, -19.30 Tue).

Soupson
£-££
Located at the rear of the building where children's lunchboxes are available as well as soup, baked potatoes,

pasta etc, as well as sandwiches and cakes. Soft drinks such as smoothies, fruit juices and water are on offer, as well as the fizzy options; and for the jaded parent, they offer 2 strengths of coffee. High chairs and booster seats available.

Museum of Scotland
Chambers Street
Tel: 247 4422
Web: www.nms.ac.uk/scotland
Opening times: Mon-Sat 10.00-17.00, Sun 12.00-17.00
Late opening Tue (to 20.00)

Admission: free
Membership available giving a variety of benefits. (see Royal Museum's entry, above)

This modern landmark was opened in 1998. The Museum presents the history of Scotland, its land, people and culture.

There are masses to engage under 5s - even the entrance foyer can prove to be a major part of the visit!
Of particular interest to children is the programme of Sunday events with activities for all the family.

In Beginnings on the lower ground level there is an experience which talks through the weather conditions, animals and habitat of Scotland. There are plenty of interactive displays here and throughout the museum. The Museum takes a journey through Early People, Kingdom of the Scots, Scotland Transformed and finally Industry and Empire. Other displays which may interest the under 5s include a thatched cottage, a coin store and the Silver Gallery – an entire room devoted to silver which sparkles when you walk in! Lift to roof terrace for views of the city.

Access to the building is easy for pushchairs and there are lifts to all floors. There are purpose built nappy changing facilities on the ground floor next to the shop and all adapted toilets on each floor have a pull down changing unit. The Tower Restaurant (£££) has more formal dining, but there are the two cafés situated on the ground floor of the Royal Museum next door.

The Writers' Museum
Lady Stair's Close
Lawnmarket
Royal Mile
Tel: 529 4901
Opening times: Mon-Sat 10.00-17.00, Sun 14.00-17.00 during Festival.
Admission: free.

Museum contains memorabilia and manuscripts relating to three of Scotland's great literary figures – Robert Burns, Sir Walter Scott and Robert Louis Stevenson. Also regular programme of temporary exhibitions covering other Scottish writers. The Museum is housed in a 17th century building with spiral stone staircases so is tricky for pushchairs. Nappy changing table in the ladies toilet which can be used by men on request. Best visited as parents of infants (perhaps in a papoose) as little of direct interest to children under 5, although there are plenty of visual items which older children will appreciate with a bit of parental interpretation - check out the trip step (a 17th century burglar alarm)!. However, the close and the courtyard outside has carved paving stones with famous lines from some of Scotland's greatest poets, and provides an interesting shortcut from the Mound on to the Royal Mile.

CLOSE TO HOME

East Lothian

Museum of Flight
East Fortune Airfield   EH39 5LF
Tel: 01620 880 308
Web: www.nms.ac.uk/flight
Getting there: museum is signposted off A1 on B1347 to North Berwick.

Opening times: daily mid-March-30 Oct 10.00-17.00; weekends only 31 Oct-mid Mar. Please check website for precise details – opening times change year on year.
Admission: adult £5; concessions £4; children (under 12s) free, plus Concorde Boarding Pass adult £3; concessions £2 and children (under 12s) £2. Admission free with National Museums of Scotland membership scheme card.

Man's fascination with flight comes to life at this list WW1 and WW2 airfield, now home to Scotland's Concorde. It's worthwhile checking the websites for information of one-off events and tie-ins with festivals etc. The museum hosts a full programme of events throughout the year.
Aviator Café, self-service, serves hot and cold snacks, including lunchboxes.
Opening times: Mon-Sun 10.00-16.30pm (1 Apr-31 Oct) In winter open during museum's opening hours. Nappy changing facilities are in the toilets for the disabled. There's also a museum shop.

Myreton Motor Museum
Aberlady EH32 0PZ
Tel 01875 870288
Getting thereto get to Aberlady, take A1 to Haddington then A6137 towards Aberlady.

Opening times: Daily 11.00-16.00 April-Oct. Nov - Mar Sat & Sun only 11.00 - 15.00.
Admission: adult £5; child £2. Under 5s free.

An interesting collection of bicycles, cars, motor cycles, and World War II military vehicles, among others. Also has displays of posters and toy cars and related memorabilia. Toilet, but no nappy changing facilities. Accessible to single but not to double pushchairs.

Midlothian

Scottish Mining Museum
Lady Victoria Colliery
Newtongrange   EH22 4QN
Tel: 663 7519
Email: enquiries@scottishminingmuseum.org
Web: www.scottishminingmuseum.com
Getting there: 10 miles S of Edinburgh on A7. From the eastern end of City Bypass, at Sherriffhall Roundabout follow signs for Newtongrange – approx 3 miles. Lothian bus no. 30, every 1/2 hr (45 mins).

Opening times: daily, 10.00-17.00 Last entry for tour 15.30. Phone for winter hours (can be shorter).

Admission: adult £4.95, child/ concession £3.30; family ticket £15. Under 5s free.

This purpose-built visitor centre has two floors of exhibitions, interactives, displays, buttons to press and magic helmets, so while young children might not understand the exhibition, there's a good chance that they'll still enjoy it. Families can enjoy Scotland's biggest steam engine and a simulated coalface, plus an Operations Centre full of activities.
Airy café is equipped with high chairs, and serves hot and cold meals throughout the day.
Children's outdoor play centre with Victorian toys (e.g. skittles). Gift shop. Toilets with nappy changing facilities (M&F), breastfeeding welcome. Pushchair access to all areas. Free car parking.

West Lothian

Queensferry Museum
53 High Street
South Queensferry
Tel: 331 5545
Getting there: First Edinburgh bus no 43 from Edinburgh Bus Station in St Andrews Square will take you there. Or follow signs for South Queensferry from the A90.

Opening times: Mon, Thu, Fri, Sat 10.00-13.00, 14.15-17.00; Sun 12.00-17.00. Last admission 30 mins before closing.
Admission: free.

The museum is dedicated to the local social history of Dalmeny and South Queensferry. There are displays on the Royal Burgh, aspects of life and leisure, the spectacular Forth Bridges and the unique local annual custom of the Burry Man. The shoreline of the Forth Estuary at South Queensferry provides a variety of wildlife, which can be explored using the museum's binoculars and the display showing the natural history of this area. There are other displays which are attractive to young children. Access is not possible with a pushchair and there are no dedicated facilities for children or for mothers who wish to breastfeed. However, there is a table with crayons and colouring in sheets.

FURTHER AFIELD

Fife

Abbot House Heritage Centre
Maygate
Dunfermline
Tel: 01383 733266
Web: www.abbothouse.co.uk

Opening times: daily all year 10.00-17.00.
Admission: adult £3.00, conc. £2.00. Accompanied children under 16 free.
The oldest house in Dunfermline: 'The People's Tardis'. Permanent displays of Dunfermline/Scottish life from the Picts to the 1960s and of famous people, such as Andrew Carnegie. Also hosts exhibitions and craft fairs. Upper floors unsuitable for pushchairs. However, the café with highchairs and the shop on the ground floor are accessible. Café has a 'sitooterie' with a view of the Abbey. Under 5s can play in the gardens and in the adjoining

Abbey grounds, but beware of attractive hazards such as the fountain.

M&F nappy changing facilities.

If you are lucky, you might see a 'royal' procession to the Abbey, as school parties can hire royal/court costumes. £1/child for school tour, plus £1/costume to fit age 9-10.

Kirkcaldy Museum & Art Gallery
War Memorial Gardens
Tel: 01592 412860

Getting there: 5 mins. from Kirkcaldy railway station
Opening times: Mon-Sat 10.30-17.00; Sun 14.00-17.00. admission: free.

This museum is lively, friendly and fully accessible to pushchairs and to disabled visitors with ramped access to main entrance and a lift to the first floor galleries. There is a local history display with some 'please touch' sections, galleries with temporary exhibitions and an outstanding collection of 18th to 20th century Scottish paintings. Gift shop. For further information, contact the Outreach Officer.

Café:
High chairs, breastfeeding welcomed. Nappy changing facility.

St Andrews Museum
Kinburn Park
Doubledykes Road, St. Andrews
Tel: 01334 412690

Opening times: Apr-Sep 10.00-17.00 daily; Oct – daily 10:30-16:00
Admission: free.

Small local museum in a park about 1/2 mile from the town centre. Previous researchers have described this as 'a great bolt-hole for a rainy day' – we arrived on a dreich day and would thoroughly agree! The exhibits are not wildly exciting for under 5s, but there is a basic activity room, for school parties (on 1st floor, lift available) which provided paper and crayons for under 5s to draw. Friendly and welcoming staff were another bonus to this visit. There is easy parking, a café in the museum, plus the surrounding parkland has putting in summer months, all-year tennis, and space to run about. The museum is totally accessible to prams & pushchairs: entry was via a ramp for the disabled located at the side of the building (you need to ask staff to open the side door). Nappy changing facilities and potties in both male & female toilets.

Café in the Park (within St Andrews Museum)
£, high chairs (2), breastfeeding welcome, non-smoking, children's menu & half portions available, provided with baby plates cutlery/cups; baby food/ bottles heated on request, unlicensed.

Ever-friendly staff in café serving very reasonably priced, wholesome, savoury food (dish of the day, light snacks, baked potatoes, vegetarian dishes) and cakes. Whilst you are unlikely to spot royalty, the carrot cake alone is worth the trek.

Falkirk

Callendar House
Callendar Park
Falkirk FK1 1YR
Tel: 01324 503770
Web: www.falkirkmuseums.gov.uk

Getting there: from M9, J5, turn left along the Laurieston Bypass. At the end, turn left, then right. Pass the grassy banking of the Antonine Wall and the park entrance is on your left, signposted, at a roundabout. For the House and Stables Tearoom, take 1st left past the high flats.

Opening times: Mon-Sat from 10.00, Sun (Apr-Sep) from 14.00. Last admissions 16.00.

Admission: adult £3.00; OAP £1.50; child (5-16 yrs) £1.00; under 5s free; family ticket (2A + 2C) £7.00.

Callendar House, the town's museum, is well worth a visit. Falkirk's location means that all sorts of Royal intrigues and battles took place here. The house is set in extensive grounds with play park and woodland trails. Inside the house are four 'interpretative areas' with costumed guides: the 1828 kitchen, the General Store, the Clockmaker's Workshop and the Printer's Workshop. You get to eat things in the kitchen and the general store and the staff are nice to everybody, including children who interrupt. There are also temporary exhibitions of art and history, as well as permanent displays . Shop selling handmade preserves and sweets and traditionally-made replicas of products from the famous Carron Ironworks. Toilets, including adapted ones suitable for disabled visitors, nappy changing unit.

Stirling

Bannockburn Heritage Centre (NTS)
Glasgow Road
Stirling   FK7 0LJ
Tel: 01786 812664

Getting there: leave M9 at J9 services and take A872 Stirling, Bannockburn HC, N for 1 mile.

Opening times: Mar-Oct 10.00-17.30; Feb-Mar and 8 Nov-23 Dec 10.30-16.00.

Admission: adult £5; child/concession £4; family ticket £14; single parent family £10. National Trust for Scotland Members free. Under 5s free.

This heritage centre is built near to the site of the Battle of Bannockburn, when the Scottish army led by Robert the Bruce defeated the English army and drove them out of Scotland. Displays, tableaux, model soldier layouts, and audio-visual presentation (lasts about 15 mins) of the build-up to the famous battle and the battle itself. Some gory bits! On certain days there is an actor who gives a living history presentation for added enjoyment although some of his weaponry and tales of bloody battles might alarm little ones. Brass rubbing. Various art materials available to make stained glass windows and Robert the Bruce's spider. Soldiers' helmets and period costumes (including very heavy chainmail for older ones and game parents) available for dressing up your very own 14th century warriors and peasants! Nappy changing facility in disabled toilet. Pushchair access and facilities for disabled people. Gift shop and small café with high chairs. Breastfeeding welcome.

The heritage centre is surrounded by grassy parkland that is ideal for children to run about on. A march up to the nearby monument to Robert the Bruce completes the visit.

OPEN TOP BUS TRIPS

City Sightseeing (all tours)
Tel: 0131 220 0770
Email: info@edinburghtour.com
Web: www.edinburghtour.com

Tours depart regularly from Waverley Bridge, give 'hop off-hop on' options and 24 hour tickets.. While the tours are all run by the same company at present, they offer slightly different experiences, and take slightly different routes round the city. You can buy tickets from the Tour bus drivers, Waverley Bridge ticket sellers, or from the Lothian Buses Travelshops at Waverley Bridge, Hanover Street & Shandwick Place.

City Sightseeing Tour
Look for the bright red buses. Tour offers an hour-long guided tour, available in 7 languages available. First tour departs 9.45 and then tours depart around every 20-30 mins.

Your ticket entitles you to discounted entry into various venues, museums and attractions. Prices from around £8.50/A, £ £2.50/C (5-15yrs). Under 5s are free. Family ticket (2A and up to 3C) from around £20.00. Prices may increase in 2006/7.

The Edinburgh Tour
This tour (on the green and cream liveried buses) offers trips round the city with a guide on-board. First tour leaves Waverley Bridge at 9.15, and then departures are every 20 mins. Tour takes in the city centre, a little bit of the New Town, and the Old Town, including the Scottish Parliament. Prices from around £8.50/A, £ £2.50/C (5-15yrs). Under 5s are free. Family ticket (2A and up to 3C) from around £20.00. Prices may increase in 2006/7. Again, there are discounts available with the ticket.

Mac Tours
This bus ride offers a similar tour to the Edinburgh Tour (with multilingual scripts in 7 languages and a live guide on-board), but this is on a vintage bus. Takes in parts of the Old and New Town of Edinburgh. For fares, see above.

The Majestic Tour
Look for the blue & gold buses. Tour includes the New Town, the Botanics, Newhaven, Ocean Terminal and the Royal Yacht Britannia, plus the Scottish Parliament building. Discounts for places and shops along the tour with the tickets, including 10% discount on entry to Britannia herself. Prices as above.

PARKS, COUNTRY PARKS and GARDENS

IN THE CITY

Calton Hill Park
Regent Road

Parking at top of hill, free for 30 mins.
Admission to park: free.

A good place for a run around, though caution is needed near road and car park. A grassy hill (355 ft) with many monuments, including the National Monument – based on the Parthenon – which was started in 1822 but never finished due to lack of funds. Fabulous panoramic views across the city. Popular kite flying spot. A large brass cannon provides enjoyable climbing for children as well as rocks to climb on and jump off. In the summer, an ice-cream van operates from the car park. Not recommended after dusk, despite the floodlit city panoramas, as the social dynamics completely change once evening falls.

There are two attractions to visit on Calton Hill, The City Observatory (Tel: 556 4365, open Easter-end Oct) and Nelson's Monument (Tel: 556 2716) though neither is really suitable for under fives.

Princes Street Gardens

The City's most famous park runs alongside Princes St under the lee of the castle. The park is a useful rest point for weary parents, mid-shopping, as there are plenty of seats and trees for shade on a sunny day.

It also provides an open space for toddlers to let off steam after the confines of the pushchair in the nearby department stores.

There are lawns, trees, flowerbeds and many statues & sculptures – to interest both parents and children. Look out for a tree with a hole through it, near the gardener's lodge in the West Gardens. The park's patrol officers will be pleased to point this out, or help you out with any other questions or problems. The gardens are locked at sunset or 22.00 (23.00 during the festival). Please note that dogs must be kept on a lead.

The presence of the railway line in the gardens is a bonus, especially the bridge behind the Ross Bandstand from which children can safely and easily see the trains coming and going and drivers usually oblige with a wave and a toot!

The gardens are a good place for a picnic: some stores on Princes St sell sandwiches, yoghurt, fruit, etc, and there are many sandwich shops on the likes of Frederick St, Hanover St and Rose St. Ice cream kiosks are dotted around the park.

The park is divided in two by the Mound. The East Gardens may be accessed from the Mound, Waverley Bridge and Princes St. Access to the lower level of the gardens is via steps at the Mound end and via a steep sloping path at the Waverley end. The Scott Monument, a Victorian, high-gothic memorial to the author Sir Walter Scott – and a convenient landmark – can be climbed for an admission fee. The spiral stairs are very steep and narrow near the top and would probably not be enjoyed by small children or mothers-to-be! Next to the Scott Monument is a kiosk selling sweets, ices, hot and cold drinks to take away. There are plenty of pigeons, sparrows and squirrels to feed and some of the kiosks sell nuts and pigeon food. The station platforms and trains can be viewed from the path at the side of the National Gallery.

The East Gardens are the venue for Edinburgh's Winter Wonderland (see Annual Events) with ice rink, children's fairground rides and food kiosks.

Nearest toilets (open 8.00-22.00) are by the Mound, ladies (with nappy-changing facilities) and toilets for the disabled to the East side, gents down steps on the West side of the Mound, near the Floral Clock.

The West Gardens can be accessed from the Mound, Princes St, Johnstone Ter and King's Stables Rd. The famous Floral Clock, next to the steps down to the park at the junction of Princes St and the Mound is a source of delight for both children and adults alike. The clock is composed of up to 35,000 small plants and functions all year round except when being replanted although this can be worth watching in itself. A cuckoo emerges briefly from a wooden house every quarter hour. It was the original idea of an Edinburgh clockmaker in 1903 and there are now copies all over the world including one in Napier, New Zealand. There are several rain shelters at the Mound end of the gardens, close to the foot of the Floral Clock steps.

Be ready to listen out the Castle's 1 o'clock gun – it is loud and might give you a fright if you're not prepared for it. There is some vehicle traffic in the gardens especially when the Ross Bandstand is being used, but many under 5s will enjoy admiring forklift trucks and the gardener's tractors.

The Ross Bandstand is situated in the middle of the West Gardens. This is used for various events throughout the year including Scottish Country Dance evenings (late May to early August). During the Edinburgh Festival Fringe there are events and entertainment usually daily. Also during the summer festivals a carousel and a bungee dome usually operate near the Ross Fountain.

Over the railway, the South side of the gardens is less formal, with a steep grassy slope leading up to the castle. The slope is covered with daffodils in the spring. There is a gate into the castle esplanade via a steep zigzag path with steps, but the gate can be locked at times (especially during the Edinburgh Military Tattoo). There is a level entrance to the Gardens from King's Stables Rd, opposite the multi-storey car park and a sloped entrance from Johnstone Ter, round the side of the castle. These paths join up and cross a railway footbridge (no view of trains) into the gardens near the playground. A path also leads from the bridge, alongside the railway to another bridge (excellent view of trains) at the Ross Bandstand and then further on along a path leading up over the railway alongside the Mound and back to the Floral Clock.

Toilets are near the playground with nappy changing facilities. The key can be obtained from the attendant on duty from 10.00-22.00 (except from 15.00-16.00 when they are closed for cleaning). Note: there is no ramp up to Princes St from these toilets. Also toilets at the Ross Bandstand (open summer only 8.00-20.00, no nappy-changing facilities).

Royal Botanic Garden
East Gate on Inverleith Row and
West Gate on Arboretum Place
Tel: 552 7171

Car parking on 3 sides of the gardens (restricted on Inverleith Row); easiest on Arboretum Pl.
Opening times: Daily, except 25 Dec and 1 Jan.
Opening times: Daily, except 25 Dec and 1 Jan.
Mar: 10.00 - 18.00 (cleared at 17.45).
Apr-Sep: 10.00-19.00 (cleared at 18.45).
Oct: 10.00 - 18.00 (cleared at 17.45).
Nov-Feb: 10.00-16.00 (cleared at 15.45).
Admission: free

An immaculate, beautifully landscaped and well sign posted garden. Dogs are not allowed so there is no problem with dog fouling. There is no cycling allowed but there are cycle racks at the west gate. Abundant grassy

areas, flat and sloped and tarred paths. There is a pond where you can feed the ducks, moorhen and swans, and where occasionally a heron can be seen. The shop at the west gate sells sunflower seeds to feed the very tame squirrels. The rockery area has a waterfall and lots of winding paths, some suitable for pushchairs. The Chinese garden has a pagoda next to a small pond and path winding up the slope with small bridges over a 'mountain stream'. Other themed areas, such as alpine, cryptogamic and herbaceous may interest the older child and parents; or just enjoy the extra space and gardens. Unfortunately no picnics are allowed.

The Glasshouse Experience
Open daily, except 25 Dec and 1 Jan
Mar & Oct 10.00-17.30
Apr-Sep: 10.00-18.30
Nov-Feb: 10.00-15.30
Admission: Adult £3.50 (conc. £3.00); Child (5-14) £1.00.
Under 5s free

There is only one entrance to the glasshouses – all other doors are exit only. Leaflets are available. Pushchairs can be left at the cash desk as the displays are on two levels – with quite a few sets of steps – and some paths between plants are quite narrow. Some ponds have no railings so hold on to active youngsters. There are old and new glasshouses, at various temperatures and humidities, and a small aquarium.

Inverleith House in the centre of the garden, houses a botanical art gallery with a programme of historical and contemporary exhibitions. No pushchairs or prams allowed.

Botanic Garden education staff lead guided tours and provide resource material for school parties. They are willing to give advice to playgroup and nursery teachers and adapt their materials to suit parties of younger children. Tel: 552 7175.

The shop at the West Gate has a range of goods suitable for younger children starting to learn about the environment. Toilets at the Glasshouses, Inverleith House and the West Gate. Nappy changing and feeding facility at the East Gate; ask the Park constabulary there to give you a key.

There is an ice cream kiosk at the West Gate and often an ice cream van parked across from the West Gate at the entrance to Inverleith Park.

The Terrace Café sits in the centre of the Gardens It's a popular meeting place for parents with small babies and toddlers, has nappy changing facilities and is a relaxed place to breastfeed. See Eating Out: Edinburgh North & Leith.

CLOSE TO HOME

East Lothian

John Muir Country Park
Contact: Bobby Anderson, Snr Countryside Ranger
Tel: 01620 827318

Getting there: take A1 or A199 towards Dunbar, turn along A1087 for 1 mile, and turn left into Linkfield car park. For Shore Rd, continue further 1/2 mile into West Barns. 1 1/2 mile walk from bus station, or take local bus to West Barns, Shore Rd.

Large country park with a lovely beach, clifftop trail, and woodland walks. Not always suitable for a pushchair – take a sling or backpack. Picnic sites at Linkfield car park and Shore Rd car park Adventure playground on grass with bark chips at Linkfield car park. Barbecues for hire. Toilets with disabled units served by radar key. There are new interpretation boards at various points throughout the park.

Midlothian

Dalkeith Country Park
Tel: 654 1666 (ranger's office)
Tel: 663 5684
Web: www.dalkeithcountrypark.com

Getting there: the park is a few hundred yards away from the town centre.

Opening times: Apr-end Sep 10.00-17.30.
Admission: adult/child £3; family ticket available. Under 5s free. Group rates also available.

Entrance near St Mary's Church. Nature trails, woodland walks, picnic benches and large children's adventure playground with supervisor. Take care with small children on the river paths and in the riverbank tunnels. N.B. All of this is under threat from a proposed new road.

Café:
£-££, high chairs (1), toilets, nappy-changing facility (M&F) available, seats 60.
Small space for prams and pushchairs. Children's menu. All facilities on ground floor. Parties hosted.

Vogrie Estate and Country Park
Tel: 01875 821990
Getting there: near Gorebridge, 12 miles South of Edinburgh
Signposted from Gorebridge (A7) and Dalkeith (A68).

Open all year, 7.00-dusk.
Admission free. Car park £1.

This country park has a garden centre, barbecue sites (book them in advance), a 9-hole golf course, woodland walks, grassy areas suitable for games, and a tree trail. There's a toddlers' playground situated next to car park for easy access. There's also an adventure playground mainly suitable for children aged 7+, with some equipment suitable for younger children. All equipment is on bark chips, so wellies are a good idea if it's been raining heavily! There is also a miniature railway which runs the second and fourth Sundays of the month in Summer.
Vogrie House has a visitor centre, displays, tearoom with children's menu and highchair, nappy changing facilities and toilets. Space to park pushchairs inside. Children's parties also hosted.
Tearoom open during the summer months only. Tel: 561 5263 for opening times.

West Lothian

Almondell and Calderwood Country Park
Tel: 01506 882254

Opening times: Visitor Centre open 7 days/week. April to October 9.00 to 17.00, November to March 10.00 to 16.00 closed for lunch 12.30 to 13.00).

Getting there: signposted off A89. The entrance is 2 miles south of Broxburn. Almondell North car park is nearest to the Visitor Centre and closes at sunset. People with walking difficulties can park next to Visitor Centre.

This country park has lovely riverside walks, and an aquarium, displays and seasonal exhibitions in the visitor centre, which also serves hot drinks and other snacks in a small seated area. The paths are suitable for both pushchairs and wheelchairs. There are also wilder tracks to explore.

The Rangers organise family events throughout the year (Adults £1.50, children £1) and host playgroup visits. There is also a wooden play area and duck pond near the visitor centre, picnic tables and a barbecue site which requires booking in advance.

Calderwood has been left as a natural area to encourage wildlife. The paths are rough tracks and there are some facilities. A new area called Oakbank also connects with Calderwood. This is an old shale mining area, which has been planted with nitrogen-fixing plants to restore it to nature. Access off A71, 2 miles before Livingston.

Beecraigs Country Park
Tel: 01506 844516
Fax: 01506 846256
Email: mail@beecraigs.com
Web: www. beecraigs.com

Getting there: 2 miles South of Linlithgow. Drive through the town centre; turn up Preston Rd and keep going, past all the houses and on up the road. It is well signposted. The 1st junction leads you to the deer park, toilets, campsite and visitor centre. Alternatively, keep on and next turn-off takes you into Balvormie area, where the play park and pond are situated.

Entry free. Please telephone Park Centre for other charges.

Woodland walks, deer farm, trout farm (you can feed the fish for a small charge), fishing reservoir, outdoor pursuit activities, caravan and camping site. Park Centre for information, refreshments, craft sales, farm shop and Countryside Ranger Service. Restaurant within the Park environs. Clean well thought out play area which suits a large range of ages. The barbecue area is nearby – bring your own charcoal, fee; £18.15 per session. Check out the website for more information.

Polkemmet Country Park
Whitburn
Tel: 01501 743905

Getting there: by car take M8, J4 then A89 to Whitburn and B7066 towards Harthill. By bus; No 12 bus from Edinburgh bus station passes park entrance on B7066.

Open all year, admission free.

Polkemmet offers a variety of facilities, including riverside walks, picnic areas, golf course, driving range and a barbecue area which can be hired by groups for £18.00; remember to bring your own charcoal. Nearby is Fantasy Forest, a well thought-out, enclosed, dog-free play area, including a separate part for young children. This sandy area contains swing, rocking animals and a climbing frame with scoops on a chain to haul up sand! Another area for older children contains enclosed slides and larger climbing frames. Equipment very tactile and colourful. Some pieces designed especially for children with disabilities. Bark chips and rubber matting throughout. Picnic tables within fenced area. Toilets in nearby stable block, nappy changing bench in Ladies'. Block also houses a Countryside Ranger's information centre and shop in the courtyard where sweets, ice cream and drinks are sold. Accessible to pushchairs. Tables outside in courtyard.

FURTHER AFIELD

The Borders

Dawyck Botanic Gardens
Tel: 01721 760254
Getting there: B712, 8 miles SW of Peebles. Signposted from A721.

Opening times: 14 Feb-mid Nov; groups by arrangement in winter.
Admission: adult £3.50; concession £3; child £1, Family ticket £8. Under 5s free.

Gardens are lovely for children to run about in. If you're going, why not consider taking a picnic, for while Dawyck has a tearoom which sells home baking and snacks (no hot food or lunches), it's very small. There's pushchair access and but no nappy changing area. Small gift shop. Toilet.

Kailzie Gardens
Kailzie Gardens
Tel: 01721 720007
Tel: 01721 722807 (Restaurant)
Web: www.kailzie gardens.com
Getting there: 21/2 miles from Peebles on B7062.

Opening times: daily 11.00-17.30.
Admission: adult £3; child (5-14 yrs) £1; under 5s free.
Honest box mid-October-mid-March.

Pretty gardens with small river running through and walled garden. There's a Blue Tit and Osprey Bird Watch (see below), as well as Red Squirrels, Fish, Badgers and Swallows. Picnics can only be eaten outside gardens – watch out for hungry ducks!

Restaurant
£-££, seats 70
Opening times: 11.00-17.00 Mon-Sun. Closed Nov.
Nappy changing mat in restaurant toilet. Restaurant can be busy in summer months so may be worth booking. Children will need close supervision at play area, especially on slide/climbing frame. Small gift shop.

Osprey Watch
Kailzie has an osprey centre, where you can watch live CCTV pictures of the ospreys, which may be seen from 10.00-17.00, daily until the end of Aug.
Admission: adults £1 for the osprey centre (children free) - other charges apply.

Central Region

Muiravonside Country Park
Tel: 01506 845311

Getting there: take the A801 from J4 (Lathallan Roundabout), then follow the B825 towards Linlithgow and Whitecross. Country Park is signposted

Set in 170 acres of the former Muiravonside Estate. The mansion house of the estate is long gone, but there's a stepped garden on its site, with picnic benches and a barked children's play area, complete with a large spider-web climbing structure. While the chute is very high, and the swaying log-walk are too advanced for most under 5s, the toddler playpark next to the barked area is much more accessible. There are swings (bucket-swings), a couple of animal-shaped buckabouts and a see-saw.
The main car park is sited next to Newparks Farm, where children can see an array of animals, including horses, Shetland ponies, guinea pigs and rabbits in abundance, sheep and goats, Tamworth pigs and a Highland bull. There are toilets at the farm site.
There are industrial relics of the estate's past scattered here and there, so don't be surprised if you come across rusting skeletal tractors.
This is a lovely place for a stroll. However, the River Avon (said as to rhyme with Gavin) flows alongside some of the

paths – and there is a weir and a mill lade, so keep a close eye on children if you take a walk along the lower paths. There's a visitor centre: park in the small overflow carpark and walk along the road – there are a couple of parking bays for disabled drivers next to the visitor centre, which is in the old farm buildings of the estate. There are toilets (clean but basic and including those for disabled visitors) next to the centre, and there's a café on the opposite side of the courtyard (teas, coffees, juice, burgers, chips etc). If you make the visitor centre your first port of call, you can pick up a really clear map of the entire estate. Contact the Ranger Service on the number above for information and updates.

Fife

Pittencrieff Park
Dunfermline

Lovely park close to Dunfermline Abbey, with wooded glen, wide open areas and play park. Animal houses, glasshouses, and pavilion selling coffee, ice cream etc. Free entry to park. Small museum in Pittencrieff House in centre of Park.

Lochore Meadows Country Park
Tel: 01592 414300

Getting there: cross Forth Road Bridge and follow M90. At J2A, take Kirkcaldy turn off. Follow Lochgelly exit from this road, then the B920 to Crosshill. Park is signposted on the left.

Opening times: buildings open 9.00-17.00 daily, park open 24 hours. Admission free.

Park offers a multitude of activities including canoeing, hillwalking, sailing, horse riding, golf/putting, and a woodland trail. Award winning facility in 1988, but would now benefit from some maintenance. The park also has an adventure playground/beach/BBQ picnic areas. Lovely safe enclosed toddler play park but wood bark on ground wearing thin. Toilets, nappy changing room (needed some attention on day of a visit – staff happily addressed issue when raised). Building all on one level.

Cafe:
highchairs (2), breastfeeding welcomed.

Craigtoun Country Park
Tel: 01334 473666
Getting there: 3 miles SW of St Andrews on B939.

Opening times: Mar/Apr w/ends, May-Aug every day, Sep w/ends 10.45-17.30 (last ticket 16.30).
Admission: child (0-3) free ;(3-5) £1; (6-15) £3; 16-adult £4; OAP £2 ; disabled visitor £1 + 1 carer free; family (2A +2C over 6) £12; family (2A +3C over 6) £15. All facilities are free after payment of entry fee.

Plenty to do for all the family including: Rio Grande Railway, trampolines, two bouncy castles, boating, putting, crazy golf, adventure play park, toddler play area, Countryside Centre and lots of parkland to roam. Calendar of events throughout the year. Indoor picnic hut available if raining – booking recommended (especially by large parties) . Most attractions are outside so unsuitable if raining.

Tearoom:
£-££, highchairs(3).
NB. Tearoom has (distracting) stands selling plastic footballs and toys.
Toilets at various points of the park. Nappy changing facilities (clean) in toilets for the disabled. . Park appeared to be well kept and was undergoing some ground maintenance on the day of our visit.

Falkirk

Callendar Park
Falkirk FK1 1YR
Tel: 01324 503770
Web: www.falkirkmuseums.gov.uk
Getting there: from M9, J5, turn left along the Laurieston Bypass. At the end, turn left, then right. Pass the grassy banking of the Antonine Wall and the park entrance is on your left, signposted, at a roundabout. For the House and Stables Tearoom, take 1st left past the high flats.

Large park with crazy golf, putting, bouncy castle, electric cars (all Apr-Sep), woodland walks and Castle Callendar – an enclosed, dog-proof play park for children of all ages and abilities, which features irresistible spiral slides, unusual tyre swings and a big sand-pit. The boating pond is inhabited by many greedy birds. Kiosk selling ice-lollies, burgers, etc. For historical interest, you can run up and down the Antonine Wall, built by the Romans, which defines the park's northern boundary.

Stables Tearoom:
In Callendar Park, near Callendar House, by east car park. £-££, high chairs, breastfeeding welcome, nappy-changing facilities (M&F).
The tearoom is small and friendly and serves children's portions of most dishes. The garden to the rear is accessible to prams and pushchairs via a lane to the left hand side of the Park Gallery and through a gate. Unfortunately the tearoom itself can't cope with prams. Sit outdoors in the herb garden in summer and watch the swallows as they fly around the picturesque ruined tower. Nooks and crannies in the garden for exploring! A pleasant place to spend time.
Next to the tearoom is the Park Gallery, a small contemporary art gallery (admission free) featuring temporary exhibitions and an art activity box to create your own artwork.
Make a day of it: see Callendar House, above in Museums.

Stirling

Stirling has lots of playparks with the usual array of play equipment. Two which are particular favourites are the playparks at King's Park and Beechwood Park.

King's Park (King's Park Road off Queen's Road and Victoria Place) has a fantastic playpark featuring lots of interesting modern equipment. Very popular and very busy! It is situated next to tennis courts, skateboard park and putting green.

Beechwood Park (St Ninian's Road) has a large play area featuring a helter skelter for brave under 5s. There is also a BMX bike track for older children which at quiet times can give the under 5s an interesting place to run about and broom cars down hills. Beechwood Park also features a Bouncy Castle during the summer months and a Bike Park (below).

Beechwood Bike Park
St Ninian's Road
Stirling
Tel: 01786 448308

Opening times: During school Easter and summer holidays daily 10.00-18.00. Between Easter and summer holidays and from end of summer holidays usually until local September holiday w/end open at w/ends only, weather permitting. Phone first.
Charge: £1.10/hr.

Excellent enclosed traffic system of roads, zebra crossing, traffic lights etc. Bikes with and without stabilisers available for hire. Trikes also available as are helmets. Some new models but some of the bikes could do with some loving care and attention. You can bring your own bikes too. Seating for adults. Park open from 9.00 for groups by arrangement via the above phone number.

Make a day of it: see Stirling Castle, above.

PICK YOUR OWN

This is a really fun thing for young children to do, whilst encouraging them to eat fruit at the same time! There are many farms offing PYO fruit and they are often sign posted from main roads, but some also have play areas and these are listed below.

CLOSE TO HOME

East Lothian

Stenton Fruit Farm
Ruchlaw Produce Ltd
Ruchlaw Mains
Stenton EH42 1TD
Tel: 01368 850378
www.stentonfruitfarm.co.uk
Getting there: on the B6370 from East Linton. Follow the fruit signs, or print off map from website.
Opening times:10.00-21.00 daily, Jul and Aug.

Pick your own fruit. Ring for crop availability. Play area with chute, climbing apparatus, trampolines and table tennis. Ducks and picnic area. Refreshments – ice cream, lemonade and tea/coffee machine. Toilets. Access for single and double pushchairs. Can also do parties with free fruit in season. Phone or email for details.

Midlothian

Lowe's Fruit Farm
Campend, Dalkeith
City Bypass at Sherrifhall, A7 junction
Tel: 660 2128

Getting there: By bus: LRT 82; First 86.

Opening times: Late June until end of fruiting season, 7 days a week 10.00-18.00, weather permitting. Advisable to phone to check at extremes of season.
Lowe's is well known for strawberry and other soft fruit picking through the summer. Apples, pears and plums later in the season. Great for giving children a sense of the seasons and some knowledge of where food comes from. Toilets and a grassy car park where you can picnic. Lowe's is fun but it is a working farm and parents should ensure their children's safety at all times.

West Lothian

West Craigie Farm
South Queensferry
Edinburgh EH30 9TR
Tel: 319 1048
Web: www.thejamkitchen.com

Getting there: head out along the A90, past Cramond Brig. Take the first sliproad off (B9080). Pass the army barracks entries. West Craigie Farm is first turning on your right: well marked.

Opening times: Apr-end Jun: just jam and frozen fruit for sale; please phone to arrange a time.
Jul-mid Aug: Mon-Fri 10.00-19.00, Sun 10.00-17.00.
Mid Aug- end Mar: open Mon, Wed-Sun from 10.00-14.00, closed Tue.

July and August are the months of the soft-fruit season. The Sinclair family plus their helpers welcome families to come and pick their own fruit. Great views over The Forth and over Edinburgh and the Pentlands. Take a picnic and make a day of it; there are picnic tables. There's also a nature detective trail.

Fife

Allanhill Farm
Grange Road (signposted from roundabout at East Sands Leisure Centre).

Farm shop and Pick-your Own strawberries, raspberries, loganberries and gooseberries. Outdoor play area with slide, swings, haystack, sandpit, maze, and a rabbit and guinea pig. Large wooden play fort near raspberries. Café with indoor and outdoor tables selling teas/coffees, cakes and sandwiches as well as produce.

Carnie Fruit Farm
Cupar

Farm shop and pick your own strawberries, raspberries, tayberries, gooseberries, blackcurrants and redcurrants. Café serving speciality strawberry teas and home baking. Play area.
Cairnie Mega Maze and Funyard includes trampolines, go-karts, haystacks, sandbox with giant diggers and 6-acre maze field. Opening times: 11th July – 4th Sept, 10.00 – 18.00. Adults £4.50, child/conc. £3.50, Family £13.50.

SEALIFE CENTRES AND AQUARIA

CLOSE TO HOME

East Lothian

Scottish Seabird Centre
The Harbour
North Berwick EH39 4SS
Tel: 01620 890202
Website: www.seabird.org

Opening times: 10.00-18.00 April - October. 10.00 - 16.00 November to Jan (17.30 weekends). 10.00 - 17.00 Feb and March (17.30 weekends).

Award-winning attraction overlooking the islands of the Firth of Forth and the beaches of North Berwick. Displays include a short film about the seabirds found in Scotland, and interactive live cameras that allow visitors to watch gannets and puffins and other nesting seabirds on the Bass Rock and Fidra. Seals and dolphins can sometimes be seen from the observation deck. A camera allows visitors to see close-ups of newborn seals on the Isle of May. Children's workshops during holidays and at weekends, and boat trips out to the Bass Rock. New Environmental Discovery Centre and Migration Tunnel. Gift shop and licensed café with indoor and outdoor seating (approx £4.50 for main meal), plenty on the menu suitable for children. Accessible to pushchairs. Toilets with changing facilities.

See also Seacliff Beach, above

FURTHER AFIELD

Fife

Deep Sea World
Battery Quarry
North Queensferry KY11 1JR
Tel: 01383 411411
Email: info@deepseaworld.com
Web: www.deepseaworld.com
Getting there: close to the north side of the Forth Road Rail Bridge, the road is very winding, but follow the signs and you'll get there!
Nearest station: North Queensferry. The road down to the aquarium is very steep.
Opening times: Apr-Oct daily 10.00-18.00, Nov-March daily 10.00-17.00. Closed 25 Dec, 1 Jan.

Admission: adult £7.95; child (3-15) £5.75; concession £4.50; families – prices vary by family size. Under 3s free. Annual adult ticket £21.95, Annual family ticket £44.95 Swim with the sharks £50.00.

This award-winning aquarium offers a spectacular fishes'-eye view of the marine environment. It's divided into various areas, including 'Krakatoa', with deadly species from around the Indo-Pacific; Amazonia which has the ever popular pirhanas; and the Underwater Safari. This is fascinating, as you stand on a moving walkway to observe the fish which swim all around the tunnel you're in. The downside is that pushchairs and prams are not allowed here, due to the walkway.
There's an opportunity to see sharks in close-up, via a high-tech exhibition. Equipped with a video camera, visitors can sit in a purpose built control capsule situated in the main exhibition area and drive a ROV (Remotely Operated Vehicle), whilst watching the live footage of the sharks on the TV screens.
The touch pools, Ray pool and Dogfish pool are particularly good for Under 5s, as you can see the creatures in very close proximity. The dogfish are great fun when they are fed, as they jump out of the water. The rays like to be tickled on their backs.
Free face painting, behind the scenes tours, animal handling sessions and family talks and activity sessions. Large car park.
Café:
£-££, high chairs, breastfeeding welcome.
Bright, spacious café, which serves a range of snacks, teas, coffees and lots of fizzy drinks. Nappy changing facilities,

ramp access except for the Under Sea section. Birthday parties by arrangement. Shop sells a wide range of toys and marine-theme merchandise.

St Andrews

St Andrews Aquarium
The Scores
Tel: 01334-474786
Web: www.standrewsaquarium.co.uk

Getting there: Take M90 to J8, then A91 East. Stagecoach operates services from Edinburgh. Train from Edinburgh to Leuchars and then local bus service into St Andrews town centre. Historic market town, famous for being the 'home of golf' and its university. Innovative Park'n'Ride runs in the summer. Free bus service running round town from well-signposted car park on outskirts.

Opening times: daily 10.00-18.00.
Re-entry all-day ticket: adult £5.50; child £3.75; concession £4.50; family £17.00/£14.00.

Special feature exhibitions include tropical fish and touch pools. The centre also rehabilitates seals for release into the wild. Access to the actual aquarium area from the pay desk is down a set of stairs, but if you have a pushchair etc, access to the lower level of the aquarium can be obtained via an external ramp.
Café with children's menu and bar open to all. Gift shop.

Make a day of it: see St Andrews Museum (see Museums)

ICE SKATING

Murrayfield Ice Rink Ltd
Riversdale Crescent
Murrayfield EH12 5XN
Tel: 337 6933

Sessions: daily from 14.30. Best times for under 5s and their families are beginners sessions Mon, Fri 17.00-19.00. Group tuition Wed 17.00-19.00 and Sun 12.00-13.45 (this is a certificated Learn to Skate session with instruction from resident coaching staff). Family skating Thu 19.00-21.00 and Sat 10.00-12.00. Groups can be taken w/day mornings by prior arrangement with resident instructor. Beginner's sessions, including skate hire cost

from £3. Group and UK Learn to Skate sessions cost £3 plus £1 for skate hire. Skates available from children's size 5. Wheelchair access and toilet facilities for the disabled. Shop sells all manner of skates and accessories. Café open most sessions serving hot drinks, hot snacks, toasties, etc. Hot drinks and snacks from machines at other times.

SOFT PLAY CENTRES

Soft play centres vary greatly in terms of size and availability of areas for younger children – where some may have some great facilities for older brothers and sisters, under 3s may be confined to a ball-pit – ideal if they're happy, not so great if they're not. It might be wise to avoid planning your first visit to a soft play centre during school holidays, or on school half-days, as they can become extremely busy, and the noise and general good-natured mayhem might overawe a young first-timer.

Many of the soft play centres are available for party hire. We have given details of these in the Birthdays & Celebrations section. What you should remember is that your groups will not have exclusive access to the actual soft play structure and in some cases, during weekends especially, parties are run on a 'conveyor belt' system, with one group after another being given access to the party-room: while it's usually clean, you may get the feeling that the birthday 'magic' is lost.

Please note that not all the soft play centres are listed: as with other sections, some venues did not respond to enquiries.

IN THE CITY

Bonnyrigg Leisure Centre
King George V Park
Park Road
Bonnyrigg
Tel: 663 7579

Opening times: phone for current times.
Admission: 90p/1/2 hr.
Pleasant soft play area with imaginative layout. Includes features such as ballpool, slide, rat run, giant castle and a multitude of play shapes.
Ideal to hire for small groups (£17.00/hr).

Castle Gyle Shoppers' Crèche and Party Centre
Gyle Shopping Centre
Tel: 476 7766
Opening times: Mon-Fri 9.30-17.45; Sat 9.00-17.45; Sun 11.00-16.45.
Admission: £3.50/hr.

Large soft play, ball pool and slide; home corner, playdough, toys
and games to suit different ages of children (ages 2-8 yrs accepted). Situated near the central entrance to the shopping centre.
Available for party hire every evening.

Clambers
Royal Commonwealth Pool
21 Dalkeith Road EH16 5BB
Tel: 667 7211
Opening times: Mon-Fri 10.00-18.00, Sat and Sun 09.00-17.00

Admission: £2.00/child for a 45 minute session.
Check availability at reception.

This multi-level play area has 3 levels of slides, tubes and lots of safe surfaces to clamber on and over. Suitable for 3-8 yrs. Parents and carers must stay in the surrounding area – or you can join your child inside the play area.
There is a toddler (under 3s) area within Clambers, where children must be accompanied by a parent or carer.

Access times for this area are: Mon-Thu 10.00-18.00; Fri 10.00-13.00; Sat & Sun 09.00-12.00. Under 3s are not admitted at all during school holidays. Available for birthday groups

NB Upgrading of the entire Commonwealth Pool complex may begin over the next couple of years. This may affect access, and may result in a new layout.

Clown Around
Units 2&3
109 Restalrig Rd EH6 7NY
Tel: 553 7676
Mob: 07976 053690
Website: www.clownaround.me.uk

Opening times: daily 10.00-18.00.
Admission: phone for current charges.

A fairly new soft play centre, which has the additional attraction (in our case certainly!) of trampolines. There's a toddler area, which has a multi-level soft play unit, along with soft shapes and interactive items, such as musical notes on one of the walls. The other multi-level area is for 4-10 yrs, and has rat runs, a slide, a large ball pit, moveable 'obstacles' etc. There's also a games consul area. Nappy-changing facilities available.

There are 2 locations with tables, from which you can see the play areas. There's a café, so you can have a tea or coffee while you watch the antics. While there are no surprises on the menu (fish & chips, burgers, filled rolls etc), it is freshly prepared. Birthday parties catered for. The unit has access for disabled visitors, and a controlled entry/exit arrangement.
Admission: phone for current charges.

Jelly Club
Peffermill Road
Tel: 652 0212
Email:info@jellyclub.co.uk
Web: www.jellyclub.co.uk

Opening times: daily, 10.30-18.30.
Admission: £3.60/0-2 yrs; £4.00/3-4 yrs; £4.60/ 5-12 yrs, No charge for adults.

The Jelly Club underwent an extensive refurbishment in 2002, and now offers more equipment and increased security (there's now an electronic entry/exit format).

The five play zones are aimed at different ages. Two soft play areas with ball pit and slides, one for 0-3 yrs (also has small chutes, soft shapes and rockers), one for 4-12 yrs. Adventure maze area for 4-10 yrs with climbing sections, walkways, slides etc. 'Jelly Village' for 2-7 yrs provides cars and tractors for pedalling around a road system. There are two large bouncy castles with slides and nets, one for 2-6 yrs, one for 6-12 yrs. There's also a small garden seating area.

There's some supervision in play zones, but children do stray into zones they should not be in, and this can be problematic if, say 8 yr olds are charging around amid 5 year olds.

Parents not allowed in bouncy castle or adventure maze. Shoes required for some zones and socks for others. Under 3s may find it a bit daunting and under 4s may be frustrated at being excluded from various zones. No booking required except for groups. Wheelchair/pushchair access to the main seating area. Nappy-changing surface in toilet for the disabled & in the ladies.

Café
£, high chairs, bottles and food heated
Seating throughout the play area so parents/carers can see their children. Usual food selection (chips, sandwiches, panini, pasta), children's menu (chips, nuggets, pasta), and snacks at reasonable prices. Birthday parties hosted in separate areas.

Junglee Fun
115 North High St
Musselburgh EH21 6JE
Tel: 653 0666
Web: www.junglee-fun.com
Opening times: 7 days/week 10.00-17.00.
Admission: £2/child and you stay as long as you like.

Soft play café, which offers a brightly coloured environment with soft play shapes, bouncy castle, educational ball pool and jungle-themed toys. Caters for children aged 0-6 yrs. Meals, snacks, homebaking and drinks available all day. Nappy-changing facilities, child-friendly toilets with potties and booster seats. Premises are accessible to pushchairs. No smoking policy throughout. Available for party hire: pre-booking required.

Meadowbank Sports Centre
139 London Road
Tel: 661 5351

Opening times: daily, 07.30-22.00.
Soft play opening times: Mon 13.30-14.30; Tue, Thu 9.30-11.30, 13.30-14.30; Wed, Fri 10.30-11.30; Sat, Sun 10.30-11.30, 12-30-13.30.
Admission: £2.00 to stay as long as you like. Group hire £40.

There is ramped access to the sports centre and the automatic entrance doors are wide enough for a double pushchair. The lift offers access to all facilities and is suitable for use by parents with young children and people with disabilities.

There are toilets on all floors and nappy-changing facilities are available.

Newly refurbished soft play area in a safe area within the sports complex; equipment is suitable for children with special needs. As this area is unsupervised, parents and carers must remain with their children at all times. The area can be booked for private parties.

Molly's Play Centre
Ocean Terminal
Ocean Drive EH6 6JJ
Tel: 0845 123 5593
Email: info@mollys.co.uk
Website: www.mollys.co.uk
Opening times: : Mon-Thurs & Sat: 10.00-18.00; Fri: 10.00-19.00; and Sun: 11.00 – 18.00.
Admission: babies up to 18 months are free; 18mths – 3 yrs - £2.50; and 3yrs upwards (max age is 12) - £3.00 per 1 hour play.

Molly's opened at the beginning of 2005. It's located on the second floor of the Ocean Terminal shopping centre, adjacent to Debenhams. Large, extravagant play structure, designed to be accessible to children with physical disabilities as well as able-bodied children. Parents/carers are required to remain in the centre and there are lots of seats and tables beside the play area so that you can watch your child. There is always at least one member of staff in the structure; the ratio goes up in relation to the number of children.
Café
£-££
Serves teas, decent coffee, cold drinks and various snacks. Huge windows offer views of Britannia and the Forth: it's a good choice if you don't like the 'warehouse-style'

soft play centres. Premises completely accessible for pushchairs and has child friendly toilets. Also available for themed parties.

Musselburgh Sports Centre
Newbigging
Tel: 653 6367

Small soft play area for under 5s, which costs £1.40/1/2 hour.

CLOSE TO HOME

Midlothian

The Happy Castle
Bankmill
Valleyfield Road
Penicuik EH26 8LW
Tel: 01968 675638
Fax: 01968 675911

Getting there: go through Penicuik town centre and after town hall on the left, follow the road round Bridge St, turn left into Valleyfield Rd, The Happy Castle is sign-posted. Then turn right and continue on under the narrow bridge, bear left and you will find the car park; the entrance is on the right.
Opening times: daily, 10.00-17.00.
Admission: £3.90 for 1 3 yr olds; and £1.60 for 1 12 yr olds.
There's a separate area for under 3s, with soft play, slides, ball pool and scramble nets – excellent fun for climbers, but less mobile babies would be happier (and more accessible) at the entrance. During busy times it would be advisable to stay close to younger children, as the older children can be boisterous if they sneak in. There's a huge multi-storied soft play extravaganza for children up to 12 yrs, containing aerial slides, rope bridges, free fall and snake slides.
Café
£, high chairs, bottles heated, nappy-changing facilities.
Private rooms for parties, special rates for group bookings.
Good seating arrangements mean that parents and carers can enjoy their tea or coffee while keeping an eye on the children. Themed selection of children's meals; also toasties, baked potatoes etc. Jugs of diluting juice available at reasonable prices.

West Lothian

Space Bugs
Linlithgow Leisure Centre
Kettlestoun Mains Road
Tel: 01506 775440

Getting there: drive through town until you come to the crossroads at Linlithgow Bridge. Take the left and continue along Mill Rd (B8029). Cross over at the roundabout.

Opening times: phone for current details.
Admission: £2.50/45 mins
Fairly new soft play on two levels. Plenty room to run about, slide, or swing on the ball-slide. Dark area, rollers and crawl tubes.
While there are times when play is supervised, parental supervision required if it is not staffed. Separate area for under 3s, with large soft shapes and ball-pit.
Part of leisure centre with pool.
Café
£, high chair, seats 40
Serving snacks and a range of hot and cold drinks.
Nappy changing (M&F)
(make a day of it: if you visit the palace, why not end the day with some soft play - also good if you go to, say Beecraigs (see Country Parks, above) and it starts raining etc)

Grangemouth
Brewsters Fun Factory
Cadgers Brae
Beancross Road
Tel: 01324 720726
Getting there: along M9. Turn off at J5 and take A9 road (almost straight ahead on roundabout). Take first entrance on the left.
Phone for current times and prices
Large multi-level soft play. Includes rollers, cargo netting, slides, crawling spaces. Area for younger children also. Part of the Brewsters restaurant.

Grangemouth Sports Complex
Abbots Road
Grangemouth FK3 8JB
Tel: 01786
Getting there: along M9. Turn off at J5 and take A905 road (3rd exit). Travel along until you come to another smaller roundabout and go down Newlands Rd. Keep going down and the centre is on your right after King's Seat Ave.

Opening times: 9.00-17.30.
Admission: £2.75/ 45 mins. £1 refundable on return of wristband.

Soft play on two levels, complete with slide. Plenty of soft blocks, ropes, hanging obstacles, rollers and nets. Its format makes it easy to retrieve any child who gets stuck.

SWIMMING

Most babies love moving in water once the initial fear of being uncovered has gone. Swimming is an excellent way of exercising the body, and more and more parents are introducing their children to the pleasures of water early in life. Safety is obviously a motivating factor. Opinions vary as to when to start your child off (6 mths is probably the average), but whenever you start, here are a few things to remember:
▶ Have a healthy respect for the dangers of water.
▶ Always stay near your child when in or near water.
▶ Allow at least 1 hour after a feed before entering the water.
▶ Respect your child's wishes. Do not force youngsters into the water if they dislike it. Wait and try again in a week or so.
▶ Babies get chilled easily. Take them out of the water at the first signs of cold. 10 mins in the water is enough for the first times, and no more than 30 mins at other times.

What to Wear
There are various companies producing swimsuits and shorts with in-built nappy, ranging from 3-36 mths. Disposable swim nappies are available, but they're expensive. Ordinary nappies are not suitable.

Buoyancy Aids
Small arm bands are available. The type with 2 or more air chambers and non-returnable valves are the safest. The triangular type with a flat section next to the body will stop your child wobbling too much. These aids are available from swim centres, sports shops, Early Learning Centre, Jenners toy dept, and so on. Other buoyancy aids, such as body vests and inflatable ring seats, are available. You might find that these are more suitable for young babies and aids such as these also come in several sizes. Remember that arm bands and inflatable rings are not lifesavers.
Early classes are intended to develop your child's

confidence and pleasure in the water. They teach some of the basic skills leading towards learning to swim, and show parents how they can help their children. As regards a proper stroke, experts say that it is better to let under 5s develop their own way of swimming through playing regularly in water: perfecting a stroke can come later. In fact, the longer you leave it, the quicker they learn. The Amateur Swimming Association offers the following useful publications by mail order:
▶ Make a Splash - £8.50 plus £1.50 p&p
▶ Teach Your Child to Swim (Usborne Pubs) – £5.99, plus £1.50 p&p

Send your order and remittance to: ASA Swimming Times Ltd, 2 Kingfisher Enterprise Park, 50 Arthur St, Redditch, Worcs B98 8LG (Tel: 0800 220 292 or 01527 514 288). Alternatively, check bookshops or the EDL service for copies.

Swimming in the Sea
Edinburgh's beaches from Cramond to Musselburgh are generally reasonably clean. However, standards can change from season to season, so always check before going into the water, and always obey the notices posted – just because it looks clean doesn't mean it's safe. The Scottish Environment Protection Agency (SEPA) monitors and reports on water quality (see www.sepa.org.uk for latest results) of other recreational waters as well as those which are EC recognised. Some of these beaches in urban areas can be affected by sewage debris and have higher bacterial concentrations during and immediately after heavy rain, caused by storm sewer overflows and run off from streets.

All the beaches in the Edinburgh and Lothians area meet EC water quality standards. The following beaches are categorised as exceptionally clean: Portobello Central (James St), Seton Sands/Longniddry, Gullane, Yellowcraigs, North Berwick (Milsey Bay), Dunbar (Belhaven and East), Thorntonloch, Pease Bay, St Abbs and Coldingham.
Other beaches away from towns are generally safe to play on but simply do not have official EC recognition because they are too sparsely used.

Beaches which are most suitable for toddlers are: Gullane, Seacliffe and Yellowcraigs. All have toilets (no charge for use), Gullane (Apr-Sept). Seacliffe Beach, non-EC, is one of the cleanest and safest beaches on the Lothian coast.

▶ Remember, sea water can be extremely cold, even on sunny days.

Family Swimming During the Summer Months

Wester Hailes runs family sessions. Schools with pools, such as Trinity Academy, Currie High, the Royal High, Queensferry High, Dr Bell's Primary, Portobello High, James Gillespie's and Gracemount High, may all offer evening family swimming sessions: contact the Community Education programme for current information, Tel: 469 3250.

Some of the city's private gyms and hotels have pools that offer swimming classes and activities for children but these can be extremely expensive. See Yellow Pages for full listings, or ask if you're a member of a club.

Swimming Pools

General Notes & Information

The pools in this section are all local authority run. For details of the City Council Leisure Access Scheme (LAC) which gives reduced admission rates to cardholders, see Activities for Parents.

▶ The water temperature ranges from 80-84°F.

▶ All pools have showers and hairdryers. Most hairdryers take 20p coins.

wIn general the admission charge entitles you to unlimited swimming time. However, when pools are busy e.g. during school holidays, they may run sessions of limited duration, usually 40 mins.

▶ The pools all sell armbands, shampoo sachets, soap, combs and goggles

wAll pools without cafeterias have hot and cold drinks machines and sweet/snack machines.

▶ Spectators are allowed into all Council pools, free of charge.

▶ During school holidays and at w/ends, most of the pools have fun play-sessions with toys, inflatables etc.

▶ Children under 9 must always be accompanied by an adult at all Council pools. The number of children whom an adult can accompany is currently in debate, and the safety ratio may differ in some pools in the near future.

At Council pools, lessons are very popular and must be booked in advance. There are three main booking periods.

▶ August – for the period August to January;

▶ December – for the period January to July;

▶ June for Summer holiday courses.

Customers who have made main bookings in either August or December are offered priority booking for any other courses, within that period. However, new customers can still apply for any remaining spaces in the new course.

▶ In August and December course places are offered on a first come first served basis. You should expect long queues which form ahead of opening time.

▶ For details of the school holiday activities and play sessions, contact the Edinburgh Leisure Head Office, Tel: 650 1001 for a current seasonal leaflet or your local sports/swim centre.

Ainslie Park
92 Pilton Drive EH5 2HF
Tel: 551 2400
Opening times: Mon-Thu 7.30-21.15, Fri 7.30-20.30; Sat 8.00-17.00 and Sun 8.00-16.00.

Free car park beside centre.

Modern leisure centre. Amenities include a large pool (25m x 8 lanes), shallow teaching pool, spa pool and splash pool, sports hall, pulse centre and crèche. There is an extensive range of activities and coaching sessions.

Changing area: mixed, with 3 large family cubicles. Coin-operated lockers (50p returnable deposit). Wall-mounted hairdryers, play pens, changing tables, and high chairs are available, as are safety seats to assist in changing with children. Not always as clean as it could be.

Learner pool starts with a gentle water-filled slope leading into a shallow pool, which is very suitable for introducing small babies and toddlers to the water. At one end there's a jet-pressurised water system, which older toddlers and children enjoy.

Entrance to the spectator area overlooking the pool is through the sitting area.

Parent and child sessions are held throughout the week and aim to familiarise the baby/toddler with the environment of water. No booking necessary. Classes are available for pre-school children. Lessons are very popular and have to be booked in advance. Full programme available from centre. Learner pool starts with a gentle water-filled slope leading into a shallow pool, which is very suitable for introducing small babies and toddlers to the water. At one end there's a jet-pressurised water system, which older toddlers and children enjoy.

Entrance to the spectator area overlooking the pool is through the sitting area.

Parent and child sessions are held throughout the week and aim to familiarise the baby/toddler with the environment of water. No booking necessary. Classes are available for pre-school children. Lessons are very popular and have to be booked in advance. Full programme available from centre.

Balerno High School
Tel: 477 7733
Contact: Vivienne Mackay, Community Manager

Bonnyrigg Leisure Centre
King George V Park
Park Road
Bonnyrigg EH19 2AW
Tel: 663 7579
Opening times: Mon-Fri: 9.00-22.00; Sat/Sun: 9.00 – 20.00. Reduced opening hours during public hols 10.00-18.00.

Pool admission: adult £2.50; child/concession £1.20. Under 3's free.
Pool available for private booking £48/50mins.
Free car parking for up to 80 cars.

This modern centre includes a leisure pool, consisting of upper and lower lagoon, and special water features such as water cannons, geysers, spa pool, slides and water mushrooms. No spectating area. Centre also has 'Knights and Princesses' soft play area, and a games hall. Programmed sessions include swimming lessons, gymnastics and martial arts mini kickers (see ballsports in Activities for Children) among others.
Crèche:
Opening times: 9.30-11.30. Costs £1.10/hour
Changing area: mixed family changing is available, with coin-operated lockers and nappy-changing facilities. There are no cafeteria facilities, but a wide range of snacks is available from vending machines. Tables, chairs, and high chairs are provided in the conservatory.
NB: parents/carers may only supervise a max of 2 children under 8 yrs in the swimming pool.

Dalry Swim Centre
Caledonian Crescent EH11 2AL
Tel: 313 3964
Opening times vary so contact centre. Ladies only swimming Tue 11.00-12.00 & 18.30-20.30. Other times also – contact the centre.
Admission: adult peak £2.90/ off peak £2.30 (Leisure Card Holder £2.30/£1.70 respectively). Under 5s and primary school children free. Older children (up to 18) £1.50.
On-street parking available, but area is very busy.

Victorian 23m (25 yd) swimming pool with changing cubicles and coin-return lockers upstairs. Nappy-changing facilities and play pens on poolside. Ample space for parking pushchairs. Purpose-built changing, shower and toilet for people with disabilities.
Antenatal swimming exercise session 9.00-9.40 and Parent and Child sessions 9.40-10.20 on Tuesdays. These sessions are supervised by friendly, qualified coaching staff, from whom advice and assistance is available. Pulse centre - full programme available from centre. Staff fully trained to service the special needs of under 5s and the parents. NB the water can be on the chilly side!

Drumbrae Leisure Centre
Drumbrae Terrace EH4 7SF
Tel: 312 7957
Opening times: Mon-Fri 7.00-22.00; Sat 9.00-16.00; Sun 9.00-21.30.

Admission: adult peak £3.30/ off peak £2.50; child £1.60. Under 5s and all children of primary school age free. All children under 8 must be accompanied by an adult.

Opened in 1999, this centre is close to various bus routes and has a good-sized car park. Built all on the same level, the large, bright swimming pool is worth visiting just for the amazing view. Centre recently won an award from Practical Parenting magazine as one of the most child-friendly pools in the UK.

Pushchair park (50p refundable). Multi-purpose hall for various activities including gymnastics, GymNippers and birthday parties. There's also a pulse centre. Numerous toilets with changing facilities throughout the centre.
Changing areas: mixed, with family and facilities for the disabled. Coin-operated lockers require 50p coins (refundable). Changing area is open to the swimming pool, so care should be taken with over-enthusiastic children: a poolside barrier is erected at certain times to prevent children charging straight out of the booths and into the water.

Adult and Child swim session Mon 9.30-10.00 and Wed 09.30-10.00: sessions to develop water safety and confidence, for children 4 mths-4 yrs, accompanied by an adult in the water.
Learn to Swim programmes for pre-school children 31/2-5 yrs who are confident in the water.
Crèche:
Opening times: Mon-Fri 9.15-12.30; Tue, Thu 13.00-15.00. £3.40/session (11/2 hrs) or £2.20 with a Leisure Card. Bookable 7 days in advance.

Cafeteria:
£, high chairs (4), serves cold snacks
Opening times: Mon-Fri 9.00-14.00. There are also vending machines selling drinks, chocolate bars etc. The seating area is near to the pool viewing area.

Glenogle Swim Centre
Glenogle Road
Stockbridge EH3 5JB
Tel: 343 6376
Glenogle Swim Centre is scheduled to be temporarily closed for one year for major refurbishment from early 2006.

Gracemount Leisure Centre
22 Gracemount Drive EH16 6RN
Tel: 658 1940
Phone for current opening times and charges.

Opened in 2000, this swimming pool and fitness centre provides swimming lessons, tots classes and ante-natal exercise – full programme available from the centre. Nappy-changing facilities (M&F). There is an area for private breastfeeding. Premises are accessible to double pushchairs. Lift access to upper floor.

Crèche:
Opening times: Mon, Wed, Fri 09.15-10.45 and 10.50-12.15 (2 sessions). £2.85/child (LAC holders £1.85). Must be booked 7 days in advance.

Leith Victoria Swim Centre
Junction Place EH6 5JA
Tel: 555 4728
Phone for current opening times and charges

Car parking: parking, including parking for disabled, at the Bonnington Rd entrance.
Lift available, changing for the disabled, and access to 23m (25 yd) Victorian swimming pool. Spectating facilities available. Variety of facilities to suit all abilities: contact reception for current details.
Crèche:
Opening times: Mon-Fri 09.15-12.15, cost: £3.40, booking system in place. No cafeteria, but drinks etc available from vending machines. Pushchair corner, where they can be locked to a rail: chain and padlock available at reception if you leave deposit.

Leith Waterworld
377 Easter Road, EH6 8HU
Tel: 555 6000
Opening times: Term time: Fri: 10.30-16.45; Sat/Sun: 10.00-17.00 (out of water by 16.15). During school holidays: Fri: 10.30- 16.45; Sat-Thurs: 10.00-16.45.
Parent and child classes: Fri 10.40-11.20; Adult aqua fit class: Fri: 11.15-12.00.

Admission: Adult: £3.80; Junior £2.60; Under 5's free; Family ticket (2 adults and 2 children) £10.00; Family ticket (2 adults and 2 under 5's) £5.25. Parent and toddler class: £3.10; Adult aqua fit class: £2.50.

Pool has sloping `beach' style entrance, wave machines, fast flow channel, spa pool, flumes for toddlers and older children, river run and bubble beds. Adult to child ratios must be observed and for under 5s these are one adult for each child. Family changing areas, including nappy changing facilities and facilities for people with disabilities. The Island soft play area for toddlers and children aged 3-8years – cost: £1.40 for 1 hour session.

Multi-sensory area for children with disabilities: This area has been designed to be both subtle and relaxing, whilst providing stimulating sounds and textures. It features a choice for a variety of disabilities and can accommodate up to 15 people (including carers) at a time. Cost: £16 for exclusive use or £1.40 per child, carers free.
Party room available for hire.
Waterworld doesn't have a café but there are vending machines available.

Loanhead Leisure Centre
George Avenue
Loanhead EH20 9LA
Tel: 440 4516
Opening times: vary considerably from day to day, and at different times of the year – contact centre for current hours.
Car parking: free car parking, with designated parent and child spaces.

Admission: adult £2.50; child £1.20. Family tickets (various combinations of adults and children) £6.00. Free for under 3's.

This modern leisure centre has a 25m pool, with adjoining toddler pool with slides and a viewing gallery. Adults may only supervise a maximum of 2 children (aged under 8)

each in the pool. Water tends to be nicely warm for children during parent and child sessions.
Changing areas:
mixed family changing is available, with nappy-changing facilities.
Crèche:
Opening times: Mon/Tue/Wed 9.30-12.30, Thu/Fri 9.30-11.30. £1.10/child, bookable in hourly sessions. When the crèche is closed, the area can be used for nappy-changing and feeding.
Drinks and snacks can be bought from vending machines, and there are tables, chairs and high chairs.

Musselburgh Sports Centre
Newbigging EH21 7AS
Tel: 653 6367
Phone for current opening hours and charges.

A modern sports centre, offering a wide range of facilities, such as a pool, health suite and café. A swim for under 5s costs 30p. Children's swimming classes, including lessons for under 5s, are available – contact centre for details. Centre also offers pre Monkees gymnastics classes (see gymnastics in Activities for Children)
There is no private area for breastfeeding.
Crèche (3months – 5yrs)
Opening times: Mon/Wed/Thu 9.00-11.00, Tue10.00-12.00 and Fri: 09.15 – 11.15. Costs £2.60/2 hours.
Café has high chairs. Centre accessible to double pushchairs.

Portobello Swim Centre
57 The Promenade EH15 2BS
Tel: 669 6888

Access is well thought out, with a ramp to front entrance, automatic doors that are wide enough for double pushchairs. Secure pushchair parking at reception (padlocks available for refundable deposit). A lift gives access to first floor/café.
Changing area:
Family changing rooms consists of a communal, family friendly 'changing village' with baby seats and nappy-changing units (not always as clean as they could be).
Swimming classes for children. Pre-school (31/2-5 yrs, confident in water); adult and child (2-4 yrs); adult and baby (4 mths-2 yrs). Classes also available for children with special needs. All lessons take place in the centre's small pool. Spectating area for parents/carers. See also

gymnastics for details of gym nippers classes for 3-5 year olds.
Crèche:
Opening times: Mon: 9.00 – 13.15; Tues - Fri 9.00-12.00 (0-5 yrs), £3.40/child (LAC holder £2.20).
Cafeteria:
Children's menu, high chairs, facilities to heat baby food and to warm milk.

Royal Commonwealth Pool
Dalkeith Road
Newington EH16 5AE
Tel: 667 7211
Opening times: Mon-Fri: 6.00-21.30; Sat: 6.00-8.00 then 10.00-21.30; Sun: 10.00-16.30.

Admission: Under 12s can swim for free and there are reduced rates for under 18s. For current adult admission prices, please phone.
Car parking: limited – the overflow car park can also be crowded at peak times, so it is advisable to leave plenty time for parking before lessons.

Built for the 1970 Commonwealth Games, facilities include a large competition-sized 50m pool, shallow teaching pool, and diving pool. Other facilities include a gym with exercise and weight machines, separate male and female saunas, a cafe and a crèche. For reasons of hygiene, pushchairs must be left in the foyer pram store – a separate (unlocked) room is provided where pushchairs can be left.. The entire building is a no smoking zone.
In both the main pool and the teaching pool children under 9 must be accompanied in the water by an adult.
Changing areas:
down a steep flight of stairs. Lift access to changing level available. Female and male changing areas have high chairs, which you can take into your cubicle. There are also play pens, nappy bins and a nappy-changing table. Hand hairdryers are available. Coin-operated lockers – 50p returnable. There is a table for dressing babies in the male changing room. Pushchairs are available downstairs for sleeping babies.
Teaching pool is usually occupied by young children, and many parents change their babies' clothes on the wide shelf with padded mats surrounding the pool, so they stay uncovered for the minimum time. The teaching pool temperature is 30°C. Chairs on the pool side for spectators.
Parent and baby sessions held every weekday am. Under 1s at 10.00 and under 2s at 10.30. Parents and babies

introduced to early water skills under the supervision of an instructor. Parent and child lessons are also available – contact centre for current information.

Swim classes for under 5s are available during term times and must be booked and paid for in advance. Pre-school classes for 3-5 year olds are held mornings and afternoons everyday. Classes for over 5s run during term times, Sat mornings and in the Summer holidays.

There is also a soft play area. 'Clambers', for 3-8 yrs, is a large multi-level adventure play area, with slides, tubes, ball pit and lots of soft surfaces. During term time, under 3s can enjoy 'Clambers' accompanied by their parent/carer. Toilets available upstairs and down.

Coffee Outlet:
High chairs (8), bottles heated, no-smoking, parties hosted
Current opening times (subject to change): Mon-Fri 1000-1800 and Sat/Sun 11.00-17.00. Hot food is available up to 17.15 during the week and 1600 at the weekend.

There is a spacious seating area in front of the coffee outlet or beside Clambers. Both areas overlook the main swimming pool and there is a relaxed atmosphere and plenty of room for children to run around. The area is also fully accessible for pushchairs and prams. The coffee outlet sells snacks and hot food and there are various vending machines selling snacks and drinks. There are toilets nearby with nappy changing facilities although these are not always as clean as they could be.

Warrender Swim Centre
Thirlestane Road
Marchmont EH9 1AP
Tel: 447 0052

Warrender Swim Centre was closed for major refurbishment at the time of publication. Due to re-open in Jan 2006. Contact Centre for information.

Wester Hailes Swimming Pool
Western Hailes Education Centre
5 Murrayburn Dr
Wester Hailes EH14 2SU
Tel: 442 2201
Opening times: Mon, Tue, Thu, Fri 9.30-21.10; Wed 9.30-18.00 (women only 18.00-20.10); Sat 10.30-16.30; Sun 9.30-16.30.
Admission: adult £2.00; child £1.00. 10p key deposit.

Modern pool with amenities including: a 25m pool; a children's pool; and a diving pool with springboard and highboard. The children's pool is graded in depth, so small children can touch the bottom at one end. There is a frog house with slide into the water. Under 4s must be supervised on the slide. Nappy-changing facilities available on the pool side. In the Summer, there's an early morning family swim 8.50-9.30. When the leisure pool is really busy it operates on session times.

Changing area:
In the female changing area, there's a separate facility which includes mats, play pen and high chairs. These items are available on request in the male changing area. Lockers lock automatically on closure, so beware of locking the key inside! There is a powder room with mirrors, and hairdryers are available. A lockable pushchair bay is also available.

Classes:
A comprehensive programme of swimming lessons for ages 3 yrs+ is available. These must be booked in advance. Details on request.

Crèche:
Opening times: Term time only Mon-Thurs: 8.15-16.45; Fri: 8.15 – 16.00. Pre-bookable. 75p/hour.

Cafeteria:
£, high chairs (2), bottles heated, parties hosted, seats 200

Opening times: Mon-Fri 9.00-21.00; Sat/Sun 10.00-16.00. Self-service cafeteria overlooking pool, offering an inexpensive range of snacks and meals. Wholefood and vegetarian options available on weekdays. The staffroom may be used on request for breastfeeding. Prams and pushchairs allowed inside. Take-aways available. Toilets by cafeteria.

THEATRES

Theatres are becoming more child friendly and there are often shows for children aged 3 years+, particularly during the Children's Theatre Festival as well as the Fringe. However be aware that theatres may not be suitable for pushchairs. If a show is advertised as being for children, it's still best to check beforehand on age restrictions and the duration of the show. Refreshments may not always be suitable for children.

Various theatre brochures and festival publications give information on facilities such as parking, toilets and access.

IN THE CITY

Assembly Rooms
54 George Street
Tel: 220 4348 (Admin)
Tel: 220 4349 (Box Office)

Used as Science Festival venue during Mar/Apr. Also hosts antique fairs craft fairs etc. Lift to 1st floor and toilets. Nappy changing facilities in toilet for the disabled in Main Foyer. Quiet area on request for breastfeeding.

Church Hill Theatre
33a Morningside Road EH10 4RR
Tel: 447 7597

Getting there: there is a bus stop in front of the theatre: served by numbers 11, 15, 16, 17 and 23. Parking in front of the theatre can be difficult but there is unrestricted on-street parking in the surrounding side streets.

Musicals, drama, and dance school shows all by amateur groups. Occasional shows for children, usually during Edinburgh Festival. Ramped main entrance. Staircase to main theatre. Parking in surrounding streets. Parking for the disabled outside theatre. Toilet for the disabled with nappy changing facilities on the ground floor. Bottle warming facilities are also available. Coffee bar.

Edinburgh Festival Theatre
13/29 Nicolson Street,
Edinburgh EH8 9FT
Tel: 529 6000 (Box Office)

Nearest car parking: George Square parking bays. Lothian Buses: 2, 3, 3A, 5, 7, 8, 14, 21, 29, 31, 33, 37, 37A, 42 and 49.
Occasional children's shows for 3 yrs and over. Level access.

Café Lucia on the ground floor is licensed for children until 20.00. Toilet with nappy-changing facilities on 1st floor (lift access). Although the façade is very modern, the actual theatre is traditional and some seats have a slightly restricted view.

George Square Theatre
George Square
Tel: 651 1930
If travelling by car, there's metered parking up to 2 hrs (free after 18.30) on George Sq itself.

A venue which is used during university holidays for shows, including children's shows. However, this is a university lecture theatre and consequently there are no specific facilities for young children or babies.

King's Theatre
2 Leven Street,
Edinburgh EH3 9LQ
Tel: 529 6000 (Box Office)
Nearest car parking: nearby streets in evenings. Lothian Buses 1, 10, 11, 15, 16, 17, 23, 24, 27, 28, 34, 35 and 45. Traditional theatre. Occasional children's shows, some specifically aimed at under 5s. Some shows with special low price tickets. Book early for a good seat. Ice cream and refreshments available. Toilet with nappy-changing facilities on ground floor.

The Netherbow
43-45 High Street EH1 1SR
Tel: 556 9579
Closed until early 2006 for extensive renovations. No definite information available at time of writing.

North Edinburgh Arts Centre
15A Pennywell Court EH4 4TZ
Tel: 315 2151 (box office)
Email: admin@northedinburgharts.co.uk
Web: www.northedinburgharts.co.uk

By bus: take Lothian Buses 27, 32A, 37, 37A, 42. Get off at Muirhouse Shopping Centre and approach through the shopping centre. Nearest parking: free parking beside the library and shopping centre.
Purpose-built arts centre. Offers a variety of performances and other arts activities for children including some for the very young.
In addition, there's a full programme of theatre and dance performances, plus weekly family Saturday workshops in a range of art forms every single Saturday. The Centre also offers Summer schools and other holiday arts activities run – some may be suitable for under 5s.
Fully accessible centre, with baby changing facilities, garden with play structure and a family friendly café.
Café:
£-££, highchairs (4), bottle and baby food heated.
Opening hours: 10.00-15.00; lunches 12.00-14.30.
Offers fairtrade coffee and plenty healthy food options.
Bright environment with access to garden area.
Nappy changing (M&F).

Playhouse Theatre
18-22 Greenside Place
Tel: 0870 606 3434 (Box Office)
A wide variety of shows including opera, musicals, ballet and rock concerts. Occasional children's shows. Toilets on ground floor. Some restricted views.

The Queen's Hall
37 Clerk St EH8 9JG
Tel: 668 2019 (Box Office -Mon-Sat 10.00-17.00)
Tel: 0131 668 3456 (Administration)
Fax: 668 2656
Email: admin@queenshalledinburgh.org
Web: www.queenshalledinburgh.co.uk
Nearest car parking: nearby streets, Buccleugh Street, or George Square.
Some concerts and events for children. Toilet for disabled with nappy changing area. There are some restricted view seats due to the pillars in the main performance space.

Royal Lyceum Theatre
30 Grindlay Street
Box Office: 248 4848
Family show at Christmas. Has also been used as a venue for the Scottish International Children's Festival in May. Lifts to all levels. Toilets for the disabled on the ground floor. Nappy changing facilities. Traditional-style theatre – very ornate and plush inside, once you are past the modern glass façade.

St Bride's Centre
10 Orwell Terrace EH11 2DY
Tel: 346 1405
Children's theatre and film shows, usually in school holidays. Tue: Arts and Crafts class (4-6 yrs). Thu: After Schools club (4-8 yrs).
Café with large, enclosed play area and reading corner. Free drop-in parent and tots group Fri 9.30-11.30. Nappy changing facilities. St Brides programmes detailing children events and classes is distributed through local schools and libraries.

Theatre Workshop
34 Hamilton Place
Stockbridge
Tel: 226 5425 (Box Office)
Web: www.theatre-workshop.com
Many shows geared for school children and occasionally under 5s. Also exhibitions, classes and workshops. Concession rates apply to children's tickets. Nappy-changing facilities. Café.

Traverse Theatre
10 Cambridge St EH1 2ED
Tel: 228 1404 (Box Office)
Tel: 228 5383 (Bar Café)
Email: boxoffice@traverse.co.uk
(for booking tickets)
Web: www.traverse.co.uk
Occasional children's shows including the Children's International Theatre Festival (May, annually). Generous discounts to most performances. The Traverse Bar Café is licensed for children until 20.00. Children's portions available all day. Lift to eating area and toilet with nappy changing facilities. See also Eating Out Central.

CLOSE TO HOME

Brunton Theatre
Ladywell Way
Musselburgh EH21 6AA
Tel: 665 2240
Getting there: situated around 4 miles from Edinburgh city centre, on the main road into Musselburgh. By Lothian bus 15, 15A, 26, 44. First 44C, 44D, 124, 129. By car: ample free parking.
Ramped access to foyer, staircase and lift to main theatre. Many shows suitable for young children. Every seat has a view. Runs a pantomime season. Spacious toilets with nappy-changing facilities. Caters for disabled patrons, with facilities such as viewing gallery, toilet, lift and easy access. Café serving children's meals, bar and kiosk open during performances.

FURTHER AFIELD

Macrobert Arts Centre
University of Stirling
Stirling FK9 4LA
Tel: 01786 466666
Web: www.macrobert.org
Located on University of Stirling campus. Follow M9 to end at Dunblane then follow signs to Bridge of Allan. Travel through Bridge of Allan and entrance to university is on left as you exit the village. Regular bus service to the university from Stirling.

Fabulous arts centre clearly designed with children in mind. Lots to interest the under 5s. Varied programme for the whole family including many children's theatre productions and current films. Panto at Christmas. Art, dance and theatre workshops for a variety of age groups. Treehouse is a crèche facility in a lovely bright space open 7 days/wk between 10.15 and 13.15 which provides arts activity and play for children aged 3 months to 12 years. You can enjoy coffee or a show or even leave the Macrobert building while your children are at the Treehouse. Costs £4 per hour. Spacious foyer area with small tables for little ones, colouring activities and toys.

Cafe with good range of food. Extensive children's menu. A popular place for kids' birthdays.

Fully accessible to pushchairs. Area for parking pushchairs near to main entrance.

Private area for feeding in baby care room. Baby changing facilities in M&F toilets and in baby care room.

TRAINS

Trainspotting

There is a footbridge which connects West Princes Street Gardens to the lower ramparts of Edinburgh Castle behind the Ross Bandstand. Its mostly transparent sides provide a perfect viewing point for the small train enthusiast. Indeed, many of them can be found gathered at this spot regardless of the weather! The bridge crosses the 4 main railway lines into and out of Edinburgh Waverley station. The trains are of various types and run to various destinations both near and far. Drivers tend to be friendly and will usually wave back to any children that are on the bridge. Some also blow their whistles.

Bo'ness & Kinneil Railway
Bo'ness Station
Union St
Bo'ness
Tel: 01506 822298 (Talking Timetables)
Tel: 01506 825855 (Office)
Web: www.srps.org.uk

Getting there: take M9 out of Edinburgh. Come off at J5 and follow the signs to Bo'ness on the A904. Alternatively, take A90 out of Edinburgh, then follow the A904 out through Newton to Champany Corner on the A904. Turn right and follow the road to Bo'ness. The railway is situated near to the shore of the River Forth, in the town centre and is signposted. Nearest train station is Linlithgow – you can

catch a bus to Bo'ness from the High St. and Bo'ness bus terminal is very close to the railway.

Opening times: Apr-Oct only Sat and Sun; July & August, daily except Mon.

Return rail travel: adult £4.50; concession £3.50; child £2.00. Under 5s free. Family ticket (2 A & 2 C) £11.00. 10% discount for groups of 12 or more paying passengers.

Steam train trips. A very pleasant outing for both children & parents. Special events are very popular e.g. Easter Egg Specials; Days Out with Thomas w/ends in May & August; Santa train trips in Dec. Special timetable and fares (incl. those for under 5s) apply for special events. Details from Scottish Railway Preservation Society on the numbers above.

Fares are available which include Caverns of Birkhill Mine (great visit, but is a very long way back up carrying your kids). The Scottish Railway Exhibition at Bo'ness station has an interesting collection of locos, rolling stock etc. with a Scottish connection. Admission: adults £1.00; children free.

VISITOR ATTRACTIONS

Brass Rubbing Centre
Trinity Apse
Chalmer's Close
The Royal Mile
81 High Street EH1 1SS
Tel: 556 4364

Opening times: Apr-Sept, Mon-Sat 10.00-17.00; during the Festival open Sun 12.00-17.00.

Admission: free, but there is a charge for the brass rubbing.

Tucked away in an old church building, between High St and Jeffrey St, the Centre is bright, warm and welcoming inside. Contains a collection of replicas moulded from ancient Pictish stones, rare Scottish brasses and Mediaeval church brasses. Of more interest to the over 5s, but a mature 4 yr old might enjoy producing a small rubbing. Materials are provided. Stop rubbings at 15.45.

Butterfly & Insect World
Dobbies Garden World
Lasswade
Midlothian
Tel: 663 4932
Email: info@edinburgh-butterfly-world.co.uk
Web: www. edinburgh-butterfly-world.co.uk

Getting there: on A7, nr Dalkeith, By bus, take LRT 3 or 29.

Opening times: Apr-Oct, Mon-Sun 9.30-17.30. Nov-Mar, Mon-Sun 10.00-17.00.
Closed 25, 26 Dec and 1 Jan.

Admission: adult £4.90; concession £3.75; child £3.75; family ticket(2A &4C) £20. Under 3s free.
Season tickets from £15; family from £47. Group rates, guided tour and talks available.

One of Europe's largest butterfly farms. Popular attraction with a minimum of 500 free-flying butterflies on display, although the numbers can escalate to 1200 at times. The butterflies live amidst a landscape of tropical plants, little waterfalls and pools, which contain fish and terrapins.
Individual displays of other creatures – bees, spiders, 'glow-in-the-dark' scorpions, snakes, lizards, beetles, stick insects etc - some of which you get a chance to touch! Also displays of 'life-cycles of butterflies' and 'insects and habitats'. Entrance is though the shop, where there's a good selection of books and gifts.
It's very humid in the butterfly area, so be prepared for this – though you might need jackets to go outside and look at the bees etc.

There's a café in the garden centre, serving meals, snacks, etc. High chairs available. Toilets and separate nappy-changing facilities are also available (go past the pay-desk and they're on the left). There are a couple of play areas – one adjacent to the café, one situated between Butterfly and Insect World and Dobbies Garden World.

Camera Obscura
549 Castle Hill EH1 2ND
Tel: 226 3709

Opening times: daily, 9.30-19.00 (British Summertime); 10.00-17.00 (end Oct-Mid Mar). Also dependent on weather and daylight.
Admission: adult £6.45; child £4.15. Under 5s free. Group concessions also available - group visits must be booked in advance.
This is the oldest purpose-built visitor attraction in Edinburgh, and adults and children alike still find it fascinating. Over 3s would probably get a lot from a visit. Under 3s usually enjoy the hologram exhibition on level 3 (though they may have to be lifted up to appreciate the effects) and the view from the rooftop terrace on

level 5 more than the camera. It has to be very dark in the camera room, so if your child is nervous of this, be aware although the sight of the streets below may take up their attention! Has a very narrow staircase, which is unsuitable for prams and pushchairs. These may be left in the shop. No specific facilities for babies or young children, but there is a public toilet directly across the road. Choose a bright day to visit!

Our Dynamic Earth
112 Holyrood Road
Tel: 550 7800
Web: www.dynamicearth.co.uk

Opening times: Apr-Jun, Sept-Oct, Mon-Sun 10.00-17.00 (last entry 15.50); July-Aug 10.00-18.00 (last entry 16.50); Nov-Mar, Wed-Sun 10.00-17.00 (last entry 15.50). (Occasionally open half-term, please phone).
Closed Christmas Eve and Christmas Day.
Admission: adult £8.95; child £5.95; disabled child £4.25. Under 5s free. Family tickets – several variations available, max (2A & 3C) £28.50. Other concessions available.

Our Dynamic Earth is an interactive tourist attraction, which tells the story of the Earth and the elements. it's not primarily designed for under 5s and you're more likely to take a young child when visiting with older children. Be prepared for the fact that they may be scared when it is dark, with the flashes of light or when the floor vibrates in the volcano experience. However many under 5s will love it! Expect to spend around 11/2 hrs, 'travelling' through time, though you can 'escape' earlier – but you might need to be shown a quick way by a member of staff.
You can meet a life-sized pterodactyl, find out what volcanic tremors feel like and touch an iceberg.
Everywhere is pushchair accessible, with lifts where necessary. Older children tend to crowd round interactive displays – so be prepared to get stuck in there if it's busy. There's a shop, Natural Selection, which sells 'earth-themed' gifts, including pocket money toys etc.
There are a variety of special events during the year, some of which will be suitable for under 5s. Phone or watch press for details.
Nappy change facilities available. Chair suitable for breastfeeding in the nappy changing room.
Food Chain Café:
£-££, high chairs (6); bottle heating/baby food warming available.
Open all day, serving hot meals, snacks, pastries and hot and cold drinks.

EATING OUT

Some new parents feel that once they have children, the type of bistro, café or restaurant they are welcome in alters. Out go, perhaps, the sleek bistros, in comes 'chips with everything'. Every style of eatery has its place, but you shouldn't feel pigeon-holed and the good news is that things are still improving in terms of dining out with children.

Everyone is different when it comes to the idea of a pleasant (or successful) meal out – we all have different tastes in food, different dietary requirements, different expectations, and so on. To reflect this, we have included a range of cafés, restaurants and bistros in Edinburgh, the surrounds and further afield, which have been tried and tested – because it's easy for a restaurant etc to say they are child friendly, but it's quite another thing to turn up and put this to the test! We have tried to give a varied selection – from the 'family-friendly' restaurant chains, to independent bistros – and even some of Edinburgh's premier restaurants.

The experience of eating out with young children often lies somewhere between fun and enthusiastic chaos! Needs vary according to age and our researchers endeavoured to check all the various requirements. A newborn will be quite content in a car seat, but in a matter of months a high chair is a priority, then, before you know it, the location of the toilet is the first requisite for toilet training toddlers – the list goes on.

Some of the places listed may not be able to accommodate all ages of children, but where there has been a positive attitude towards dining out with a child, we have included them, and have noted that they might be better suited to, say an 'older 'under 5, say 3-5, where we felt this appropriate.

If you are choosing a meal for a special occasion you are always best to book first, mentioning that you will have children under 5 yrs (and that you found the restaurant listed in this book). Check that the facilities you need will be available (high chairs may be reserved, for example). Several hotels and family restaurants have special promotions at the weekend, such as under 5s eating free or special children's entertainment, so it's worth checking.

Hours

We have listed the opening hours. For those restaurants that open late into the evening, we've listed the 'curfew' times for children, where the venue noted them.
If you're booking for a party including children, it's

worthwhile mentioning the fact when booking, as some places have earlier 'curfews' than others, although 20.00 is a popular cut off point, and when it comes to eating out with young children, their personal 'cut-off point' should always be considered, for your own sake as well as the other diners.

Pricing

We have used the pound symbol (£) to represent the approximate price of an adult main course: £: under and up to £5; ££: £5-10; £££: over £10. This usually refers to lunch, rather than dinner options.

High chairs

We have asked how many high chairs, clip-ons and booster seats there are, but bear in mind that the high chairs may well all be occupied. Make sure that staff know you require one so that they can help you; they might not always notice you struggle with a small fractious tot! And don't be afraid to mention any problems with the high chair to the staff – you might be surprised how many do not have restraints.

Nappy-change surface

What constitutes a 'good changing surface' to a parent and to a manager with no children may be very different. A shelf with a rim is easy to install and does not take up much space, and is much more acceptable than crawling around on the floor of a public toilet. On the other hand, it is a pleasant surprise to find that an increasing number of places keep a supply of disposable nappies and wipes tucked away in case of emergencies – ask if you are desperate, and you may strike lucky!

With the role of fathers increasingly acknowledged, more places are trying to offer changing facilities outwith the female toilets. So, within the lists we've tried to specify where the nappy change is: (F) indicates female toilets; (M) indicates male toilets, (D) indicates toilet for the disabled; and (M&F) indicates facilities accessible to either parent/carer – which can often be a dedicated nappy change room.

Licenses

Generally, restaurants can only serve alcohol with food.

Parties hosted – Contact management for details, or see Birthdays and Celebrations.

Prams

Some places do not allow prams or pushchairs. The entries indicate if there is space inside to store them (perhaps folded).

Toilet Access
Access should be reasonable; we have said if there are stairs or other hazards.

Play and Provisions
Details of special provisions for young children were included in the questionnaire and are indicated in the listings, e.g. children's menus or half portions, baby foods, the availability of play equipment, toys, etc.

Fast Food
Details of the most popular chains are at the end of Eating Out. As these chains are pretty much the same no matter which country, city or town you are in, we haven't gone into any great detail – you know what to expect.

You Tell Us
Please let us know of any other places where your family have enjoyed a meal, and of any good or bad experiences in places included here – management or staff changes can change a venue for the better or for the worse.

Email us via our website www.edinburghforunderfives. co.uk or write to PO Box 012345, Edinburgh, EH9 2YB.

It may be that you have a favourite restaurant or café that has always been great to visit because they are attentive and positive to families and individuals with young children, but they might not be in the book – not every venue we contacted wanted to be listed, for one reason or another.

Smoking, No Smoking and Breastfeeding Welcomed
Unlike past editions, this edition does not include specific information whether a venue welcomes breastfeeding or whether it is non-smoking. This is due to recent legislation passed in Scotland, which is currently different to the rest of the UK.

From March 18 2005, it has been a criminal offence in Scotland for a mother to be harassed or otherwise prevented from breastfeeding her child (defined as a child under the age of 2 yrs) in a public place or licensed premises where children were previously welcomed (e.g. 'family-friendly' pubs). This law also covers other carers feeding children (as defined above) milk.

From 26 March 2006, the Smoking, Health and Social Care (Scotland) Bill will come into force. This bill bans smoking in enclosed public places such as restaurants, pubs and workplaces.

We've listed the restaurants and cafés geographically, and then alphabetically - enjoy!

CENTRAL EDINBURGH

Including restaurants, bistros and cafés from:
Queen Street-Chambers Street
Grassmarket
West End-London Road

Always Sunday
170 High Street
Tel 622 0667

Opening hours: Mon-Fri 8.00-18.00; Sat-Sun 9.00-18.00 (daily to 19.30 in Jul, 22.00 in Festival).
£ / ££, clip-on seat (1), bottles heated, nappy changing mat in F toilet but can be accessed by fathers, licensed, seats 40 (+16 outside in summer).
Airy, bright self-service café/restaurant with friendly and accommodating staff in a super location on the Royal Mile. Aims to give visitors 'that Sunday feeling' by offering a varied menu in relaxed and arty surroundings. The wide choice ranges from full breakfasts to home baking via soups, salads and hot dishes and is particularly strong on healthy and vegetarian options. The imaginative fruit smoothies were a highlight on our visit. No separate children's menu but half portions available on request. Clear labelling for special diets. Space to park two or three pushchairs unfolded.
Toilets in basement down a flight of steep stairs.

Agua Restaurant
Apex City Hotel
61 Grassmarket   EH1 2JF
Tel: 0845 365 0002 (Restaurant Hotline)
Web: www.apexhotels.co.uk
(menus and online booking)
££-£££, highchairs (5), licensed, will warm up bottles/baby food, seats 56.
Stylish restaurant with views over the Grassmarket. Open daily for lunch, dinner & snacks in the bar area. Children's portions taken from main menu. The restaurant offers an eat early deal 16.00-18.30, 7 days a week.
Nappy changing (F).

Bean Scene
67 Holyrood Road
Tel: 557 6549

Opening hours: Mon-Sat 8.00-20.00; Sun 10.00-20.00
£, high chairs (3), baby food and bottles heated, seats 30.

Trendy but chilled out coffee house near the site of the new Parliament and Holyrood Palace. It sells a variety of light snacks and tapas. Kid's lunch bags are no longer available and most of the food is geared towards adult tastes, but if your child likes olives and goat's cheese this may be the place for you! The atmosphere is relaxed (there are several large sofas) and aims to be child friendly. A limited range of toys are provided and there are free baby wipes and nappies in the changing room. There is a side entrance if you want to avoid steps at the door. Limited space to park prams inside.
Nappy changing (M&F).

Bella
7 Hanover Street
Tel: 225 4808
Opening hours: Mon-Sat 10.30-23.00; Sun 12.00-23.00.
££, high chairs (6), can provide hot water for heating bottles and baby food, licensed, seats 114.

Popular city-centre eatery. Friendly, attentive service and child friendly staff. Good value children's menu of Italian favourites, dessert and unlimited juice. Crayons and colour-in mat provided and children's seasonal pictures may be displayed. Pushchairs can be taken in and stored.
Nappy-changing facility (F only) in upstairs toilet,

BhS Restaurant
64 Princes Street
Tel 226 2621
Opening hours: Mon-Wed 9.00-18.15; Thu 9.00-20.00; Fri-Sat 9.00-18.15; Sun 11.00-17.00.

£, high chairs for babies (5) & toddlers (5), breastfeeding welcome, bottles heated, nappy-change surface, seats 200.

Large, spacious self-service café/restaurant. Level access from Rose St entrance but can also be accessed from main store via escalator to centre of eating area. Offers an extensive choice from snacks to lunches, including vegetarian dishes and carry out items; large children's menu and half portions available for under 12s. Children's meals come in decorative lunch/picnic boxes for under £3. Baby food available, or will warm food brought in by parents.
Toilets and feeding and nappy-changing room (M&F) one floor up (3 flights of stairs).

Brodies Coffee Houses
Ottakar's Bookshop (1st floor)
57 George Street
Tel: 220 2943
Opening hours: Mon-Sat 9.00-17.00; Sun 11.30-16.30.

£, high chairs (4), bottles heated, nappy-change surface, seats 90.

Handily located self-service café on 1st floor of Ottakar's bookshop, accessed by stairs or a lift. Offers a varied menu and accommodates most tastes, includes light snacks and home baking (including some of the best scones in Edinburgh). Child portions and carry-out food available. Tables in corners and balcony offer some privacy to breastfeeding mothers as do the large, comfortable sofas. Illustrations from children's books brighten the walls. Willing and friendly staff. Ample space to park pushchairs unfolded.
Toilets with a basic changing shelf (F) on same floor.

Browns Restaurant and Bar
131-133 George Street
Tel: 225 4442
Opening hours: Mon-Sun 11.00-23.00.
££-£££, high chairs (8), children's menu, baby food and bottles heated, , licensed, seats 270.

Spacious restaurant at the West end of George St that has become a firm favourite with many families. Owing to licensing laws children are not allowed in the bar area, but under 5s are welcome in the restaurant. The food prepared especially for children is good quality, and children are served with a free portion of ice cream at the end of their meal. A dining experience that doesn't compromise on adult appeal, while remaining child-friendly. Attentive and friendly staff, keen to accommodate children.
Nappy-changing facilities (M&F) in ground floor toilet

Café Rouge
43 Frederick Street
Tel: 225 4515
Opening hours: Mon-Sun 9.00-23.00.

££, high chairs (8), breastfeeding welcome, nappy-changing facilities, no-smoking area, licensed, seats 140

A few steps up to entrance, then all on one level. As the name suggests, there's a French accent to the menu of this spacious restaurant. Table-service and daily specials. 'Menu pour les enfants' includes choice of items, juice and dessert for one price. Half portions also available. Nappy-changing in toilet for disabled.

Centotre
103 George Street
Tel: 225 1550
Opening hours: Mon-Fri 8.00-22.00 (22.30 Fri), Sat-Sun 11.00-1700 (22.30 Sat).
£££, highchairs (4), baby food/bottles heated, children's menu, licensed, seats 120.

Table service restaurant in the elegant setting of an 18th century townhouse with a very central location. The ballroom style restaurant is light and airy and appeals to adults and children alike. Under fives are welcomed in the restaurant area (children are not allowed in the bar area). Children's menu offers quality Italian dishes and children may also enjoy lighter choices or half potions from the adult menu. The motto here is 'fresh, simple, Italian', with a commitment to family values. Staff are friendly and service is efficient, although waiting periods may be longer during peak times. Quickly becoming a favourite with families. Possibly the best hot chocolate in Edinburgh!
Nappy-changing M&F (ground floor),

Chisholms Restaurant
Caledonian Hilton Hotel
Princes Street, West End
Tel: 222 8900
Opening hours: Mon-Sun breakfast and dinner; Mon-Sat lunch (please telephone to confirm restaurant's current hours).
£££, high chairs (4), bottles heated, licensed, seats 120.

Table-service in plush newly refurbished surroundings. Family Sunday Roast every Sunday 12.00-15.00 – great for a special family occasion (£££). Large range of food and snacks throughout day. Space to park pushchairs and prams. Crayons and paper provided if requested. During off peak hours entry is gained through main hotel door.

Debenhams
4th Floor, The Castle View Restaurant
Princes Street
Tel: 08445 616161
Opening hours: Mon-Fri 9.30-16.00; Sat 9.00-17.00; Sun 11.00-16.30.

£, high chairs (7), booster seats (2), bottle-warmer and microwave, nappy-change surface, seats 96. Free "Baby VIP" kits including feeding bowl, bib, spoon and wet wipe.

Large self-service restaurant with friendly staff and (as its name suggests!) stunning views of castle. Impressive range of highchairs to suit both babies and toddlers. Varied menu including hot food (with children's options), salads, baking and baby food. Children's menu plus 'fun sheet' and crayons for colouring-in. Children's pick and mix, and packed lunch boxes came with free fruit offer when we visited.
Toilets and baby changing facilities (in disabled toilet) nearby at lifts.

The Elephant House
21 George IV Bridge
Tel: 220 5355
Opening hours: Mon-Fri 8.00-23.00; Sat, Sun 9.00-23.00
£, high chairs (2)

A useful café stop on the way into town from the Meadows. The Elephant House is a self-service coffee house with good range of coffees, baking and lunches. Staff happy to accommodate children's tastes and will prepare a plain sandwich for a fussy eater! Wonderful display of all things 'elephant' to keep toddlers amused; they also love the elephant seats at the front of the café in the no-smoking area. Magazines and children's books at rear. Space may be limited at busy times.
Toilets on the same level as the café and nappy-changing (M&F) in the toilet for the disabled.

Est Est Est
135 George Street
Tel: 225 2555
Opening hours: Mon-Sun 12.00-23.00.
££, high chairs (12), bottles heated, licensed, seats 200.

This eatery aims to combine great food, cool surroundings and a positive attitude towards families. Popular with people without children too, the restaurant manages to cater for all ages. There is a children's menu, although half portions of the main pasta dishes always go down well, and they can draw while waiting for their food (crayons and paper provided).
Children can also make their own pizzas.
Nappy-change surface in (M &F).

The Filling Station
235 High Street
Tel: 226 2488
Opening hours: Mon-Sun 9.00 – 11.15; 12.00-00.00.

££, high chairs (4), tables suitable for clip-on chairs, bottles heated, licensed, seats 122.

Children welcome in the eating area of this bar/restaurant. Car theme throughout, fun atmosphere, TV and video. American, Mexican and Italian food. Children's menu with the usual culprits – pasta options are good value but lack vegetables. Attentive, child friendly service; balloons and children's activity pack provided, including seeds for children to collect and plant.
Nappy-changing area adjacent to toilet for the disabled (on the ground floor). Excessively busy during August and the adjacent bar area can be rowdy towards evening. Nappy-change surface (M&F),

Frasers Restaurant
5th Floor, 145 Princes Street
Opening hours: Mon, Wed, Fri 9.00-17.00; Tue 9.30-17.00; Thu 9.00-19.00; Sat 9.00-17.30; Sun 11.00-16.30.
£, high chairs (3), bottle and food warming items provided, seats 116.

Self-service restaurant with easy access from lifts. Spacious eating area, children's menu. Toilets located adjacent to the restaurant.

Garfunkels
29-31 Frederick Street
Tel: 225 4579
Web: www.garfunkels.co.uk
Opening hours: Mon-Sun 12.00-23.30.

££, high chairs (12), tables suitable for clip-ons, bottles heated, nappy-change surface (in F toilets only, but alternative arrangements can be made for men with under 5s), licensed, parties are hosted on weekdays.

Comfortable, table-service restaurant serving a wide range of American-influenced food. Also offers a children's menu. All children under 10 receive a bag containing 'goodies'.
Toilets downstairs in basement.

Gennaro
64 Grassmarket
Tel: 226 3706
Opening hours: Mon-Sun 12.00-00.00.
££, clip-ons (2), bottles heated, licensed, seats 90.
Traditional, long-established Italian restaurant which welcomes families. Varied menu with children's portions available. No prams, pushchairs folded. Seating outside continental style. If not too busy, waiters like to entertain children, allowing parents to enjoy their meal in peace. Carry-out food available.

Gurkha Brigade
9a Antigua Street
Tel: 556 6446
Opening hours: Mon-Fri 12.00-14.30, 17.30-23.00; Sat 12.00-14.30, 17.30-00.00.
£-££, high chair (1), licensed, BYOB, seats 40.
Friendly Nepalese restaurant welcomes families at all times. Children's snacks and meals such as chicken salad, fish and chips also available, but the menu, unsurprisingly concentrates on Nepalese cuisine: Chinese and Indian influences, but with an emphasis on coriander, ginger, chilli, and garlic. Garden at rear for summer visits. Chef welcomes children in the kitchen to see food being prepared. Space for pushchairs.
No nappy-changing facilities.

Hard Rock Café
20 George Street
Tel: 260 3000
Opening hours: Mon-Sat 12.00-late, (under 14s must be seated by 20.00)
££, high chairs (6), booster seats (6), bottles heated, licensed, seats 150.
Busy and informal family restaurant, with a focus on US and Tex/Mex food. Reasonable access for prams, and there are small booths available for family gatherings or if you prefer some privacy for breastfeeding. Colour-in books, crayons and balloons for children, also plasma screens and fairly loud music to keep them amused. Staff friendly, very attentive, and welcoming to children.
Nappy-change facilities (M&F).

Hendersons
94 Hanover Street
Tel: 225 2131
Email: info@hendersonsofedinburgh.co.uk
Web: www.hendersonsofedinburgh.co.uk

Opening hours: Mon-Sat 7.30-22.30; Sun 12.00-21.00.
££, high chairs (4), tables suitable for clip-ons, bottles heated, nappy-change surface (M&F), licensed, seats 180.

Basement buffet restaurant (access down several stairs), serving broad range of vegetarian and vegan food. Children's menu for £4.50. Healthy food displayed so children can choose what they want – not the most visually appetising if your child isn't used to it. No chips! Several dishes contain nuts, so do check if allergies are an issue. Quiet alcoves make pushchair access tricky, but they're good for breastfeeding if you prefer some privacy. Staff available to help with pushchairs. Carry-out service available.
Books and crayons can be provided.

The Hub
Castlehill
Tel: 473 2067
Email: thehub@eif.co.uk
Opening hours: Sun, Mon 9.30-18.00; Tue-Sat 9.30-22.00.
£, high chairs (3)

Fixed menu and light snacks. Children's portions of most adult meals available as well as very reasonably priced children's menu offering good quality food. Spacious inside, with a mix of low sofas and regular tables and chairs. There's also seating outside on the terrace, which is great in summer. Children may appreciate having lunch beside the castle. Pushchairs and prams welcome.
Toilets and nappy changing facilities near to restaurant, towards the rear of the ground floor.

Jenners
48 Princes St
Tel: 225 2442
Web: www.jenners.com
Jenners is popular, but can be daunting when negotiated with a pushchair. For easiest access, enter by Rose St next to the Barber's Shop and take the lift up. If this takes you too far from the areas you want, or you don't want the perfumery/beauty dept first, enter the store by the side entrance of S St David's St. As with all entrances (except the Rose St lift option), this involves negotiating a few steps. This brings you into Menswear. Go towards the rear of the store (Men's Designer Dept) and this gives you access to the large lift, which makes for easier pushchair transport.

There are 4 restaurants to choose from in store.

Toilets, nappy-changing and feeding room all located on 3rd floor.

Café 2
Ground Floor
Opening hours: Mon-Wed, Fri, Sat 8.30-17.30; Thu 8.30-19.30; Sun 11.00-16.30.
£, no high chairs.

Coffees, teas, soft drinks, sticky pastries etc. Small café on entrance-level mezzanine above Menswear dept. Ideal for a quick bite, but it can be busy and the stools aren't ideal for small children.

Kenningtons Restaurant
1st Floor
Opening hours: Mon, Wed-Sat 9.15-17.30; Tue 9.30-17.30.
££-£££, high chairs, bottles heated, licensed.

Most formal of the store's restaurants and can be slightly quieter. Access through the baby clothing department. Table-service. Child's menu available. Offers a range of goodies for, say, afternoon tea, as well as full menus.

Princes Street Restaurant
2nd Floor
Opening hours: Mon, Wed, Fri, Sat 9.00-17.30; Tue 9.30-17.30; Thu 9.00-19.30; Sun 11.00-16.30.
£-££, high chairs, bottles heated, licensed. Access through the food hall.

Busy self-service restaurant on two levels with splendid views of Scott Monument etc. Choice of salad bar and hot dishes of the day.
Good selection of teabreads and cakes.

Bistro on 5
5th Floor
Opening hours: Mon, Wed-Sat 9.00-17.30; Tue 9.30-17.30
£-££, high chairs, bottles heated, licensed.

Self-service café/bistro. Can be accessed by 3 lifts (the largest comes opens on to the hair salon – turn right for the restaurant). Selection of snacks, soup and dishes of the day. Cakes and scones, etc. Some tables are set up on a dais area, but the few steps are negotiable by a pushchair. The made-to-order hot dishes are brought to your table. This café can be quieter when the others are busy, outwith weekends and Xmas period.

The Place to Eat - John Lewis
St James' Centre
Tel: 556 9121

Opening hours: Mon-Wed 9.00-17.45; Thu 9.45-19.45; Fri 9.00-19.45; Sat 9.30-18.15; Sun 11.00-16.30.

£-££, high chairs (6), bottles and baby jars heated, feeding and changing facilities available (M&F) on same floor, licensed, seats 280.

Large, busy self-service restaurant and espresso bar on level 4. Fantastic views over the city from large windows. Vegetarian dishes available, as well as children's portions and children's lunchboxes. Small selection of baby food available to buy. Plenty of room for prams and pushchairs. Staff will assist with getting trays to tables. Bibs, bowls and spoons available if required. Easy access from lifts. Also easy access to fantastic baby facilities, 'the loos with the views' for the under 5s. Children made most welcome everywhere, but the smaller espresso bar with its temptingly low furniture and glass walls is probably more suitable for babies and older children than lively toddlers.

Lower Aisle Restaurant, St Giles Cathedral
Parliament Square
High St
Tel: 225 5147
Web: www.stgilescathedral.org.uk/shop.asp

Opening hours: Mon-Fri 8.30-16.30 (18.00 during the Edinburgh Festival); Sun 10.00-14.00; Sat 10.00-16.30 during the Festival

£, high chair (1), tables suitable for clip-ons, bottles heated, seats 70.

Spacious self-service restaurant down a flight of stairs, uncluttered with simple furniture. Soup, rolls, light snacks, variety of vegetarian dishes, vegan diet catered for. Children's portions available. Fraternised by the legal profession. It often gets very busy, especially after services. Friendly staff.
Toilets: Gents on ground floor, no nappy-changing facilities, but bench in (F) toilet – down five steps.

Marks and Spencer's Café Revive
91 Princes Street
Tel: 225 2301

(M&S Ladieswear Shop)
Opening hours: Mon-Wed, Fri, Sat 9.00-18.30; Thu 9.00-19.30; Sun 11.00-17.30

££, high chairs (3), breastfeeding welcome, seats 80; nappy-changing room (M & F), toilets, mother and baby room on the ground floor.

Self-service café at the rear of the basement floor, accessed by lift or stairs. Large selection of tempting sandwiches, cakes, scones and light snacks. No baby food or children's portions available, but jugs of hot water are provided to heat jars or bottles and children's lunchboxes are available for £2.95. The café is adjacent to displays of clothes, and although it is partially screened off, lively toddlers (with sticky fingers) can be a bit of a liability. Toilets and nappy-changing are up one floor (lift), where there is also a mother and baby room for mothers to breastfeed in private if desired. Space for prams and pushchairs.
See main entry under Shopping.

also at

54 Princes Street
Rose Street Level

(M&S Menswear, Children's Wear, Food and Home Shop)
Opening hours: Mon-Wed, Fri, Sat 9.00-18.30; Thu 9.00-19.30; Sun 11.00-17.30.

££, high chairs (3), breastfeeding welcome; fully no smoking; seats 60; nappy-changing unit (M & F), toilets adjacent to the café.

Café situated at the back of the store, accessible by lift from the main store or by automatic door entrance from Rose St. Serving similar snacks and sandwiches to the main café at 91.
Nappy changing room is cramped, and can be awkward for larger pushchairs: it's more or less impossible to access with a traditional pram or double pushchair.

Metro Brasserie
Apex International Hotel
31-35 Grassmarket EH1 2HS
Tel: 0845 365 0002 (Restaurant Hotline)
Web: www.apexhotels.co.uk (menus and online booking)

££-£££, high chairs (5), bottles and baby food heated, licensed, seats 80.

Chic brasserie in the centre of the city. Open daily for lunch and dinner and snacks in the Bar area. Children's portions taken from main menu. Offers an eat early deal 16.00-18.30, 7 days a week. Changing facilities (M&F).

National Portrait Gallery
Queen Street Café
1 Queen Street
Tel: 624 6200

Opening hours: Mon-Sat 10.30-16.30; Sun 14.00-16.30.
£, high chairs (2, no reins), licensed, seats 60.

Self-service café with light snacks and vegetarian dishes. Prefer pushchairs folded. Toilets on same floor. Nappy-changing facilities in the larger toilet for the disabled.

Pizza Hut
46 North Bridge
Tel: 226 3038
Web: www.pizzahut.co.uk
Opening hours Mon-Thu 11.30-22.30; Fri, Sun 11.30-23.30; Sat 11.30-00.00.
££, high chairs (4), bottles heated, nappy-change surface, licensed, seats 150.
Ground floor seating. Some seating downstairs. Access by staircase. All restaurants have a children's menu, which has suggestions from the adult menu plus a salad bar option. Games and comic free with every child's meal/ salad bar. . Selection of toys for babies and children. Carry out food available.
Toilets are down 2 flights of stairs.
See also Eating Out - West.

Spoon
15 Blackfriars Street
EH1 1NB
Tel: 556 6922
Opening hours Mon-Sat 8.00-18.00. Festival 8.00-22.00
£, highchair (1), bottles and baby food heated, fully no-smoking; seats 24.
Welcomes children with open arms. Paper, crayons, felt tips and finger puppets can be provided. Space to park pushchairs unfolded. Snacks and variety of larger dishes, including vegetarian offered with an emphasis on fresh seasonal ingredients. Space for baby changing in toilets but no specific facilities.

Valvona & Crolla Vincaffe
11 Multrees Walk
Tel: 557 0088
Opening hours: Mon-Sat 8.00-22.00 (lunch 12.00-15.30/dinner 17.00-22.00) Sun 10.00-18.00.
£££, booster seats for children over 6 mths (5), (private room for breastfeeding may be available), baby food/bottles heated, children's menu, no-smoking, licensed, seats 120.
Table-service restaurant serving fresh Italian food. A contemporary, stylish setting for relatively formal dining, which manages to be child-friendly at the same time. Under fives are welcome, with Sundays a particularly good day for family dining. Children's menu with healthy, appetizing Italian dishes that children are sure to love. Friendly staff, although you may have to avoid peak times for quick service. Location is ideal for a break from shopping! Paper and pencils provided for children (you may have to ask). Pushchairs can be taken in, folded or unfolded. Dining is on ground and first floor, with lift access; toilets are on ground and first floor.
Nappy-changing (M&F).

NORTH EDINBURGH & LEITH°

Most points North of Queen Street, including venues in:
Broughton Street
Canonmills
Leith Walk
Stockbridge
The Shore and Greater Leith

NORTH EDINBURGH

Brewer's Fayre with Fun Factory
51-53 Newhaven Place
Tel: 08701 977093
Opening hours: Mon-Sat 11.00-23.00; Sun 12.00-23.00. Fun Factory Sun-Thu 12.00-20.00; Fri-Sat 12.00-21.00.
££, high chairs (9), booster seats (5), bottles heated, nappy-changing room (M&F), licensed, parties hosted, seats 200.

Large 'family-themed' restaurant near the Travel Inn on Newhaven Harbour. Children's menus for under and over 5s. Usually have special meal deals: can include visit to the ice cream factory to choose their own sweets to top the ice cream, but have also introduced fruit salad options. Baby food available to buy. Large choice for adults. The restaurant is on one floor. One area adjacent to the bar is a 'child free zone', but with Bewster's Fun Factory on site there is plenty to keep toddlers occupied. Generally child-pleasingly loud and lively. Operates system of ordering and paying, then table service is provided.

Circle Café and Bakery
1 Brandon Terrace
Tel: 624 4666
Email: brysonscatering@hotmail.co.uk
Opening hours: Mon-Thu 8.30-17.30, Fri/Sat 8.30-20.30, Sun 9.00-17.00.

£-££, high chairs (2), table service, licensed, seats 35. Accessible to pushchairs. Can accommodate a couple of travel systems and folded pushchairs.

This table-service café has a relaxed and welcoming atmosphere. Menu is changed regularly but is usually along the lines of modern British bistro food. Also offers a range of vegetarian options and light snacks. They also carry a breakfast and an afternoon tea menu. Circle also offers a take-away sandwich menu, plus a range of coffees and soft drinks. All food is made to order.

Friendly and efficient staff provide half portions on request, and can provide hot water for heating baby food & bottles.

The toilet is small and has no changing table.

Dean Gallery: Café Newton
Belford Road
Tel: 624 6200
Email: enquries@natgalscot.ac.uk
Opening hours: Mon-Sun 10.00-16.30.
£-££, high chairs (3), licensed, seats 30.
Art deco style ground floor café, with good coffee and very lovely cakes! And there's also a tasty and interesting lunch menu with dish of the day and a variety of vegetarian dishes. Half portions available for children. Toilets in basement – very colourful decor. Lift access

Giuliano's
18/19 Union Place
Tel: 556 6590
Opening hours:Mon-Sun 12.00-00.00.
££, high chairs (7), bottles and baby food heated, children's menu and child portions, licensed, table-service, carry-out available, seats 170.
This large, very friendly Italian restaurant has a relaxed atmosphere and is welcoming to children and babies. Colour-in books and crayons provided. Tables near the entrance have room to park pushchairs. Nappy-change facilities (F only).

Hamilton's Bar and Kitchen
Hamilton Place
Stockbridge
Tel: 226 4199
Email: info@hamiltonsbar.com
Opening hours: Mon-Fri 12.00-15.00, 18.00-22.00; Sat/Sun 10.00-17.00, 18.00-22.00.
££, high chairs (2), licensed, changing area (in toilet for the disabled), seats 40.

A gastropub which has a dining area away from the bar throroughfare – up a couple of steps. Menu has a range of influences and always has a range of vegetarian options. Offers a set lunch menu or a la carte options. Portions tend to be large – as are the wedge cut chips! Staff have always been friendly and accommodating during our visits.

Toilets on ground floor.

Lauriston Farm Restaurant
69 Lauriston Farm Road
Tel: 312 7071
Opening hours: Mon-Sat 11.00-23.00; Sun 12.00-22.00.
££, high chairs (16), bottles heated, changing area (M&F), seats 240.

Large and spacious restaurant which is part of the Brewer's Fayre chain, with very wide-ranging children's menu (including healthy options), and using the order and pay at once system, which means you can leave quickly if you have to! Toddler size cutlery is a nice touch too. There is a small indoor play area, and a bigger outdoor one, although under 5s will probably need adult supervision on it. There are also tables outside next to the play area, which are great for sunny summer days.

Café Mediterraneo
73 Broughton Street
Tel: 557 6900
Opening hours: Mon-Thu 8.00-17.30; Fri & Sat 8.00-21.00; Sun 9.00-16.00.
££, high chairs (1), licensed, seats 40.

If you like a coffee, Mediterraneo serves some of the best in town! The food is also good – the menu is varied and draws on French, Italian and Mediterranean influences. Half portions available on request. Overall, the cafe is quite small, though, so pushchairs are better folded. However, it's airy and bright in the rear eating area. Take away options are available.

No nappy change facilities.

Dionika
3-6 Canonmills Bridge
EH3 5LF
Tel: 652 3993
Email: info@dionika.com
Opening hours:Tue-Sat, Sun phone for current opening hours - closed Mon.

Spanish restaurant and delicatessen in Canonmills. The tapas section of the menu works especially well, letting children share a range of dishes with their accompanying adults. Seafood a speciality, and cakes temptingly displayed at toddler level in the deli. Toilets are down a flight of stairs – and although it's fairly spacious, there are no specific nappy changing facilities.

Olive Branch Deli
1 Howard Street
Tel: 557 4265
Email: info@theolivebranchscotland.co.uk
Web: www. theolivebranchscotland.co.uk
Opening hours: Mon-Fri 8.00-17.00, Sat/Sun 9.00-17.00.
£-££, highchairs (2), licensed, accessible to pushchairs, seats 36.

Table-service bistro-style café which also offers take away options. Menu includes salads, pasta, and a selection of large open sandwiches, wraps or crepes. Also offer cakes, pastries, teas, coffees and a selection of soft drinks. Nappy changing in (F), but is accessible to male carers. Friendly staff.

Pizza Express
1 Deanhaugh Street
Tel: 332 7229
Opening hours: Mon-Thu 11.30-23.00; Fri-Sun 11.30-00.00.
££-£££, high chairs (10), nappy-changing facilities (M&F), licensed, seats 110 inside, 50 outside by Water of Leith.

Pizzas galore in stylish surroundings by Water of Leith walkway, plus nice desserts, which do have a ice-cream theme going on; having said that, the cheesecake is great! Crayons and paper usually materialise on the table pretty quickly if you have a toddler, and balloons sometimes are a 'goodbye' gesture. Friendly staff. Toilets with changing facilities downstairs – only accessible via a flight of stairs.

NB refurbished Oct 2005 - changes to times, facilities etc may result.

Scottish National Gallery of Modern Art Café
72 Belford Road
Tel: 332 8600
Opening hours: Mon-Sun 10.00-16.30.
£-££, high chairs (3), clip-ons (1), feeder beakers, licensed.

Access by lift to self-service café in basement. Delicious home-cooked soups, hot meals, salads and great cakes.

Also vegetarian meals. Half portions of soup and meals available. Outdoor terrace for fine weather, where children can enjoy the garden. The only downside is that it can be very busy during lunch-time.

Telford Arms
78 Telford Road
Tel: 332 4647
Opening hours: Mon-Sun 11.00-20.30, Sun 12.30-20.30. 20.00 curfew.

££, high chairs (4), tables suitable for clip-ons, children's menu, nappy-changing surface (M&F), licensed, seats 200.

Families are welcome in the lounge area of this bar. There is a fixed but varied menu plus a children's menu, with table-service. Accessible to wheelchairs.

Terrace Café
West Gate, Royal Botanic Garden
Tel: 552 0616
Website: www.rbge.org.uk
Opening hours: Mon-Sun 10.00-17.00 (Apr-Aug 9.30-18.00).
££, high chairs (7), bottles heated, nappy-change surface (M&F), licensed, seats 80 inside, 80 outside.

A very popular meeting place for parents and toddlers, situated next to Inverleith House. The menu includes hot meals, salads, filled focaccias, plus children's options. In summer 2005, the Terrace Café introduced a till-point selling selection of nuts, popcorn and the like separate to the main point of sale for meals. Pushchairs allowed in the café but it is courtesy to leave them just inside the door when it is very busy. Often extremely busy at lunch-time, and the fairly inefficient queuing/payment system can result in a long time spent queuing with a hungry child in tow if you're by yourself.

Nappy-changing facilities in toilet for the disabled.

Ye Olde Peacock Inn
Lindsay Road, Newhaven
Tel: 552 8707
Opening hours: Mon-Sat 12.00-21.45; Sun 12.30-21.45.
££, high chairs (6), breastfeeding welcome, licensed.

Large table-service family room in this inn on the Forth. Extensive bar menu including soup, salads, fish, steak. Children's menu. Haddock and chips very good!

LEITH

Giuliano's on the Shore
1 Commercial Street, Leith
Tel/Fax: 554 5272
Opening hours: Sun-Thu 12.00-22.30; Fri-Sat 12.00-23.00.
£££, high chairs (12), tables suitable for clip-ons, breastfeeding welcome, bottles heated, nappy-changing room, licensed, parties hosted, seats 120. Carry-out food available.

Children very welcome in this attractive, lively Italian restaurant where they can even make their own pizzas, but grown-ups are well catered for too! Half portions available and they promise they can cater for any diet. Crayons and books available. Access good and the restaurant has its own parking, although you may need to look slightly further afield at busy times. Toilets on ground floor.

Malmaison Brasserie
1 Tower Place
Tel: 468 5000
Opening hours: Mon-Sun 10.00-22.00.
££, high chairs (2), licensed, seats 65 (Brasserie) 40 (Café).

Friendly hotel by Leith Docks, helpful and welcoming to children, but posh enough to please the grandparents. Varied menu with good choice for vegetarians. Half portions available. Good access. Space for prams and pushchairs.
Nappy-changing table in (D) toilet.

Mariachi Mexicana
72 Commercial Quay, Leith
Tel: 538 0022
Opening hours: Mon -Thurs 12.00 - 14.30, 17.30 - 22.30; Fri - Sun 12.00-23.00.
££, high chairs (2), bottles and baby food heated, licensed, seats 150.

Bright, glass-fronted Mexican restaurant with relaxed atmosphere facing Victoria Quay in semi-pedestrianised area. Spacious with plenty of room for pushchairs. Staff have always been welcoming and helpful, positive towards under 5 diners, with quick service an added bonus. No

specialised changing facilities but toilets are roomy and clean. They do an 'all you can eat' Buffet lunch (£5.95) on weekdays, 12.00-14.30. Children's food including drink and ice cream £3.95. Parties hosted.

Pizza Express
38 Waterview House
The Shore, Leith EH6 6QU
Opening hours: Mon-Sun 11.30-00.00.
££-£££, high chairs (4), nappy-changing facilities (M&F), licensed, seats 82.
Pizzas that are just a little bit different from other pizza chains, with views overlooking Water of Leith and The Shore. Nice desserts, which do have a ice-cream theme going on; having said that, the cheesecake is great! Crayons and paper usually materialise on the table pretty quickly if you have a toddler, and balloons sometimes are a 'goodbye' gesture. Friendly staff. Toilets on same level as restaurant.

The Raj on the Shore
5-91 Henderson Street
Leith EH6 6ED
Tel: 0131 553 3980
Web: www.rajontheshore.com
Opening hours: lunch Sun-Sat 12.00-14.30; dinner Sun-Thu 17.30-23.30, Fri & Sat 17.30-00.00.
££, licensed

Welcomes children of all ages with their friends and family. Waiters will advise parents on the suitability of dishes and size of portion. They will offer platters of different milder dishes more suitable to younger palates. The price is in the range of starters and side dishes.
Lunch, express lunch and dinner menus available.
A free soft drink/bottled water or ice cream is offered to each child diner.
No nappy change or high chairs, so better for older under 5s!

Skippers Seafood Bistro
1a Dock Place, Edinburgh EH6 6LU
Phone: 0131 554 1018
Fax: 0131 553 5988
Email: info@skippers.co.uk
Web: www.skippers.co.uk
Opening hours: Mon-Fri 12.30-14.00, 19.00-22.00; Sat 12.20-14.00, 18.30-22.00; Sun 12.30-14.30, 19.00-22.00.
££-£££, high chairs (4), licensed, seats 50 (incl. outdoor seating).

Popular and long-established bistro with a definite emphasis on seafood, so expect the likes of mussels, halibut, sole and sea bass to take centre stage – although there is usually game, poultry and a vegetarian option on offer too. It's a bit of a warren inside, with tables set in small rooms, which children may love or loathe: it was a hit with our daughter! Booking is recommended.

No nappy change facilities: owners also have the Waterfront Bistro which is more or less adjacent and say diners are welcome to use the nappy change in there – not ideal but useful if you've finished eating and are 'going' before you go.

The Waterfront Wine Bar & Grill
1c Dock Place EH6 6LU
Phone: 0131 554 7427
Fax: 0131 555 6060
Email: info@waterfrontwinebar.co.uk
Web: www.waterfrontwinebar.co.uk
Opening hours: Mon-Thu 12.00-15.30, 18.00-22.00.
££-£££, high chairs (4), . licensed.

While the bar area is very traditional – dark wood and stone, with old maps and advertising posters on the wall, the conservatory eating area is bright and airy. All day dining menu, á la carte, all day dining and express lunch menu (Mon-Fri 12.00-16.00) available. Menus have a strong emphasis on fish dishes (this bar complements Skippers restaurant). Children's menu. Room for prams & unfolded pushchairs. No stairs. Nappy changing unit in (D).

EAST EDINBURGH

Points Eastwise of London Road, excluding Leith. Includes venues in or near to:

Fort Kinnaird
Musselburgh
Portobello

Chiquito
6 Kinnaird Park
Fort Kinnaird
Tel: 657 4444
Opening hours: Mon-Sat 12.00-23.00; Sun 12.00-22.30.
££, high chairs (4), booster seats (3), nappy-change facilities (M&F), licensed, seats 103.
Spacious, bright restaurant with relaxed atmosphere and

a Tex-Mex theme. There is comfortable booth seating available, handy for babies in car seats. Staff are welcoming and will happily heat baby food and bottles. There is a children's menu which includes wraps as well as nuggets, fish fingers etc and includes a free soft drink (fruit juices or milk). Staff will sing 'Happy Birthday' if you are celebrating. Children's birthday parties hosted.

Costa Coffee
WH Smiths
Fort Kinnaird
Tel: 669 1351
Opening hours: Mon-Fri 10.00-19.00; Sat 10.00-17.30; Sun 11.00-17.00.
£-££, high chairs (2), bottles and baby food heated, nappy change (M&F), seats 60.

This small self-service coffee shop is located on the first floor within WH Smiths, with easy access by lift. It offers a variety of hot and cold sandwiches including panini and toasties, and also has a large selection of pastries and cakes. Ample room for prams and pushchairs next to your table. The staff are friendly and helpful and will take trays to the table for you – often without having to be asked. Take-away food available if you are in a rush!

Café Noire
Clinton Cards
Fort Kinnaird
Tel: 669 5019
Opening hours: Mon Fri, Sun 10.00 18.00; Sat 0.900 18.00.
£, high chairs (4), bottles and baby food heated, seats 50.

Bright, modern café situated on a mezzanine floor above the shop floor of Clinton's Cards: lift access at the rear of the store. As well as a range of coffees, they sell fruit juices, soft drinks and water. We didn't try all their cakes, but those we did have were yummy! Sub rolls, panini, plus old-fashioned rolls with bacon or sausage available. Toilets on same level; nappy change facilities (M&F).

Luca's
32-38 High Street
Musselburgh
Tel: 665 2237
Mon-Sat 9.00-22.00; Sun 10.30-22.00.
£, high chairs (5), breastfeeding welcome, nappy-change facilities (M&F) seats 115.

An East Coast institution. As well as the famous ice cream, to eat in or take out, the café serves full menu from toasties and panini to pizzas and all day brunches. Children's portions available. Spacious two floored premises – ground floor has capacity to seat 72. Easy pushchair access to ground floor.

Starbucks Coffee Company
Borders Books
Fort Kinnaird
Newcraighall
Tel: 657 9768
Opening hours: Mon-Sat 09.00-21.30; Sun 10.00-19.30.
£, no high chairs, clip on seats (1), bottles and baby food heated, nappy change (M&F) , seats 80.
Usual Starbucks' options including sandwiches and panini, muffins, biscuits, cakes etc. It is situated on a mezzanine level with easy lift access, and looks over the bookshop below – you can sit and look at your new purchase(s) in total comfort if one of the leather sofas or armchairs is free! Space for folded pushchairs, prams can be placed in hallway. Service can be frustratingly slow. Carry out food is available. Nappy change (M&F).

Vittoria Restaurant
113 Brunswick Street (Leith Walk)
Edinburgh
Tel: 556 6171
Opening hours: Mon-Sat 10.00-23.00; Sun 12.00-23.00.
££, high chairs (6) , bottles and baby food heated, licensed ,seats 200.
Friendly Italian restaurant happy to serve anyone anything, from a coffee to a full meal. Pizzas and pasta available, vegetarian meals, burgers, chips, sandwiches, ice-creams. Children's menu and half portions available. Carry-out food available. There's space for prams outside, folded pushchairs inside. Full disabled entrance and toilet. Parties hosted and welcomed.
Nappy change facilities (M&F).

SOUTH EDINBURGH

Imagine Chamber St as our 'cut-off point' between Central and south Edinburgh, so South includes venues in and South of:
Chambers Street
Nicolson Street
Bruntsfield-Morningside
Newington

Annabelle's
27 Sciennes Road
Tel: 667 0700
Opening hours: Mon-Fri 8.30-17.00; Sat 10.00-15.00.
£, high chairs (2), nappy-changing facilities, seats 30.

Friendly café with fresh food for lunches, snacks and afternoon tea. Space for folded pushchairs, but not prams. There are large windows so pushchairs and prams can easily be seen if left outside. Carry-out service.

394 Café/Bistro
394 Morningside Road
Tel: 447 9287
Opening hours: Mon-Sat 9.45-17.00.
££, high chairs (2), half portions for children, licensed, seats 40.

At the moment this is a café/bistro serving wholesome food. Basement area, room for pushchairs if folded. There is an alcove table which seats 6 and is slightly away from the main customer area – phone in advance to book it! Friendly staff who always seem happy to help to carry pushchairs downstairs to the large seating area there. This bistro may also be opening in the evening in the future, which may or may not change the feel of the daytime café: time will tell.

Braid Hills Hotel
Buckstone Bistro
134 Braid Road
Tel: 447 8888
Opening hours: Mon-Sat 11.00-20.00; Sun 12.30-20.00.
££, high chairs (3), bottles and baby food heated, nappy-changing surface (F), licensed, seats 70.

Families are welcome in the Buckstone bistro. Children's menu available. A wide choice of food in lovely surroundings without being too costly. Waitress-service. No prams.

Café Grande
184 Bruntsfield Place
Tel: 228 1188
Opening hours: Mon-Wed 9.00-22.00;Thu-Sat 9.00-23.00; Sun 10.00-22.00.
££, high chairs (1), clip-ons (2), bottles heated, changing mat and potty provided, accessible to pushchairs, licensed, seats 50.

Friendly waitress-service café/bistro where children are welcome. Breakfasts, coffees, cakes and light meals served, full lunch and dinner served. Children's menu available. Pushchairs allowed (folded) but prams must be left outside. Box of toys, books and crayons provided.

Café Lucia
Edinburgh Festival Theatre
13/29 Nicolson Street
Tel: 662 1112
Opening hours: Mon-Sat 10.00-17.30; depending on shows; Sun 16.00-20.00.
£, high chairs (2), licensed (for children until 20.00), accessible to pushchairs, parties hosted, seats 60.

This self-service café offers light snacks and half portions for children. It is part of the theatre and has show material displayed like 'Playdays' and 'The Singing Kettle'. Toilets and nappy-changing room (M&F) are one floor up, lift available.

Elephants and Bagels
37 Marshall Street
Tel: 668 4404
Website: www.elephant-house.co.uk
Opening hours: Mon-Fri 08.30-17.00; Sat-Sun 09.30-17.00. (Later closing in summer).
£, high chairs (1), bottles heated, seats 40.

The sister café of The Elephant House, this is Edinburgh's first and foremost bagel shop, serving a variety of bagels with all kinds of fillings, as well as other light snacks. Crayons, pens and paper provided, children's art exhibited – and there's a large collection of elephants. Space for pushchairs. Toilets are downstairs. Additional seating outside in the summer. Children's parties by prior arrangement.

The Engine Shed Café
19 St Leonard's Lane
Tel: 662 0040
Opening hours: Mon-Thu 10.30-15.30; Fri 10.30-14.30. (Check opening hrs during holiday periods).
££, high chairs (5), tables suitable for clip-ons, breastfeeding welcome, bottles heated, nappy-changing surface (M&F), no-smoking, seats 60.

Run by Garvald Community Enterprises, the café houses a bakery, as well as bright, cheerful vegetarian café on the

1st floor, accessed by lift or stairs. Reasonably priced menu changes daily and children's portions are available. All the food is made on the premises. Carry-out service, delivery within the City and outside catering available. Children made very welcome. Relaxed atmosphere and friendly staff.
Toilet for the disabled on the ground floor and toilets adjacent to café. Moveable nappy-changing unit suitable for use in (F) or (M).

Kaffe Politik
146 Marchmont Road
Tel: 446 9873

Opening hours: Mon-Sun 10.00-22.00

££, high chairs (1), carry-out service, nappy-changing facilities (M&F), bottles and baby food heated, licensed, seats 30.
Table-service café/bistro with fixed menu, light snacks and vegetarian dishes. Children can have half portions of menu items. Space for folded pushchairs only.

Monster Mash
4A Forrest Road
Tel: 225 7069
Web: www.monstermashcafe.co.uk
Opening hours: phone for current times
£-££, high chairs (2), carry-out service, licensed, seats 40.

Given the name, its formica topped tables and the Beano for reading, this sounds – and looks a bit – like a novelty-based eaterie, but it isn't. The food is stubbornly 70's retro on paper – the mainstays being sausage and mash (Crombies sausages and always a vegetarian option), choice of gravies, fish and chips, shepherd's pies (again, always a vegetarian option) etc. There are ice creams, crumble or sponge puddings for afters. Child's menu on offer – more of the same as the adults', with fish fingers and the like. Space for pushchairs, but best folded. Staff are always enthusiastic and entertaining.
Nappy changing shelf in (F) toilets – down a steep flight of stairs.
New branch will be opening on Thistle St in 2005/6.

Luca's
16 Morningside Road
Tel: 446 0233
Opening hours: Mon-Sun 9.00-22.00.
£, high chairs (4), breastfeeding welcome, bottles heated,

nappy-changing facilities (M&F), no-smoking, seats 50 upstairs and 15 on ground floor.

Homemade pizza, pasta, milkshakes and the 'famous' ice-cream; children's menu available with half portions of some dishes. Access to upstairs is by a spiral staircase; prams and pushchairs can be left downstairs. Toilets are located on the ground floor. Recently awarded Eat Safe award from Food Standards Agency promoting excellence in food hygiene.

Parrots
3 Viewforth
Tel: 229 3252

Opening hours: Tue-Thu 18.00-22.30; Fri 17.30-22.30; Sat 17.00-22.15 (no curfew for children, parents' judgement accepted!)

££, booster seat.

Families welcome, relaxed approach to parties including children. 723 parrots (counted by a little boy!) of different shapes and sizes to entertain children. Table-service with a large variety of ethnic dishes, fixed menu items, pasta, vegetarian dishes and snacks. Staff very friendly to children. Limited floorspace for pushchairs. If booking, it is helpful to mention that your party will include children as some tables are more suitable for them than others.

Stop Press: Parrots is currently up for sale, so changes may occur.

The Square Centre Café
Nicolson Square Methodist Church
25 Nicolson Square
Tel: 662 0417

Opening hours: Mon-Fri 8.30-15.30.

£, high chairs (4), clips-ons (1), booster seats (2), tables suitable for clip-ons, bottles heated, nappy-changing facilities (M&F), seats 100.

Spacious, if a bit basic, self-service café. Scones, cakes and filled rolls served throughout the day. Cooked breakfast 8.30-11.00. Hot meals, salads and vegetarian option served from 12.00. Smaller portions available for children. Disabled/pram access round the back of the café.

The 1924 Café and Cards
The Eric Liddle Centre
15 Morningside Road, Holy Corner
Tel: 446 3325

Opening hours: Mon-Sat 9.30-17.00; Sat 9.30-16.00

£, high chairs (2), tables suitable for clip-ons, bottles heated, nappy-changing surface (M&F), disabled access, seats 40.

Friendly café serving homemade soups, snacks and homebaking. Plenty of room for pushchairs and prams. Located within Eric Liddell Centre, focus for community care, arts and education projects. A range of children's activities run in the centre, such as Jo Jingles, Gymini and Messy Monsters – phone no. above for information regarding current groups.

Ti Amo Restaurant
16 Nicolson Street
Tel: 556 5678

Opening hours: Mon-Sun 12.00-23.30.

££, high chairs (2), clip-ons (1), bottles heated, licensed, seats 140. Curfew: 19.00.

Families welcome in this Italian restaurant before 19.00. Books, crayons, paper, toys and lollipops available and children can help to make their own pizza. The fishpond is an additional attraction!

WEST EDINBURGH

Taking the West End as the start of this area, West incorporates:
West End
Haymarket
Lothian Rodd
Corstorphine
Ingliston

Metro West End
Apex European Hotel, Haymarket
90 Haymarket Terrace, EH12 5LQ
Tel:0845 365 0002 (Restaurant Hotline)
Web: www.apexhotels.co.uk (menus and online booking)

Opening hours: Mon-Sun 10.00-14.30, 19.00-22.00.

££-£££, high chair (1), bottles and baby food heated, licensed, sits 44.

Stylish, modern hotel in the west of the city offering brasserie-style menu. Open daily for lunch, dinner & snacks in the bar area. Children's portions taken from main menu. Offers an eat early deal between 16.00-19.30 7 days a week.

Nappy changing rooms (M&F).

Bar Roma
39A Queensferry Street
Tel: 226 2977
Opening hours: Sun-Thu 12.00-00.00; Fri-Sat 12.00-01.00.
££, high chairs, two nappy-changing facilities, seats 200.

Friendly and spacious Italian restaurant. Children's portions are available. It can be very busy at lunchtimes. Friendly staff who love children.

Brasserie at Norton House
Norton House Hotel, Ingliston (opp showground)
Tel: 333 1275
Opening hours: Mon-Sun 12.00-14.30, 18.00-21.30.
££, high chairs (8), breastfeeding welcome, bottles and baby food heated, no smoking, licensed, seats 72.

Contemporary styled restaurant with large conservatory overlooking the hotel grounds. Children's menu available.

Coffee and Cream
235 St John's Road
Tel: 539 7008
Opening hours: Mon-Sat 8.30-17.00.
£, high chair (1), feeder beakers available.

Children of all ages are welcome. Coffee shop offers scones, toasties, etc. Children's menu and child portions available. Friendly staff are happy to help out and table-service is a bonus.

Cuba Norte
192 Morrison Street
Tel: 221 1430
Opening hours: Mon-Sun 12.00-20.00.
££, bottles heated, licensed, seats 150.

Spacious, friendly bar/café decorated in Cuban style. Serves Cuban and vegetarian (including vegan) food. Chef will cook to order for special requests. Toilets are down one flight of stairs. No nappy-changing facilities.

Filmhouse Café Bar
88 Lothian Road
Tel: 229 5932
Opening hours: Mon-Sun 10.00-21.00 (for food).
££, highchairs (2), nappy-changing facility (M&F), licensed, seats 150.

Busy café/bar serving light snacks, vegetarian and vegan food with a fixed menu and a daily special. A relaxed and informal atmosphere; well suited to families, although seating for peoples with children is limited to an area well away from the bar. Limited space for pushchairs.

Gyle Shopping Centre

Food Court
Tel: 539 9000
Opening hours: Mon-Wed, Fri, 8.30-20.00; Thu 8.30-21.00; Sat & Sun 8.30-18.00.
£-££, high chairs (10), breastfeeding welcome, bottles heated, nappy-changing room (M&F), self-service, no-smoking, seats 680.

The food court is upstairs and is accessible by a lift, stairs and an escalator. There are five franchises serving food: Mathieson's Patisserie; Singapore Sam's; Burger King; Spud-U-Like and Pizza Hut. The up side is that there's choice, the downside is that you may have to queue a couple of times. All cutlery, cups, plates etc are now disposable.
Toddler seats with play tables are situated at the far left of the area from the lift, as is the nappy changing room. Food/bottle heating facilities on the left-hand wall.

Café Revive
Situated in Marks & Spencer.
Two café areas, serving a range of sandwiches, wraps, cakes and pastries. Teas, coffees, plus a range of soft drinks. Nappy changing area near both cafés – there is also a room where parents can feed a baby in privacy near the larger café - but despite the signage on the doors, there is no private feeding area in the toilet areas near the car park.

Starbucks
Situated towards East end of the shopping centre. Wireless internet connection.

Morrisons
In-store self-service café.

Holiday Inn – Edinburgh North
Queensferry Road
Blackhall
Tel: 311 4920
Opening hours: Mon-Sun 18.30-22.00.

£££, high chairs (5), tables suitable for clip-ons, bottles heated, feeding and changing room, family area, garden, licensed, seats 80.

Inventive children's menu provides plenty of choice. There is an outdoor play area for use at Sunday lunch times with chute, tunnel, etc.

Khukuri
8 West Maitland Street
Tel: 228 2085
Opening hours: Mon-Thu 12.00-14.00, 17.30-23.30; Fri & Sat 12.00-14.00, 17.30-24.00; Sun 17.00-23.00.
££, high chairs (2), bottles heated.

Friendly Nepalese restaurant serving a range of Indian and Nepalese food: lunch-time fixed menu available. Chef can adapt dishes. Children's portions available. Staff welcome family dining. Take away available.
Toilets downstairs.

Lazio Restaurant
95 Lothian Road
Tel: 229 7788
Opening hours: Monday 17.00-24.00, Tues, Wed, Thu and Sun 12.00-24.00, Fri-Sat 12.00-02.00.
££, high chairs (3), breastfeeding welcome, bottles heated, baby changing facilities on ground floor, licensed, seats 60.

Families are welcomed at this restaurant. Varied menu, children's portions available. Folded pushchairs only. Crayons and pencils supplied so children can add drawing to the 'gallery'.
Toilets on ground floor.

Pizza Express
32 Queensferry Street, West End
Tel: 225 8863
Web: www.pizzaexpress.co.uk
Opening hours: Mon-Sun 11.30-00.00; 20.00 curfew.
££-£££, high chairs, bottles and baby food heated, nappy-changing facilities (M&F), licensed, seats 90.

Pizzas with all sorts of toppings – including sultanas; dough balls and ice creams that are just a little bit different. Crayons, paper and balloons are available to distract impatient young diners. Children's portions available. Restaurant can cater for children's parties if given prior notice. Friendly staff. – live jazz most Mon evenings 19.30-22.00. See Also Eating Out – Central & North & Leith.

Pizza Hut
113-117 Lothian Road
Tel: 228 2920
Web: www.pizzahut.co.uk
Opening hours: Mon-Thu 12.00-22.30; Fri-Sat 12.00-23.00.
££, high chairs (6), booster seats (2), bottles heated, licensed, seats 96.

Family restaurant. Crayons, toys and balloons available. Toilets on ground floor. Ice cream factory very popular with young ones.
Nappy-change surface (M&F)
Hosts children's parties. See also Eating Out – Central.

St. Bride's Community Centre
10 Orwell Terrace
Tel: 346 1405
Opening hours: Mon-Fri 10.00-15.30; Sat 10.00-16.00.
£, high chairs (2), bottles and baby food heated, children's parties hosted, nappy changing (M&F).

Café offering hot meals and home bakes at great prices. There is a large soft play area, reading corner and toys for children. Plenty space for pushchairs. Nappy changing (M&F).

St. George's West Church
Shandwick Place
Tel: 225 7001
Email: gwest@dircon.co.uk
Opening hours: Mon-Sat 10.00-15.30.
£, high chairs (4), baby food and bottles heated, parties hosted, seats 90.

In addition to great value hot meals and cakes, – children's menu is available –this restaurant now has a children's play area. Access also by lift at side entrance on Stafford St. Space for multiple push chairs, no need to fold them up. nappy-changing surface (F).

Traverse Theatre and Traverse Bar Café
10 Cambridge Street
Tel: 228 5383
Opening hours: Mon-Sat 10.30-20.00; Sun 17.00-20.00.
£, high chairs (2), bottles heated, licensed, seats 80.

Centrally located, a large, open bar café with friendly and welcoming staff. Wide range of vegetarian dishes and home-baking; children's portions are available. Lift to café, bar and theatres. Newspapers. There's a good wine list and American and continental beers are available at the bar. The atmosphere is very relaxed; an ideal place for parents with young children to enjoy a drink, a coffee and something to eat. Space for prams and pushchairs. Nappy-changing room (M&F).

Verandah Restaurant
17 Dalry Road, Haymarket
Tel: 337 5828
Opening hours: Mon-Sun 12.00-14.30, 17.00-00.00.
£££, high chairs, tables suitable for clip-ons, bottles heated, licensed, seats 44.
A friendly Indian restaurant with a very high culinary standard. Varied menu including vegetarian options. Special lunch menus available. Children's portions served, and crayons and colouring books provided to keep little ones amused. Carry out food available. Free home delivery service.

OUT OF TOWN

Here you'll find a selection of bistros cafés and restaurants which are located out of the Edinburgh area, but which have proven to be welcoming to parents and carers with young children.

CLOSE TO HOME
The Bridge Inn
The Edinburgh Canal Centre, Ratho
Tel: 333 1320
Opening hours: Mon-Sat 12.00-20.00; Sun 12.30-20.00
££, high chairs (8), clip-ons (5), bottles heated, nappy-change surface licensed, seats 120. In addition, there are 2 canal boats, each of which seat 36 passengers.
Inn has a family area, a play area and patio. There's a varied bar-style menu, plus a children's menu. There is also an a la carte restaurant (££-£££). Three course set menus (££-£££) on the canal boats. Outdoor play area with parent-powered carousel. Resident family of ducks live beside the canal. Rosie and Jim Canal Safety Campaign promoters. Parties hosted.
also:

Pop Inn
Opening hours: Mon-Sun 12.00-18.00.
Informal lounge bar with relaxed and friendly family dining, part of the Bridge Inn.

West Lothian

The Park Bistro & Eating House
Park Farm
by Linlithgow EH49 6QY
Tel: 01506 846666
Getting there: on the East side of Linlithgow. Located along the Philipstoun turnoff from the B9080, just after Kingscavill.
££, licensed, high chairs (3), bottles and baby food heated, seats 100+.

Recently opened restaurant near to Linlithgow. Large portions of freshly cooked favourites, including home-made burgers, pasta, baked potatoes, panini etc. Daily specials. Fixed price children's menu. There's a well-equipped playroom to the side of the eating area. Nappy changing (M&F), plus the toilets have toddler seats. Outdoor seating is pleasant on sunny days. It's enclosed, so there should be no escapes into the carpark, plus there are some pedal cars to keep under 5s happy. You can watch barges and boats sailing by on the Union Canal.

FURTHER AFIELD

Stirling

Corrieri's Café
7/9 Alloa Road
Causewayhead
Stirling FK9 5LH
Tel: 01786 472089
Opening times: 10.00 - 21.30 (closed Tue).
£-££, high chairs, M&F changing facilities.

A family run and family orientated café/restaurant beside the roundabout on the way to the University/the Wallace Monument. Italian food (pizza, pasta) but also great Scottish breakfasts, snacks and vegetarian food throughout the day. Very friendly & fun place to eat with small portions for children. Quick service and fast cooking adds to the appeal for parents of under 5s! Ground floor access with room for pushchairs. On-road parking along Alloa Rd. Wide range of ice creams. Very busy at weekends!

If you just fancy an ice cream – why not buy one and go to the playpark just along the road. There's a tyre swing, a tyre-balance, and a multi-level sandpit cum climbing frame. There are bucket swings and a double covered tube slide.

Next to the playpark is a basketball/football court. Plenty of grass to run about on too.
See also the Macrobert Centre, in Where Shall We Go Today

COFFEE FRANCHISES

Caffe Nero
A relatively new but fast-growing franchise in Edinburgh. The venues listed below have seating on ground floor level, although some – such as the Rose St branch – has additional seating on other levels.
Relaxed atmosphere. Serving a range of juices, smoothies, panini, muffins, plus some hot meal options. They also – unsurpisingly – serve a wide range of coffee.
Caffe Nero locations:

Blackwells Bookstore
53-59 Southbridge EH11YS
Opening hours: Mon, Wed-Fri 9.00-19.30; Tue 9.30-17.30; Sat 9.00-17.30; Sun 12.00-17.30.

Stockbridge
4-6 Glanville Place
Opening hours: Mon, Wed-Fri 9.00-19.30; Tue 9.30-17.30; Sat 9.00-17.30.

Lothian Road
43-45 Lothian Road EH1 2DJ
Opening hours: Mon-Fri: 7.00-19.00; Sat 8.00-19.00; Sun 9.00- 18.00.

Morningside
177 Morningside Road EH10 4AY
Opening hours: Mon-Fri 8.00-19.30; Sat 8.00-19.00; Sun 10.00-18.00.
Wireless internet connection.

Rose Street
58 Rose Street EH2 2NN
Opening hours: Mon-Sat 7.30-21.00; Sun 9.00-21.00.
Incorporating EasyEverything, which offers banks of computer terminals for email access.

Starbucks Coffee Company
There are more than 14 outlets (as we go to press) in Edinburgh! In the city centre the following outlets offer coffees, fruit smoothies, muffins, panini and a lively atmosphere. Facilities vary at each one and the following are possibly more convenient if you are in town with babies and young children.

Opening hours vary, with the majority open between 8.30-19.00 Mon-Sat and Sun 9.00-17.00.

East End
30a George Street (Corner of Hanover and George Street) and Castle Street.

Haymarket
Palmerston Place – has wireless internet connection.

Ocean Terminal
Level I – has wireless internet connection
Old Town – 124 High St at the corner of the Tron – has wireless internet connection.

Princes Street
120a Princes Street – has wireless internet connection.

Stockbridge
Bakers Place

West End
106 George Street

Some (including Princes St and Castle St) have nappy-changing facilities and high chairs.
Of all these branches, the Princes St outlet at 120a has a wonderful view and is a relaxing place to spend time with visitors; particularly if the armchairs at the window are free as you have a wonderful view of Edinburgh Castle. The back area is more private and has very comfortable chairs for breastfeeding. However, the café is up two flights of stairs and there are no plans at present to install a lift. Staff are welcoming and friendly, and if you are able to leave a pram or pushchair downstairs to go up and ask for help, they will assist.

Also at:

85 George St; Lothian Rd and Exchange Cres. These outlets are more focused on the office market and do not have high chairs. The last two listed do have wireless internet connection.

FAST FOOD

There are many fast food outlets in Edinburgh. We have listed Burger King, McDonald's and Kentucky Fried Chicken outlets below. The universal nature of these eateries means that you know what to expect in terms of food, environment etc. Most offer children's themed meals, nappy-changing facilities, and may host children's parties: contact venue for more details. All offer sit-in and take-away meals. Where 'drive-thru' is available, we have also noted this.

BURGER KING

£, highchairs, tables suitable for clip-ons. All have nappy-changing facilities.
The outlet at the Gyle has the advantage of the good toilet and nappy-changing facilities of the centre.

Gyle Shopping Centre
Tel: 317 1561
Opening hours: Mon-Wed, Sat 9.00-19.00; Thu, Fri 9.00-20.00; Sun 9.00-17.30.

Milton Road (at Woolworths)
Tel: 669 0558
Opening hours: Mon-Sun 8.00-22.00.

10-15 Princes Street
Tel: 557 4575
Opening hours: Sun-Thu 8.00-23.00; Fri, Sat 8.00-00.30.

Waverley Station (inside main travel centre area)
Tel: 557 9128
Opening hours: Mon-Sat 6.00-00.00; Sun 8.00-00.00.

KFC

£, highchairs, breastfeeding welcomed, tables suitable for clip-ons, no-smoking areas, nappy-changing facilities.

Craigleith Retail Park
South Groathill Avenue
Tel: 343 3101
Opening hours: Mon-Fri, Sun 11.30-22.30; Sat 11.00-23.00.
'Drive-thru' available.

36 Nicolson St
Tel: 662 9533
Opening hours: Sun-Thu 11.00-23.00; Fri, Sat 11.00-00.00.

McDonald's

£, highchairs, tables suitable for clip-ons, bottles heated. Some have a children's area, with small tables and chairs, some with tvs showing Cartoon Network etc. Most have nappy changing facilities.

1 Glasgow Road, Corstorphine
EH12 8HW
Tel: 334 9789
'Drive-thru' available. Wireless internet connection.

99 Gorgie Park Road
EH14 1NG
Tel: 337 1869
'Drive-thru' available. Wireless internet connection.

Kinnaird Park
Newcraighall EH15 3RD
Tel: 657 5363
Mon-Sun 8.00-00.00.
'Drive-thru' available.

59 London Road
EH7 6AA
Tel: 659 5841
Mon Sun 8.00 00.00.
'Drive-thru' available. Wireless internet connection.

Unit 12, Princes Mall
Princes Street EH1 1BQ
Tel. 556 6597

137-138 Princes Street
EH2 4BL
Tel: 226 3872

Seafield Road
63 Craigentinny Avenue North EH6 7LJ
Tel: 555 5196
'Drive thru' available. Wireless internet connection.

3-5 South St Andrew St
EH2 2AU
Tel: 558 9348

74 Telford Rd EH4 2NF
Tel: 315 3447
Mon-Sun 8.00-23.00.
'Drive-thru' available. Wireless internet connection.

Accessible Edinburgh and Beyond

INTRODUCTION

This is a new section for Edinburgh for Under Fives and hopefully one that will be developed over the years.

While there are many publications dealing with the special task of parenting a child with disability or special needs, none look specifically at 'the Edinburgh experience', so the purpose of this section is to offer advice, hints and information about caring for a child with additional support needs in and around the Edinburgh area.

The information shared is not all inclusive, but it is hoped Accessible Edinburgh – And Beyond will help families have fun days out, as well as find the support they need.

My daughter, Maya, and I have had many experiences together in this diverse city. Like any other carer of a young child, I've always been keen to get involved in doing things. In getting out there and enjoying the city and beyond, carers of young children with additional needs may have to be that little bit more organised, that little bit more resourceful and have just that little bit more energy!

The experiences we've had have been positive, heart warming, frustrating, difficult, amusing, thought provoking: we've been stranded at the bottom of the steep steps in Princes Street Gardens at midnight after the September fireworks; we've been treated like VIPs when we visited Edinburgh castle; we've been refused access to the bus unless we 'fold the chair' – only to have a group of passengers get off the bus and help us on (I ended up carrying nothing!); we've done the gastrostomy feed in the National Portrait Gallery (and giggled when my daughter's wind caused a bullet of milk to shoot from the feeding tube, narrowly missing a painting); we've skipped the queue for the big wheel at Winter Wonderland; we've been taken backstage at theatres to avoid the stairs (we've met the Singing Kettle!); we even managed the 'radical road' – just.

We've been refused entry; we've been welcomed. It's not just about access – but about attitude too. One of the most positive experiences we've had was go-karting at the Noah's Ark Centre in Perth. There was a short distance to carry Maya to the karts – a task made more difficult for the fact she had to wear a large helmet and we had many bags. The man working the go-karts was very eager to assist us. He said: 'you just tell me what you need me to do – I'll do whatever you need me to.' Friendly, helpful staff can make all the difference to a day out. Similarly, a visit to Edinburgh Castle is proof that with a little bit of creative thinking and a team of helpful staff with a positive attitude to inclusion, even the most difficult of venues can be made accessible and can be enjoyed by all.

This section is in three parts: 'What shall we do today?' 'Out and About' and 'Support and Services'. The first part gives advice and information about various venues and activities. It also lists music classes, places to visit, annual events, etc. Many of these venues are listed above in the Where Shall We Go Today section, but here we have focused on the resources which make a visit with a child with additional support needs enjoyable for all concerned.

The second section deals with day-to-day aspects aspects such as shopping and getting around the city.

The third part lists information regarding support and services which may be available to families of children with additional support needs.

Research has shown that for families with disabled children, information needs may not be met and many families may experience difficulty in finding out information about support and services available to them.

While we haven't been able to cover all of the support and services available to families, it is hoped that the advice and information given may be useful – do remember that a number of advice and information services are listed that families can contact for further information. SNIP (Special Needs Information Point), for example, are a very valuable resource for parents of children with special needs in the Edinburgh area looking for information or support.

Comments or suggestions about this section are most welcome. Contact Edinburgh for Under Fives at:
Edinburgh for Under Fives
PO Box 012345
Edinburgh EH9 2YB
Or
info@efuf.co.uk

Enjoy Edinburgh!
Nicola Coates

WHERE SHALL WE GO TODAY?

CERAMIC CENTRES

The Ceramic Experience
Ocean Drive
Britannia Quay EH6 6JB
Tel: 554 4455
Web: www.theceramicexperience.com

Bright, spacious studio area with small café and soft play area.
The soft play area may suit a good climber as entry to the slide is quite high and it's not possible for adults to accompany children. High chairs available for additional support for children wishing to paint, although no booster seats. Ceramics are displayed at a low enough level that children using a wheelchair can view them. Parking is available at Ocean terminal nearby.
Good toilet facilities for the disabled.

Doodles Ceramics Work Shop
29 Marchmont Crescent EH9 1HQ
Tel: 229 1399
Web: www.doodlesscotland.co.uk

Friendly, helpful staff who will bring paints to the table for you if you can't leave your child, which can be a great help. A moulded booster seat is available (without sides) for extra seating support. Very difficult access to the toilet which is downstairs.

CINEMAS

It's worth knowing that most cinemas in Edinburgh admit a carer free of charge – some may have an 'Access for All' type card that you need to apply for (very brief application procedure) to enable you to gain free entry. When choosing seats consider whether or not you would like to book the seats reserved for wheelchair users – see the entry above on theatres for more information on these type of seats. Some cinemas will operate a 'no pushchairs' rule but should be accommodating to children in wheelchairs (although storing wheelchairs in the aisle may be a no-no for health and safety reasons). All new build cinemas are wheelchair accessible, with the older cinemas accessible to varying degrees. The Cameo has two of its three screens fully accessible to wheelchair users (screens 1 and 2) and the bar area is accessible by the side entrance (there is also a toilet for the disabled). The Filmhouse is fully accessible and has toilet facilities for the disabled. The Dominion (a listed building) has steps into every screen so is not accessible.

FARM PARKS, ZOOS & ANIMAL PARKS

In the City

Edinburgh Zoo
134 Corstorphine Road
Tel: 334 9171

If you can cope with hills, the zoo can be a great day out. All enclosures and animal houses are accessible and a courtesy vehicle, with wheelchair access, runs about every 15 minutes and goes up to the top of the zoo where the wild cats and zebras live (not together!). Unfortunately, the courtesy vehicle is very popular – even with those who are able to walk up the steep hill and would probably benefit from doing so, so you may have to wait in long queues during peak times. At present, there is no priority given for those who can't manage the walk, which can be a little frustrating. Parking is nearby and there are blue badge parking bays, which may not always be available during peak times. Parking is free for members. Carers get in free and it's worth knowing that if you buy an annual membership for your child, their card should state 'plus carer' on it; this can be an affordable option if you plan to visit fairly regularly. There are several cafes, all of which are accessible, although the café on the lower floor of the member's house has a 'no pushchairs' rule. This can be quite strictly enforced and may cause difficulties if your child has a 'buggy' style wheelchair that passes for a pushchair – be prepared to explain this to staff if you visit this cafe. Overall, an enjoyable day if the weather's nice and it's not too busy – two things that often go together. A visit during the day in school term-time might be best.

Gorgie City Farm
51 Gorgie Road
Tel: 337 4202

Parking is limited but convenient for the farm if you can get a space. There's disabled access to all facilities, although the terrain is slightly rough in parts and the play park area has a bark ground covering. There are toilet facilities for the disabled. If you consider having a birthday party here for your child, they will be happy to change from the usual party room to one that is more accessible.

Close to Home

Almond Valley Heritage Centre
Millfield, Livingston
Tel: 01506 414 957

The majority of The Almond Valley Heritage Centre is accessible to wheelchair users. Due to the nature of the land – with its hills and bumps – access may be a little tricky, but everything that can be done to make the centre accessible has been. While the terrain near the animal enclosures may be rough, it should be accessible to pushchairs and wheelchairs, and ramps have been provided to assist access.

Santa Specials

The narrow gauge railway trip to the 'North Pole' is a feature of the Santa special weekends. While there is no ramp access to the carriage and a child may need to transfer from their wheelchair to the carriage seats, staff are more than willing to assist with the storing of chairs and equipment. Ask for help if you need it – it's part of the staff ethos to assist parents where they can. There are toilet facilities for the disabled and blue badge parking bays – parking shouldn't be a problem.

East Links Family Park and Narrow Gauge Railway
By Dunbar
Tel: 01368 863607

Ample parking. Toilet for the disabled provided. Ask about a carer's discount – carers get in to the park for the price of a child. All of the park is accessible by wheelchair, including the small animal barn and the animal feeding activities. The narrow gauge railway has ramp access to a carriage that can accommodate a wheelchair so access shouldn't be a problem. All in all – top effort!

If combining a visit to East Lothian with a trip to the beach – beware the dunes of Gullane!

PARKS & PLAY AREAS

For details of play parks and outdoor play areas please see the main section. Design of play parks in the Edinburgh area now takes into consideration the needs of wheelchair users and of children with a wide variety of special needs. There are, how- ever, still many parks in the Edinburgh area that were designed before access for all was considered. It's rather a case of trial and error – there may be some parks that are particularly good for your child and others that offer them little in the way of play opportunities. If you feel your local park is unsuitable for your child's needs it may be worth contacting you local council (you can also do this to report glass or other dangerous litter in the park). If you are looking for more information on which parks are currently accessible or on plans to improve accessibility in Edinburgh, then it may be worth contacting Mr McLeod on 529 7898 in the Parks Division of the City of Edinburgh Council.

The Yard: Scotland Yard Adventure Centre
22 Eyre Place Lane EH3 5EH
Tel: 476 4506

Aims to provide creative and adventurous play opportunities for children and young people with additional support needs. While many of the clubs are geared towards older children, the family days (Saturdays and Thursday evenings) may provide a stimulating play environment for younger children and their siblings. Equipment includes: a wide range of adapted bikes, a large bedswing and ballcone, an enormous sandpit and a soft play area. There is also a sensory garden, a music trail, a stream, musical instruments, an art room and a calming sensory room. The yard is staffed by professional play-workers and volunteers, who will assist your child in play. The environment may be daunting for younger, less mobile children at times when there are lots of older children and young people playing. Phone prior to your first visit so that someone can meet you on arrival. Parking can be problematic due to the central location but there should be yellow line parking available nearby if you have a blue badge. There is no charge for families, although donations are welcome. Toilets and facilities are accessible. The Yard hosts a variety of community events including a bonfire night and community summer festival.

SOFT PLAY

Clambers
Royal Commonwealth Pool
Dalkeith Road EH16 5AE
Tel: 667 7211

Adults can go in to all areas with children who need additional help. There are three levels, with the lower level offering a challenging environment for younger children or those learning to crawl. Depending on the height of the child, the ball pool area may be deep enough to allow supported standing, although this area can be busy at peak times. Access to the upper levels is difficult and suited only for good climbers. It may be possible to access upper areas by carrying your child up the 'staff only' steps if a member of staff agrees (this may be a relatively informal practice that has insurance issues!). Cold water is available. Ask about a discount for your child, particularly if they can only access the lower area. Blue Badge parking bays are available but the car park can get very busy and these are in high demand.

Clown Around
Units 2&3
109 Restalrig Rd EH6 7NY
Tel: 553 7676
Web: www.clownaround.me.uk
Different areas for different age groups. The 0 – 3 area may be enjoyed by children with limited mobility. Parents can go into this area and some thought has gone in to the provision of equipment for sensory experience, including low placed music notes that sound when pressed. There is a slide in this area, however entry is quite difficult and the slide isn't wide enough for an accompanying adult. In the main area, for ages 4 – 10, the two entry points are difficult and relatively steep. Adults are not allowed in this area, a rule that is particularly enforced during busy times. There is an additional trampoline area with six trampolines with soft surrounds and covered gaps. Older children tend to jump between the trampolines and adults are not allowed to go on with their child (although may rescue them if needed!). The party room can accommodate children with additional needs and wheelchair access can be created at party tables, or chairs with sides provided. Similarly, in the café area, some tables will accommodate a wheelchair – although space may be an issue. It may be necessary to call in advance to check how busy the centre is. There are no blue badge parking bays so parking may be an issue. The exit from the soft play leads directly onto the car park. No discount at the time of visit for children with disabilities and some reservation about parents/carers accompanying children on equipment.

Jelly Club
Peffermill Rd EH15 5UY
Tel: 652 0212
Web: www.jellyclub.co.uk
No blue badge parking bays, although the car park is fairly large. Significant reduction on entry fee for children with

disabilities. Different areas for different age group. The area for younger children is large with plenty to occupy crawling or walking children, and plenty of soft shapes that may be suitable for children needing sitting support. The tables next to this area may be useful for keeping an eye while allowing some independence. The two slides in this area are accessible by ledges that may be crawled up or accessed by a child with limited climbing ability (adult assistance is possible). The area for older children has a tube slide that may be accessible to a crawling child and may allow for some independence (and if necessary an adult can easily access to assist). The remaining slides have difficult access to them (rope ladders, steep inclines) and adults may not be able to accompany due to space restrictions. During quiet times, the bouncy castles may be suitable, although adults are discouraged from going on. Floor area between the different play zones may be dirty and unsuitable for a crawling child. Toilet for the disabled provided. The increased security at the entry/exit doors may suit a child prone to wandering off!

Leith Water World
377 Easter Road EH6 8HU
Tel: 555 6000

A small soft play area, usually fairly quiet. Most suitable for a child with the ability to pull themselves to stand and to climb ledges to reach the upper level. The ball pool area is at the bottom of the slide so may not be suitable for a less mobile child. Adults sit very close to the play area, which may suit. There is a sensory facility for children with special needs that can be booked in advance. The sensory room is close to the soft play area and is a great facility for children who enjoy multi-sensory experience. Call in advance to check availability.

Molly's
Ocean Terminal
Ocean Drive EH6 6JJ
Tel: 0845 123 5593
Web: www.mollys.co.uk

This soft play centre opened in 2005 and is proving to be very successful. There's a small area for the very young, including a small ball pool – this may not be suitable for a larger child due to the small access point. The main play area can offer stimulation and a lot of fun. There are three entry points to the play area – a steep rope net that may suit good climbers but be tricky to others, a sloped padded entry point that may suit a crawling child who can manage steps, and a series of stairs going up the inside of the play tree. The stairs are wide and not too steep and the unit has been designed so that a child can transfer straight from a wheelchair onto the bottom of the steps. A crawling child should be able to manage these steps independently and access the long wave slides at the top. Adults are not allowed on the play equipment, although a child requiring extra support may be accompanied at most times. The friendly staff have a positive attitude to inclusion and have been known to assist children on a one-to-one basis during quiet times. There's plenty of parking at Ocean Terminal – level E is best for Molly's. A toilet for the disabled is provided and a discount is available for children with disabilities.

Close to Home

The Happy Castle
Bankmill
Valleyfirld Road
Penicuik EH26 8LW
Tel: 01968 675638
This soft play centre may provide good stimulation for a child with reasonable ability to climb and for older/more able bodied children. The easiest entry point to the main area is by climbing a series of ledges – about half a metre high each. This may pose a good challenge for a child improving climbing skills, but may be a barrier to a child not able to pull him/herself to stand or climb. An adult must accompany children with special needs; adults are allowed in all areas. Slides are located at the upper level of the equipment and are large enough for an adult to accompany a child (and quite good fun!). In most areas, an adult may be able to assist a child with climbing due to the design. Play equipment is, in parts, worn and ripped and carpets may be dirty due to the size and popularity of the centre. There is one blue badge bay and no discount for children with disabilities.

Junglee Fun
115 North High Street
Musselburgh EH21 6JE
Tel: 653 0666
Web: www.junglee-fun.com
This small soft play area allows for easy supervision with seating directly next to the play section. Entry to the play area is, however, down a few steps and can often be crowded – space for wheelchair storage is very limited. Although there's no designated blue badge parking, on

street parking should be fairly plentiful nearby. Monday and Tuesday am are the quietest times and it may be that the size of the venue is reassuring to children who are overwhelmed by large play areas. The small bouncy castle may appeal and the age limit is restricted to children under six – although this rule may not be strictly enforced. Plans are being developed to start a parent and child group for children with disabilities/special needs so keep an eye out for those. Toilet for the disabled provided.

Further Afield

Noah's Ark
Glendevon Farm
Western Edge
Perth, PH1 1QE
Tel: 01738 445568
2 disabled spaces. Reduced entry fee for children with disabilities. There are 3 different areas for different age groups. The one for the under 3s may be enjoyed by children with limited mobility or children enjoying a less busy area. Adults can accompany and there is plenty room and soft shapes to support sitting or to provide stimulation for crawling and limited climbing. The under fives area offers more opportunity for the development of crawling and climbing skills – with a child who is able to crawl independently potentially able to access all the area without assistance. If assistance is needed, adults are allowed to accompany. The area for older children offers excitement and stimulation for more able-bodied children and may be useful for families visiting with older siblings. The café area is large, with seating beside the under 3s area, which may be useful for parents needing to keep an eye. Door handles are high to prevent young children escaping and doors have finger-safe hinges. Toilet for the disabled.
As well as soft-play, the centre also has go-karting and indoor bowling. The karting may suit a child with sitting ability but the seats are deep and there is a seatbelt so a child with balance difficulties should still be able to ride. If you need help to get to the cart – do ask. The staff are very friendly and willing to help.

SPORTS & SWIMMING

Gymnastics

Unlike Glasgow, Edinburgh doesn't have a gymnastics-style class specifically for disabled children. The best advice we can give, if you want your child to try out a mainstream gymnastics class, is to speak to the coach to get an idea of how your child might best be included and what they might gain from the class. Again, it may be best to organise a trial session to ensure that the club activities will be suited to your child's needs.

Tumbletots
Edinburgh East
Contact: Jo Letelier-Lobos
Tel: 01875 320066
Email: joletelier.lobos@virgin.net
Edinburgh West
Contact: Julia Kerr
Tel: 313 3556
Web: www.tumbletots.com/edinburgh
Although there is no class specifically for children with additional support needs, children are welcome to attend a class suited to their developmental stage. If your child is happy to attend a class with younger children, then this might suit. Parents/carers can stay with their child (all parents/carers accompany children under 3 years old) or, depending on the needs of the child, may be able to leave.

Horse-Riding – Riding for the Disabled
Riding for the Disabled offer horse-riding for people with disabilities, including young children.

There are two centres in Edinburgh and the Lothians:
West Lothian & District Group, tel: 0845 450 6952
Ravelrig Group, tel: 0845 450 6725

Waiting lists can be extremely long so consider putting your child's name down as soon as you possibly can – but the wait can be well worth it. Volunteers and are friendly, enthusiastic and dedicated and your child may gain a lot from the experience of regular riding. Places are in high demand and the level of support offered to cater for a child's needs is commendable.

Swimming pools
Remember to ask for a carer's discount! Children under five and accompanying carers should get into any Edinburgh City Council swimming pool free of charge. If you're phoning in advance of taking your child swimming, it may be worth asking about equipment available (and whether it is clean and in working order!).
Equipment that can be helpful, if not vital for some

families, includes: a height adjustable changing bed, a shower chair that doesn't couple as a toilet chair (that is, it doesn't have a large hole in the seat area), and a hoist for pool entry (although you may not choose to use this with younger children). While all such equipment will be geared towards disabled adults, it is often suitable for use with children too.

While all swimming pools and leisure centres should have facilities for the disabled, equipment varies between venues with some pools not having a shower chair and others not having a working changing bed. Venues also differ with reference to cleanliness of facilities for the disabled. If a pool doesn't have a chair that your child can use to gain access to the poolside, do ask about taking a wheelchair in if your child needs to. Listed below are details of some of the swimming pools that may be suitable.

Dalry Swim Centre
Caledonian Crescent EH11 2AL
Tel: 313 3964
Disabled parking at main entrance to reception and pool, both of which are at street level. Hoist available with staff trained to operate it. Toilet, changing and showering accommodation for people with disabilities is provided, as is a shower chair and smaller benches that may be suitable, depending on your child's needs.

Drumbrae Leisure Centre
Drumbrae Terrace EH4 7SF
Tel: 312 7957
A good sized car park with blue badge parking bays near the door. The changing facilities for the disabled are accessed by key, which you'll need to ask for at reception (you'll be required to leave a car key or similar as a deposit). The staff are very helpful – do ask if you need assistance. The disabled changing area is near the poolside – the facility is large and clean with lockers, adapted toilet and shower and a very good height-adjustable changing bed. A shower chair is also provided, however it couples as a toilet chair so may not be suitable for children – ask about taking your child's wheelchair onto the poolside if you need to. There's a small seat with a grab rail in the communal shower area beside the pool.

Leith Waterworld
377 Easter Road EH6 8HU
Tel: 555 6000
A favourite with many children. Parking is in the nearby car park shared with Scotmid. Blue badge parking bays are

available but are in high demand at peak times. Changing facilities for the disabled are accessed by a key, available from reception. Large family changing rooms are also available which might suit. There is no shower chair but wheelchairs can be taken close to the poolside and staff are happy to store a wheelchair securely while you are in the pool. There's a small seat in the communal shower area beside the pool. The sloping beach style entrance to the pool means non-swimmers can enjoy the waves too. Staff are helpful and experienced in accommodating disabled visitors.

Musselburgh Sports Centre
Newbigging EH21 7AS
Tel: 653 6367

A good sized car park with blue badge parking bays close to the entrance. The facilities for the disabled – adjustable changing bed, adapted toilet and shower area - are clean and shower chairs (2) are available. A hoist is available for entry to the pool and the shower chair can be taken right up to the poolside. The children's area of the pool (which is quite deep at 0.8m) may be busy at peak times or during swimming lessons. It can be a little cool in the pool. Staff are friendly and helpful. It's sometimes easier just to shower at the poolside rather than in the disabled changing area unless your child can transfer to the seat (without sides) provided in this area.

Portobello Swim Centre
57, The Promenade EH15 2BS
Tel: 669 6888

Parking can be problematic and is in high demand. The facilities for the disabled – shower area, adapted toilet and shower chair – are close to the pool. Staff are helpful and can take you a short cut to the pool from the changing room. The shower chair can be taken to the poolside and a hoist is available if needed. There's a lift to access the upstairs level (where the café is) and ramps leading up to the automatic main doors of the venue.

Royal Commonwealth Pool
Dalkeith Road EH16 5AE
Tel: 667 7211

Large car park that is usually crowded with blue badge parking bays that are in high demand too. Access to the lower floor for changing and swimming is by lift.

Close to Home

Dunbar Splash Centre
Dunbar, East Lothian
Tel: 01368 865 456

Disabled parking bays provided a little distance from the entry to the centre, no larger than other bays so may prove tricky. Carer and an under five swim for 30p.
One disabled changing area is provided next to two family cubicles on the poolside. Unfortunately the disabled cubicle seems to get used as an additional family cubicle and, indeed, doesn't provide any extra facilities. A shower chair is available, you need to ask for it. Benches in the changing area are quite small, with no changing bed provided. Pool has a ramp access and a beach style entry to the water – so non-swimmers can enjoy the waves too.

There are a variety of animal water features, a shallow bubble pool area and reasonably warm water. The spectating area is on the poolside so another adult not swimming may be able to assist if needed. A small soft-play area (£1.40 half an hour) accessed from the poolside may be enjoyed by a child with limited mobility or a child improving on crawling/early walking skills. Toys available in the soft play. Disabled toilet in the wet area beside the pool, as well as downstairs (lift access) in the dry area.

Not far from the pool is Lauderdale Park which has outdoor play facilities for children of a variety of ages and abilities. A lot of thought has gone into the design of the park and it may be enjoyed by older/able bodied children as well as less mobile children. Facilities that may be enjoyed by children with limited mobility include a very large diaphragm-shaped swing, water and sand features and a roundabout with a seat with back and sides on it. There's plenty for everyone and nearby picnic seats have spaces for wheelchairs and some seats with back and sides. Walkway access to the park is good and the nearby public toilet facilities are fantastic ('loo of the year 2005'!) – disabled toilet key is held by attendant.

The recently opened Junglee Fun on Dunbar High Street is also worth a visit. The café serves good food, the disabled toilet facilities are excellent and there's a quiet room if it all gets too much! The soft play facilities could suit a young or non-mobile child (ball pool area tends to be quiet) as well as older, more mobile children. Some climbing ability is needed to get up to the highest level (adult assistance would be difficult), and the reward for getting there is an exciting steep slide down. Café area has a variety of seats, including high chairs and seat with backs and sides. Most parents leave their pushchairs outside, which can benefit wheelchair storage inside. Nearby street parking is unrestricted so tends to be in demand but you should get something reasonably nearby.

Further Afield

Perth Leisure Pool
Glasgow Road
Perth, PH2 0HZ
Tel: 01738 635454

10 blue badge parking bays and accessible entrance via an extensive ramp. Helpful reception staff and carers and under fives get in for free. Lift access to changing area with family changing rooms large enough to accommodate a wheelchair as well as facilities for the disabled: adapted toilet, a shower with pull down seat and a changing bed. The changing area is on the poolside and you can request use of the shower chair to take your child to the poolside if needed. There is a separate pool area for younger children, which may suit children of limited mobility. There are a number of water features in this 'Monkey Jungle' activity area. In the main pool area there are inflatable rings, wild water and whirl pools, a spa area with 'lots of bubbles' that children might enjoy, and an outdoor area. Water should be quite warm – particularly in the outdoor area!

There is also a park adjacent to Perth Leisure Pool – the Boomerang Play Area. This has been thoughtfully designed to include wheelchair access to the slides and may prove to be a hit!

SWIMMING CLUBS & CLASSES

Depending on your child's needs, they may be able to access one of the many mainstream swimming classes on offer. The Swim4All programme, for example, does offer classes specifically for children with special needs, although these are limited to children with relatively mild disabilities.

Council-run classes for children who require one-to-one support are not available at present, although class sizes are reduced in those classes aimed at children with additional support needs. In these classes, the instructor is not usually in the water. These classes are offered at a variety of venues – call the venue before booking the class to make sure they have the facilities you need; not all swimming pools have shower chairs and some have very long walks to the pool side! It may be advisable to arrange a trial session to check that the class will be suitable for your child's needs.

Lothian Waves Swimming Club
Contact: Heather, Tel 445 2987
Contact: Elma Morrison, Braidburn School 312 2320

Classes held:
Braidburn School
107 Oxgangs Road North
Term-time, Thu 16.20-18.00 (3 classes)
This swimming club aims to provide the opportunity for children with physical disabilities and/or visual impairment to: have confidence in water, learn to swim to the best of their abilities and desire and to progress or move on to another more appropriate club as is their wish. Children learn to swim in a fun, safe and enjoyable environment. The club works with children on a one-to-one basis and welcomes children of all abilities. A team of dedicated volunteers work with the swimming teachers to encourage each child to develop their swimming ability as best they can. Parents don't go in the water with their child, but sit close by (and chat!). The swimming pool is warm and the changing facilities geared towards additional needs. This swimming club comes highly recommended! Contact the nos above for more information.

THEATRES

City centre theatre venues have good access for the disabled (this may not be the case in the festival when everything but your granny's living room turns into a venue). When booking tickets ask about a carer's discount – some venues will give carers a concessionary rate – and consider whether or not you wish to book the seats allocated for wheelchair users. Sometimes these seats can be in a good location, with plenty room around them for ease of access, although this is not always the case. If you book these seats your child will be expected to stay in their chair (or can sit on your knee) and a seat will be provided for a carer next to the wheelchair space. If you don't need this facility, it should be possible to book end of row seats, which may make things easier for you. If your child has a 'buggy' style wheelchair, you may be asked to leave it outside and may need to explain to staff that it is a wheelchair.

VISITOR ATTRACTIONS

Edinburgh Castle
Tel: 225 9846

Top marks for accessibility! You may not believe it, given that the castle was not built with ease of access in mind, but a trip to the castle can be fun, educational and easy! If you have a blue badge you can park on the esplanade. A courtesy vehicle will then transport you and your child through a 'secret tunnel' that cuts through the rock and up the steep cobbled hill to the top area of the castle. The wheelchair accessible courtesy vehicle can transport you up and down again although, if you can brave the cobbles, you may wish to walk back down. Truly VIP treatment! Almost all of the exhibitions, including the crown jewels and the prisoner of war exhibit/dungeons, have alternate wheelchair access (although note that the accessible entrance to the dungeons may be closed in high winds and that there are a small number of steps within the dungeons). The staff are fantastically helpful – do ask if you need assistance. There are toilets for the disabled at various levels. Carers and under fives get in free so, if it's just the two of you, it may not cost you anything! A visit comes highly recommended.

Close to Home

Bo'ness and Kinneil Railway
Bo'ness Station
Tel: 01506 822298 (Talking Timetables)
Tel: 01506 825855 (Office)

Day out with Thomas; Wizards and Witches rides; Santa Steam trains.
Disabled parking is available close to the station, although may be popular at the busy 'Day out with Thomas' events. If you're having difficulty, ask a member of staff for advice. There's a ramp up to the main building. On busy days expect long queues, although it may be possible to use the side ramped entrance instead of waiting in the queue. If your child has a special need that makes waiting in the queue a difficulty, explain this to staff who should be happy to help. There is access from the platform to the train carriage via a ramp and a carpeted area in one of the carriages suitable for a child wishing to stay in their wheelchair, with a seat beside for a carer. The carriage for the disabled is not available on the Santa Steam trains,

however, although staff will be very happy to assist and wheelchairs may be stored and delivered back to you after the journey. Ask about a carer's discount. Toilet for the disabled provided.

ANNUAL EVENTS

Edinburgh Festival Fringe
Due to the large number of venues throughout the city, it's not possible to list those that may be accessible or not. The advice would be to book directly with the venue if you can rather than through the box office (particularly for late bookings) – as booking with the box office may mean having to pick up tickets from a different location before heading to the venue. Check with the venue beforehand about access. Some buildings may have an alternative wheelchair access that you may need to arrange use of in advance. While most venues will have done their best to ensure accessibility, forward planning may still be needed. There may be a strict 'no pushchair' rule in small, busy venues so explanations may be necessary and staff should be able to accommodate your needs by allowing you to go into the show first with your child. This can be really helpful (and may even result in a sneaky detour backstage for ease of access!). If your child transfers out of a wheelchair for the duration of the show, the staff may store their chair in a safe place and should deliver it back to you at the end of the show.

Edinburgh Military Tattoo
Access for the disabled has been fully considered. On Monday to Friday performances a vehicle pass facility is operated so that drop-offs by taxi or private car can be made right up at the esplanade. If you need to bring your car, the nearest disabled parking is St Giles Street at the top of the Mound (the disabled parking on Johnston Terrace is restricted during August and it usually isn't possible to park there after 4pm). A carer will be free when accompanying a disabled adult or child. The North stand has wheelchair spaces with carer seats next to them on the ground level. Toilet for the disabled provided.

The Edinburgh Canal Centre
Ratho
Tel: 333 1320
Santa Barge Trips

The Bridge Inn, which incorporates the Edinburgh Canal Centre, is wheelchair accessible – unlike the canal boats!

Children who use a wheelchair would have to transfer from their chair and be carried into the boat, where they would then sit in one of the standard seats. If you can manage this then the Santa Barge Trips may be an option. Staff will assist with transfers in and out of the boat (although transfer equipment is not in place) and should be happy to help you if you need any other assistance

Festival Fireworks

These are impressive and usually very loud – so not for everyone! Parking for blue badge holders is available on Kings Stables Road and this is the best entry point for wheelchair users (other entry points can be difficult to say the least). Remember that if you choose to sit at the east end of the gardens, it may be difficult to get back to the west end King's Stables Road exit point once the fireworks finish. This entry/exit point tends to be closed earlier than the rest so you may find yourself without an easy exit (and a steep flight of stairs carrying a tired child, a wheelchair and the remnants of a picnic may not be what you fancy at midnight!).

MUSIC FUN

The Boogie Bunch
Contact: Orla O'Neill
Tel: 01506 418 940
Lothian Downs Syndrome runs several clubs for children with Downs Syndrome and their brothers and sisters. The club for children aged up to 10 is held on the 3rd Saturday of every month, and the club for over 10s is every second Tuesday evening. Contact Orla O'Neill for more details.

Daisy's Music Time
Contact: Di Maguire
Tel: 662 1243
Held in Wardie Parish Church.
Di will welcome children with additional needs into her music and fun classes and has experience of working with deaf children. The parent/carer stays with their child for the session. Parking is good and the hall is accessible and has a toilet for the disabled.

Jack and Jill – Music fun for Tots
Contact: Jill Reeves
Tel: 667 9664
Children with special needs are very welcome at these music fun classes, held in Marchmont St Giles Church,

Kilgraston Rd. Jill, a qualified teacher and music therapist, has a very positive attitude to inclusion and will work to make sure no children are left out of the activities. There is a small step up to the property, which can be avoided by using the main church door. Parking is in high demand so it's advised to arrive early! These classes come highly recommended.

Jo Jingles
Contact: Joanne Goodall
Tel: 443 4196
Web: www.jpjingles.co.uk/edinburghwest
Classes are held in a variety of venues so contact Joanne for details of each one.

Mini Minstrels
18 Bonaly Crescent
Contact: Hazel Stewart
Tel: 441 3750
Children with special needs are welcome. There are three steps up to the property. Parking is unrestricted but you may wish to get there early as the street can become a little busy when classes are on. Hazel has previous experience of working in a special needs environment.

Stepping Stones
Orcadia Creative Learning Centre
3 Windsor Place
Portobello EH15 2AJ
Orcadia run an integrated programme of dance and creative movement for children aged 4-8 with special needs and learning disabilities. Dance, creative movement, music, mime, mask and puppetry are all on the agenda. Classes are held on Mon, Wed & Thu from 16.00-17.00. Contact Orcadia for more information.

OUT AND ABOUT

GETTING AROUND

Traveline Scotland has a website (www.travelinescotland.com) featuring a journey planner and a helpline (0870 608 2 608).

Buses

Information may not be available from the Traveline Scotland helpline on which buses are accessible.

Lothian Buses
Tel: 555 6363

If you're looking for information about access on Lothian Buses, it may be worth contacting the head office on 0131 554 4494. They should be able to direct your call to customer services. Lothian Buses are moving towards having 100% of their buses accessible (low floor for getting on and off and space for wheelchair users). At the time of writing around 50% of their fleet is accessible. Some routes are more likely than others to have accessible buses – and there are routes that have such buses for the majority of the time (but this can not be guaranteed).

Routes that sometimes have accessible buses are currently: 2, 10, 11, 24, 35 and 36.
Routes that have accessible buses most of the time are currently: 22, 26, 29, 30, 37, 38, 44 and 49.

As there is limited space for pushchairs and wheelchairs on these accessible buses, you may find you cannot get on the bus if someone is already sitting in the wheelchair space (often, it has to be said, with a pushchair). Wheelchair users are given priority and the driver can ask someone who is not a wheelchair user (including someone with a pushchair) to move, however there is no obligation for them to do so. If you feel that the person occupying the space would be able to move to accommodate you and your child, then it may be worth asking. This situation can be frustrating for all – especially if the bus is busy. It's also worth knowing that you will not be able to get on a bus that doesn't have wheelchair access and space with an unfolded pushchair. This can be a very difficult situation if your child cannot stand or walk and you have bags to carry.

First Edinburgh
Tel: 08708 727271

First Edinburgh were unable, at the time of writing, to state which of their routes would be serviced by accessible buses.

Taxis

Your child may be entitled to a taxi card (from aged 2) which could help with the cost of travelling around the city by taxi. Holders of the card are entitled to travel with selected taxi companies for a reduced fare (a £3 discount on fares up to £5, you have to pay the extra on fares above £5 but still get the £3 discount).

Contact Travel Concessions for further information, Tel: 469 3891/3540/3840.

Handicabs
Web: www.handicabs.org.uk

Handicabs offer a door-to-door transport service for people unable to use ordinary public transport. Two services are provided – Dial-a-Ride and Dial-A-Bus. The Dial-A-Ride service may be useful if your child uses a wheelchair as all buses are adapted to carry wheelchair users. This service offers door-to-door transport seven days a week. The fare is reasonable, particularly for longer journeys. May be used for holidays or for getting to the airport. Bookings need to be made in advance. Contact Dial-A-Ride, Tel: 447 9949.

By Car

Your child may be entitled to parking concessions under the blue badge scheme. You can get a blue badge if you receive the higher rate of the mobility component of Disability Living Allowance or if you have a permanent and substantial disability which means you are unable to walk or have considerable difficulty in walking.
Although children under the age of three years are not entitled to receive the mobility component of Disability Living Allowance, children aged two years may still qualify to receive a blue parking badge if they have considerable difficulty walking caused by a permanent or substantial disability. Your child may have to be assessed to check that they qualify.
For further information contact Travel Concessions – Tel: 469/3891/3540/3840.

Many parents with children who are entitled to the higher rate mobility component of DLA choose to surrender this part of their award and pay a non returnable deposit (for some cars this deposit is nil) in return for the hire of a new vehicle of their choosing. Insurance and repair costs are met over the three year rental period. There are a wide variety of cars to choose from, with MPVs being a popular choice among families with younger children. The cost of the deposit varies depending on the car chosen. For more information on the schemes available, how to apply and current prices have a look at the motability website: www.motability.co.uk

If you need a disabled parking bay outside your home, contact Clarence, Tel: 0800 232323.

Trains

National Rail produce a rail map for people with reduced mobility, which can be helpful when planning your journey.

Of the train stations in and around Edinburgh, those where wheelchair access to all platforms without having to use any steps is possible and where staff are available to assist are: Edinburgh Waverley, Inverkeithing, Kirkcaldy, Falkirk High, Stirling, Glasgow and Perth.

Those stations where there is wheelchair access to all of the platforms but staff may not be available to assist are: Musselburgh, Wallyford, Longniddry, Drem, North Berwick, Dunbar, Aberdour, Dunfermline, Cardenden, Bridge of Allan, Drumgelloch and Shotts.

Those stations where there are steps to some or all of the platforms are:

Edinburgh (Haymarket), Prestonpans, Carstairs, Dunblane, Markinch, Ladybank, Springfield, Cupar and Gleneagles.

For travel to or from Edinburgh Haymarket - only platform 1 is wheelchair accessible, platforms 2, 3 and 4 are not wheelchair accessible and there are a large number of steps to the platforms.

These details were correct at time of writing but may have changed since. Call Scotrail on 08456 015929 for information on accessibility at particular stations.

Walking

Edinburgh is a city of hills and cobbles, both of which contribute to Edinburgh's appeal as a historic city. Cobbles don't bide particularly well with the pushing of wheelchairs, nor the wearing of high heels (particularly hazardous if these two activities are combined!) and hills can be a work-out at the best of times – not least when pushing a pushchair or wheelchair up them! If you can manage the hills then you can enjoy the city by foot and get a good work out in the meantime (an extreme Sunday workout involving the 'radical road' up Arthur's seat, an excited child in a wheelchair, two dogs, a kite may not be for all!). If you can't manage the hills, then there are plenty of areas that have good access and pathways. The Meadows area has good views of Arthur's seat, extensive and well kept grasslands and good parking if you have a blue badge. The play park areas are not particularly suitable for children with additional needs but there may be plans to change this in the near future so watch this space! Inverleith Park and The Botanics have good parking and toilet facilities (the Botanics has disabled

toilet facilities) and the choice of completely flat walkways or some gentle hills. Lots of animal feeding opportunities and good ice-cream on site. Inverleith Park offers a safe environment for a child learning to use a cycle – with wide flat walkways. Although bikes are not permitted in the Botanics, the rule may be overlooked if your child uses a special needs trike with a pull bar. For a sea-side walk, Portobello Promenade is flat, wide and has good parking facilities close by.

Water of Leith Visitor Centre
Tel: 455 7367
Web: www.waterofleith.org

Getting there: Lothian buses 44, 34 and 28 are best (the 44 is most likely to be accessible).
The Water of Leith walkways are accessible in parts. Contact centre for further information.

Water of Leith Buggy Scheme

'Borrow a Buggy' is a scheme to provide disabled and other children who have limited mobility the means to access the countryside. The aim of the project is to enable users to enjoy previously inaccessible places, like the water of Leith Walkway, visits to the countryside, beaches and hill-walking. It's a free service, registration is required. The 5 all terrain buggies come in three sizes, with one available in the small 'ranger' size – suitable for children up to 11 years. They're kept at the Water of Leith Visitor Centre, Slateford, and Craiglockart Tennis Club. The parent/carer must first register by taking along 2 forms of identification (one photo ID and one with a home address). After a familiarisation session, which lasts about 15 minutes, then you will be able to borrow a buggy. The buggies are available for half day, full day or weekend hire (subject to availability) and once you are a registered user all you need to do is call in advance to reserve your buggy for the day.

Edinburgh Canal Centre
Tel: 333 1320

Some of the entry points and most of the walkway areas of the Caledonian Canal are accessible in the Edinburgh area. For more information on walking on the Caledonian Canal walkways contact the Centre.

See also www.thewaterwaystrust.org.uk/lowlandaccess and go to section 4.9 on Edinburgh.

For information on walking around the Pentland Hills area have a look at:
www.edinburgh.gov.uk/phrp/disabledaccess/disabledaccess.html

For information on disabled access to walks in other areas throughout Scotland have a look at the Walking Scotland website:
www. walking.visitscotland.com (and click on disabled access)

LIBRARIES

For details of libraries, including special needs toy libraries, please see the listing in the main section.

Currently those libraries accessible to wheelchair users are: Blackhall, Central, Currie, Fountainbridge, Gilmerton, Moredun, Muirhouse, Newington, Oxgangs, Piershill, Ratho, Sighthill, Westerhailes.
Rarely would those libraries that are not classified as completely accessible have more than three steps. If you need assistance, do ask – there may be an alternate access.

Listening Books
Web: www.listening-books.org.uk

This is a charity that provides a postal audio book library service to anyone who has an illness or disability that makes it impossible or difficult to hold a book, turn its pages, or read in the usual way. They provide audio books for both leisure and learning - providing important support for the National Curriculum at Key Stages 2, 3, 4 and A-level, as well as a large adult library. The service caters for those with physical disabilities, visual impairment and specific learning difficulties, including dyslexia, for which reading print is frustrating, even impossible. Their catalogues include many titles for children of primary 1 age that may be suitable for slightly younger children. For more information, visit their website.

SHOPPING

Supermarkets
If your local supermarket doesn't already have a 'disabled child' trolley then you could request that they purchase one; this has been known to work in the past. These trolleys will usually be kept within the store as apparently they disappear easily! The most common type of disabled child trolley is one that has a single large box seat, with some soft padding for comfort, fitted with a five point harness; your child will face towards you once seated and should be able to reach some produce if they want to help with the shopping. If your child needs extra seating support then this kind of trolley may not be suitable. There are trolleys that have seats for disabled children who need extra seating support (car seat style) but these are a rare species! The following details were correct at the time of writing, but things change – if you're having difficulty shopping in your local supermarket, it may be worth requesting the kind of trolley you need, preferably in writing.
Sainsbury's: The Blackhall store has 2 disabled child trolleys with large box seats and front opening 5 point harnesses. These are usually kept beside the customer service desk.
Asda: None of the Asda stores currently have disabled child trolleys. Trolleys were available at The Jewel store but have not yet been replaced since they were stolen. Asda are currently working to rectify this so it may be worth checking with them.
Morrison's/Safeway: None of the stores currently have disabled child trolleys.
Tesco: None of the Edinburgh stores currently have any disabled child trolleys, although Tesco stores in other areas of the UK do have very good provision for disabled children; with some stores having the two different types of disabled child trolley. There are plans to provide such trolleys at stores in Edinburgh, excluding Tesco Express and Tesco Metro stores, but this is not yet in place.
Other stores: Unfortunately, some of the low cost stores may not have specialist trolleys – and beware that they may not have baskets either, which can make shopping with your child very tricky.
Those stores that do not have disabled child trolleys may offer a member of staff to accompany you as you shop. Avoid Saturdays for this service, which is less likely to be available at peak times.

Toys & Equipment

We have listed some selected providers of toys and equipmen.t plus details of where to get advice about toys and equipment. Remember that even if you're buying a toy or a piece of equipment privately it's worth speaking to your child's physiotherapist or occupational therapist, who should be able to offer advice on what would be suitable.

Babyjr
Tel: 01732 455947
Web: www.babyjr.co.uk

Manufactures unique front opening wrap vests for babies designed for easy changing – no need to pull over the head so may suit a child on oxygen therapy. Call or visit for more information.

Cyclone
Tel: 0800 180 4850
www.cyclonemobility.com

Manufacture an attractive sports style child's wheelchair.

DCS Joncare
Contact: 01505 702 403 (Mr Bill Slack, Scotland Rep)
Web: www.dcsjoncare.freeserve.co.uk

A company dedicated to mobility for disabled children offering a range of equipment including powered and self-propelled wheelchairs, standing and seating systems, and trikes.

Disabledaccessories.com
Tel: 01480 494 417
(Head Office - Co. is part of Pupa Ltd)
Tel: 0800 389 5534 (24 hr Orderline)
Web: www.disabledaccessories.com

A range of aids and equipment, including paediatric aids and equipment

G & S Smirthwaite
Tel: 01626 835552
Web: www.smirthwaite.co.uk

For furniture and equipment for special needs and conductive education. Wide range of products.

Hug it
Web: www.hug-it.co.uk

Manufacture seat harnesses for ages 12 to 28 months to be used on buggies, highchairs, wheelchairs to ensure better tightening of straps. It can also be used on adult seat belts to improve positioning. It's designed to stop young children 'escaping' their shoulder straps and may be especially useful for children with special needs as it offers extra support for the upper body. See website for more details. Offer 10% discount to NCT, NCMA and TAMBA members.

JCM Seating Solutions Ltd
Tel: 01775 766664
Web: www.jcmseating.co.uk

Paediatric equipment including seating systems, sleep systems and car seats. They have friendly, trustworthy reps who travel to Edinburgh on a regular basis.

Lomax
Tel: 01382 503000
Web: www.lomaxmobility.com

Independent wheelchair manufacturer based in Dundee. They manufacture wheelchairs for children and adults (their Kidactive chairs come in a variety of colours – including pink!)

Nottingham Rehab Supplies
Tel: 0845 120 4522
Web: www.nrs-uk.co.uk

Daily living aids for adults and children. Wide range of products.

Theraplay Ltd
For foot pedal tricycles, hand crank tricycles, gait trainers and toileting/shower chairs. The tricycles may be particularly popular with children who need additional support for cycling – the Imp tricycle comes in colours that appeal to children (including pink!) and suits children from about 2 1/2 years. Adapted tricycles can be quite expensive – if you're applying for funding to buy one for your child remember the SNIP fundfinder service!

Details of Theraplay Ltd products can be found at:
www.triaid.com
Tel: 0141 876 9177

If you're interested in a product, a rep will be able to come to your home to assess the kind of trike your child needs. You could also consider trying out a tricycle with your child before you purchase one – the special needs toy library may have one available for loan or you could visit the Scotland Yard Adventure Centre where they might have one for your child to try.

Sunrise Medical
Tel: 01384 44 66 88
Web: www.sunrisemedical.co.uk

Manufacturers of wheelchairs for adults and children. Child friendly designs available.

The Whistling Tortoise
42A Hamilton Place, EH3 5AX
Tel: 225 6365
Web: www.whistlingtortoise.com
A disability equipment shop in Edinburgh

The Disabled Living Foundation
Tel: 0845 130 9177 (Helpline)
Web: . www.dlf.org.uk
The website contains a huge amount of information and resources on equipment for people with disabilities. There are also fact sheets available for download – including fact sheets on choosing equipment for children

Edinburgh City Council
A new booklet from the City of Edinburgh Council shows all the equipment you can get free without the need for an occupational therapy assessment (although your child should also be assessed by an occupational therapist if they need to be). All you have to do is fill in the form included in the book, send it to the council and they will send or deliver the equipment to you. You can get a free copy of the booklet, called "Equipment for use at home: simple solutions that you can choose" by calling 313 2435.

SUPPORT AND SERVICES

Childcare and Early Education

See the listings in the main section on pre-school play and education, parent and toddler groups, playgroups, private nurseries, nursery classes in local authority and independent schools.

Parents with disabled children can experience difficulties trying to find appropriate and affordable childcare for their child. If you are experiencing problems finding childcare for your child do remember that you are not alone and that it is not an impossible task! Parents of children who need one-to-one care may find organising childcare particularly difficult. The current situation is that many childminders may not feel they are in a position to accommodate a child with additional needs as they may have to limit their numbers if they do so, or they may feel they do not have the appropriate training. It is also unusual for additional support to be available for children with special needs in private nursery settings. There are,

of course, childminders and nurseries who are willing and able to accommodate children with additional needs – so how do you go about finding them?

Edinburgh Childcare Information Service can provide information on childminders, nurseries and play-schemes that accommodate children with special needs. This information, however, is currently very limited and no information is given on the kind of special needs the childcare provider can accommodate or on the special needs training and experience of the staff. Also, while some of the providers indicate that they can accommodate special needs, they may also indicate that their premises are not wheelchair accessible. Parents can, however, use this information as a starting point in exploring options for their child and can contact providers listed for further information and to arrange a visit. Contact the City of Edinburgh Childcare Information Service on 0800 032 0323 or visit their website to have a look at the childcare available in your area (www.childcarelink.gov.uk)

Funds may be available (depending on the age of the child and the local authority) to enable mainstream childcare providers to cover the extra costs of looking after a disabled child (these funds may be restricted to parents who are in work, training or education). Don't assume that the childcare provider you're interested in is aware of these funds! The Edinburgh Childcare Partnership (0131 270 6061/6064) may be able to advise on such funds – they have an Inclusion Officer who deals with funding applications from providers seeking to provide care for children with additional support needs. The Edinburgh Childcare Partnership also has a website with a database of providers available to search online: www.edinburghchildcare.co.uk

If your child attends a local authority nursery school, it may be that they are provided with additional support to enable their inclusion. The support may be for a few hours a week or for all of the time they attend, depending on their needs. If the nursery you choose for your child offers wrap-around care (9am to 3pm) then your child may be entitled to a funded full-time place to enable them to access the full curriculum – again, depending on their needs. You should put your child's name down for your chosen nursery school as soon as you can.

Other options and specialist provision for early education include:
Children and Family Centres – there are a variety of children and family centres throughout the city (providing respite rather than childcare services). Child and Family

Centres offer support to vulnerable and disadvantaged families with children under five. Work with the child and the family may take place within the centre (which offers good quality nursery style care) or the family home, or in other appropriate settings such as a nursery class. Respite day care within the centre may be offered as part of the family work. As well as offering day care to the child, the Centres offer a range of services to support the family for example mother and toddler groups and community groups. Children with disabilities can attend the Centres, which are supported by community occupational therapists and physiotherapists and have access to a range of medical and social work services. Ask your social worker (if you have one or the duty children and families social worker if you don't) for further information.

The Barrie Nursery
Canaan Lane
Tel: 446 3120

Partnership nursery with the City of Edinburgh Council and is based at the Canaan Lane Campus of the Royal Blind School. The Canaan Lane Campus of the Royal Blind School is a purpose built educational and residential facility for children and young adults with multiple disabilities in addition to their visual impairments.

The Barrie Nursery offers: small group and individual teaching; high staff ratio; elaborated and adapted 3 - 5 curriculum for visually impaired; therapists as an integral part of teaching team; access to specialist teaching for all pupils in mobility, music therapy and physical education; adapted and accessible outdoor play area. The nursery offers early education to children aged 2 years 11 months to 4 years. The Early Years Play Group meets weekly in the Barrie nursery and includes a toy library, access to hydrotherapy pool and the services of parent counsellor. For further information contact the nursery.

The Westerlea Early Education Centre
Ellersly Road, Murryfield
Tel: 337 9467
www.capability-scotland.org.uk

An early learning Capability Scotland support service for children with additional support needs. It is open to anyone who feels their child will benefit from any of the services on offer. These services include group and individual work on play, movement, communication and sensory development, massage, hydrotherapy and music therapy (for music therapy see below). Westerlea offers centre based work and outreach, as well as a playscheme.

They cater for children from birth to 3 years and are based at for more information. For more information, see contact details above, or ask your child's physiotherapist.

Capability Scotland also provide music sessions for children every Thursday at Westerlea. There are two groups for children and parents/carers and some 1:1 sessions. The music is used as a therapeutic intervention, and the long-term targets for all who take part concentrate on achieving social skills and group interaction while having fun. The main aim of the 1:1 sessions is to enable each child to interact with their peers.

If you would like to find out more:
Contact: Leanne Gray
Tel: 337 9467
Email: westerlea.sure-start@capability-scotland.org.uk

Bright Sparks
Contact: Liz Charles
Tel: 01875 823699

Midlothian Special Needs Playgroup takes place every Tuesday and Thursday from 9.30 to 11.30am at Brown Buildings in Gorebridge. Everyone is welcome. Activities include a soft play area and music therapy (monthly); transport can be provided.

Spectrum
St Giles Centre
Broomhouse Crescent EH11 3UB
Tel: 0131 443 0304

Offers teaching programmes for preschool children with autism and helps families to use them with their child. Support can be either at home, a children's centre or nursery depending on the child's and the family's needs.

Edinburgh Visiting Teaching and Support Service
154 McDonald Road   EH7 4NN
Contact: Lindi MacWilliam
Tel: 469 2850

This specialised early intervention and support service may be able to offer a home visiting teacher for your child, to work on a one-to-one basis with them to support them in pre-school learning.

A new service, Bright Start – for children with complex needs– is also being developed, so you could ask about this too!

Advice for working parents of disabled children

Parents at Work aims to help children, working parents and their employers find a better balance between responsibilities at home and work. Their Children with Disabilities Project produces a newsletter - "Waving not drowning", for parents of disabled children who work or want to work. Their website has a wide range of information, including factsheets to download about things like tax credits and flexible working. See www.parentsatwork.org.uk or call them on 020 7253 7243.

HOLIDAYS – ADVICE AND INFORMATION

Access Travel
Tel: 01942 888844
Web: www.access-travel.co.uk
Provides holidays for disabled people. They can arrange wheelchair accessible properties, special aids, nursing and care services and adapted vehicles.

The Calvert Trust
Tel: 01434 250232
Web: www.calvert-trust.org.uk
Specialises in outdoor activity holidays for people with disabilities. There are sites at Kielder, Keswick and Exmoor. They also have a bursary fund for financing holidays to Kielder.

Holiday Care
Tel: 0845 124 9971 (helpline)
Web: www.holidaycare.org.uk
Holiday Care is the UK's central source of travel and holiday information for disabled people, their families, friends and carers. They have information on hundreds of accessible hotels and visitor attractions in the UK and a range of information sheets on overseas destinations.

Special Families Homeswap Register
Tel: 01752 347577
Web: www.mywebpage.net/special-families/
Set up for physically disabled people of all ages to enable them to swap homes in a two-way or one-way swap for holidays or breaks at any time of the year.

Trefoil House
Tel 339 3148
Web: www.trefoil.org.uk

Trefoil House is a specially adapted mansion in Edinburgh that provides holidays for adults and children with all levels of disability. While Trefoil House is currently closed for holidays, parents can apply for funds (usually a maximum of £250) to take their child on holiday elsewhere.

HOUSING – ADVICE AND INFORMATION

City of Edinburgh Housing Department

Part of the official council website devoted to housing issues. Links to sections on adaptations, information for tenants and details of houses available for exchange: www.edinburgh.gov.uk/CEC/Structure/Web/Housing/Housing.html

Ownership Options In Scotland
Tel: 661 3400
Web: www.oois.org.uk

A charity providing information, advice and other support (although not financial) to disabled people, carers and professionals to improve access to housing in the owner occupied sector. This service is also provided for parents of disabled children and may be useful if you considering home ownership or seeking more information on whether home ownership is a possibility for your family.

Council Tax Reduction

To qualify for the council tax reduction (which would move your council tax bill down by one band), households must include a child or adult who is substantially or permanently disabled. They must also either: use a wheelchair indoors; need a second bathroom, toilet or kitchen; or be the main user of one room, as a living space, for treatment or to store equipment.
The reduction is granted regardless of income or savings, and claims can be backdated indefinitely if applicants can prove that they met the criteria in the past. Contact your local council tax office for further information, you can do this by phoning your local council switchboard (for City of Edinburgh Council call 0131 200 2000).

INFORMATION ABOUT ACCESS

DisabledGo Edinburgh
Web: www.disabledgo.info

A free internet guide offering people with different access concerns information about access to shops, pubs, restaurants, cinemas - all goods and services - throughout Edinburgh. The purpose of the guide is to empower people to get out and do what they want to do by making it much easier to check which places are accessible. Hundreds of shops, pubs, restaurants and other venues are taking part. It's hoped that this new guide will help open up Edinburgh to its thousands of disabled residents, and also make the area more accessible to Britain's 8.7 million disabled people.

WHEELCHAIR TRAINING AND PROVISION

If your child may need a wheelchair they should be referred to ETC – Enabling Technology for Children, for assessment. Speak to your child's physiotherapist for more information. ETC are based in the RES department at the Eastern General Hospital, Seafield Street, Edinburgh, EH6 7LN. You can contact them on 536 4681.

The Association of Wheelchair Children
Tel: 0870 121 0050
Email: headoffice@wheelchairchildren.org.uk
Web: www.wheelchairchildren.org.uk

Specialist national charity providing expert mobility training and advice to wheelchair-using children and their families across the UK and Ireland. They teach children useful, practical skills, such as the management of kerbs, slopes and steps enabling them to move safely and confidently about their homes and neighbourhood. All courses are free of charge and are in a variety of locations throughout the UK (including Scotland).

Whizz Kidz
Tel: 020 7233 6600 (Children's Services Administrator)
Email: kidzservices@whizz-kidz.org.uk
Web: www.whizz-kidz.org.uk

Provide customised wheelchairs, tricycles and other specialised mobility equipment, wheelchair training,

information and advice to change the lives of disabled children across the UK. They also are working to raise awareness of the need of disabled children so that they get the support they deserve from the general public and from the Government. Their website has factsheets for parents and carers on a wide range of subjects, including choosing mobility equipment for children The waiting list is currently very long.

Remember SNIP's 'funder-finder' if you wish to apply for funds to privately purchase a piece of mobility equipment for your child!

THERAPY CENTRES IN CENTRAL SCOTLAND

Bobath Scotland
Tel: 0141 435 3270
Web: www.bobathscotland.org.uk

Bobath Centres specialise in the treatment of cerebral palsy and acquired neurological conditions in children & adults. There are centres throughout the UK, including The Scottish Bobath Centre in Glasgow. If you feel your child would benefit, speak to their consultant and physiotherapist. You can also call the Centre directly for more information.

Craighalbert Centre
Tel: 01236 456100
Web: www.craighalbert.org.uk

The Scottish Centre for Children with Motor Impairments, known as the Craighalbert Centre, is Scotland's national centre for young children with cerebral palsy. The centre is a nursery and a school, although children can also attend the centre on periodic placement or join one of the clubs that runs regularly – for example the Saturday group. This is conductive education therapy, based on methods devised at the Peto institute. For more information contact the centre on or have a look at their website.

Westerlea Early Education Centre
(see above)

Help and advice – benefits, finances, support groups, advocacy and counselling, useful contacts and organisations.

See the main healthcare section and help and information section for details of: emergency care, general practitioners services, hospital services, antenatal care, antenatal classes and support, postnatal support, dental care, complementary health care, benefits/social security information, advice services, media listings, support organisations for lone parents and step families, guides to Edinburgh and other support groups. The following are listings of some additional websites, organisations and useful contacts for parents/carers of children with additional support needs.

HELP & SUPPORT

EDINBURGH & THE LOTHIANS

In addition to the many support groups listed in the Help and Information section, the following local groups may be able to provide families affected by disability with support.

AFASIC Edinburgh
Contact tel: 557 9755
Email: afasic.edinburgh@afasicscotland.org.uk
Local support group.

The Action Group
Norton Park, 57 Albion Road, Edinburgh, EH7 5QY
Tel: 475 2315
Email: advice@actgroup.demon.co.uk
Web: www.actiongroup.org.uk
The Action Group is a voluntary organisation that has developed a range of services for people with support needs and learning disabilities - and their carers throughout Edinburgh and the Lothians. They offer a family info and support service, playschemes, welfare rights advice, holidays, leisure schemes, sitter service, information and newsletters.

BEMAS
Black and Ethnic Minorities Advice Service
The Action Group
Norton Park
57 Albion Road EH7 5QY
Contact: Jean Ye or Surjit Chita
Tel: 475 2315
The BEMAS team in the Action Group provide practical advice and assistance regarding social work services, education, health and housing to Black or Ethnic Minority families who care for children and adults with additional support needs. The service is free and confidential. Interpreters can be arranged upon request.

Child Brain Injury Trust
Contact: Jenny Hill
Tel: 229 1852
Web: www.cbituk.org
CBIT works with children who have an acquired brain injury and their families. They have a number of new parents groups which meet to talk about brain injury, to share ideas and to have a night out. There are groups in Edinburgh, West Lothian and Glasgow.

Edinburgh Adders
Email: edinburghadders@aol.com
A group of parents have set up an ADHD/ADD support group in Edinburgh. If you are interested or would like to know more, please email them.

FAIR
(Family Advice and Information Resource)
25-27 West Nicolson Street EH8 9DB
Tel: 662 1962
Email: fair@fairadvice.org.uk
Web: www.fairadvice.org.uk
Information and advice service for people with learning disabilities, parents, carers and people who work with them in Edinburgh. Call them or pop into their office.

Family Support Group
Queensferry, Dalmeny & Kirliston area
Contact: Lee McCombie
(Prinicipal Teacher of Additional Support Needs)
Tel: 319 3200
A group of parents of children with additional learning needs have started this support group for parents and relatives of children with additional learning needs, no matter what age. The aim of the group is for parents to get together, chat and exchange information.

Firsthand
39 Broughton Place
Edinburgh EH1 3RR
Tel: 557 3121
Email: admin@1sthand.org.uk
Web: www.zen38434.zen.co.uk
A voluntary organisation that runs services for one parent families, families affected by disability and young disabled people. Their services include a sitter service for parents of disabled children or young people. They offer a regular sit so that parents who have no other reliable sitter can

count on a break. They work within the city of Edinburgh and are staffed by paid staff as well as volunteers (paid staff usually sit for children with complex needs). Firsthand can also be contacted via e-mail enquiry on their website.

Grapevine
Norton Park
57 Albion Road EH7 5QY
Tel: 475 2370
Email: grapevine@lothiancil.demon.co.uk
Web: www.lothiancil.org.uk
Opening hours: Mon-Fri 09.30-16.00.
Provides free, confidential information to disabled people, their supporters and any organisation or individual looking for disability-related information in Edinburgh and Lothian. You can contact Grapevine about a wide variety of issues, including: disability benefits, transport, aids and equipment, access issues, community care and direct payments, housing and adaptations, holidays and leisure, education and employment, and the Disability Discrimination Act.

Link Support Group
PO Box 1883
West Calder EH55 8WB
Contact: Lynne McKeag
Tel: 01506 873650
Email: linksupport.wl@btinternet.com
Web: www.linksupport.wl.btinternet.co.uk
Support group situated in West Lothian who are dedicated to providing information to parents of children with special educational needs.

Lothian Autistic Society
66a Newhaven Road
Tel: 554 9362
Runs a monthly under 5s support meeting.

North West Carers Centre
Contact: Liz Thomson
Tel: 315 3130
Offers a free, flexible sitter service for people living or caring for someone in North West Edinburgh. Trained paid support workers give people a short break from their caring responsibilities by providing support either to the carer or to the person being cared for.

The Roundabout Group
Contact: Jan Anderson or Corinne McGinley
Tel: 01875 615415

Parents whose lives are affected because family members have dyslexia, Asperger's syndrome, DAMP, dyspraxia, autistic spectrum disorders and ADD can attend a support group in Tranent. The Roundabout group was set up to support parents having to deal with the problems associated with these conditions. The group meets every second Thursday evening between 6.30-8.30pm in the Early Years Centre.

Siblings of Children with Autism
Scotland Yard Adventure Centre
70 Eyre Place
Tel: 557 8199

A parent and toddler group for children 3yrs and under who have a brother or sister with autism. First Thursday of the month, 10.00-12.00.

SNIP
Tel: 536 0583 (helpline)
SNIP run therapeutic support groups in Edinburgh for parents/carers of children with special needs. Contact the helpline on 0131 536 0583 for further information.

VOCAL - Voice of Carers Across Lothian
Tel: 622 6666
Web: www.vocal.org.uk

A carer-led organisation which campaigns for carers and their needs, giving them a real voice. It provides information and advice to carers & professionals and an advocacy and counselling service is available to carers free of charge. VOCAL also run courses for parents on lifting and handling   these can be very useful for parents and are provided free of charge.

West Lothian parent group for children with communication difficulties or autism
Contact: Louise Jarman
Tel: 01506 777598
Email louise.jarman@wlt.scot.nhs.uk

Meeting times: Tue (term-time) 09.30-11.30, Child Development Centre, Beatlie Campus, Craigshill, Livingston

At this group parents of children with communication difficulties or autism have the opportunity to discuss various topics, including using a variety of visual strategies to improve communication. There is also a library with appropriate books on autism available and a creche.

SCOTTISH SUPPORT & INFORMATION GROUPS

Capability Scotland Advice Service (CSAS)
11 Ellersly Road EH12 6HY
Tel: 313 5510
Text phone: 346 2529
Fax: 346 1681
Email: ascs@capability-scotland.org.uk
Website: www.capability-scotland.org.uk
Provides information and advice on any disability matter.

Children In Scotland
Web: www.childreninscotland.org.uk
National agency for voluntary, statutory and professional organisations and individuals working with children and their families in Scotland. It exists to identify and promote the interests of children and their families and to ensure that relevant policies, services and other provisions are of the highest possible quality.

Down's Syndrome Scotland
158-160 Balgreen Road EH11 3AU
Tel: 313 4225
Fax: 313 4285
Email: info@dsscotland.org.uk
Web: www.dsscotland.org.uk
Aims to provide support and information to parents of children with Down's Syndrome. Local branch activities include parent and toddler groups, music and drama workshops, computer club and outings.

Enlighten Action for Epilepsy
5 Coates Place EH3 7AA
Tel: 226 5458
Email: info@enlighten.org.uk
Web: www.enlighten.org.uk
Offers information, advice, support and counselling to parents of children with epilepsy and parents with epilepsy who have young children.

Enquire
Tel: 0845 123 2303
(Mon 9.00-17.00; Tue 9.00-17.00, 19.00-21.00; Wed 8.00-17.00; Thu 9.00-17.00, 19.00-21.00; Fri 9.00-17.00)
Web: www.enquire.org.uk
Enquire is the Scottish advice and information service for additional support for learning. The service is available to parents and carers of children and young people with additional support needs, to children and young people themselves, and to professionals working with them.

Enquire offers special educational needs advice and information, including advice and information to parents and carers of children attending nursery.
The telephone helpline is attended by trained advisors. Outwith these times there is an answering service.
Written responses will also be made to their online email forms and enquiries via the website. Enquire also offers training and talks, produces a range of free publications and has a legal subscription service.

Epilepsy Action Scotland
48 Govan Road, Glasgow
Telephone 0141 427 4911 (Office)
Tel: 0808 800 2 200 (Confidential helpline; Mon-Wed,Fri 10.00-16.00;Thu 10.00-18.00)
Web: www.epilepsyscotland.org.uk
Provide information on the causes and treatment of epilepsy and campaigns for more Epilepsy services in Scotland.

Independent Special Education Advice (ISEA) Scotland
164 High Street
Dalkeith EH22 1AY
Tel: 454 0096 (general)
Tel: 454 0082 (helpline)
Tel: 454 0144 (advocacy and representation service)
Fax: 454 0096
Email: iseascotland@whsmithnet.co.uk
Web: www.isea.org.uk
Provides advice, information, advocacy and representation to parents throughout Scotland who have a child or young person with additional support needs.

RNIB Scotland
Dunedin House
25 Ravelston Terrace, Edinburgh EH4 3TP
Telephone 0131 311 8500
email rnibscotland@rnib.org.uk
Web: www.rnib.org.uk
RNIB offers practical support and advice to anyone with a sight problem.

Scottish National Federation for the Welfare of the Blind
Redroofs, Balgavies, Forfar, Angus DD8 2TH
Contact: Hon. Treasurer Mr Duncan
Tel/fax: 01307 830265
Email: snfwb@care4free.net
Co-ordinates organisations working for blind people in Scotland.

Scottish Society for Autism
Hilton House
Alloa Business Centre
The Whins
Alloa   FK10 3SA
Tel: 01259 720 044
Email: autism@autism-in-scotland.org.uk
Web: www.autism-in-scotland.org.uk
Seeks to ensure the provision of the best possible education, care, support and opportunities for people of all ages with autism in Scotland.

Scottish Spina Bifida Association
190 Queensferry Road
Tel: 332 0743 (national office)
Tel: 08459 111112
(family support service - phone for local contacts)

Sleep Scotland
Tel: 651 1392
Tel. 0845 0031212 (support line, Mon-Fri 9.30-23.30)
Email: sleepscotland@btinternet.com
Web: www.sleepscotland.org
Provides support to families of children with special needs and severe sleep problems.

SNIP (Special Needs Information Point)
Freepost SCO5846
Edinburgh EH9 0BR
Tel: 536 0583
(Mon- Fri 10.00-16.00, answering machine all other times)
Email: snip@btinternet.com
Web: www.snipinfo.org
An important contact for parents and carers of children with special needs. Based up at Rillbank Terrace, next to the Royal Hospital for Sick Children, Edinburgh – SNIP offer a variety of very valuable services. They provide advice and information on services available to children with special needs and their carers and welcome calls from parents, carers, professionals and anyone else with an interest in special needs. They don't charge for information and will call you back if you contact them by phone. As well as a helpline service they also run support groups, produce a monthly newsletter, have a very informative website and can carry out a 'funder finder' for families of children with additional support needs to apply for grants to purchase things like equipment and holidays.
Keep SNIP's contact details at hand – you're likely to need them!

NATIONAL SUPPORT GROUPS

Advice guide
Web: www.adviceguide.org.uk
This is the online advice service of the National Association of Citizens Advice Bureaux, offering online advice on a variety of topics.

AFASIC
Tel: 0845 3555577 (helpline Mon-Fri 10.30-14.30)
Web: www.afasic.org.uk
Web: www.afasicscotland.org.uk
Web: www.talkingpoint.org.uk
Charity supporting children and young adults with speech, language or communication impairments and their parents/carers.

Barton Hill Advice Service
Web: www.bhas.org.uk
This voluntary sector agency offers free online guides to claiming disability living allowance, attendance allowance and incapacity benefit.

Benefit Enquiry Line
Tel: 0800 88 22 00
A confidential telephone service for people with disabilities, their representatives and their carers.

Benefits Now
Web: www.benefitsnow.co.uk
Their website has detailed information about claiming DLA, along with discussion lists where parents can exchange advice and information, as well as links to equipment suppliers and information about the Motability scheme. The site also contains the full text of the Disability Handbook, used by the Benefits Agency when assessing claims and which has useful information about the appeals process.

Muscular Dystrophy Group
Prescott House, Prescott Place
London
Tel: 020 7720 8055

Contact A Family
Tel: 0808 808 3555 (helpline; Mon- Fri 10.00-16.00)
Web: www.cafamily.org.uk
Contact a Family is the only UK charity providing support and advice to parents whatever the medical condition

of their child. Their web-site has information on a huge number of specific conditions and rare syndromes, along with details of support groups. They have a very useful helpline (see above) for information relating to parenting a child with additional needs; they aim to be a one-stop advice service for parents. Advice and information can be given on a wide range of topics, including: medical conditions affecting children (including very rare disorders), funding for holidays, benefits, putting you in touch with other parents with children with the same condition and details of local support groups for families of children with any disability.

Department for Work and Pensions
Web: http://www.dwp.gov.uk/lifeevent/benefits/index.asp

Website gives details of the different types of benefits available and how to make a claim.

Disability Rights Commission
Tel: 08457 622 633 (Helpline)

The Disability Rights Commission (DRC) is an independent organisation with the goal of 'a society where all disabled people can participate fully as equal citizens'. The DRC Helpline is there to give advice and information about the Disability Discrimination Act (DDA) 1995. If you feel your child has been treated unfairly because of their disability and want to talk to the DRC, then contact the helpline.

The Family Fund
PO Box 50
York YO1 9ZX
Tel: 0845 130 45 42
Web: www.familyfund.org.uk

Helps families of disabled or seriously ill children under 16. They give grants related to the care of the child including holidays, leisure, laundry equipment, driving lessons and lots more. They also provide a range of information on benefits, holidays, transport and lots more. If your income is £21,500 or less they may be able to help. Apply by phone on, online at or in writing. You'll need to give your child's name, date of birth, their disability and details of the help you need.

Mosaic Down's Syndrome UK
Web: www.mosaicdownsyndrome.org

This website offers support and information for parents of children and adults with Mosaic Down's Syndrome.

One Parent Families
Web: www.oneparentfamilies.org.uk
Web: www.opfs.org.uk (Scottish site)

One Parent Families has published a free guide "The Lone Parent Guide to Caring for a Child with Additional Needs" which includes sections about accessing support and financial help. They have also worked with Contact a Family to develop a telephone advice service. The advice service can be contacted on 0800 018 5026.

SOCIAL WORK SERVICES

Social Work provides a range of services to support children with disabilities and illness. For more information about any of these services, contact your nearest Social Work Centre (see the following listing). Services and support offered may include:

Share the Care - links families to carers who can offer regular care in their own home to give the families of children with disabilities a break.

Family Focus - offers care at the child's own home. It might be help with bathing, toileting or feeding or accompanying the family on outings. Sometimes Family Focus staff "sit" to allow parents to go out alone or with other children.

Residential Respite Care - is offered at Seaview, a centre where children with profound disabilities can go and receive the specialist care they need. Places are in high demand and are generally offered only to children who are unlikely to be matched to a Share the Care family.

Community Occupational Therapists (OTs) - help people with disabilities make the most of their abilities. They teach people new ways of doing things, provide equipment and practical help where necessary, and give support and advice. They help people overcome the limiting factors of disability and help them to be as independent as possible.

Direct Payments – Direct payments allow people, including parents of disabled children, to purchase services to meet their community care needs instead of the local authority arranging services for them. If your local authority decides that you need community care or children's services, they must offer you direct payments as an alternative to arranging the services for you. Parents of a disabled child who has been assessed as needing children's services are now eligible for direct payments to enable them to purchase these services, however in reality few parents in some local authorities (including City of Edinburgh) are currently able to make use of direct payments, for a variety of reasons. If your child has not had a formal assessment of need carried out by a social worker, then contact your local social work centre and request that this happens. Once this assessment is completed, you may then be offered services for your child. If you are offered services you should also be given the option to receive direct payments to purchase these services yourself, if you are able to and choose to do so. You can contact Direct Payments Scotland for advice on receiving direct payments.

Direct Payments Scotland
27 Beaverhall Road
Edinburgh   EH7 4JE
Tel: 558 5200
Tel: 558 3450
Email: info@dpscotland.org.uk
Web: www.dpscotland.org.uk
Can give advice by telephone. also publishes a variety of useful factsheets on direct payments related issues, including 'A guide to receiving direct payments in Scotland'. Contact them if you're having difficulties trying to access direct payments or if you wish to know more about purchasing services with direct payments.

SOCIAL WORK CENTRES

Muirhouse Crescent Social Work Centre
34 Muirhouse Crescent   EH4 4QL
Tel: 343 1991
Opening Hours: Mon-Fri 8.30-16.40.

West Pilton Gardens Social Work Centre
8 West Pilton Gardens   EH4 4DP
Tel: 529 5400
Opening Hours: Mon-Fri 8.30-16.40.

Westfield House Social Work Centre
5 Kirk Loan EH12 7HD
Tel: 334 9933
Opening Hours: Mon-Fri 8.30-16.40.

Springwell House Social Work Centre
I Gorgie Road   EH11 2LA
Tel: 313 3366
Opening Hours. Mon-Fri 8.30-16.40.

Murrayburn Gate Social Work Centre
5 Murrayburn Gate EH14 2SS
Tel: 442 4131
Opening Hours: Mon-Fri: 8.30-16.30.

Oxgangs Path Social Work Centre
4 Oxgangs Path EH13 9LX
Tel: 445 4451
Opening Hours: Mon-Fri: 8.30 16.40.

Victoria Street Social Work Centre
11 Victoria Street EH21 2HE
Tel: 226 6731
Opening Hours Mon-Fri 8.30-16.40.

Giles Street Social Work Centre
9-11 Giles Street EH6 6DJ
Tel: 553 3835
Opening Hours: Mon-Fri 8.30- 16.40.

Leith Social Work Centre
St John's House
71 Constitution Street EH6 7AF
Tel: 553 2121
Opening Hours: Mon-Fri 08.30-16.40.

Craigentinny Social Work Centre
Loaning Road EH7 6JE
Tel: 661 8291
Opening Hours: Mon-Fri 08.30-16.40.

Captains Road Social Work Centre
40 Captains Road EH17 8QF
Tel: 529 5300
Opening Hours: Mon-Fri 8.30-16.40.

Craigmillar Social Work Centre
171 Duddingston Park South EH15 3EG
Tel: 656 9800
Opening Hours: Mon-Fri: 08.30-16.40.

See also Help & Information.

Toilet Stops

TOILET STOPS

There are 29 public toilets in Edinburgh, for which the Council's Environmental and Consumer Services are responsible.

For any comments or more info on them, contact:

City of Edinburgh Council
Environmental and Consumer Services
Tel: 529 3030
Email: env.con.svs@edinburgh.gov.uk

Please note that the Council reserves the right to alter opening times etc. There are other, automated, loos (at eg. St Andrew's Sq) but you'll need to spend much more than a penny to operate them!

Key:
D= facilities for people with disabilities. These toilets are part of the national key scheme.

Toilets in Edinburgh

8.00-18.00
St James

8.00-20.00
Castlehill (8.00-18.00 in Winter)
Castle Terrace (D)
Haymarket (D)
Ross Band Stand ((D)Summer only)

8.00-22.00
Hunter Square (D)
The Mound – Gents only (D)- Ladies are within **Weston Link**

10.00-18.00
Bruntsfield
Canaan Lane
Canonmills
Colinton
Cramond
Currie
Hamilton Place
Hope Park
Joppa
Juniper Green
Middle Meadow Walk
Nicolson Street
St John's Road
Taylor Gardens

10.00-20.00
Ardmillan
Bath Street
Hawes Pier (18.00 in Winter)
High Street (18.00 in Winter)
London Road
Pipe Street (Summer only)
Tollcross

Toilets with Nappy Changing Facilities

Ardmillan Terrace, Gorgie
10.00-22.00

Canaan Lane
10.00-20.00

Castle Terrace Car Park
10.00-20.00

Cramond
10.00-18.00

Canonmills
10.00-18.00

Haymarket
10.00-22.00

High Street, South Queensferry
10.00-22.00

Hunter Square (D)
8.00-22.00

Joppa
10.00-18.00

St James
10.00-20.00

Taylor Gardens, Leith
10.00-22.00

Tollcross
10.00-22.00

Weston Link
10.00-18.00

Travel and Transport

As with most things, getting out and about with small children requires a lot of energy and a certain amount of planning ahead. It needn't turn into a military operation, but being prepared is the key, although it also makes sense to be prepared for things not going according to plan!

The aim of this chapter is to give you as much information as is currently available to enable you to be prepared as you get out and about in Edinburgh.

Over the years there have been proposals to upgrade the public transport system serving the city. The recent developments have not proved popular and plans are now afoot to alter the traffic management one again, so it is unlikey that we will see changes such as the proposed tram link from the city centre to the airport in the near future. So, for now, your options are walking, cycling, or taking a car, bus, taxi or train.

TRAVELINE & NADICS

Traveline
Tel: 0870 608 2608 (every day 8am-8pm, except 25, 26 Dec and 1 Jan: national call rates apply)
Web: wwwtraveline.org.uk
For information about public transport, such as timetables, details of available concessions, or details of transport for people with disabilities, contact Traveline, where you'll receive impartial advice, based on current published timetables. The website can direct you to many others, and help you plan a journey in Scotland, Wales or England.

NADICS
Web: www.nadics.org.uk
Run by the Scottish Executive, the NADICS (NAtional Driver Information and Control System) site provides up-to-date information on roadworks, delays etc, and can help when planning a journey.

AIR TRAVEL

Edinburgh Airport
Edinburgh EH12 9DN
Tel: 333 1000
Web: www.edinburghairport.com
The airport is located 8 miles west of Edinburgh.

Getting There
The airport is easily accessible by car, just off the A8 dual carriageway to the west of the city.

PARKING
Edinburgh Airport currently has 2 short-stay car parks and 1 long stay one: there is also a long-stay NCP car park nearby. The short stay ones are located metres from the terminal itself; in the ground floor of the multi-storey car park, there are also spaces for parking up to a max. of 2 hrs.

Both of the long stay car parks are linked to the terminal by courtesy buses.

Car Park Rates
1 hour – £1.50/30mins; £3.00/1 hr
Short term – £7.50 for up to 2-3 hours or £11.00/ day. Weekend rate are available. Special rates are also available if you pre-book (Tel: 0870 000 1 000)
Long term - £5.40/day (min 4 days parking); a courtesy coach to terminal building included. Pre-booking discounts are available. Tel: 0870 000 1 000 or book online.
NCP is currently £5.20/day or £36.40/7days. The longer you stay, however, the more economical it becomes. Further park and ride facilities available near airport, Tel: 335 3666.

Bus Links
Lothian Buses operate a service called Airlink, Tel: 555 6363. The service runs to and from Waverley Bridge to the airport. The journey time is approx. 25 mins with buses leaving Waverley Bridge every 10 mins during the day. At the time of writing, the fares currently stand at £3.00 single/ £5 open return for an adult traveller, with Child fares at £2/£3. There is an option for a saver ticket which incorporates travel on the Airlink and also on regular fleet buses.

Taxis
Black cabs and private hires can take passengers out to Edinburgh Airport (expect to pay around £16 or so), but it's a point of great contention what happens then. There are dedicated Airport Taxis (in white livery) which have an official rank, but there is an ongoing battle of wits and legalities waged by some black cab operators …
Airport taxis available for hire are saloon or estate cars. Approximate cost to the City Centre is £16-20. Child seat belts are available in the back, if advance notice is given.
For full details of all airline numbers and website addresses please contact the Airport Switchboard on 333 1000.

The Airport Terminal

While Edinburgh Airport has many facilities, one thing which did succumb to the building improvements in recent years was the spectators' gallery; however, while junior plane-spotters can no longer watch the arrivals and departures from the terminal, there are several children's play areas throughout the Terminal and Departure lounges. There is also the landmark 57 m high air traffic control tower to look out for as you travel to the airport.

There are four baby care rooms in the airport. The one before security is situated next to Costa in the UK and Ireland Arrivals area.

The ones after Security are next to Gate 11 and also of the 1st floor by Books etc. For people arriving, here is also a baby care room in International Baggage Reclaim.

Most rooms are fitted with vending machines supplying nappies and have a private nursing room. They contain nappy-change surfaces, sink unit, a playpen, a comfy chair and an activity wall hanging. An en suite toilet and a small room with a chair for feeding complete the facilities.

All toilet areas are facilitated with unisex and wheelchair accessible toilets. If you are travelling with a child of the opposite sex to yourself and need to use the toilets, then you can use the unisex accessible toilets.

There are also children's play areas called Fingerbox, nr gates 2, 4, 9 and 11.

The eating areas have been moved and now have a view of the Pentland Hills. Apart from Costa Coffee on the ground floor, the whole food court has been relocated to the east end of the first floor. Accessible by escalator, lift or stairs the food court boasts a wide selection of both snacks and full meals. There are plenty of highchairs and a selection of tinned baby food is available. Bottles can be warmed on request.

Airport & Tourist Information

The Airport & Tourist Information Desk can be found in the International Arrivals area. The staff will help you with details on airport facilities, places of interest, accommodation and car hire. The car hire firms are based within the Domestic Arrivals Hall.

Shopping

A number of shops selling gifts, clothes, books, magazines, confectionery, etc can be found on the first floor. All retail outlets are easily accessible for all passengers by escalator or lift.

Travelling by Plane with Babies or Toddlers

Always let the airline know in advance that you are travelling with a baby or toddler and check out the facilities available when booking. If you have a lively toddler, it may be worth finding out if you can use a car seat on board. You may have to pay for the seat, depending on the airline and how busy the aircraft is. Car seats can also travel in the hold – but check your baggage allowance! On British Airways international flights of +1hr, you can pre-book your child's meal. The cabin crew will also heat bottles or baby food you bring along - check with other airlines.

British Airways have recently unveiled a new airline seat for the under 2s. Initially these seats will be fitted into Boeing 747s for long-haul flights, but there are plans to extend the service. They also have skycots.

Skycots are available on long-haul flights. Attached to the bulkhead, they provide respite for tired arms by holding sleepy babies.

Other major international airlines offer similar services, such as bassinets, nappy change units, children's meals and so on.

Booking is essential for all these facilities, no matter which airline you travel with, so check when booking flights.

Pushchairs can either be taken on as hand luggage or brought to you when you disembark. Ask when booking or checking in. Take tried and tested snacks and toys for in flight entertainment. During take-off or landing, swallowing food or drinks will help prevent earache arising from changes in cabin pressure. Nappy-changing facilities vary with each aircraft; you may have to resort to your knee. If in doubt, ask. Staff will probably be more than happy to help, particularly if the alternative is having miserable passengers on board.

Travelling by Plane while Pregnant

Travelling whilst pregnant need some planning ahead. Airlines usually accept women up to 36 weeks pregnant (32 with a multiple pregnancy). They require a medical certificate at check-in. If there are complications, further forms are need in advance of the flight.

Extra care must be taken on long-haul flights and equally, due to the risk of hypoxia, excessive flight travel is best avoided in the early weeks.

TRAVELLING BY BUS

Two companies – Lothian Buses and First Bus – provide the majority of services in and around Edinburgh, although other operators provide localised transport.

Lothian Buses still have some maroon and white double deckers which have been part of Edinburgh for years, but updated livery has gold and red squares joining the maroon and white.

First Edinburgh operates fewer routes in the city centre, but has more buses which service the outlying zones of the city. First's livery is white, indigo and red for the majority of the fleet – though you also see green and gold liveried First buses, especially operating outside the city.

Both companies have introduced lower-chassied single deckers, which are easier to board than the older style buses, and which have more space for pushchairs inside.

Under 5s travel free on buses of both companies, on the understanding that they will surrender their seat for a fare-paying passenger. A maximum of two under 5s may accompany one adult, and a standard child fare must be paid for further children.

Fares are similar on both services, based on a stage principal for both adults and children; there's a flat fare for concessionary travel: currently, adults can expect to pay around 80p for 1-2 stages. A 'half-fare' in Edinburgh is actually 60p.

At the time of writing, people who have concession passes for Edinburgh, East Lothian and Midlothian can travel free after 9.30, Mon-Fri and all day Sat and Sun.

Both companies sell bargain day tickets which means you can hop on and off their buses as you require. As well as the day tickets, there's a raft of saver options available, so if you use buses frequently, it might be worth taking the time and working out what's your best option: weekly, monthly and even yearly passes are available. Lothian Buses offer a SmartCard ticket, paid by direct debit, which allows the bearer nigh-on the freedom of that network (excepting the company's tour buses).

Frequency of buses varies depends on the route. However, a 15-20 minute frequency is usual on most main routes during weekdays 7.00-19.00. Off peak bus services vary enormously, so always check a current timetable, available from the respective bus offices or websites, or phone the enquiry lines, otherwise, you could be in for a long wait. In addition, when it comes to route changes, be aware that alterations can occur with what appears to be little public notification, so, again, if in doubt, contact the companies.

Contact Details

Lothian Buses
Lothian Buses plc
Annandale Street   EH7 4AZ
Tel: 0131 554 4494
Fax: 0131 554 3942

Email: info@lothianbuses.co.uk
Web: www.lothianbuses.co.uk

Bus Times & Information
Tel: 555 6363 (24 hrs)
Lothian buses are also introducing a text information service, which will allow you to find out when the next bus will arrive etc. For more information, see: www.travelinescotland.com/smsBusTimes.htm

Lothian Buses Travelshop
27 Hanover Street EH2 2DL
Opening times: 8.15-18.00; closed Sun
Shandwick Place
Opening times: 8.15-18.00; closed Sun
and
31 Waverley Bridge
Opening times: 8.15-18.00; Sun 9.30-17.00

Lost Property
Tel: 558 8858

First Bus
Carmuirs House
300 Stirling Road
Larbert FK5 3NJ
Tel: 01324 611 111
Fax: 01324 611 287
Web: www.firstgroup.com/firstedinburgh

Edinburgh Busline enquiries
Tel: 08708 727271

General Timetable enquiries
Tel: 0870 6082608

Travelling Further Afield
Long distance buses operate out of St Andrews Square. There are services to many parts of Scotland, London and other parts of England. The main operators are Citylink, National Express and Stagecoach. Although fares tend to be cheaper than rail fares, a long distance coach trip with small children can be difficult, so the pros and cons should always be weighed up carefully.

Edinburgh has a new bus terminal, which is much sleeker – and much less draughty – than its predecessor. One thing to watch out for are the automatic doors which screen the waiting area from the bus ranks.

The following companies provide coach travel from Edinburgh to various destinations. If you're not sure which company goes where, try Traveline for information (see above).

Express coach services within Scotland

Scottish Citylink
Buchanan Bus Station
Killermont Street
Glasgow G2 3NP
Tel: 08705 50 50 50 (Contact Centre)
Tel: 0141 332 9644 (head office)
Fax 0141 332 4488
Email: info@citylink.co.uk
Web: www.citylink.co.uk
NB: One child under five years of age not occupying a seat, and accompanied by an adult fare-paying passenger, will be carried free of charge. Any additional child or children under five years of age, accompanied by the same adult, and all children aged 5 to 15 years inclusive can get discounts of up to 30% off normal fares.

Stagecoach Buses
Stagecoach have several locally managed companies in Scotland in Glasgow, Perth and Fife. The Head Office contact address is:

Stagecoach UK Bus
10 Dunkeld Road
Perth Scotland PH1 5TW
Web: www.stagecoachbus.com
Information regarding Stagecoach Fife is available in Travel Shops, such as:
Bus Station
Kingsgate
Dunfermline
Tel: 01383 621249
Bus Station
Church Street
Glenrothes
Tel: 01592 610686
Bus Station
Hill Street
Kirkcaldy
Tel: 01592 642394
Bus Station
City Road
St Andrews
Tel: 01334 474238

Megabus
Web: megabus.com
Stagecoach also provides the Megabus.com inter-city service. Tickets are bookable online: book online and take you booking reference when you travel.
NB: Children under 3 years of age go free, but they are not guaranteed a seat – unless a specific seat has been purchased for them and the reference number provided. All children under 14 yrs of age must be accompanied by an adult (someone aged 16 years old or over). These buses cannot accommodate people travelling with bikes. They also have no wheelchair access.

Express coach services throughout the UK and Ireland:

National Express Limited
Ensign Court
4 Vicarage Road
Edgbaston
Birmingham B15 3ES
Tel: 08705 80 80 80 (Bookings & information)
Tel: 0121 4238479 (Disabled Persons Travel Helpline)
Tel: 0121 455 0086 (textphone)
Web: www.nationalexpress.com

CYCLING

Given the numbers of hills in and around Edinburgh, cycling may not be the first thing you think of doing with your baby or toddler, but with a wealth of off-road routes in and around the city, maybe you will be inspired! Your child will certainly be thrilled by feeling the breeze and watching people and objects speed by.

Before taking off, a few guidelines. Firstly, get your bike checked over at a specialist shop and keep it well maintained, especially the brakes and the wheels, as they will be under greater strain than normal. Next, buy the best child seat you can afford. See Shopping - Bicycles for details and availability. Finally, wear a helmet and ensure that your baby, toddler or child wears a helmet at all times both on road and off road.

Whether you cycle alone or with your child, dress brightly and make use of fluorescent strips to maximise visibility and if it may get dark while you are out, remember to have working front and back lights. The use of a flashing red rear light in addition to the legally required steady red light is recommended. Beware of the effect other road users' actions may have on you, such as car doors opening unexpectedly, and of the effect your actions may have on other road users, such as overtaking a stationary queue of traffic at a junction. Never jump the red lights at pedestrian crossings – if you can't obey the rules designed to protect pedestrians, why should vehicle drivers obey the rules designed to protect cyclists?

Compared with cycling alone, you will find that the bike feels heavier with a child on or attached to your bike. That's what those low gears are for. If using the more common rear-mounted child seat, it is advisable to carry any necessary luggage in front panniers to balance the weight front and back. You may find that wider handlebars give better control over the steering, but if you are using a mountain bike, change the knobbly tyres for smooth ones to reduce resistance on off-road paths and tarmac surfaces.

Although some keen cyclists have been known to tow babies as young as a few weeks old in child trailers, it is advisable not to take them cycling until the baby can support its head and sit up unassisted, usually around 6 mths. Babies and toddlers can be taken cycling in a child trailer towed behind the bike or in a rear-mounted child seat which clips into a bicycle's rear rack. There are pros and cons to both and what is most suitable for you will depend on the type of cycling you intend to do and your budget. Once the trailer or child seat have been outgrown (3-4 yrs depending on size), the choice is a trailercycle which attaches to your bike or a tandem bicycle. Again there are pros and cons to both. See Shopping - Bicycles for further details and for fully comprehensive information you could try a book such as Bicycling with Children by Trudy E. Bell.

Bikes on Trains

All ScotRail trains are fitted with bike accommodation, although the space can vary from 2-6 bikes/train, depending on the service. On some services, pre-booking is required, on others it is to be recommended and on the rest it's not possible. While ScotRail no longer operate a bike charge, some other companies still do and some require bike spaces to be reserved. Note that tandems, tricycles and trailercycles are not carried on ScotRail services. Full details are on their website at www.scotrail. co.uk/cycle.

Child Safety

It is not advisable to allow children under 9 into traffic. Cycle training for primary age children (usually at Primary 6/7) should be available through schools under a scheme run by Lothian and Borders Police. If your child's school does not offer training, ask them to consider doing so. Spokes offshoot, Lothian Safe Routes, can offer advice. Basic cycle training and safety should be promoted to under 5s, in addition to making sure that all their cycles and equipment are well maintained. All cyclists should wear a helmet at all times.

Cycling in Pregnancy

If you are reasonably fit and used to cycling, there is probably no reason not to keep cycling during pregnancy – but do follow your doctor's advice. Consider lower gears and inverting dropped handlebars to enable a more upright sitting position for greater comfort. Be aware that your balance may change as your bump grows.

Contacts

CTC (Cyclists Touring Club)
Cotterell House
69 Meadrow
Godalming, Surrey GU7 3HS
Tel: 0870 873 0060
Email: cycling@ctc.org.uk
Web: www.ctc.org.uk
The Cyclists Touring Club is Britain's largest national cycling organisation. It campaigns for all cyclists regardless of age, ability or type of bike. Members receive a range of services, including a bi-monthly magazine, touring information and technical advice, public liability cover and legal claims advice. The CTC offers a range of insurance policies designed for cyclists.

There is a local group, the CTC Lothians District Association. There are occasional rides for parents with children – on child seats, tandems, pushchairs, own bikes.

Local contact:
Mike Harrison (Secretary)
11 Stead's Place
Edinburgh EH6 5DY
Email: secretary@ctclothians.org.uk
Web: www.ctclothians.org.uk

Spokes
St Martin's Church
232 Dalry Road EH11 2JG
Tel: 313 2114
Web: www.spokes.org.uk
A Lothian cycle group which campaigns for cyclists, Spokes is an entirely voluntary organisation. It produces Cycle

Maps of Edinburgh, Midlothian, East Lothian and West Lothian. These detailed and easy to follow maps show alternative routes to your destination along cycle tracks made from disused railway lines, river valleys, minor roads etc, avoiding busy and cobbled roads. Steep gradients, schools and parks are clearly marked. Available from bike shops, bookshops or post-free from Spokes, £4.95 per map or all four maps for the price of three. Lothian Safe Routes is an offshoot set up to encourage and advise projects that will allow more children and families to walk, cycle or take the bus to school and improve local road conditions.

Sustrans
National Cycle Network Centre
2 Cathedral Square
College Green
Bristol BS1 5DD
Tel: 0117 926 8893
Web: www.sustrans.co.uk

Sustrans Scotland
16a Randolph Crescent
Edinburgh
EH3 7TT
Tel: 0131 539 8122
Fax 0131 539 8123
Email: scotland@sustrans.org.uk

A charity working on sustainable transport projects, the flagship project being the National Cycle Network: a 10,000-mile network of cycle paths combining a mixture of off-road routes and traffic calmed streets. National Route 1 from Dover to John O'Groats, the Orkneys and Shetland passes through Edinburgh and Aberdeen and there are now several regional routes starting in Edinburgh. Up to date details are on the website. Sustrans maps and guides are available from bike shops, bookshops or direct. Sustrans also offers advice on Safe Routes to School projects.

TRAVELLING BY CAR

There's no doubt that Edinburgh is becoming increasingly convoluted. As more roads become one way, and building programmes cause lane closures and restrictions, it can seem that drivers are persona non grata: however, the controversial congestion charging was rejected by public note in 2005, and that is now off the agenda in Edinburgh at least.

However, despite what it feels like when you're crawling along Queen Street at peak times, the city doesn't really suffer from gridlock. Getting from a-b isn't too much of a chore, if you keep to the limits and don't have to travel at absolute peak times.

Parking

The main headache in Edinburgh is not driving, but parking.

If you choose to visit one of the outlying shopping complexes, this problem is negated by the provision of ample and free parking at centres such as the Gyle, Fort Kinnaird, Straiton, Hermiston Gait etc. See Shopping for more details.

However, sometimes parking in or near the city centre cannot be avoided. In the last few years parking restrictions have become tighter and charges have become steeper. There are now 8 zones. Zones 1-4 are within the the central area of the city: they run from the West End-Waterloo Place and from Heriot Row to Melville Drive. Zones 5-8 are peripheral to the others.

In the Central zones, restrictions generally apply Mon-Sat 8.30–18.30. In the peripheral zones restrictions run Mon-Fri 8.30–17.30

NB: These zones may be extended in 2006.

Expect to pay no less than 40p/15 mins: in prime locations, such as George St, the charge can be around 50p/15 mins.

The alternative is to use one of the various multi-storey or one-level car parks within the city's environs. They have a combined total of 5975 spaces, so with fingers crossed, you should find one. The problem with several multi-storeys, such as Castle St (nr Princes St West End), is that they don't have lifts. You either have to tackle narrow stairs or ramps with cars approaching you – neither of which is really suitable for parents with children in pushchairs. Currently, one of the most pushchair friendly multi-storey car parks is at Greenside Place. New Street car park is all on one level, and isn't too much of a hike with a pushchair from Princes St, if you cut along Market St and on to Waverley Bridge., though it can be a bit on the gloomy side. Parking options in the Old Town include the Grassmarket, which is often very busy, George Square (ticket machines), while Chalmers St NCP is also handy for the Meadows and Tollcross areas.

For more information about city parking, click on to: www.edinburgh.gov.uk, and follow the links from the 'Transport' page.

Safety

Safety while driving with small children is a priority. Accidents can be easily caused by unrestrained children, often with dreadful results. Since Sept 1989, if seat belts or child restraints are fitted in the rear of a car, it is the driver's responsibility to ensure that children under 14 use them – no matter how short the journey is. Further information on child car safety and the seatbelt laws can be obtained from The Scottish Executive, Victoria Quay, EH6 6QQ.

Get in the habit of regularly checking your baby or child's seat, especially the restraints. Ensure that all adults securing it in a car are following the manufacturer's instructions on fitting. Why not visit www.childcarseats.org.uk, run by RoSPA, for up to date advice and information.

The law regarding child restraints and seat belts will be changed in May 2006: it's good to keep one step ahead.

City Car Club

An alternative to owning a car in Edinburgh is to join the City Car Club. This is run by a private company, but has the support of the City of Edinburgh Council. You pay for the time you use a car for, plus a mileage charge. There is a monthly membership fee, a refundable security deposit (£100 at the time of writing) and Insurance Excess (£100). You can hire a car for as little as an hour up to a few days (although this is usually through a hire-car company). You can book a car a few weeks in advance, or even as little as half an hour before you need one – although the location and type of car available may obviously be restricted in this case. The Club has 20+ cars, of various sizes, and they are located in dedicated parking bays round the city, such as Marchmont, Bruntsfield, Canonmills, Gorgie, Stockbridge and Portobello. All cars are less than 3 years old and have 5 doors.

The Club does not provide car seats for children, so you would need to provide your own.

Contact:

Smart Moves
31 Argyle Place EH9 1JT
Tel: 0845 458 1784
Email: edinburgh@smartmoves.co.uk
Web: www.smartmoves.co.uk

Car Hire and Child Seats

Most local car rental firms offer car seats for 9 mths-4 yrs, but cost and availability varies considerably. It is recommended to book the car seat at the same time as hiring the car.

See Yellow Pages for contact details or log on to www.yell.com.

ON FOOT

Built on seven hills, Edinburgh is pretty steep in places! It's not always the easiest city to negotiate with pushchairs or prams, or with young children in tow. It always helps if you give yourself plenty of time and have some idea of the route you plan to take. In the city centre much has been done to encourage the pedestrian, such as widening pavements and adding crossings.

Road Safety

When out with small children it makes a lot of sense to emphasise basic road safety even from an early age, and in particular to set a good example. It is well known that road accidents are the major cause of death and injury to children and they are most at risk when on foot and alone. The Royal Society for the Prevention of Accidents (RoSPA) teaches the following basic rules of road safety to children:

Never go out without an adult. Always hold an adult's hand. STOP, LOOK, and LISTEN before you cross the road.

The Children's Traffic Club in Scotland is a free club for children and parents of three-year-olds living in Scotland. Invitations to enrol are sent out by the local Health Board and parents/carers enrol their child by completing the registration card and returning it in the free post envelope provided. The invitation arrives shortly after the child's third birthday. Once enrolled, the child receives a membership certificate and a series of booklets, which contain activities designed to explore road safety. Advice is given on key points and suggestions are given for practice when out and about with the child. The materials are designed for use by parents with children. The club is administered by the Scottish Executive via the Scottish Road Safety Campaign from whom further information can be sought (see below). For advice about other road safety education matters. contact your local Road Safety Training Officer at Lothians and Borders police, Tel: 316 6400.

Scottish Road Safety Campaign
Heriot-Watt Research Park (North)
Riccarton, Currie
Edinburgh EH14 4AP
Tel: 0131 472 9200
Fax: 0131 472 9201
Email: enquiries@srsc.org.uk
Web: www.srsc.org.uk

Road Safety Units and Contacts

Fife Police Headquarters Road Safety Unit
Detroit Road
Glenrothes
Fife KY6 2RJ
Tel: 01592 418 510
Fax: 01592 418 444
Email: Jane.Greer@fife.pnn.fife.police.uk

Lothian and Borders Road Safety Unit
Fettes Avenue
Edinburgh EH4 1RB
Tel: 316 6400
Fax: 316 6401
Email: paul.richardson@lbp.pnn.police.uk

Contacts for other areas in Scotland can be found on **www.srsc.org.uk.**

Problems with Roads, Pavements, Lighting etc
If you have experienced any problems with pavements, crossings or whatever, whether it is in the city centre or your local area, it's worth trying to do something about it. Write to, and encourage friends to write to, your local councillor, pointing out the dangers you and your children face and putting forward your preferred solution, or call CLARENCE (council helpline) on 0800 23 23 23.

TAXIS

Taxis are a fairly expensive way to travel in Edinburgh. Black cabs can be hailed in the street or at taxi ranks, and all charge standard fares. They take a maximum of 5 passengers. Not all black cabs are designed to accommodate wheelchairs, but those which are have the recognisable wheelchair logo prominently displayed. All black cabs are licensed with the City Council and their licence no. will be prominently displayed within the cab itself.
There are a variety of radio cab companies in Edinburgh

for hire, details in the Yellow Pages. Some of these companies offer a range of vehicles, although unless you state how many people it's for, the vehicle in question will probably be a saloon, licensed to carry four passengers.

Points to Note
All cabs and taxis should have licenses displayed and the drivers usually have ID badges.
Use the rear seatbelts: it's the law. Some styles of cabs have a pull-down child seat in the middle of the rear seat. Irrespective of vehicle-type, they should operate under a meter system – so make sure your driver uses it, no matter what form of taxi or hire it is.

TRAVELLING BY TRAIN

For all train times and fare enquiries, call the National Rail Enquiry Service, Tel: 08457 48 49 50
This a 24 hr service. operates a call-rotation system, so hold on if you don't get an answer straight away. Alternatively, visit www.nationalrail.co.uk.
If you are planning a journey, you could also check out Traveline (see above).
There are currently three main passenger service operators in and around Edinburgh. Their Customer Service numbers are as follows:

First ScotRail Tel: 0845 601 5929

GNER, Tel: 08457 225 333 (Mon-Fri 08.30-18.00)

Virgin, Tel: 0870 789 1234

Stations
Although there are around 10 stations in the Edinburgh area, there is limited use for trains within Edinburgh due to the current lack of suburban services. The following is an outline of the stations and the routes they serve.

Edinburgh Park
Edinburgh's newest station, this is situated at the Edinburgh Park Business Park on the Western bounds of the city. It creates a stop between Haymarket and Linlithgow, as well as being a new stop on the Edinburgh-Bathgate route.

Edinburgh Waverley
The main station in Edinburgh and a principal station in the rail network. Trains run south from Waverley to England, and also serve other cities such as Glasgow, Aberdeen and Inverness. There are also connections to other routes, as well as busy local services to East and West Lothian and Fife.
The main station access for pushchairs is from Waverley

Bridge. Other entrances, such as those from Market St and the station car park, have long flights of steps. Access to several of the platforms is by stairs or lifts. There is no drop off/pick up point for private cars.

The station provides many amenities on one level: the travel centre is inside the large, airy Victorian waiting hall – a great place for restless children, but it is always busy and there are automatic doors which allow easy exit! Within the bounds are the ticket and reservation counters, station, toilets, food court (including M&S Simply Food), cash machines etc. Out in the main concourse, there is WH Smiths, Boots the Chemist, Bureau de Change, hotel reservations desk, Hertz car rental (platform 7), luggage lockers, sandwich shops etc.

There is a charge to enter the toilets. There is a separate mothers' room for feeding and nappy-changing. The latter is usually kept locked, so ask the attendant for access. Fathers can have access to the toilet for the disabled for nappy-changing.

The main platforms have got ticket-operated barriers. You can buy tickets within the waiting hall or from one of the machines around the station.

Haymarket

This station serves all points west and north. There are lots of steps to the platforms. The short trip between Waverley and Haymarket is popular as a playgroup outing. Snack bar, Pumpkin, on Platform 4.

South Gyle

A suburban halt serving all Fife trains. Tickets are obtained from the train conductor. Large car park on the southside, but quite a walk to the Edinburgh platform. Could be a struggle with a pushchair to get from one side to the other. Trains run regularly to Waverley.

Slateford, Westerhailes, Kingsknowe and Curriehill stations have hourly services to/from Glasgow Central via Shotts. Restricted Sunday services.

Musselburgh Station is served by services to/from North Berwick. Trains hourly, with a reduced service on Sunday.

The Trains

Facilities on the trains themselves are improving. Most now have external and internal push buttons for sliding doors, so boarding with a pushchair and toddler in tow has become easier. There is usually adequate luggage space and pushchairs can be left folded up. Toilets on board are few, but at least one per train should include a fold-up nappy-change table.

One of the best ways to keep a child happy on board on a longer train journey is to feed him or her. Buffet trolleys operate on First ScotRail Express and longer distance routes, but there are few on local services. These offer hot/cold drinks, sandwiches, crisps and confectionery. However, the range available can be extremely limited and everything is very expensive. It's far cheaper to take your own provisions.

Fares

As a general rule, under 5s travel free, on the understanding that they will give their seats up to fare paying passengers. An adult can be accompanied by up to two free under 5s.

A variety of special fares are available for families, including saver, cheap day returns and family railcard. Always ask to check the cheapest way to travel before buying your ticket. There is usually an abundance of leaflets with special deals available.

USEFUL POINTS OF CONTACT

Edinburgh and Scotland Tourist Information Centre
3 Princes Street   EH2 2QP
Telephone: 0845 22 55 121
Web: www.edinburgh.org

Opening times: vary extensively throughout the year. Mon-Fri it's open at least 9.00-17.00; Sun 10.00-17.00. Times extended in the summer season.

The friendly staff are happy to share and swap local knowledge with tourists and local people and can also draw on a huge database of attractions, tours and events. You'll glean lots of ideas for days out, activities and sports from the range of leaflets, guides and information sheets. They also stock a free monthly 'What's On' guide for Edinburgh and the Lothians. The web site has a special section for children put together by real experts — the pupils of the Royal High Primary School. Parents will find it useful too!

Scottish Booking & Info Centre
visitscotland.com
Fairways Business Park
Deer Park Avenue
Livingston   EH54 8AF
Tel: 0845 2255 121
Website: www.visitscotland.com

Tourist information for the whole of Scotland. Phone calls and letters only.

Walks and Country Places

WALKS AND COUNTRY PLACES

INTRODUCTION

Edinburgh is blessed with over 4500 acres of green space – parks, open spaces and woodlands where children and adults can relax or let off steam, without having to travel miles out into the country. The walks in this section range from carefully tended public gardens to wild open hillsides.

We have tried to give some indication of the terrain in terms of accessibility for pushchairs and small bikes; of course, children can also be carried in a packpack or sling. Remember that conditions can vary on non-surfaced paths, dependent on the season or the weather: what can be a pleasant stroll on a dry summer afternoon, can be a mire on a November morning!

More detailed information and maps can be found in Edinburgh City libraries and also local bookshops. A map of the city's cycle paths, published by 'Spokes', the cyclists' organisation, is useful for walks where pushchair accessibility is needed. Happy tramping!

PARKS, HILLS, ESTATES & WOODS

THE BRAIDS

Grassy slopes and hills, good for kites, walking and sledging. Access and parking at the entrance to the Braid Hills Public Golf Course on Braid Hill Approach and along Braid Hill Dr. There are usually horses to be seen in fields nearby at Liberton Tower Farm.

Braidburn Valley Park
Pentland Terrace, Comiston Road

A stream runs through the middle of hilly slopes (which are well used for sledging during snow). Paths suitable for pushchairs. No play equipment. There is a 'fairy ring' of trees, ideal for children to run around and wear themselves out. The stream is suitable for fishing for tiddlers and is shallow enough for supervised paddlers near the 'fairy ring'.

The Hermitage of Braid and Blackford Hill Local Nature Reserve

The Hermitage of Braid: offers a taste of the countryside in the city and is ideal for pushchairs. A good flat entrance from Braid Rd (south of the mini roundabout) leads through a beautiful wooded valley beside the tumbling

Braid Burn. There is a map at the entrance. At the heart of the valley is Hermitage House, a Ranger Centre with maps, leaflets and imaginative and informative activities for children of all ages. The Centre is open all year, Mon - Thur 14.00 - 17.00, Fri & Sun 14.00 - 16.00 (closed Sat). Picnic table on a flat grassy area in front of the house. Toilets inside the house and outside (although these are best used only in an emergency). If you take the right fork past the house there are a few steps up to an old icehouse, used to store ice in bygone days. The path follows on over bridges, excellent for 'Pooh Sticks', to the Lang Linn Bridge. Here you emerge from the wooded valley and can continue along to Blackford Glen Rd and eventually the foot of Liberton Brae. This is also an excellent walk for pushchairs. There are often cows in the fields across the burn and lots of bird life.

For those without pushchairs the Hermitage is riddled with steep twisty paths that are wonderful to explore. Bluebells in spring, bird boxes and inquisitive squirrels are all easy for tots to spot. At Lang Linn Bridge there are steps with a gate (tricky for pushchairs) and a stony path up to your left that will take you around the side of Blackford Hill to the pond.

The Ranger Centre often organises interest walks for families and can take playgroups and nurseries at quiet times. Contact the Countryside Ranger Service for details:
Tel: 447 7145
Email: ranger@cecrangerservice.demon.co.uk

Blackford Hill

Car parking at the Royal Observatory, Braid Rd and Midmar Dr; limited street parking at Cluny Gdns for the pond, and at Blackford Glen Rd, Liberton. Maps of walks at the entrances.

Several picnic sites, sledging in winter and popular for kite flying. Beware of the cliffs at the old quarry. Unfortunately the area is badly fouled by dogs, especially around the Observatory and at entrances.

The beautifully situated Blackford Pond, to your right as you enter from Cluny Gdns, contains ducks, moorhens, geese, coots and swans. The swans and geese can be very enthusiastic so keep children behind the low rail on the path. Sometimes there are squirrels to be seen too. There is a shelter on a landscaped path to the east side of the pond. Dogs are not allowed around the pond.

BRUNTSFIELD LINKS AND THE MEADOWS

Parking on various nearby streets; some are metered, some are single yellow lines, some are not.

Acres of space to run in the middle of town. During the summer, the area is popular with all sorts of people, from dog walkers to frisbee throwers and football players: most of the walkways have cycle ways on them, so try to stay on the pedestrian side of the line.

There are 'emergency' toilets on Middle Meadow walk – no nappy changing though.

See also Playgrounds and Parks

CAMMO ESTATE

Main gate and Visitor Centre at Cammo Road
Tel: 317 8797 (Barnton Ranger Service)

The estate was left to the National Trust in 1975. They made the house safe and feuded the estate to the City of Edinburgh Council. It is now managed to enhance the plant and wildlife environment, for use as a teaching resource and by the general public.

Cammo House is now just ruined remains, but its 100 acres of wildlife habitats in woodlands, meadows and marshes leave an estate of unusual character. There are snowdrops in spring and lots of butterflies in summer. Look out for nest boxes and their inhabitants in spring. The pond, originally built for curling, has a good range of pond life, including frogs, toads and insect larvae. At the far end of the pond reeds and other vegetation grows, providing cover for moorhen, mallard and very occasionally a kingfisher. There is also a walled garden. Most paths are accessible for pushchairs; a wheelchair and pushchair accessible trail has been created around approximately 1km of the estate. Other main paths have been upgraded.

The Visitor Centre in the lodge has toilets, including disabled, but no nappy changing surface; maps and leaflets about the park and displays. The Centre is not often open as the Ranger is usually out and about, but is usually open on Sunday afternoons courtesy of the Friends of Cammo.

Cammo and the River Almond

Cammo Road, Barnton

The paths along the River Almond can be joined from Cammo. These routes are not really suitable for pushchairs, as they are narrow, uneven and overgrown.

Start the walk on Cammo Rd. A signpost leads you through a gate on the right and down a rough wide path to the river. Here the riverbank is very steep. The path continues to follow the river upstream towards the airport, it can be very overgrown.

There are stepping stones about halfway along or turn up that path to the left near the bridge and you will eventually rejoin Cammo Rd again. Along this path you pass Craighall Temple – a locked tower, or turn right over Grotto Bridge. The river is very narrow here and looks spectacular after rain as the water thunders underneath. Just over the bridge is a cattle grid, which has been known to capture clambering youngsters! The path follows the river downstream and can be rough with some steep steps down to the water. It ends near the Cramond Brig Hotel. For a walk further downstream see Cramond, south: the River Almond Walkway. The Cammo Park leaflet mentioned in the previous entry also covers this area.

CORSTORPHINE HILL LOCAL NATURE RESERVE

Panoramic views of the city and beyond are offered at the 530ft summit. The terrain is varied, with a rocky and steep section – which includes a flooded quarry – between the Queensferry Rd and Clermiston Rd entrances, and large areas of woodland. Flora and fauna include conkers, acorns and pinecones, squirrels, badgers and foxes. There is also Clermiston Tower, built in 1851 to commemorate the centenary of Sir Walter Scott's birth. Access to the tower by arrangement with the Ranger Service or during Sundays in the summer courtesy of Friends of Corstorphine. Between the tower and the entrance on Clermiston Rd opposite Queen Margaret College, is the Walled Garden. The Friends of Corstorphine have restored the overgrown garden into a woodland walk for the community, allowing the less physically fit to be able to appreciate the garden as a microcosm of the vegetation found on the hill.

There are several routes to the summit of the hill: Clermiston Rd (3 paths: the one near the Best Western Hotel is rough and steep); Queensferry Rd (steep and rugged); Craigcrook Rd (a long push, between new houses, up a fairly steep gradient, but a reasonably smooth path); Ravelston Dykes Rd (near Mary Erskine School and about 200 yards North of Murrayfield Golf Clubhouse) and from Cairnmuir Rd, at the junction with Kaimes Rd. This latter route is easiest for pushchairs, although muddy after rain, and there is car parking. There is a grassy slope on the left near this entrance – also good for sledging. The path to the summit follows the edge of the zoo where some animals may be seen before it joins the paths from Ravelston Dykes and Craigcrook entrances.

CRAIGLOCKHART

Craiglockhart Dell and Colinton Dell

Beautiful wooded glens with the Water of Leith and its walkway running through the centre (see separate entry). Plenty of paths to explore although those with pushchairs will have to search for flat routes. Cycling is only permitted on the main Water of Leith Walkway. Bridges for 'Pooh Sticks' and open grassed areas next to the river are ideal for picnics and games. Access includes Dell Rd, Colinton, Katesmill Rd, pathway from Lanark Rd near Dovecot Pk and behind the Tickled Trout pub on Lanark Rd at Slateford.

Craiglockhart Hill

Street parking is available at Craiglockhart Ter, Lockharton Cres and at Craiglockhart Sports Centre.

Level paths from the sports centre and from Craiglockhart Ter are suitable for pushchairs and take you to the pond. The pond holds swans, ducks, moorhens and coots, the nests of some of which can be seen in early summer. There is a map of the area at Craiglockhart Ter and at the pond. Many interesting and attractive plants have been established to improve the area for bird and insect life. Off the level path steep paths, some with steps, go up through semi-natural woodlands to the top of the hill. The highest part is open and gives impressive views of the city and countryside beyond.

CRAMOND

The village is situated at the mouth of the River Almond. There are swans and seagulls to feed and lots of small boats to look at. Walks radiate in all directions from the yachting centre. There is a large car park on Cramond Glebe Rd, below Cramond Kirk and above the Cramond Inn. A ramp leads down to the esplanade. Below the Inn are public toilets. There are also two cafes serving teas and ice creams.

Cramond was home to an established Roman settlement. There is a partially excavated site in the upper car park, beside the 17th Century Cramond Kirk.

North – To Cramond Island

There is a newly upgraded causeway across the tidal mudflats out to Cramond Island, which is negotiable at low tide. Tide charts are pinned up at the start of the causeway monthly but often get torn down. Check the tide times with Forth Ports or the Ranger Service before

setting out. Take a picnic to your own small uninhabited island. Good views of the Forth Bridges but keep an eye on the time for returning before the tide comes in again.

South – The River Almond

About 1 1/2 miles, the walkway starts on the esplanade, near the yachting centre, and follows the river upstream on a wooded path. The path is wide and on the level, and is suitable for pushchairs and bikes, but can be muddy. The river is tidal up to Cockle Mill Cottages, where the path opens out into a grassy area, watch out for dog fouling. There is also a small car park, access from Whitehouse Rd via School Brae. The path continues up to Fair-a-Far Mill where there is a waterfall and a fish ladder. The mill is now a ruin and children will enjoy running through the arches and up a few steps. The river is railed at this point but toddlers can get underneath quite easily. People throw pennies into the top of the fall and children collect them later! The path continues up to the Cramond Brig Hotel and Haugh Park, but there is a steep flight of steps and pushchairs would have to be carried. See also Cammo and the River Almond, for a description of the route further upstream.

East – the Esplanade

A broad paved footpath runs for 2 miles from Cramond through Silverknowes to Granton Point West Shore Rd. An attractive area for promenading with the pram, roller-skating or for learning to ride a bike. Plenty of seats and shelters. Superb views across to Fife on clear days. Suitable for picnics on the Grassy Banks at Silverknowes where there is parking along Marine Drive – but look out for dog mess. You can also walk up to Lauriston Castle from Silverknowes.

Tide charts are available for reference in summer. Ice cream vans, pipe bands and entertainment over some summer weekends. The beach itself is sandy at Cramond and stony elsewhere. It can be oily and there are often pollution warnings about collecting shellfish. The beach is gently sloped but the tide can come in fast and maroon you on a sandbank – be prepared to paddle!

West - across the River Almond

There is no bridge across the Almond at Cramond, and unfortunately the passenger ferry which used to operate is no longer there. At present there are no plans to reinstate it. The land on the west bank of the river belongs to the Dalmeny Estate, and is accessible from the Shore Walk described in the next section.

DALMENY HOUSE AND ESTATE
Tel: 331 1888
Web: www.dalmeny.co.uk
Take the A90 and then B924. There is a bus service from St Andrew Sq to Chapel Gate, 1 mile from the house.
House and estate are open from 14.00 to 17.30, Sun, Mon and Tue afternoons in July and August. While we'd not recommend Dalmeny House as a place to visit with young children, the estate itself is pleasant to walk around – fields, shore and woodland with cows, sheep, pheasants and a statue of a horse. There is a sheltered woodland walk through the rhododendrons and azaleas of the garden valley. No dogs allowed. Picnics only by prior arrangement. No fires.
The house can also be reached by the 4 1/2 mile Shore Walk from Long Craig Gate in South Queensferry, east towards Cramond (as the ferry is closed you can no longer go all the way to Cramond this way). The path is open all year round to pedestrians only. It is negotiable with a pushchair or manageable with small children in backpacks, and passes through several designated Sites of Special Scientific Interest – including nesting and feeding grounds for several rare species of birds, as well as giving wonderful views of the Forth. There are lovely beaches in the estate, particularly the ones near Barnbougle Castle and also just past Dalmeny House, known to locals as the 'shell-beds'. Gate closes 21.00 summer, 18.00 winter.

FIGGATE BURN PARK
Entrances at Duddingston Road,
Mountcastle Drive and
Hamilton Drive behind Portobello High School.
A strip of parkland with trees and grassy slopes along the Figgate Burn in Duddingston. The paths are easily negotiated and ideal for bikes. On Figgate Pond there are plenty of tame wildfowl to be fed. On raised ground to the north-east of the pond there is a children's playground where most of the equipment is better suited to school age children. Next to the Burn are the Craigentinny Carriage sidings, off the main railway line, which can be interesting for junior trainspotters, particularly when shunting is in progress. See Playgrounds and Parks.

HOLYROOD PARK
Park Rangers' Office
Tel: 556 1761
Car parks at Dunsapie Loch, near the entrances at Duddingston Loch, Holyrood Palace and Meadowbank Terrace.
A rugged park, including Arthur's Seat (823ft), Salisbury Crags, and three small lochs. A surfaced road, Queen's Dr runs around the park for approximately 3 miles. Apart from a small stretch of surfaced path from the Holyrood Palace entrance up Haggis Knowe towards St Anthony's chapel (about 200yds), all the other routes are rocky or on grass. The climb to Arthur's Seat is a steep one for youngsters (shortest route from Dunsapie Loch) but there is an excellent view at the top with a Trig Point indicating surrounding sites of interest. Lower down there are good views from Dunsapie Hill (523ft). It is possible to walk round St Margaret's Loch with a pushchair and there are ducks, geese and swans to be fed here. Rowing boats can be hired in the summer. In the south east of the park is Duddingston Loch, a bird sanctuary, where the geese and swans can be quite aggressive.
Leaving Queen's Dr, below Salisbury Crags and to the south-east of Pollock Halls is a cycle track and footpath, suitable for prams, known as the Innocent Railway (see Railway Paths and Cycle Tracks, below).

INCH PARK
Old Dalkeith Road,
near the Cameron Toll Shopping Centre
A large area of grassland, with playing fields, deciduous trees, slopes for sliding, paved paths for pushchairs and learning to ride a bike. Ideal for letting off steam after a shopping session at Cameron Toll (there is an entrance from the car park). Large play area. See Playgrounds and Parks.

THE PENTLAND HILLS

Regional Park HQ
Tel: 445 3383
Email: rangerservice_phrp@yahoo.co.uk
A beautiful range of hills spreading along Edinburgh's southern edge. Supported by City of Edinburgh, Midlothian and West Lothian Councils and Scottish Natural Heritage. The Pentland Hills regional park consists of 2 country parks, reservoirs (no swimming permitted), nature reserves and other private areas. Within the Regional Park there are several areas of interest to parents with young children.

Bonaly
Where Bonaly Road crosses the city bypass there is a fork in the road. The right turn, Torduff Rd (public vehicle access for only a few hundred yards and limited parking at the end) leads up to Torduff Reservoir and is surfaced but is a long push for prams and small cyclists. At the reservoir

you can turn left for a walk across to Bonaly Country Park (see below) – steps and a grassy path, but good views over the city. For pushchairs, a better walk is to follow the west side of the reservoir along to the end where there is a short push up to Clubbidean Reservoir, 3/4 mile. Here there is more space for picnics and there are sometimes anglers in boats to watch. The path alongside Clubbidean is rougher for pushchairs but energetic parents with backpacks may like to continue on to Currie, 1 1/2 miles.

Following Bonaly Rd, from the city bypass as far as it will go, brings you to a car park. This area is know as Bonaly Country Park and from here you can walk up into the hills. There is an information board with maps and a picnic area. Of the three paths up from here, the left is too steep for youngsters, the right takes you over Torduff Reservoir (see above) and up into the heather. The middle path, possible with pushchairs and for reasonable walkers leads up through a plantation of trees to Bonaly Reservoir.

Glencourse Reservoir

On the A702(T) Biggar Rd, 7 1/2 miles from the city centre; turn right at the Flotterstone Inn.

An Information Centre with displays and maps in the car park. The road up to Glencourse Reservoir is closed to public vehicles. Ideal for prams and cyclists. As you leave the car park, on your left next to the burn is a barbecue and children's area, dog free. Further along, off to the left across a footbridge is a wooded picnic area, and another up the hill in woods on the right. Several paths fork off across fields and up into the hills. At the reservoir, anglers in boats can often be seen. It is possible to follow the northern edge along to the end on a surfaced road. The water is fenced or walled off. Paths branch off to the right at intervals up to Castlelaw firing range and across the hills to Harlaw (unsuitable for youngsters). Lambs can be seen over the fences in spring.

Harlaw and Threipmuir Reservoirs

Harlaw Reservoir car park is reached by leaving Currie on Kirkgate (follow signs for Currie Old Kirk) or Balerno on Harlaw Rd; turn off at Harlaw Farm. There is an information board here. At the gate, turn right and follow a surfaced road about 100 yards to the reservoir. The former waterkeeper's cottage and garden are open as a Ranger Centre with maps, displays and leaflets. Toilet available. Picnic benches and pond in the wildlife garden. The path around the south side of Harlaw Reservoir has been upgraded and is ideal for pushchairs and bicycles. On the north side is a track (occasionally used by council vehicles), which can be reached by a small metal bridge

or across the overflow in summer – fun for paddlers. The track (with paths off through the trees to explore), continues to the end of Harlaw Reservoir where it joins up with Threipmuir Reservoir by way of another overflow. To continue on around Harlaw, cross the footbridge here and turn left through the gap in the wall. The track follows the wall and over the bank on your right is Threipmuir Reservoir, not fenced. Turn left at the end of the wall to continue on around the south side of Harlaw. Those without pushchairs may like to negotiate the stiles further on for a walk back to the car park, along a lane across the fields.

It is possible to walk along Threipmuir from the overflow, keep to the right and do not cross the footbridge. This is an easy walk for pushchairs but you cannot link up with the car park at Red Moss (see below) as there are a series of kissing gates at the other end. It is not possible to walk all around the Threipmuir Reservoir. A variety of birds can be seen on this walk, keep your eyes peeled for herons and cormorants.

Car parking available also at Threipmuir and Red Moss Nature Reserve. Take 1st left in Balerno Village after the High School. Follow the road for approximately 2 miles out of the village past the animal sanctuary to the car park.

Hillend Country Park

Follow the Biggar Rd out just beyond Lothianburn Golf Course on the right and turn up to Hillend. The No 4 bus stops on the main road and there is a long path up to the ski centre. There are picnic tables up to the foot. There is a notice board with maps and general information on the Pentland Regional Park. At the top of the road there is the Hillend Ski Centre and a large car park. A chairlift at the artificial ski slope here may be used by non skiers. It is open 7 days a week, but check for opening (Tel: 445 4433) as it closes in poor weather. Adults - £1.80, Under 17s - £1.10p, Family Ticket (2 adults, 2 juniors)- £5.20; generally children taking a seat pay. No pushchairs. There are several bench type seats so you can tuck tots in between adults, a bar comes down to lap and foot height and keeps you safely in. Very active toddlers should not use the chairlift. There is a stop half way up to get off if a child becomes frightened. The ride up is exhilarating, sailing over skiers and golfers below. At the top there is a viewfinder on a cairn and there are paths through the heather which energetic tots, or parents with backpacks could cope with. The weather can change quickly though so don't stray too far from the chairlift. At the top of the lift are cameras and a tannoy so that the operators can check everybody is safely in before moving. Toilets in the ski centre reception and refreshments are available from the 'Hut on the Hill' portakabin.

Red Moss Wildlife Reserve and Bavelaw Bird Reserve, Balerno

Parking at Threipmuir — see Harlaw and Threipmuir Reservoirs.

There is a picnic table here and information board with maps. A short footpath, unsuitable for pushchairs leads down to Threipmuir Reservoir and along to Harlaw (see relevant section). With a pushchair the best route is to turn left out of the car park and follow the road along towards a bridge. On your right is the Red Moss Nature Reserve. This area is boggy so keep to the boardwalk. Continue over the bridge and up a steep, tree lined hill. Bavelaw Bird Reserve is on your right and there is a bird hide on the shore, over a stile and along to a narrow boggy path. Note: the key is held at Balerno Post Office.

A signpost at the top of the hill gives walking options. Only the left continues to be suitable for pushchairs until you reach the stile opening onto the Pentland Hills. This walk is exposed and can be cold but worth it on a clear day for the views. There are sheep and cattle in the fields, waterfowl and fishermen on the reservoir below.

Swanston Village Farm

Access from Oxgangs Rd, by Swanston Rd over the city bypass.

A small picturesque village at the foot of the Pentlands near Fairmilehead. RL Stevenson lived at Swanston Cottage from 1867 to 1880. The whitewashed, thatched cottages of old Swanston village date from the 17th century and there is a mid-19th century farm with steadings. Beyond the village are grassy slopes with sheep grazing and lambs in springtime. Higher up is rougher ground. It is possible to walk over to Hillend but not with a pushchair. Nice for picnics.

Meadows Yard

Local Nature Reserve

A small quiet reserve near Seafield (1 hectare). Access is via a steep flight of steps off Fillyside Rd, along which there is a regular bus service (Lothian 2/12). The site has a narrow mulched path (so not great for pushchairs), running around an area of grasses, scrub and emergent trees. Unfortunately the pond in the centre is now completely overgrown, and no longer a haven for damselflies and butterflies, but a new Ranger is due to start soon, so hopefully the reserve will be tidied up.

Portobello Beach and Promenade

The paved promenade runs for 1 3/4 miles from Seafield Rd to Esplanade Terrace in Joppa. The west end of the beach is reached from Bath St (Lothian Buses 2/12, 15, 26, 42/46; FirstBus 129). Here you will find an indoor amusement arcade with some children's rides, including a carousel, as well as the usual take away snacks. There is a car park in Bridge Street. The quieter end of the beach is reached from Brunstane Rd, where you can park. The beach is sandy, the City Council cleans it regularly and there is a no dog policy, but as on all beaches, vigilance is required and sandals are advisable for children. There are toilets at regular intervals along the promenade and information boards, including an electronic display outside the Portobello Swim Centre which advises on water quality (summer months only). Playgrounds can be found along the promenade at Straiton Place and at Tower Bank. See Playgrounds and Parks. At the time of writing a new public garden is being developed at the foot of John Street.

RAILWAY PATHS & CYCLE TRACKS

Railways were developed through Edinburgh by rival companies. The remains of some of these tracks have been developed into a network of cycle and footpaths which obviously supply flat walking, ideal for pushchairs. Spokes, the cyclists' organisation, publishes a map which shows them all. They include parts of the Water of Leith Walkway and the Innocent Railway. This is so called because horses, not steam engines, initially pulled the carriages. It runs from Holyrood Park (east of the Pollock Halls) to Craigmillar, walled between Prestonfield Golf Course and Duddingston Loch Nature Reserve; then on through Bingham to Musselburgh, following the main East Coast railway line, approximately 6 miles.

Another ex-railway cycle track starts from Balbirnie Pl in Roseburn where there is a map of the route. This metalled track crosses the Water of Leith with steep steps down to join the walkway and continues north to the old Barnton railway junction at Craigleith, where it divides. One branch goes to Davidson's Mains and the other branches again to Leith and Trinity. Here the cycle path passes along side St Marks Park which has a playground, and then through the centre of Victoria Park, which has two playgrounds. (see Playgrounds and Parks).

For Spokes' contact details, see Travel and Transport.

ROYAL BOTANIC GARDEN
Tel: 552 7171
East Gate on Inverleith Row and West Gate on Arboretum Place
Car parking on 3 sides of the gardens (not Inverleith Row); easiest on Arboretum Place
Opening times: Daily, except 25 Dec and 1 Jan
Mar: 10.00 - 18.00 (cleared at 17.45)
Apr-Sep: 10.00-19.00 (cleared at 18.45)
Oct: 10.00 - 18.00 (cleared at 17.45)
Nov-Feb: 10.00-16.00 (cleared at 15.45)
Admission: free

An immaculate, beautifully landscaped and well sign posted garden. Dogs are not allowed so there is no problem with dog fouling. There is no cycling allowed but there are cycle racks at the west gate. Abundant grassy areas, flat and sloped and tarred paths. There is a pond where you can feed the ducks, moorhen and swans, and where occasionally a heron can be seen. The shop at the west gate sells sunflower seeds to feed the very tame squirrels. The rockery area has a waterfall and lots of winding paths, some suitable for pushchairs. The Chinese garden has a pagoda next to a small pond and path winding up the slope with small bridges over a 'mountain stream'. Other themed areas, such as alpine, cryptogamic and herbaceous may interest the older child and parents; or just enjoy the extra space and gardens. Unfortunately no picnics are allowed.

The Glasshouse Experience
Daily, except 25 Dec and 1 Jan
Mar: 10.00-17.30
Apr-Sep: 10.00-18.30
Oct: 10.00-17.30
Nov-Feb: 10.00-15.30
Adult £3.50 (conc £3), chiildren 5-14 £1, under 5s free

There is only one entrance to the glasshouses – all other doors are exit only. Leaflets are available. Pushchairs can be left at the cash desk as the displays are on two levels – with quite a few sets of steps – and some paths between plants are quite narrow. Some ponds have no railings so hold on to active youngsters. There are old and new glasshouses, at various temperatures and humidities, and a small aquarium.

Inverleith House in the centre of the garden, houses a botanical art gallery with a programme of historical and contemporary exhibitions. No pushchairs or prams allowed.

Botanic Garden education staff lead guided tours and provide resource material for school parties. They are willing to give advice to playgroup and nursery teachers and adapt their materials to suit parties of younger children. Tel: 552 7175.

The shop at the West Gate has a range of goods suitable for younger children starting to learn about the environment. Toilets at the Glasshouses, Inverleith House and the West Gate. Nappy changing and feeding facility at the East Gate; ask the Park constabulary there to give you a key.

There is an ice cream kiosk at the West Gate and often an ice cream van parked across from the West Gate at the entrance to Inverleith Park. There are two cafés: The Terrace Café at the centre of the Gardens and Rachael's Tearoom at the East Gate. The Terrace Café is a popular meeting place for women with small babies and toddlers, has nappy changing facilities and is a relaxed place to breastfeed. See Eating Out: Edinburgh North.

WATERWAYS

Union Canal
The Union Canal runs from the Lochrin Basin in Fountainbridge, access from Gilmore Pk and Leamington Rd. Alternatively there is a signposted car park just before the bypass at Calder Gdns off Calder Rd, from where you can walk into the city or out into the countryside. Hermiston also provides a convenient place to park. Thanks to the Millennium Link project the Union Canal now runs right through to Falkirk where the Millennium Wheel carries boats on to the Forth & Clyde Canal, thus connecting Edinburgh and Glasgow. The towpath through the city is on the north bank and is suitable for pushchairs, obviously children need close supervision. From the centre of the city and industrial buildings the canal passes suburban gardens and parks, and nesting swans can be seen. You may also see oarsmen from the rowing club. The canal is carried by the 12 arch Slateford Aqueduct over the Water of Leith and a long flight of steps lead down to the Water of Leith Walkway (see below). Beyond the bypass the canal offers an easy and delightful walk through open countryside, although you may have to negotiate steps to reach it.

The Water of Leith Walkway
The Water of Leith rises in the Pentland Hills and runs through the villages of Balerno, Currie, Juniper Green and Colinton and into the heart of Edinburgh before flowing

into the Firth of Forth at Leith. In its 24 miles it flows through wooded dells, past abandoned mills, elegant Georgian terraces and new housing developments, before opening up into a broad river surrounded by the buildings of Leith docks. It is designated an Urban Wildlife Site by the City of Edinburgh Council. Look out for herons, especially near weirs.

The walkway runs along most of the river in the City and most parts are negotiable with a pushchair. Unfortunately access is not always so easy and we have tried to list alternatives to steps, where they exist. Some sections are well used by dogs too. Keep an eye on young cyclists as the banks can be steep and there are not always railings, and watch out for exuberant cyclists racing ahead; pedestrians and dogs are not always aware of bikes behind them, and this can lead to collisions.

The brown water is due to peat. Giant hogweed a tall plant (up to 3m) with tiny white flowers has established itself on several stretches. Touching this plant or blowing through sections of its hollow stem may cause an allergic reaction and photosensitivity of the skin. These plants are routinely treated with weedkiller and hacked down but return each year. Along stretches of the river are raspberries and blackberries which should be safe to eat, but remember that dogs may have been there before you – pick high!

A comprehensive guide to the walkway complete with map and historical notes is available from:

The Water of Leith Conservation Trust
24 Lanark Road
Tel: 455 7367
Edinburgh City Libraries stock a good selection of books on the Water of Leith.

If you want to access parts of the route by bus, First Bus 66 and LRT 44 follow the Water of Leith from Balerno to Slateford along the A70 Lanark Rd.

Balerno to Juniper Green
The walkway begins to the north side of Balerno High School, Bridge Rd and follows the track of an old railway, making it ideal for pushchairs and cyclists. There are a number of access points along the route to Currie, Waulkmill Loan is easiest for pushchairs. At Currie Kirkgate there are steps up to the walkway, next to the bridge. Here it is better for pushchairs if you continue under the bridge and up the road to Currie Baptist Church, where there is access to the walkway via an old goods yard; you can park here too. The walkway continues for approx 1

1/2miles to Juniper Green. Easiest access is at Kinleith Mill, through the industrial estate off Blinkbonny Rd. There are also steps up from the walkway to Blinkbonny Rd bridge. There is a section here where a 20 feet wall drops sharply down to the river below so hold on to wandering tots. The path then crosses to the north side of the river again. Access in Juniper Green is from Baberton Loan, next to the Post Office where you can park.

Juniper Green to Slateford
Including Craiglockhart Dell and Colinton Dell
Along this attractive and peaceful section of the river, the walkway continues on the old railway, passing under the city bypass and into a wooded dell; crossing the river several times. Good access next to Post Office in Juniper Green (see previous entry), West Mill Rd, Gillespie Rd by the bridge, or through Spylaw Park, Colinton where there is a good play area. Continuing on, the walkway enters an old railway tunnel, dimly lit but not as long as it looks and a superb place for echoes. Look out for a silhouette on the wall of a Balerno pug, the small engine specially designed for the steep sided Colinton Dell. The path emerges way above the river with other paths below. From Dell Rd, Colinton, down past the church, the walkway runs through the wooded Colinton and Craiglockhart Dells. This section is difficult for pushchairs as there are steps every so often (see separate entry). Access points include Katesmill Rd, at Redhall Mill and behind the Tickled Trout, on Lanark Rd at Slateford.

Slateford to Roseburn
The Water of Leith Heritage Centre is located on the Lanark Road A70 at Slateford opposite the Tickled Trout pub. There is an exhibition where children can listen to the sounds of some of the wildlife they may see and look down onto a video of the river. Admission: Adults - £1.90, Conc £1.40, Children - £1.20 ,Under 5s free, Family Ticket - £5.00, Tel: 455 7367. Toilets and nappy changing facilities. There is limited parking at the centre. It is open 10.00-16.00 everyday from April to September; Wed – Sun, October to March. There is a flight of steps up to the Union Canal from Slateford for those without pushchairs. A flat pathway runs from Slateford to Gorgie Road and the river can be followed through Saughton Park. See Playgrounds and Parks. The section beside Murrayfield Rugby Ground and Ice Rink can be accessed from Baird Drive and Riversdale Road and provides an easy walk for pushchairs.

Roseburn to Dean Path

From Roseburn the path is accessed from Roseburn Cliff where shallow steps lead to a concrete path right next to the riverside. It is easy to follow to Belford Bridge. There are steps at the bridge so it is easier to leave the path by the back of the Belford Hotel. There is also access to the Gallery of Modern Art via a steep and stepped path. From Belford Bridge the Dean Bank footpath follows a slow moving loop running in a deep and wooded glen. The path is surfaced and runs on the riverbank, a precarious few feet above the water. Some sections have a handrail about 3 ft high – useful for adults but small children can slip underneath quite easily. Access is from Dean Path, with steps a little way up the hill from Dean Village or for pushchairs a better option is at the footbridge along from Sunbury Mews in a modern housing development. There is access from an alleyway beside Damside in Dean Village but the cobbles can be slippy after wet weather and the walkway here is liable to flooding.

Dean Path to Stockbridge

This well railed and paved section runs along the south bank from Miller Row in Dean Village, to Saunders St in Stockbridge. As the river gushes beneath the dramatic Dean Bridge, it is hard to imagine the urban bustle only 10 mins walk away at the West End of Princes St. The depth of the steep wooded valley is emphasised by the views of the backs of Moray and Ainslie Pl. St Bernard's Well, a Georgian statue and temple, is halfway along the path and there are several flights of steps down to paddling and fishing spots. There are upper and lower routes between St Bernard's Well and the bridge at Saunders St. A new curved sloping path has been created to allow pushchair access direct to Saunders St.

Stockbridge to Warriston

There are steps down to the Deanhaugh Footpath from Deanhaugh Street in Stockbridge. Easier access from Haugh St or Falshaw Bridge at the other end of the pathway. At Falshaw Bridge turn left and immediately right onto Arboretum Ave. At the end of Arboretum Ave you reach the Rocheid Path with views across the river of the Colonies. Easiest exit from this path is via Inverleith Terrace Lane onto inverleith Row. If you cross the river the path becomes rather overgrown and there are steps up to Canonmills.

Warriston to Leith

If you want to continue to follow the river take Warriston Rd and follow the riverbank at the bridge. It is possible to take a pushchair along this path but hard pushing is sometimes required. An easier but less scenic route is to access the Warriston Cycleway from the corner of Canonmills and Broughton Rd. The two routes join at Connaught Pl where you can continue along the old railway line and rejoin the river after 500 metres. Or take the flight of steps up to Newhaven Road, cross the road, turn right and walk towards town, and after 50 metres a recently completed section of the walkway will take you across the river to Anderson Pl. Upon exiting at the road, turn left then right along West Bowling Green St and then rejoin the walkway where the sign indicates on the left side.

The scenery changes yet again as the now broad river enters the docks of Leith and you can treat yourselves to a well earned cup of coffee. There are plenty of buses to various destinations from the bottom of Leith Walk.

This section has dealt with suggested walks within the City of Edinburgh or at least very close by. All Edinburgh bookshops stock a wide selection of books and pamphlets describing the huge numbers of walks and country places in the wider Lothian area. It is all relatively easy to access – just get out there, and let us know of your particular favourites.

PART TWO – THE DIRECTORY

PART 2 – THE DIRECTORY

Welcome to the Directory section. Here you'll find listings for activities and classes, information about schemes, support groups' names and addresses, nursery information and so on.

Many of the chapters refer to areas of Edinburgh. This edition, we have defined them either geographically (using main thoroughfares to define areas) or by postcode: we thought this would be most relevant in the Private Nurseries listings; you should be able to work out, at a glance, which nurseries are nearest to you. We have also expanded on the introduction to the Private Nurseries, which may prove helpful if you have relocated to Scotland from England or Wales.

On that note, can we remind you, once again, that:
From March 18 2005, it has been a criminal offence in Scotland for a mother to be harassed or otherwise prevented from breastfeeding her child (defined as a child under the age of 2 yrs) in a public place or licensed premises where children were previously welcomed (e.g. 'family-friendly' pubs). This law also covers other carers feeding children (as defined above) milk.

And, in addition:
From 26 March 2006, the Smoking, Health and Social Care (Scotland) Bill will come into force. This bill bans smoking in enclosed public places such as restaurants, pubs and workplaces.

Activities for Children

ACTIVITIES FOR CHILDREN – ART & CRAFT

ART & CRAFT

Although they are not numerous, there are art and craft classes available for under 5s in Edinburgh, outside a nursery environment. The following venues run classes for younger children.

Edinburgh Rudolph Steiner School Parent and Toddler Group
60 Spylaw Road
Edinburgh EH10 5BR
Tel: 337 3410

Opening times: Mon-Fri 10.15-12.30,
Mon-Thu 13.30-15.30
See Parent and Toddler Groups for further information. This parent and toddler group offers a range of baking and simple crafts as well as other nursery/parent and toddler activities. Breastfeeding, naturally, is welcome, although there is not a private area for feeding.

Messy Monsters
Contact: Sarah Smith
Tel: 656 6758
Email: sarah.smith@messymonsters.co.uk
Web: www.messymonsters.co.uk

Messy Monsters art club is primarily a parent and toddler group that allows children, accompanied by their parents or carers, to spend one hour of quality time in messy, creative activities. Classes are available for children aged 6 months upwards are held in various venues, typically community centres and church halls. Also available for birthday parties and other special occasions. See also Birthdays

BALL SPORTS

Ainslie Park
92 Pilton Drive EH5 2HF
Tel: 551 2400

Mini Kickers classes for 3-5yr olds. Held on Weds (during school terms): 16.15-17.00 and 17.15 – 18.00. Costs £24.80/8week block.

Bonnyrigg Leisure Centre
King George V Park
Park Road
Bonnyrigg EH19 2AW
Tel: 663 7579

Mini Kickers classes for 3-4yr olds are held on Wednesday afternoons. Costs £2/class payable on a 6 week block.

Enjoy-a-Ball
Various venues through city
Contact: Warwick Dredge
Tel: 08452 26 26 94
Email: dredge@enjoy-a-ball.com
Web: www.enjoy-a-ball.com

Sports coaching programme for 3-9 year olds. No more than 10 children per class. The programme is divided into four stages. Stage 1 – Bee Bops is for 3 and 4 year olds and introduces them to a formalised sports environment. Fun and creative games are used to enable the children to learn basic sporting skills in a non-threatening and unintimidating sporting environment. Also aims to develop the child's confidence, concentration and social skills. Children are presented with a certificate at the completion of a stage and reports are given to parents. All equipment is provided. Children attend one hourly class per week.

Classes are held in local sports, church and community centres on Mon-Fri afternoons and on Sat mornings. Free trial lesson available.

Socatots/Brazilian Soccer School
Contact: Bryan Robertson
Tel: 663 0140
Mobile: 07732774563
Email: b.robertson@cfds.com
Web: www.socatots.com/edinburghnel&elothian

Socatots is a soccer-specific physical play programme for children from 6 months – 5 years old. Sessions are held in various venues in Edinburgh and East Lothian and feature parent/carer participation. The emphasis is on fun and structured play.

Tots' Tennis
Edinburgh Leisure runs tots' tennis classes for children aged 3-5yrs. Classes teach young children basic hitting, movement and co-ordination skills for tennis. The coaching is by qualified and experienced coaches in a fun and encouraging environment. Parents/carers must accompany children during the session.

Classes are available at the following Edinburgh Leisure venues. Contact the venue direct for class times and booking.
Craiglockhart Tennis Centre, Tel: 444 1969
Drumbrae Leisure Centre, Tel: 312 7957
Ainslie Park Leisure Centre, Tel:551 2400

COMPUTERS

Whizzkidz
Multimedia Learning Centre
19 Morningside Drive
Edinburgh EH10 5LZ
Tel: 447 5893

Fun and educational computer classes for children aged 3+ yrs. Computer based activities are used to teach pre-school children basic language and maths skills. Classes are held on an individual or small group basis at £5/1/2 hr. Classes are booked in monthly blocks.

COOKERY CLASSES

Cookery classes for younger children can be fun with enjoyable results!

Balerno High School
Contact: Vivienne MacKay,
Community Manager
Tel: 477 7733

Fun with Food, for 3-5 yrs. Classes run for 8-10 weeks and must be booked and paid for in advance. Days and times may vary from term-to-term. Places are limited. Telephone contact for more details.

DANCE

Classes for younger children (i.e. 21/2-41/2 yrs), usually teach music and movement. This may include nursery rhymes and simple dancing – hopping, skipping, toe-pointing, mime and moving in time to music. Socialising, learning to wait your turn etc, are key elements in all dancing classes. Footwear is sometimes light shoes, available from any decent shoe shop, more often ballet shoes. There are many local dance classes, some of which are listed here, others may be found through friends' recommendations, ads in local libraries, community centres, shop windows and the local press.

Choosing the right class for your child can be difficult; it's worthwhile investigating the teacher's qualifications, class content, studio facilities etc. The Royal Academy of Dance has a registration system for teachers. Contact the RAD for a list of local registered teachers. Tel: 020 7326 8000 or contact them by email via their website: www. rad.org.uk.

DANCE TEACHERS REGISTERED WITH THE ROYAL ACADEMY OF DANCE

Buckstone Youth Dance
Tel: 445 3892 (waiting list secretary)
Ballet (RAD) from pre-school year. Modern and Tap (ISTD) from primary 1. Jazz from primary 4. £2.00/class for girls and boys living in the Buckstone area.

Dance for All at the Theatre School
106 St Stephen St EH3 5AQ
Tel: 226 5533
Dance classes for children.
2-4 yrs. General nursery dance; a fun introduction to dance steps, rhythm and co-ordination, mime, songs and creative dance.
4-5 yrs pre-primary Ballet; a gentle introduction to more structured dance steps and sequences, alongside free expression and creative dance, rhythm and co-ordination exercises.
Tap dancing classes from 4 1/2 yrs. Jazz classes available from 5 yrs.
No private breastfeeding location. Accessible by single pushchairs.
After-school classes and all day Saturday. Phone for full details.

Edinburgh Dance Academy
20 St Bernard's Crescent EH4 1NS
Contact: Susie Galloway
Tel: 343 1015
Email: edinburghdance@aol.com
Web: www.edinburghdanceacademy.co.uk
Ballet from 3yrs+. Classes are held in venues throughout Edinburgh and the Lothians. Contact for current details, venues and requirements.

EH Dance UK
TF3, 4 Kings Road EH15 1EA
Mob: 07976 585479
Email: Ehdance@gmail.com
Web: www.ehdance.co.uk
Classes in ballet, tap and jazz in the Craigmount and Granton areas. Classes start at age 3 where the emphasis is placed on fun and the children are encouraged to learn the basics of balance, movement and interaction with other children. Phone for current prices.

Jane Goulding School of Dance
Mob: 07740 585614

Classes in ballet (RAD), tap and modern (ISTD) for children 3+ years. Edinburgh classes for under 5s are held on Tue-Fri at Balerno Community Centre.
Dress: all pupils wear leotards and correct footwear. Phone for current prices.

Lothian Dance Academy
2 Rosefield Avenue Lane
Portobello EH15 IDT
Contact: Morag Phillips
Tel: 669 9073

Pre-school ballet, tap and creative music classes for 3 – 5year olds. The main studio is in Portobello but classes are also held in various other locations throughout the city. Phone for current prices and locations.

Manor School of Ballet
Tel: 334 0399
Contact: Mrs Noel Platfoot, Mrs Claire Smith or Miss Jacqueline Casey, (Directors)

Music and movement for ages 2 1/2-4 yrs. Ballet (4 1/2+ yrs). 45 min classes £4.50/class.
Classes are held at:
Marchmont St Giles Church, Kilgraston Rd; Old Parish Church, High St, Corstorphine; Belgrave Hall, Belgrave Rd, Corstorphine; St Serf's Church, Goldenacre; Inverleith Church, Ferry Rd; St Anne's Church, Murrayfield.
In terms of dress, the youngest pupils wear normal clothes, plus ballet shoes, which the school sells at a reasonable price. Children start to wear leotards at age 3 1/2 yrs. The school employs several teachers who are all RAD and ISTD registered. See also Activities for Parents.

Morningside Dance Academy
Contact: Sonja Messer B.Phil (Hons), Principal
Tel: 668 4977or 477 4344

Classes held at The Grange Studio, 9b Grange Road and 11-23 Morningside Dr. Ballet, Tap, Modern, Drama and Jazz dancing from age 3 to Majors. RAD and BTDA syllabus to Examination Standard.

OTHER DANCE TEACHERS
Pamela Allam AISTD, BTDA
Tel: 01259 742973

Nursery Ballet and Tap classes for children aged 3+yrs are held on Thursday afternoons in St Columba's Church, Blackhall. All classes accompanied by a pianist. Fully qualified staff. Registered teachers recognised by the Council for Dance Education and Training. British Theatre Dance Association syllabus taught to examination standard. Enrolment by phone.

Dance Base
National Centre for Dance
14-16 Grassmarket EH1 2JU
Tel: 225 5525
Web: www.dancebase.co.uk
Email: dance@dancebase.co.uk

Dance Base is a fully accessible building offering state-of-the-art facilities, with four dance studios.
Creative Movement for under 5's and 'Dance a Story' classes run throughout the year and encourage children to express themselves through movement games, facial expressions, using props, action songs and story-telling in a non-competitive environment. Children under the age of 5 must be accompanied by an adult. Adults are encouraged to take their socks and shoes off and join in with their children. Phone or email centre for details of class times and prices.
Dance for 2-5 yrs, Wed 11.00-12.00, Thu 14.30-15.30.
Through simple games children and parents explore movement together, using stretching, facial expressions and hand gestures.
Saturday class 2-5 yrs 10.00-11.00. This is for the whole family to enjoy; bring brothers and sisters too! Children can join in as soon as they can walk! All classes £20 for block of 4 classes, or Pay-on–the-day £2.50 (£1/extra child). Creative Movement Outreach classes also available. See also Activities for Parents.

Dancercise
Portobello Swim Centre
Contact: Louise Mackinnon
Tel: 669 9916

Dance classes for all ages. Under 5s Fri 16.00-17.00.

Mhairi Hogg School of Dancing
Contact: Mhairi Hogg MBATD
Tel: 449 3035

Classes held in Colinton Mains Community Centre and Oxgangs Neighbourhood Centre. Nursery Tap classes are held for 3-5 yrs. A class leotard is worn, plus appropriate footwear. Enrolment by phone.

DRAMA

Brou Ha Ha
Tel: 07870 529491
Contact: Siobhan Wyman
Pre-school drama activity classes held for 4-5 yr olds. Classes involve music, dance, performance skills and aim to develop children's confidence in articulating themselves and interacting in a social environment. Classes are held in Molly's Soft Play Centre, Ocean Terminal on a Wed – 14.00-15.00. Cost: £4/child. Classes may become available in other venues – contact for more info.

The Drama Studio
19 Belmont Road EH14 5DZ
Tel: 453 3284
Email: thedra@thedramastudio.co.uk
Contact: Julie McDonald
Drama workshops for 3-4 yr olds are held at Juniper Green Church Hall on Tuesdays 13.30-14.15 and for 4 yr olds at Fairmilehead Church Hall on Tuesdays 4-5pm. Contact centre for prices.

Edinburgh Acting School
15 Orwell Place EH11 2AD
Tel: 337 5155
Email: annatinline@hotmail.com
Contact: Anna TInlIne
Drama classes for 4-6 yr olds are held on Saturdays 12.15 – 1.15pm at The Pleasance (part of the University) There are no specific waiting areas although there is a bar where food, coffees, teas etc are available. Contact School for further information.

ENVIRONMENT

Balerno High School
Contact: Vivienne Mackay, Community Manager
Tel: 477 7733
Green Tots course for 3-5 year olds, which explores nature and the environment. Involves arts and crafts work and activities such as growing woodland boxes. Courses run for 8-10 weeks and must be booked and paid for in advance. Days and times may vary term-to-term. Crèche available if booked in advance. Phone contact for current prices and times.

GYMNASTICS

Gymnastics classes are popular for the under 5s and classes accommodating this age group are generally available in Edinburgh. When choosing a class, convenience is usually the prime consideration. However, it is well worth checking on the teacher's qualifications for teaching pre-school children, the facilities available and on their insurance cover, in the event of an accident.

All British Amateur Gymnastics Association (BAGA) coaches will charge a set amount to all children who attend their classes. This is paid to the Association for insurance purposes. This sum will be paid irrespective of the cost of the course. Anyone working with young children, ie nursery groups etc, might be interested in taking the Scottish Gymnastics Coaching Award for pre-school gymnastics and movement. For information, a copy of the syllabus, and general advice on gymnastics classes, contact Scottish Gymnastics Association, via their website: www.scottishgymnastics.com

Ainslie Park Leisure Centre
92 Pilton Drive
Tel: 551 2400
Gym Nippers programmes for under 5s. Run on block course. Contact centre for details.

Craiglockhart Tennis & Sports Centre
177 Colinton Rd
Tel: 443 0101 Sports Centre
Tel: 444 1969 Tennis Centre
Gym Nippers pre-school programme for under 5s. Under 3s must be accompanied by an adult. Course is run on a 9-12 wk block. Priority is given to children already on the programme. There is a Gymnastic Link Transition Programme to allow children to progress from Pre-school to 5+ yrs gymnastics, Wed 15.30-16.30. Classes run by qualified staff.
Crèche Mon, Tue, Wed, Thu 9.15-10.45 & 10.45-12.15; pre-booking essential. See Activities for Parents.

Drumbrae Leisure Centre
30 Drumbrae Ter
Tel: 312 7957
Gym Nippers classes on Saturday mornings for 18mths-3yrs and 3-5yrs . Costs £21/6 week block. Gymnastics for older children also. Must be booked. Contact centre for details.

Gracemount Leisure Centre
22 Gracemount Drive
Tel: 658 1940
Gym tots Wed 10.00-10.45, 10.45-11.30 £24.80/8 wk block. Mini gymnastics available for 3-5 yrs Mon, Wed 13.00-14.00 and 14.00-15.00, £24.80/8 wk block. Possible waiting list. Crèche Mon, Wed and Fri 9.15-10.45 and 10.50-12.15. Sports Camp during school holidays.

Gymini
Eric Liddell Centre
Morningside Road
Contact: Fiona
Tel: 334 3657
Gymnastics classes for toddlers onwards. Classes are held in a large, bright room with rubber matting, lots of equipment and friendly and imaginative teachers. Room is on top floor of building – lift available. Nappy changing facilities available. Not much space for pushchairs but these can be left downstairs. Café on ground floor of centre for parents waiting for 3-5year olds.
Parent and toddler classes: Tue 9.30-10.10 and 11.05-11.45; Thu 9.30-10.10.
Classes for 3-5year olds: Tue 10.15-11.00, 13.00-1345, 13.50-1435; Thu 10.15-11.00, 11.05-11.50, 13.00-13.45 and 13.50-14.35.

Jack Kane Sports Centre
208 Niddrie Mains Rd
Tel: 669 0404 or 664 4710
Pre-school gymnastics Tue 9.45-10.30 (18 mths-3 yrs); 10.45-11.30 (18 mths-3yrs). Further details from centre.

Kirkliston Leisure Centre
Kirklands Park Street
Kirkliston
Tel: 333 4700
.Gymnastics classes for under 5s held on Mondays. Parent and toddler class (18 mths or older): 11.00-11.45. 3 and 4 year olds class: 10.00-10.45 and 14.15-15.00. Classes usually booked in a block of 6-8 weeks. Contact centre for current prices.
Crèche available but must be booked in advance and costs £3.40/session (or £2.20 with a LAC).

Meadowbank Sports Centre
London Road
Tel: 661 5351
Gym Nippers programme offers young children the chance to learn balance, movement and co-ordination along with

music and action songs, all in a fun, creative environment. Classes are available for: 18mths-3 yrs (children must be accompanied by an adult), 3-5 yrs, 4-5 yrs, P1, P2. Courses are arranged via block bookings and can be booked in advance. Contact venue for further details.

Musselburgh Sports Centre
Newbigging
Musselburgh EH21 7AS
Tel: 653 6367

Gym Monkeys classes Wed 15.30-16.15, Fri 13.30-14.15 (18mths-3yrs, parents must stay); Wed 16.15-17.00 and 17.00-17.45, Fri 14.15-15.00, 15.00-15.45 (3-5 yrs). £2.35/class booked in advance. Waiting list. Teacher is BAGA approved coach. Crèche £2.60 /2 hrs. Details from centre.

Oxgangs Kindergym
Pentland Community Centre
Oxgangs Brae EH13 9LS
Tel: 445 2871

45 min session for children accompanied by parent/carer. Meets Mon-Thu 9.30 and 10.30 and some afternoons. Booking in blocks of 4 weeks. £2.00 annual centre membership and £2.00/session. Concessionary rates and some free places available. Children with special needs / disabilities especially welcomed.

Portobello Indoor Bowls and Leisure Centre
20 Westbank Street
Portobello EH15 1DR
Tel: 669 0878

Gymnastics classes for 18 mths-3 yrs (children must be accompanied by parent/carer): Mon 10.30-11.15; Fri 9.30-10.15, 10.20-11.05. Ages 3-5 yrs - Fri 11.15-12.00. £3.10/session.

Portobello Swim Centre
57 The Promenade EH15 2BS
Tel: 669 6888

Gym Nippers classes for 3-5 year olds. Run on block course. Contact Centre for details.

Ready Steady Play
Contact: Deborah
Tel: 664 8894
Email: Deborah@readysteadyplay.co.uk
Web: www.readysteadyplay.co.uk

New physical activity classes for children aged 18mths-3yrs. Classes last 45 minutes and begin with a warm up followed by various activities, such as: ball play; hula hoops; running; relay games; balloon play; tug of war; creative movement and fun dancing. Activities end with a cool down and children receive a weekly reward sticker as they leave the class. Children are given a sports bib to wear during the class.

Classes are held on Weds in Fairmilehead Church Halls – 9.30-10.15 and on Fridays in Liberton Kirk Halls – 9.30-10.15. Costs: £3.95/class, payable in block terms plus £1.75/term insurance fee.

Royal Commonwealth Pool
Dalkeith Road
Newington EH16 5AE
Tel: 667 7211

Gym Nippers classes for under 5s. Run on an 8 week block. Cost: £3.80/class. Classes held on Weds, Thurs and Fri. 18months-3 years: 09.30-10.15; and 3-5yrs: 10.30-11.15. Parents/carers of 18mths – 3 year olds are required to stay with their child.

Tumble Tots
Web: www.tumbletots.com/edinburgh
Contact (Edinburgh East): Jo Letelier-Lobos
Tel: 01875 320066
Email: joletelier.lobos@virgin.net
Contact (Edinburgh West): Julia Kerr
Tel: 313 3556

Classes held at: Cluny Church Centre, Cluny Dr, Morningside – Mon, Tue, Fri
Inverleith Church Hall, Ferry Rd – Tue
Murrayfield Parish Church – Wed
St Michael's Church Hall, Linlithgow – Thu
Cramond Kirk – Wed
Mary Erskine School, Ravelston – Sat
Livingston - Mon

The Tumble Tots specially designed programme is divided into 3 age ranges, which helps develop co-ordination, balance, climbing skills and agility. All with appropriate equipment. Supervision is by specially trained staff. Parents assist with under 3's.

There are 2 different ability levels for under 5's: Gymbabes – crawling - walking. Play, exploration and learning in a safe environment; and Tumble Tots - for children up to 5 yrs who can walk confidently. Sessions based round 'activity stations'.

Membership and insurance £19.00/yr (includes t-shirt, 'Right Start' magazine 6 issues/yr; insurance cover and a gift). £5.10 per 45 min session, paid in advance in 5-8 week blocks, after a paid trial session.

Wester Hailes Education Centre
5 Murrayburn Drive
Tel: 442 2201

Toddler gymnastics classes for 3-5 year olds held on Saturdays 12.00-13.00. Cost £1. A waiting list applies. Contact the centre for more details.

HORSE RIDING/ PONY TREKKING

Edinburgh and Lasswade Riding Centre
Kevock Road, Lasswade
Midlothian EH18 1HX
Tel: 663 7676
Contact: Marjory McNaughton

Half hour pony treks for under 5s. Small Shetland ponies and older, quieter ponies are used with this age group. There is no minimum age limit – as long as a child is happy to sit on the pony s/he can be taken on a small trek. The ponies are on leads and one member of staff is allocated to each child. Costs £13/half hour. Children should wear wellies/boots. Protective hats are available for hire - £1/ hat. The Centre also hosts children's parties (minimum 10 children) and these include a pony trek, the opportunity to feed and groom a pony and then party food and grassy play area.

JUDO

Shishi Kai Judo
Eric Liddell Centre
15 Morningside Rd
Contact: Jim Syrett
Tel: 447 7859
Email: jim@shishikai.co.uk

Judo classes for children aged 4 years onwards. The class for 4-5 year olds is held on Fridays 16.00-16.45. There is a waiting area for parents/carers and it's possible to view the class. First session free. Child/coach ration is 8:1. All coaches qualified, registered and child protection vetted. Contact Club for prices and more information.

MUSIC FUN

Young children love music. However, in most cases under 5s are not able to specialise in a particular instrument – their hands are not big enough, they don't have the lung power etc. Most of the music classes mentioned below, therefore, teach listening skills and moving in time to music. It is highly advisable to book in advance for all classes.

Baby Music
Contact: Jenny Newland
Tel: 2293667 (Birth Resource Centre)
Email: info@birthresourcecentre.org.uk

Action songs, rhymes and lullabies for babies up to 1yr. These are very popular classes , so places are limited: please call for venue, times, cost and to reserve a place. Concessions are available. Also offers courses in baby shiatsu, baby massage and parent and baby yoga.

Daisy's Music Time
Held in Wardie Parish Church Hall
Primrose Bank ROAd EH5 3JE
Contact: Di McGuire
Tel: 662 1243

Fun music sessions for babies and toddlers aged 3 months-3 1/2 yrs. Singing, rhythm activities, movement, listening and playing percussion instruments. Lots of props. Classes run during school term time by an experienced teacher. Accessible and child friendly venue. Phone for current times and further information.

Dough-Doh Music Club
3 Seaforth Drive
Contact: Carol Freeman
Tel: 332 4540

Educationally motivated music club for ages 2-5 yrs. Established 1994, this club is taken by Carol and Laraine, two experienced teachers. Meet the Dodo family! Listen, learn and move to unique Dodo stories, tongue twisters, rhymes and songs. Children develop natural rhythm through use of percussion instruments (eggs, bells, sticks) and to love music with our keyboard. Classes last 40-50 mins. Information pack and testimonials on request. This is a mobile service and is suitable for schools, nurseries, playgroups etc.

Edinburgh Young Musicians
Contact: Jean Murray
Tel: 226 3392
Email: admin@e-y-m.org.uk
Web: www.e-y-m.org.uk

Musical play classes for children, starting in their final pre-school year, leading to instrumental tuition, choirs and orchestras for older children. Classes provide a general introduction to music, developing the child's sense of rhythm, sense of pitch, listening skills, co-ordination and imagination.

Classes are held at James Gillespie's High School, Lauderdale St on Sat mornings during term time.

Jack and Jill – Music Fun for Tots
Contact: Jill Reeves (MusBHons, PGCE, Music Therapist)
Tel: 667 9664 / mob. 07729 719756

Lap rides, finger plays, action songs, dancing, playing simple percussion instruments, and listening to live music – interactive musical fun and learning for tots (ages 3 mths-5yrs) and their accompanying adults. Classes run by qualified and experienced music teachers. Children with special needs welcome. Classes are held in St Catherine's Argyle Church, Grange Rd, Marchmont, on Wed and Fri mornings during term time. £3.60 /class, payable termly.

Jo Jingles
Contact: Joanne Goodall
Tel: 443 4196
Web:www.jojingles.co.uk/EdinburghWest

Music and movement classes for various age ranges from 6 months to 5yrs. Includes action songs, nursery rhymes and playing of musical instruments. Some songs are familiar, others are new, so there's something to keep the participating parent/carer on their toes. Also available for Birthdays (see Birthdays & Celebrations)

Current classes held in various venues throughout the city, including Murrayfield, Juniper Green, South Queensferry, Trinity, Morningside, Linlithgow, Bo'ness, Craiglockhart, Corstorphine, Cramond, Blackhall and Oxgangs. Different classes for different age groups: classes are tailored to those children who attend, so you might find groups such as 6 mths-walking, 9 mths-2 yrs, 2-3 yrs, 3-5 yrs and so on. Contact Joanne Goodall for current times and class groups. More venues may be included in 2006/7. Classes are also held in nurseries and playgroups across the city. Nappy changing facilities available.

Mini Minstrels
18 Bonaly Crescent
Contact: Hazel Stewart
Tel: 441 3750

Music sessions for 3-6 yrs. Singing, musical games, instruments, and development of musical skills through fun.

3 yrs: various times on Tue, £2.50/30 mins. Max 6 in class.

Pre-school year; Wed or Thu £3.00/45 mins. Max 8 in class.

P1:Wed or Thu 16.00, £3.25/50 mins. Max 10 in class.

Music with Mummy
8 Greenbank Loan EH10 5SH
Contact: Carolyn Watson
Tel: 447 7033
or
25 Morningside Park EH10 5HD
Tel: 07751 699084
Contact: Carole Clegg

Lively approach to music for children aged 3 and under. Structured programme that encourages listening skills, sense of rhythm through music and games – and having fun! Has been running since 1992. Weekly 1/2 hr sessions, limited to 8 children (accompanied by parent/carer). £3.00/session, payable 1/2 termly in advance. Please phone for current times.

Music for Fun
5 Willowbrae Avenue
Contact: Nina Craighead
Tel: 620 0685

Finger rhymes, action songs and musical games, and percussion playing for children from 3 yrs to school age. Run by former primary school teacher in her home. Classes are on Weds and Thurs 13.45-14.30. £2/class. Payment is by class each week — there's no payment required if the child is absent. A cup of tea/coffee is provided in the kitchen for whoever brings the child to the class.

Musical Minis
Contact: Jenni Taylor
Tel: 665 1811
Email: jenni@musicalminis.co.uk
Web: www.musicalminis.co.uk

Fun-time musical group for children aged 6months-pre-school. Sessions introduce children to music and percussion, with an emphasis on rhythm, song, sound and music and includes action songs and nursery rhymes. The range of music is diverse, from classical to modern. Max. 15 children/group.

Sessions run: Mon – Trinity 9.45-10.30, 10.45-11.30, 13.45-14.30, 14.45-15.30. Thu – Morningside 9.15-10.00, 10.15-11.00, 11.15-12.00. Fri – Port Seton 10.30-11.15, 11.30-12.15

ACTIVITIES FOR CHILDREN – SIGNING & SWIMMING

St Mary's Music School
25 Grosvenor Crescent
Contact: Monica Wilkinson
Tel: 538 7766

Music classes for children in their final pre-school year, including musical games, singing, listening, and use of simple percussion instruments. Classes are on Sat 9.00-13.30. £6.50/class.

Also classes for older children, including group instrumental lessons for beginners. There is generally a waiting list.

SIGNING

Sing and Sign
Contact: Dee Armstrong
Tel: 07831 409459
Email: signedinburgh@aol.com
Web: www.singandsign.com

Classes are aimed at 7-18 month olds (& their mums/dads etc!) and run in a course of 10 weeks (during term times). Classes last 45 mins, and signs are taught through songs & rhymes which are specially written or adapted to target signs relating to babies routines & interest. Musical instruments, props, puppets & pictures are used to capture babies & mums' attention & the aim of the classes is to enhance parent-baby communication by using signs (as well as having a bit of fun along the way). Classes held in the West End and also Trinity/Leith. Telephone or email for further information.

SWIMMING CLASSES

Edinburgh Leisure offers classes in their pools (see Swimming in Where Shall We Go Today for contact details). In addition, there are a number of private swimming teachers who run classes at various venues throughout Edinburgh.

Many of these have long waiting lists and have preferred not to be listed in this guide. The following offer classes for under 5s.

Swim Easy
Tel: 466 0764
Web: www.swimeasy.co.uk

Classes run in pools throughout Edinburgh and the Lothians. Small groups (4-5) for pre-school, non-swimmer and beginner young children. Instructors work in the water with younger age groups to aid confidence. Games are incorporated into learning programme to keep the process as much fun as possible. Check site or call for current fees.

Swimming Nature
Tel: 0870 0949597
Web: www.swimmingnature.co.uk

Swimming classes held in Edinburgh University Aquatics Centre, Holyrood Rd Mon-Sat. Class sizes are small and instructors work in the water following a modular programme that can be easily followed by children and their parents. Fun, games, stories and rewards are used to encourage and stimulate the children to love the water. Free trial lesson offered. Intensive courses offered in school holidays. Call centre for information and to make a booking.

Waterbabies Edinburgh
Contact: Hugh Davidson
Tel: 312 7520
Mobile: 07958 631220
Email: hugh@waterbabies.co.uk
Website: www.waterbabies.co.uk

Swimming classes for babies from birth onwards. Fully qualified STA instructors teach water confidence and safety techniques with babies swimming above and below the water's surface. Classes are small and held throughout Edinburgh in private, warm-water pools. Contact Waterbabies for information about prices and course times.

YOGA

Aditi Yoga Centre
5 Alva Street (1st floor) EH2 4PH
Tel: 226 2601

Yoga for Children; Fri 16.00-16.45. For children aged 2-5 yrs. Classes are a blend of active and passive poses, and are a combination of playful yoga postures, animated breathing exercises and imaginative relaxation and meditation activities. See also Activities for Parents & Carers.

Activities for Parents & Carers

PARENTS & CARERS – COMMUNITY EDUCATION

INTRODUCTION

Making time for yourself as well as for your children is very important, for everyone involved.

The aim of this section is to provide you with some starting points and ideas of the types of community classes and groups, education and training opportunities, and sports facilities in the area.

Many of the centres listed have crèche facilities and we have listed those we know about – but it is always worth checking with the venue.

There are many possibilities open to parents with young children, thanks to evening classes, open/flexible learning opportunities and a wealth of community-based initiatives to help parents extend their horizons and have a break from childcare. If the venues are unable to provide childcare, there is a range of private crèches/nurseries that can offer flexible childcare. For full listings, see Childcare and Pre-school Play and Education.

COMMUNITY EDUCATION CENTRES

These centres provide a broad range of formal and informal activities and classes. There are opportunities to study for qualifications, keep fit, or learn a new craft or skill. Many provide a crèche. The majority of these centres are schools, community schools or resource centres. Many run programmes under the management of the City of Edinburgh Council's 'Adult Community Education Programme'. Classes start in September, January and April. For further information on classes, contact Community Education head office, tel: 469 3250. See also Sport and Leisure in this section.

Cameron House Community Centre
Cameron House Avenue EH15 5LF
Contact: Susan Ferguson
Tel: 667 3762
Daytime classes Yoga and keep-fit.
Toddler Group on Fridays 10.30-12.30; small friendly group. Centre membership £2/£1, then 20p admission weekly plus tea/coffee 30p, juice 10p. Phone venue for further information on classes etc.

Carrickvale Community Education Centre
2 Saughton Mains Street EH11 3HH
Tel: 443 6971
Fax: 455 7362
Parent and Toddlers Mon, Tues, Thur, Fri 9.30-11.30. Crèche can be negotiated for use with courses, events etc. Phone centre for information on any class or group.

Castlebrae Family Centre
Castlebrae Community High School
2a Greendykes Road
EH16 4DP
Centre Leader: Lyn Tarlton
Tel: 661 1282
Centre providing range of activities for babies and young children, but also adult education classes. Contact centre for current details.

Clovenstone Community Centre
54 Clovenstone Park EH4 3EY
Tel: 453 4561
Variety of social and educational activities which cater for local residents of all ages. Free crèche – mainly for women's activities. Programmes on request.

Craigmount Community Wing
Craigmount High School
Craigs Road EH12 8NH
Tel: 339 1884/8278
Wide range of activities, including arts and crafts, alternative therapies and miscellaneous groups. Women's discussion group. Free crèche (under 5s), usually staffed by two people. Also: Sat 9.00-13.00, there's a class for Japanese children (3+ yrs) in their own language and culture, and an English class for their parents, with crèche (0-3 yrs).

Craigroyston Community Centre
1a Pennywell Road EH4
Tel: 332 7360
Various classes – with crèche provision – run throughout the year. Full details are available from centre.

Craigroyston Community High School
Pennywell Road EH4 4QP
Craigroyston Early Years Centre
Contact: Linda McDonald
Tel: 477 7801
Early Years Centre where people may come to play and learn with their children. Adult day and evening classes also run, with cover provided for the children of adult learners as appropriate.

Currie and Balerno High Schools
Contact: Vivienne Mackay, Community Manager
Tel: 477 7733 or 449 5922

Comprehensive programmes of learning and recreational opportunities are offered throughout the year at the dual sites of Currie and Balerno high schools. The combined resources of the schools allow for the provision of a wide range of day, evening and weekend classes, courses and community activities. Crèche places are available at both schools for children of adult students attending morning classes/activities. Please book crèche requirements when enrolling for day class. Contact the above nos for details of current classes etc.

Drummond High Community High School
41 Bellevue Place EH7 4BS
Tel: 556 2651

Wide variety of day and evening classes. Vocational courses also available. Contact venue for availability of crèche.

Duncan Place Resource Centre
4 Duncan Place EH6 8HN
Contact: Rohan Seilman
Tel: 554 1509

A range of adult education classes, daytime and evening. Crèche facilities for daytime classes. Adult clubs are also run, as are Fri afternoon classes for older children. Contact centre for more information.

First Step Community Project
37 Galt Avenue
Musselburgh EH21 8HU
Contact: Prisca Kemp or Cathy Carstairs
Tel: 665 0848

Variety of classes and courses, such as: computing; cookery; stress management; assertiveness; art; women's group; Dad's group; and positive parenting. Crèche available on Wed 9.30-11.30 (£1 charge) for class participants. Contact project for more details.

Fort Community Wing
North Fort Street, Leith EH6 4HF
Contact: Nancy Richardson (9.30-13.00)
Tel: 553 1074

Various classes run throughout the year. Phone to find out what is currently available and whether crèche facilities are available.

Gilmerton Community Centre
4 Drum Street, Gilmerton EH17 8QG
Contact: Helen Bouquin
Tel: 664 2335

Groups specific to women are run, such as a women's interest group, and also a support group. Free crèche with experienced staff. A playgroup also runs Mon-Thu: contact centre for all current details or playgroup application form.

Lasswade High School Centre
Eskdale Drive
Bonnyrigg, Midlothian EH19 2LA
Contact: David Hand
Tel: 663 8170/7171

Various discussion and interest groups from the area meet in the centre. New members are welcome, so phone centre for current information.

Lochend YWCA
198 Restalrig Road South EH7 6DZ
Contact: Morag Demarco (Crèche Coordinator)
Sarah Cross (Centre Manager)
Tel: 554 3400
Email: lochend.ywca@care4free.net

Activities vary depending on need and demand, but include lifelong learning opportunities, training courses, support groups and general interest groups.
Parent/carer and baby/toddler groups are held during the week and are well attended. A flexible crèche is available Mon-Fri, 8.30-13.00.
Please phone centre for current information.

St Bride's Centre
10 Orwell Terrace EH11 2DZ
Contact: Faye Ward
Tel: 346 1405

Programme of classes, activities, shows and popular films during term time and holidays. Crèche available with some morning adult classes. Café with enclosed children's play area open Mon-Fri 10.00-16.00. Nappy changing facilities. After school club for 4-8 yrs, Thu 17.00-18.30 during term time.
Classes available vary, so contact centre for current information.

South Bridge Resource Centre
Infirmary Street
Edinburgh EH1 1LT
Tel: 556 2944
Daytime classes in computing, dressmaking, pottery and some others. Crèche available. Other classes may be available. Phone for details.

South Queensferry Community Centre
Joint Sites:
Community Centre,
Kirkliston Road, South Queensferry
Rosebery Hall, South Queensferry
Contact: Steve Stewart
Tel: 331 2113
Various classes and playgroups (pottery, yoga, ballet & tap classes, childminders group, soft play). Contact centre for details and times.

Southside Community Centre
117 Nicolson Street
Edinburgh EH8 9ER
Contact: venue
Tel: 667 0484
Web: www.southside.edin.org
Class with free crèche (0-5yrs); must be pre-booked: Yoga Tue 10.00-12.00; Southside Sunshine Club (for 0-3 years) Wed 10.00-12.00. Other classes available. Classes can vary from term to term, so phone for information. Other groups, such as Parents and Tots may also meet – phone for current information.

Centre Cafeteria
Opening times: Mon-Fri 10.00-14.30, Sat 11.00-14.00
£, high chairs (2), bottles heated

Cafe serving snacks and wholesome lunches. Menu incl. dish of the day. Meals served 12.00-14.00. Children's portions; vegetarian dishes.

Stevenson College
Edinburgh Community-based ESL Section
Duncan Place Resource Centre
4 Duncan Place EH6 8HW
Tel: 535 4630
Fax: 535 4633
Community-based classes (held in schools and community centres all over the city) for adults permanently resident in Edinburgh who speak English as a second language. Crèche (0-5) for some classes.

Tollcross Community Education Centre
Tollcross Primary School
Fountainbridge EH3 9QG
Contact: Sarah Sibbert
Tel: 229 8448/221 5800
Web: www.tollcross.edin.org
General day activities, including lip reading, craft classes, multi-cultural activities, Community-based English as a Second Language, Gaelic Mother and Toddlers Group, Tollcross Parents Group. Free crèche for some daytime Adult Education classes.

Wester Hailes Education Centre
5 Murrayburn Drive
Edinburgh EH14 2SU
Tel: 442 2201
Modern community school providing opportunities for all ages to study or play. Amenities include library, art, drama and music studios, technical workshops, swimming pools, games hall, gymnasium, racquet sports hall, and cafeteria. Variety of classes including typing, computing, languages, SQA subjects etc; adults may be integrated with older school pupils. Recreational classes are adult only. There is the Rainbow Crèche (0-5yrs) for children of parents or guardians who are taking classes/activities. Early registration for the crèche is recommended.

YWCA Roundabout Centre
4b Gayfield Place EH7 4AB
Tel: 556 1168/557 4695
Web: www.ywca.scotland.org
This is a women's community centre committed to the elimination of racism and to empowering women to develop their full potential.
Providing training and support for volunteers. Rainbow People – friendship network and support group for parents and carers of children of mixed race/dual heritage.
Advice and Information for anyone seeking advice on volunteering, adult education, training events. Also runs a 'Budget Cookery and women's health issues' course. Intercultural Crèche for children 2-5. Intercultural Summer School for children aged 5-12 and young women aged 12-16 in July. Contact centre for details.

EDUCATION & TRAINING

Edinburgh offers a huge variety of education, training and 'new direction' courses. There are also opportunities to learn a practical skill, craft or sport through the Adult

Community Education Programme run by the City Council at schools throughout the city. If a venue has a crèche available, this is always mentioned in the entry.

Adult Learning Project
184 Dalry Road
Edinburgh EH11 2EP
Contact: Stan Reeves
Tel: 337 5442
Courses, programmes, projects and events. Linking adult education and social action, including social and national politics, history, women's studies, language and writing, multicultural work and literacy.

Careers Scotland
Cairncross House
25 Union Street EH1 3LR
Tel: 556 4110
Fax: 557 6736
Information on careers, education and training. Individual career counselling services for employed and unemployed adults. Children welcome. Other premises are used, on an outreach basis, for those who are out of town. Write or phone for an appointment.

Edinburgh College of Art
Lauriston Place EH3 9DF
Tel: 229 9311
Courses in art and design, architecture and town planning. Some evening classes available.

Edinburgh University Settlement
Community Learning Centre
New Parliament House
5-7 Regent Road
Edinburgh EH7 5BL
Tel: 550 6805
Courses for adults with few or no qualifications who want to return to work or find a new direction for their lives. Courses include SQA modules in communications, numeracy and IT. Courses in child development, parenting, behaviour and play (all SQA) also available. Other venues at Craigmillar, Wester Hailes, Pilton and South Edinburgh.

Edinburgh's Telford College
Crewe Toll
Tel: 332 2491
Tel: 332 2424
(Course Information Line – 24 hr service)
Email: mail@ed-coll.ac.uk
Web: www.ed-coll.ac.uk

Wide range of courses in general education, vocational skills and general and recreational interest suitable for preparing to go back to work or wishing to maintain skills and interests. Large open learning programme and a range of other attendance patterns – ask if shorter hours are possible. Some subject areas have 'drop-in' facilities which increases flexibility.
Nursery has 80 places, split into 4 rooms of 20 children (2-5 yrs). Opening times are 8.30-16.30 during term-time only. For more information phone 315 7476 and ask for Lynn McNair or Mike McMillan.

Employment Service
Disability Service Team
24-26 Torphichen Street   EH3 8JP
Contact: Jane Bruce (DST Manager)
Tel: 456 5330
Primarily for individuals with disabilities or health problems looking to return to work. Services include assessment, work preparation, job matching and practical assistance to take on employment through Access to Work.

Heriot-Watt University
Riccarton Campus EH14 4AS
Tel: 449 5111
Web: www.hw.ac.uk
Established university with excellent reputation in science, engineering, mathematics, computer science, management, finance, languages and built environment. Check website for details of courses available at undergraduate & postgraduate level.
Pinocchio's Nursery at Heriot-Watt is open Mon-Fri (0-5 yrs): Tel: 451 5236. See Pre-School Play and Education for more information.

Jewel and Esk Valley College
Milton Road Campus,
24 Milton Road East, EH15 2PP
Eskbank Campus, Newbattle Road,
Dalkeith, EH22 3AE
Tel: 660 1010 for sites
Tel: 0845 850 0060 for a prospectus
Web: www.jevc.ac.uk
email: info@jevc.ac.uk

Wide range of educational, vocational and leisure courses. Scottish Wider Access Programmes for mature students moving on to higher education. Swimming pool and gymnasium at Milton Rd. Open learning options available. No crèche facilities.

Lasswade High School Centre
Eskdale Drive
Bonnyrigg
Contact: Community Education Worker
Tel: 663 7171/8170
A variety of daytime/evening classes for adults. Contact centre for current syllabus.

Learn Direct Scotland
Freephone: 0808 100 9000
Web: www.learndirectscotland.com
Offers careers advice and course information. Advisors can give objective course information and subjective advice over the phone. LDS also provides details of other similar organisations and can forward individuals' details regarding the Government's Individual Learning Account, and can advise and explain about other sources of course funding.

Moray House Institute
Faculty of Education,
University of Edinburgh
Old Moray House, Holyrood Road EH8 8AQ
Tel: 651 6138
Courses leading to qualifications in teaching, community education and sport and leisure. Undergraduate and post-graduate courses available. University has nursery provision.

Napier University
10 Colinton Road EH14 1DJ
Tel: 0500 35 35 70
Email: info@napier.ac.uk
Web: www.napier.ac.uk
Full-time undergraduate, postgraduate and part-time prospectuses available from the Information Office. Flexible learning through Credit Accumulation and Transfer Scheme (CATS), as well as open learning facilities and courses, summer school and a wide range of short courses.

NISUS Scotland
121 Giles Street EH6 6BZ
Tel: 554 5656
Full-time courses in Information Technology for unemployed women aged over 25 with low or no qualifications. ESF and CEC funded in partnership with Edinburgh's Telford College. NISUS also offers 'Quaytech' training – cost-effective IT skills training to both voluntary and private sectors, which is open to men and women. In addition, NISUS provides 'Flexit' – a drop-in IT training programme in hourly blocks for men or women with disabilities or health concerns.

The Number Shop
188-190 The Pleasance EH8 9RT
Tel: 668 4787
The Number Shop is part of the City of Edinburgh Council's Community-Based Adult Education Service and provides free help with arithmetic and maths. Tuition is available to adults who want to improve their numeracy skills and to feel more confident with numbers for everyday use. Just drop-in or phone for an interview with a member of staff.

The Office of Lifelong Learning
University of Edinburgh
11 Buccleuch Place EH8 9LW
Tel: 650 4400
Email: OLL@ed.ac.uk
Web: www.lifelong.ed.ac.uk
Offers a Return To Learning programme. Courses specifically designed for adults or those who fall into the 'mature student' category: course structures include 'New Horizons' and 'Access'.
For more information contact RTL secretary Lorna Ketchion at the above address. Evening classes on a wide range of subjects also run – contact centre for prospectus and information.

The Open University in Scotland
10 Drumsheugh Gardens EH3 7QJ
Tel: 225 2889
Web: www.open.ac.uk/scotland
The OU offers a wide range of courses, diplomas, degrees and professional qualifications. With the support of a personal tutor, you study by part-time open learning, which fits around your family and work commitments. For many OU courses, you don't need to have any previous qualifications. Contact the Course Choice Team for further information and a prospectus.

Play Scotland
Midlothian Innovation Centre
Pentlandfield
Roslin, Midlothian EH25 9RE
Contact: Helena Brown

Tel: 440 9070
Fax: 440 9071
Email: helenabrown@playscotland.fsnet.co.uk
Web: www.playscotland.org
A charitable organisation which provides advice and information to both its members and the public about play, funding opportunities, play provision and play training. Also acts as a pressure group to persuade others that play is important for children and young people and conducts and stimulates research into play provision in Scotland.

Queen Margaret University College
Clerwood Terrace EH12 8TS
Admissions contact: Lorna Kemp or Jenny Thacker
Tel: 317 3247
A range of full-time, part-time, distance learning, post-registration and continued professional development courses. Undergraduate and postgraduate degrees are available in the areas of health care, theatre arts and cultural management, communication and information, business and management and social sciences.

Scottish Pre-school Play Association (SPPA)
Head Office
45 Finnieston Street
Glasgow G3 8JU
Tel: 0141 221 4148
Fax: 0141 221 6043
Web: www.sppa.org.uk
SPPA provides practical help with all aspects of running your pre-school group. It provides information and advice on setting up and running your group, competitive group insurance, and a range of pre-five publications and training opportunities. For membership information contact SPPA Centre.

Office covering City of Edinburgh:
111 Union Street
Glasgow G1 3TA
Tel: 0141 227 3922
Fax: 0141 2273923
Email: joyce.waddell@sppa.org.uk
Local support service for playgroups, toddler groups, under fives groups and nurseries.

Scottish Wider Access Programme (SWAP)
25 Buccleuch Place
EH8 9LN
Tel: 650 6861
Freephone: 0800 731 0949
Email: swapeast@ed.ac.uk

Web: www.swap2highereducation.com
Wide range of access courses to prepare adults, over 21, who do not have the standard entrance qualifications for study in further or higher education. Successful completion of an access course at an appropriate level guarantees a place at a range of colleges and universities. Part-time and flexible programmes may be available.

Stevenson College of Further Education
Bankhead Avenue EH11 4DE
Tel: 535 4700 (Information Centre)
Email: info@stevenson.ac.uk
Web: www.stevenson.ac.uk
Offers a wide range of courses on a full-time, part-time, evening and flexible learning basis. Courses are designed to help achieve your ambitions whether they involve returning to work or education, gaining formal qualifications or developing your career. Student support team can arrange childcare and may be able to help with fees for after schools clubs, nurseries and childminders. Contact the information centre on the above number for further information.

University of Edinburgh
Old College, South Bridge EH8 9YL
Tel: 650 1000
Special prospectus for mature students. Entrance qualifications for degree courses may differ for mature students. The University has a nursery (6wks-5yrs). Tel: 667 9584, for information from nursery manager. See also Centre for Continuing Education.

Women onto Work (WOW)
137 Buccleuch Street EH8 9NE
Tel: 662 4514
Email: mail@womenontowork.org
Courses in Craigmillar, greater Pilton, Wester Hailes, South Edinburgh and citywide. For women who have been out of paid employment, to look at options for employment or further study. Also for women from an ethnic minority or with a disability. Full childcare provided.

Workers Educational Association (WEA)
34b North West Thistle Street Lane
EH2 1EA
Contact: Elizabeth Bryan or Tim Green
Tel: 225 7772
Email:lothian@weascotland.org.uk
Scottish-wide voluntary adult education organisation which works locally to encourage access to learning through life.

Free, friendly and informal courses in confidence building, returning to learning, social and political studies, and the arts. Courses can be tailored to meet needs of groups.

SPORTS & LEISURE

Firstly, we have listed the centres that are run by local councils and offer reasonably priced facilities, membership and regular crèches. After this, we have a short list of private sports and leisure centres, which we know have good family facilities.

There are a number of health, fitness and sports centres the length and breadth of the city. These usually charge a joining fee, and thereafter have a monthly payment scheme. Full details in the Yellow Pages. It's worth checking local press for up-to-date information, or indeed phoning around, as this market is very competitive and many clubs run short-term special offers for new memberships.

Check the crèche facilities – there have been past examples of crèches running only for a short time and then being closed down, as a means of membership recruitment: if documentation mentions a crèche is planned, again proceed with caution. However, many established private clubs have established crèche facilities – which are as popular as those run within the centres run by local councils: always book your crèche place in advance.

LEISURE ACCESS SCHEME

Edinburgh Leisure, which runs facilities for the City of Edinburgh Council, offer this scheme, giving access to a wide range of benefits and discounts to all Edinburgh Leisure facilities, including sports, swim and golf centres. Currently, the scheme's Leisure Access Cards cost £43 (at time of writing); concessionary rates are available. There are different rates for activities for cardholders and non-cardholders at peak and off-peak time. Children always pay the lowest price available. You do not need a Leisure Card to use facilities but if children (under 18s) or adults want to book in advance they must have one. Application forms are available from all sport and swim centres, local libraries and Edinburgh Leisure Head Office – 54 Nicolson St, Tel: 650 1001, Fax: 651 2299.

Parents and carers who are Leisure Cardholders are entitled to use on-site crèche facilities at reduced rates. For information about the crèches contact the Crèche Co-ordinator on the number above. All centres can provide information about their prices, current activities

and the coaching they offer. Programmes do tend to vary throughout the year, so it is advisable to check details in advance.

Edinburgh Leisure's Sports and Service Development Section, based at Meadowbank Sports Centre provides an information point for sport and recreation opportunities within Edinburgh. Will advise on classes, crèche facilities etc, Tel: 652 2178.

DANCE

Dance Base
National Centre for Dance
14-16 Grassmarket EH1 2JU
Tel: 225 5525
Web: www.dancebase.co.uk
Offers classes and workshops in a wide range of dance styles, from ballroom to belly-dancing! All ages and abilities. Also classes in Tai Chi, yoga, Pilates and Alexander Technique. See Activities for Children for main entry.

Edinburgh Dance Academy
65 Orchard Brae AveNUE
EH4 2UR
Tel: 343 1015
Email: edinburghdance@aol.com
Web: www.edinburghdanceacademy.co.uk
Ballet, modern, jazz and tap lessons. Pilates-based body conditioning classes for mothers. See also Activities for Children.

Manor School of Ballet
Contact: Mrs Noel Platfoot (director)
Tel: 334 0399
Fax: 334 0399
Tap classes for beginners up to advanced. Keep-fit classes and ballet classes for beginners up to advanced. See Activities for Children for full entry.

SPORTS & LEISURE CENTRES

Ainslie Park Leisure Centre
92 Pilton Drive EH5 2HF
Tel: 551 2400
Wide range of coaching and activity classes, including aerobics, body conditioning and sculpture, body

systems, circuit training, fitness/weight training (recently refurbished gym), badminton, gymnastics, judo, step, yoga and swimming lessons for children and adults of all ages and ability. Antenatal, postnatal and aquafit exercise classes. 'Women Only' evening every Mon 18.00-22.00. Programme available from centre.

Crèche:
Mon, Tue 9.00-13.00; Wed 9.00-13.30; Thu, Fri 9.00-12.30: Leisure Access Cardholders can benefit from a concessionary rate. Must be booked in advance. Staffed by qualified crèche workers.

Bonnyrigg Leisure Centre
King George V Park
Bonnyrigg EH19 2AD
Tel: 663 7579
Opening times: Mon-Sun 9.00-22.00 incl. most public holidays (reduced opening hours 10.00-18.00)
This centre offers a leisure pool consisting of upper and lower lagoon and special water features, and exercise studio, fitness suite, sauna and outdoor 5-a-side and tennis courts. Programmed sessions include aerobics, step, martial arts and fitness classes. Leisure Access Card scheme in operation offers discounts for concessionary groups. Crèche Mon-Fri 9.45-11.15; pre-booking essential up to 7 days in advance. Free parking. Range of snacks available from vending machine. Mixed family changing available. Coin-operated lockers and nappy changing facilities.

Countryside Ranger Service
Hermitage House
Hermitage of Braid
69a, Braid Rd, Morningside EH10 6JF
Tel: 447 7145
Email: ranger@cecrangerservice.demon.co.uk
Web: www.cecrangerservice.demon.co.uk
Guided walks and special events programme based on various themes for all the family all year round. Phone for information and programme – rangers are very helpful. Details of women's walks programme advertised in local notice boards and local press – especially 'Herald and Post'.

Craiglockhart Tennis & Sports Centre
177 Colinton Rd EH14 1BZ
Tel: 443 0101 (Sports Centre)
Tel: 444 1969 (Tennis Centre)
Opening times: Mon-Thu 9.00-23.00; Fri 10.00-23.00; Sat, Sun 9.00-22.30

City's main public centre for racquet sports, with indoor tennis, badminton and squash. Coaching in aerobics, step, weight training, keep-fit and trampolining. Well equipped weights gym. Outdoor facilities include tennis courts and boating pond. Easy access for pushchairs. Programme available from centre. The tennis facilities include 6 indoor courts and 8 outdoor, with a main centre court. Tennis coaching classes available by block booking or drop in for 'women only' sessions: Mon, Wed 9.30-11.00, 11.00-12.30 and Fri 10.30-12.30. Free car parking at the tennis centre; short walk down two flights of stairs to the main centre. There are crèche facilities at the main centre for under 5s only, run by qualified staff, must be booked in advance: a small cost applies. Phone centre for details.

Dalry Swim Centre
Caledonian Crescent EH11 2AL
Tel: 313 3964
Range of exercise and aquafit classes and swimming classes. Antenatal class Tue 9.00-9.40. Sauna. Full programme available from centre. No crèche facilities.

Drumbrae Leisure Centre
30 Drumbrae Terrace EH4 7SF
Tel: 312 7957
Modern leisure centre offering a wide range of activities, including sports coaching and swimming lessons, exercise classes, women-only sessions. There is a Pulse Centre with easy to use equipment. Centre is all on one level, which makes for all-round easy access. Full programme with current times etc available from centre. Crèche facilities available – best to book ahead. Centre also has a small café and vending machines.

Glenogle Swim Centre
Glenogle Road EH3 5JB
Tel: 343 6376
Glenogle Swim Centre is scheduled to be temporarily closed for one year for major refurbishment from early 2006.

Gorgie Dalry Community Association
22 McLeod Street EH11 2NH
Contact: Jim Young
Tel/Fax: 337 3252
Mon-Sat 9.00-18.00 (plus some evenings); Sun 11.00-19.00 (staffed only when classes are on).
Formed from an amalgamated sports centre/community association – activities include football, basketball, tennis,

hockey, badminton cricket, self-defence and general keep-fit classes. Can also host one-off social and community events. Crèche (under 3s). Call centre for full details.

Gracemount Leisure Centre
22 Gracemount Drive EH16 6RN
Tel: 658 1940

Facilities include multi-purpose games hall hosting badminton, basketball, 5-a-side football, volleyball, gymnastics, trampolining, indoor hockey, short tennis, table tennis, martial arts, and fitness studio. Crèche. A wide range of fitness classes for all ages and abilities are available. 'Women only' evening Wed 18.00-21.00. Sports camps during school holidays. Programme available from centre. Good access with lift and ramps to all floors. Crèche Mon, Wed and Fri 9.15-10.45, 10.50-12.15; cost £2.50, Leisure Access Cardholders £1.50. Must be booked (up to 7 days in advance). Café and vending machines on site.

Inch Community Education Centre
255 Gilmerton Road EH16 5UF
Tel: 664 4710

Exercise class Fri 9.15-10.15, £1.50/class. Free crèche.

Jack Kane Sports Centre
208 Niddrie Mains Road EH16 4NB
Tel: 664 4710 or 669 0404

Centre has facilities for badminton, martial arts, football, basketball, pulse centre, free weights, hockey, gymnastics. Programme available from centre. No crèche.

Kirkliston Leisure Centre
Kirklands Park Street EH29 9ET
Tel: 333 4700

Multi-purpose sports hall. Outdoor tennis and 5-a-side facilities. 'Women only' sessions. Crèche available and breastfeeding welcome. Nappy changing facilities. Good access, all on one level. Free car parking. Play area for older children to the rear of building.

Lasswade High School Centre
Eskdale Drive
Bonnyrigg, Midlothian EH19 2LA
Tel: 663 7171 (Main Office)
Tel: 663 8170 (Community Education)
Tel: 660 1933 (Sports Centre)

Facilities include main sports hall, 2 squash courts, weight training room, fitness suite, activities studio, gymnasium, lounge, cafeteria, outdoor facilities, indoor football and rugby. Also a variety of daytime/evening classes for adults.

Kiddie Trampers and Kiddie Kartwheels are available for ages 21/2-5 years. Crèche morning sessions Mon-Fri 9.00-12.00; afternoon sessions 13.00-15.00/15.45; staffed by qualified nursery nurses, £1.20/session.
Shoppers' Crèche available at a higher cost of £2.30. Book 7 days in advance from 9.00 am daily.

Leith Victoria Swim Centre
Junction Place EH6 5JA
Tel: 555 4728

Swimming pool, sauna, pulse centre, fitness programme including women only sessions, beauty therapy and a variety of relaxation classes. Hot and cold vending machines. Crèche available Mon-Fri 9.00-12.00 (phone to book). Car parking, including disabled parking, at Bonnington Rd entrance. Lift available with disabled access to pool and Pulse Centre. Full details of current hours and programme of events available from reception.

Leith Waterworld
337 Easter Road EH6 8HU
Tel: 555 6000

Adult aqua fit classes Fri 11.15-12.00; £2.00/class
Parent and toddlers classes Fri 10.15-11.00 ; £2.60/class

Loanhead Leisure Centre
George Avenue
Loanhead EH20 9LA
Tel: 440 4516

This modern leisure centre has a swimming pool, fitness suite, exercise studio and outdoor 5-a-side and tennis courts. Contact centre for details of exercise classes and other activities. Crèche facilities available.

Meadowbank Sports Centre
139 London Road EH7 6AE
Tel: 661 5351

Opening times: Mon 9.30-22.30 (last booking 21.30), Tue-Sun 9.00-22.30.
Excellent centre on 3 floors. Facilities for over 30 sports including badminton, squash, yoga, aerobics, step, fitness centre and running track. Ramped access and automatic doors wide enough for a double pushchair. Lift for disabled centre users and parents with small children. Full programme available from centre.

Musselburgh Sports Centre
Newbigging
Musselburgh EH21 7AS
Tel: 653 6367

Modern leisure centre offering squash, multi-purpose sports hall, bodyworks gym, meeting room, dance studio and lounge area, plus swimming pool, health suite with sauna, steam room, spa and café. Wide range of activities, including: hockey, volleyball, badminton, squash, table tennis, basketball, trampolining, and judo. Fitness classes include step, aerobics, aquafit and body conditioning. Programme available from centre.

Crèche coincides with step and aerobic classes, although parents can use any facilities at these times. Advisable to book up to 7 days in advance.

Portobello Indoor Bowls and Leisure Centre
20 Westbank Street
Portobello EH15 1DR
Tel: 669 0878
Winter: indoor bowls and fitness classes. Adults' and children's classes in a wide range of activities.
Summer: indoor bowling and a wide range of activities for adults and children. Good access, with lift to first floor. Nappy changing facilities. Catering -contact centre for function / bar / cafeteria details.

Portobello Swim Centre
57 The Promenade
Portobello EH15 2BS
Tel: 669 6888
Wide range of facilities, including Turkish baths. Also pulse centre with cardiovascular and resistance equipment. Make an appointment for induction. Alternatively, you can just go for a swim. Aquafit ante /postnatal classes. Pay as you go swim lessons for adults. Cafe on 1st floor, accessible by lift.
Crèche (0-5 yrs), Mon-Fri 9.00-12.00. Cost £3 (non-leisure cardholders and £2 Leisure Access Cardholders). Always 2 experienced crèche workers on duty. During crèche times, centre offers adult swimming classes for all abilities and fitness classes (including step and aerobics) for men and women in the fitness centre.

Queensferry High Recreation Centre
30 Ashburnham Road
S Queensferry EH30 9JN
Tel: 319 3222
Opening times: Mon-Thu 16.30-22.00; Fri 16.00-22.00; Sat 10.00-17.00; Sun 9.00-17.00. For opening hours during school holidays, please contact centre.
Casual bookings welcomed for badminton, table tennis, 5-a-side football, basketball, short tennis, pool and Pulse

Centre. Adult coaching lessons in swimming, aquafit, aerobics, step, fitness training, subaqua and badminton. Contact centre for details of times, prices and booking information.
Children's activities include swimming lessons, tots tennis, short tennis, holiday activity camps. See also Birthdays & Celebrations.

Ratho Community Centre
1 School Wynd
Ratho EH28 8TT
Contact: Dave Stewart
Tel: 333 1055
Keep-fit, Fri 9.30-11.00. £2.50/session. Crèche (under 5s) £1/child or £1.50 for 2 or more. Staffed by the appropriate no. of crèche workers. Coffee bar facilities available.

Royal Commonwealth Pool
21 Dalkeith Road EH16 5BB
Tel: 667 7211
The pool offers a wide range of activities/swimming sessions with something to suit all the family. Programme available from centre. Crèche (5 and under); Leisure Cardholder £2, non-holder £3. (Mon-Fri 9.00-12.00). Two experienced crèche workers on duty at all times. Can be booked in advance if you are attending a course of activity/swimming lessons.
You can also use the crèche, if there are spaces available, when using pool or fitness room. See Activities for Children for full entry.

Saughton Sports Complex
Stevenson Drive, Balgreen EH11 3HB
Tel: 444 0422
Sports complex with outdoor facilities for football, 5-a-side football, tennis, hockey and running track with floodlights; run in safety and meet new training partners. Suitable for all levels and supervised by a qualified coach. Small pulse gym.

Warrender Swim Centre
Thirlestane Road
Marchmont EH9 1AP
Tel: 447 0052
Full range of classes available including aquafit, antenatal, parent and child. Masters swimming lessons also available. Sauna. Yoga classes, Pulse Fitness Suite with full range of resistance and cardiovascular fitness equipment. Full programme available from centre. No crèche facilities.

Wester Hailes Education Centre
5 Murrayburn Drive
Edinburgh EH14 2SU
Tel: 442 2201
This community leisure centre offers a programme of aerobics, aquafit and other activity classes for adults. Women-only swimming on Wednesday evenings. Crèche available (only open term times, not open in the evening). Phone for details.

YOGA

Aditi Yoga Centre
5 Alva Street (1st floor)
EH2 4PH
Tel: 226 2601
Email: info@aditiyogacentre.com
Web: www.aditiyogacentre.com
Please contact centre for current costs for all classes

Prenatal Yoga
Mon 16.15-17.15, Tue 19.15-20.15, Wed 18.00-19.00, Thu 16.15-17.15. Emphasis on breathing and relaxation, and preparing the body and mind for labour.

Postnatal Yoga
Wed 10.30-11.30. Classes can be attended as soon as 4-6 weeks after birth. Classes promote good posture and specifically focus on regaining physical strength, suppleness and tone in the neck, shoulders, abdominal, low back and pelvic areas. Breathing and relaxation techniques also taught.

Astanga Yoga Centre
25 Rodney Street
EH7 4EL
Tel:558 3334
Fax: 558 3830
Email: reception@astanga yogacentre.com
Web: www.astangayogacentre.com

Pregnancy Yoga
Mon, Wed 17.00-18.00. Classes welcome complete beginners to those women who are experienced in yoga. The emphasis is on gentle postures, breathing and relaxation. While the classes may benefit post-natal women, no babies can be brought to the classes.

Annual Events

ANNUAL EVENTS

There are some events which you only have one chance a year to enjoy – some have a long history, others are more recently established events; some can provide a whole day's worth of entertainment, others can help pass a pleasant hour or so.

To help you plan ahead, we've divided the list into monthly sections, and then, if relevant, into those events which are 'in the city', 'close to home', and 'further afield'.

For more information, why not go online – the following sites may prove helpful:

www.edinburgh.org
www.edinburgh-festivals.com
www.eventful-edinburgh.com

JANUARY- MARCH

The start of the year can be a bit of an anti-climax: Christmas is over, the lights are down in the city and the outlook – and the weather - can seem a bit bleak. However, there are events and attractions to go and see …

IN THE CITY

Pantomimes and Plays

The panto season extends through the Winter season. If you are thinking about going to one, why not consider waiting until after Christmas, otherwise the outing might just become part of the exciting blur leading up to Santa's visit. while venues such as the King's Theatre and the Playhouse stage traditional pantos, other theatres such as the Royal Lyceum, North Edinburgh Arts Centre, Theatre Workshop and the Netherbow have offered more contemporary – or certainly less traditional shows – in past years.

Although many of the pantos have famous names heading the bill, they tend to appeal to an older audience and they far too long for many under fives. Plus remember that the jokes tend to become more adult in the evening performances!

Probably more suitable for under 5s are shows such as those from The Singing Kettle: www.singingkettle.com or another form of children's show.

See press or go online for tour and performance information.

CLOSE TO HOME

Snowdrops at Dalmeny House
Dalmeny House
South Queensferry EH30 9TQ
Tel: 331 1888
Web: www.dalmeny.co.uk

Still in private ownership, Dalmeny house is only open for 3 afternoons a week in July and August. However, the gardens are opened specially on a Sun during Feb/Mar for 'Snowdrop Day' – the exact date depends on when the snowdrops come out!

Impressive display on Mons Hill. Backpacks, wellies and warm socks recommended. Refreshments available in the tearoom.

This is a charity event and all funds raised benefit St Columba's Hospice, The Queen's Nursing Institute of Scotland and The Garden Fund of the National Trust for Scotland. Try going online for current information.

Almond Valley Heritage Centre
Millfield
Livingston Village
Tel: 01506 414957
Web: www.almondvalley.co.uk

February events. There's usually some kind of family discovery session on offer over February. It may be 'Nasty Niffs', it may be something else, but older under 5s may enjoy it – as may parents, grandparents etc. Check website, or call, for current information.

See Where Shall We Go Today - Farms, Zoos & Animal Parks for more details

EASTER EVENTS & EASTER BREAK LEISURE SCHEMES

IN THE CITY

Easter Event
Historic Scotland Ranger Service
Holyrood Park Education Centre
1 Queen's Drive Edinburgh EH8 8HG
Tel: 652 8150

The Ranger Service organises an Easter event within the bounds of Holyrood Park. A family-orientated event, there is usually something of interest for under 5s, such as a teddy bears picnic.

Information is available from the ranger service (Tel. no. above) or on information boards in the park.

Easter Festival
Princes Street Gardens
Web: ww.edinburgheaster.co.uk

Easter weekend. A festival which includes events such as a street cavalcade, an Easter egg hunt, open-air concerts, the chance to try out some circus skills and face painting. Toilet facilities in Princes Street Gardens.

Craiglockhart Tennis & Sports Centre
177 Colinton Road EH14 1BZ
Tel: 443 0101

Tots tennis (3-5 yrs) £6.50/4 days. During Easter holidays. Booking essential.

Currie and Balerno Community Schools Partnership
Tel: 477 7733
Contact: Vivienne Mackay, Community Manager

Offers several programmes, usually for 3-4 yr olds and 4yrs–immediate pre-school aged children. For the younger age range, the programme usually incorporates early learning skills in a range of creative and physical activities; for older children, there is a variety of fun, educational and recreational activities for children about to start primary school in the Autumn of the current year. Mid-morning juice and biscuits are included in course fees.
It is recommended that all children wear old clothes in case of paint spillage etc. All children must be toilet trained.
Also pre-school swimming classes for children who will be starting primary school in the Autumn of the current year. Parents are not required to be in the pool.
Booking recommended, although activities may also be booked on a daily basis.

Edinburgh Zoo – Easter Treasure Trail
134 Corstorphine Road EH12 6TS
Tel: 334 9171
Web: edinburghzoo.org.uk

Easter Sunday, Monday. Two age groups: 7 and under, 8 and over. 'Follow the animal clues and find a chocolate surprise'. No extra charge. No booking necessary. Zoo holds other special events on a daily basis during school holidays, such as brass rubbing, touch tables and information talks.

St Bride's Centre
10 Orwell Terrace EH11 2DZ
Tel: 346 1405

Contact centre for current information regarding Easter children's programmes. Events are usually run for children aged 4+ years

CLOSE TO HOME

Almond Valley Heritage Centre
Easter 'Eggcitement'
Livingston Village
Tel: 01506 414957
Web: www.almondvalley.co.uk

During a fortnight over Easter, 10.00-17.00.
Lambs, chicks and other baby animals to see; egg painting, bonnet making and an Easter Trail. Standard admission charges apply (see Animal Parks, Farm Parks & Zoos).

Bo'ness and Kinneil Railway
Easter Egg Specials
Tel: 01506 822298
Tel: 01506 824356 for information on this special event
Web: www.srps.org.uk

From Edinburgh, travel along the M9, leave at J3 and follow the A904 to Bo'ness. The railway is situated near the town centre, behind Tesco's car park.
Easter w/end, Fri-Mon, 7 journeys per day, starting at 10.30. Last train 16.30
This event has slight variation each year, but includes the likes of face painting, children's entertainment, a colouring competition, a hunt-the-easter-egg game and an easter bonnet competition. During the train ride, the Easter Bunny distributes eggs. Charges vary from usual rates – adult/ child c. £7, under 2s free; family saver (4 seats) ticket usually available c. £25. Phone to check if advance bookings are being taken.

FURTHER AFIELD

Traquair House – Easter Egg Extravaganza
Innerleithen EH44 6PW
Tel: 01896 830323
Web: www.traquair.co.uk
Email: enquiries@traquair.co.uk
Easter Sunday, 13.30 onwards.
Over 6000 mini eggs hidden in the maze for under 10s to

hunt out and eat! The house usually organises three egg hunts: one for under 5s, one for 5-6 yr olds and the last for 7-9 yrs. Other entertainment also available, which varies from year to year, but usually includes the likes of a bouncy castle and face painting. Ground admission charges apply. Refreshments available from the house's restaurant. Please check current year's start times.

New Lanark Visitor Centre – Easter Fun
New Lanark, by Lanark
Tel: 0155 566 1345
Email: trust@newlanark.org
Easter Sunday and Monday 12.00-16.00. Activities usually include a treasure trail and Easter Bunnies distributing eggs around the centre.

APRIL – MAY

IN THE CITY

Edinburgh International Science Festival
Web: www.sciencefestival.co.uk
This is the largest science festival in the world. Various venues throughout the city, including the Science Play Centre at the Assembly Rooms. Programme becomes available at the beginning of March. Events for all ages from 3yrs upwards. Although the programme always looks as if there's loads for younger children, there is much, much more for 5+yrs, and while these children might have loads to do, you might find yourself (plus an under 5) pacing around waiting – or standing in long queues: forwarned is forearmed! Pay on the door events may also charge additional fees for specific attractions.
See programme for details of shows - pick one up from bookshops throughout the city or from The Hub, tel: 473 2070. Best to book well in advance.

NCT SALES
NCT Centre
University Health Service
5th Floor
5 Bristo Square EH3 9AL
Tel: 668 3257
Web: nct-edinburgh.freeserve.co.uk
Edinburgh North and South Branches hold annual sales of nearly new nursery equipment, children's and maternity clothes and toys. A small percentage from the sale goes to NCT funds, the rest to the seller. First sale of the year is usually in Spring and sales are held approximately 8 times a year. Venues vary. Contact the NCT centre, or see local press for details.

Balerno Children's Gala
Tel: 449 3847
Contact: Mr D Donaldson
Last week in May. Week starts with a procession of floats and crowning of the Gala Queen. Many events held around the village during the week leading up to the gala day, including bike races for all ages and a pet show. There are children's races, bouncy castles, a disco magic and puppet shows and many stalls representing local clubs on the day. 13.00-17.00 in Malleny Park (or the High school, if raining).

Lauriston Castle
Lauriston Castle grounds,
2 Cramond Road South EH4 1AB
Tel: 336 2060
Lauriston Castle hosts a series of Summer events. To keep everything dynamic, the programme usually changes from year to year, so contact Castle for information. However, for the last few years, they have hosted a teddy bears picnic every second year: next one due 2007. Usual charges for castle itself.

Scottish International Children's Festival
Imaginate
45a George Street
Edinburgh EH2 2HT
Tel: 225 8050
Web: www.imaginate.org.uk
Held at various venues around the city for one week (Mon-Sun) May/June. This is Britain's largest performing arts festival for children. Aimed specifically at 3-14yrs, with weekend afternoon shows programmed so that the majority of the family can be catered for ie. a show for ages 3-6yrs will run simultaneously with one for, say, 5-12yrs. Venues are chosen for child friendliness. Venue cafés provide child orientated menus during festival run. Free crèche for under fives – book your place(s) when you book a performance; details of crèche available on booking. Programmes available beginning of April, or check online.

CLOSE TO HOME

Bo'ness and Kinneil Railway
Day Out with Thomas
Tel: 01506 822298
Tel: 01506 824356 for information on this special event.
Web: www.srps.org.uk
From Edinburgh, travel along the M9, leave at J3 and follow the A904 to Bo'ness. The railway is situated near the town centre, behind Tesco's car park.

Over a long weekend in mid-May. First train leaves at 10.30, last train leaves at 16.30. Engines wear a 'Thomas' type face. There's a bouncy castle, a children's roundabout, face painting, an inflatable slide – and the Fat Controller is usually around just to keep everyone on their best behaviour! There's no advance booking so it's probably best to get there early. Adult/child c.£7; under 2s free; family ticket (4 seats) c.£25.

FURTHER AFIELD

Links Market
Town House, Kirkcaldy
Contact: John Haggart
Tel. 01592 417843
Web: www.fifedirect.org.uk (look under 'Leisure')
Kirkcaldy Esplanade. This historic fair lasts 6 days, starting on Wed before 3rd Fri in April. Reputedly the longest street funfair in Europe - perhaps in the world, and April 2004 saw its 700th anniversary. Expect attractions along the lines of Mediaeval, craft or farmers' markets, stalls, a funfair, and falconry displays. Numerous rides and stalls for under 5s. Wed from 14.30, Thu-Mon from 13.00. Well worth the 40 min drive across the Forth Bridge. Trains from Waverley and Haymarket.

Summerlea Heritage Park
Spring Fling
Coatbridge
Tel: 01236 431261
3 day festival for children on May Bank Holiday w/end. Free entry.

JUNE – JULY

IN THE CITY

Currie and Balerno Community Schools Partnership
Contact: Vivienne Mackay, Community Manager
Tel: 477 7733
Summer break programmes for toddlers through to pre-school age. Also offer swimming classes. See 'Easter' entry for full information.

Edinburgh Zoo
134 Corstorphne Road EH12 6TS
Tel: 334 9171
Web: edinburghzoo.org.uk
Special events throughout the Summer. Check the zoo's website for up-to-date details.

Royal Highland Show
Royal Highland Centre, Ingliston
Edinburgh EH28 8NF
Tel: 335 6200
Web: www.royalhighlandshow.org.uk
Thu-Sun 3rd week in June.
Showground open 8.00-20.00 Thu-Sat, 8.00-19.00 Sun.
Approximate admission prices: £18 for adults (£13 student/ senior citizens concessions). Discounts available on advance bookings – see details online. Accompanied children under the age of 16 free. Reduced prices after 16.00. Disabled visitors are not given concessionary rates but their carer receives free entry.. Car parking is around £5 per vehicle per admission.
Lothian Regional Transport usually operate a special bus service (no 98) for the four days of the show. Picks up/ drops off at the East Gate entrance to the showground. (phone Traveline for details: 225 3858)
There's a huge range of attractions available within the showground and the show does offer specific activities etc especially for children, although the very size of the place might be a little overwhelming for them at first. It makes no difference to children that the cattle, sheep, horses, poultry etc are the country's finest – it's fun just to see them up close! Each year there are unique attractions, so the show has an individual input every year. There's also usually an indoor activity centre, where children can try the likes of seed planting, willow weaving, food science activities, design and technology challenges, healthy eating

activities and so on – some activities may be attractive to under 5s.

The show has a crèche with registered staff, and also provides a breastfeeding area, along with bottle warming facilities.

St Bride's Centre
10 Orwell Terrace EH11 2DZ
Tel: 346 1405

Contact centre for current information regarding children's Summer programmes. Events are usually run for children aged 4+ years.

CLOSE TO HOME

Lifeboat Week
Contact: North Berwick Tourist Information
Tel: 01620 892197

Take A198 to N Berwick. Regular bus and train services. North Berwick, last week in July. All kinds of fundraising.

Museum of Flight
East Fortune Airfield, East Lothian
Tel: 01620 880308
Web: www.nms.ac.uk/flight

There's usually a festival of flight show in mid-July, with rare/vintage planes, flypasts etc – spectacular events for anyone interested in aviation. July plays host to Scotland's largest civil air show with fantastic air displays. Recent inclusions included an evening event with flights choreographed to music. Peripheral attractions usually include stalls, bouncy castle, refreshments etc. The museum recommends ear plugs for young children. Only guide/hearing dogs permitted entry.

Ticketed events, expect to pay around £12/adult. A family ticket (2A + 3C) costs approx £34. Under 5s free. Discounts available on advance online bookings and for NMS members.

In general, the Museum of Flight has ample car parking facilities. There are nappy changing facilities in the toilet facilities for the disabled visitors. The Aviator café offers a range of fresh snacks and light bites.

Hopetoun House
The Hopetoun Summer Fair
South Queensferry
Tel: 331 2451
Web: www.hopetounhouse.com

Last Sunday in July, 11.00-17.00.

Admission (these prices are approximate): Adult £6, child £4 (under 5s free) family £18.

The stately home's major fundraising event aimed at families. The event is hosted on the house's West Lawn. Attractions include crafts marquees, environmental themed demonstrations and an arena programme.

Queensferry High Recreation Centre
30 Ashburnham Road
S Queensferry EH30 9JN
Tel: 319 3222

Centre runs holiday activity camps. Contact venue for details.

GALAS/FESTIVALS

Many local Galas that are held in the city and the Lothians take place in June. These may be the principal annual event that annually draws a community together and they are well worth supporting – although due to changing local demographics, insurance requirements, and funding difficulties many are finding it hard to continue. We have listed just a few of them.

Clermiston and Drumbrae Children's Gala
Contact: Karen Keil (chairperson of committee)
Tel: 339 4149

Location: Drum Brae Leisure Centre. Usually held on the 2nd Sat in June. Attractions and events usually include a parade, a fun fair, magicians, clowns etc. Day finishes with a children's disco.

Corstorphine Fair
Contact: Corstorphine Fair Committee
c/o 178/2 South Gyle Wynd
Edinburgh EH12 9HN
Email: corsfair@hotmail.com
Web: www.corstorphinefair.org.uk

Main location: St Margaret's Park. Biennial event on 1st Sat in June - due 2006/2008. A large, extremely well-supported community event with many stalls and attractions such as a bouncy castle, pony rides, face painting, funfair rides, puppets, dancers and displays, plus a handy NCT feeding and changing tent. The celebrations last around a week and include a duck race event on the days running up to the fair day itself.

Davidson's Mains Gala Day

Contact: Susan Robertson (committee chairperson)
Tel: 336 2572
Web: www.dmainsgala.org.uk
Location: Lauriston Castle grounds. 3rd Sat in June. A traditional gala, complete with a parade along Davidson's Mains Main Street, leaving the War memorial at 11.30, with the Gala Queen-elect riding in a horse-drawn carriage. After the Queen's crowning there's plenty of family orientated entertainment laid on, including pony rides, a bouncy castle, 'Thomas' rides, children's races and many stalls. There are also events in the week running up to the Gala Day.

Gorgie Dalry Gala Day

Tel: 337 3252 (community centre)
Contact: Jim Young
Murieston Park. 2nd w/end in June, Sat 12.00-16.00. Puppet shows, children's entertainers, clowns, theatre for children and many shows free.

Kirkliston Gala

Contact: Leisure Centre
Tel: 333 4700
Kirkliston Leisure Centre. 2nd Sat in June. Parade through village. Displays, bands, model railway and races.

Leith Festival

Web: www.leithfestival.com

Leith Festival is a Community Festival for the people of Leith and North Edinburgh. The festival runs from Sun-Sat at the beginning of June.
In recent years the Festival has grown and now offers something for the under-fives throughout the week, mostly during the day, in various venues in Leith. You can find out more about the festival by listening to Leith FM, the Festival's own radio station which broadcasts on 87.7fm during the festival week (subject to licence). The Festival ends with a walking parade down Leith Walk commencing at noon. The parade finishes at Leith Links with a traditional gala day with stalls, funfair, hot air balloon, football competitions, a tug of war and live music.
Look out for the programme usually published just after Easter or go online.

Meadows Festival

Contact: Meadows Festival Association
PO Box 1053
Edinburgh EH7 5YA
Tel/fax: 620 9108 (24 hrs)

Sat and Sun beginning June. A popular festival, with stalls, funfair, puppets, children's competitions, face painting, live music etc. Free crèche. Feeding / changing tent run by NCT. This is a long-running event but various set-backs always seem to threaten its ongoing existence.

Stockbridge Festival

Over a week of events at end of June. Street party in St Stephen St all day Sat. On Sun at 15.00 the famous duck race takes place – ducks are launched off the bridge across the river – stand down on the river path beside Pizza Express to get a close-up view! Ducks for sale in the previous weeks in local shops such as Stockbridge Bookshop and the Baillie pub. Events during the preceding week such as quizzes, fun fair in Inverleith Park etc.

CLOSE TO HOME

Bo'ness Fair Day

Take M9 out of Edinburgh. Come off at J3 and follow the signs to Bo'ness on the A904. Alternatively, take A90 out of Edinburgh, then follow the A904 out through Newton to Champany Corner on the A904. Turn right and follow the road to Bo'ness.
2nd Fri in July. Reputedly the largest fair in the UK. Extremely well supported and a good example of a traditional 'Fair-day'. It's worthwhile taking a trip through prior to the actual fair, to see the impressive house frontages which decorate the homes of the children involved. The Queen is chosen from one of the town's schools, so the focus is on a different part of the town each year.

AUGUST – SEPTEMBER

August is Edinburgh's busiest month of the year, as people from all over the world descend upon the city for the Edinburgh International Festival and the Fringe. The city's population is said to double in August.

There are breathtaking numbers of official events – and almost the same amount of street entertainers, although licensing is reducing their numbers year on year. Free snippets of acts can be seen on the main stage in Princes Street gardens during the day and evening. So hold on to your toddler, turn up and enjoy yourselves!

IN THE CITY

Edinburgh Fringe
180 High Street EH1 1QS
Contact: Fringe Office
Tel: 226 0026
Email: admin@edfringe.com
Web: www.edfringe.com
Cited in the Guinness Book of Records as the largest Arts Festival in the world! A myriad of events, such as puppet shows, magic, drama and music at venues throughout the city. The programme lists events by age group. Programme free from the Fringe Office and other venues round the city - bookshops are the best bet for picking one up.

Fringe Sunday
180 High Street EH1 1QS
Contact: Fringe Office
Tel: 226 0026
Email: admin@edfringe.com
Web: www.edfringe.com
Location: The Meadows. 2nd Sun of Festival 11.00-17.00. This is an exuberant melange of what's on offer throughout the Fringe: it's bright, loud and tends to reflect the essence of what the Fringe is about. It's also extremely busy, so hold on to small hands! There is normally a handy NCT feeding and changing tent.

Edinburgh International Book Festival
Scottish Book Centre
137 Dundee Street Edinburgh EH11 1BG.
Tel: 228 5444
Tel: 624 5050 (box office)
Email: admin@edbookfest.co.uk
Web: www.edbookfest.co.uk

Location: Charlotte Square. Mid Aug. 9.30-21.30 daily. Europe's largest book event. Plenty for children of all ages, including events especially for 0-5s. There's a dedicated Children's Bookshop, workshops, storytelling from favourite authors, demonstrations from illustrators and even visits by well loved characters. Tickets can be booked in advance or on the day, but popular events do sell out very quickly. Some events are free. Several cafés on site, as well as the ice cream trike. Log on to the website, where there's specific info about the Children's Book Festival.

Edinburgh International Festival
The Hub,
Castlehill, Royal Mile EH1 2NE
Tel: 473 2015 (the Hub)
Tel: 473 2001 (information line)
Web: www.eif.co.uk
Held in venues throughout the city. The reputation has taken Edinburgh's name to all parts of the globe. Events include theatre, puppet shows, dance, opera and music – some shows may be suitable for under 5s, it all depends on the programme. Full programme available from end of March onwards – again, check your nearest bookshop for a copy. What might be of more interest is the Fireworks Concert, held at the end of the Festival (see below).

Festival Cavalcade
Procession of floats, pipe bands, members of Tattoo etc on 1st Sun of festival. Starts at Waterloo Pl at around 14.30, proceeds along Princes St and arrives at the Grassmarket at approx 16.00. Very popular, so arrive early to secure good viewpoint. May be a little long and loud for some under 5s. See local press for information.

Festival Fireworks
A spectacular farewell to the Festival! Music, 'son et lumière' fireworks display free to the public. The castle and the castle rock provide a dramatic backdrop. For a seat at the concert performed by the Chamber Orchestra in Princes St Gardens, book very early at The Hub (it's done by postal ballot and the closing date is in May). Small children may be wary of the loud noise and the crowds, which can be very heavy around Princes St, George St and The Mound. Quieter locations, still with great views, are around Bruntsfield Links and Inverleith Park - take a radio as at least one local station has coverage - so you can hear the music while watching.

Edinburgh Mela

Contact: The Arts Quarter
Gateway Theatre, Elm Row
Edinburgh EH7 4AH
Tel: 557 1400
Email: info@edinburgh-mela.co.uk
Web: www.edinburgh-mela.co.uk
Location: Pilrig Park. Last weekend in Aug / 1st weekend in Sept. The Edinburgh Mela is a long established celebration of multiculturalism. The park is transformed with stalls, sculptures and artworks. Music, puppet shows and performers. Children's workshops vary each year, but they are mostly best suited to older children. The fun is for all the family however and most events are free. Other events around city in week running up to w/end. For information, try going online.

Edinburgh Military Tattoo

Tattoo Office, 32 Market Street
Edinburgh EH1 1QB
Tel: 8707 555 118 (Box Office)
Fax: 225 8627
Email: edintattoo@edintattoo.co.uk
Web: www.edinburgh-tattoo.co.uk
Location: Edinburgh Castle Esplanade. First 3 wks in Aug. Famous event including pipes, drums and massed bands, as well as international music, theatre and dance. There's a different theme each year. Performances start late; Mon-Fri 21.00, Sat 22.30, but there's additional early shows on Sat at 19.30 (book early as it's very popular). Quite ambitious event to take under 5s to, due to the length of show and the bangs and crashes that can be part of the displays, but they go free if they sit on an adult's knee. Seating is hard and can be cold – take a cushion along! Tickets half-price at dress rehearsal. Blankets and refreshments advised.

NCT Sponsored Toddle

NCT Centre
University Health Service
5th Floor
5 Bristo Square EH3 9AL
Tel: 668 3257
Web: nct-edinburgh.freeserve.co.uk
A fun event for families with pre-school children, to raise funds for Edinburgh NCT.

CLOSE TO HOME

Almond Valley Heritage Centre

Millfield
Livingston Village
Tel: 01506 414957
Web: www.almondvalley.co.uk
'Yesterday's Harvest'. Last Sun in Aug. 10.00-17.00. See how the harvest used to be gathered, as some of the old machinery is dusted off and put to work. Join in with tattie howkin and stookin hay. You can try making your own corn dollies ... rolling in the haystacks available too!
'Railway Shuntabout', last weekend in Aug. See the special trains on the narrow-gauge railway and keep your eyes peeled for some of the centre's more unusual engines.

Bo'ness and Kinneil Railway

Day Out with Thomas
Tel: 01506 822298
Web: www.srps.org.uk
Fri, Sat and Sun in Aug. Fares as in May entry. Contact Scottish Railway Preservation Society for exact dates.

Vogrie Festival Day

Contact: Yvonne Anderson
Tel: 271 3353
Located on the B6372 between Pathhead and Gorebridge.
Vogrie Country Park. 2nd Sun in Aug. 11.00-17.00. Large event throughout grounds includes puppet shows, magicians, music, model railway, funfair and much more! Phone for current entrance prices.

FURTHER AFIELD

Traquair Fair

Traquair House
Innerleithen EH44 6PW
Tel: 01896 830323
Email: enquiries@traquair.co.uk
Web: www.traquair.co.uk
1st weekend in Aug. Entertainment for all the family. Recently, themed fairs have opened up new dimension to this well-established event. Entertainment on offer includes the likes of theatre, live music, street entertainers, clowns, workshops, crafts etc. Children's entertainment includes well known children's musicians (the likes of Mr Boom, Jo Jingles etc), magicians, face painting, art workshops, a mini

train, swing boats and so on. Special entrance prices for this weekend. Expect to pay in the region of £14/adult, £8/child. £38/family (2A & 3C). Under 5s free . Advance purchase discounts available.

OCTOBER – NOVEMBER

IN THE CITY

Scottish International Storytelling Festival
43-45 High Street EH1 1SR
Contact: The Netherbow
Tel: 557 5724
Fax: 557 5224
Email: scottishstorytellingcentre@uk.uumail.com
Web: scottishstorytellingcentre.co.uk
Various venues throughout the Lothians, end Oct-mid Nov. A two week feast of storytelling from the oral tradition for all the family. Booking essential.

Fireworks Extravaganza
Meadowbank Sports Centre
139, London Rd, Edinburgh, EH7 6AE
Tel: 661 5351

Large well organised display on 5 Nov , which is usually enjoyed by a capacity audience. Popular with an older audience but may prove a bit overwhelming for under 5s. Charges apply – expect to pay around £4-£5 dependent on whether you want to stand in the grounds or sit in the stands.
Smaller fireworks displays organised by local Scout or Round Table groups are advertised locally. See press for details. For information on firework displays, phone City of Edinburgh Council Recreation Dept, tel: 529 7844.

CLOSE TO HOME

Almond Valley Heritage Centre
Spooky Happenings
Tel: 01506 414957
Web: www.almondvalley.co.uk
Runs for 2 weeks during Oct. Open 18.00-21.00 on Hallowe'en. Special events include ghost hunts, a 'trail of terror', monster masks makes, and other Hallowe'en horrors. Certain to scare the adults! Standard admission charges.

Bo'ness & Kinneil Railway
Wizards and Witches Rides
Tel: 01506 822298
Web: www.srps.org.uk
The weekend nearest Hallowe'en. £7 per person. Children under 2 free. Family ticket (4 seats) £25. Trains run from 10.30 and run every hour until 16.30. Enjoy (or otherwise!) a train ride, complete with a visit to the Witches' Cavern. There's also a magic show, and prizes awarded throughout the weekend for the best fancy dress. Check whether advance bookings are being taken.

FURTHER AFIELD

Traquair Christmas Fair
Traquair House, Innerleithen,
Peeblesshire, EH44 6PW
Tel: 01896 830323
Email: enquiries@traquair.co.uk
Web: www.traquair.co.uk
Last Sat & Sun in Nov.
An opportunity to combine Christmas shopping with a day out (if you are so inclined!). Santa usually has a presence here, and there are other attractions for children such as a puppet show. Ease yourself into the festive shopping spree, with a mooch around craft stalls and some mulled wine. Free entry to the house and grounds. For information, contact Traquair house.

DECEMBER

IN THE CITY

Edinburgh's Capital Christmas
Tel: 529 4310
Web: www.capitalchristmas.co.uk
End of Nov-24 Dec. A varied programme of street theatre, a parade, shopping opportunities in the themed Christmas market in Princes Street Gardens, and perhaps best of all for under 5s, the switching on of the Christmas lights. See local press near the time for details. The city's Hogmanay celebrations run-on almost seamlessly from this event (see 'After Christmas' section).

Edinburgh Zoo
134 Corstorphine Road EH1 6TS
Tel: 334 9171
Web: www.edinburghzoo.org.uk

Usually hosts a Santa weekend, the weekend before Christmas, with Santa roaming around the Zoo, 11.00-16.00. Children can get a gift from his sack for £1.However, it is not certain whether this weekend may run in future. Please check with the Zoo.

CLOSE TO HOME

Edinburgh Canal Centre – Santa Barge Trips
27 Baird Road, Ratho EH28 8RA
Tel: 333 1320
Email: info@bridgeinn.com
Web: www.bridgeinn.com
Santa Cruises run each weekend from the beginning of Dec until Christmas week when they become daily. Cruises are 1 hr long and times vary from early morning until evening. Santa comes on-board and and distributes gifts for the children: there are mince pies and coffee for parents so you don't feel too left out. Booking is essential! Cost: around £8.50

Almond Valley Heritage Centre
Santa Special Weekends
Livingston Village
Tel: 01506 414957
Web: www.almondvalley.co.uk
Four weekends prior to Christmas. Visit Santa's farmyard cottage, enjoy a nativity scene with the animals, and make traditional Christmas decorations. There are also narrow gauge railway trips to the 'North Pole'. Standard admission prices apply with extra charge for Santa visit.

Bo'ness and Kinneil Railway
Santa Steam Trains
Tel: 01506 822298
Web: www.srps.org.uk
Four weekends leading up to Christmas. Sat and Sun 10.30; 12.00; 13.30; 15.00. Santa visits each child with a gift during the 50 min journey,. Tea/coffee and mince pies for adults, fruit for children. Trains are well decorated and friendly staff lead the festive singing. An enjoyable outing for all. Booking essential. Contact railway for prices.

AFTER CHRISTMAS

Edinburgh's Hogmanay
Email: hogmanay@edinburgh.gov.uk
Web: www.edinburghshogmanay.org
Venues all over the city centre. 29th Dec-4th Jan. This event has become Britain's biggest (and busiest!) street party. Includes a carnival and funfair and other indoor and outdoor events, some ticketed and some free. There's also the torchlight procession, kids' Hogmanay, a food fair and live music. Events around Princes St and the High St on Hogmanay can be extremely crowded, require street passes (which are in limited number), and would probably prove overwhelming for an under 5.

Sled Dogs
Holyrood Park
1 Jan. Afternoon. Wrap up warmly and take a trip to Holyrood Park where you can watch sled dog racing. The dogs themselves seem very attractive to young children – maybe it's because of their eyes – many have blue or mis-matched ones. The races are for fun, and there's a relaxed, friendly atmosphere.

dreamy

Birthdays & Celebrations

BIRTHDAYS & CELEBRATIONS

POINTS OF INTEREST

Parties whether at home, in a local church hall or at an all-inclusive venue do need some forward planning and if you need to book a venue, most places recommend doing this at least 8 weeks in advance.

Many church halls, public halls, schools, community centres and sports clubs will hire out their premises for an afternoon. Remember weekends tend to be busier.

Soft play centres also offer birthday packages, often with use of a party area: the actual soft play structures are usually open to everyone. However, some do offer times when you can book the soft play for your party's exclusive use for an extra cost.

Younger children may be quite frightened if it is too crowded, especially in the more energetic venues.

We have listed party venues, and also offered some ideas regarding party entertainers, products and services that might come in handy, whether you decide to host the party at home or in a venue.

Please note that there are many more party entertainers in and around Edinburgh than we have listed: some are so busy that they did not feel further note of their businesses was necessary, others did not respond.

PARTY VENUES

BOATS, CANALS & RIVERS

CLOSE TO HOME

The Children's Party Cruise
Edinburgh Canal Centre
The Bridge Inn, Ratho
Tel: 333 1320/1251
Email: info@bridgeinn.com
Web: www.bridgeinn.com

A children's party on board a cruising canal boat restaurant. A CD disco is provided just take your own CDs (a disco can be organised for extra cost). A video player is available at no extra cost and there is plenty of space to play. Bridge Inn can supply the food or you can bring your own. Min 20 people, max 36. A 2 hr cruise on the Union Canal costs £11/person.

CERAMIC CENTRES

IN THE CITY

The Ceramic Experience
Ocean Drive EH6 6JB
Tel: 554 4455
Email: edinburgh@theceramicexperience.com
Web: www.theceramicexperience.com
Each child paints an item which can be taken away on the day thus eliminating the need for a party bag. Alternatively the item can be fired and picked up a day or so later. Party lasts 1 1/2hr and includes a play in the soft play and ball pool. Venue can provide the birthday tea; just bring the cake. This package costs £5/child for food and starts from £4.99/child for item to be painted.

Doodles Ceramics Work Shop
29 Marchmont Crescent EH9 1HQ
Tel: 229 1399
Email: doodlescw@aol.com
Web: www.doodlesscotland.co.uk
Opening times: Tue-Thu 11.00-21.00, Fri, Sat 10.00-18.00, Sun 12.00-18.00
Doodles can cater for parties of any age group, from first birthdays (for example a plate with their foot print) and beyond. Max 25 children. Contact centre for prices.

DEDICATED VENUES & HALLS TO HIRE

IN THE CITY

The Fairy Shop
37-39 Morningside Road
Tel: 466 7474
Parties themed around the magical world of fairies and wizards. A fairy queen welcomes guests to one of the two party rooms (one large, one small depending on size of group). Parties last 1 1/2 hrs and include invitations, wizard and fairy costumes, games (with prizes), party tea and party bags; just take the cake. Party concludes with a fairy story and each child gets to make a magical wish. Staff include nursery nurses and trainee teachers. Suitable for 3-8 yrs. Min 10 and max 18 children. This package costs £7.99/child.

Play Action Team
Tel: 311 7073/7077
Octobus is a colourful, fun-filled play activity bus, available for private hire for events such as children's birthday

parties, fairs and gala days. Age and number restrictions apply and hire charges vary according to the event, location and day required.

St Ninian's Church Hall
St Ninian's Road, Corstorphine
Tel: 539 6204 (Tues-Fri 9am – noon)
Venue only. Large Hall with adjoining kitchen which can accommodate up to 30 children. £40 for 2 hour party. Included is _ hour for setup and _ hour for tidy up.

FURTHER AFIELD

Biggar Puppet Theatre
Puppet Tree House
Broughton Road
Biggar
Lanarkshire MI12 6HA
Tel: 01899 220631
Email: admin@purvespuppets.com
Web: www. purvespuppets.com
Special birthday party option is offered by this well-established company. Parties take place at 12.30, followed by a performance. Birthday tea is provided; just bring the cake. Invitations, balloons and a finger puppet for each guest are also provided. Min. 10 people but that can include the adults. This package costs £13/head.

FARMS, ZOOS, ANIMAL PARKS & SEALIFE CENTRES

IN THE CITY

Edinburgh Zoo
Tel: 314 0337(for party information)
Web: www.edinburghzoo.org.uk
Party lasts 2hrs and includes invitations, a mini tour of the zoo, games and crafts, birthday tea with personalised cake and party bags. Min 8 and max 24 children. 1 adult per 4 children is required to stay with party. This package costs £15/child.

Gorgie City Farm
51 Gorgie Road
Tel: 337 4202
Email: gorgiefarm@compuserve.com
The party includes a visit to see and feed animals, music and games, a birthday tea and for an additional charge,

pony rides around the farm (weather permitting). Please take appropriate clothing if weather is bad. Adult supervision is provided throughout the party and only 2 parents/carers are required to stay for the duration (due to lack of space in the party room). Balloons and party bags are also provided; just bring the cake. Min 10 and max 15 children. This package costs £6.50 or £7.50/child (dependent on menu option) with pony rides an additional £10 per party.

CLOSE TO HOME

Almond Valley Heritage Trust
Millfield
Livingston Village
Tel: 01506 414957
Web: www.almondvalley.co.uk
Special birthday party package includes admission to all features of Mill Farm and the Heritage Centre (include. free admission to all adults helping at the party), exclusive use of party room for 2 hrs (time to organise your own games too), your own tractor & trailer ride and an exclusive 1/2hr booked session in the soft play area. Traditional birthday tea is provided; just bring the cake. Vegetarian and special diets can be catered for. Disposable tableware, tooters, balloons and badges are also provided. Partygoers are welcome to stay on at the farm afterwards. Parents can buy teas/coffees in the café next door. Min 10 children. This package costs £5/child and £2.50/party bag.

FURTHER AFIELD

Deep Sea World
Battery Quarry
North Queensferry KY11 1JR
Tel: 01383 411880
Email: info@deepseaworld.com
Web: www.deepseaworld.com
The party includes a 1 hr guided tour of the centre with a dedicated party host, touching starfish and sea anemones in the rock pools with the divers, a journey along the world's longest underwater tunnel to view the sharks, fish, eels and the birthday board displaying the birthday child's name and age. Look out for the divers at feeding time. The last 1/2 hr is spent in the Lagoon café, with live appearance by Shaky the Shark, where there is a choice of hot or cold food and a surprise gift for the birthday child. All children are given face painting, floating balloons

and themed goodies. Remember to bring your own cake. This package costs £9.95/child (2 adults get in free, min 10 children). Members get a 10% discount.

Jedburgh Deer and Farm Park
Camptown
Jedburgh TD8 6PL
Tel: 01835 840364
Email: mervinslaw@ecosse.net
Website: www.aboutscotland.com/jedforest
Party includes entrance to the farm park and facilities, feeding the reindeers and a birthday tea; just bring the cake. This package costs £6.50/child.

SOFT PLAYS

IN THE CITY

Castle Gyle
Gyle Shopping Centre
Tel: 476 7766
Available: Mon-Sat 18.15-19.45, Sun 17.15-18.45
Party lasts 11/2 hrs. Large soft play, ball pool and slide; home corner, toys and games to suit different ages of children (ages 2-8 yrs accepted). The whole room can be booked for parties. Max 24 children. Either take your own food or order from Burger King. Room hire is £50 Mon-Thurs and £55 Fri-Sun.

Brewsters Parties
Brewsters
Newhaven Quay
Tel: 555 1570
Party lasts 1 1/2hrs and includes time in the soft play area, party games, choice of main course and juice, visit to the ice cream factory and a special birthday cake (for parties of more than 8). Invitations, balloons, goodie bags and thank you cards are provided. This package costs £5.95/child.
Exclusive use on Saturday or Sunday morning is available at an extra cost of £40.

Clambers
Royal Commonwealth Pool
Tel: 667 7211
Fax: 662 0265
Two party options are offered at the Royal Commonwealth Pool. The soft play option is held in Clambers, which has 3 levels of soft play. The other option is a pool visit.

The RCP staff will provide the catering and the invitations. A dedicated party host for the day is also provided and if requested in advance, will do face painting as well as play party games. A visit from Edi B (Edinburgh Leisure's bear mascot) can also be arranged at £13. Clambers party costs £7.50/child: pool parties – price on application. Parties must be booked in person, at reception: a non-refundable deposit of £30 is also required at time of booking.

Clownaround
109 Restalrig Road
Tel: 553 7676
Party lasts 1 1/2 hrs with 1hr in play facilities including soft play (separate areas for 0-3 and 3-10) and trampolines and 1/2hr in party room for birthday tea; just take the cake. Min 10 children. Prices start from £5/child and are cheaper midweek; hot food option not available for cheaper prices.

Jelly Club
Tel: 652 0212
Website: www.jellyclub.com
Party lasts 2hrs and includes play in the play centre and a birthday tea; just bring the cake. Parental supervision is required in a ratio of 1 adult to 5 children. There are different play areas according to age. Those suitable for under 5s include a ball pit and slide (0-3 yrs), an adventure maze (4-10 yrs) and the Jelly Village (3-7 yrs). Min 10 children.   Individual needs and special diets catered for. There are various safety rules about children's dress to be considered. Please note at weekends that the Jelly Club can get very busy and noisy with as many as 5 parties going on simultaneously. This may be daunting for nervous youngsters. If you are not hampered by pushchairs, try and book the balcony area to allow you a better view of the vast ground floor as the children scatter in all directions! This package costs £6.75/child and £1.35/party bag.

Molly's
Ocean Terminal
Leith
Tel: 554 0102
Soft play party with choice of 16 themes lasts 1 1/2hrs and includes themed invitations, two party leaders, reserved tables in play area, private themed party room with themed tableware, bubble machines and birthday tea. Min 10 and max 30 children. Themed cake available for £15. This package costs £8/child and £2/themed party bag.

CLOSE TO HOME

Happy Castle
Penicuik
Tel: 01968 675638
Party lasts 2hrs in two private rooms with a castle theme and includes time in play facilities, birthday tea and party bags. Min 10 and max 40 children. This package costs £7.50/child.
See also under 'close to home' Sports Centres for details of leisure centre soft plays in Bonnyrigg, Broxburn, Livingston and Linlithgow.

Junglee Fun
115 North High Street
Musselburgh
Tel: 653 0666
Party lasts 11/2 hrs and includes 1hr in soft play (suitable for 0-6 yrs), birthday tea, balloons and party bags. Min 10 and max 25 children. This package costs £7.50/child and exclusive hire costs an extra £25.

FURTHER AFIELD

Play Planet
Donibristle Industrial Estate
Dalgety Bay
Tel: 01383 822288
Getting there: 5 mins from Forth Bridge
Party lasts 2hrs and includes 1hr in soft play (3 separate areas for 0-3, 3-5 and 5-12 yrs) and 1hr in themed party rooms. Live appearance by Zinny the alien, birthday tea and party bags are all provided. Min 10 children. This package costs £7.25/child.

SPORT & COMMUNITY CENTRES

IN THE CITY

Ainslie Park Leisure Centre
Tel: 551 2400
Party last 2 hrs with 1 hr in the games hall with bouncy castle and 1 hr eating – bring your own food. Max 20 children. Facillity hire is £30.50.

Gorgie/Dalry Community Association
22 Mcleod Street EH11 2NH
Tel: 337 3252
Fax: 346 0772

Party lasts 2hrs and offer the options of a traditional party with games or an activity-based party (football, unihoc or basketball). Centre will provide party food, with staff on hand to help serve refreshments. Min 10 and max 30 children. Contact centre for prices.

Craiglockhart Tennis & Sports Centre
177 Colinton Road
Tel: 443 0101
Parties last 2 hrs and can include hire of bouncy castle and trampolines. This facility is only available at weekends. You take your own food and entertainment. Party price starts from £50.

Drumbrae Leisure Centre
Tel: 312 7957
Party lasts 2hrs and includes 1 hr in hall with bouncy castle or ball games and 1hr in party room with tables for the birthday tea; bring your own food. This package costs £50.

Gracemount Leisure Centre
Tel: 658 1940
Party lasts 2 hrs with 1 hr in the hall with bouncy castle or ball games then 1 hr for eating and party games in the function room. Bring your own food. Max 20 children. Facility hire costs £40.

Jack Kane Centre
Tel: 669 0404
Birthday party facilities available Friday afternoon and weekends for a 2 hr period. There is a separate room with tables laid out; just bring the food. Facility hire includes hall with bouncy castle and costs £42.

Meadowbank Sports Centre
Tel: 661 5351
Newly refurbished soft play room can be booked for private parties at £40/hr. Sports hall with bouncy castle costs £50/hr. The café (3 party menus) upstairs can reserve tables or you can bring your own food.

Portobello Swim Centre
Tel: 669 6888
The small pool is available for exclusive use on Sat, Sun for £35/hr. Spectating area. Café can provide the party food at £3.50/child.

Royal Commonwealth Pool
Tel: 667 7211
Fax: 662 0265

Two party options are offered at the Royal Commonwealth Pool. The soft play option is held in Clambers, which has 3 levels of soft play. The other option is a pool visit.

The RCP staff will provide the catering and the invitations. A dedicated party host for the day is also provided and if requested in advance, will do face painting as well as play party games. A visit from Edi B (Edinburgh Leisure's bear mascot) can also be arranged at £13. Clambers party costs £7.50/child; pool parties – price on application. Parties must be booked in person, at reception: a non-refundable deposit of £30 is also required at time of booking.

Wester Hailes Education Centre
Tel: 621 8303

Exclusive hire of soft play area costs £12/hr. Max 10 children. A birthday tea can also be provided for your swimming party. The coffee lounge is available for your own catering or food can be provided. Contact centre for details.

CLOSE TO HOME

Balerno High School
Tel: 477 7733

Swimming parties (lifeguard supplied, balls, floats and goals available) or football and ball games in the gym. Parents supply the food and drink and organise the games. Contact centre for prices.

Bonnyrigg Leisure Centre
Tel: 663 7579

Hall and soft play room can be hired for parties. Children spend 1 hr in soft play, and then 1 hr in hall, eating and playing party games. A bouncy castle can also be set up in the hall. Self-catering – a kitchen is available for preparing food and they tidy up the mess! Party costs £46.50.

Broxburn Swimming Pool
Tel: 01506 775680

Soft play and pool parties hosted. The soft play option is hosted in the 'Pirates Cove' soft play area. Max 20 children. Party price of £40 ensures 2 hrs exclusive use; just bring your own birthday tea. A blend of soft play and swimming is also available, costing £50 for 2 hrs.

Bubbles
Livingston Leisure Pool
Tel: 01506 777870

'Space Bugs' soft play party, for children up to age 7, includes two hours of fun on slides, chutes, ball pool and a birthday tea; just bring the cake, in a designated eating area. Invitations, party bags and thank you cards (voucher for free admission) are provided. This package costs £6.35/child.

Kirkliston Leisure Centre
Tel: 333 4700

Party lasts 2hrs with 1hr in hall with bouncy castle and 1hr in room with tables; just take the food. Max 20 children. Facility hire cost £40 for two rooms or £24 for 1 1/2 hr hire of party room.

Linlithgow Leisure Centre
McGinley Way
Tel: 01506 775440

A soft play party followed by use of the dance studio area for your own catering. Max 20 children. Facility hire cost £40.

Loanhead Leisure Centre
Tel: 440 4516

Two party options available. The Bouncy Fun Party (costs £44.50) includes use of a bouncy castle and a multitude of soft play shapes. Tables and chairs can be set out for your party tea; you provide the food. Adjoining kitchen is also available.

Swimming parties can also be held, with giant inflatables and play shapes. Cost £60.50 for max 40 children. The hall can be hired simultaneously to cater for your party.

Musselburgh Sports Centre
Newbigging
Tel: 653 6367

Soft play party costs £30.60/hr. Max 20 children. Food can be provided by centre's café, contact centre for prices. Alternatively, take your own food; charge for room for own catering £10.20/hr.

Queensferry High Recreation Centre
Ashburnham Road
South Queensferry
Tel: 319 3222

The High School has facilities which can be hired out at

evenings or weekends. Party deals include bouncy castle parties or 5 aside parties. The Recreation Centre can offer the hire of a room for your own entertainment. Facility hire costs £40.

FURTHER AFIELD

Mariner Leisure Centre
Camelon
Tel: 01324 503750
Party lasts 1 1/2hrs and includes soft play and a birthday tea; just bring the cake. This package costs £4.20/child.

North Berwick Sports Centre
Tel: 01620 893454
Birthday parties available, contact centre for details.

PARTIES AT HOME

Throwing your own party can be a lot of fun with a little planning. Remember to send out invitations at least 4 weeks ahead. 1-1/2 hrs is long enough for young ones' parties. Useful party planning books are available in libraries and the following points may provide you with some ideas. Asking guests to come in fancy dress can help get everyone in party mood.

Enlist adult help – ask other parents or grandparents to stay and help but make sure you let them know that you want them to do this.

Games – make a list (in the excitement you may just forget all those great ideas!) of lots of quick games as concentration spans are short; and organise music. Giving a sweet to each child when they are put out a game can prevent anyone feeling upset! Also contriving to have each child win a game and awarding them a 'medal' keeps everyone happy.

Here is a list of party games:

Corners – best in the garden. Designate a colour (e.g. red, blue, yellow, green), attribute (broomstick corner, cauldron corner, spiderweb corner, witch's hat corner) etc to each corner (and mark them with pictures, paper etc). The children stand in the middle of the area. You call out the attribute (ie. red corner) and the children run / hop/ skip whatever to the corner. Last one there is out
Musical bumps
Musical chairs/cushions
Musical statues

Paper islands (run around until music stops and then jump onto pieces of paper on ground)
Roll-along – roll mashmallows with your nose along a piece of plastic
Simon says: Pass the parcel (2 parcels going at the same time works well as everyone does not have to wait too long for a turn – try putting a sweet or a small gift inside each wrapping
Passing balloons from child to child (no hands!) in rows.
Craft session – stickers and crayons to decorate their own paper plate or cheap wooden photo frame. Do avoid pens and glue so as not to spoil party clothes and to minimise mess! Remember some children will finish in two minutes while others may take 20 mins so have another adult on stand by to take the quick finishers for some more games and try to keep the session short only 10-15 mins to stop children getting bored.
Birthday tea – having a picnic on the floor can work well – keep food simple and in small portions as children are usually too excited to eat much. Have another adult on hand armed with a roll of kitchen paper and a pack of wet wipes to help with any accidents! Put out the savouries first (e.g. small sandwiches, sausages, crisps, cherry tomatoes, carrot sticks, cheese sticks etc) then bring out some small cakes, chocolate crispy cakes, mashmallow top hats, fruit chopped into small pieces and then finally the birthday cake.
Finale – instead of handing out party bags try making a lucky dip or a piñata. For the lucky dip fill a box with shredded newspaper and hid enough small gifts for everyone. If you have the time small children love helping to make a piñata. Cover a balloon with strips of papier mache (newspaper soaked in a mixture of flour and water) and leave to dry for a couple of days then paint in bright colours. When fully dried burst the balloon, fill piñata with small named gifts or sweets (nothing too heavy!) and thread some string through so that you can either hang it up or hold it up for them all to take a turn at whacking it with a wooden spoon until it breaks and all the contents came tumbling out.

BUYING & HIRING

Bennetts Bouncy Castles
9 Meadowplace ROAd   EH12 7TZ
Tel: 334 4545 (24hrs)
Email: bennettshire@blueyonder.com
Web: www.bennettshire.co.uk

Bouncy castles delivered and set up from £45. All sizes

from 10' x 10', suitable for indoor use or in your garden with a shower cover. Specialised designs for under 5s.

Kidbounce
9 Scarlett Park, Musselburgh
East Lothian EH21 8BY
Tel: 0131 653 6243
Operating throughout Edinburgh and the Lothians, we are hirers of bouncy castles and soft play equipment. This company has a number of products specifically designed for children under 5.

Jenners
Good selection of hats, masks and other dressing-up requirements. Also lots of small gifts. See Shopping.

John Lewis
Large choice of paper tablecloths, serviettes, cups, plates. Also good selection of small gifts and stationery stocking fillers. See Shopping.

Monkey Business
167 Morrison Street
Tel: 228 6636
Opening times: Mon-Fri 9.30-17.30; Sat 10.00-17.00
Quality costumes to buy or hire, plus a large selection of hats, masks, wigs and jokes, and novelties (although many are geared towards a more adult market). Fireworks stocked all year round.

Party Land/Birthdays
Unit 9
Gyle Shopping Centre EH12 9JY
Tel: 339 7309
Unit 30
Cameron Toll Shopping Centre EH16 5TB
Tel: 0131 664 8076
Unit 9
Fort Kinnaird, EH15 3RH
Tel: 669 9905
115 Princes St EH2 3AA
Tel: 2261906
Good selection of tableware, themed party ware, gifts, balloons – including helium ones. Also stock wigs, party bag fillers, soft toys etc.

Party Mania
30 West Nicolson Street
Tel/Fax: 667 6020
Website: www.partypartyparty.co.uk
Opening hours: Mon-Sat 9.00-18.00
Tableware, party bag fillers, decorations, poppers, confetti,

wigs, hats and helium balloon table decorations. Helium gas tanks (from £25) can also be hired to fill your own balloons. Accessible with pushchairs.

Party Pieces
Freepost (RG910)
Child's Court Farm
Ashampstead Common
Berkshire RG8 7BR
Tel: 01635 201844
Fax: 01635 201911
Web: www.partypieces.co.uk
Colour catalogue with around 500 products to choose from, including: invitations, games, balloons, party bag fillers and tableware (including themed boxes with a cup, straw & napkin) at very reasonable prices. Next day delivery service available if orders received before 2pm. Order by post or online.

The Party Shack
140 North High Street
Musselburgh
Tel: 665 4287
Specialises in ordering items for themed parties. Stocks lots of party accessories, balloons and children's fancy dress.

The Finishing Touch
See Catering and Cakes section in this chapter.

Toys R Us
Party bag gifts, cups, plates, etc on various themes. Party bag fillers. See Shopping.

Woolworths
Party bag gifts, tableware, sweets, toys and other party accessories. Range varies in terms of choice from branch to branch. See Shopping.

CATERING & CAKES

Most parents provide their own food for 'home hosted' parties (see above for ideas) and there are books in the library to inspire you but do keep it simple as children are usually too excited to eat much. Most of the supermarkets can, with prior warning, provide trays of buffet food, such as sandwiches. Or why not try your local deli or sandwich shop? Cakes are usually the centrepiece of any party tea and again libraries often have books with easy to follow recipes and ideas. A number of shops hire out cake tins and instructions. However, if you don't feel ambitious enough to tackle one, Edinburgh seems to be teeming with people with novelty cake making businesses. Local bakers, confectioners and many supermarkets can supply cakes with your photo of choice turned into edible icing. The following firms have something special to offer:

The Cake and Chocolate Shop
12 Bruntsfield Place
Tel: 228 4350
Website: www.cakeandchocolateshop.co.uk
Opening times: Mon-Fri 9.00-17.30 Sat 9.30-17.00
Will make cakes to any design (the only limit is your imagination) and there are lots of books of photographs to give you ideas.

The Finishing Touch
17 Patrick's Square
Tel: 667 0914
Mon-Sat 10.00-17.30
Over 40 novelty tins to hire, plus numbers, letters, squares, hexagons, etc. Good instructions. £1/night., with a £10 refundable deposit/tin. Also every imaginable utensil and ingredient for cake decorating. Lots of other party paraphernalia too including party toys, masks, wigs and an extensive range of ribbons.

Paper Lace
29 South Street
Dalkeith EH22 1AH
Tel: 663 2491
Email: Place138@aol.com
Novelty cake tin hire. Also balloons and balloon delivery. Accessible to pushchairs.

Studio One
71 Morningside Road
Tel: 447 0452
Email: studioonecookshop@yahoo.co.uk
Opening times: Mon-Fri 9.30-18.00 Sat 9.30-17.30 Sun 12.00-16.00
Tin hire: £2/night, £10 deposit. Letters, numbers, hearts, squares, etc.

ENTERTAINMENT

Many of the entertainers we contacted felt that their acts weren't suitable for under 5s and stressed that there was nothing worse than adults giving a running commentary to tots. It is most important when looking for an act to tell them the age span of the children and whether you have seen them before, as many entertainers have several routines. Some may even run the whole party if you want. Those listed below have acts/services suited to the under 5s age group.

Carries-Matic Theme Parties
Contact: Carrie Todd
Tel: 0131 336 3673
Mob: 07952 945 749
Email: carriesmatic@yahoo.co.uk
Specially designed party entertainment to suit your occasion, using stories, poems, song, dance, puppets, face-paint, balloons and games to give an interactive and educational experience. Using your own venue, prices are £50 for one hour and £60 for two hours. Parties suitable

BIRTHDAYS & CELEBRATIONS

for all ages from tiny tots to teens and there are a wide variety of themes available including; Ballet, Wizards, Posh Princesses, Native American Indian and animals. Carrie is a professionally trained dancer, dance and drama teacher, children's theatre director, member of equity and mother. She has been vetted by Disclosure Scotland and passed to work with children.

Gary James and Stone the Crow
46 Easter Drylaw Bank EH4 2QN
Tel: 332 8321
Mobile 0793 272 8695
Email: g.james@blueyonder.co.uk
Children's entertainer, magic, balloon modelling, 'Punch and Judy' style show. Full (2 hour) party packages are also available.

Flotsam and Jetsam Puppets:
The Blue Dress Shows
24 Blackwood CresCENT
Contact: Aileen Finlay
Tel: 662 9834
Mob: 07813 705 840
Email:
flotsam_and_jetsam_theatre@btopenworld.com
Lively puppets and gentle stories specially designed to appeal to younger children (ages 2 and upwards). Puppeteer and storyteller Aileen Finlay will come to your party wearing her magical blue 'story dress'. The dress has many pockets and in each one are puppets and props waiting to come out and tell their stories. Lots of joining-in fun and a special surprise for the birthday child. Call for a brochure and current prices. Educational shows based around the seasons are also available to playgroups and nurseries.

Gordon's Magic and Puppet Show
Gordon Morris
7 Royal Park Terrace
Tel: 652 2189
Email: gordonhunt1@btinternet.com
Entertainment for birthday parties and other events with puppets, magic, balloon animals and organised games. Packed with chances for party guests to participate in the action.

Jimmy Craig
11 Barry Rd
Kirkcaldy
Tel: 01592 261706
This experienced fun magician provides prize winning fun

filled magical entertainment for children. He specialises in shows suitable for children of playgroup age and up.

Jo Jingles
Contact: Joanne Goodall
Tel: 443 4196
Web: www.jojingles.co.uk
Jo Jingles is available for birthday parties, for children up to 5 yrs old. Sessions last 30 or 45 mins, and include musical instrument playing, nursery rhymes and action songs. Contact for current prices.

Kids & Co
Contact: Fiona
Tel: 334 4309
Mobile: 0771 8919125
Fiona specialises in stress free parties. She can organise everything from the venue, birthday cake, catering and party bags. You can choose from various themes and her team will supervise the games and entertain the children. Best of all the tidying up is included in the price.

Magic Bob
Main Street, Gordon
Tel: 01573 410363
Email: magicbobquiletti@btinternet.com
Website: www.magicbob.co.uk
This popular magician performs a variety of colourful, cheerful shows which children and adults love. Lots of good humour and audience participation with souvenirs for all partygoers. Traditional yet innovative.

Mr Boom
Contact: Andy Munro
The Old Repeater Station
Libberton
South Lanarkshire
Tel: 01555 841168
Email: info@mrboom.co.uk
Website: www.mrboom.co.uk
The children's one-man band from the moon has been visiting Planet Earth for some 21 years now. He's written a wealth of science based songs well known to several generations of youngsters. He's a popular draw at fund raising concerts and visits schools and nurseries with his enchanting singing and dancing show for young children. Sing along all together now! Dance in a pixie ring! Be a planet going round the sun! If Mr Boom's there, you'll have lots of fun.

176

Story Teller Scotland
Contact: Linda Bandelier
Tel: 554 8771
Email: info@storytellerscotland.co.uk

Song and storytelling programmes for children's parties and nursery schools. Probably most suitable for 4+. Contact Linda for fees and to discuss content.

Tricky Ricky
Ricky McLeod
41 Broomhall Place EH12 7PE
Tel: 334 7671
Email: ricky@trickyricky.com
Web: www.trickyricky.com

Multi award-winning children's entertainer & magician. Magic, songs and lots of fun, including Bingo the real puppet dog!

CHILDCARE

CHILDCARE

INTRODUCTION

The search for – and selection of – the right type of childcare for you and your family can be extremely stressful, and the aim of this section is to try to provide some information on childcare options if you return to work, studies, or need some help looking after your child. Choices include taking your child to a childminder, employing someone to come to you, or enrolling your child in a nursery: we have listed some of Edinburgh's nurseries in our Pre-school Play and Education section.

Irrespective of the type of childcare you are considering, try to give yourself as much time as possible to check out the options; the more time you have, the less likely you are to feel that you've been unnecessarily pressured into making a decision. However, do bear in mind that while everyone has an idea of what they want for their particular child, and while you should be clear about your preferences, you may find that you have to make unexpected compromises in order to get suitable childcare.

Talk to as many people as you can about their experiences of childcare: their good accounts will reassure you and their 'horror stories' will help you be aware of what to look out for.

There is an informal local network of nannies and childminders and you may find what you are looking for via word of mouth.

If you feel happy and relaxed about your childcare arrangements, then you can use your time away from your child much more effectively. While your child may seem so vulnerable and to need only you, remember that other adults outside the family can be a very positive part of their life.

For impartial and comprehensive advice on local childcare of all forms. contact:

Edinburgh Childcare Information Service
PO Box 777
Edinburgh EH4 4JY
Tel: 270 6061 (Mon-Fri 08.30-16.00)
Fax: 270 6069
Freephone: 0800 032 0323
Email: info@childcarepartnership.org
Web: www.edinburghchildcare.co.uk

As part of the Government's National Childcare Strategy, the City of Council runs the Childcare Information Service. The service aims to provide impartial advice and information to parents and carers in or seeking to return to employment or training and requiring childcare provision.

Parents and carers can contact the Service to find out about the most suitable childcare for their family's needs Information is available on all different types of registered childcare – whether provided by the independent, voluntary or statutory sectors, including: childminders; independent nurseries; local nurseries; out of school care; playgroups; crèches and holiday play-schemes. Lists and profiles of childcare provision can also be tailored to meet each family's specific needs, such as services for a particular age group or geographical area. Information is regularly updated.

For information and support about returning to work, your local NCT branch may have a working mothers' group, or you could contact:

Working Families
1-3 Berry StREET
London EC1V 0AA
Tel: 020 7253 7243
Tel: 0800 013 0313 (helpline for low income families)
Fax: 020 7253 6253
Email: office@workingfamilies.org.uk
Web: www.workingfamilies.org.uk

Working Families help children, their parents and employers with information about childcare and flexible working; advise on workplace violence, maternity rights and tax credits, and benefits, tax credits and childcare for parents of children with disabilities.

If your circumstances are particularly difficult, your local Social Work Department may be able to assist.

Social Work Department
Tel: 556 6787

The Social Work Department can help with childcare in the form of Children's Centres, day carers and places at specially approved private nurseries. The service is free but is only available to families who are in need of help for social, financial or health reasons.

AU PAIRS & 'MOTHER'S HELPS'

If you do not need someone to take full responsibility for your child/ren on a regular basis, but feel that you need some help in the home with general work as well as childcare, a mother's help may fit the bill. Mother's helps do not need any qualifications or experience and you can specify what you want them to do to help you, but remember the emphasis is on the word 'help'.

AU PAIRS

An au pair is a young, single person (aged between 17 and 27) who comes to the UK in order to learn English. They live with an English-speaking host family, and should have the opportunity to study, and in return for board and lodging with a room of their own and a reasonable allowance (about £55+/wk), they should help in the house for up to 5 hours a day 5 days a week. So, there should be at least 2 full free days per week, and the help can include light housework and childcare.

These conditions are laid down by the Home Office. The official au pair scheme includes nationals from the following countries: Andorra, the Faroe Islands; Monaco; San Marino; Greenland; Romania; Bosnia-Herzegovina; Bulgaria; Macedonia; Turkey; and Croatia. European Economic Area nationals are not included in the official au pair scheme, but they are free to come to the UK as au pairs.

Au pairs from the European Union do not need work permits;

au pairs from outside the EU (such as those from Bosnia-Herzegovina, Bulgaria; Croatia; Macedonia; Romania and Turkey) must apply for a visa that is valid for two years. Call the Home Office Immigration Department on Tel: 0870 606 7786 (www.ind.homeoffice.gov.uk) for more details.

An au pair can stay in the UK for up to two years. They do not need to remain with the same family, but they must ensure that all families they stay with fulfil legal requirements.

You will probably find when you are looking for childcare, that many well-meaning acquaintances suggest having an au pair. However you should think very carefully about whether this form of help would suit you. Au pairs are not qualified in childcare and their main reason for being with you is to learn about the language and the country, not to care for your children. Whilst many au pairs have extremely successful placements, you must remember that you have a responsibility as a host family: many au pairs are desperately unhappy as they are asked to work very long hours, and are treated as a servant rather than as one of the family. Their English may be limited on arrival; they can be very young and inexperienced, not only in domestic matters, but in life in general. You may find yourself having to explain to them the most basic elements of childcare, as well as possibly having to deal

with unanticipated issues, such as anti-social behaviour, romantic dramas, homesickness, etc.

Many parents find that, although they have help with housework, childcare and babysitting, they have also acquired the equivalent of an extra (teenage) child with all the responsibilities that entails!

Au pairs are not a cheap solution for regular childcare if you have very young children, but they can be perfect as a help around the house or for part-time care for older children.

Au pairs can be found through agencies or contacts with the language departments of local schools, colleges and universities.

Captial Au Pairs
4 Forthview Road
Blackhall
Edinburgh EH4 2DE
Tel/fax: 332 4008
Emails: capitalaupairs@blueyonder.co.uk
Opening hours: Mon-Fri 9.00-12.00
Specialiase in au pairs placements; long or short term
The au pairs are male and female, and mainly come from

Poland, The Czech Republic, Sweden, Germany, France, and Spain. Company offers a personal matching service and after placement support throughout stay, as well as offering an entertainment programme for the au pairs.

The Edinburgh Au Pair Agency
Carrick Cottage, The Walled Garden
Rosewell
Midlothian EH24 9EQ
Contact: Anne Hunter
Tel: 440 0800
Email: aupairs@rosewell.co.uk

This agency may answer your queries on au pairs. Their au pairs (male and female) are between 20 and 27 years of age, with a basic/average level of spoken English, completed Secondary School education (many are graduates), and with evidence of having a genuine interest in children and some experience of caring for them. Three types of placements are available depending on the amount of hours you would like your au pair to work. There is a small registration fee and a one-off placement fee.

BABYSITTERS

Some nanny agencies can help you find babysitters, although this is an more expensive option than the traditional options of friends, family or neighbours. You can, if you wish, employ a neighbouring teenager to babysit but bear in mind that he or she must be over sixteen. Current rates are around £4.75+/hr, more after midnight and if you are out late you should ensure that they get home safely.

Babysitting Circles
These are groups of parents who get together to provide a babysitting circle. To find out about circles in your area ask neighbours, parent and toddler groups, local parents, your Health Visitor, or your local NCT group. All these circles are organised on a purely informal basis and it is up to you to decide if you are happy with the way the circle is run. Many arrange for the parents and the children to meet together at regular intervals so that you can get to know each other better and if the circle is large enough similar families are matched together so that a new mother with one baby, for example, can avoid the happy bedtime chaos of a larger family with toddlers and older children!

Babysitting Agencies
(see also Nanny Agencies in this chapter)

Babybusters
Contact: Natalie - n.sutton@blueyonder
Contact: Sue -suemarhim@tiscali.co.uk

This is a small group of women qualified and/or experienced in childcare who are available for babysitting evenings and occasional daytimes. Full information sheets, FAQs, rates etc, all available via email. Parents pay a registration fee at the beginning, but rates thereafter are very reasonable.

firsthand
39 Broughton Place
Edinburgh EH1 3RR
Tel: 557 3121
email:
mail@1sthand.org.uk/admin@firstahnd.org.uk

firsthand is a voluntary organisation providing services to lone parents, carers, children, and young disabled adults. Formerly known as Edinburgh Sitters, one of firsthand's services is a Sitter Service for lone parents and carers of disabled children. Families are matched with a volunteer or paid sitter who looks after the child(ren) in the family home, for up to four hours at a time, on a regular basis. The aim is to give a regular break to lone parents and carers who may not otherwise have one. firsthand offers support to families with children under 3 through Sure Start funding. There is a waiting list but eligible parents or carers should contact firsthand to ask for an application form.

CHILDMINDERS

Childminders care for children in their own homes. They can offer a child a homely, family environment; most will have had first-hand experience with their own children, and may well be involved with the local toddler/play groups and schools, which may be an advantage for your child later on.

Childminders are self-employed and are legally required to register with the Scottish Commission for the Regulation of Care. Registration involves health, police, fire and home safety checks and is reviewed regularly. Registration is not, however, an evaluation of their skills as a childminder – these are for you to assess.

Childminders are approved to care for a maximum of six

children up to and including the age of 16 yrs, of whom no more than three are under 5 yrs and only one is under 1 yr; these figures include their own children. You must use a registered childminder: if in doubt ask to see a registration certificate, and check that it is up to date.

How to Find a Childminder

A list of all registered childminders is available from the Childcare Information Service (270 6060 or Freephone 0800 0320323). Your health visitor may have a list (check it is up-to-date) and other parents who use a childminder may know of any local vacancies.

How Much Will it Cost?

Rates vary according to area, but across Edinburgh the average rate is around £3.50/hr per child. Rates for part-time places may carry a premium, and some minders offer a reduced rate for siblings. Childminders are responsible for their own tax and National Insurance payments and also for Public Liability and Accident Insurance cover. You should check that they are either covered by their domestic insurance or that they have a special childminder's insurance policy. Payment for holidays and sick pay vary: often a childminder will not charge if unavailable due to holidays or illness, but if you do not attend you should pay the normal rate or at least a percentage of it.

Choosing a Childminder

You will need to decide where you want your childminder to be based: someone close to home may mean that your child can make friends locally which will carry on to school, and enforced change in the long term is less likely to be necessary if your childminder is willing to continue caring for your child once he or she has started school. It is also more convenient to have someone nearby who can take your child, if, say, you are ill. Alternatively, you may prefer a childminder who lives closer to your place of work.

Once you have selected the names in your chosen area from the list, you will need to phone around to find out who has vacancies. Be prepared to find few vacancies – in many areas in Edinburgh demand outstrips supply. Most childminders are very helpful in telling you of any vacancies they are aware of, so do ask. Always visit anyone who sounds suitable in their home and prepare yourself with a list of information for the childminder about you and your child and also questions you want to ask about the childminder. You need to establish the practicalities of hours, rates, holidays, sick pay, overtime (if required) and notice and whether you need to provide

food and nappies. You might also want to think about the following during your visit: Will your child have plenty of play opportunities – indoors and outdoors? Will there be outings to the park, playgroup, library etc? Will your child be able to rest during the day? If so where? What are the arrangements for meals and snacks? Are there other children for your child to play with and are they happy, settled and busy? What time will be set aside for you to discuss your child with the childminder? Will your wishes for the care of your child be accepted and respected? When you do decide ensure you have a written contract summarising your agreement with the childminder.

Scottish Childminding Association
Suite 3
7 Melville Terrace
Stirling FK8 2ND
Tel: 01786 445 377
Tel: 01786 449 063 (advice line)
Fax: 01786 449 062
Web: www.childminding.org
The only Scottish dedicated support organisation for registered childminders. It promotes good quality childcare within a home environment. It provides support, advice and information to all who are interested in childminding. It produces several useful publications for parents and childminders, some of which are free of charge, some of which are not. The SCMA also has comprehensive guides and advice sheets available online.

NANNIES

You may prefer to employ someone to look after your children in your own home. Nannies may 'live in' or 'live out'. The choice between these options will depend on the nature of your childcare needs, your available accommodation, how you feel about having someone in your home and also on your financial resources. Nannies are not required to be registered in the same way that childminders are, so you must follow through on references thoroughly; a recent Which? investigation in England and Wales showed that agencies there were not always checking references. It is worth thinking beforehand about the sort of person you are looking for and to specify your requirements with regard to training and qualifications, experience, age and so on.

Conditions of Service
Be clear in your own mind about your conditions of service in terms of hours, holidays, pay, duties, sick pay

Remember too the additional cost to you of National Insurance contributions and income tax payments, which can equal up to one third of the person's take-home pay. When you do appoint someone, it is up to you to contact your local Inland Revenue office to let them know you are an employer, and they will send you the necessary paperwork for you to fill in.

Finding a Nanny

The following suggestions may help you find the right person:

Local contacts or friends may be able to recommend someone suitable – nannies usually know other nannies, or parents with children at private nurseries may hear that a member of staff is looking for a move. Take advantage of anyone's experience of employing a nanny – ask them about what they like about their nannies, and if there is anything they would have done differently.

You can place advertisements in the Scotsman and/or the Evening News on Fridays (contact the papers at least two days in advance). Be prepared for a good number of responses, but if response is by phone in the first instance have a short list of questions handy to filter out unsuitable candidates quickly and only interview those who meet your criteria of experience and qualifications. You could also place notices in health centres where they have a general notice board, or you could look further afield by placing an advert in e.g. The Lady.

If you seek someone with childcare qualifications, but don't mind if they do not have experience, contact the local colleges which offer childcare training (Jewel & Esk Valley, Tel: 660 1010; Stevenson, Tel: 535 4700; West Lothian College Tel: 01506 418181) – the final term (Apr/May) is the best time to do this.

You may also wish to use an employment agency and there are a few in the Edinburgh area which specialise in finding nannies. They usually charge a registration fee and then once they have your details they try to match you with someone suitable. If you are looking for a part-time nanny, some will try to set up a nanny-share scheme with other clients. All candidates should have been thoroughly interviewed and references checked by the agency, but the final responsibility to ensure the nanny's suitability and to double check references is with you. If you do appoint someone, you then pay a substantial appointment fee to the agency. If you use an agency, find out before signing up what they offer in terms of service to you: some provide useful fact packs on registration which will help you with interviewing, contracts, conditions of employment, tax and National Insurance etc. They should also give some sort

and so on. Must your nanny: be able to drive; be a non-smoker; understand a vegetarian diet; understand allergies; observe certain religious practices – and so on? In the case of live-in help you should also think about any restrictions you wish to place upon the use of your home, such as having friends to stay, using the phone, etc.

Apart from looking after the children, duties can include babysitting, cooking, light housework and so on. Be realistic: if you have one young child who sleeps for a couple of hours each day then it is reasonable to ask the nanny to fill that time with light housework, but if there are active toddlers or young children around then they must take priority with the nanny over time-consuming domestic chores.

Rates vary widely depending on qualifications, age and experience: full-time live-out care can range from £280-350/wk net, or around £6-£8+/hr part-time. Live-in pay can be less (£200-300/week), but don't forget to take account of the 'hidden' domestic costs. When deciding what to pay take into account training, experience, number of children and level of responsibility required.

of guarantee to find a temporary cover if you need it. Go for an agency that you feel will give you a dependable service, but remember it can only be as good as the nannies on its books, and if, as can sometimes be the case, they cannot come up with anyone suitable, it will be back to you to find someone.

Interviews

Ask all candidates to send you their CV in advance or, if that's not possible to bring it with them to the interview – this will give you a good starting point. Prepare your list of questions in advance and don't feel embarrassed to ask searching questions – you need to find out as much as you can in a very short time! Don't forget to give the candidates a chance to ask you questions and to tell you about themselves – they need to assess whether you will be the right family for them too and you can find out a lot about someone by listening carefully to what they have to say. Be sure to obtain references from previous employers or from college tutors and follow them up (even if it means
phoning Australia!) – again have a short list of questions ready to ask referees but also give them an opportunity to volunteer their own information.

Contract

It is important to have mutual expectations clear at the outset. A written contract stating the terms and conditions of service and the duties and responsibilities of the job is very helpful in preventing problems later on, or at least making them easier to sort out, for both parties and the law requires employers to provide certain written particulars.

The following agencies do not reflect the entire range of agencies available in the area, but they did provide full information regarding contact details and the services they provide.

NANNY AGENCIES

Butterfly Personnel
7 Earlston Place
Edinburgh EH7 5SU
Tel: 659 5065
Email: enquiries@nanny-agency.net
Web: www.nanny-agency.net
Established in 1998 and registered with the Care Commission, this agency specialises in providing permanent/temporary nannies, babysitters, and also maternity nurses.

It also provides emergency cover staff to many nurseries and private homes. Staff are fully interviewed, reference checked and cleared through Disclosure Scotland. They carry photo ID cards. No registration fee required.

Family Circle Recruitment
22 Tower Street
Edinburgh EH6 7BY
Tel: 554 9500
Fax: 554 9504
Mobile: 07970 442428
Email:mail@familycircles.org
Web: www.familycircles.org

The childcare division provides all aspects of temporary and permanent childcare cover including nannies, babysitters, emergency cover, nursery staff, maternity nurses, child friendly housekeepers and also 'after school club' help.

Flying Pig Childcare Management Co. Ltd
13A Abercromby Place
Edinburgh EH3 6LB
Tel: 0845 062 4453
Email: info@flyingpigchildcare.com
Web: www.flyingpigchildcare.com

An innovative childcare company which provides services to both private and corporate clients. Services available throughout Scotland and many parts of the UK. Flying Pig focuses on providing solutions to their customers' childcare issues, whatever they may be. The company aims to offer a professionsal, personal service which meets their clients' specific requirements.
Services available are: night nannies; flying nannies; emergency nannies; nanny recruitment; nanny screening; babysitting; hotel babysitting; and corporate childcare.

OTHER SOURCES OF HELP WITH CHILDCARE

Edinburgh Crèche Co-op
297 Easter Road
Edinburgh EH6 8LH
Tel: 553 2116 (Mon-Fri 9.00-16.00)
Specialises in delivering flexible, professional childcare services including setting up and running crèche facilities, training, consultancy and staff cover. You need to provide a suitable room and the crèche workers are vetted, trained

and experienced in organising stimulating and educational play activities, with an emphasis on child-centred care. It has full public liability insurance and complies with all relevant legislation and can be fully operational with only a few days notice.

Mother to Mother
Post-Natal Doula Support
Contact: Clare Bartos
Tel: 445 4445
Email: clare@mothertomother.co.uk
Web: mothertomother.co.uk
A post-natal doula will work with a mother and her family for a mutually agreed period of time – usually about 6 weeks after the birth of a baby, although the extent of the support can vary according to the mother and her family's needs. This will usually be a set number of hours each day for a set number of days each week.
A post-natal doula provides physical and emotional support to a mother and her family. She will also help a mother to locate information and support from other sources. She can also free the mother from some domestic chores so that the mother has time to meet her own and her baby's needs.

firsthand
39 Broughton Place
Edinburgh EH1 3RR
Tel: 557 3121
email: mail@1sthand.org.uk/admin@firstahnd.org.uk
firsthand is a voluntary organisation providing services to lone parents, carers, children, and young disabled adults. Formerly known as Edinburgh Sitters, one of firsthand's services is a Sitter Service for lone parents and carers of disabled children.
See full entry under Babysitters earlier in this section.

Family Circle Recruitment
See Nannies in this chapter.

North Edinburgh Childcare
Crèche Services
18b Ferry Road Avenue
Edinburgh EH4 4BL
Contact: Helen Stoker
(Crèche Services Team Leader, tel: 311 6933)
Contact: Donna Purches
(Customer Care Manager, tel: 332 8001)
Tel: 311 6934

A childcare facility which gives quality, affordable crèche cover, to enable parents to access either leisure or business opportunities. The crèches provided are safe, stimulating and above all, fun. Available for bookings by any group or organisation which is planning an event – anytime, anywhere, on a one-off booking or cover for a regular event. North Edinburgh Childcare can accommodate up to 12 children between the ages of 0-12yrs (under 1s can be catered for if there are less than 6 other children). Rates vary, depending upon staffing ratios and the venue

One Stop Childcare
17 Calder Grove
Edinburgh EH11 4LZ
Tel: 476 7800
One Stop Childcare's crèche service is designed to respond to the needs of a broad range of clients: they can assist with childcare for events such as AGMs, family fundays, weddings etc.   Crèches are tailor-made to meet the needs of clients, including play and care for children with special needs. Childcare can be provided in and outside Edinburgh, either on a long or short term basis or for a one-off event. One Stop will provide, or come to, a suitable location and supply play materials and a healthy snack.

HELP IN THE HOME

Home Agency
36 McLaren Road
Edinburgh
Contact: Sarah Somner
Tel: 468 4200
Email: enquiries@thehomeagency.co.uk
Web: www.thehomeagency.co.uk
The Home Agency provides regular household services, such as cleaners and ironers, and can also find you tradesmen etc. for specific home maintenance. Registration fee for use of service - you pay the tradesmen/women directly.

For Free & Rainy Day Ideas

This section is a quick-reference guide to having fun for free or filling in time when the weather isn't that great.

It's always good to remember that a trip out doesn't have to cost an arm and a leg. Indoors and out, there are lots of places to go with Under 5s that don't cost anything, excepting, perhaps, your transport there and back.

Likewise, an afternoon making (and eating) some biscuits or chocolate crispies can go down just as well as a trip out - and it doesn't have to be raining to get the junk box out!

FOR FREE

Museums & Galleries

The following museums and galleries have free entry

Brass Rubbing Centre
(There is a charge for rubbings)

The Dean Gallery

Dunbar Under Ground

Museum of Childhood

Museum of Scotland

National Gallery of Scotland

Newhaven Heritage Museum

North Berwick Museum

The People's Story

Prestongrange Industrial Museum

Queensferry Museum

Royal Museum
(check whether there are free children's arts events on)

Scottish National Gallery of Modern Art

Scottish National Portrait Gallery

Although some of these are more suited to older under 5s, places like the Royal Museum or The Museum of Scotland are packed with things to catch young children's eyes. Remember too that the Royal Museum and the Museum of Scotland have a dedicated area for eating packed lunches. Although this is used by schools during visits, it's also available to the public, so you don't have to eat in the cafés.

Art galleries can prove fascinating for some children – the Lichtenstein, with its bright colours, in the ground floor corridor of the Scottish National Gallery of Modern Art always grabs the attention on our visits!

OUTDOORS

Gorgie City Farm

Trainspotting – from the bridge in Princes Street Gardens

Royal Botanic Garden: we always have fun searching for the dinosaurs that (apparently!) live there. No luck in spotting them yet, but the nosy squirrels and the ducks seem to be a good substitute

Looking at the boats at Cramond, Musselburgh, Granton, South Queensferry and Leith harbours. If it's cold, you can always do this from the relative warmth of Ocean Terminal.

Vogrie Country Park.

Dalkeith Country Park

Parks & Playgrounds – if it's a nice day (and it's feasible!) why not walk a little bit further and visit a less familiar playpark.

Holyrood Park, Salisbury Craggs and Arthur's Seat: loads of space to run, run, run. There are signets at some points of the year, frogs crossing the roads at others. On Ne'er Day, there's sled dog racing.

Lauriston Castle grounds.

Why not have a glance through Annual Events – many of the events listed in this section have free entry.

Shopping centres

This isn't as half-baked as it sounds! Some of the larger centres such as the Gyle or Ocean Terminal organise attractions which are specifiically for younger children. Usually timed to co-incide with bank holidays, summer holidays and weekends, it's always worth checking at information points or online.

What's on offer can vary, but you may find that there are storytelling sessions, card or poster design competitions, face painting and suchlike.

Ocean Terminal also has a large chess board on level 2, which has toddler size pieces.

RAINY DAY IDEAS

The saying 'always put something by for a rainy day' suddenly takes on a whole new meaning when you have to entertain boisterous or restive youngsters. We've included some ideas which might help fill 10 mins here or 40 mins there – or hopefully even more.

Why not start a collection of toilet roll/ kitchen roll tubes, yoghurt pots, shiny paper (sweet wrappers, gift wrap etc), lolly sticks (cleaned up or bought from craft sections of larger stationers or art shops), cereal boxes and so on? You can make trains, robots, rockets, monsters, fairy tale castles – anything your under 5 wants to!

MESSY STUFF

Make a Snowman

Snowmen are popular in our house all year round. You need a toilet roll tube (or a cut-to-size kitchen roll tube), cotton wool balls, glue and some other oddments. Cover the tube with the cotton wool balls, then decorate it. Either use sticky label dots for eyes, buttons etc, or use some dots made from card or paper and a paper-punch. Decorating a colourful paper scarf with crayons, stars etc extends this pastime.

Pasta

Pasta is great if you're under 5, since it's one of those foodstuffs which offers many more options than just eating it. You can stick it down in collages , you can string it to make necklaces, and you can seal it inside a tube and make a shaker. Under 5s don't seem to care about painting it but if you do have tricolore and don't mind sacrificing it, you can have instant colour.

Play Dough Recipe

1 cup flour
1/2 cup salt
2 teaspoons cream of tartar
1 cup water
2 teaspoons of oil

Heat the oil in a saucepan. Add other ingredients and cook for 3 minutes stirring constantly. Drop the ball of dough in waxed paper till cool enough to handle. Knead the dough, separate into portions and add food colouring if desired. Will stay soft if kept in fridge in a polythene bag.

Tray/Table Art

Shaving foam (as cheap as you like)
In homage to Tony Hart – or if you're too young to remember him, Art Attack. Spray the foam over a melamine or plastic tray or over a table top and make messy patterns. If you cover the top with cling film first, there should be less mess! You can achieve the same basic effect with some sand.

Printing

Potatoes, carrots, onions, old sponges etc etc

Paper

Paints

You'll need something to squeeze the paint on to or into – paper plates, empty margarine tubs etc. Cut the stampers into shapes (they don't have to be fancy). Stand back and let your under 5 at it (cover the tables, floor etc with newspaper or splashsheet before they commence!).

FOOD

Cress Heads

(best for older under 5s)
You need cress seeds, a cleaned out egg shell, cotton wool and some water. You'll also need an egg cup and some card to go round it, or a piece of card rolled into a tube, which will hold the egg shell.

The egg shell can be decorated as a monster, person, animal – anything your under 5 wants, ditto with the card which forms the body of said character. Fill the egg shell with dampened cotton wool, place in a dark, warm place and it should sprout within 5 or 6 days. The cress then makes the 'hair' of the character drawn on the shell.

Alternatively, patterns, letters or names can be created by cress seeds on some dampened kitchen towel set on a plate or lid. Place in a dark, warm place. The cress will sprout into shapes, names etc – which you can bring out a week later when the activity has been forgotten about, cut it and eat on sandwiches

Chocolate Crispies

100g chocolate
50g butter
4 tablespoons syrup
75-100g corn flakes or crispies – you might need more dependent on the brand and tye of cereal
Cake cases
Decorations – cherries, chocolate chips, angelica – anything you or your under 5 fancy or have to hand
This should be enough for about 10-12, but it all depends on the type of chocolate and cereal used.
Melt chocolate, butter and syrup in a pan on a low heat. Remove from heat and stir in the corn flakes or crispies. Children can help with this part onwards – drop some mixture into each case. Decorate any way you want. Chill in fridge. Eat.

Funky Toast

Make some toast. Cut out various shapes with cookie cutters (time is usually spent choosing the cutters). Spread with whatever you like. Eat.

Tea Biscuit Decoration

Raid the kitchen cupboards for hundreds and thousands, chocolate vermicelli, sugar flowers, sweeties etc. Make up some water icing. The biscuits get iced and then get decorated. And – perhaps – eaten.

Keeping a favourite character cake mix in the cupboard can also be popular on wet days. Bob the Builder, Tweenies etc have baking merchandise.

NOISY STUFF

Music Shakers

Put some dried pulses in a yoghurt pot or into a toilet roll tube with one end sealed with paper or card. Cover the open end. Shake vigorously (and probably repetitively). Older children might like to decorate their instrument: every little thing that adds to the experience can get your under 5 past the critical boredom theshhold and back into a better mood!

Bubblewrap

If you get a parcel etc with a sheet of the large-sized bubble wrap, keep it. Bring it out, lay it on the floor and have a manic 5-10 mins stomping about on it. The bigger the bubbles, the noisier the 'pop'. Why not play your favourite music at the same time?

GOING OUT

Soft plays are a popular choice (though bear in mind that many other parents will have the same idea), as is the Royal Museum on Chambers Street. Check the Where Shall We Go Today chapter or see above in 'For Free' for more ideas, both indoor and outdoors.

Or get your wellies on, find the biggest puddles you can and jump right in!

Healthcare

This section includes local NHS, voluntary and complementary health care facilities. Although it cannot claim to be comprehensive; it should, however, be able to direct you to sources of more detailed information.

EMERGENCY CARE

If your child requires urgent medical attention:

Dial 999 or 112
or,

Contact your GP
or

Out of hours, phone

NHS 24 Scotland
Tel: 08454 24 24 24

Or go direct to:

Royal Hospital for Sick Children
Sciennes Road
Tel: 536 0000

GENERAL PRACTITIONER SERVICES

If you think your child has a medical problem the normal first contact is your GP. As well as treating most common conditions and referring your child on to a specialist (should this be necessary), most GPs in Edinburgh provide special services for under 5s. These include a Child Health Surveillance Programme, often in conjunction with your health visitor, in which your child will be called for routine medical and developmental checks. In addition, your GP is likely to undertake your child's basic immunisation programme.

New to the Area?
Lothian Health Board (see 'Useful Addresses' in this chapter) or Capital Information Points (in libraries and throughout the city) can provide a list of local GPs.

Want to change your GP?
You can do so by registering and completing a form with a new doctor of your choice. If you have difficulty finding a GP who will accept you as a patient, contact the Health Board (see 'Useful Addresses' in this chapter) which has an obligation to find a GP.

Out of Hours / Night Care
GPs offer 24 hr care but you may not always be seen by a GP from your own practice if you require treatment between 18.00 and 8.00, or at weekends or public holidays. Many local GPs utilise an out of hours service at these times which means that the duty doctors attend the patients of several different surgeries.
The number to call in this event is that of NHS 24: 08454 24 24 24
You'll be put through to a call handler, who will take your details. Only then will you be forwarded to a nurse advisor, who'll assess the condition of you or your child. You may have to wait for a call back, though. The NHS 24 Contact will then offer advice and, if necessary, they'll advise you what type of medical attention is available:

NHS 24 works with the:
Scottish Ambulance Service
GP out of hours services
Accident and Emergency departments

You may be asked to attend a local treatment centre rather than receive a home visit. If you need to attend A&E, NHS24 will call ahead and forward your details.

In emergencies, dial 999 or 112

HOSPITAL SERVICES (Excluding Maternity)

Royal Hospital for Sick Children
Sciennes Road
Tel: 536 0000
Orientated to the needs of children in all areas of the hospital. Clinics, waiting areas and the accident and emergency department are all stocked with toys and books etc for all ages.
Resident facilities are available for parents wishing to stay with their child in hospital. These comprise of separate areas, which are not directly part of the clinical setting and some accommodation on the wards, including a small number of child and parent cubicles with en suite facilities. All parents who wish to stay with their child can do so and attempts will be made to find beds for as many as possible. Priority is given to parents of very sick children, parents who travel long distances and breastfeeding mothers. Parent sitting rooms, kitchen, laundry and bathroom facilities are all available.

Visiting is permitted on a 24hr basis for parents/guardians. Other visitors are welcome until 19.00 at the discretion of the ward charge nurse. An adult must accompany visiting children at all times and take responsibility for their behaviour.

Play staff are available in all the clinical areas to ensure that play is encouraged and maintained during a child's stay in hospital. The play specialists within the team can assist the child to understand the treatments and investigations they are undergoing while in hospital. Volunteers support professional staff within Sick Kids. For example, they may support the play specialists to ensure that the children's recreational needs are met. They guide families around the hospital, take the mobile library around the wards, befriend a child, read bedtime stories to the children in the evenings or even assist with fundraising.

Preoperative Play Coordinators run pre-admission visits for children who are due to have surgery. These are recommended in order to alleviate stress and anxiety surrounding a hospital admission. Visits can also be organised for small groups of nursery/primary school children wishing to find out more about hospitals.

With prior arrangement the hospital nursery can accommodate a number of young children of parents visiting the hospital. The nursery is open Mon-Fri 8:00-18.00.

For further information contact Play Services Coordinator, Tel: 536 0000, Bleep: 241.

St John's Hospital at Howden
Howden Road West
Livingston
Tel: 01506 419 666

West Lothian Healthcare (NHS) Trust offers a holistic approach to ill children aged 0-16 yrs and their families. Parents are welcome to stay and their needs are accommodated where possible on the ward. Siblings are welcome but appropriate adult supervision is appreciated. Visiting times for parents are open. For friends and relatives the hours are 11.00-19.00 and at the discretion of the Ward Sister.

There is a playroom staffed by play leaders during the week and open at the weekend, nursing staff permitting.

There is a wide range of clinics where your child's condition, treatment and care is assessed by paediatricians and nursing staff. There are play facilities coordinated by play leaders when available.

Children's Community Nursing provides specialist nursing care for children in their own homes. They work closely with hospital staff, GPs, health visitors, special schools

and many other agencies to help provide the child and family with holistic care. The team comprises of 4 specially trained nurses who cover the whole of West Lothian, one of whom is based in the Child Development Centre and specialises in caring for children with neuro developmental problems.

ANTENATAL CARE

As soon as you think you are pregnant you should visit your GP. Usually you will be asked to choose where you would like to have your baby, at home or in hospital. A home birth can be arranged with the community midwives in your local area.

Basic facts to bear in mind are your preference and comfort and your medical history.

Simpson Centre for Reproductive Health
Royal Infirmary of Edinburgh – Little France
51 Little France Crescent
Tel: 536 1000

Maternity services in Lothian are now community based, with most women receiving care in their local area. Antenatal care is provided by the local midwifery team, your GP or, if necessary, a consultant obstetrician. This means that most women only attend hospital for the birth of their baby.

Postnatal care is provided at home by the local midwifery team.

Information
The midwives based in your local area will provide advice in relation to all aspects of pregnancy, birth and postnatal care. In addition, a leaflet 'Your Baby – Your Choice' is available in the community to help you make decisions about your care. The midwives at your local clinic will be able to provide you with any further information you require in relation to your care.

Parent Education Sessions
Provided by the midwifery team (with the support of other healthcare professionals) within your locality, parent education sessions cover various aspects of pregnancy up to and including the birth of your baby. The midwife will also discuss the arrangements for your care following the birth of your baby.

Feeding Your Baby

Information about feeding your baby will be provided by the midwifery team as part of your antenatal care; breastfeeding is encouraged. The Simpson Centre for Reproductive Health has 'Baby Friendly' status awarded by UNICEF for its support of breastfeeding. There is a weekly drop-in clinic on a Tuesday from 1200-1600 on the ground floor of the centre, for those with breastfeeding problems, or contact the NCT Centre, Tel: 668 3257.

Facilities for Childcare

There are two play areas situated on the ground floor of the centre. A selection of toys and children's books are available. Parents are asked to keep children under supervision at all times.

Neonatal Unit

The unit provides specialist care for 44 babies. Parents are encouraged to visit and to participate in their baby's care; siblings are also welcome. There is accommodation available for parents, with priority given to those whose babies are acutely ill or whose babies have been transferred to the unit from another hospital. There is a play area for children stocked with toys and books. Parents are asked to keep visiting children under supervision at all times.

Simpsons Special Care Babies

A voluntarily run charity set up by parents and friends who have had babies in the unit. Raises funds to provide equipment and facilities for the unit, to complement and enhance those provided by the NHS.

St John's Hospital at Howden
Howden Road West
Livingston
Tel: 01506 419 666
West Lothian Healthcare (NHS) Trust offers a holistic approach to midwifery care encompassing a full range of maternity services, as well as water birth, home and hospital birth.

Antenatal appointments

At your first appointment with the midwife at the health centre, a full range of written information relating to health in pregnancy, screening tests, parenting skills and options for delivery will be discussed and given to you. Your midwife will also plan with you the frequency and content of antenatal visits for the rest of your pregnancy.

Antenatal Classes

Antenatal classes both at your local health centre and at the hospital will be offered to you. Community midwives facilitate these with other health professionals such as health visitors and physiotherapists. Courses vary from: women only classes, women and partner classes, teenage classes, aqua natal classes and hypnotherapy classes.

Special Care Baby Unit

The unit provides holistic care for 14 babies. Breastfeeding is encouraged and necessary facilities are provided. Parents and siblings may visit anytime but supervision of children is required. Parents may stay if accommodation is available.

ANTENATAL CLASSES AND SUPPORT

Association for Improvements in the Maternity Services (AIMS)
40 Leamington Terrace EH10 4JL
Contact: Nadine Edwards
Tel: 0131 229 6259
Tel: 0870 765 1433 (Help line)
Web: www.aims.org.uk
AIMS provide information and support to parents about their choices in maternity care. A range of booklets on how to make the right decision for you, the second and third stages of labour, the pros and cons of induction, VBAC, breech birth, home birth, water birth, twins etc, plus quarterly journal are available. Send SAE for free publications list.

Birth Resource Centre
18 St Peters Place
Viewforth EH3 9PH
Contact: Co-ordinator
Tel: 229 3667
Web: www.birthresourcecentre.org.uk
The centre provides classes for parents during pregnancy and after birth, including yoga for pregnancy, birth preparation workshops for women and their partners, postnatal discussion groups, baby massage, baby music, toddler music, baby shiatsu, postnatal yoga for parent and baby, breastfeeding support group and other events. The weekly yoga classes provide practical skills including breathing awareness, relaxation, yoga poses suitable for

pregnancy and time for discussion. The day workshops prepare women and their partners to meet the challenge of labour and birth with confidence and the postnatal groups support women and their families after birth. All sessions provide parents with the information they need to enable them to make decisions about their pregnancies, birth and care of their babies, as well as an opportunity to meet others in similar circumstances. Birth pools, birth balls, library and newsletter available.

National Childbirth Trust
NCT Centre – Edinburgh
University Health Service
5th floor
6 Bristo Square EH8 9AL
Tel: 668 3257
Tel: 0870 444 0907 (NCT Breastfeeding Line 8.00-22.00)

NCT antenatal classes give parents the chance to discuss and to become informed about all aspects of pregnancy, birth and life with a new baby. Relaxation, breathing techniques, massage and different birth positions are practised and explained, enabling parents to approach the birth confidently. Breastfeeding education is included as part of the antenatal class package and support continues postnatally.
Venues vary. Couples Course £142, Refresher Course £89, Short Course £89 Concessionary fee is half full fee.

Scottish Birth Teachers Association
Contact: Nadine Edwards
Tel: 229 6259

2 year training and occasional study days. List of SBTA teachers available.

Lothian Home Birth Support
Contact: Ruth Kirkpatrick
Tel: 445 1507

Offers support and information through a network of parents

POSTNATAL SUPPORT

Community Midwives
Community midwives visit you at home after the birth of your baby and will attend the delivery if you have a home confinement. They will visit every day until the baby is 10 days old (or for longer if there are any problems).

Health Visitors
Health Visitors are all registered nurses who have undertaken further extensive training to enable them to deliver family and community focused care in the community. The focus of much of their work is centred on families and children offering assessment, advice, information and support on health, social and environmental matters.

The health visitor is able to offer antenatal contact and ongoing support throughout the child's pre-school years. This is achieved through home visits, clinic contact and parenting programmes, and involves helping parents develop an understanding of their child's health and development as well as offering wider support for the family. They have a sound knowledge of the local community and the resources available and can therefore direct families to relevant agencies, e.g. Children and Families Services, and local groups to obtain the help and support they might require.

Working with health visitors within the Health Visiting team there are also staff nurses, nursery nurses and health assistants who will work with the health visitor offering support to families. The health visitor also works closely with other members of Primary Health Care teams such as midwives, doctors, practice nurses, district nurses, community psychiatric nurses and school nurses.

Doulas
Essentially, a doula (say doo-la) provides emotional and practical support for the mother/parents before, during and/or after the birth of their child. She is also a mother's advocate in whatever situation she chooses to give birth, be it in hospital, at home, with or without medical intervention.

A doula will assist the woman, and will work within her chosen environment as a birth assistant, adapting to the woman's changing needs during labour and birth. Doulas do not offer medical advice. For more information see the websites listed below, or go to www.doula.org.uk

Edinburgh Doulas
Contact: Kim Bradie
Kim: 0131 554 6620 or 07947 493 234
Email: kim@edinburghdoula.co.uk
Contact: Sian Scott
Tel: 01875 870262
Email: sian.scott1@btinternet.com

Contact: Nicola Goodall
Tel: 0131 4423064
Email: nicolagoodall@postmaster.co.uk
Web: www.edinburghdoulas.co.uk
Edinburgh Doulas provides ante- and post- natal support for women.
The doula will be on 24 hour call for the mother for four weeks: two weeks before your due date and two after. When you go into labour they are to be called at any time, and can be with you as soon as you feel you need support. They can be with you at home during the early stages of labour or can meet you at the hospital (if you are planning a hospital birth) but some first time mums may find it useful to have someone beside them to help them decide when to leave for the hospital.
Edinburgh Doulas state that their most important role during birth will be a nurturing presence. They can offer advice and help regarding breathing, movement and positioning if needed but, most importantly, continuous emotional support and comfort.

Mother to Mother
Post-Natal Doula Support
Contact: Clare Bartos
Tel: 445 4445
Email: clare@mothertomother.co.uk
Web: mothertomother.co.uk
A post-natal doula will work with a mother and her family for a mutually agreed period of time – usually about 6 weeks after the birth of a baby, although the extent of the support can vary according to the mother and her family's needs. She will work for about 3 hours each morning for an agreed number of days
each week.
A post-natal doula provides physical and emotional support to a mother and her family. She will also help a mother to locate information and support from other sources. She can also free the mother from some domestic chores so that the mother has time to meet her own and her baby's needs.

Health All Round
Springwell House, Ardmillan Terrace
Tel: 537 7530
Local project identifying and responding to a range of health needs and issues within the local community. Offers counselling, complementary therapies exercise groups and yoga. Parent support group meets weekly and includes general activities and health promoting events. Multicultural womens group also meets weekly. Children welcome to attend with parent/carer.

La Leche League
Tel: 01875 320991, contact: Sandra
Tel: 01506 414010, contact: Caron
Tel: 01899 810348, contact: Hazel
Tel: 01383 731644, contact: Ingrid
Web: www.laleche.org.uk
E-mail: llledinburgh@cbahowden.icuklive.co.uk
Breastfeeding support and information. Monthly group meetings for pregnant and breastfeeding mothers and their babies in both Edinburgh and Livingston. Telephone counselling from trained volunteers who have personal breastfeeding experience. They also run a toddler group for mothers breastfeeding older children.

NCT Centre
University Health Service
5th floor
6 Bristo Square EH8 9AL
Tel: 6683257
Tel: 0870 444 0907
(NCT Breastfeeding Line 8.00-22.00)
Web: www.nct-edinburgh.freeserve.co.uk
Please phone for new hours
The NCT offers extensive postnatal support in the form of local groups of parents who meet on a regular basis. If you go to NCT antenatal classes your name will be given to your local group representative who should contact you around the time your baby is due, if not before. She will give you details of local meetings and may be able to advise you whom to contact if you have any specific problems. The NCT centre will tell you who your local group representative is if you are not an NCT member. You are welcome to join a postnatal support group even if you have not been to NCT antenatal classes. Activities include coffee mornings or afternoons, evening talks, discussion groups, bumps and babies groups, fund-raising events, picnics, local newsletter, etc. Members receive the quarterly magazine 'New Generation'.
The NCT also provides information, support and encouragement for breastfeeding through its network of breastfeeding counsellors who have all breastfed their own children and been through intensive training. They can also arrange the hire of electric breast pumps and valley cushions

POSTNATAL DEPRESSION

It is not uncommon for women to feel depressed any time in the first year postnatally. Do not hesitate to ask for help; contact your GP or health visitor for support and advice. Support groups are frequently run for mothers with postnatal depression and your health visitor will be able to advise you.

Postnatal Depression Project
Wallace House, 3 Boswall Road
Tel: 538 7288
8a Palmerston Pl
Tel: 220 3457

St Philips Church
Joppa
Tel: 657 9844
Email: pnd@crossreach.org.uk
Web: www.bluebellday.org.uk
You can contact the project direct, via a health visitor, GP or other health professional referrals. It offers a range of services to families suffering with postnatal depression including: couple and individual counselling, women's therapy groups, art therapy and baby massage classes. All services supported with crèche facilities.

Dental Care
All dentists providing NHS care may be found on a list held by Lothian Health Board (see Useful Addresses in this chapter), or at a post office or library. The majority of children go to a family dentist for treatment but in certain circumstances your child could be treated by the Community Dental Service. Community Dentists also have a responsibility to provide oral health education and to monitor the dental health of school children through the National Inspection Programme.

Mothers are entitled to free dental treatment throughout pregnancy and until the baby's first birthday. Children under 18 yrs are also entitled to free treatment. Babies may be registered with a dentist from birth and should certainly be registered before their second birthday. If you take your child along to your own dental visits he/she will become used to the surgery from an early age.

The water supply throughout Lothian does not contain sufficient fluoride to benefit teeth. Teeth should be cleaned as soon as they appear using a small headed brush and a fluoride toothpaste containing no less than 1000 parts per million fluoride. Only a smear of paste

should be applied to the brush. For children at high risk of dental decay dentists may prescribe fluoride tablets or drops.
For further information please contact:
Mrs Christine Wight
Duncan Street Dental Centre
16 Duncan Street
Edinburgh EH9 1SR
Tel: 0131 667 7114
Email: christine.wight@lpct.scot.nhs.uk

COMPLEMENTARY HEALTH CARE
There is a wide range of complementary/alternative therapists offering a variety of therapies in the Edinburgh area but not all of these would be suitable for children or pregnant women. Individual practitioners offer most of these services privately and fees for consultation and treatment vary widely. Practitioners advertise in local directories or can be located via their national professional body. It is strongly recommended that you check that any therapist is registered with their appropriate professional body. Please remember that an entry is not necessarily a recommendation.

It is also sensible to advise any therapist of any conventional medical treatment you are undergoing prior to commencing therapy and vice versa. It would not be practical to attempt to include an exhaustive list of therapies/therapists in a publication such as this. If you are unable to find a local practitioner or a particular therapy your local library will be able to direct you to a national organisation you can contact.

You may also be able to obtain further information from the following local resources. And remember, you can also request an NHS referral to the Homeopathic hospital if you think this would be helpful for you or your child. While the hospital is in Glasgow, it operates outreach clinics in St John's at Howden. However, the waiting list may be extensive.

Baby Massage Classes
3r Therapies
Contact: Claire Lumsdaine
Tel: 07941 393170
Email: claire@3rtherapies.co.uk
Web: www.3rtherapies.co.uk
Baby massage helps parent and baby to bond and relax and may ease babies' digestion and sleep. Regular scheduled classes provide a chance to meet other parents. Alternatively, group classes at your own venue or individual sessions. Also ante-natal sessions to prepare

HEALTHCARE

you to massage your newborn. Classes suitable up to crawling. Call, go online or email for prices and more information.

Baby Massage /Homeopathy
Contact: Linda Bendle RSHom
Tel: 447 3060

Baby massage can help to relieve colic and constipation; reduce restlessness aiding sleep; soothe and comfort a fractious child; improve the health and vitality of your baby. Classes, one-to-one sessions and gift vouchers available. Homeopathy is a safe, gentle and highly effective system of medicine, which uses natural substances to treat the whole individual. Linda specialises in working with women in pregnancy, with children and with their families. Consultations and workshops on how to prescribe remedies in first aid situations; in labour and post natal; and with children available.

Discover Chiropractic
240 Queensferry Road
Tel: 332 0063
Email: blackhall@discoverchiropractic.co.uk

Opening hours: Mon,Wed 8.00-11.30 and 14.30-18.10; Tue,Thu 14.00-18.10, Fri 8.00-11.30; 3rd Sat each month 10.00-12.00.

Chiropractic care may help with many childhood ailments such as sleeplessness, hyperactivity, vomiting, ear/nose/throat infections, Erbs Palsy and Shaken Baby Syndrome. Child friendly family run business, focused on family care. Consultations available from birth. Toys/books/videos available. Nappy changing room with nappies provided. Breastfeeding welcome, premises accessible to pushchairs. Usually a member of staff can look after children during a parent's consultation.

The Edinburgh Natural Health Centre
1 St Colme St (behind Charlotte Square) EH3 6AA
Tel: 220 8205 (switchboard)
Tel: 0800 298 7015 (freephone)
Web: www.enhc.co.uk

Opening hours: Mon-Fri 9.00-18.00.

Acupuncture, Homeopathy, Acupressure massage, Chinese herbal medicine and Nutrition are available with advice on and treatment for vaccinations. Consultation by appointment.

Glovers Integrated Healthcare
10 William Street
Tel: 225 3161
Email: gloversIHC@aol.com
Web: www.glovers-health.co.uk

Opening hours: Mon-Fri 10.00-17.00.

Homeopathic consultations, remedies and mail order available.

Homeopathic Clinic
Dalkeith Medical Centre
24 St Andrew Street
Dalkeith EH22 1AP
Tel: 561 5510

Homeopathic treatment is available on the NHS at clinics held at both Dalkeith Medical Centre and the Firrhill Medical Centre in Edinburgh. Patients referred by their GPs are able to consult homeopathically-qualified doctors. Treatment is free. All enquiries and referrals to Dalkeith Medical Centre.

Ewan Kenny, Craniosacral Therapist
Energetics
14a Broughton Street Lane EH1 3LY
Tel: 557 9567
Web: www.ewankenny.com

Craniosacral therapy is a gentle 'hands on' treatment. Suitable for all ages, this therapy may prove particularly useful for many infant problems such as colic, breathing difficulties, restlessness and irritability.

Medicalternative
Waterside House
19 Hawthornbank Lane EH4 3BH
Tel: 225 5656
Email: reception@medicalternative.com
Email: julie-anne.taylor@virgin.net
(for advanced hypnotherapy)

Opening times: 8.00-19.00.

Private health care centre, which encompasses both conventional and alternative care. You can walk in off the street and see a qualified GP (no referral or appointment needed). There are numerous alternative therapists, all highly qualified and specialists in their own field. Breastfeeding welcomed. Nappy changing facilities.

Massage Therapies
30A Hermitage Gardens
Edinburgh EH10 6AY
Contact: Benedetta Gaetani d'Aragona
Tel: 447 4421
E-mail: massage@easynet.co.uk
Web: www.massagetherapies.co.uk

Opening hours: 9.00-21.00.

Pre and postnatal massage; massage instruction for partners to assist in labour. Prices £35 /50 mins.

Napiers Dispensary
18 Bristo Place
Tel: 225 5542
Web: www.napiers.net

Opening hours, shop: Mon 10.00-18.00; Tue-Fri 9.00-18.00; Sat 9.00-17.30; Sun 12.30-16.30.

Parent baby/child herbal clinic: Fri 10.00-17.00 (fortnightly) by appointment.
£20 for first consultation; thereafter £18.
Baby/child homeopathic clinic: Wed 9.30-12.30 (fortnightly) by appointment
£30 for first consultation thereafter £25. Approx £3/ remedy.

also at:
35 Hamilton Place
Stockbridge, EH3 5BA
Tel: 315 2130
Web: www.napiers.net

Opening hours, shop: Mon 10.00-18.00, Tue-Fri 9.00-18.00, Sat 9.00-17.30, and Sun 12.30-16.30.
Parent /child herbal clinic: Fri 9.45-16.30 by appointment.
£20 for first consultation; thereafter £18.
Baby/child homeopathic clinic: Wed fortnightly 9.30-12.30 by appointment.
£30 for first consultation thereafter £25. Approx £3 per remedy.

Consultations in herbal medicine, aromatherapy, osteopathy, homeopathy, acupuncture and counselling. The parent and child herbal clinics provide dedicated support for pregnant women, babies and children. Herbal medicine is especially gentle for babies and children and may prove useful in treating, for instance, colic, sleep problems, cradle cap, glue ear, coughs and catarrh.
Specialists in women's health problems also available – please call for details.
The shops stock a range of traditional herbal remedies, nutritional supplements, aromatherapy products and organic skin care as well as their own mother and baby range.
For mail order call 0131 343 6683 or visit www.napiers. net

The Osteopathic Practice
1 Wester Coates Avenue EH12 5LS.
Contact: Tom Kelman
Tel: 346 0134
Mob: 07866 299 250
Email: tom_kelman@hotmail.com
Practice times: Mon to Fri: 9.00-18.00.
Tom Kelman is a Registered Osteopath who holds a postgraduate Diploma in Paediatric Osteopathy and who specialises in paediatric and family care. He offers experienced advice, treatment and management for many childhood problems ranging from: unsettled, crying or colicky symptoms following a difficult birth, to children with developmental delay, cerebral palsy, autism or epilepsy. May also help mums with gentle and effective relief from aches and pains before or after a birth.

The Whole Works Complementary Therapy and Counselling Centre
Jackson's Close
209 Royal Mile
Edinburgh EH1 1PZ
Contact: Rob Ritchie (Manager)
Tel: 225 8092
Web: www.thewholeworks.co.uk
Opening hours: Mon – Fri 9.30-19.30; Sat 9.30-16.30.
Offers a range of complementary health therapies and counselling, including craniosacral therapy, massage, homeopathy, chiropractic, acupuncture and herbal medicine.

USEFUL ADDRESSES
This list is not intended to be exhaustive but it may help point you in the right direction if you are seeking further information locally. See also Support Groups in Help & Information section. For further information check with your local health professional, NCT Group, library or community centre.

Action for Sick Children (Scotland)
172 Leith Walk EH6 5EA
Tel: 553 6553
Email: asc2k@lineone.net

A charity for all children in hospital and for adults caring for them. Information for parents with babies in special care units. Parent packs to help children prepare for a hospital visit. Hospital play box for loan to local playgroups which helps parents to prepare children (3-6 yrs) for a hospital visit; includes toys, books, real medical equipment and mini uniforms.

CAPT – Child Accident Prevention Trust
Tel: 020 7608 3828
E-mail: safe@capt.org.uk
Web: www.capt.org.uk
A national charity committed to reducing the number of children and young people killed, disabled and seriously injured as a result of accidents.

Chatterbox – Private Speech Therapy Services
Contact: Jane Armstrong
Tel: 445 7385
Email: janec.Armstrong@virgin.net
Web: www.chatterbox-speechtherapy.co.uk
Chatterbox offers a range of assessments which can be used to determine what is wrong with a child's speech and/or language skills. It is a mobile service, coming to your house where a thorough investigation is made of your child's communication skills.

Family Planning Centre
18 Dean Terrace
Tel: 332 7941 or 343 6243

Home Start
35 Guthrie Street, Edinburgh
Tel 0131 226 1331
E-mail: homestartedinsc@btconnect.com
Tel: 0800 068 63 68 (freephone)
Web: www.home-start.org.uk
Informal and friendly support for families with young children who are finding it hard to cope.

Lothian NHS Board Library and Resource
Deaconess House
148 The Pleasance
Tel: 536 9451/2/3
Opening hours: Mon 13.00-16.30; Tue-Wed 9.30-16.30; Thu 9.30-18.30; Fri 9.30-13.00.
Can provide leaflets and posters on a wide range of health issues free of charge. Resources for teaching and training purposes are also available for loan. The centre has several databases, which have information about specific conditions and related support and self-help groups. These are updated regularly and information can be printed out on request.

NHS Direct Scotland
Tel: 08454 24 24 24
Text Phone 18001 08454 24 24 24
Web: www.nhs24.com
NHS direct is a 24 hour telephone health advice and information service.

NHS Lothian
Stevenson House
555 Gorgie Road, EH11 3LG
Tel: 537 8400

Parentline Scotland
Tel: 0808 800 2222
Web: www.parentlinescotland.org.uk
Parentline Scotland is a free, confidential, telephone helpline for parents and anyone caring for a child in Scotland. You can call about any problem, however big or small.

Royal Life Saving Society UK
Contact: Linsey Watson
Scottish Eastern Branch
17 Station Road, Loanhead EH20 9RQ
Tel: 07834 705431
Provides courses in baby resuscitation called 'Save a Baby's Life'. These are invaluable to any parent, carer, babysitter or grandparent, or anyone who will be in sole charge of an infant. They are organised periodically and for a small fee, currently £5, you will be taught life saving skills on a manikin, (it is recommended that you attend without children). Courses last 2 hrs and cover action in an emergency, drowning, choking, breathing stopped, heart stopped. Additional instruction for technique required for children aged 1+ yrs can be provided in the form of a short display at the end. Contact the above phone number for details of these or their other life saving courses, or send an SAE to Linsey Watson. If you have 10 or more people interested, Linsey would be able to provide you with your own training session or for individuals advise when the next organised course will take place.

Scottish Health Council – Lothian Office
21 Torphichen Street EH3 8HX
Tel: 229 6605
Fax:229 6220
Email: Jackie.mackenzie@lhc.lothian.scot.nhs.uk
Web: www.scottishhealthcouncil.org
The Scottish Heath Council is an official body set up
to ensure that the views of patients and the public are
taken into account by NHS Boards. The council has local
offices in each NHS Board area where local people are
appointed to serve on an advisory council for each local
office.
The fundamental purpose of the Scottish Health Council
is to promote improvements in the quality and extent of
patient focus and public involvement in health services.

Sick Kids Friends Foundation
Royal Hospital for Sick Children
20 Millerfield Place,
Tel: 0131 668 4949
Web: www.edinburghsickkids.org
Raises funds to further interests of the child health
services in the RHSC.

SNIP - Special Needs Information Point
Royal Hospital for Sick Children
14 Rillbank Ter
Tel: 0131 536 0583 (helpline)
Tel: 0131 536 0360 (office/text phone)
Email: Snip@btinternet.com
Web: www.snipinfo.org
Information, advice and support for parents, carers and
professionals about children with special needs.

Help and Information

INTRODUCTION

This section is meant to be a starting point if you are looking for help or advice. It is not all-encompassing, but we have tried to list the names and addresses of organisations that can provide you with information, advice and support.

HEALTH

For help with specific medical conditions or services available to children with special needs and their carers please refer to the chapter on Health Care or contact SNIP (Special Needs Information Point based at the Sick Kids Hospital in Edinburgh) who can provide information, contact addresses and support.

Special Needs Information Point (SNIP)
14 Rillbank Terrace
Royal Hospital for Sick Children
Edinburgh EH9 ILN
Tel/Fax: 536 0583
Text phone: 536 0360
Email: Snip@btinternet.com
Website: www.snipinfo.org

BENEFITS / SOCIAL SECURITY INFORMATION

There's a good deal of information online. Two helpful websites are:

Parents at Work
Web: www.parentsatwork.org.uk
Has a wide range of information including factsheets about things like tax credits and flexible working.

Department for Work and Pensions
Web: www.dwp.gov.uk/lifeevent/benefits/index.asp
Provides details of the different types of benefits available and how to make a claim.

Other sources of information are:

Benefits Agency
38 Castle Ter
Tel: 229 431 1
General information and advice about social security and child benefits.

LOCAL SOCIAL SECURITY OFFICES

City Centre
38 Castle Terrace EH1 0QG
Tel: 229 4311
For Postal Districts EH1-4, 8, 10

Edinburgh East
275 Portobello High Street EH15 2AQ
Tel: 657 7400
For Postal Districts: EH15-16, 21, 31-36, 39-42

Leith
199 Commercial Street EH6 6QP
Tel: 555 8000
For Postal Districts: EH4-7

Edinburgh West
8 Clifton Terrace
Tel: 01506 638000
For Postal Districts: EH11-14, 28-30

South
158/160 Causewayside EH9 1QJ
Tel. 552 5500
For Postal Districts: EH9, 16-20, 22-26, 37

Wester Hailes ESJ/Social Security Office
Westside Plaza EH14 2SP
Tel. 456 4300
For Postal Districts: EH11-14, 28-30

Jobcentre Plus Offices
In some areas Jobcentre Plus offices offer/will offer a fully integrated work and benefits service. The integration process is currently underway. Benefits can be claimed at the Jobcentre Plus offices listed below, as well as the addresses given above. For more detail and up-to-date information see www.jobcentreplus.co.uk.

Torphichen Street Jobcentre Plus
24-26 Torphichen Street EH3 8JP
Tel. 456 5200

Leith Jobcentre Plus
1-3 Leith Walk EH6 8TD
Tel. 456 4200

Portobello Jobcentre Plus
21-23 Windsor Place EH15 2AF
Tel. 456 4800

Edinburgh High Riggs Jobcentre
20 High Riggs EH3 9HU
Tel. 456 4000

Edinburgh City Centre Jobcentre Plus
11-13 South St Andrew Street EH2 2BT
Tel. 456 3300

Child Tax Credit
For help or information regarding child tax credit, contact the helpline or write to the office (addresses given below). You will need your NI number (and your partner's if the claim was joint). The help line can be extremely busy, but it's still quicker than writing.

Tax Credits Helpline
(for those living in GB)
Tel: 0845 300 3900
Textphone: 0845 300 3909
(for those living in NI)
Tel: 0845 603 2000
Textphone: 0845 607 6078
Helplines are open daily, 8.00-20.00 (except Christmas Day, Boxing Day, New Year's Day and Easter Sunday). See also HM Revenue and Customs website: www.hmrc.gov.uk
For information regarding Child Benefit, there's a national number: 0845 3021444.

The City of Edinburgh Council Advice Shop
85-87 South Bridge   EH1 1HN
Tel: 225 1255
Consumer advice, debt advice and advice on welfare benefits.

SOCIAL WORK

The City of Edinburgh Council Department of Social Work HQ
Shrubhill House
Shrub Place, Leith Walk EH7 4PD
Tel: 553 8395
Tel: 0800 731 6969 Emergency Social Work Service - out of hours

As well as the HQ listed above, There are 12 social work centres throughout the city, all open Mon-Fri 8.30-16.40. Social workers are also based at hospitals.

Social Work Centres

Central

Victoria Street Social Work Centre
11 Victoria Street EH1 2HE
Tel: 226 6731

North East

Giles Street Social Work Centre
9-11 Giles Street EH6 6DJ
Tel: 553 3835

Craigentinny Social Work Centre
Loaning Road EH7 6JE
Tel: 661 8291

Leith Social Work Centre
St John's House
71 Constitution St EH6 7AF
Tel: 553 2121
North West

Westfield House Social Work Centre
Westfield House
5 Kirk Loan EH12 7HD
Tel: 334 9933

Muirhouse Crescent Social Work Centre
34 Muirhouse Crescent EH4 4QL
Tel: 343 1991

West Pilton Gardens Social Work Centre
8 West Pilton Gardens EH4 4DP
Tel: 529 5400

South East

Craigmillar Social Work Centre
171 Duddingston Park South EH15 3EG
Tel: 657 8500

Captain's Road Social Work Centre
40 Captains Road   EH17 8QF
Tel: 529 5300

South West

Springwell House Social Work Centre
I Gorgie Road   EH11 2LA
Tel: 313 3366

Oxgangs Path Social Work Centre
4 Oxgangs Path   EH13 9LX
Tel: 445 4451

Murrayburn Gate Social Work Centre
5 Murrayburn Gate   EH14 2SS
Tel: 442 4131

Advice centres

Citizens Advice Bureaux
Web: www.adviceguide.org.uk
A free, confidential service providing general advice and information on topics such as housing, family, employment, benefits and consumer issues. Offers money advice and debt negotiation, representation at employment and social security tribunals, some court representation. Appointments usually last 45 minutes. Most offices have legal clinics on a weekly basis. See www.cas.org.uk for information specifically about the Citizens' Advice Bureau in Scotland.

Edinburgh Central
58 Dundas Street
Tel: 557 1500 (public line)
Tel: 558 3681 (appointments)
Fax: 557 3543
Opening times: Mon, Tue 9.30-16.00; Wed 9.30-12.30, 14.00-18.00 (money advice), 18.30-20.00 (general and legal enquiries), Thurs 9.30-16.00, Fri 9.30-11.30 (money advice).

Gorgie/Dalry
137 Dundee St (above Fountain Bridge Library)
Tel: 474 8080 (advice line)
Tel: 474 8081(to make appointments)
Opening times: Mon 13.30-16.00, 17.00-19.00; Tue 10.15-12.45, 13.30-16.00; Wed 13.30-16.00; Thu 10.15-12.45,13.30-16.00. Closed Fri.

Leith
166 Gt Junction St
Tel: 554 8144
Opening times: Mon, Tue 9.30-15.30; Wed closed; Thu 9.30-15.30, 18.00-19.30, Fri 9.30-15.30.

Pilton
661 Ferry Road
Tel: 332 9434
Opening times: Mon, Wed, Fri 9.30-12.30; Tue and Thurs 9.30-15.30.

Portobello
8a-8b Bath Street, Portobello
Tel: 669 7138 (advice)
Tel: 669 9503 (appointments)
Opening times: Mon, Tue, Thu 9.30-15.30; Wed 9.30-12.00, 18.30-19.45. Closed Fri.

Gingerbread Edinburgh and Lothians Project Ltd
Gingerbread House
19 Chester Street EH3 7RF
Tel: 220 1585
Email: GINGERBREADEDIN@aol.com
Opening times: Mon-Fri 10.00-16.00.
Information and advice centre for lone parent families. It also provides 4 after school clubs (in Dalry, Leith, Tollcross and West End), and cover for in-service days, school holiday play schemes, and holiday information packs for lone parents.

Granton Information Centre
134-138 West Granton Road
Tel: 552 0458
Email: info@GIC.visps.com
Information and advice on benefits, debts, housing, employment etc. Also available for development of local self-help/support groups. Youth and disability rights.

The Rights Office
Southside Community Centre
117 Nicolson St   EH8 9YG
Tel: 667 6339
Advice sessions: Mon and Wed 10.00-15.30.
Independent advice and representation on welfare benefits, disability rights, employment rights, debt and housing.

MEDIA LISTING

The Scotsman Group
108 Holyrood Road
Tel: 620 8620 (reception)
Tel: 620 8888 (advertising)
Website: www.scotsman.com

The Scotsman
National daily morning paper, carries birth announcements. Has daily section with details of exhibitions, theatres, art galleries, etc. Church Service information on Sat. Weekend section on Sat with 'What's on' information.

Evening News
Daily afternoon and evening paper full of local news. 'Daily Plan-It' has details of events. Also carries daily cinema programmes. Theatres, sales, fetes etc also listed, especially on Fri.

Scotland on Sunday
Scottish Sunday paper. Has events page.

Edinburgh Herald and Post
Tel: 620 8888 (advertising)
Tel: 620 8705 (editorial)
Email: edinhp@scotsman.com
Published every Thu and delivered free to most homes in the city. Cinema listings and details of local arts and community events, sales, fetes etc. Large 'For Sale' columns. If given sufficient notice, usually at least two weeks, the Herald and Post can publish details of your playgroup fair or other fundraising activities free. A different edition is printed for West Lothian, Tel: 01506 503400 for enquiries or editorial.

Families Edinburgh
Tel. 624 0049 (distribution information)
Web: www.familiesmagazine.co.uk
Free bi-monthly magazine for families with young children. Distributed at playgroups, nurseries, lesiure centres, etc. Local listings, advertisements, features.

The List
14 High Street EH1 1TE
Tel: 550 3070
Fax: 557 8500
Email: editor@list.co.uk
Web: www.list.co.uk
Published fortnightly and includes a small section 'Kid's List'

which provides information about events in and around Edinburgh and Glasgow. It's worthwhile checking with the specific venues regarding times etc, as information can change after the publication has gone to press. Available at newsagents.

Radio Forth
Forth House, Forth Street
Tel: 556 9255
Web: www.forth1.com
Web: www.forth2.com
Daily 'What's On' slot in the morning show on Forth 1, with information on forthcoming local events. Events page on the websites.

GUIDES TO EDINBURGH

Council libraries have books, files and on-line information for reference purposes. These include:

Capital Information Point (CAPINFO)
Website: www.edinburgh.gov.uk
CAPINFO is a free council-run information service, which provides information about your local community and council departments: education, children, young people and families, leisure and health care. You can access Capinfo on the internet, on the above address at home or in libraries throughout Edinburgh.

Citizens' Advice
Published by Citizens Advice Bureau.
Website: www.adviceguide.org.uk
Edinburgh Information Pack including information on childcare, nursery education, local and regional councillors, local churches, etc.
List of local clubs and organisations.
Reference books about Edinburgh.
A-Z guide produced by City Of Edinburgh Council, listing contacts, community updates, council lists, and general information regarding the city.

Two websites are also worth mentioning:
www.netmums.com/edinburgh
Includes information on events, activities and meeting local mothers.

www.edinburghmums.co.uk
A yahoo discussion group. Members also meet regularly, both with their children (usually including one monthly outing) and for mums only evenings.

SUPPORT GROUPS

This section contains listings for organisations and voluntary groups who offer support and assistance on a wide range of issues.

For more comprehensive information on Women's Groups, contact the City of Edinburgh Council Equality Unit, 12 St Giles St, Tel: 469 3603. Your local Community Education Centre and some of the Community High Schools also arrange Parents' Groups with creche facilities; see Community Education Centres in Activities for Parents.

AFASIC
Tel: 0845 3555577 (helpline Mon-Fri 10.30-14.30)
Web: www.afasic.org.uk
Web: www.afasicscotland.org.uk
Web: www.talkingpoint.org.uk
Charity supporting children and young adults with speech, language or communication impairments and their parents/carers.

AFASIC Edinburgh
Contact tel: 557 9755
Email: afasic.edinburgh@afasicscotland.org.uk
Local support group.

Allergy UK
No 3 White Oak Square
London Road
Swanley
Kent BR8 7AG
Tel: 01322 619864 (helpline)
Web: www.allergyfoundation.com
UK charity providing information on all aspects of allergy.

Asthma UK Scotland
(formerly Asthma Campaign Scotland)
4 Queen Street EH2 1JE
Tel: 226 2544
Tel: 08457 010203 (helpline Mon-Fri 9.00-17.00)
Email: enquiries@asthma.org.uk
An independent UK charity, based in London and Edinburgh, which works to conquer asthma. It works in partnership with people with asthma and all who share their concern, through a combination of research, information, support and campaigning.

Capability Scotland Advice Service (ASCS)
11 Ellersly Road   EH12 6HY
Tel: 313 5510
Text phone: 346 2529
Fax: 346 1681
Email: ascs@capability-scotland.org.uk
Website: www.capability-scotland.org.uk
Provides information and advice on any disability matter.

The Compassionate Friends
53 North Street, Bristol BS3 1EN
Website:www.tcf.org.uk
A self-help group for parents and their families who have suffered the loss of a child of any age through any cause. Lending library and link scheme available.

Contact a Family Scotland
Norton Park
57 Albion Road EH5 7QY
Tel: 475 2608
Fax: 475 2609
Email: scotland@cafamily.org.uk
Web: www.cafamily.org.uk
Opening times: Mon-Fri 10.00-16.00.
Introduces and links families whose children have special needs through local mutual support and self-help groups. Offers nationwide support and links individual parents of children with very rare disorders.

Couple Counselling Lothian
9a Dundas Street
Tel: 556 1527
Email: cclothian@btopenworld.com
Web: www.cclothian.btinternet.co.uk
Opening times: Mon-Thurs 9.00-21.00; Fri 9.00-16.00; Sat 10.00-13.00.
Confidential counselling service for those who are experiencing disharmony and tension in their marriage or personal relationships. Also at Sighthill Health Centre; Dalkeith Medical Centre; Dedridge Health Centre, Livingston and Howden Health Centre, Livingston.

Cruse Bereavement Care Scotland
3 Rutland Square   EH1 2AS
Tel: 229 6275
Web: www.crusescotland.org.uk
In addition to counselling, advisory services and friendship groups for adults and offers bereavement counselling to children.

HEALTH & INFORMATION – SUPPORT GROUPS

DAPeND Helpline
Tel. 0845 1203746 (Mon-Fri 19.00-22.00)
Offers support to those suffering from postnatal or antenatal depression. Run under the auspices of Depression Alliance.

Dosti Muslim Groups
172 Leith Walk EH6 5EA
Contact: Audrey Peacock/ Wendy Spencer
Tel: 553 2189

Opening hours: Mon-Fri 9.30-17.00
Provides: support groups for Muslim women and children; information service to Muslim families and also the wider community. Muslim mothers with pre-school children can access training (with creche), plus family activities and events. Premises have nappy changing facilities (M&F).

Down's Syndrome Scotland
158-160 Balgreen Road EH11 3AU
Tel: 313 4225
Fax: 313 4285
Email: info@dsscotland.org.uk
Web: www.dsscotland.org.uk
Aims to provide support and information to parents of children with Down's Syndrome. Local branch activities include parent and toddler groups, music and drama workshops, computer club and outings.

The Edinburgh Miscarriage Support Group
Tel: 657 5377
Contact: Sue

The group provides emotional support for anyone suffering the effects of miscarriage and pregnancy loss. Meetings held second Wednesday of every month 19.30-21.00 at Craiglockhart Sports Centre, 177 Colinton Rd. (see also the Miscarriage Association, below)

Edinburgh Twins Club
Tel: 01506 416412
Contact: Karen Winfield

Support group for families with twins, triplets etc, providing help, advice and friendship. Bumps and babies, babies and toddler groups, soft play sessions, informal evening meetings, regular newsletters, discounts and library of twin related publications. Meetings in Edinburgh, East Lothian and West Lothian. See also TAMBA, below.

Edinburgh Women's Rape and Sexual Abuse Centre
PO Box 120
Brunswick Road EH7 5WX
Tel: 556 9437 (answerphone out of office hours)
Email: support@ewrasac.org.uk
Email: info@ewrasc.org.uk
Information, practical and emotional support for women who have been raped or sexually assaulted at any time in their lives. Run by women for women.

Enlighten Action for Epilepsy
5 Coates Place EH3 7AA
Tel: 226 5458
Email: info@enlighten.org.uk
Web: www.enlighten.org.uk
Offers information, advice, support and counselling to parents of children with epilepsy and parents with epilepsy who have young children.

ERIC - Enuresis Resource and Information Centre
34 Old School House
Britannia Road
Kingswood
Bristol BS15 8DB
Tel: 0117 960 3060 (helpline, Mon-Fri 10.00-16.00)
Email: info@eric.org.uk
Web: www.eric.org.uk
ERIC provides advice and information to children, young people, parents and professionals on bedwetting, day-time wetting and soiling. Can advise you on the location of your local enuresis clinic. The charity also sells washable duvet and mattress protectors, literature and alarms.

Family Care - Birthlink Adoption Counselling Service
21 Castle Street, EH2 3DN
Tel: 225 6441
Email: mail@birthlink.org.uk
The adoption contact register for Scotland. Counselling, support and advice for adopted people, birth parents and adoptive parents.

Family Mediation Lothian
37 George Street EH2 2HN
Tel: 226 4507
Email: Lothian@familymediation.freeserve.co.uk

Helps separating and divorced parents to make arrangements for the future care of their children. Also runs several 'Contact Centres' where children can spend time with the parent and other relatives with whom they do not live or see regularly. Also provides support for older children.

firstHand
(formerly known as Edinburgh Sitters)
39 Broughton Place EH1 3PR
Tel: 557 3121
Email: mail@1sthand.org.uk
A voluntary organisation providing services to lone parents, carers, children and young disabled adults. Firsthand also runs Saturday Groups for children (7-14 years old) from one parent families and families affected by disability. Please see under Childcare or Accessible Edinburgh for information on the Sitter Service, and firsthand direct.

First Step Community Project
37 Galt Avenue
Musselburgh EH21 8HU
Tel: 665 0848
Project for families with young children offering many services for parents as well as the children. Services include home visiting, play visiting, confidential counselling, classes and groups for adults and information library. Has a special needs playgroup. Also runs a group for teenagers with babies.

Homelink
Unit 5, Abbeymount Techbase
2 Easter Rd EH7 5AN
Tel: 661 0890
Email: homelink@tinyworld.co.uk
Provides emotional and practical support to young families, using trained befrienders. Operates in South East and South West Edinburgh and Midlothian.

Homestart Leith and North East Edinburgh
172 Leith Walk EH6 5EA
Tel/Fax: 553 7819
Email: homestartleith@btconnect.com
Web: www.homestartleith.co.uk

Homestart Edinburgh South Central
35 Guthrie Street EH1 1JG
Tel: 226 1331
Email: homestart.edinsc@btconnect.com

Volunteers offer regular support and practical help in the home to young families who have at least one child under 5.

Humanist Society of Scotland
26 Inverleith Row EH5 5QH
Contact: Ivan Middleton
Tel: 0701 071 4778
Email:ivan@humanism-scotland.org.uk
Information about non-religious ceremonies including baby naming ceremonies.

Hyperactive Children's Support Group
71 Whyke Lane
Chichester, West Sussex PO19 2LD
Contact: Sally Bunday
Tel: 01243 551313
Fax: 01243 552019
Web: www.hacsg.org.uk
The HACSG considers non-drug therapies (dietary ones in particular) especially important for under 6s. Provides information for parents and professionals.

Independent Special Education Advice
(ISEA) Scotland
164 High St
Dalkeith EH22 1AY
Tel: 454 0096 (general)
Tel: 454 0144
(advocacy and representation service)
Fax: 454 0096
Email: iseascotland@whsmithnet.co.uk
Provides advice, information, advocacy and representation to parents throughout Scotland who have a child or young person with additional support needs.

LIBRA
4 Norton Park EH7 5RS
Tel: 661 0111
LIBRA provides free counselling and support to women who are concerned about their own or someone else's drinking.

Lochend YWCA
198 Restalrig Road South EH7 6DZ
Tel: 554 3400
Community cafe; children welcomed and catered for. Full access for prams and pushchairs; nappy-changing facility; bottles can be warmed on request.

Lothian Autistic Society
66a Newhaven Road
Tel: 554 9362
Runs a monthly under 5s support meeting.

Lothian Racial Equality Council
14 Forth Street
Tel: 556 0441
Email: admin@lrec.org.uk
Aims to work towards the elimination of racial discrimination, to promote racial equality and equal opportunities for all and promote good race relations.

MAMA - Meet a Mum Association
7 Southcourt Road
Linslade
Leighton Buzzard
Beds LU7 2QF
Tel: 0845 120 6162
Email: meet_a_mum.assoc@btinternet.com
Web: www.mama.co.uk
Friendship and support to mothers and mothers-to-be through local groups or individual contacts. Support and information on postnatal illness.

The Miscarriage Association
c/o Clayton Hospital
Northgate
Wakefield, West Yorkshire
Tel: 01924 200799

Muscular Dystrophy Group
Prescott House
Prescott Place
London
Tel: 020 7720 8055

National Childbirth Trust
NCT Centre - Edinburgh
University Health Service
5th floor
6 Bristo Square EH8 9AL
Tel: 668 3257
Tel: 0870 444 8708
(NCT breastfeeding line 8.00-22.00)

Provides classes, groups and counselling services, offering parents information and support during pregnancy and the early years of parenthood.

National Domestic Violence Helpline
Tel. 0808 808 9999 (24 hours)

National Eczema Society
Hill House, Highgate Hill, London N19 5NA
Tel: 0870 241 3604
(information line, Mon-Fri 8.00-20.00)
Web: www.eczema.org
An independent UK charity which runs a helpline and produces a quarterly journal keeping members up-to-date with the management and treatment of eczema.

One Parent Families Scotland
13 Gayfield Square EH1 3NX
Tel: 556 3899
Tel. 0800 0185026 (National Lone Parent Helpline)
Email: info@opfs org.uk
Web: www.opfs.org.uk
Information and help for lone parents. Publishes newsletter, a 'Rights Guide' and factsheets including 'Reflections of a Changing World: a list of children's books portraying different families'. Free publications list and membership details. Child-friendly office.

Parentline Scotland
Tel: 0808 800 2222 (free helpline no. Mon, Weds, Fri 9.00-5.00; Tues, Thurs 9.00-21.00)
Web: www.children1st.org.uk/parentline
Information, advice, or someone to listen to you on the telephone.

Parentwell
Tel. 467 6745
Email: parentwell@blueyonder.co.uk
Web: www.parentwell.co.uk
An advisory and support home visiting service. Offers individual home consultations and parenting courses for parent/toddler groups. Topics covered include child behaviour, sleep, nurturing the parent/child bond, toilet training, and healthy eating.

The PF Counselling Service
Eric Liddle Centre
15 Morningside Rd   EH10 4DP
Tel: 447 0876
Email: info@pfcounselling.org.uk
Counselling is available for individuals and couples (over 18 yrs) on a wide range of problems and difficulties. Open to all, on an ability-to-pay basis.

Positive Help
13a Great King Street
Tel: 558 1122
Voluntary organisation for families and children affected/ living with HIV. Provides driving service, decorating, gardening, childcare and children befriending service.

Prison Advice and Care Trust Family Support Service
254 Caledonian Road
London N1 0NG
Tel: 0800 0853021
Email: familysupport@pact.uk.net
Advice, information and support for the families of those in prison. Overnight accommodation for those travelling long distances to visit London prisons. Very close to Pentonville and Holloway Prisons.

Roundabout Centre (YWCA Scotland)
4b Gayfield Place
Contact: Emma Crawshaw
Tel: 556 1168/557 4695
Email: roundaboutywca@care4free.net
Web: www.ywcascotland.org.uk
Runs a multicultural creche for 2-5 yrs (Tue-Thu 9.30-12.00, 12.30-15.30). Various classes. Volunteer training and opportunities in anti-discrimanatory campaigning and international creche and summer school. Fortnightly meeting of friendship, support and networking group for parents of children of dual heritage. Resource and information library.

Saheliya
10 Union Street   EH1 3LU
Tel: 556 9302
Contact: Pat Elsmie and Samina Digpal
Email: saheliya@connectfree.co.uk
Opening times; Mon-Fri 9.00-17.00.
Well-being and mental health project for black and minority ethnic women.
Provides counselling, couples counselling, one to one support, complimentary therapies and befriending. Languages spoken: Arabic, Punjabi, Singhalese, Bengali, Cantonese, Urdu, French, Italian and Hindi. Accepts self-referrals and also referrals from other organisations and professionals.

Scottish Cot Death Trust
Royal Hospital for Sick Children
Yorkhill, Glasgow G3 8SJ
Tel: 0141 357 3946
Web: www.sidsscotland.org.uk
Gives personal support to bereaved families by letter, telephone and leaflets and puts parents in touch with other bereaved parents.

Scottish National Federation for the Welfare of the Blind
Redroofs, Balgavies, Forfar, Angus DD8 2TH
Contact: Hon. Treasurer Mr Duncan
Tel/fax: 01307 830265
Email: snfwb@care4free.net
Co-ordinates organisations working for blind people in Scotland.

Scottish Society for Autism
Hilton House
Alloa Business Centre
The Whins
Alloa   FK10 3SA
Tel: 01259 720 044
Email: autism@autism-in-scotland.org.uk
Web: www.autism-in-scotland.org.uk
Seeks to ensure the provision of the best possible education, care, support and opportunities for people of all ages with autism in Scotland.

Scottish Spina Bifida Association
190 Queensferry Road
Tel: 332 0743 (national office)
Tel: 08459 111112 (family support service - phone for local contacts).

Sexual Health Information Line
Tel: 0800 567 123

Shakti Women's Aid
Norton Park
57 Albion Road EH7 5QY
Tel: 475 2399
Fax: 475 2301
Email: info@shaktiedinburgh.co.uk
Web: www.shaktiedinburgh.co.uk
Offers information, practical and emotional support and safe, temporary accommodation to all black and ethnic

minority women and their children who are being abused either physically or mentally by their partners, husbands or families.

Simpson House Drugs Counselling and Related Services
52 Queen Street EH2 3NS
Tel: 225 1054/6028
Opening times: Mon-Fri 9.00-17.00
Free and confidential counselling service to drug users, friends and families. Creche available. Drugs education. Sunflower Garden Project for children affected by family drug use offers play therapy, infant massage, storytelling, home visits, children's and grandparents' groups, art therapy.

Sleep Scotland
Tel: 651 1392
Tel. 0845 0031212
(support line, Mon-Fri 9.30-23.30)
Email: sleepscotland@btinternet.com
Web: www.sleepscotland.org
Provides support to families of children with special needs and severe sleep problems.

Smokeline
Tel: 0800 848484 (7 days 12.00-24.00)
Freephone number offering help and support from trained counsellors. Leaflet available.

Special Needs Information Point (SNIP)
Royal Hospital for Sick Children
14 Rillbank Terrace EH9 1LN
Tel/Fax: 536 0583
Email: snip@btinternet.com
Web: www.snipinfo.org
Provides information and support to parents/carers of children with special needs about the services available to them. This can be about benefits, equipment, play and leisure activities, education, respite care etc.
Monthly newsletter and regularly updated website. Fully accessible office.

Stepfamily Scotland
5 Coates Crescent EH3 7AA
Tel: 225 5800
Tel. 0845 122 8655 (helpline)
Email: info@stepfamilyscotland.org.uk
Web: www.stepfamilyscotland.org.uk

Opening times: Mon, Tue, Wed 11.00-15.00;Thu 13.00-19.00.
Offers support and information to all members of stepfamilies and those working with them.

Stepping Stones (North Edinburgh)
10 Wardieburn Road EH5 1LY
Tel: 551 1632
Opening times: Mon-Fri 9.00-16.00.
A chance for young parents who live in the Greater Pilton area to meet together and participate in various activities. Large well-staffed and equipped playroom for under 5s. Counselling, home visits, welfare advice and support.

TAMBA Twinline
Tel: 0800 138 0509 (helpline)
A confidential listening support and information service run by trained volunteers all of whom are parents of twins or triplets. Provides information and support for parents of twins, triplets etc., and the professionals involved with their care.

Wellspring
13 Smith's Place EH6 8NT
Tel: 553 6660
Web: www.wellspring-scotland.co.uk
Provides psychotherapy and counselling service. Fees payable on sliding scale according to circumstances.

Libraries

LIBRARIES

The good news is that libraries welcome under fives! In fact, libraries welcome everyone. They have a wide selection of stimuli for you and your child to enjoy – such as books, books on tape, CDs, toys, games, magazines, comics, computers, plus organised activities and events.

How to Join

It's free to join and children can join at any age if they live or go to school in Edinburgh. Fill out a children's membership form and take along proof of your current address (e.g. driving licence, child benefit book). Children are given their own library card and can borrow 12 items from the library for up to 3 weeks.

Adults who live, work or study in Edinburgh can join and must fill out a membership form and show 2 forms of identification, one of which must show your current address (such as a bank statement), and one which must show your signature, such as a driving licence.

Parents/guardians are responsible for the books borrowed on their child's card, and for handing them back in good condition and on time. There are no fines on overdue books issued on a child's card and it's free for children to reserve books. Items borrowed can be returned to any public library in Edinburgh.

Books – and much more

All libraries have designated children's areas. They all have kinderboxes with a wide range of interactive and fun baby board books, picture books and story books for babies and toddlers. There are also books on tape & CD, cartoons, poetry books, chapter books, stories for older children, information books and reference books which are great for homework. All libraries also have dual language picture books and books in large print. In all libraries children's books are arranged by subject, interest and reading level. Shelves are clearly marked and there is a leaflet available explaining the system. If you can't find what you want – or need information, there are always staff on hand.

Under Fives' Events

Libraries within Edinburgh's bounds have specific events for Under fives, such as Baby Bookcrawl, where you can receive a certificate for your child with every 4 visits to the library. Other things to look out for are 'Bounce and Tickle Rhymetimes' throughout the city, which incorporate action songs and rhymes, listening to stories and looking at books. Look at the website to find out about regular storytimes for under fives.

Bookstart

Bookstart puts books into the hands of babies and their families throughout the city. At their baby's 8 month health check parents receive a free book bag containing 2 books, nursery rhyme cards and an invitation to join the library. A further Bookstart pack is given to parents at their children's 23 month health check.

Activities and Events

For information about activities such as storytimes, author visits and craft events check the website and look out for posters in the library. Look out for special events during the school holidays.

Toys and Games

Every library has toys, colour-ins and a selection of games and puzzles for children.

Children's Multilingual Picture Book Collections

Dual-language picture books are available in Arabic, Bengali, Chinese, Farsi, French, Gaelic, German, Gujarati, Hindi, Italian, Japanese, Portugese, Punjabi, Pushtu, Shona, Spanish, Turkish and Urdu. A booklet which lists holdings of dual-language picture books is available in all libraries. Single language books are available in Arabic, Bengali, Chinese, Japanese and Urdu. The Ethnic Services Library at McDonald Road Library has extensive collections. Smaller collections are available at some community libraries.

For further information and for details of bilingual storytimes contact Ethnic Services on 529 5636.

Music CDs

Most libraries provide a range of music CDs to borrow. Children pay 30p to borrow each CD. All music CDs are listed in the library catalogue and can be reserved at any library in Edinburgh.

Music CDs are currently available in the following libraries:

Balgreen, Blackhall, Central Music, Corstorphine, Craigmillar, Currie, Gilmerton, Kirkliston, Leith, McDonald Rd, Morningside, Muirhouse, Newington, Oxgangs, Piershill, Portobello, Ratho, Sighthill, South Queensferry and Wester Hailes.

Parents' Collections

Parents can borrow books from this section to help their child deal with difficult topics such as the death of a parent or grandparent, bullying, a new baby, starting school etc. Collections are available at the following libraries but titles can be reserved from any library:

Blackhall, Central Children's, Corstorphine, Currie, Fountainbridge, Gilmerton, Kirkliston, Leith, Morningside, Muirhouse, Newington, Oxgangs, Piershill, Portobello, Sighthill and Wester Hailes.

Computers, Internet and the Council Website

Computers with free internet access and word processing facilities are available in all libraries. Most libraries have PS2s and a selection of games and CDROMs for children to use. All computers have a link to Wizard Websites, a collection of child-friendly websites. Information about other council services is available via the Council's web site www.edinburgh.gov.uk and you can now renew your library books online. Check out www.edinburgh.gov.uk/events for a listing of events for children and families throughout the city.

Local information

Library notice boards can be a great source of both local and general information and are well worth keeping an eye on. Some libraries keep a diary of forthcoming local events or folders with local information.

Access and Toilets

Standards of access vary; new and refurbished libraries usually have good all-round facilities. All of the libraries, apart from the Music Library, have wheelchair access, but not all libraries have toilets for the disabled and a few – notably the Central Children's Library – do not have public toilet facilities at all. The library staff will allow use of staff toilets if possible. Many have nappy changing facilities and these are listed in the entries.

Library Opening Hours

Full-time libraries:
Central, Blackhall, Corstorphine, Leith, Morningside, Muirhouse, Newington, Oxgangs, Piershill, Portobello, Wester Hailes:
Opening times: Mon, Tue, Wed, Thu: 10.00-20.00: Fri: 10.00-17.00: Sat: 9.00-13.00

Part-time libraries:
Balerno, Balgreen, Central Children's, Colinton, Craigmillar, Currie, Fountainbridge, Gilmerton, Granton, Kirkliston, McDonald Rd, Moredun, Ratho, Sighthill, South Queensferry, Stockbridge :
Opening times: Mon, Wed: 13.00-20.00: Tue, Thu, Fri: 10.00-17.00: Sat: 9.00-13.00

Libraries Open all day Saturday and Sunday Afternoons:
McDonald Road, Muirhouse, Newington, Oxgangs, Portobello, Wester Hailes.
Opening times: Sat: 9-5pm, Sun: 1-5pm

CENTRAL LIBRARIES

Edinburgh Central Library
George IV Bridge   EH1 1EG
Tel: 242 8000

Comprehensive public reference and information services, major collections of local history material, a large stock of adult fiction and non-fiction, and the largest local collection of books about children e.g. parenting, play, education, problems etc. Books for young children are available to borrow from kinderboxes in the general lending department. Extensive Music, Fine Art and Scottish collections. A Kurzweil reading machine, media aids and PC access software for people with disabilities are available in the Resource Centre (Tel: 242 8135).

Toilets in basement, access by lift with stairs to negotiate. If the toilets are not open, a notice is posted at the top of the stairs. On Tuesdays a crèche is run by the Edinburgh Crèche Co-operative between 10.00-12.00. Children 0-5 years are welcome. Staff are trained and qualified, and are registered with Disclosure Scotland. It is situated upstairs in the Board Room.

Central Children's Library
George IV Bridge EH1 1EG
Tel: 242 8027

Situated next door to the Central Library. Level access. Compact library that is attractively decorated and laid out to appeal to young children, although if your child needs the toilet you have to leave the building and use the facilities next door in the Central Library. Collection of children's books and audio books, including dual-language picture books in Urdu, Chinese, Arabic and French, as well as books in Gaelic. There are also games, toys and colour-in sheets. There is one internet PC for children's use only, and a selection of CDROM games. Free activities and story-telling sessions run during school holidays. Crèche facilities are available in the main building, please call for current details.

LIBRARIES

COMMUNITY LIBRARIES

Balerno Library
1 Main Street EH14 7EQ
Tel: 529 5500
Email: balerno.library@edinburgh.gov.uk

Ramp access. Small library, part of primary school annexe. Good selection of children's books and story tapes. Drawing table and small selection of toys available. Photocopier, PC, internet access. No public toilets.

Balgreen Library
173 Balgreen Road EH11 3AT
Tel: 529 5585
Email: balgreen.library@edinburgh.gov.uk

There is ramp access to this small library. Wide range of children's books, with a selection in large print and books on tape & CD. Paper, crayons, toys and board games are also available. Photocopier and 2 PCs with internet access. No public toilet.

Blackhall Library
56 Hillhouse Road EH4 5EG
Tel: 529 5595
Email: blackhall.library@edinburgh.gov.uk

Ramp access and car park. The children's section is roomy and newly refurbished. 'Family Collection' of books and videos to support parents and carers. Toys, games and CDROMs for use in library. Photocopier, PCs and PS2. Regular story times for under 5s - contact library for more details. Out of hours book return letterbox so you can return library items even when library is closed. Self-issue terminals so you don't have to wait in a queue! Toilet facilities (including toilet for the disabled). Nappy change unit.

Colinton Library
14 Thornburn Road EH13 0BQ
Tel: 529 5603
Email: colinton.library@edinburgh.gov.uk

Car park and access with double pushchair. Children's area with books, books on tape, games, toys and colour-in books available. For details of regular story-telling and other children's events contact library. Photocopier. PCs with free internet access, e-mail, CDROMs and word processing. Staff toilet is made available for use.

Corstorphine Library
12 Kirk Loan EH12 7HD
Tel: 529 5506
Email: corstorphine.library@edinburgh.gov.uk

Ramp access. Access with single pushchair only. Wide range of children's books with a selection in large print, books on tape & CD. Paper, crayons, toys and board games are available. Photocopier. Children's PC. Staff toilet is made available for use.

Craigmillar Library
7 Niddrie Marischal Gardens EH16 4LX
Tel: 529 5597
Email: craigmillar.library@edinburgh.gov.uk
Web: http://www.craigmillarbooksforbabies.org.uk

Welcoming rainbow mural on external library wall. Ramp access. Designated under fives area with lovely furniture and picket fence. Good selection of children's books, books on tape, toys and games. Photocopier. Two PS2s and 11 PCs with access to internet. For details of storytimes, games and competitions contact the library. 'Books for Babies' a national reading initiative is based at the library and holds regular storytimes and drop-in sessions. Check 'Books for Babies' website or call the library for details. Toilet (key at the desk). Nappy change unit.

Currie Library
210 Lanark Road West EH14 5NN
Tel: 529 5609
Email: currie.library@edinburgh.gov.uk

Car park and access with double pushchair. Children's area with collection of books, toys, games, colour-in books, audio CDs and books on tape. Ethnic picture book collection.
Story-telling and children's events are advertised, or contact the library for details. Photocopier. PC. Toilet facilities. Nappy change area.

Fountainbridge Library
137 Dundee Street EH11 1BG
Tel: 529 5616
Email: fountainbridge.library@edinburgh.gov.uk

Murdoch Terrace entrance has ramp access. Large selection of children's books, toys, books on tape and games (ask at the counter). PS2. Community Room available. Photocopier. PCs with free internet access. For storytimes and other events call library for details. Toilets with disabled access. Nappy change unit.

Gilmerton Library
13 Newtoft Street EH17 8RG
Tel: 529 5628
Email: gilmerton.library@edinburgh.gov.uk
Ramp access and car park at rear of the building. Small but bright library with a pleasant children's area, toys plus books on tape. Games are available at the desk. PS2. Community Room and computer centre. Photocopier. Free internet access. Children's events in the library - ask for details. Toilets. Nappy change unit.

Granton Library
Wardieburn Terrace EH5 IDD
Tel: 529 5630
Email: granton.library@edinburgh.gov.uk
Recently refurbished. Access for double pushchairs. Collection of books, toys, colour-ins, audio tapes/books, ethnic picture books. Storytimes. PS2. Homework Centre. North Edinburgh Bookstart runs rhymetimes – contact the library for details. Photocopier. PCs. Toilet facilities.

Kirkliston Library
Station Road
Kirkliston EH29 9BE
Tel: 529 5510
Email: kirkliston.library@edinburgh.gov.uk
Access with double pushchair. Collection of books, toys, colour-ins, audio tapes/books. Regular storytimes – contact library for details. Photocopier. 5 PCs with internet access. Toilet facilities and nappy change area.

Leith Library
28–30 Ferry Road EH6 4AE
Tel: 529 5517
Email: leith.library@edinburgh.gov.uk
Access with double pushchair. Small car park at rear of building. Children's section with comfortable seating. Books, toys, colour-in sheets, audio tapes/books available. Regular storytimes and events - contact library for details. Photocopier. PC designated for children only or parent with child. Learning Centre with free access to internet and email. Toilet available for under 5s - ask librarian.

McDonald Road Library
2 McDonald Road EH7 4LU
Tel: 529 5636
Email: mcdonaldrd.library@edinburgh.gov.uk
Recently refurbished. Ramp access; lift access to all 3 levels; and large collection of children's books, books on tape, music cds, and ethnic and dual-language titles. PS2. Photocopier. Twenty PCs including free internet access and community language software. Public toilets. Nappy changing facilities.

Mobile Library Service
Service based at:
Access Services HQ
343 Oxgangs Road EH13 9LT
Tel: 529 5683
Email: access services@edinburgh.gov.uk
The Mobile Library Service visits about 60 locations in the Edinburgh area ranging from small villages such as Dalmeny, to large urban locations such as Wester Hailes. Other stops include East Craigs, Inch, Barnton, Juniper Green, Buckstone, Cramond, Clermiston, Prestonfield, Liberton and Gracemount. A wide variety of books are available, including an ever-changing selection of children's books. Most vehicles have powered ramps for easier access. Contact Access Services for mobile van timetable.

Moredun Library
92 Moredun Park Road EH17 7HL
Tel: 529 5652
Email: moredun.library@edinburgh.gov.uk
Ramp access. Small friendly library with bright children's area. Lots of board games available. Photocopier. PCs with internet access. PS2. Toilets for the disabled – ask for key at the desk. Nappy change unit.

Morningside Library
184 Morningside Road EH10 4PU
Tel: 529 5654
Email: morningside.library@edinburgh.gov.uk
Ramp access. There is a large, separate children's section with a wide range of story and information books and books on tape & CD. Colour-ins, toys, board games, CDROMs, PS2, PC with internet access. Photocopying. No toilet facilities. Nearest public toilet in Canaan Lane.

Muirhouse Library
15 Pennywell Court EH4 4TZ
Tel: 529 5528
Email: muirhouse.library@edinburgh.gov.uk
Specially designated area for under 5s with toys and soft seating. Good selection of books for all ages. Games available for use in the library. Videos, CDs and books on tape available. Community Room. Learning Centre. PCs with internet access. Photocopier. Toilets with disabled access. Nappy changing facilities.

Newington Library
17–21 Fountainhall Road EH9 2LN
Tel: 529 5536
Email: newington.library@edinburgh.gov.uk
Spacious and attractively decorated, with a large collection of picture books, fiction and non-fiction. Regular storytimes for pre-school children – please contact library for details. See noticeboard for details of events and activities for children. Car park. Photocopier. Toilets for the disabled. Nappy change unit.

Oxgangs Library
343 Oxgangs Road EH13 9LY
Tel: 529 5549
Email: oxgangs.library@edinburgh.gov.uk
Level access. Good selection of picture books, fiction and non-fiction. For details of children's events contact the library. Toys, games, colour-in sheets and crayons are available on request. Carpeted Community Room with kitchen facilities available. Photocopier and Fax available. PCs with internet access for both adults and children. Toilets with disabled access. Nappy change unit.

Piershill Library
30 Piersfield Terrace EH8 7BQ
Tel: 529 5685
Email: piershill.library@edinburgh.gov.uk
Level access and excellent facilities. Bright children's area with extensive range of books and books on tape. For details of children's events and storytimes contact the library. Toys and board games. PCs and photocopying. Toilet and nappy change unit.

Portobello Library
14 Rosefield Avenue EH15 1AU
Tel: 529 5558
Email: portobello.library@edinburgh.gov.uk
Bright library with ramp access and two parking spaces for the disabled. Large children's and teenage sections with study tables. Toys and games available. Story-telling sessions for nursery groups can be arranged - apply to the library. PCs for internet and word-processing and games. PS2. Photocopier. Toilet and nappy change unit available on request. These facilities are upstairs and require a member of staff to unlock the door. See also Toy Libraries in this chapter.

Ratho Library
6 School Wynd EH28 8TT
Tel: 333 5297
Email: ratho.library@edinburgh.gov.uk

Access with single pushchair. Visitors car park. Good selection of books, books on tape, toys and colour-in sheets. Photocopier. PCs with internet access. Toilet facilities and nappy change area available.

Sighthill Library
6 Sighthill Wynd EH11 4BL
Tel: 529 5569
Email: sighthill.library@edinburgh.gov.uk
Spacious library with level access and automatic doors. Good stock of children's books, supplemented by books on tapes, comics, toys, and games. 'Bookstart 0–3' project based at the library - runs stories, songs and rhyme events for parents and children aged 0-3yrs. Family collection of books, videos, leaflets and magazines. Photocopier. Two PS2s. PCs and Learning Centre offering free internet access for parents and children. Toilets (key at the desk). Nappy change unit available.

South Queensferry Library
9 Shore Road EH30 9RD
Tel: 529 5576
Email: southqueensferry.library@edinburgh.gov.uk
Level access. Bright children's area with picture books and board books, toys, colour-in sheets and books on tape. Regular storytimes – contact library for details. Photocopier. PCs with internet access. Staff toilet may be used for young children – ask the librarian.

Stockbridge Library
Hamilton Place EH3 5BA
Tel: 529 5665
Email: stockbridge.library@edinburgh.gov.uk
Access by ramped entrance. Bright and friendly children's area with toys and comfortable seats for adults. Large selection of children's books, books & CDs on tape, comics and games. Monthly storytelling for the under fives. Check with the library for children's activities during school holidays. Community room available for hire. Photocopier. PCs with free internet access and Learning Centre. Toilet and Nappy change unit.

Wester Hailes Library
1 West Side Plaza EH14 2FT
Tel: 529 5667
Email: westerhailes.library@edinburgh.gov.uk
Access with double pushchair. Collection of children's books including ethnic picture books. Toys and colour-in sheets available. Community room available on first floor

(access by lift). Storytimes in library – contact the library for details. Bookstart worker based at the library. Weekly rhymetimes run - contact the library for details. PCs with internet access. Youth Library and Learning Centre. Photocopier. Toilets. Nappy change unit.

TOY LIBRARIES

As the name suggests, toy libraries are centres which lend toys to families, carers, and to children with special needs. Most of them are run as drop-in centres, and as such, guidance can be given on the toys best suited to your child.

There is generally a joining fee and depending of the toy library, toys can be borrowed for little or no charge. It is wise to check with each individual project.

Opening times tend to mirror school terms, but some do stay open during school holidays.

The two main contacts are:

National Association of Toy and Leisure Libraries
First Floor, Gilmerton Community Centre,
4 Drum Street, Edinburgh, EH17 8QG
Tel: 0131 664 2746
Fax: 0131 664 2753
Email: natll.scotland@playmatters.co.uk
Web: www.playmatters.co.uk
Edinburgh Toy Library Group, which supports toy libraries formerly run by WRVS

Edinburgh Toy Library Group
Tel: 441 1925

SPECIAL NEEDS TOY LIBRARIES

Barrie House Toy Library
Barrie House
Canaan Lane
Tel: 446 3136
Opening times:Fri 10.00- 11.30 term time only, but available other times: phone for information.
A division of the Royal Blind School and, as such, the toy library is primarily for parents of children who attend the playgroup there. However, the library welcomes other enquiries.

SPLATT Toy Library - Special Needs
Keycomm
St Giles Centre
40 Broomhouse Crescent
Tel: 443 6775
Opening times: Mon-Fri 10.00-16.30
Switch Play, learning and technology for parents and professionals. Also adapts family toys

Homestart South Central Toy Library
66A Gorgie Road (opposite Gorgie City Farm)
Contact: Val Goodwin
Tel: 226 1331
Opening Times: 10.30-14.30 every Wednesday

Play Plus Toy Library
Inch House Community Centre
225 Gilmerton Road
Contact: Helen Anderson
Tel: 657 2380
Opening times: Tue 9.30-12.30
Play sessions, quality toys for families, groups, carers etc., including toys for children with special needs. Audio books and ethnic picture book collection.
Nappy-changing facilities. Accessible to double pushchairs.

Portobello Toy Library
Portobello Community Library (upstairs)
Rosefield Avenue EH15 1AU
Contact: Carol Strang
Tel: 529 5558
Opening times: Wed 10.00-11.00 during term time.
Available for children from 1-5 yrs.

Oxgangs Toy Library
Pentland Community Centre
Oxgangs Brae EH13 9LU
Tel: 334 2463
Thursdays 10 - 11.30 term time only

BOOKSTART
Bookstart Edinburgh, launched in February 2000, works with Health Visitors to put books into the hands of babies and their families across the city. At their baby's first year health check, parents receive a free book bag containing two books, nursery rhyme cards and an invitation to join the library. A further Bookstart pack is given to parents at their child's toddler health check. Parents who think they

may have not received a Bookstart pack can get one by contacting the address below.

Over 40,000 books have been given to families throughout Edinburgh, and hundreds of babies have joined their local library.

Bounce and Tickle sessions are offered at libraries and outreach venues across the city. These are fun sessions of action rhymes and songs for parents/carers and their children aged 0-3 years. Parents and babies can also take part in the Bookstart Book Crawl, collecting stickers each time they visit the library and receiving a colourful certificate when they have four stickers.

Contact: Eric Brennan, Bookstart Coordinator
Youth Services
Central Library
George IV Bridge EH1 1EG
Tel: 242 8162
Email: eric.brennan@edinburgh.gov.uk

Bookstart Edinburgh's citywide scheme is complemented by three local Bookstart projects:

North Edinburgh Bookstart Project
Muirhouse Library
15 Pennywell Court EH4 4TZ
Tel: 529 5530

Sighthill Bookstart Project
Sighthill Library
6 Sighthill Wynd EH11 4BL
Tel: 529 5571

Wester Hailes Bookstart Project
Wester Hailes Library
1 West Side Plaza EH14 2FT
Tel: 529 5693

and our partner organisation:

Craigmillar Books for Babies
Castlebrae Community High School
2A Greendykes Road EH16 4DP
Tel: 621 2621

All you have to do is go along to a rhymetime at a library near you. For more information contact your local Bookstart Project or the citywide scheme, or visit their web pages at:
www.edinburgh.gov.uk/bookstart

Playground & Parks

INTRODUCTION

Edinburgh is well provided for in terms of the number of playparks in and around the city: there are over 150, ranging from small housing estate play areas to larger city park playgrounds.

We have not listed all of them. Instead, what we have done in this chapter is to offer some information regarding those playprks we feel offer the best experience for you ad your children, in terms of equipment type, cleanliness, access and so on.

We have divided the city in terms of Central, North , East, South and West. Then under these headings, we've listed our favourite playparks, others of note, and also others in the vicinity.

New or upgraded playgrounds nearly always have brightly coloured multiplay units which incorporate a variety of activities. Edinburgh City Council is also keen to encourage imaginative play through thematic playgrounds with multiplay units in the form of castles, trains, boats etc. The Castle at Inch Park, the Piate Ship at Inverleith Park and the Juni Train at Broomiehall Park, Juniper Green are examples.

Other recent playpark features are the ground level panels with bells, chimes, spinning spirals, beads and noughts and crosses. Children of all abilities can enjoy these and although there is generally no specialised equipment for children with special needs, a number of playgrounds do have low decks, ramps and handrails.

Scotland Yard Adventure Centre is a notable exception to this and provides play opportunities for children and young people with a special need or disability.

Priorities for redeveloped playgrounds include: play area within a fenced-off area with self-closing gates; safer surfacing under all play equipment (e.g. wood chips, rubber tiles or sand); if a playground includes equipment for a variety of age groups then age-relevant equipment should be grouped together; and increased inspection of playgrounds by council representatives. Other improvements include putting up notices displaying the name of the playground and a contact number to report any damage to. Many of the newer playgrounds have equipment made from tough plastic designed to be hard wearing and to withstand vandalism – although sadly this can mean that the vandals become more inventive.

Remember, if your local playpark is vandalised etc, contact the Council (Tel: 529 7913) – that way you know that they are aware of the damage and repair may be more quickly effected.

NB. While lack of nearby toilets are still a problem at many playgrounds, the Recreation Department has no say in the allocation of public toilets.

CENTRAL EDINBURGH

Taking in playparks from Queen St (N) - Lauriston Pl (S), London Rd (E) - Shandwick Pl (W).

Princes St Gardens Playpark

The nearest entrance is from Princes St; the second gate from the West end is best, as the first gate has a long flight of steps. Also level access from King's Stable Rd or through St Cuthbert's Churchyard.

The multiplay unit is loosely based on a castle theme, with ramps, tunnels, slides and walkways suitable for toddlers, eventually leading up to a higher tower with a wavy slide and scramble netting, interesting for older children. Be careful near the drop at the fireman's pole especially at busy times. There is also an octagon of low-level panels with perspex drums, metal chimes and crazy mirrors accessed by a low ramp on wooden boards suitable for wheelchairs. Other activities include a 'television', noughts and crosses an abacus, an animal buckabout and a small roundabout.

Although the playground is unfenced, dogs in the gardens are supposed to be kept on leads and it is relatively clean. There is just one bench within the playground but there are plenty of benches nearby with a good view of the playground, however younger children will need to be watched closely, especially when the equipment is crowded.

Toilets are near the playground with nappy changing facilities. The key can be obtained from the attendant on duty from 10.00-22.00 (except from 15.00-16.00 when they are closed for cleaning). Note: there is no ramp up to Princes St from these toilets. Also toilets at the Ross Bandstand (open summer only 8.00-20.00, no nappy-changing facilities).

The Piazza Open Air Cafe
West Princes Street Gardens
Tel: 225 5533
Opening times: 7 days, Apr-May 11.00-18.00; June-Aug 9.30-21.30; Sep-Oct 11.00-17.00; Nov-Mar closed.
Handy spot to grab a coffee, soft drink, or snack near to the playground.
Large groups can be catered for by prior arrangement.

NORTH EDINBURGH & LEITH

From the shore of the Forth (N)-Queen St & Leith Walk (S). Cramond Brig (W) -Leith Links (E).

OUR FAVOURITES
Inverleith Park and Playground

Entrances on Arboretum Pl, Inverleith Pl, East Fettes Ave and Portgower Pl.

A large park (61 acres) with allotments, a rose garden (between the playground and the boating lake), a boating lake, a cricket pitch, football pitches and rugby pitches. The boating lake is near the Edinburgh Academicals Ground on Comely Bank Road. This is a good place to feed the ducks, watch the tractors mowing the sports fields and watch remote controlled boats on Sundays.

The playground, near the south end of Arboretum Place, was fully rebuilt in early 2004. The centrepiece is a large ship in three sections: the wheelhouse, mast and bow, incorporating a slide, rope ladders, rigging, and crow's nest. There is also a smaller multiplay with slide, steps, mini climbing wall and gangway, 2 bucket swings, 4 swings, seesaw, sit-in wobbly whale, and a high revolving disc for older children to hang on and swing about. The playground is fenced off from the main park. It has seating and litterbins and is generally clean and tidy. All equipment is set on rubberised surface with fun coloured pictures.

There is an ice cream van just outside the park's entrance on Arboretum Pl from late Spring into early Autumn, which sells a great range of ice creams, lollies and also offers soft drinks, teas and coffees.

Other potential points of interest are the Inverleith Petanque Club who play on Wednesday afternoons and Sundays, and the bowling green both of which are close to the playground.

King George V Park

Eyre Place, entrances off Logan Street (level access) and Royal Crescent (steep and bumpy path), nr Canonmills.

Somewhat hidden away, this small park has three playgrounds: KVG for toddlers; another one for older children; and a third for children and young people with special needs (see The Yard in Adventure Playgrounds subsection). The toddler playground is fully fenced and has a small multiplay incorporating a wide slide, a 'look-out post', a climbing frame and a small ramp with rock-face grips on it. There is a hemispherical climbing frame, 2 bucket swings, 2 swings and a mini-roundabout. Everything is set on a deep covering of woodchips, with rubberised surfaces under the swings. There are 5 benches, a litter bin and a small grass area within the fencing.

The junior playground, in comparison, is rather more old and run-down, although a good time can still be had: the woodchips are more sparse, there's evidence of graffiti, and there are more abandoned bottles and litter. There is a very long slide set into the hill at the back of the park, accessed by a scrambling wall; 2 climbing frame areas; and 4 swings. To the side of the playground, there is a basketball court. This playground is only partly fenced.

The park is popular for picnicking, sunbathing and toddler ball games. It is also popular with dog walkers although any fouling is generally minimal.

Leith Links and Playground
Links Place, Leith

48 acres of grass, trees and spring bulbs complete with hillocks which are the remains of 16th century gun emplacements. There are benches and paths, which are lit in the evenings, suitable for pushchairs. The fenced playgrounds are to the North West of the park.

The toddler area has a Noah's Ark themed multiplay complete with slide and rope ladder, 4 bucket swings, a sit-on animal roundabout and 2 horse buckabouts, all set on rubberised surfaces. There's a picnic table and other seating, a litterbin and also a fenced grass area to the side of the playground for running around and picnics, this has an interesting carved wooden bench.

The junior area set on bark chips, which seem to be good and deep, has a large multiplay climbing frame with chain scramble netting, slide, steps, ladders and monkey hoops. There is also a tyre commando slide and a tyre swing (tyre missing at time of visit). Some of this is suitable for under 5s under close supervision. Again, seating is provided.

There's a third area which has an 'Eiffel Tower' climbing net and a basic balancing frame. This area is set in sand. The equipment is only really suitable for older children but all ages can enjoy the sand. These playgrounds are extremely popular, and are usually in pretty good condition, but there is some graffiti here and there. Dog fouling does not appear to be a problem in the immediate surrounding area.

Ravelston Park and Playground
Craigcrook Road, Blackhall

An enclosed playground surrounded by a grassy park lined with trees and spring bulbs. There are paths up through Ravelston Woods for those interested in a small nature expedition. The playground was recently upgraded; it has 2 bucket swings, 2 swings, a roundabout, a seesaw, 2 4-seater buckabouts and a large multiplay. The multiplay has a high slide, a medium slide, climbing wall, hanging rope tube, steps, dangling rope seat. At ground level there is a car dashboard with steering wheel and gear lever and also a colourful spinning 'picture-maker' game.

The equipment is set on rubberised surface with interesting coloured pictures, there is a hopscotch game marked on the tarmac. This decent-sized playground is ideal for toddlers and older children, and is popular with families. Easy parking on Craigcrook Rd. There are 2 benches within the playground and 3 more just outside. There is a litter bin. There is a fenced tarmac area (old tennis court) next to the playground useful for football, bat and ball etc. The park is popular with dogwalkers but fouling does not appear to be a problem.

Victoria Park and Playgrounds
Between Newhaven Road and Craighall Road, Newhaven
A lovely 18-acre park with 2 excellent playgrounds. The first is near Newhaven Rd and is suitable for toddlers. This enclosed area includes; a multiplay unit with a slide, 2 bucket swings, a small hemispherical climbing frame, a 4-seat buckabout, and a roundabout – all set on rubberised surfaces. There are benches and a litter bin.

The second playground is near to Craighall Rd. This is more suitable for 3+ years although younger children will enjoy some of it if closely supervised. The playground is very popular and so under 5s will need careful supervision when the equipment is crowded as there are some high drops in places. The playground is made up of modern tough plastic equipment. It has interlinked climbing frames, bridges, walkways and slides – one with a roller surface – a small helter-skelter slide, a larger tube helter-skelter slide and a whole variety of climbing, swinging and bouncing equipment. This is all fenced off and set in wood chips with a couple of picnic tables and benches nearby.

You may wish to avoid it at lunchtime, as pupils from nearby Trinity Academy tend to swarm all over it. Minor graffiti in both play areas.

The park also has a floodlit, all-weather, five-a-side football pitch and a basketball court. There are several cycle paths running through the park.

THE BEST OF THE REST
Davidson's Mains Park
East Barnton Avenue
Playground within large grassy park.

Granton Mains
Granton Mill Crescent, off West Granton Road
Playground with two multiplays, plus other stand alone equipment: adjacent basketball court.

Granton Crescent Park
Granton Crescent
Playground with multiplay unit and stand-alone equipment. Surrounded by sloping grass area.

Henderson Gardens
Henderson Street, behind Great Junction Street, Leith
Playground with boat-shape multiplay, plus stand-alone equipment. Adjacent basketball and football area.

Keddie Gardens Playground
Largo Place, off Ferry Road
Playground with toddler multiplay and other equipment includes helter-skelter slide. Adjacent grass area, close to steps down to Water of Leith walkway.

Pilrig Park and Playgrounds
Pilrig St,reet other entrances off nearby streets
Large park with 2 playgrounds situated at east and west corners of park. Both have been recently upgraded.

Redbraes Park
Broughton Road
Playground with multiplay plus swings. Surrounded by grass area.

St Mark's Park
Warriston Road
Playground with two multiplay units, plus a roundabout. Grassy area within and round the playpark.

OTHER PLAYGROUNDS AND PARKS

Beaverbank Playground
Broughton Road near to Beaverbank Place
Playground only. Some older-style equipment.
NB. Plans for refurbishment shuold be put into action in 2006, changing this area into a playpark, complete with a garden. Check www.efuf.co.uk for progress updates.

Corstorphine Hill Playpark
Craigcrook Road just north of Hillpark Green.
Playground only, but close to path leading up to Corstorphine Hill.

Craigleith Retail Park
South Groathill Avenue or Queensferry Road.
Playground only located behind trees at the exit from Sainsbury's petrol station, close to the carwash.

Cramond Walled Garden
Cramond Glebe Road, behind Cramond Kirk, follow sign for the Roman Fort.
Playground and grass area. Rather secluded which can lead to vandalism

Dalmeny Street Park
Entrances on Dalmeny Street, Iona Street, Sloan Street and Dickson Street.
Playground and adjacent grass area.

Hopetoun Street Development
McDonald Road.
Playground only (small).

Muirhouse Linear Park and Playground
Near Muirhouse Drive and Muirhouse Park.
Playground with adjacent grass area, basketball court and skateboard park.

Pennywell Gardens
At east end of Pennywell Gardens
Playground only.

Pennywell Road
Between Pennywell Grove and Pennywell Gardens
Playground only.

Sandport Street
Off Commercial Street, Leith.
Playground only.

EAST EDINBURGH

London St (W)-Portobello (E); Easter Rd/Clare-mont Pk (N)-Joppa (S)

OUR FAVOURITES

Figgate Park
Portobello, entrances on Duddingston Road and Hamilton Drive
A strip of parkland, which run alongside the Figgate Burn. The playpark is to the Northeast of the area. There is a toddler multiplay and bucket swings. For older children, there is a junior multiplay, with a curved slide, a scramble tube, a ramp and walkways.
Figgate pond is good for feeding ducks, but be aware of the water.

Joppa Quarry Park
Off South Morton Street, Portobello
The old small playground has been replaced with a brand new and larger play area. For under fives there are bucket swings, springy seats, puzzles and sensory boards, and a slide and scramble net on the smaller end of a large multiplay unit. For older children the multiplay unit has a fireman's pole, climbing wall and monkey rings. There are also bigger swings, a roundabout and a whirling 'hanging on' roundabout which is very popular with our older young ones. All is set in rubberised matting and the whole area is fenced to keep out dogs.
A good mixture of equipment to please the family, with the added benefit of trains close by for small enthusiasts.

Montgomery Street Playground
Montgomery Street, Elgin Street, Hillside
A popular fenced playground with level access from Elgin St. It has a tractor-shaped climbing frame with slide; a fort-shaped multiplay unit with slide, bridge, tunnel and rings; a traditional roundabout; a rocking rocket; a tall helter-skelter slide; and 4 swings. The toddler area is partly fenced off from the main playground and has a small slide; a mini roundabout; a 'spider' climbing frame; and 3 bucket swings. All equipment is set on rubberised matting. There is a hard surface area beside the playgrounds with small goal posts, as well as a basketball court with hoops and a ball-play unit. There is a separate grassy park area. The playground is generally clean, with litter bins and benches.

Prestonfield Park
Prestonfield Road, next to the Bowling Green
Playground has separate toddler and junior areas. Toddler equipment includes 3 bucket swings plus a low level multiplay with 2 slides, curved and rope ladders, a fireman's pole and activity panels. Junior area has climbing structures, plus a hand slide and a helter skelter. There's also good old-fashioned hopscotch.

Rosefield Park and Playground
Rosefield Place, Portobello
This is a small, pretty park with a bridge over the Figgate Burn. The playground is suitable for toddlers and juniors

and consists of a large multiplay unit with a slide, scramble net, low level double sike, walkway and pole, 2 animal rockers, 2 bucket swings, 2 larger swings and a roundabout. All the equipment is set in rubbersized matting, and there are trees and bushes for extra running around and hide and seek games, including a lovely long hedge for the especially intrepid under fives. The area is fenced off to keep out dogs.

BEST OF THE REST

Lochend Park and Playground
Lochend Road
Fenced playground set within the 23-acre park. Playground equipment includes a multiplay unit which is suitable for both toddlers and juniors. Park has fenced-off pond.

Magdalene Community Centre
Next to Brunstane Primary School
Playground has two multiplay units for juniors/older toddlers. The partitioned toddler area has a play PO/bank counter, a bead panel and smaller seats.
Accessible to the public out of school hours and school holidays, except Sundays

Straiton Place
Portobello
This is a small toddler playground with a boat shaped multiplay unit and some springy animals on rubber matting. There are also bushes and ornamental grasses for extra exploring, and the fence and grid at the entrance mean that it is dog free. A handy stop off point on the way to or from the beach, and there is now a new 'superloo' right next door, which usefully is roomy enough for a double buggy, two toddlers and a parent!

Tower Bank
Off the promenade, by Tower Bank Primary School, Portobello
Multiplay unit, plus stand-alone equipment.

OTHER PLAYGROUNDS AND PARKS

Craigmillar
Niddrie House Square
Multiplay plus other equipment.

Mount Lodge Park
Mount Lodge Place, off Windsor Place, Portobello

Northfield Broadway
Next to Northfield Community Centre
Toddler playground

EDINBURGH SOUTH

Areas South of Lauriston Place, Slateford Road,

OUR FAVOURITES

Falcon Gardens
Near St Peters School, Morningside, entrance from Falcon Road
A park set in a walled area, back from the road. There are 3 bucket swings, a seesaw, a chute and a multiplay unit. There are benches and litterbins.

The Meadows and Bruntsfield Links
The Links border Bruntsfield Place and Whitehouse Loan, while the Meadows extend along Melville Drive from Brougham Place to Buccleuch Street.
These are open, leafy and well-maintained parkland areas, often busy with people playing sport, games and picnicking. There are 3 fenced playgrounds, tennis courts and wide, safe paths suitable for inexperienced cyclists.

Meadows East
Corner of Buccleuch Street and Melville Drive
A fenced-in playground, which is very popular with families. It has a helter-skelter slide, 4 swings a multiplay which incorporates a slide, a bridge and a low-level playhouse. There are benches and bins. Due to its location, it can be busy and sometimes there's litter.

Meadows West
Corner of Leven Terrace and Melville Drive
A compact, fenced-round playground which has imaginative equipment which should appeal especially to younger children. This includes, frames, bridges, rope ladders and crawl tunnels. There are also 2 bucket swings, a roundabout and a slide. Benches and litterbins are provided.

Meadows Toddlers
Towards East end of Melville Drive, next to the tennis courts
A fenced, grassy playground, with toddler-friendly

equipment which includes a multiplay, bucket swings, a seesaw and a roundabout.

Seven-Acre Park
Stanedykehead, Liberton

The access road was in poor state of repair, and the playground can seem a bit isolated as it's set in parkland. However, the playground itself is bright and modern, with bucket swings, a toddler-safe roundabout, and a multiplay which includes a helter-skelter, towers and a climbing ramp. There's also a basketball shooting ring and a 'hanging' seesaw for older children.

BEST OF THE REST

Buckstone Park
Buckstone Circle

Fenced playground, with mature woodland on either side. Two multiplays, high-back bucket swings (to avoid wraparound), plus other stand alone equipment.

Colinton Mains Park
Oxgangs Road North, junction with Redford Road, behind the huts

Two multiplays, plus other stand-alone equipment including 3 bucket swings. Flanked by playing fields on 2 sides.

Glenvarloch Crescent
Glenvarloch Crescent, Liberton

Bright, enclosed playground set in the centre of a grassed area, with estate roads on four sides. Two multiplays – smaller one is best for under 5s. There's also stand-alone equipment.

Harrison Park
West Bryson Road, Watson Crescent

Fenced park with tree-lined walkway along the banks of the Union Canal. Set near tennis courts, playing fields and a bowling green.
There are 4 bucket swings, a seesaw, a slide and a small climbing frame

OTHER PLAYGROUNDS AND PARKS

Camus Park
(also known as Fairmilehead Public Park)
Entrance from Camus Avenue and Pentland View

Gracemount Leisure Centre
Captain's Road, entrance of Gracemount Drive, to rear of car park

Playground only

Inch Park and Playground
Access from Glenallen Drive

Playground and parkland.

EDINBURGH WEST

From Cramond (N&W)-Crewe Rd N&S (E), and Balerno (S)

OUR FAVOURITES

Clermiston Park
Clermiston Gardens

This park has been completely renovated within the past few years and has mostly new equipment. There are 2 bucket swings, separated from the rest of the playground by a metal fence, 4 other swings, a multiplay with rope climbs and slides, roundabout, seesaw, and 2 springy animals, all set on rubber matting. New benches and litter bins have been added. The surrounding park is grassy with lots of new trees. There is a hard surface area next to the playground with basketball nets. There is minimal graffiti.

Bloomiehall Public Park
Juniper Green

This park is situated at the end of Juniper Park Rd, and accessed from Baberton Ave, opposite the entrance to Baberton Golf Course. Pushchair access can be found on a track that goes round the edge of the park. This excellent playground, situated in large grassy area, has a range of equipment to suit all ages. The toddler area multiplay is based on a train theme with carriages, a station and a ticket office all on a coloured track. To the side of this there are 2 bucket swings on rubber surfacing. The section for older children is behind this and separated by red metal fencing. It has a large amount of multiplay equipment with slides, rope climbing, bridges, balancing beams and large tyre slide. For the more advanced there is a large rope pyramid structure. The park is encircled by a fence, has benches, and is generally well maintained.

Gyle Park
Accessed from Wester Broom Pl

A redeveloped public park providing five football pitches, two rugby pitches, artificial cricket square, wheels area and roller hockey. The enclosed playground lies at the Gylemuir Primary School end of the park, and is best accessed by foot from Wester Broom Pl, along a path that runs beside Gylemuir Primary School or by parking at the David Lloyd leisure centre and walking along the open pathway. Equipment includes 2 bucket swings, and a special toddler zone unit with rubber decks, wide slide and game panels. For older children there are swings, an extremely imaginative multiplay including a straight and twisty slide, tunnel and rope climbs, and cableway. All equipment is set on colour safety surface, which incorporates children's artwork. There is a picnic table provided on a dog-free grass area within the playground, along with cycle racks and seating for adults. This is a quiet park and one of the best kept and with some of the best facilities.

Fort Saughton
Saughton Park
Entrances on Gorgie Road, Balgreen Road, Stevenson Drive

This is a 47 acre park mostly designated as football pitches and a putting green. Fort Saughton Playground, which is accessed from Balgreen Rd and has its own car park, is easily one of the best playgrounds in Edinburgh since being rebuilt in 1999. The large enclosed playground has sections that cater for all ages. The toddler play area has 4 bucket swings, a seesaw, roundabout and a great sand play area, where the children can enjoy many scooping and pouring activities around two multiplay areas and some low play tables. The rest of this extensive playground is set on wood chips and has a large multiplay with a tube slide, a hanging rope roundabout, 7 swings, a separate large slide, a large climbing net, springy animals, lots of balancing games, and a cableway. There are also several benches and 2 picnic tables. There is minimal graffiti. Opposite the entrance to the playground is Saughton Gardens. These gardens have been developed especially for the blind, with an emphasis on scented plants. They are attractive and well paved. There is also the Winter Gardens, an attractive heated greenhouse with tropical plants. Opening times: Mon-Wed 10.00-16.00; Thu-Fri 10.00-15.30; Sat-Sun 12.00-16.00. The cafeteria is open weekdays from 10.00 -15.30, however best to check it's definitely open before you go. Toilets area available during opening hours.

Haugh Park
Brae Park Road, Barnton

A leafy and quiet playground located close to the River Almond Walkway. Must be one of the most beautifully situated in Edinburgh. The equipment is mostly wooden and includes a climbing frame with 2 swings and a slide, a bucket swing, another 4 swings and a wooden rope bridge. All are set on a bark chip surface. However the equipment could do with a lick of paint. There is a car park specifically for this playground close by, as parking on Brae Park Rd can be difficult and there is a picnic table and benches. There are often ponies grazing in the paddock next to the park.

Spylaw Public Park & Playground
Spylaw Street/Gillespie Road

This large playground can be accessed from either Spylaw St, past Spylaw House, or by turning sharp left at the bottom of Gillespie Rd.

The playground is beautifully situated in a leafy green park by the Water of Leith. It is very well maintained and comprises a toddler multiplay, 2 swings, a tractor and trailer climbing frame, tyre swing, slide with platform and fireman's pole, and 4-seater buckabout. There are 2 seats and the playground is fully fenced. The nearby water of Leith Walkway is good off road cycling for beginners and there is also an exciting tunnel nearby to whiz through on bikes.

Stewart Terrace Park
Off Gorgie Road

Enclosed toddler park which is bright, clean and inviting. There are 2 bucket swings, 2 springy animals, plus a multiplay unit which has tunnels, a slide and climbing structures. There are also grassy areas and benches.

BEST OF THE REST

Curriemuir End Park
Off Wester Hailes Road

This playground has to be approached by foot, using either the path that leaves Wester Hailes Rd close to the junction with Viewfield Rd, or the underpass beneath Wester Hailes Rd that links the Clovenstone estate to the park.

Playground with mainly wooden equipment. Surrounding park is grassy and hilly, and there are several picnic tables nearby.

Dean Park
Balerno
Situated next to Dean Park Primary School. Access by car via Dean Park Pl.
Compact park with equipment which includes a toddler multiplay, a springy motorbike and tractor.

Pentland View Park
Currie
Situated on the busy Lanark Rd, but it's fully fenced and the access gate doesn't lead directly on to the road. Playground contains 2 toddler multiplays, 2 bucket swings, plus 4 other swings. Two benches for adults.

Fauldburn Park
East Craigs
Multiplay plus buckabouts. There are children's goal posts on grass next to the park.

Sighthill Park
Fort Broomhouse, Broomhouse Road
Playpark with two areas: toddler area equipment includes a sit-down roundabout, a multiplay and 2 bucket swings on a special low frame to help eliminate the disappointment of swing wrap round. The junior area includes a multiplay & more adventure style equipment., incl. a 'Space Climbing' net.
Next to the playground on the surrounding grass there are two small goal posts and a skateboarding ramp area.

OTHER PLAYGROUNDS & PARKS

Corstorphine Park
The Play Station, Carrick Knowe Drive
Multiplay unit playpark and grassy area

Murieston Park
Murieston Crescent
Playpark and some grass

Roseburn
Roseburn Crescent
Multiplay unit, situated next to open playing fields

St Margaret's Park
Corstorphine High St
Playground and grassy park
Also within St. Margaret's park there is the Heritage Centre that has a cafe open from 10.00- 12.00: there

is also a putting green, tennis courts, football area and a bowling green. There is very limited on street parking on Orchardfield Avenue.

Wester Hailes
This area has very few large playgrounds, but it has benefited from a programme to create a number of small play centres within individual estates for children.

White Park
Gorgie Road
Situated opposite the Hearts Football Ground Gorgie Road entrance. Playground plus grassy area.

ADVENTURE PLAYGROUNDS

Adventure playgrounds are less formal than the playgrounds described above and offer greater opportunities for creative play, making them harder work for parents. Some adventure playgrounds are really only suitable for older children but Vogrie Estate and Country Park can cater for all ages. There is also an adventure playground specifically created for children with a special need or disability at the Scotland Yard Adventure Centre

Dalkeith Country Park
Tel: 654 1666/663 5684
Web: www.dalkeithcountrypark.com
The park entrance is near St Mary's Church, a few hundred yards from the town centre
Opening times: Apr-end Sep 10.00-17.30
Admission: adult/child £3.00; group and family rates also available.

See Where Shall We Go Today: Parks, Country Parks & Gardens for full entry

Vogrie Country Park
Tel: 01875 821990 (ranger service)
Near Gorebridge, 12 miles South of Edinburgh
Signposted from Gorebridge (A7) and Dalkeith (A68)
Open all year.
Admission free. Car park £1.

See Where Shall We Go Today: Parks, Country Parks & Gardens for full entry

The Yard
70 Eyre Place EH3 5EJ
Tel: 557 899

The Yard provides adventure play opportunities for children and young people with specific care requirements. It aims to provide exciting, challenging and adventurous play for children in a safe and supportive environment. The centre has outdoor and indoor facilities. It's wheelchair accessible, and there's space for car parking. The Centre is open to families on Thu 18.00-20.30 and Sat 10.00-15.30. While there's no fee for families (brothers, sisters and friends are also welcome), it is essential to phone The Yard before visiting. See also Accessible Edinburgh - And Beyond for more info.

Pre-school Play and Education

PRE-SCHOOL PLAY & EDUCATION

INTRODUCTION

There are many opportunities for under 5s to meet with others in the same age range.

From the outset of family life, informal groups for parents and babies/toddlers can often provide a welcome break for both from the home and usually offer a larger range of toys and space than at home. This becomes particularly valuable once you are past the baby stage and want to meet others in a similar situation.

Moving on at around 2 1/2 yrs, playgroups provide a more structured environment. Many nurseries and playgroups are now in partnership with the City Council. From April 2002, under the Standards in Scotland's Schools Act 2000, Local Authorities have been under a duty to provide a funded part-time pre-school education place for every 3 and 4 year old whose parents wish it. The entitlement is for 412 1/2 hours per year, which is equivalent to one 2 1/2 hour session per day in practice.

As well as listing some of the toddler groups and playgroups in and around the city, we have also listed private nurseries; some of these provide daycare from 3 months. Many private nurseries are also in partnership with the City Council to provide funded places for 3 yrs. For 3+ yr olds, there are details of nursery schools and classes. We have also included details of nursery provision in the independent sector.

Finally in this section, there is so   me brief information on starting school.

Progression is usually:

Up to age 1 | Parent and Baby group
Age 1-2 1/2 | Parent and Toddler group
Age 2 1/2 -5 | Playgroup, Home Playgroup, Private Nursery
Age 3-5 | City of Edinburgh Council Nursery, Private Nursery, Independent School Nursery
or
Age 0-5 | Private Nursery, Independent School Nursery

If you are looking for full/part-time day care for your child, you can refer to 'Private Nurseries' in this section and also to the Childcare section, which covers nannies and childminders.

Details of multi-lingual groups and groups for children with special needs may be obtained from the Scottish Pre-School Play Association and the Education Department. This section has the following layout:

Sources of Information
Parent and Baby Groups
Parent and Toddler Groups
Playgroups and Home Playgroups
Private Nurseries
Nursery Schools
Nursery Classes in Schools
Independent Schools
Starting Schools

SOURCES OF INFORMATION

With regards to informal groups, information is usually posted on notice-boards in libraries, supermarkets, toy shops, church halls etc. Many groups meet in church halls; you do not need to be a member to attend. Another good place to check for information regarding local groups is health centre notice boards – or ask your health visitor.

Edinburgh Childcare Information Service
PO Box 777
Edinburgh   EH4 4JY
Tel: 270 6061 (Mon-Fri 08.30-16.00)
Fax: 270 6069
Freephone: 0800 0320323
Email: info@childcarepartnership.org
Web: www.childcarelink.gov.uk
Web: www. www.edinburghchildcare.co.uk

For full details of the service please see under Childcare.

To receive a list of registered children's centres, nurseries and childminders, contact:

The Scottish Commission for the Regulation of Care
Stuart House
Eskmills Business Park
Musselburgh   EH21 7PB
Tel: 0131 653 4100
Tel: 0845 600 8335

National Childbirth Trust
NCT Centre – Edinburgh
University Health Service
5th floor, 6 Bristo Square   EH8 9AL
Tel: 668 3257
Tel: 0870 444-8708
(NCT Breastfeeding Line 8.00-22.00)
Opening times: Mon-Thu 9.30-12.30, Fri 9.30-11.30.

Pupil Support Services Group
Education Department
City of Edinburgh Council
Wellington Court
10 Waterloo Pl   EH1 3EG
Tel: 469 3000.

Scottish Pre-school Play Association (SPPA)
14 Elliot Place Glasgow
Tel: 0141 221 4148
At time of publication, there is no Lothian/East of Scotland office.

Gaelic Medium Groups
At the time of writing, the established nursery class in Tollcross Primary School has been joined by a Gaelic playgroup (Croileagan) in Corstorphine, and some parent and toddler groups (Parant is Paisde). There is no requirement for parents to have any knowledge of Gaelic. For more information, contact Norma Martin on 469 3307.

POINTS TO CONSIDER
Lists: we have compiled our lists from questionnaires sent to groups registered with the Social Work Department, those sent to groups listed in the last edition of Edinburgh for Under Fives and information supplied by the authors and members of the National Childbirth Trust. There are other groups in and around the Edinburgh area. A listing is not necessarily a recommendation.

Contacts: these have been given where possible, but please bear in mind that contacts do change frequently, especially those of mother and toddler groups.

Play Environment: all groups which care for children under 8 for more than 2 hours without a parent or guardian in attendance are inspected and registered by the Social Work Department. This does not apply to baby and toddler groups, so it is advisable to check personally for the atmosphere and safety standards. In particular, check large outdoor equipment – for example, if there's a climbing frame, is it on a safe surface such as woodchip, rubber matting or grass, and so on.

PARENT & BABY GROUPS

These groups cater for parents and babies, and are genrally held in health centres or in someone's home. Your health visitor, clinic or the National Childbirth Trust (Tel: 260 9201, Mon, Wed, Fri 9.30-11.30, Tue, Thu 14.00-17.00) will put you in touch with other parents in your area.

PARENT & TODDLER GROUPS

These groups are generally set up by local parents and are held in church halls, community centres, or schools, and cater for babies and toddlers. The carer (parent, guardian, nanny or childminder) stays with the child throughout the session. Some groups separate the babies and the toddlers by age and have specific days for specific age ranges.

Facilities and standards vary, but most have a selection of toys and puzzles, books, crayons and some larger pieces of equipment, such as climbing frames, chutes, play cookers, ball pits, Wendy houses etc. Princes range from nothing to approximately £5-7/term, with a small charge for tea, coffee, juice, biscuits and so on. There's usually a rota for making tea etc, and carers help set up and tidy away the toys. Where we know that outdoor play is available, this has been mentioned.

NB If you are looking for information on supportive groups, please also refer to Activities for Parents – Community Centres.

Balerno

Balerno Toddlers
Balerno Parish Church Hall (Opposite Scotmid)
3 Johnsburn Road, Balerno
Contact: Maureen Harmer, Tel: 476 7851
or Kirstie Armsworth, Tel: 466 1253
Thu 9.45-11.15 (Not last Thu of the month)

St Mungo's Minis
St Mungo's Church, Ladycroft
Balerno
Contact: Andrea Brewster
Tel: 449 7030
Tue, Wed 10-11.30.
Brunstane, Magdalene & Joppa

Caring for Kids
Magdalen Community Centre
106b Magdalene Dr
Contact: Jacqui Cairney
Tel: 661 3109
Thu 10.00-12.00. Part of Magdalene Sure Start project.

St Philip's Church
Brunstane Road North
Contact: Debbie Smith
Tel: 669 1794
Fri 9.45-11.15.

Bruntsfield
Barclay Bruntsfield Church Hall
Barclay Place
Contact: Katherine Ellis
Tel: 228 4136
Tue 10.00-12.00.

Carrick Knowe
Carrick Knowe Church
Main Hall, situated to the left of the church
Saughton Rd N
Contact Christine Stewart
Tel: 334 5459 or Church 334 1505
Thu, Fri 10.00-11.30.

Clermiston
Parkgrove Parent & Toddler Group
The Munro Centre
Parkgrove Street
Tel: 539 7179
Thu 10.00-11.30.

Colinton
Colinton Toddler Group
St Cuthbert's Church Hall
Westgarth Avenue
Mon 9.30-11.30.

Stableroom Toddler Group
Colinton Parish Church Hall
Spylaw Bank Rd
Contact: Margaret Maxwell
Tel: 477 9494
Thu 9.30-11.30.

Corstorphine

Corstorphine Gaelic Medium Mother and Toddler group
Corstorphine Youth and Community Centre
Kirk Loan, Corstorphine
Contact: Norma Martin, Early Years Gaelic Development Officer
Tel: 469 3307
Email: Norma.Martin@educ.edin.gov.uk
Mon 10.30-12.30. The group is open to any to join. Parents do not need to be Gaelic speakers. There is normally a playleader in place for language input.

Gylemuir Primary School
Wester Broom Place
Contact: venue
Tel: 334 7138
Thu 10.00-11.30, 13.00-14.30.

Jack and Jill Mother and Toddler Club
St Anne's Church Hall
Kaimes Road
Contact: Frances Tennant
Tel: 316 4740
Wed 9.30-11.30.

St Ninian's Church Hall
St Ninian's Road
Contact: Sue McLean
Tel: 339 4773
Tue 10.00-11.30; Fri 10.00-11.30.

St Thomas Church
79 Glasgow Road
Contact: church
Tel: 316 4292
Tue 10.00-11.30.

Craiglockhart

Craiglockhart Church Hall
Craiglockhart Drive North
Contact: Rachel Carlyle
Tel: 4440852
Mon 10.00-11.45.

Craigmount
Craigmount School
Craigs Road
Contact: Community Education Office
Tel: 339 8278
Mon 13.45-15.15: all welome.

Cramond
Parent & Toddler Group
Cramond Kirk Hall
Cramond Glebe Road West
Tue 10.00-11.30.

Dalkeith
Woodburn Community Centre
6 Woodburn Road
Contact: Terri
Tel: 663 3958
Wed 9.30-11.00.

Dalry/Gorgie
Gorgie Memorial Hall
Gorgie Road
Contact: Wendy Duffy
Tel: 337 9098 (9.00-12.00)
Drop-in groups run throughout the week: Mon 9.30-13.30; Tues, Wed Thu 9.30-14.30; Fri 9.30-13.00.

Gorgie Parish Church
190 Gorgie Road
Tel: 337 9098
Thu 9.30-11.30.

St Bride's Centre
Orwell Terrace
Contact: centre
Tel: 346 1405
Fri 9.30-11.30.

Davidson's Mains
Davidson's Mains Parish Church
Quality St
Contact: Julie Brodie
Tel: 336 5385
Thu 9.15-11.15.

Holycross Mother & Toddler Group
Holycross Church Hall
Davidsons Mains
Contact: Juliet Pound
Tel: 336 3642
Mon 9.30-11.30. Birth to Nursery age. Mums, dads, grandparents and Carers welcome. Call for further details.

East Craigs
East Craigs Playgroup
East Craigs Church Centre
Bughtlin Market
Contact: venue
Tel: 339 8336
Mother and Toddler group: Tue 10.00-11.30, Thu 10.00-11.30.

Easter Road
Calton Centre
121 Montgomery Street
Contact: venue
Tel: 661 5252
Tue, Thu 10.00-12.00.

Fairmilehead
Fairmilehead Parish Church
Frogston Road West
Contact: Jennifer Saker, Tel: 445 1787
Mon, Tue, Thu, Fri 10.00-11.30.

Gilmerton & Inch
Gilmerton Community Centre
4 Drum Street
Contact: venue
Tel: 664 2335
Various groups run throughout the week: all welcome to toddler groups.
Mon: Spinney Tots, 9.15-11.30; Parent & Toddler Group, 12.45-15.00.
Wed: Adult & Toddler Group, 10.00-12.00.
Thu: Spinney Tots, 12.45-15.00.
Centre also runs a Daycarers obly group, Tue 9.30-11.30.
Playgroup also runs Mon-Fri 9.15-11.15.

Inch Community Centre
255 Gilmerton Road
Tel: 664 4710
Mon: Parent & Toddler, 9.30-11.30.
Wed, Thu: Daycarers-only groups 9.30-11.30.

Other parent/carer groups may also be running. Contact venue for current information.

Inverleith

Mother and Toddler Group
Inverleith Church
Ferry Road
Contact: venue - drop in on Wed
Wed 9.30-12.00. Large, informal group. Home-baking, tea, coffee, soft drink or water for children.

The Acorn Club
Inverleith Church
Ferry Road
Contact: drop-in at venue during group's times
Thu 9.45-11.15. Activities for 18+ mths.

Kirkliston

Kirkliston Community Education Centre
Queensferry Road
Contact: Jackie McNab
Tel: 332 9351
0-4s groups: Mon 9.00-11.30, 12.30-15.00. Wed 9.00-11.30.

Leith

Parent & Toddler Group
Fort Community Wing
North Fort Street
Tel: 553 1074
Wed 9.30-11.30.

Liberton

Liberton Kirk
Kirk Gate
Contact: Jackie Tait
Tel: 664 4205
Mon, Thu, Fri 9.30-11.30.

Loanhead

Loanhead mother & Toddler Group
Loanhead Community Learning Centre
Mayburn Walk
Loanhead
Mon, Wed, Fri 9.30-11.00. £1 entry, refreshments 50p. All welcome, just drop-in.

Lochend

Lochend YWCA
198 Restalrig Road South
Contact: venue
Tel: 554 3400
Mother & Baby group Wed 11.00 - 13.00. Carer & Toddler group Fri 9.30-11.30. Toy Library Wed 10.00-11.00.

Ripple Project Parent and Toddler Group
St Margaret's Church Hall
Restalrig Road South
Contact: Ripple Project
Tel: 554 0422
Tue 9.30-11.15.

Toddle-In Group
Pilrig Child and Family Centre
102 Pilrig Street
Contact: Pat Southall
Tel: 554 3040
Tue 13.00-14.30. Other groups can be arranged, contact Centre for details.

Piershill Under-3 Project
New Restalrig Church
Willowbrae Road
Contact: Jacqui Cairney
Tel: 661 3109
Wed, Fri 9.45-11.30. Part of Magdalene Sure Start project.

Marchmont

Marchmont St Giles Parish Church
Kilgraston Road
Contact: venue
Tel: 446 9217
Thu 10.00-12.00.

St Catherine Argyle Church
61 Grange Road
Contact: venue
Tel: 667 7220
Tue 10.00-12.00.

Meadowbank

Holyrood Abbey Baby and Toddler Group
Dalziel Place, London Road
Contact: Jean Archer
Tel: 653 2314
Mon 10.00-11.30.

Merchiston

Next Step Parent & Toddler Group
Rudolph Steiner School
60 Spylaw Road
Contact: Anne Reijnierse
Tel: 441 5977
Mon-Fri 10.15-12.30. 13.30 - 15.30. Baking, crafts, games.

Morningside

Morningside Parish Church
Cluny Centre
Cluny Drive
Contact: venue
Tel: 447 6745
Mon, Thu 9.30-11.30.

Greenbank Church Mother and Toddlers Group
Braidburn Terrace
Contact: venue
Tel: 447 9969
Thu 9.45-11.15. Mothers, fathers, grandparents and carers welcome.

Morningside Baptist Church
Morningside Road
Contact: venue
Tel: 447 9787
Thu 10.00-12.00. Mother and Under 1s group Fri 10.30-12.30.

The Old Schoolhouse
140 Morningside Road
Contact: Adele Thomson
Tel: 445 5726
Thu 9.45-11.30.

Muirhouse

Craigroyston Community Centre
1a Pennywell Road
Contact: Christine Docherty
Tel: 332 7360
Mon-Thu 9.30-11.15.

Newington

Duncan Street Toddler Group
Duncan Street Baptist Church
Duncan Street
Contact: no co-ordinator at time of writing.
Contact via Duncan Street Playgroup
(Lorraine Adam, Tel: 667 8097 (pm only))
Tue 10.00-12.00. Age 0-2 1/2 yrs.

Niddrie

Greengables Toddler Group
8a Niddrie House Gardens
contact: Kate Frame
Tel: 669 9083
Thu 12.30 2.30 (term time). See also 'Nursery Schools'.

Old Town

High School Yards Nursery
High School Yards, off Infirmary Street   EH1 1LZ
Contact: Alison Conroy
Tel: 556 6536
Sure Start Parent & Toddler Club on Wednesdays 9.15 - 11.15, for families with under 3s.

St Ann's Community Centre
6 South Gray's Close
Contact: venue
Tel: 557 0469
No group running from centre at time of writing, but contact venue for current details.

St. Columba's Free Church
Johnson Terrace - entrance by hall door at Victoria Terrace.
Contact: Catriona Lamont
Tel: 228 3782
Tue 9.30-11.30. No charge.

Oxgangs
Edinburgh Twins' Club's Bumps & Babies/ Toddlers' Group
Oxgangs Neighbourhood Centre
Firrhill Dr, off Oxgangs Cres
Contact: Karen Winfield
Tel: 441 7558 (centre number)
Tue 15.00-16.30; Thu 10.00-11.30.
Only open to families with twins or more.

Pentland Community Education Centre
Oxgangs Brae
Tel: 445 5559
Fri 10.00-12.00. A self-supported group of parents/carers come together for crèche and a chat while children are able to play together in a safe and secure environme. Call Gary Rose for full details, tel: 445 5559.

Oxgangs Sure Start Project
Colinton Mains Community Centre
1 Firrhill Loan
Contact: Sue Christie
Tel: 441 7318
A community-based project offering support and guidance for families and carers with children who are aged 0-3 yrs. Session days and times may vary: phone for up-to-date information.

Children's Activity Group
Pentland Community Education Centre
Oxgangs Brae
Contact: Heather Levy
Tel: 445 5559
For children with special needs/disabilities who live in Oxgangs and surrounding areas. Meets Friday afternoons 14.00-15.50. Offers a range of activities are available in safe surroundings. Meetings during school term-time only at the moment. Contact team leader for more information. Age range is 4-14, but group will welcome younger children.
There is also a group on Wed 15.30-17.00, primarily for older children.

Pilton
Forthview Primary School
West Pilton Place
Contact: Tracey Berry
Tel: 332 2468
Tue 9.30-11.00 (term time only)
Mother and Toddler group. A Parents' Group also runs – please contact venue for current details of this. Both run by an Educational Home Visitor who is teacher trained.

Polwarth
Polwarth Parent, Baby and Toddler Group
Polwarth Church Hall
Polwarth Terrace
Email: welcome@polwarthtoddlergroup.org.uk
Web: www.polwarthtoddlergroup.org.uk
Tue, 10.00-12.00; Thu, 14.30-16.30.

Portobello
Portobello Old Parish Church
Bellfield Street
Contact: Heather Gray
Tel: 669 7512
Tue 9.15-11.15.

Prestonfield
Cameron House Community Centre
Cameron House Avenue   EH15 5LF
Contact: Susan Ferguson at venue
Tel: 667 3762
Fri 10.30-12.30.

Ratho
Ratho Community Centre
1 School Wynd
Contact venue
Tel: 333 1055
Tue & Thu 10.00-12.00.

St Leonards
St Peter's 0-5s
St Peter's Church
Lutton Place
Contact: venue
Tel: 667 9838
Mon, Thu 9.30-11.00. Well established group. 50p charge to cover refreshments.

South Queensferry

South Queensferry Community Centre
Rosebery Hall site
Rosebery Hall, High Street
South Queensferry
Contact: venue
Tel: 331 2113
Parent& Toddlers – Mon 9.30-11.30; Wed 9.30-11.30.
Childminders' group Thu 9.30-11.30.

Stenhouse

Carrickvale Community Education Centre
Stenhouse Street West
Edinburgh EH11 3EP
contact: venue
Tel: 443 6971
Mon, Tue, Thu, Fri 9.30-11.30.

HUT Parent & Toddler Group
9 Hutchisopn Crossway
St Cuthbert's Primary School
Stenhouse Child & Family Centre
Tel: 443 1207
Wed 9.30-11.30

Stockbridge/Comely Bank

Comely Bank Toddlers
St Stephen's Comely Bank Church
10 Comely Bank Road
Contact: Helen Bennett
Tel: 343 4616
Thu 9.30-11.15. Term-time only. 0-3 yrs.

International Playgroup
St. Stephen's Centre
St. Stephen Street, near Howe Street
Contact: Jonelle McArdle
Tel: 556 5467
Mon & Fri 10.00-11.30 for babies and toddlers until 4th birthday. Admission £2 per family. Tea, coffee, children's snacks provided.

Stockbridge Library Baby and Toddler Group
Stockbridge Library
Hamilton Place EH3 5BA
Tel: 0131 529 5665
Contact Debs
Email: debs3d@yahoo.com
10.00-12noon every Thursday. A relaxed and informal playgroup for babies and toddlers up to 4 years old. Playgroup runs throughout the year even the summer months. Singing at 11am, so no-one misses out! Snacks provided for the children and group organises a coffee run to the local coffee shop for the adults. Price £1.50 per family.

Tollcross

Tollcross Gaelic Medium Mother and Toddler Group
Tollcross Community Centre
Tollcross Primary School
117 Fountainbridge, Edinburgh
Contact: Norma Martin,
Early Years Gaelic Development Officer
Tel: 469 3307
Email: Norma.Martin@educ.edin.gov.uk
Wed 9.00-11.30. The group is open to any to join. Parents do not need to be Gaelic speakers. There is normally a playleader in place for language input.

Trinity
Trinity Toddler Group
School Buildings
Craighall Gardens
Mon 10.00-12.00; Tue 10.00-11.30; Wed, 10.00-12.00, 12.00-14.00 (first-time mums), 14.00-16.00; Fri 10.00-12.00, 14.00-16.00.
£1/ session, plus £5 per quarter. There is currently no group on Thu, but there are plans for one in the future. To join, just drop-in during one of the sessions.

West End
St Mary's Episcopal Cathedral
Walpole Hall
Chester Street
Contact: Jane Tupper
Tel: 667 8978
Fri 9.30-11.30, incl. school holidays.

PLAYGROUPS

Balerno
The Village Playgroup
Community Centre, Main Street, Balerno
Contact: Alice Anderson (owner)
Tel: 451 5756
Private playgroup. 34 places am. Mornings 8.30-16.00. Ages 2-starting primary school. Open 50 weeks/year. Contact playgroup for current fees. Also offers a lunch club provision 12.00-13.00 for a small additional fee. Breakfast Club from 08.00

Compass Playgroup
Deanpark Primary School
31 Marchbank Gardens
Balerno EH14 7ET
Contact: Mrs Sally Foster (playleader)
Tel: 449 4530
20 places. Mon-Thu 9.00-11.45. Ages 2&3 mainly. Grassy outdoor play area. Duty rota. Contact venue for current fees.

Blackhall
Blackhall Nursery
18 Keith Terrace
Craigcrook Rd
Contact: Tina Woolnough
Tel: 332 8296
30 places am, 30 places pm, Mon-Fri 9.00-11.30 and 12.15-14.45. 3-5 yrs. Outdoor play. Free – all places are partner provider status.

Blackhall Playgroup
St Columba's Church
Hillhouse Road
Contact: Heather Keenan
Tel: 339 3995
24 places. Mon, Wed, Thu 9.30-12.00; Tue 13.00-15.30. Ages 2 1/2-5 yrs.

Broomhall
Broomhall Playgroup
Broomhall Scout Hall
81A Broomhall Avenue
Contact: Linda Aitken
Tel: 07749765104 (during playgroup's hours)
28 places. Mon-Fri 9.15-11.45. 2-5 yrs. £12.50/week. Duty rota.

Bruntsfield
Bruntsfield Playgroup
Lower playground,
Bruntsfield Primary School
Contact: Fiona Anderson
Tel: 228 1526 (9.00-11.45)
Mon-Fri 9.00-11.45. In partnership with local authority, therefore all places funded from 3rd birthday. Nominal fee up to that age. Outdoor play area.

Calton
Calton Playgroup
Calton Centre
Contact: venue and ask for play managers
Tel: 661 5252
20 places. Mon-Fri 9.15-11.45. Ages 2 1/2 – 5. £15/week. No outdoor play area, but does organise visits to parks etc.

Church Hill
Holy Corner Community Playgroup
Christ Church
6 Morningside Road
Contact: venue
Tel: 228 2768 (between 9-11.30)
24 places, Mon-Fri 9.15-11.45. 21/2 -5 yrs. £4.50/morning: partner provider with City of Edinburgh Council. Duty rota, outdoor play area.

Clermiston
Parkgrove Playgroup
The Munro Centre, Parkgrove Street
Contact: playleaders at venue
Tel: 539 7179
24 places. Mon, Wed, Fri 9.15-11.30. 21/2 -4 yrs. £2/ session. Outdoor play.

Colinton
Cranley Nursery
Paties Road Pavilion, Katesmill Road
Contact: Vikki Connolly
Tel: 441 3804
Email: enquiries@ cranleynursery.co.uk
Web: www.2webmonkeys.co.uk/cranley
25 places. Mon-Fri 8.00-18.00. Ages 2-5 yrs. In partnership with City of Edinburgh Council. Large, secure outdoor play area. Contact nursery for current fees.

Stableroom Playgroup
Colinton Parish Church
Colinton EH13 0JW
Contact: venue
Tel: 477 9494
16 places/session. Mon, Wed, Fri 9.15-11.45; Mon, Wed 12.30-14.30 (Afternoon session Easter term only). Ages 21/2 -5 . Partner provider with City of Edinburgh Council. Duty Rota.

Colinton Mains Playgroup
Colinton Mains Community Centre
Firhill Loan
Contact venue
Tel: 441 6597
Sure Start group runs from venue. Call for current details.

Corstorphine
Craigsbank Playgroup
Craigsbank Church Hall, Craigsbank
Contact: Mrs Walls
Tel: 476 1707
24 places. Tue-Fri 9.15-11.45. 21/2 -4 yrs. Some outdoor play. Minimal fees – contact playgroup for current fees.

East Craigs Playgroup
East Craigs Church Centre, Bughtlin Market
Contact: Mrs Walls
Tel: 476 1707
24 places. Tue-Fri 9.15-11.45. 21/2-4 yrs. Some outdoor play. Small charge – contact playgroup for current fees.

Fox Covert Nursery
Fox Covert Primary School
Clerwood Terrace
Contact: the playleaders (9.00-13.00)
Tel: 467 7294
40 places. Mon-Fri 9.00-11.40. 3-5 yrs. Partner Provider with City of Edinburgh Council. Outdoor play area. Duty rota.

Corstorphine Village Playgroup
Old Parish Church Hall
Corstorphine High Street
Contact: Mrs Jean Howe
Tel: 07707 695 426
24 places Tues – Thurs 18 places Mon and Fri 9.15-11.45. Ages 21/2 -5. Small daily fee. Fees payable/term. Advised that child's name is put down from 1st birthday on waiting list.

Craigentinny
Craigentinny/Lochend Social Centre Playgroup
Loaning Road
Contact: venue
Tel: 661 8188
16 places. Mon-Fri 9.10-11.30. Ages 21/2-5. £12/week. Outdoor play area.

Craiglockhart
Craiglockhart Playgroup
Craiglockhart Church
Craiglockhart Drive North
Contact: Maureen Sloan
Tel: 455 8229
20 places. Wed-Fri 9.15-11.45. 2-4 yrs. Duty rota. Outside area used daily

Cramond
Cramond Kirk Hall
Cramond Glebe Road West
Contact: waiting list secretary
Mon-Fri 9.00-11.55. Ages 2-5. Staffed playgroup. No parental rota. Contact playgroup for current details regarding partner provider info and outdoor play.

Currie
Currie Playgroup
16 Kirkgate
Currie EH14 6AN
Contact: venue
Tel: 449 2016
20 places. Mon-Fri 9.00-11.45. 2-5 years. Partner provider nursery. Duty Rota. New garden area.

Jubilee Playgroup
Youth Club, 280 Lanark Rd W
Contact: Joan Baillie
Tel: 449 6224 (centre no.)
12 places. Mon-Fri 9.30-11.45. Ages 2 -5 yrs. Outdoor play. Small numbers – may be helpful for children who do not settle in larger playgroups.

Dalry
Nari Kallyan Shangho Project
Darroch Annexe
7 Gillespie Street
Contact: project
Tel: 221 1915
Email: nks@nkshealth.co.uk
Web: www.nkshealth.co.uk
Full-time childcare facility. 10 places. Mon-Fri 9.00-11.45, 12.15-15.00. 2-5 yrs. £3/session or £6/day. Small outdoor area.

St Martin's Playgroup
St Martin's Church, Murieston Crescent
Contact: venue (am only)
Tel: 337 9714
20 places. Mon-Fri 9.15-11.30. Ages 2-5. Duty Rota.

Davidson's Mains
Reindeer Playgroup
Holy Cross Church Hall
Quality Street
Davidson's Mains EH4 5BT
Contact: the playleaders
Tel: 07906 518 747
Tue-Fri 9.15-11.45. Ages 21/2-4. Children should be potty-trained. No rota.

Goldenacre
Edzell Nursery Class
St James Church Hall
Inverleith Row
Contact: venue
Tel: 551 2179
3 yrs. 12 places. Mon, Wed, Fri 9.00-11.45. 4 yrs. 12 places. Mon-Fri 9.00-11.45. Outdoor play in enclosed garden. Partner Provider.

Wardie Nursery
Wardie Residents Club
125 Granton Road   EH5 3NJ
Contact: the playleaders
Tel: 07969 099 340
30 places. Mon-Fri 9.00-11.45. Ages 21/2-5. Partner provider. Outdoor play area.

Gilmerton
Gilmerton Community Centre
4 Drum Street
Gilmerton
Contact: venue
Tel: 664 2335
Mon-Fri 9.15-11.15: contact centre for all current details or playgroup application form.

Inch
New Life Nursery
70 Dinmont Drive
Contact: Christine McPake
Tel: 666 1826
20 places. Mon-Fri 9.30-12.00, Accepts children 21/2 -5 yrs. Outdoor play. Contact nursery for current details, session costs etc.

Juniper Green
Juniper Green Nursery Playgroup
Juniper Green Community Centre
Juniper Park Road
Contact: venue
Tel: 453 4427 w/days am
30 places. Mon-Fri 9.15-12.00. 2-5 yrs. Group accepts children in disposable nappies. Nappy changing facilities. Outdoor play.

Kirkliston
Kirkstyle Playgroup
Thomas Chalmers Church Centre, The Square
Correspondence add: 28 Kirklands Park Crescent
Kirkliston West Lothian EH29 9EP
Contact: Mrs Goodall
Tel: 333 3725 or venue, 333 4088
24 places. Mon, Wed, Thu, Fri 9.15-11.45. 2-5 yrs. Duty rota.

Leith
Leith Academy Nursery
Leith Academy School
20 Academy Park   EH6 8JQ
Contact: Amy Heron
Tel: 554 0606
Accepts children 0-5yrs. Open Mon-Fri 8.15-16.15. The crèche can be accessed by students participating in community education classes within the school or within

the local area, although it can also be accessed by school students, staff and working parents. Offers activites and equipment incl. water and sand play, music and movement, and arts & crafts.

Liberton
Liberton Northfield Playgroup
Liberton Northfield Church, Gilmerton Road
Contact: Sonya Adelman
Tel: 664 1910
23 places. Tue, Thu, Fri 9.15-12.15. 2-5 yrs. Duty rota. Outdoor play. £3/morning. Registered charity.

Marchmont
Marchmont St Giles Playgroup
Marchmont St Giles Church Hall
1A Kilgraston Road
Contact: venue
Tel: 446 9217
24 places. Tue-Thu 9.30-12.00. Ages 21/4-5. Duty rota. Outdoor play.

Morningside
Greenbank Preschool Playgroup
Greenbank Church Hall, Braidburn Terrace
Contact: Church Office
Tel: 447 8068
25 places. Mon-Fri 9.00-11.45. 3-5 yrs. Outdoor play. Duty rota. Organic snacks. Partner provider.

Nile Grove Community Playgroup
Morningside Parish Church
Braid Centre
1 Nile Grove
Contact: Enrolment Secretary
Tel: 447 9430
24 places. Mon-Fri 9.15-11.45. Ages 21/4 -5. Duty rota. Outdoor play.

Muirhouse
Craigroyston Project
Craigroyston Community Centre
1a Pennywell Road
Contact: Christine Docherty
Tel: 332 7360 (venue)
16 places. Mon-Thur 9.15-11.15. Ages 21/2 -5 years. Outdoor play area.

Murrayfield
Montessori Nursery School
Good Shepherd Church Hall, Murrayfield Avenue
Contact: Mrs Park
Tel: 346 8921
24 places. Mon-Fri 8.45-12.30. 3-5 yrs. Outdoor Play. In partnership with City of Edinburgh Council.

New Town
Doune Terrace Playgroup
9c Doune Terrace
Tel: 225 3805
Contact venue for new details: finalised details unknown at time of writing.

St Mary's Playgroup
St Mary's Primary School
63 East London Street
Contact: Gail Dempster
Tel: 556 1634 (during playgroup hours)
20 places. Mon-Fri 9.00-12.00. 21/2-5 yrs. £3/session. Duty rota. Outdoor play.

Newington
Duncan Street Pre-school Playgroup
Baptist Church Hall, Duncan Street
Contact: Lorraine Adam
Tel: 667-8097 (pm only)
18 places. Mon-Fri 9.15-11.45. Part wk places available. Ages 21/2-5. In partnership with City of Edinburgh Council. Funded places available for over 3s, otherwise £5/morning. Outdoor play. Duty Rota.

Pilton
Funtime Playgroup
Royston Wardieburn Community Education Centre
Pilton Drive North
Contact: Frances Wallace or Eileen Harrison
Tel: 552 5700 (during playgroup hours)
20 places. Mon-Fri 9.15-11.45. Ages 21/2 -5 – child must be toilet-trained. Outdoor play. Duta rota. £1/session.

The Prentice Centre Playgroup
The Prentice Centre, 1 Granton Mains Avenue
Contact: Elizabeth Campbell
Tel: 552 0485

2 sessions of 10 places. Mon-Thu 9.00-11.30, 12.15-15.00. Ages 2-5 yrs (must be toilet trained). £1 annual membership for child: parent must also have membership £2/year. £1/session (includes snack). Outdoor play. . Also bookable crèche on Fri, 9.15-11.45.

Polwarth
Harrison pre-school Playgroup & Mother and Toddler Group
Phoenix Youth Club, Harrison Gardens
Tel: 337 2171
28 places. Mon-Fri 9.30 -11.30 (term time only). Ages 2-5 yrs. Outdoor play. Separate quiet room. Please phone for current fees.

Portobello
Portobello Toddlers Hut
28 Beach Lane
Portobello
Contact: Karen Wilson
Tel: 669 6849
18 Places. Mon-Fri 9.00-11.30. 2 1/2-5 yrs. Outdoor play area. Duty rota.

St. James's Playgroup
Parish Church Hall, Rosefield Place
Contact: Mrs Peden
Tel: 669 6277
21 places. Mon, Tue, Thu 9.00-12.10, Fri 9.00-12.00. 2 1/2-5 yrs. Outdoor play. In partnership with City of Edinburgh Council. Contact for current fees.

Saughton
Balgreen Playgroup
Balgreen Bowling Club
Pansy Walk, Balgreen Rd
Tel: 313 5097 (am only)
16 places. Mon-Wed 9.00-11.45. Ages 2-5 yrs. Indoor soft play room. Outdoor play area in enclosed garden. Contact group for current costs.

Slateford
Cafe Boo
Slateford Green Community Centre   EH11 3HS
Tel:
(down from The Dell sorting office, off Slateford Road - or up the hill behind McDonalds/Somerfield off Gorgie Road. Big green and white building with the community centre being at the Slateford Road end)
Wed, Thu 10.30-14.00 (term-time only). Community Cafe & Playspace for Under-5's and their Grown-Ups.
Range of toys, softs play and boooks, plus occasional storytelling, craft, dance or music sessions. Cafe Boo's playspace and cafe open to everyone who has a little one. Entry is free, (but there is a 'subs' tin for donations), and the cafe is keenly-priced and full of homebaking and homemade foods. Children's portions 1/2 the price of the adults (£))

South Queensferry
Rosebery Playgroup
Rosebery Hall, High Street
S Queensferry
Contact: the playleaders
Tel: 331 2113
30 places. Mon-Fri 9.15-11.45. Ages 2-5 yrs. Partner provider; otherwise £4/session for ages 2-3. Outdoor play area. Contact playgroup for current fees.

Trinity Nursery
Wardie Church
Primrose Bank Road   EH5 3JE
Contact: the playleaders
Tel: 551 3847
20 places. Mon-Fri 9.00-12.00. Ages 3-5. Outdoor play. Partner provider.

Willowbrae
Northfield Playgroup
Northfield Community Centre
Northfield Rodd
Contact: Brenda Devlin
Tel: 661 5723
30 places. Mon-Fri 9.15-11.45. Duty rota. Outdoor play. Partner Provider.

PRIVATE NURSERIES

In Scotland, all private nurseries should be registered with the Care Commission, which can provide a list of registered groups, including nurseries, childminders and other daycare provision for children. For anyone relocating from England or Wales, Ofsted has no jurisdiction in Scotland. The Care Commission Regional Office address is:

PRE-SCHOOL PLAY & EDUCATION – PRIVATE NURSERIES

The Care Commission
Stuart House
Eskmill
Musselburgh EH21 7PB
Tel: 0131 653 4100 or 0845 600 8335
Web: www.carecommission.com

Nursery premises etc. are inspected once a year and reports are compiled after the inspection. These reports are compiled with the nursery in mind, rather than the potential parent, so they may seem dry and full of point-system references, but you can access them via the Care Commission website.

The Care Commission update the registration list regularly and if you cannot find a suitable nursery in your preferred area, it is worth phoning them.

The Edinburgh Childcare Information Service can also provide information:

Edinburgh Childcare Information Service
Tel: 0800 0320 323
Web: www.childcarelink.gov.uk

Partner Providers
From April 2002, under the Standards in Scotland's Schools Act 2000, Scottish local authorities have been under a duty to secure a funded part-time pre-school education place for every 3 and 4 year old whose parents wish it. You are entitled to a funded part-time place for your three or four year old from the beginning of the term starting after their third birthday, in accordance with guidelines laid down by the Scottish Executive. The entitlement is for 412 1/2 hours per year. This is usually delivered daily as a 2 1/2 hour session, morning or afternoon, during school term times. You may be able to get a different pattern of sessions to suit your child or your pattern of work.

Choosing a Nursery
If possible, get recommendations from other parents, then, in order to get a realistic picture of a nursery, drop in unannounced perhaps on more than one occasion at different times of the day. Visit several alternatives and take a list of questions to ask and points to consider. Ultimately the choice is a personal one but you might like to keep the following in mind:

Activities
How is the day structured? What are the children doing during your visit? What activities are available if it is a free play period? Are there lots of books in evidence? Do children have access to a TV, or is a radio on during your visit – and how do you feel about this? What trips and visits are provided?

Facilities
Does the nursery seem pleasant, spacious and light? Is it brightly decorated with children's paintings? Is there room for a variety of activities? Is there a peaceful room set aside for naps? What sleeping facilities are provided for babies? Is there a garden or safe outdoor play area?

Feedback and Communication
What sort of report do parents receive at the end of the day (nappies, sleeps, meals, activities) – is this verbal or written? Is your child assigned a key worker with whom you can discuss daily matters and general progress? What opportunities do parents have to discuss their child's needs and other matters with the nursery staff and management?

Financial Considerations
Does the weekly charge include meals, milk and nappies? Are any free settling-in sessions provided? Are there any discounts available for students, families on low incomes, companies and siblings?
Remember, if you spend money on childcare while you work and you qualify for the Working Tax Credit, you might be entitled to financial help with childcare costs. Called the childcare tax credit element, more information can be found on various websites, such as:

www.childcarelink.co.uk
or
www.inlandrevenue.gov.uk/taxcredits

Leaflets available at main Post Offices, or from the Inland Revenue Tax Credits helpline on 0845 300 3900 (open Sunday to Saturday. 8am–8pm)

Practicalities
Who is in charge of the nursery – are they in evidence during your visit? Are staff/child ratios being complied with? What is the staff turnover like? How long is the waiting list if any? Will they welcome expressed milk?
If meals are provided, ask to see a week's menu, and ask about the preparation facilities and the sourcing of the food. What provision is made for vegetarian children or those with allergies etc? Is fruit provided at snack time? Initial steps are underway to provide guidance for nurseries etc as to healthy eating, to bring pre-school

education into line with primary schools' food standards, but at the time of writing it is up to the nursery to choose what is provided, so that may be biscuits, a little sandwich etc every day for snack – are you content with that: it's up to you to decide.

If you're enquiring about part-time sessions, does the fee include snack and lunch?

Does the nursery accept children wearing real nappies? In this guide nurseries that accept real (non disposable) nappies are indicated with RN.

Do you envisage your child using the nursery aged 3? If so is it (or applying to be) a partner provider?

Timetable

Do opening times fit in with your schedule? Are pick-up times flexible? Is there an after school club for older children? Is there parking available at busy times? Remember, you don't have to (or shouldn't have to) drop-off at precisely opening times – you're paying for the service, so if, say, 9.30 suits you better as a drop-off time than the opening time of 8.30, drop off at 9.30, but remember you'll still have to pay the same for the session.

Section Information

Nurseries are listed by area: Central, North, South, East, West and alphabetically within area. We have listed the relevant post code areas at the head of each section. We have omitted fees/ prices, as up-to-date information can be given by the nurseries. However, do remember that fees are higher for under 2s, as the ratio of staff to children is higher.

The following at-a-glance information is a referred to in the listings:

❖ These nurseries offer places for children under the age of 2. Places for the under 2s can be hard to find so try to register with the nursery as soon as possible, even before the baby is born.

✪ Partner pre-school providers. Please note that this list is updated regularly: if in doubt refer to the Care Commission, or Edinburgh Chidcare Information Service. The City of Edinburgh Council offers funded part time pre-school education to all children in the year before they start primary school, and to all 3 year olds from the term after their 3rd birthday, see 'Nursery Education'. This can be in either a local authority nursery or a partner provider – which is usually a private nursery or community playgroup. As soon as your child is 2 yrs you can put his/her name on the waiting list for the nursery or partner provider of your choice. You register directly with the nursery and may put your child's name down

on more than one waiting list. The nursery you choose will not affect the primary class your child moves on to. If you wish additional hours and any other services including outwith term time, you will be charged for these. Each nursery will have arrangements about payment and you should discuss this with them before accepting a place. Nurseries selected under this scheme must meet HMI standards, have a qualified teacher and be prepared for HMI Inspections.

RN These nurseries accept children who wear real nappies. While some nurseries do provide disposable nappies, be prepared to provide your choice of real nappy, and perhaps a storage bin.

Please remember that a nursery entry in Edinburgh for Under Fives is not necessarily a recommendation; facilities, type of care and safety standards must be checked personally. Please also remember that unlike primary schools, there are no catchment areas for nurseries – you can choose one anywhere in the city that suits you.

CENTRAL EDINBURGH

Includes Nurseries in the following postcode areas: EH1, EH2, EH3, EH12

❖✪ Bright Horizons The Birrell Collection
17 Walker Street   EH3 7NE
Contact: Sheila Thorpe
Tel: 225 8031
25 places, Mon-Fri 8.15-18.00. 12mths-5yrs. Part time available. Snacks and lunch provided. Outdoor play.

❖✪ Bright Horizons Family Solutions
4a Rutland Square EH1 2AS
Contact: Shona Watters
Tel: 229 8888
Fax: 229 9503
Email: rutland@brighthorizons.com
46 places, Mon-Fri 8.00-18.00. 3mths-5yrs. Discounts for 3yrs+ if 5+ sessions attended each week.Snacks provided. Music, dance & French taught. Outdoor play.

❖✪ Careshare - Port Hamilton Nursery
69 Morrison Street   EH3 8BW
Contact: Lesley Brown
Tel: 228 1221
100 places, Mon-Fri 7.45-17.45. 0-5yrs. Fees on application. Nappies, snacks, lunch, suncream, birthday cake and

Christmas present included in fees. Investors In People award. Music & language lessons. Outdoor play.

❖ Doune Terrace Nursery
9c Doune Terrace EH3 6DY
Contact: Catherine Quinn
Tel: 225 3805
Email: douneterracenursery@btconnect.com
35 places, Mon-Fri 8.00-18.00. 0-8yrs. Full-time sessions only . After school club. French, dance and literacy classes. Snacks and lunch provided. All-weather outdoor play area and garden.

❖ Early Days Nursery
36 Palmerston Place EH12 5BJ
Contact: Maureen Crandles
Tel: 226 4491
Email: earlydaysnursery@btconnect.com
Web: www.earlydaysnursery.co.uk
50 places, Mon-Fri 8.00-18.00. 0-8yrs. Full-time sessions only. Offers school holiday care and after school club.

French, dance and literacy classes. Snacks and lunch provided. All-weather outdoor play area.

❖❂ RN New Town Nursery Too
4 Forres Street EH3 6BJ
Contact: Mark Loughton
Tel: 226 5692
35 places currently; expansion due. Mon-Fri 8.00-17.45. Partner Provider. Outdoor play/activities.

❖ Primetime Nurseries Ltd
29 Queen Street EH2 1JX
Contact: Janet Kellalib
Tel: 226 7340
Email: info@primetimenursery.com
65 places for 0-5 yrs. 15 places for after-school club for 5-8yrs. Mon-Fri 7.30-18.00, 8.00-18.00 Sat. Part-time places available. Breakfast, morning snack, lunch, afternoon snack, tea. All food is prepared on site. Organic menu. Outdoor play, with safety surfacing and soft play equipment. Partner provider with the education department

The Royal Infirmary Day Nursery
1-3 Lauriston Park EH3 9JA
Contact: Elaine Brown
Tel: 476 3978
Email: rie.nursery@virgin.net
Web: www.riedaynursery.co.uk
43 places, Mon-Fri 07;00-17.45. Full and part-time places. Discount for NHS staff. Snacks provided. Gardens.

❖ Royal Mile Nursery
Old Stamp Office Close
215 High Street EH1 1PX
Contact: Michelle Wainwright
Tel: 226 6574
20 places, Mon-Fri 8.00-18.00. 3mths-5yrs. £140-145/wk. Outdoor play.

❖ Uni-Tots Nursery
University of Edinburgh
7 George Sq EH8 9JZ
Contact: Audrey Cameron
Tel: 650 3448
24 am places, 16 pm places. Mon-Fri 8.30-17.30. 21/2-5yrs. Morning session, lunch (12.00-13.00) and afternoon sessions offered on a full-time and part-time flexible basis as available. Snacks provided. Large new outdoor play area.

NORTH EDINBURGH

Includes Nurseries in the following postcode areas: EH4 EH5 EH6 EH7 EH8 EH15

❖ Bright Horizons Family Solutions
Elsie Inglis Nursery School
1 Waverley Park
Spring Gardens
Edinburgh EH8 8EW
Contact: Vanessa Constable
Tel: 661 8551
Fax: 661 8567
Email: elsies@brighthorizons.com
62 places, Mon-Fri 8.00-18.00. 3mths-5yrs. Morning and afternoon snacks provided. Dancebase classes, music & French taught. Outdoor play area with safety matting.

❖❍ RN Bright Horizons Nursery
The Scottish Executive
Victoria Quay   EH6 6QQ
Contact: Beth Pearce
Tel: 244 0782
Email: victoriaquay@brighthorizons.com
36 places, Mon-Fri 7.30-18.30. 0-5yrs, cost on application. Scottish Executive employees only. Morning and afternoon snacks provided. Outdoor play, access to gym hall for pre-school room.

❖❍ RN Careshare - Newhaven Nursery
Next Generation Club
Newhaven Place   EH6 4LX
Contact: Morag Gall
Tel: 467 4647
55 places, Mon-Fri 8.00-18.00. 0-5yrs. Fees on application. Disposable nappies, snacks, lunch, suncream, birthday cake and Christmas present included in fees. For children in real nappies, parents are requested to supply nursery with the nappies and a bin to store them in until they take them home. Investors In People award. Outdoor play area.

❖ RN Crewe Road Nursery
122 Crewe Road South EH4 2NY
Contact: Lorraine Suggitt
Tel: 332 8392
Email: crewerdnursery@tiscali.co.uk
46 places (22 under 3s), Mon-Fri 8.00-17.45. 3mths-5yrs. Meals and snacks not included in fees. Waiting list. Part time places available. Two outdoor play areas, one for under 2s, one for over 2s.

❖❍ RN Dolls House Nursery
9 Wardie Crescent EH5 1AF
Conact: Cally McCann
Tel: 552 9001
Email: cally.dollshouse@blueyonder.co.uk
25 places, Mon-Fri 8.15-17.45. 0-5yrs. Outdoor play. Please contact nursery for current fees.

❖ RN Edinburgh Nursery Crèche
13 East London Street EH7 4BN
Contact: Clare Brown
Tel: 557 9014
Email: edinburghnursery@aol.com
Web: www.edinburghnursery.com
18 places, Mon-Fri 8.00-17.45. 3mths-2yrs, Investor in People. SINA quality assured. Outdoor play area. Please contact crèche for current fees.

also at:
71a Broughton Street
Contact: Laura Grieve
Tel: 556 3373
Email: edinburghnursery@aol.com
Web: www.edinburghnursery.com
9 places, Mon-Fri 8.00-17.45. 3mths-2yrs. Investor in People. SINA quality assured. Outdoor play and nursery garden.
Please contact crèche for current fees.

❖✿ RN Edinburgh Nursery
3 Beaverhall Road EH7 4JQ
Contact: Nursery Manager
Tel: 556 9252
Email: edinburghnursery@aol.com
Web: www.edinburghnursery.com
31 places, Mon-Fri 8.00-17.45. 18mths-3yrs. Half and full days available: contact nursery for current fees. Investor in People. SINA quality assured. Breakfast and home-cooked lunches and afternoon tea inclded. All weather outdoor play and nursery gardens.

❖ Edinburgh Nursery School
129 Broughton Road EH7 4JH
Contact: Karen Fairlamb
Tel: 557 5675
Email: edinburghnursery@aol.com
Web: www.edinburghnursery.com
20 places, Mon-Fri 8.00-17.45. 3-5yrs. Breakfast, home cooked lunch and afternoon tea included. Investor in People. SINA quality assured. Outdoor play and nursery garden. Please contact nursery for current fees.

❖✿ RN Forbes Childrens' Nursery
12 Claremont Park
Leith Links   EH6 7PJ
Tel: 553 5068
50 places, Mon-Fri 8.00-18.00. 3mths-5yrs. Please contact nursery for current fees: discount on 2nd child on 4 sessions or more. Lunch, snacks, disposable nappies and formula milk provided. Parents who use real nappies are requested to provide their own. Large enclosed garden for outdoor play.

❖✿ Headstart Nursery School
16 Queen Charlotte St, Leith
Contact: Chris Slater
Tel: 555 0700

59 places, Mon-Fri 8.00-18.00. 3mths-5yrs, Full and part time places. Partner Provider. Snacks provided, child brings own lunch if required. Nursery teacher. Computer, French and dance classes for over 2s. Outdoor play.

❖✪ RN Heriothill Nursery
32-34 Heriothill Terrace EH7
Contact: Charlie Wardill
Tel: 557 9907

29 places: pre-school unit has 60 places, under 3s unit has 69 places. Partner Provider. Separate sleep room for infants.Hot home-cooked lunch provided every day. Morning and afternoon snacks. Additional classes include yogabugs, music and movement, and Sprights. Nursery has achieved Scotland's Health at Work Bronze Award

❖✪ RN New Town Nursery
12 Dean Terrace EH4 1ND
Contact: Mark Loughton
Tel: 332 5920

55 places, Mon-Fri 8.15-17.45. 3mths-5yrs, please contact nursery for current fees. Fully qualified staff. Outdoor play area.

❖✪ RN North Edinburgh Childcare
18b Ferry Rd Avenue EH4 4BL
Contact: Allison McDonald
Tel: 332 8001
Email:
allison.mcdonald@northedinburghchildcare.co.uk
Mon-Fri 8.00-18.00. 0-5yrs (open 50wks/yr). Part time available. Lunches and snacks provided. Outdoor play.

❖✪ RN St Columba's Hospice Nursery
Challenger Lodge
15 Boswall Road EH5 3RW
Tel: 551 7709
Contact: Brenda Ward
13 places, Mon-Fri 8.30-15.00. 21/2-5yrs, £3.00 per hr. Lunch and snacks provided.All NNEB qualified staff. Large, specially-built secure garden play-area.

❖ Summerside Kindergarten
1 Summerside Street EH6 4NT
Tel: 554 6560
Contact: Carol-Anne McLeod
19 places, Mon-Fri 8.00-18.00. Open 50 weeks/year. 0-5yrs. Lunches and snacks provided, tea in the evening. Separate sleep room.

❖ RN Waterside Nurseries
(formerly Edinburgh Telford College Nursery)
Crewe Toll
Tel: 315 7476
40 places, Mon-Fri 8.30-16.30. 0-5yrs. Open 50 weeks. 10% discount for second child. Separate sleep room for babies and toddlers. Outdoor play. This nursery will be moving to a purpose built facility in July 2006, as part of Telford college's expansion. Then nursery will have 2 rooms of 21. The outdoor area will be a mix of garden and all weather play surface. Open to students, staff and members of the public.

EAST EDINBURGH

Includes nurseries in postcode areas: EH15, EH21

❖✪ RN Bus Stop Nursery
17 Bridge Street
Musselburgh EH21 6AA
Contact: play leader
Tel: 653 2714
44 places, Mon-Fri 8.00-18.00. 0-5yrs. Snacks included. Partner Provider. Children bring own lunches. Outdoor play area.

❖✪ RN Butterflies Nursery
11-15 Stoneybank Terrace
Musselburgh EH21
Tel: 665 5353
Contact: Jane Bergin
Email: hapitotsbtf@aol.co.uk
Web: www.happitots.com
122 places, Mon-Fri 8.00-18.00. 0-8yrs, £22.75-£24.50 per day. Quiet room. Sleeping area. Lunch provided. Partner Provider. Outdoor play, all weather surface / woodchipped play area. After school club available.

❖ RN Hamilton House Nursery
7 Brunstane Road North
Portobello EH15 2DL
Contact: Jennifer
Tel: 669 1067
Email: hamiltonhousenursery@hotmail.com
60 places. Mon-Fri 8.00-18.00. 3mths-5yrs. Waiting list. Meals and snacks included. Sleep facilities.10% discount for second child. Discount also available for 5 sessions or more/week. Secure outdoor play.

❖✪ RN Links Nursery
8 Balcarres Road
Musselburgh EH21 7SD
Contact: Michelle Austin
Tel: 665 0008

79 places, 24 under 2s, 55 2yrs+. Accepts children 3mth-5yrs. 7.30-18.00, Mon-Fri. Part-time sessions available. 10% discount on full-time place, 10% on siblings attending. Music (Dough-Doh Club) and dance classes available. Parents of children in real nappies should provide a appy bin. Nappy bags provided. Separate sleep room, with cots and travel cots. Children also sleep in prams. Cooked lunches provided, AM and PM snack provided. Lunch included in p/t AM session. Garden for outdoor play.

❖✪ RN Little VIPs
2 Windsor Place, Portobello   EH15 2AA
Tel: 669 5040

54 places, Mon-Fri 8.00-18.00. 3mths-5yrs, Separate sleeping room for babies – travel cots and conventional cots. Snacks provided. Food heating facilities available. Parents can provide breakfast, lunch and dinner. Garden play area.

❖✪ RN Little Acorns Nursery School
1c Duddingston Park EH15 1JN
Contact: Frances Kay
Tel: 669 0405 or 699 0706
Web: www.littleacornsnurseries.co.uk

100 places, Mon-Fri 8.00-17.30. 3mths-8yrs. French & music taught. Outdoor play.

❖ RN Mr Squirrels Nursery School & Wraparound Day Care
27 Cargil Terrace
Tel: 552 0499

Phone for current numbers. 8.15-12.45. Open 50 weeks/year. Snacks provided. Children bring packed lunch. Full and part time session available.Outdoor play.

❖✪ RN The Pelican Nursery
225/227 North High Street
Musselburgh EH21 6AP
Contact: Sharon Thomson or Jennifer Condie
Tel: 653 6882

51 places, Mon-Fri 8.00-18.00. 3mths-5yrs. 10& discount for second child. Snacks included. HMI inspected. Outdoor play area.

❖✪ Rocking Horse Nursery
60a Duddingston Road
Contact: Fiona Schulte
Tel: 669 0819

29 places, Mon-Fri 7.45-18.00. 3mths-5yrs. Separate quiet room. Sleeping facilities. Meals and snacks provided. After school club for 5-8yrs with qualified staff. Partner Provider. Enclosed outdoor play area.

❖✪ RN Seabeach Nursery
27 Straiton Place
Portobello EH15 2BA
Contact: Jeanne Macmillan
Tel: 657 3249

25 places, Mon-Fri 8.00-18.00. 0-5yrs. Partner Provider. Sleeping facilities. Snacks provided. Secure outdoor play area.

SOUTH EDINBURGH

Includes Nurseries in the postcode areas EH3 EH10 EH13 EH16

❖ RN The Busy Bees Nursery
20 Valleyfield Street   EH3 9LR
Contact: Jess Van Lieshaut
Tel: 229 7889
Email: info@busybeesnursery.co.uk

13 places, Mon-Fri 8.15-17.45. 2-5yrs, Nursery provides wipes and nappy bags. Bilingual nursery (French and German speaking staff). Snacks provided, parents provide lunches, but provision for heating food. Part time available. Secure garden play area. Please contact nursery for current fees.

❖✪ RN Child's Play
8 Falcon Road   EH10 4AH
Contact: Kimberley Morris
Tel: 447 0077
Email: childsplaynursery@btconnect.com
Web: www.childsplaynurseries.com

59 places, Mon-Fri 8.00-18.00. 0-5yrs. No waiting list. Home cooked lunches and 2 snacks per day included. Separate outdoor play area for under and over 2s. 10% discount off all fees if two or more children attend nursery.

❖✪ RN The City Nursery
47 Greenbank Drive EH10 5SA
Contact: Julie Henderson
Tel: 446 0088

73 places. Mon-Fri 7.30-18.00. 3mths-5yrs. Part-time available. Lunch included with am sessions. Purpose-built building, large outdoor play area, approx 3/4 grass: 1/4 paved area for trikes etc. Separate sleep room for infants; nursery uses cots and travel cots. Children aged 2-3 also have separate sleep room.

Please contact nursery for current fees: 10% discount on current fees for any child who is full-time. A further 10% discount on the eldest child for any two or more children from the same family attending the nursery. Discount also available off fees for any two children from the same family using 5 sessions or more each week

❖✪ RN Colinton Private Nursery
22 Dreghorn Loan   EH13 9QL
Contact: Marion Towers
Tel: 477 7330

59 places, Mon-Fri 8.00-18.00. 3mths-5yrs. Snacks provided. Outdoor all-weather play area.

❖✪ RN The Corner House Day Nursery
2 Spylaw Road EH10 5BN
Contact: Jacqueline Drinkwater
Tel: 229 1500

64 places, Mon-Fri 8.00-18.00. 3mths-5yrs. Separate sleep room with cots for infants. Part time available – minimum 2 full days for under 2s, 3 sessions for 2yrs+. Meals provided, prepared by nursery cook. Separate garden play areas for under and over 2s.

❖✪ RN Corner House Day Nursery
2 South Gillsland Road EH10 5DE
Contact: Jacqueline Drinkwater
Tel: 447 4050

58 places. Mon-Fri 8.00-18.00. 3mths-5yrs. Separate sleep room with cots for infants. Part time available – minimum 2 full days for under 2s, 3 sessions for 2yrs+. Meals provided, prepared by nursery cook. Separate garden play areas for under and over 2s.

❖✪ RN Chapter One Childcare
1b Drum Street   EH17 8QQ
Contact: Diane Pearson
Tel: 664 5376
Email: info@chapteronechildcare.com

42 places, Mon-Fri 8.00-18.00. 0-5yrs. Part time available. Snacks provided. Packed lunch service available. Separate garden play area for under and over 2s. Separate sleep room with cots for infants.

❖❂ RN Forbes Childrens Nursery
5 Forbes Road   EH10 4EF
Contact: Andrea Whyte
Tel: 229 5511

25 places, Mon-Fri 8.00-18.00. 3mths-5yrs. Discount on second child attending nursery. Lunch, snacks, nappies and formula milk provided. No separate sleep room. Large (around 1/2 acre) outdoor play area.

❖ Grange Private Nursery
180 Grange Loan EH9 2EE
Contact: Stacey Gilchrist
Tel: 667 9547

20 places am & pm, Mon-Fri 8.00-18.00, 3mths-5yrs. Snacks provided. Secure outdoor play area.

❖ Headstart Nursery School
64-66 Morningside Drive
Contact: Christopher Slater
Tel: 447 4778

40 places, Mon-Fri 8.00-18.00. 2-5yr. Full and part-time sessions. Snacks provided. Nursery teacher. Partner provider. Computer, French and Dance classes.

❖❂ RN The Hermitage Day Nursery
2 Hermitage Terrace EH10 4RP
Contact: Mary Cumming
Tel: 447 5202

32 places, Mon-Fri 8.00-18.00. 0-5yrs. Morning and afternoon snacks provided. Heating-up facilities for lunches. CCTV in all playrooms and in sleeproom. Monitored sleeproom with cots. Nursery has own transport. Music & Movement, yoga and French lessons on offer. Swimming lessons in term time. Garden play, around 1/2 of which is safety surfaced.

❖❂ RN Kath's Kindergarten
14 & 27 Angle Park Terrace EH11 2JT
Contact: Kath Stewart
Tel: 337 7793 or 337 4157

35 places, Mon-Fri 8.00-17.30. 3mths-5yrs. Snacks provided. Separate sleep room for infants, with cots and travel cots. All weather play area at both locations.

❖❂ RN Little Monkeys
28 Kilmaurs Road EH16 5DP
Contact: Grace Kerr
Tel: 667 5544
Email: info@little-monkeys.net

44 places, Mon-Fri 7.00-19.00. 3mths-5yrs 0-2 Part time available. Nursery can provide all meals (breakfast, lunch and dinner). Separate sleep room for infants, with cots. Outside all-weather soft top playground and climbing frames. There is a physical education development teacher in-house.

❖❂ RN Meadows Nursery
5 Millerfield Place EH9 1LW
Contact: Jennifer Hegarty
Tel: 667 5316
Email: info@meadows-nursery.co.uk
Web: www.meadows-nursery.co.uk

35 places, Mon-Fri 8.15-17.30. 3mths-5yrs. Part time available. Snacks provided. No separate sleep room. Outdoor all-weather soft surface play area. Registered with Eco Schools Programme, so actively welcome children in real nappies.

❖❂ RN Playdays Kindergarten
17 East Suffolk Road EH16 5PH
Contact: Ashira
Tel: 662 0010

27 places, Mon-Fri 8.00-18.00. 0-5yrs. Part time available. Lunch provided for over 2s, and as part of p/time sessions. Separate sleep room with cots. Large outdoor all-weather play area. Unrestricted parking.

❖ RN Royal Hospital for Sick Children Nursery
11 Millerfield Place EH9 1LW
Tel: 536 0682
Contact: Rosie Allanson

22 places, 12 under 2s, 10 2yrs+. Accepts children 3mths-5yrs. 08.00-18.00, Mon-Fri. Part-time sessions available. Discounts available for parents who work for the hospital trust and earless than £18 000/year. Separate sleep room, with cots. Also provide sleep provision in Silver Cross prams in outdoor pram shelter. Parents of children in real nappies are requested to provide nappy sacks and liners. Bring own lunches- heating provision available. AM and PM snacks provided. Lunch included in p/t sessions. All weather soft surface outdoor play area.

❖ Small World Nurseries
1 Claverhouse Drive
Contact: Patricia Stefanovic
Tel: 664 3434

40 places, Mon-Fri 8.00-18.00. 0-5yrs, under 2s £25 per day, over 2s £23 per day. Part time available. Quiet room. Sleeping facilities. Cooked meals provided. Outdoor play. Extra curricular classes for 2-5 yrs.

❖ Stepping Stones Nursery
1 Chalmers Crescent   EH9 1TW
Contact: Carolyn Bennett
Tel: 662 0364
Also:
21A Millerfield Place   EH9 1LW
Tel: 668 4249

15 places, Mon-Fri 7.00-18.00. Separate quiet room. Sleeping facilities. Snacks provided. Enclosed outdoor play. Baby unit at Millerfield Pl.

❖ RN Strawberry Hill Nursery
13 Minto Street   EH9 1RG
Contact: Pamela Ellis
Tel: 668 3300

59 places, 7.45-18.00. 0-5yrs. Sleeping area with cots. Home made meals and snacks provided. Nappies provided. Large garden with grass and playtop rubber surfacing. Car park.

WEST EDINBURGH

Includes Nurseries in the postcode areas: EH4, EH11, EH12, EH14 & EH30

❖❂ RN Asquith Nursery
c/o David Lloyd Health Club
Glasgow Road, EH12 8LH
Contact: Claire Barr
Tel: 334 8055
Web: www.asquithcourt.co.uk

68 places (25 under 2, 43 2+), 08.00-18.00, Mon-Fri. 3mths-5yrs. £33 per day approx. Part time places available. Offers 10% sibling discount. AM and PM snack provided, 2 course cooked lunch provided – lunch included in part-time sessions. Music and Swimming Academy classes for 3-5 yrs available, as is French class for pre-school group. Parents must provide all necessary accessories for children in real nappies. No separate sleep room – cots and nursery sleep mats for 1yr+ provided. Outdoor play area with childsafe surface, climbing frame and cars/bikes.

❖❂ RN Barnton Nursery
534 Queensferry Road EH4 6EE
Contact: Alison Bruce / Tracy Jackson
Tel: 339 6340

61 places (28 under 2, 33 yrs+). 07.30-18.30 Mon-Fri. 3mths-5yrs. Part-time sessions available. 10% discount for full-time children. Offers school holiday care provision. Offers music classes (Wed AM). Parent of children in real nappies should provide bags and liners. Nursery provides cream – and disposable nappy bags. Separate sleep room with cots and travel cots – outdoor in-pram sleeping area also available. Provides cooked lunches; also heating provision for brought-in lunches. AM snack provided. Outdoor play area incorporating garden and all-weather soft surface, as well as indoor soft-play area..

Bright Horizons Family Solutions
❖❂ RN Ardmillan Terrace Nursery
11 Ardmillan Terrace   EH11 2JW
Contact: Debbie McKay
Tel: 337 5940
Fax: 346 4767
Email: ardmillan@brighthorizons.com

28 places, 9 under 2s, 19 2yrs+. Accepts children 3mths-5yrs. 8.00-18.00, Mon-Fri. Part-time sessions available. Snacks provided. Parents of children wearing real nappies should provide bags, liners etc. Music and French classes (under review at time of writing). No separate sleep room – 2 cots, but 1yr+ children all have own sleep mat. Bring own lunch – heating provision available. Am and PM snack provided. Bring own lunch for AM p/t session. Outdoor all-weather soft surface play area.

❖❂ RN Careshare Nurseries – Edinburgh Park
1 Lochside Place,
Edinburgh Pk   EH12 9DF
Contact: Fiona Fairley,
Also: Kirsty Gibson (baby building),
Neil Craig (pre-school children)
Tel: 339 1245

142 places in total, Mon-Fri 7.45 to 5.45. 6wks-5yrs. Baby building is for age group 6 weeks to 2,toddlers for children 18mths to 3years, pre-school for 3 to 5yrs. Parents are requested to provide all necessary items for use and storage of real nappies. Fees include nappies, snacks, lunch, suncream, birthday cake and Christmas present. HMI Inspected. Outdoor play areas. Please contact nursery for current fees.

❖❍ RN Croilegan Nursery
6A Featherhall Avenue EH12 7TQ
Tel: 334 2960
Contact: Chris Sinclair

55 Places - 15 places 0-2yrs, 40 places 2-5yrs, 08.00-17.45, Mon-Fri. Full day and full time places. 10% discount to eldest child if attending the same sessions as siblings. Bags required for children in real nappies. Music classes – Singing with Liza - and Dance Base classes available. Separate sleep room, equipped with cots and travel cots – children can also sleep in prams. Am and PM snack provided – heating facilities for children's packed lunches. Qualified staff. Nursery has its own transport. Outdoor garden play area with safety matting.

❖❍ RN The Gyle Nursery
Gyle Shopping Centre
Contact: Karen Fairlamb
Tel: 539 7099
Email: edinburghnursery@aol.com
Web: www.edinburghnursery

40 places, Mon-Fri 7.30-18.00. 0-5yrs. Purpose built nursery. Provides breakfast and home-cooked lunches. SINA quality assured. Investors in People. Outdoor play area. Please contact nursery for current fees.

❖ Juniper Green Private Nursery
8 Woodhall Drive EH14 5BX
Contact: Moira McLean
Tel: 458 3003
Web: www.scottishnurseries.com

30 places, Accepts children aged 2-5yrs. 08.00-18.00, Mon-Fri. Part time session available. Discounts available to full-time children. Nursery offers school holiday care and after-school club provision. Music and French classes available

❖❍ Murrayfield Nursery
52 Saughton Crescent EH12 5SP
Contact: Maxine Simpson-Smith
Tel: 346 4459
Email: Maureen.murray@btinternet.com

64 places, 24 under 2s, 40 2yrs+. Accepts children 6wks-5yrs. 08.00-18.00, Mon-Fri. Few part-time places available. Some discounts available – contact nursery. Music (Doh-Doh Club), French and swimming classes available. Home cooked lunches. AM and PM snacks provided. Parents with children in real nappies are required to supple a 'sangenic'

cassette bin. Separate sleep room, with cots and travel cots, also sleep mats. Garden and all-weather soft surface area for outdoor play.

❖❍ RN Nippers Nursery
Scotstoun Avevue
South Queensferry EH30 9TG
Contact: Janice Robertson
Tel: 331 7635
Email: nippers.nursery@btinternet.com

42 places – 15 under 2s, 27 2yrs+. 07.30-17.30 , Mon-Fri 7. Accepts children aged 3mths-5yrs. No part time places. 5% discount if two children from same family attend. Lunch provided for 2yrs+. Am and PM snack provided. Music (Jo Jingles) and Enjoyaball classes available. Parents of children in real nappies are required to provide own bags. Cream, disposable nappy bags provided. Separate sleep room with cots. Outdoor garden play area.

❖❍ RN Orchard Nursery
Royal Victoria Hospital
13 Craigleith Road   EH4 2DN
Tel: 343 6617
Contact: Melanie Aspen

56 places – 21 under 2s, 35 2yrs+. 07.00-18.30/19.00 Mon-Fri. Part-time sessions available. Discounts available to Western General Hospital staff. Snacks provided. Music classes (Doh-doh club), Yogabugs and Dance (tap) classes available. Facilities provided for real nappy storage: cream, bags provided for disposable nappies also. Separate sleep room, with cots. Sleep mats for older children. Heating provision for brought-in lunches. AM and PM snack provided. Children required to bring own snack for part-time AM sessions. Large garden and all-weather play area, which includes play houses, a sensory garden and a wild garden. SINA quality assured. Investors in People.

❖❍ RN Peek-a-Boo Nursery School
12 Parkgrove Loan EH4 7QX
Contact: Sally-Anne Peek
Tel: 339 9161
Email: sally-annep@virgin.net
Web: www.scottishnurseries.com

55 places - 22 under 2s, 33 2yrs+. Minimum age 6mths. 08.00-18.00, Mon-Fri. Part-time sessions available. 10% discount offered for second child. AM, PM snack provided. Heating provision for brought-in lunches. French, music specialist and Dance Base classes all once a week, fit kid club twice a week. Parents of children in real nappies are

requested to provide bags. Separate sleep room, with cots. Soft play area designated for sleep post-lunch for 3yrs+ requiring sleep. Large, mature secure garden for outdoor play. Also includes multi-sesnory area, a vegetable patch and rockery – separate garden for under 2s. Nursery also offers: a designated parents area; storyback initiative for parents; pta monthly meeting; unlimited parking; unlimited settling-in sessions. Nursery accepts all childcare vouchers as payment.

❖✪ RN Pinocchio's Nursery @ Heriot Watt University
1st Gait
Riccarton Campus   EH14 4AS
Contact: Tracey Gilhooley-Rutherford
Tel: 451 5236
Email heriot-watt@pinocchiosnursery.co.uk
Web: www.pinocchiosnursery.co.uk
55 places, Mon-Fri 8.00-18.00. 3mths-5yrs. Part time places available. Partner Provider. Separate sleep room, with cots, bouncy chairs and prams. All meals provided, cooked by qualified chef – no salt or sugar added. Nappies, wipes cream provided. Welcomes children wearing real nappies. Large enclosed, secluded garden. Areas for under 2s and over 2s. There are plans to change from grass to all-weather 'Astroturf' in the near future. Open to the public as well as Uni staff and students.

❖✪ RN Playhouse Nursery
20a Old Kirk Road EH12 8HT
Contact: Karen Brown
Tel: 334 5859
15 places – 6 under 2s, 9 2yrs+. Nursery accepts children 3mths-5yrs. 8.00-17.45, Mon-Fri. Part-week sessions available. Discounts available to 3 children from same family. Music classes (Dough-Doh Club) available. Nursery has own transport. Parents of children wearing real nappies are required to provide bags. No separate sleep room – children can sleep outside in covered pram area. Am and PM snack provided. Bring own lunches – heating provision available. Large enclosed garden and patio area for outdoor play.

NURSERY EDUCATION IN EDINBURGH

The City of Edinburgh Council has 17 nursery schools, 1 under 5s centre, nursery classes based in 79 primary schools and 12 child and family centres.

Children are eligible for a free, part-time place in a nursery, 5 mornings or afternoons during school term, usually from the term after their 3rd birthday depending on when their birthday falls and available places. Some nurseries offer the option to purchase additional hours or wraparound care.

There are no catchment area restrictions for nursery schools and classes. This means you can send your child to any nursery in the city if a place is available. There may be a waiting list for your nursery of choice and you should put your child's name down as soon as possible after their 2nd birthday. You can put your child's name down on more than one nursery waiting list and are able to visits the nurseries before making your decision. Your child does not need to subsequently attend the primary school to which the nursery school is attached. Children with special needs are integrated in all nursery classes.

Partner Provider Centres include private, workplace and community-run nurseries and playgroups, as well as independent schools. These centres have been commissioned to provide pre-school education and this means you are able to receive a refund on all or part of your fees once your child is eligible. For details of these providers, see 'Playgroups' and 'Private Nurseries' in this section.

The council produces a helpful guide called "Pre-school Education in Edinburgh" which can be picked up at locations such as nurseries and libraries or contact your local council:

Children and Families Department
The City of Edinburgh Council
Wellington Court
10 Waterloo Place
Edinburgh EH1 3EG
Tel: 0131 469 3000
Web: www.edinburgh.gov.uk

East Lothian Council

East Lothian Council Department of Education & Children's Services

John Muir House
Haddington
East Lothian, EH41 3HA
Tel: 01620 827631
Web: www.eastlothian.gov.uk

Midlothian Council

Midlothian Council, Education Division

Midlothian House
Buccleuch Street
Dalkeith
EH22 1DN
Tel: 0131 270 7500
Web: www.modlothian.gov.uk

Below is a list of nursery schools and primary schools with nursery provision.

NURSERY SCHOOLS

EAST LOTHIAN

Levenhall
Moir Place
Musselburgh   EH21 8JD
Tel: 655 7599

North Berwick
Law Road
North Berwick EH39 4PN
Tel: 01620 8930782

Prestonpans
Kirk Street
Prestonpans EH32 9DY
Tel: 01875 811440

Tranent
Sanderson's Wynd
Tranent EH33 1DA
Tel: 01875 610 899

EDINBURGH

Balgreen
175 Balgreen Road   EH11 3AT
Tel: 337 1454

Calderglen
Wester Hailes Road   EH11 4NG
Tel: 453 5754

Cameron House
Cameron House Avenue   EH16 5LF
Tel: 667 5117

Children's House
Wauchope Terrace   EH16 4NU
Tel: 661 1401

Cowgate Under 5's Centre
172 High Street,
7Assembly Close EH1 1QX
Tel: 225 7251

Grassmarket
11/15 The Vennel
Grassmarket   EH1 2HU
Tel: 229 6540

Greengables
8a Niddrie House Gardens   EH16 4UF
Tel: 669 9083

High School Yards
High School Yards   EH1 1LZ
Tel: 556 6536

Hope Cottage
Cowans Close
East Crosscauseway   EH8 9HF
Tel: 667 5795
Web: www.hopecottage.edin.sch.uk

Kirkliston
Queensferry Road Kirkliston   EH29 9AQ
Tel: 333 2336
Web: www.kirkliston-ns.edin.sch.uk

Liberton
Mount Vernon Road   EH16 6JQ
Tel: 664 3155

Lochrin
West Tollcross   EH3 9QN
Tel: 229 7743

Princess Elizabeth
Clearburn Crescent   EH16 5ER
Tel: 667 0946

St Leonard's
6 West Adam Street   EH8 9SY
Tel: 667 4674

Stanwell
Junction Place   EH6 5JA
Tel: 554 1309
Web: www.stanwell.edin.sch.uk

The Spinney Lane
13A The Spinney   EH17 7LD
Tel: 664 9102

Tynecastle
McLeod Street   EH11 2NJ
Tel: 337 5461

Westfield Court
Westfield Court   EH11 2RJ
Tel: 337 4914
Web Site: www.westfieldcourt.edin.sch.uk
Mainstream nursery with provision for 8 special needs places.

NURSERY CLASSES IN PRIMARY SCHOOLS

East Lothian

Aberlady Primary
Moor Road Aberlady EH32 0RQ
Tel: 01875 870232

Athelstaneford Primary
Athelstaneford EH39 5BE
Tel: 01620 880241

Campie
3 Stoneyhill Farm Road
Musselburgh   EH21 6QS
Tel: 665 2045

Cockenzie Primary
Osbourne Terrace Cockenzie
EH32 0BX
Tel: 01875 811327

Dunbar
Lammermuir Crescent
Dunbar   EH42 1DG
Tel: 01368 863773

East Linton
School Road
East Linton   EH40 3AJ
Tel: 01620 860216

Elphinstone
Elphinstone
Tranent   EH33 2LX
Tel: 01875 610358

Gullane
Muirfield Terrace
Gullane   EH31 2HW
Tel: 01620 843455

Haddington Infant
Victoria Road
Haddington   EH41 4DJ
Tel: 01620 823 271

Humbie Primary
HumbieEH36 5PJ Tel:
Tel: 01875 833247

Innerwick
Innerwick
Dunbar   EH42 1SD
Tel: 01368 840227

Law Primary
Haddington Road
NORTH BERWICK EH39 4QZ
Tel: 01620 893775

Longniddry
Kitchener Crescent
Longniddry   EH32 0LR
Tel: 01875 853 161

Loretto RC
20 Newbigging
Musselburgh   EH21 7AH
Tel: 665 2572

Macmerry Primary
Macmerry
TRANENT   EH33 1QA
Tel: 01875 610234

Musselburgh
Kilwinning Street
Musselburgh   EH21 7EE
Tel: 665 3407

Ormiston
Meadowbank
Tranent   EH35 5LQ
Tel: 01875 610 382

Pencaitland
The Glebe
Pencaitland EH34 5EZ
Tel: 01875 340 260

St Gabriel's RC
South Grange Avenue
Prestonpans EH32 9LH
Tel: 01875 811062

St Martin's RC
High Street
Tranent   EH33 1HJ
Tel: 01875 610211

St Mary's RC
Tynebank Road
Haddington   EH41 4DN
Tel: 01620 823 298

Saltoun
East Saltoun
Pencaitland
Tranent   EH34 5DY
Tel: 01875 340318

Stoneyhill
Off Clayknowes Way
Musselburgh   EH21 6UL
Tel: 665 3119

Wallyford
39 Salters Road
Wallyford EH21 8LB
Tel: 665 2865

West Barns
West Barns
Dunbar   EH42 1TZ
Tel: 01368 863209

Whitecraig
44a Whitecraig Crescent
Musselburgh   EH21 8NG
Tel: 665 3278

Yester
Walden Terrace
Gifford EH41 4QP
Tel: 01620 810435

Edinburgh

Abbeyhill
Abbey Street   EH7 5SJ
Tel: 661 3054
Web: www.abbeyhill.edin.sch.uk

Bonaly
Bonaly Grove
Edinburgh   EH13 0QD
Tel: 441 7211
Web: www.bonaly.edin.sch.uk

Bonnington
Bonnington Rd   EH6 5NQ
Tel: 554 1370
Web: www.bonnington.edin.sch.uk

Broomhouse
Saughton Road   EH11 3RQ
Tel: 443 3783

Broughton
Broughton Road   EH7 4LD
Tel: 556 7028

Brunstane
Magdalene Drive   EH15 3BE
Tel: 669 4498
Web:www.brunstane.edin.sch.uk

Buckstone
Buckstone Loan East   EH10 6UY
Tel: 445 4545
Web: www.buckstone.edin.sch.uk

Burdiehouse
Burdiehouse Crescent   EH17 8EX
Tel: 664 2351

Canal View Primary School
Dumbryden Gardens EH14 2NZ
Tel: 453 5686

Carrick Knowe
Lampacre Rd   EH12 7HU
Tel: 334 4505

Castleview
2D Greendykes Road   EH16 4DP
Tel: 661 6429

Clermiston
Parkgrove Place   EH4 7NP
Tel: 336 3361
Web: www.clermiston.edin.sch.uk

Clovenstone
54 Clovenstone Park   EH14 3EY
Tel: 453 4242
Web: www.clovenstone.edin.sch.uk

Colinton
Redford Pl   EH13 0AL
Tel: 441 1946
Web: www.colinton.edin.sch.uk

Corstorphine
Corstorphine High Street   EH12 7SY
Tel: 334 3865
Web: www.corstorphine.edin.sch.uk

Craigentinny
Loganlea Drive   EH7 6LR
Tel: 661 2749

Craiglockhart Primary School
Ashley Terrace EH11 1RG
Tel: 337 1407

Craigour Park
Moredun Park Road   EH17 7HL
Tel: 664 7594
Web: www.craigourpark.edin.sch.uk

Craigroyston
Muirhouse Place West   EH4 4PX
Tel: 343 6465

Cramond
4 Cramond Crescent   EH4 6PG
Tel: 312 6450

Currie Primary School
210 Lanark Road West   EH14 5NN
Tel: 449 3359

Dalry
Dalry Road   EH11 2JB
Tel: 337 6086

Davidson's Mains
Corbiehill Road   EH4 5DZ
Tel: 336 1184
Web: www.davidsonsmains.edin.sch.uk

Dean Park
31 Marchbank Grdens
Balerno   EH14 7ET
Tel: 449 4529
Web: www.deanpark.edin.sch.uk

Drumbrae
Ardshiel Ave   EH4 7HP
Tel: 339 5071

Duddingston
Duddingston Road   EH15 1SW
Tel: 669 5092
Web Site: www.duddingston.edin.sch.uk

East Craigs
79 Craigmount Brae   EH12 8XF
Tel: 339 7115
Web: www.eastcraigs.edin.sch.uk

Ferryhill
Groathill Road North   EH4 2SQ
Tel: 538 7382
Web Site: www.ferryhill.edin.sch.uk

Flora Stevenson
Comely Bank   EH4 1BG
Tel: 332 1604
Web: www.florastevenson.edin.sch.uk

Fort
North Fort Street   EH6 4HF
Tel: 467 7131
Web: www.fort.edin.sch.uk

Forthview
West Pilton Place   EH4 4DF
Tel: 332 2468
Web: www.forthview.edin.sch.uk

Gracemount
Lasswade Road   EH16 6UA
Tel: 664 2331
Web: www.gracemount-pri.edin.sch.uk

Granton
Boswall Parkway   EH5 2DA
Tel: 552 3987

Gylemuir
Wester Broom Place   EH12 7RT
Tel: 334 7138
Web: www.gylemuir.edin.sch.uk

Hermitage Park
Hermitage Park   EH6 8HD
Tel: 554 2952
Web: www.hermitagepark.edin.sch.uk

Hillwood
Station Road Ratho Station   EH28 8PT
Tel: 333 1210

Holy Cross RC
Craighall Road   EH6 4RE
Tel: 552 1972

James Gillespie's
Whitehouse Loan   EH9 1BD
Tel: 447 1014
Web: www.jamesgillespies-ps.edin.sch.uk

Juniper Green
Nursery Department
1 Woodhall Terrace   EH14 5BS
Tel: 467 7984

Leith
St Andrew's Place   EH6 7EG
Tel: 554 4844
Web: www.leith-pri.edin.sch.uk

Leith Walk
9 Brunswick Road   EH7 5NG
Tel: 556 3873

Liberton
229 Gilmerton Road   EH16 5UD
Tel: 664 2337
Web: www.liberton-ps.edin.sch.uk

Lismore
1 Bingham Avenue   EH15 3HZ
Tel: 669 4588

Longstone
Redhall Green   EH14 2DU
Tel: 443 4743
Web: www.longstone.edin.sch.uk

Lorne
Lorne Street   EH6 8QS
Tel: 554 2308
Web: www.lorne.edin.sch.uk

Murrayburn
Sighthill Loan   EH11 4NP
Tel: 453 5339
Web: www.murrayburn.edin.sch.uk

Newcraighall
Whitehill Street Newcraighall   EH21 8QZ
Tel: 669 3598

Niddrie Mill
267 Niddrie Mains Road   EH15 3HG
Tel: 468 7025

Oxgangs
60 Oxgangs Road North   EH13 9DS
Tel: 441 3649
Web: www.oxgangs.edin.sch.uk

Parson's Green
Meadowfield Drive   EH8 7LU
Tel: 661 4459
Web: www.parsonsgreen.edin.sch.uk

Pentland Primary School
Oxgangs Green EH13 9JE
Tel: 445 1510

Pirniehall
West Pilton Crescent   EH4 4HP
Tel: 332 5256

Prestonfield
Peffermill Road   EH16 5LJ
Tel: 667 1336

Ratho
1 School Wynd
Ratho   EH28 8TT
Tel: 333 1293

Roseburn
Roseburn Street   EH12 5PL
Fax: 0131 476 7810
Web: www.roseburn.edin.sch.uk

Royal Mile
Canongate   EH8 8BZ
Tel: 556 3347
Web: www.royalmile.edin.sch.uk

Royston
Boswall Parkway   EH5 2JH
Tel: 552 4534

St Catherine's RC
Gracemount Drive   EH16 6RN
Tel: 664 4257

St David's RC
West Pilton Crescent   EH4 4EP
Tel: 332 3500

St Francis' RC
Niddrie Mains Road   EH16 4DS
Tel: 621 6600
Web: www.stfrancis.edin.sch.uk

St John's RC
Hamilton Terrace   EH15 1NB
Tel: 669 1363
Web: www.stjohns.edin.sch.uk

St John Vianney RC
Ivanhoe Crescent   EH16 6AU
Tel: 664 1742

St Joseph's RC
Saughton Road   EH11 3RQ
Tel: 443 4591

St Mark's RC
63 Firrhill Crescent   EH13 9EE
Tel: 441 2948
Web: www.stmarks.edin.sch.uk

St Mary's RC (Leith)
Links Gardens   EH6 7JG
Tel: 554 7291
Web: www.stmarys-pri.edin.sch.uk

St Ninian's RC
Restalrig Rd S   EH7 6JA
Tel: 661 3431

St Peter's RC
10 Falcon Road   EH10 4AH
Tel: 447 5742
Web: www.stpeters.edin.sch.uk

Sighthill
1 Calder Park   EH11 4NF
Tel: 453 2464

South Morningside
116 Comiston Road   EH10 5QN
Tel: 447 5446
Web: www.southmorningside.edin.sch.uk

Stenhouse
4 Saughton Mains Street   EH11 3HH
Tel: 443 1255
Web: www.stenhouse.edin.sch.uk

Stockbridge
Hamilton Place   EH3 5BA
Tel: 332 6109
Web: www.stockbridge.edin.sch.uk

The Royal High
Northfield Broadway EH8 7RX
Tel: 669 3200
Web: www.royalhigh-pri.edin.sch.uk

Tollcross
117 Fountainbridge   EH3 9QG
Tel: 229 7828

Towerbank
Figgate Bank   EH15 1HX
Tel: 669 1551
Web: www.towerbank.edin.sch.uk

Westburn
55 Sighthill Road   EH11 4PB
Tel: 442 2997

SOUTH QUEENSFERRY

Dalmeny
Carlowrie Crescent
Dalmeny EH30 9TZ
Tel: 331 1447
Web: www.dalmeny.edin.sch.uk

Echline
Bo'ness Road
S Queensferry   EH30 9XJ
Tel: 331 3397
Web Site: www.echline.edin.sch.uk

Queensferry
Burgess Road
S Queensferry   EH30 9NX
Tel: 331 1349
Web: www.queensferry-ps.edin.sch.uk

PRE-SCHOOL PLAY & EDUCATION – INDEPENDENT

INDEPENDENT SCHOOLS

The independent schools in Edinburgh with nursery departments are listed below with fees for 2005/06. Most offer the choice of a morning, afternoon or whole day placement.

The Scottish Council of Independent Schools (SCIS) will send you a free booklet containing basic information about all the Independent Schools in Scotland. Contact them at:

Scottish Council of Independent Schools
21 Melville Street
Edinburgh EH3 7PE
Tel: 220 2106
Fax: 225 8594
Email: information@scis.org.uk
Web: www.scis.org.uk

INDEPENDENT SCHOOLS WITH NURSERY DEPARTMENTS

Cargilfield School Prep School
Barnton Avenue West   EH4 6HU
Tel: 336 2207
Email: secretary@cargilfield.com
Web: www.cargilfield.edin.sch.uk
Co-educational. £991(am), £848 (pm)/ term. Before & after school care available.

Clifton Hall School
Newbridge   EH28 8LQ
Tel: 333 1359
Email: office@cliftonhall.org.uk
Web: www.cliftonhall.org.uk
Co-educational. Full day £1325/ term including lunch. Minimum 5 mornings £655 per term.

The Compass School
West Road
Haddington EH41 3RD
Tel: 01620 822642
Email: office@thecompassschool.co.uk
Web: www.thecompassschool.co.uk
Co-educational nursery, £1005-£1375/term.

Edinburgh Academy Nursery
The Edinburgh Academy Junior School
10 Arboretum Road   EH3 5PL
Tel: 552 3690
Email: Juniorschool@j.s.edinburghacademy.org.uk
Web: www.edinburghacademy.org.uk
Co-educational. £480-£1600/term. Part-time places for 2-3 year olds. Before and after school care available.

George Heriot's School
Lauriston Place
EH3 9EQ
Tel: 229 7263
Email: admissions@george-heriots.com
Web: www.george-heriots.com
Co-educational. £4,896 annually. After school and holiday care available.

George Watson's College
Colinton Road   EH10 5EG
Tel: 447 7931
Email: info@gwc.org.uk
Web: www.gwc.org.uk

Co-educational. £3,033 (am), £2,265 (pm), £5,304 (full day) annually. Before and after school and holiday care available.

Loretto Junior School
North Esk Lodge,
Musselburgh, EH21 6JA
Tel: 0131 665 2628
Email: juniorschool@loretto.com
Website: http://www.loretto.com

Co-educational. £1529 /term

The Mary Erskine and Stewart's Melville Junior School
Queensferry Road   EH4 3EZ
Tel: 331 1111
Email: jssecretary@esmgc.com
Web: www.esms.edin.sch.uk

Co-educational. £5325/session or approx £4107 including local authority preschool grant (£1650–£2139 per term). After school and holiday care available.

The Edinburgh Rudolf Steiner School (Kindergarten)
60 Spylaw Road EH10 5BR
Tel: 337 3410
Email: office@steinerweb.org.uk
Web:www.SteinerWeb.org.uk

Co-educational. £646 per term. Children start kindergarten at the age of 3 1/2 and stay until they are 6. The emphasis is on play and on learning by doing. The school's aim is to facilitate the development of physical, as well as social skills and to nourish a healthy emotional life and a rich imagination. Artistic and creative activities take the place of formal learning, which does not begin until the children enter the main school at the age of 6.

St George's School Early Years Department
Garscube Terrace   EH12 6BG
Tel: 311 8000
Email: office@st-georges.edin.sch.uk
Web: www.st-georges.edin.sch.uk

Early Years (3-5 yrs) £880-£1465 /term. Little Nursery (2-3yrs), Mon -Fri 9.00-12.00 or 13.00-15.00. Before and after school care available.

St Margaret's School
East Suffolk Road   EH16 5PJ
Tel: 668 1986
Email: admissions@st-margarets.edin.sch.uk
Web: www.st-margarets.edin.sch.uk
Care and education from 3mths-5 yrs. 3-5s £890(am)/ term, 1,445.00/term all day. Before & after school and holiday care available.

LOOKING FORWARD TO STARTING SCHOOL

The entry date for children starting primary school in Scotland is August. Children starting P1 in August must have either celebrated their 5th birthday in the preceding 6 months (from 1 March onwards) or are due to celebrate their 5th birthday in the following 6 months (birth dates up to 28 February). You should contact the Council if you have just arrived from England or Wales, where the admission ages differ.

Parents can choose not to send their child to primary school until the session after their child's 5th birthday. Children with birthdays in January & February have the right to deferred entry and a free pre-school education place for any extra year. Children with birthdays after the start of the autumn term to 31st December also have the right to delay the start to school but the allocation of a free pre-school place is not automatic and is at the discretion of the Children and Families Department. If you are concerned about your child's entry into school speak with your child's nursery teacher in the first instance.

To enrol your child at the school in your catchment area, telephone the Head Teacher and arrange an appointment. If you wish to send your child to a school outside your catchment area, your application will be considered, provided there is a place available. You must apply for a place at a non-district school between November and 15 March for the following August. Registration, however, is normally dealt with in early December. A form for this purpose may be obtained from the school or nursery or from Pupil Support Services at the Children and Families Department. You must also inform the Head Teacher of your catchment school that you have applied to a school outwith their area.

A list of all primary schools may be obtained by contacting your local council. A prospectus should be available from the school.

If you feel that your child may benefit from attending a special school contact Pupil Support Services.

For details of school uniform stockists, see Shopping – Children's Clothes.

Shopping

INTRODUCTION

Shopping when pregnant or with small children requires a completely different approach from shopping you may have been used to. Browsing at leisure can become a distant memory, you have to discover good sources of maternity, baby and children's equipment and clothing, and you may also find that planning, timing, and toilet stops become of the utmost importance – for you and your child!

In this section, we've tried to offer some ideas where to shop for yourself and your children's needs, plus information for planning a less stressful shopping experience (why not check out Eating Out too). As with any expedition, planning is the key and knowing the easiest entrance and department locations can lessen some of the hassle.

Feeding and changing rooms are now considered a standard requirement in large department stores and shopping centres. They are available to male and female carers, although if you encounter a combined feeding/changing room, and you are male, it might be prudent to ask an assistant to check the room: some breastfeeding mothers may feel uncomfortable with a male stranger sharing the facility. Some stores have anticipated this, and have secondary rooms for male carers. These rooms should be separate from customer toilets, but it is an advantage to be near toilets, especially if you have an older child with you. The standard of parent and baby rooms in the centre of Edinburgh is generally high, but should you find them lacking in facilities, or not clean, it is worth mentioning this to a manager or supervisor (some rooms have a comments book), as it is only through such information that store managers are aware of customer requirements.

Urgent toilet stops for expectant mums and young children can be a great problem when shopping. Our research is done by questionnaire, and if an entry indicates that use of a staff toilet is permitted, we have included the information – and if you find opposition, mention that fact. See also Toilet Stops and Eating Out sections.

Useful Information

▶ Most city centre shops have late night shopping on Thursday. Some stores use Tuesday and Wednesday mornings for staff training and open at 9.30.
▶ Tuesday or Wednesday is usually half-day closing in the outlying areas.

▶ Many stores open longer in the summer and during the Festival, as well as the run-up to Christmas.
▶ Many city centre shops have Sunday trading hours (usually opening at 11.00 or mid-day). Sunday trading in suburban areas is almost standard practice.

Section Contents

▶ Key information on chemists, crèches, department stores, malls and supermarkets.
▶ Clothes and shoes, baby and children's wear, make-your-own, maternity and second-hand clothes.
▶ Specialist shops – books, bikes, hairdressers, nursery equipment, photography and toys.
▶ Real Nappy Services
▶ Hiring
▶ Shopping from home

We have used 'baby' to describe clothes for under 2s and 'children's' for over 2s.

Where we have listed shops with several branches, the description generally refers to the flagship or main stores, and you may find that smaller branches do not have the same choice of goods: if you know what you're looking for, why not phone ahead for confirmation.

NB: Please remember that the opening hours listed should be taken as a guide: stores can change their opening hours at short notice.

CHEMISTS AND PHARMACY SERVICES

NHS Lothian Primary Care Division keeps a list of chemists and operates a rota in order to provide pharmaceutical services outside normal shopping hours. Their contact details are as follows:

NHS Lothian Primary and Community Division
St Roque
Astley Ainslie Hospital
133 Grange Rd Edinburgh Eh9 2HL
Tel: 537 9000 (main number)
Tel: 537 8424
(for more details about your local GPs, NHS Dentists, Pharmacists or Opticians near you)

Chemists Open After 18.00

Asda Pharmacy
Asda Wal-Mart
The Jewel
Edinburgh EH15 3AR
Tel: 669 3550
Late closing: Mon-Fri 21.00; Sat 20.00

Boots the Chemist
Cameron Toll Centre
6 Lady Road   EH16 5PB
Tel: 666 1111
Late closing: Thu, Fri 20.00

Craigleith Retail Park
24 South Groathill Road   EH4 2LN
Tel: 332 6114
Mon-Fri 9.00-20.00, Sat 9.00-18.00

Unit 10
Gyle Shopping Centre   EH12 9JS
Tel: 317 1288
Late closing: Mon-Wed, Fri 20.00; Thu 21.00; Sat 19.00

207-209 Morningside Road
Tel: 447 6188
Late closing: Mon-Fri 19.00

101-103 Princes Street
Tel: 225 8331
Late closing: Thu 19.30, Sat 21.00

48 Shandwick Place
Tel: 225 6757
Late closing: Mon-Fri 20.00; Sat 18.00

St James' Centre
Tel: 556 1062
Late closing: Thu 19.00

Straiton Retail Park
Straiton EH20 9NL
Tel: 440 3419
Mon-Fri 9.00-20.00, Sat 9.00-19.00

Morrisons Pharmacy
1 Bughtlin Market
Maybury Craigs
Tel: 339 1188
Late closing: Mon-Fri 20.00

38 Comely Bank Road
Tel: 332 5573
Late closing: Mon-Fri 20.00

Sainsburys Pharmacy
Straiton Mains
Straiton Retail Park
near Loanhead   EH20 9PW
Tel: 448 2181
Mon-Fri 8.00-22.00, Sat 8.00-21.00
To date, this is the pharmacy which is open latest in Edinburgh

Southside Pharmacy
79 Nicolson St
Tel: 667 4032
Late closing: Mon-Fri 20.00

Chemists Open on Sunday

Asda Pharmacy
Edinburgh EH15 3AR
Tel: 669 3550
Sunday opening: 9.00-18.00

Boots the Chemist
Cameron Toll Centre
6 Lady Road
Tel: 666 1111
Sunday opening: 11.00-17.00

Craigleith Retail Park
Tel: 332 6114
Sunday opening: 10.30-17.30

48 Shandwick Place
Tel: 225 6757
Sunday opening: 10.00-17.00

Straiton Retail Park
Straiton EH20 9NL
Tel: 440 3419
Sun 10.00-18.00

SHOPPING – CRECHES WHILE SHOPPING

Morrisons Pharmacy
1 Bughtlin Market
Maybury Craigs
Tel: 339 1188
Sunday opening: 9.00-18.00

38 Comely Bank Road
Tel: 332 5573
Sunday opening: 10.00-14.00

Sainsburys Pharmacy
Straiton Mains
Straiton Retail Park
near Loanhead   EH20 9PW
tel: 448 2181
Sunday opening 8.00-20.00

Southside Pharmacy
79 Nicolson Street
Tel: 667 4032
Sunday opening: 12.00-17.00

CRECHES WHILE SHOPPING

Edinburgh has an all-year-round crèche at The Gyle Shopping Centre. In addition, there are sometimes 'one-off' crèche facilities provided for particular annual events, dependent of availability of funds and an appropriate venue. These include the Edinburgh Book Festival, Edinburgh International Festival and Festival Fringe. See Annual Events – and Childcare for more information on the Edinburgh Childcare Co-operative, which runs many of these crèches.

The Edinburgh Crèche Co-op
297 Easter Road   EH6 8LH
Contact: Pam or Brenda
Tel: 553 2116

The Gyle Creche
Gyle Avenue
South Gyle Broadway
Tel: 476 7766
Opening times: Mon-Fri 9.30-17.45; Sat 9.00-17.45; Sun 11.00-16.45

Located beside main bus stop at Gyle Shopping Centre entrance. Shoppers' crèche for children aged 2-8 incl. £3.50 per hr. Max time 2 hrs for 2-year-olds, 3 hrs for older children. Fully indoor and similar to a nursery with ball pit, art corner, house corner, wide selection of toys etc. Can be booked for children's parties in evenings.

IKEA Crèche
Straiton Road
Loanhead, Midlothian
Opening times: Mon-Sun 10.00-17.45 (last entry 16.45). £2/child
Located at the entrance. Available to children aged 3-7 yrs old. Parents or carers can shop for an hour (1/2 hr for last entries) while the qualified staff supervise children's play in the play area. As well as a huge ball-pool, there is a wide range of play equipment, including paint, drawing materials, musical play and a reading corner.
See under Department Stores, also Nursery Equipment and Toys.

DEPARTMENT STORES

Due to High Street competition and legal requirements regarding access, as well as any sense of customer care, large shops are increasingly family and child friendly.
Automatic doors, lifts, and in-store nappy changing facilities are just some of the things which have become of the standard contents of department stores, as has the presence of a café or restaurant which has high chairs, may offer a bottle and a baby food warming service, and recognises the requirements of people with young children.
Some other things don't change: large stores do alter their layout fairly often, so always check information against a store guide. If you have something to return, ask as soon as you enter the store for the correct procedure: you may be directed to a Customer Service Desk, which may save you a trek to the wrong department.

Argos & Argos Extra
Web: www.argos.co.uk
Easy shopping. Stores carry a range of home goods. Stores also have clothing catalogues. All catalogues free to take away and choose purchases at leisure. Some items on display in-store.
Fill in catalogue no. on a slip and hand it to the cashier: goods are collected from the stockroom for you. You have 16 days to return goods if not satisfied. Argos also offers a

ring and reserve service, if you have a catalogue at home and want to check that your store has what you want before you make the journey. Good value.

11-15 North Bridge EH1 1SB
Tel: 558 1474
Mon-Sat 9.00-18.00, Sun 11.00-17.00

52 Kinnaird Park
Newcraighall Road   EH15 3RD
Tel: 657 3574
Mon, Wed-Fri 9.00-20.00, Tue 9.30-20.00; Sat 9.00-18.00; Sun 10.00-17.00

Unit 7
Craigleith Retail Park
S Groathill Rd
Tel: 332 3762
Mon, Wed-Fri 9.00-20.00, Tue 9.30-20.00; Sat 9.00-18.00; Sun 10.00-18.00

Unit 3
Pentland Retail Park
Straiton Mains
Straiton   EH20 9QY
Tel: 0845 1657806

Mon-Fri 9.00-20.00; Sat 9.00-18.00; Sun 10.00-18.00

BhS
Web: www.bhs.co.uk

64 Princes Street EH2 2DJ
Tel: 0845 8410180

Opening times: Mon-Wed 9.00-17.30; Thu 9.00-20.00; Fri/Sat 9.00-18.00; Sun 12.00-17.00

Access: good from Princes St, with central escalators giving access to all floors. Small lift halfway along left hand side - you won't get a double pushchair in it.
From Rose St through restaurant, escalator down to Ground Floor.
Basement: children's clothes – have ranges for ages 2-6 and 6-13 yrs: these tend to follow fashion colours and trends. Home department stocks special children's bedding range, with accessories in various bright colours and character ranges. Night lights too.
Rose St Restaurant - see Eating Out
Feeding & changing room and toilets are on 1st Floor, upstairs from restaurant. No lift access. Toilet for the disabled on restaurant level.

Also at:
Cameron Toll Shopping Centre
6 Lady Road   EH16 5PB
Tel: 0845 8410155
Opening hours: Mon-Wed, Sat 10.00 18.00; Thu Fri 10.00 17.00; Sun 11.00-17.00
Stocks a selection of the ranges in the Princes St store.

Ocean Terminal
Ocean Drive   EH3 6DZ
Tel. 0845 8410218
Opening hours: Mon-Fri 10.00-20.00; Sat 10.00-19.00; Sun 11.00-18.00
Store has lift access from carpark levels. Capsule selections of the type of stock sold in Princes St, such as a range of children's clothes, incl. schoolwear.

Boots the Chemist
Web: wwww.boot.com; www.wellbeing.co.uk
NB Boots' store hours may change in 2006. Please phone ahead if unsure, or check online.

101-103 Princes Street
Tel: 225 8331/2/3
Opening times: Mon-Sat 9.00-18.00; Thu 9.00-19.30; Sun 12.00-17.00
Access: two automatic doors. Public lift and escalator, both on the left hand side of the store. Staff lift available for double pushchairs.
Store has wide, clear aisles, although the ground floor can be very busy at lunchtime, due to sandwich and snack sales.
Ground floor: personal care, beauty, dispensing chemist. Mother and Baby Room at rear of floor. No access for double pushchairs. Bottle warmer, wipes, nappies etc usually available.
Men are welcome to use this room, but should ask first, in case a mother is feeding.
1st floor: baby toiletries, baby food. Babitens to hire. Baby consultant available for advice. Also stocks toys, photographic dept.

Also at:
Gyle Shopping Centre
Tel: 317 1288
Opening times: Mon-Wed 9.00-20.00; Thu 9.00-21.00; Sat 9.00-18.00; Sun 10.00-18.00
Store all on one level. Baby equipment, located towards the back of the store, but no clothing. Demonstrations of Babitens, which are available to hire. Nappy collection

service. Store is near the centre's main entrance, which provides ease of parking for large purchases i.e. bulk buying of nappies. Staff toilet is available. No nappy-changing facility in-store, Gyle Parenting Room is nearby: go up to the Food Court and it's on the far left.

Craigleith Retail Park
Tel: 332 6114

Opening times: Mon-Fri 9.00-20.00; Sat 9.00-18.00; Sun 10.30-17.30

Access: automatic doors. Parent and child parking directly outside (2 bays).

Store all on one level. Toilets with nappy changing facilities, usually including emergency supplies of nappies, on the left as you enter the store. Good range of baby accessories , toys and clothing are situated towards the rear of the unit. Also beauty, personal grooming, photographic developing and chemists.

Fort Retail Park
Tel: 669 4428

Store all on one level. Good range of baby accessories , toys and clothing are situated towards the rear of the unit. Also beauty, personal grooming, etc

Straiton Retail Park
Straiton EH20 9NL
Tel: 440 3419

Mon-Fri 9.00-20.00, Sat 9.00-19.00

Store all on one level. Good range of baby accessories and clothing are situated towards the left of the unit. as you enter. Also beauty, personal grooming, etc

Stores (with smaller ranges of products) also at 48 Shandwick Pl, St James' Centre, North Bridge, and various suburban locations (see Phone Book). See also Chemists with Extended Hours.

Debenhams
Web: www.debenhams.com

109-112 Princes Street
Tel: 08445 616161

Opening times: Mon-Wed, Fri 9.30-18.00; Thu 9.30-20.00; Sat 9.00-18.00; Sun 11.00-18.00. Times may extend during Festival

Access: Main access from Princes St, with lifts to left of main entrance. Escalators to all floor.

Also access from Rose St. There's a lift into the main Princes St building.

Store can be rather daunting, as there are several sublevels due to the size. If in doubt, ask!

This store operates the VIP Baby Service, which relates to their restaurant. It includes: baby food (they carry Organix range) for 55p/jar; bottle and baby food warming; stay-warm plates; baby wipes; high chairs.

Store also has Customer Order and Home Shopping services. There's also a free Personal Shopper Service.

Basement: menswear

Lower Ground: children's wear

Ground: Beauty, perfumery, accessories, jewellery

1st floor: Casual wear, maternity wear (Dorothy Perkins), designer wear

2nd floor: Ladies' wear, including lingerie where nursing bras are sold

3rd floor: bedding and soft furnishing

4th floor: Restaurant. See Eating Out

Toilets: on 4th floor opposite main lift. Toilet for the disabled is small, but there is a small changing shelf.

Also at:
Ocean Terminal
Ocean Drive
Leith   EH6 7DZ
Tel: 08445 616161

Opening times: Mon-Fri 10.00-20.00; Sat 10.00-19.00; Sun 10.00-18.00

Store is on two floors. It has a capsule selection of those ranges available at the large Prince St store. It's fairly easy to walk round, with wide walkways. Escalators are placed in the centre of the shopfloor. There are 2 lifts to access one floor from the other (lifts serve the entire centre). Store stocks various ranges of children's clothing, along with homeware, menswear and women's wear. Has a reasonable range of lingerie, which includes limited maternity ranges. Also has beauty, perfumery, accessories, and jewellery sections

Frasers
145 Princes Street   EH2 4DL
Tel: 0870 160 7239
Web: www.houseoffraser.co.uk

Opening times: Mon-Wed, Fri 9.30-18.00; Thu 9.30-19.30; Sat 9.00-18.00; Sun 11.00-17.00

Access: Two entrances from Princes St to Ground floor, one from Hope St side of building. Lift at rear, escalators on right to all departments. Ground floor is on a split level, with a few steps between. Perfumery is best accessed via Princes St, Accessories via Hope St (where the lift is). Basement: Oasis, fashion and diffusion lines

Ground: beauty and accessories
1st floor: ladies wear
2nd floor: ladies' fashion, plus lingerie. Including maternity wear and nursing bras. Lingerie fitting service available.
3rd floor: menswear
4th floor: homewear
5th floor: restaurant
Toilets: on 5th floor, with feeding and changing room nearby.

Harvey Nichols

30-34 St Andrews Square   EH2 3AD
Tel: 524 8388
Fax: 524 8399
Web: www.harveynichols.com
Opening hours: Mon-Wed 10.00-18.00; Thu 10.00-20.00; Fri, Sat 10.00-17.00; Sun 12.00-17.00
Access also via Multrees Walk
Store on 4 floors, with stylish concession areas.
Store carries children's wear by various designers in a compact area on 3rd floor. Buckle My Shoe stockists.
There's a juice bar on the ground floor and The Forth Floor bar and restaurant is on the fourth floor – get the pun?
The store's very chi chi, but unfortunately it has to be said, it's probably best visited without little ones in tow. The layout on the ground floor is not given over to easy negotiation with a pushchair and it's a toddler's dream of shiny, feathery, sleek (and expensive) things to grab at. They often have great window displays, so you might find yourself spending some time outside the store while your child's imagination is taken up with the displays.

IKEA

Straiton Mains
Straiton, Loanhead EH20 9PW
Tel: 440 6600 (customer services)
Web: www.ikea.com
Opening times: Mon-Fri 10.00-22.00; Sat 10.00-19.00; Sun 10.00-18.00. Bank Holiday opening 10.00-18.00
Take the Straiton exit from the bypass on to the A701 and follow the signs. Various bus stops nearby.
There are parent and child parking bays, but these can be busy: it's best to try and go at off-peak times if you want to avoid congestion in the car parks and the lifts.
Huge store on the outskirts of Edinburgh: a shopper's delight – or a nightmare if you like to just shop and go! Unsupervised play area for older toddlers outside at entrance.
Crèche/ballroom inside; see Crèches while Shopping.

Pushchairs available, as are trolleys for a toddler plus a store carry bag (£1 coin required, refundable). There are also normal single and double supermarket-style trolleys (from the first floor, take the lift or stairs down to the marketplace where trolleys are stored, then bring it back up before you begin the trip round the store).

Trolleys are not allowed in the car park – if you have bulky items, cars must be brought to the pick-up point and your purchases loaded from there. You can take your child/ren to the car and leave the trolley in one of the secure lock-up points (£1 coin, refundable) - but be warned, they don't always work: however, we've always found that staff will 'mind' a trolley – with or without child/ren – while you fetch your vehicle.

The route round the store is mapped out, staff are usually   friendly and accommodating. Should you wish to deviate from the path, watch out for the 'shortcuts' marked throughout the store. There are play areas on the first floor in the children's furniture and toy area (a real try-before-you-buy experience for under 5s), and also in the café (see below). In other areas, there are little play zones for young children, with chairs and tables, bricks, bead mazes etc.

Large room on the ground floor, near the entrance for breastfeeding and changing, with comfy chairs and screen. There is also a smaller nappy-changing room. Nappies are available in vending machine in all nappy changing areas. There are also changing facilities on the first floor adjacent to the café, and also near the snack bar after the pay point on the ground floor.

NB IKEA is one of several Edinburgh stores which charges for plastic bags – buy one of their re-usable bags, or remember to take something to put your shopping in.

Café
Opening times: Mon-Fri 9.30-19.30; Sat-Sun 9.30-17.30
£, highchairs (20), nappy changing facilities (M&F), licensed, seats 306.
Extensive café/restaurant with self-service and amiable staff. Unsupervised children's play area in one corner, with a selection of toys overlooking the stairs on 1st floor. Menu with snacks and main courses including vegetarian and Swedish options. Children's options and boxed meals available: sometimes children's meals are supplemented by a free piece of fruit. Limited selection of organic jarred baby food. Bottle heaters and microwaves available to heat bottles and baby food.

Jenners

48 Princes Street
Tel: 225 2442
Fax: 260 2240
Web: www.jenners.com

Opening times: Mon, Wed, Fri, Sat 9.00-18.00; Tue 9.30-18.00; Thu 9.00-20.00; Sun 11.00-17.00

Access: Both Princes St entrances have stairs up to the doors, as does South St David St – though there are less here, and there's also a revolving door which some older toddlers might like. For easiest access, enter by Rose St next to the Barber's Shop and take the lift up.

Traditional store with large, galleried well and many different levels. Because of its design, the building can be awkward to negotiate, although there are many (small) lifts to the various floors: the largest lift is that situated towards the rear of the store – ground floor access via Men's Designer Dept.

It's worth persevering in the store, as it is very attractive, with friendly staff on the whole. There are store guides posted on the walls near the lifts, or you can request one. The store has undergone various refurbishments in recent times and there's a good mix of the traditional and the contemporary. At Christmas time a huge tree is erected in-store which can be viewed from the gallery – look out for the robin singing in the branches!

Store offers a delivery service (free to EH postcodes 1-22 and 24-30; there's a small charge outwith this area), an alteration service (free to its cardholders) and a 'left shopping' service (based on level 2) so you can wander round at least unhindered by shopping bags. House of Fraser recently bought over Jenners, and while they say there are no plans to alter Jenners, there have been some minor changes to stock availability etc already, so please use the following only as a guide.

Key locations are:
Basement: toys, children's books (lift behind perfume dept on ground floor). See Toyshops.
Lower ground: jewellery, toiletries, hair accessories, accessories
Midway/1st floor: ladies' wear, including lingerie.
1st floor: Kids at Jenners (recently refurbished).
Restaurants: Five to choose from. See Eating Out.
Toilets: on 3rd floor. Parent and baby rooms adjacent to ladies' toilets. Clean, comfortable and pleasant — and usually not too busy. The changing room and the feeding room are separate and have sofas and chairs.

See also Baby and Children's' Wear and Nursery Equipment.

John Lewis

St James' Centre   EH1 3SP
Tel: 556 9121
Fax: 550 3000
Email:JL_Edinburgh@johnewis.co.uk

Opening times: Mon-Wed, 9.00-18.00; Thu 9.30-20.00; Fri 9.00-20.00; Sat 9.00-18.30; Sun 11.00-18.00

Access: from Leith St, opposite Greenside Car Park which takes you into the store via the flooring department. Glass lift to other floors is hidden behind the escalators. Two entrances in the St James' Centre. Entrance into basement and Customer Collection Point from Little King St, adjacent to St James' Centre Car Park.

Large department store providing a wide range of goods and services. Store is on several levels, with roomy lifts and escalator access in the main store area. Customers can ring and reserve items, plus the store offers free delivery throughout Edinburgh and parts of Central Scotland, Fife and Borders.

This is a sleek, stylish store, which still has loads of room to access the various departments and concessions with pushchairs or prams.

Points of interest:
Store offers a personal fashion advisor: service is free of charge.
Extensive Nursery section. Store stocks prams, pushchairs, cots, car seats, accessories, as well as a range of babies' and children's clothing (own brand, plus branded items).
Basement (Leith St): carpets & flooring
Lower Ground: computing, hi-fis etc, kitchenware, fabrics, soft furnishings
Ground: Beauty, ladies accessories, stationery, haberdashery, accessories, toys
1st floor: women's wear, menswear, lingerie, children's wear, children's shoes, nursery equipment. Café nr menswear.
2nd floor: home furnishing, restaurant, see Eating Out

Toilets on 2nd (Changing trolley in F toilets).
Feeding and changing room. Automatic door to ease access. There are 4 nappy changing areas, 3 of which are static, 1 of which is a pull-down unit. In the toilets inside the feeding/changing area, there's a toddler height loo. The breastfeeding area has views out over N Edinburgh and over to Fife. While there's a partition wall, there isn't a screen between the entrance door and the breastfeeding area, so if you need a bit of privacy, settle yourself at the window side of the room.

See also Toys, Outdoor Toys and Bicycle Shops.

Marks and Spencer
Web: marksandspencer.com

91 Princes Street EH2 2ER
Tel: 225 2301

Opening hours: Mon-Wed, Fri 9.00-19.00; Thu 9.00-20.00; Fri 9.00-19.00; Sat 8.30-18.00; Sun 11.00-17.00. Stores extend opening hours over the Christmas period.
Access: via Princes St: automatic door nr The Body Shop. Extensive department store on 4 levels. Good lift access. Self-service café at the rear of the basement, see Eating Out. Toilets and nappy-changing on ground floor to the left hand side of store as you enter. There's also a mother and baby room for mothers to breastfeed in private. Space for prams and pushchairs. Toilets are in the same area - they can be very busy.
Basement: ladies' wear/lingerie, including nursing bras (M&S have a bra fitting service), maternity underwear etc: Store also offers ordering and alteration services.

54 Princes Street EH2 2DQ
Tel: 225 2301
Fax: 459 7802

Opening hours: Mon-Wed, Fri 9.00-19.00; Thu 9.00-20.00; Fri 9.00-19.00; Sat 8.30-18.00; Sun 11.00-17.00. Stores extend opening hours over the Christmas period.
Access: easy access from Princes St. There are lifts and escalators to all floors. Two entrances from Rose St – left hand side has automatic door and level access.
Menswear, home furnishings, M&S foodhall and Childrenswear are in this branch. It's best to access the Childrenswear by Rose St. At the time of writing, the children's clothing was in a very compact space, which doesn't offer much manoeuvring of pushchairs and prams.
Toilets also on Rose St level. 'Collect by car' food service available from this store.

Gyle Shopping Centre
21 Gyle Avenue EH12 9JT
Tel: 317 1333
Fax: 317 1444

Opening times: Mon-Fri 9.00-22.00; Sat 8.00-20.00; Sun 9.00-18.00. Store has extended opening hours during the Christmas period

Access: from car park, where parent and child parking bays are nearby, or through the Gyle Centre.
Extremely spacious store, all on one level. Children's wear, including some nursery equipment, ladies' wear, lingerie (including underwear and nursing bras: bra fitting service

in-store), men's wear and home furnishings. Cash machine in-store (near menswear).
Two cafés, one nr the car park entrance, the other nr Children's wear. There are nappy changing facilities near both cafés, along with toilets, but the larger facilities are nearer Children's wear and also have a room for those mothers who wish to breastfeed in private (don't believe the logos on the door nr the carpark toilets; there is no feeding area, just toilets).

Simply Food
Craigleith Retail Park
Tel: 343 3461

Opening times: Mon-Fri 9.00-20.00; Sat 9.00-19.00; Sun 10.00-18.00
Despite the name, this is not only a food store. It also carries limited ranges of lingerie, hosiery, babywear, toys and accessories.

Unit 31-33
Kinnaird Park EH15 3RD
Tel: 669 7695
Fax: 669 7893

Opening hours: Mon-Fri 9.00-21.00; Sat 9.00-19.00; Sun 10.00-18.00
Foodhall, with an in-store bakery. There's also a Cafe Revive, and a small range of general merchandise, including cards & wrap, hosiery, cosmetics & makeup and homeware gifts.

Ocean Terminal
Unit 3, Ocean Terminal
Ocean Drive EH6 6HW
Tel: 225 2301

Opening hours: Mon-Fri 9.00-20.00; sat 9.00-19.00; 10.00-18.00
Foodhall, with small Café Revive.

Mothercare World
Web: www.mothercare.com

Unit 6
Hermiston Gait Retail Park
31 Cultins Road EH11 4DG
Tel: 453 1383

Opening times: Mon-Fri 9.00-20.00; Sat 9.00-18.00; Sun 10.00-17.00
Store all on one level. Stocks clothes (Mothercare brand) and maternity wear. Also stocks a range of nursery goods & bedding (own brand), car seats, pushchairs (various brands) and toys.

Convenient parking and shopping trolleys (£1 coin returnable charge). Nappy-changing facilities (M&F), toilets and private breastfeeding area available. See also Baby and Children's Clothes, Maternity Wear, Nursery Equipment, and Toys.

Also at:
Unit 11C
The Fort Retail Park
New Craighall Road EH15 3HH
Tel: 657 4050
Opening hours: Mon, Wed, Thu, Fri 9.00-20.00; Tue 9.30-20.00; Sat 9.00-18.00; Sun 10.00-17.00
Similar layout and range as store at Hermiston Gait. The store has nappy changing facilities and toilets. There's also a public telephone located in-store.

Toys'R'Us
Kinnaird Park
Newcraighall Rd   EH15 3RD
Tel: 657 4121
Opening times: Mon-Sat 9.00-22.00; Sun 10.00-18.00. Operates Bank Holiday hours.
Huge store which sells more than just toys: see other listings below. The Babies'r'Us area stocks baby food, toiletries, and nappies in bulk quantities, as well as nursery equipment. Store directory guides to different areas, and there's a pick-up point for
bulky items and electrical toys. Reward card scheme.
See also Toys, Outdoor Toys, Bicycles, Children's Clothes.

Woolworths

170-174 Constitution Street
Leith
Tel: 554 3872/0210

142 Lothian Road
Tel: 229 4644

25 Milton Link Milton Road
Tel: 0131 669 1298
Fax: 0131 669 4937
This megastore has a vast array of goods, including children's clothing, outdoor toys, toys and games.

36-38 Raeburn Place
Stockbridge
Tel: 332 2613
Sunday opening: 10.00-16.00

181 St John's Road
Corstorphine
Tel: 334 6644
Sunday opening: 12.00-16.00

91-93 High Street
Musselburgh
Tel: 0131 665 2910
Fax: 0131 665 3819

At time of writing, all stores open Mon-Sat 9.00-17.30

Stores stock selection of own-brand and other brand toys, party supplies, stationery, DVDs, as well as sweets, homeware and haberdashery. The 'Ladybird' clothing brand is Woolworths', as is Chad Valley Games. See also Baby and Children's Wear and Toys.

SHOPPING CENTRES, MALLS & RETAIL PARKS

If mall shopping is your thing, or you prefer having the big names all in one place, Edinburgh has a good selection of shopping centres, both in and out of town. Many of the malls offer hire of small pushchairs and toddler straps. We have listed the general opening hours of the centres: they may operate restricted hours on Bank Holidays and longer hours in the run-up to Christmas.

Almondvale Shopping Centre
87 Almondvale South
Livingston   EH54 6HR
Tel: 01506 432961
Opening times: Mon-Wed, Fri, Sat 9.00-17.30, Thu 9.00-19.00, Sun 11.00-17.00. Public holidays 11.00-17.00. Some stores may operate longer hours.

Accessible from M8-A71 (parent/child parking) or by bus from St Andrews Square. NB the car parks may have a 'maximum stay' policy.

Accessorize, Adams, Asda Wal-Mart, BhS, Boots, Claire's Accessories, Clarks Shoes, JNR Station, Mothercare, WH Smith, Superdrug Woolworths.
Places to eat, include Aulds Bakers, Rendezvous Cafe, Bakers Oven, BhS Café, and the Mall Café Bar.
Mothercare have a good feeding and changing room located at the back of store (M&F). The nappy-changing area is locked (key from assistant).

The whole mall is one level so it's easy to navigate. The toilets are located near Boots and Symingtons Jewellers. There are two nappy changing areas, a shopper's crèche and bottle warming facilities available from the cafes and restaurants. There are also various coin-operated children's rides around the centre.

Almondvale Childcare
Tel: 01506 436474
Shopper's Crèche

Opening Times Mon-Sat 10.00-17.30; Sun 12.00-17.00. Sliding scale of charges. £3.30/h. Maximum stay is 2 hours.

There's also a nursery based at Almondvale.

Full/part time places available between 8.00-18.00, Mon-Fri.

Call no. above for more information.

Cameron Toll Shopping Centre
Lady Road
Tel: 666 2777

Opening times: Mon-Wed, Sat 10.00-18.00, Thu-Fri 10.00-19.00; Sun 11.0-19.00. Stores operate Sunday hours on Bank Holidays etc.

Hours of individual shops vary – Sainsbury's operates longer hours – but generally all open late on Thu and also on Sun afternoons.

Two large car parks serve both front and rear entrances. Can be very busy on Fri and w/ends.

Keep a tight grip on small children in car parks. Pedestrian access from Lady Rd but closely set bollards and a rollbar designed to prevent shoppers from taking trolleys out mean large prams and pushchairs need careful manoeuvring.

Self-opening doors, seats, public phones in a leafy mirrored mall. Petrol station and taxi rank. A variety of trolley designs to accommodate various ages of babies and small children. Many smaller shops do not allow trolleys inside. A variety of shops include Adams Children's Wear, BhS, Boots, Clarks, Mackays, Ottakar's, Dorothy Perkins, Sainsbury's, Claire's Accessories, jewellers, travel agents, banks and building society – all on the main shopping floor. On the 1st floor, there's the foodcourt, including Burger King, Cafe Select and 3 Potato More. Bottle warming facilities available

The centre usually hosts activities for Easter, Mother's Day etc, such as puppet shows, magicians and other children's entertainers.

Toilets on ground (near JJB Sports) and first floor (nr Headlines Hairdressers – lift on left outside entrance to Sainsbury's). There's a separate nappy-changing room with 2 changing units and enclosed area for feeding.

Craigleith Retail Park
South Groathill Road

Compact shopping centre with good parking.
Sainsbury's supermarket is open Mon-Fri 7.00-00.00; Sat 7.00-22.00; Sun 7.00-20.00.

Boots has pharmacy. Other shops include Mamas & Papas, Curry's, Homebase, TK Maxx, Holiday Hypermarket and Marks & Spencer simply Food.

Easily accessible toilets in Sainsbury's include a toilet for the disabled – useful if taking combinations of children/babies to toilets/nappy-changing. Boots has a nappy-changing area in the ladies toilets. Simply Food also has toilets.

Expansion of this retail park is underway, of 6 further retail premises, which should see an expansion in the range of stores.

Fort Kinnaird
(formerly Kinnaird Park and the Fort)
Newcraighall Road
Tel: 669 9242
Access from A1

Around 55 outlets set around 3 large car parks (watch the arrows on the roads – the negotiation around the car parks can be quite tight) . Opening hours of individual shops vary but most open late on Thu and all day Sun.

In what was Kinnaird Park, shops include Argos, Borders, Early Learning Centre, Gap, H&M, Toys 'R' Us, Curry's, and M&S Simply Food hall. The Early Learning Playstore has plenty of options to 'try before you buy', as well as planned activities.

Also in Retail Park are the UCI 10-screen cinema and Megabowl, a 10 pin bowling alley which welcomes families.

In the area which was formerly the Fort there are more outlets, including:

Boots, Mothercare World, Dorothy Perkins, Adams, Next, Birthdays, New Look etc.

Restaurants/cafés/fast food: Chiquitos, McDonald's 'Drive Thru', Costa Coffee (in WH Smiths), Cafe Noire in Clinton's Cards, Starbuck's in Borders, Café Revive in M&S, Frankie & Benny's and Pizza Hut. There are bottle warming facilities in: Borders, Chiquitos, ELC, Frankie & Benny's, the management suite and McDonald's.

Toilets: Mothercare has a good feeding and changing room, Borders Books café has a changing room, while Cafe Noire and Boots also have nappy-changing rooms (M&F). Early Learning Playstore has an excellent baby changing facility and children's toilet facility, and a baby 'dining-room' with seats for breastfeeding and bottle warmers.

Gyle Shopping Centre
Gyle Avenue
South Gyle Broadway
Tel: 539 9000
Getting there: LRT 2, 12, 18, 21, 22, 24, 58, 58A, X66 all go to the Gyle. Entrance is situated off the South Gyle roundabout.
Opening hours: Mon, Tue, Wed, Fri 9.30-20.00; Thu 9.30-21.00; Sat 9.00-18.00; Sun 10.00-18.00. Certain individual stores, such as Marks & Spencer and Morrisons, have longer hours, and hours extend at Christmas.
Large colour coded car park, with parent and child parking, and parking for the disabled at all entrances. Maximum stay is 3 hrs. Taxi rank outside main entrance. Petrol station near main entrance. There are other entrances, which give easy access to Morrisons and Marks and Spencer. Single and double pushchairs and child reins available to hire free (ID required) at Customer Services Desk in mall opposite main entrance. Small outdoor play areas with climbing frames etc.
Self-opening doors, seats, public phones in a spacious well-planned centre, with around 60 shops all on one level. A variety of trolleys to accommodate various ages of small children (available at Morrisons & M&S).
Lift and escalator to upper level where the 500-seater Food Court offers a range of snacks, meals and drinks. There are bottle/baby food heating facilities. Also situated on 1st floor is a fully-equipped Baby Room (M&F). There are toilets on the ground floor beside the main entrance and also on the 1st floor - both include facilities for disabled visitors. M&S and Morrison's also have cafés, plus there's Starbuck's on the ground level.
Shops include: Accessorize, Body Shop, Boots, Clarks, Disney Store, Early Learning Centre, Gap, Mackays, Monsoon, Monsoon for Children, Marks and Spencer, Next, and WH Smith. There are also jewellers, a building society, travel agents etc.

Hermiston Gait Retail Park
Take 1st exit marked Glasgow off A720 City Bypass coming from South Gyle.
Do not follow sign to Glasgow, go straight on which will take you to traffic lights. Turn left and follow signs.

Mothercare World open Mon-Fri 9.00-20.00 Sat 9.00 18.00 Sun 10.00-17.00.
Opening hours of other shops vary.
Large car park: keep a close eye on mobile youngsters - as the car park is usually quite quiet, drivers have a tendency to cut across parking bays rather than using the road layout.
Shops include: Curry's, Office World, JJB Sports, and Homebase.
Toilets: Feeding and changing room located in Mothercare World.

McArthur Glen Designer Outlet Livingston
Almondvale Avenue
Livingston
West Lothian   EH54 6QX.
Tel: 01506 423 600 (automated information line)
J3 off M8 - follow signs to Designer Outlet Centre. Regular buses from Edinburgh - bus station is directly in front of the Centre.
There is also a taxi rank.
Centre opening times: Mon-Tue, Sat-Sun 10.00-18.00; Wed-Fri 10.00-20.00. Individual stores' opening hours may vary.
Various car parks (there's 2000 spaces in all) although easiest access seems to be Centre West.
Large shopping centre on two levels. Mixture of designer and casual clothes shops including Aquascutum, M&S Outlet, Ice Blue, Gap, Clarks, and various sports shops. Other shops include ELC, The Toyworld Store and At Home. Various cash dispensers.
8-screen Circuit Cinema located on the 1st level.
Various options for food such as: Ashoka Shak (Indian 'tapas'), Caffe Nero, McDonald's, Rollover Pizza Express, Spud-u-Like and Refresh. Various coffee shops located on the ground floor.
Toilets: 2 nappy changing areas with 3 changing units in each, plus closed feeding area. One is located opposite Gap and the other one is in the Boulevard.

Meadowbank Shopping Park
Just off London Road before Meadowbank Stadium.
Sainsbury's open Mon-Fri 8.00-22.00; Sat 07.00-22.00; Sun 8.00-20.00.
Opening hours of other shops vary.
Large car park with Parent Child Parking.
Shops include Sainsbury's, JJB Sports, T-K Maxx, Brunswick Warehouse, Brantano, Kingdom of Leather, Poundstretcher, KFC and Au Naturale.
Toilets and nappy changing facilities in Sainsbury's.

Newkirkgate Shopping Centre
Off Great Junction Street
Leith

Opening times of individual shops vary. Closed Sun. Large car park.

Some shops around open square, others in recently refurbished covered mall. Shops include Woolworths, Lidl, Boots (small store with pharmacy). Various other shops. No toilets in centre.

Ocean Terminal
Ocean Drive
Leith   EH6 7DZ
Tel: 555 56
Web: www.oceanterminal.com

Opening times: Mon-Fri 10.00-20.00; Sat 9.00-19.00; Sun 11.00-18.00.

Getting there: Follow signs for Leith / North Edinburgh and brown tourist signs for Britannia. Lothian Buses 1, 11, 22, 34, 35 & 36. 1600 parking spaces – 2 multi-storey and 1 surface car park adjacent to Debenhams, with direct access to mall on all three floor, and stair or lift access on all.

Airy, modern mall on 3 levels, with wide walkways and plenty to take youngsters' attention, whether it's the huge propellers on display, or the sight of boats in the River Forth from the eateries. Lifts and escalator access to 1st and 2nd floors.

As well as the more usual High Street names such as GAP (with GAP kids), Boots, Waterstones and Claire's Accessories, Ocean Terminal offers a selection of clothing and lifestyle stores, such as Okaidi (children's clothes), Fat Face (with children's ranges), Junior Station, and the Bear Factory. Ocean Terminal is also home to Debenhams' and Bhs, which both carry a good range of children's clothing and accessories. Debenhams have an extensive lingerie dept, which includes maternity bras.

There is a Drop and Shop - Molly's Village, which costs £5/h (max. 2 hrs), as well as Molly's Soft Play (c. £3/h).

It also houses a day spa – Pure – , Charlie Miller's hairdressing, plus a tourist centre and shop for the Royal Yacht Britannia, which is moored alongside the shopping centre.

It has parenting suites on two of the 3 floors, which have baby changing facilities and seating for breastfeeding mothers.

There's a wide range of places to eat, including: Baxter's café, Ocean Kitchen, O'Brien's, Terence Conran's stylish Zinc bar, Zizzi, Café Revive (in M&S) and Ma Potters. Vue Cinemas operate a kids club cinema screening on weekend mornings at around 10.00 am, although it can sometime screen a PG certificate film – check press for details – for the price of £2 for an adult and child (babies under 2 go free). See Where Shall We Go Today for more details.

Princes Mall
Corner of Princes Street and Waverley Bridge
Tel: 557 3759

Opening times: Mon-Sat 8.30-18.00; Thu 8.30-19.00; Sun 11.00-17.00.

Hours for individual shops vary and not all shops open on Sun.

Built on 3 levels with 6 entrances, 2 with access ramps; Waverley Bridge and Princes St, next to Waverley Steps, which leads to the small, busy lift which serves all floors. Busy mall with Tourist Information Centre located on the rooftop (access ramp from Princes St available).

There are over 50 businesses, including Oasis, New Look, Quiksilver and The Natural World.

Food outlets include: McDonald's, KFC, Rollover, O'Brien's, Spud-u-Like, Something Thai, Coffeestop and Costa Coffee on the roof.

Toilets: Two sets both on lowest level at opposite ends. Washrooms beside the Food Court, 20p. Free nappy changing room and toilet for the disabled to the right of the washrooms (easy access with pushchair).

Toilets with a separate nappy-changing room inside the ladies' toilets through a set of doors market 'Exit' at the other end of Princes Mall.

St James' Centre
Princes Street / Leith Street
Tel: 557 0050
Web: www.stjamesshopping.com

Opening times: Mon-Wed, Fri-Sat 9.00-18.00; Thu 9.00-20.00; Sun 11.00-17.00. Some shop hours vary

Pedestrian access from the corner of Leith St, Princes St and Elder St via Multrees Walk, which connects St James to the Harvey Nichols complex. Vehicular entrance to St James' multi-storey car park from Leith St and Elder St (lift access to centre via this car park), a but an alternative is to park in Greenside car park, on Leith St, and enter via the main door or by John Lewis.

Large shopping centre. Shops include Adams, Boots, John Lewis, Mackays, Dorothy Perkins, Thornton's etc. Cash dispensers, seats and public phones.

The eating area – Food on 1 – is on the upper floor, along with the toilets for the disabled and the nappy changing facilities. This is accessible via a lift near the Princes St end of the mall. John Lewis has excellent changing/feeding room with a separate male changing/feeding room (on the store's 2nd floor, near to The Place to Eat). There are also cookie and juice stands. St James operates a pushchair hire service, which can be booked at the customer Information desk, or on 557 0500.

Westside Plaza Shopping Centre
Wester Hailes Road
Tel: 442 3123
Opening times: Mon-Sat 8.30-18.00 (19.00 Thu and Fri). Opening hours of individual shops vary, some close Wed pm. Large car park, plus railway station, bus terminal and taxi rank nearby.
Indoor shopping centre on 2 levels with lift and escalators. Shops include Iceland, Poundstretcher, Lloyds (chemist), Browns (opticians), Post Office and a variety of other food, gift, toy, hardware, newsagent and charity shops, plus an indoor market on the ground floor. Odeon multiscreen cinema, library, Citizens Advice Bureau, Job Centre and City of Edinburgh Council Local Housing Office nearby. Toilets: located on ground floor – separate nappy-changing area (M&F).

FAIRS & MARKETS

Assembly Rooms
54 George Street
Tel: 220 4348
Box Office: 220 4349
Lift to all floors at rear left of main entrance
Hosts regular craft and collectors fairs – there's always a few in the run-up to Christmas. Forthcoming events advertised in local press and in the building's window space. Christmas Charity Hypermarket held in December. Craft Fairs usually include baby and children's clothes, wooden toys, patchwork etc. Fairs tend to get very busy especially at lunchtime, which renders pushchairs and small children a liability. Occasional children's shows presented during school holidays. Toilets: back left of ground floor, down a few steps or at the right of the 1st floor (nappy changing facilities) .

Christmas Village
Princes Street Gardens East
A seasonal event. Stalls sell a range of goods and Christmas orientated merchandise. There's also food stalls. See Annual Events.

Edinburgh Farmers' Market
Castle Street
Web:www.scottishfarmersmarket.co.uk
1st and 3rd weekend of the month, Sat 10.00-14.00
A selection of stalls, where you can buy meat, poultry, game, fish, dairy products and more. Much of it is organic. The stall-owners, being the farmers and manufacturers, know their stuff about what they're selling. As well as the raw food stalls, there are stalls selling baking, drinks, fruit and veg, as well as some knitwear. The range seems to grow every week. As well as the samples which are on offer at many of the stalls (a good way to find out if your child likes what you're about to buy!), there are beverages and snacks along the lines of freshly cooked 'real' crisps, wild boar burgers and roast suckling pig rolls on sale. There is sometimes an entertainer, such as a juggler, clown etc.

SUPERMARKETS

No one would ever say that doing the weekly shop with young children is easy, but hopefully this chapter will give you an idea of the most suitable places for you and your child to shop.

Hours:
We have not listed these, as they are so varied, and in the ongoing 'supermarket wars', they change fairly regularly. Most are open Mon-Sat, from at least 9.00-19.00 or 20.00, although many of the larger stores are open to midnight, and some have 24 hr opening. Sunday hours are around 12.00-17.00, and most are open all year, only closing on Christmas and New Year's Days.

Car parks:
Most stores listed have car parks and many now offer 'parent and child' spaces, usually near to those for disabled drivers. These are usually situated near to the store entrance – but don't expect other people to respect their role!

Trolleys:
We have listed the types of trolleys provided by the store. Safety instructions for each type of trolley should always be followed. These are often found on the bar or handles. Always use the restraints – and if you find the trolleys on offer do not have functioning restraints, why not report the matter to the store management. Remember, too, that once they are loaded with shopping and children, trolleys can become unwieldy, so be aware of your own physical limits! As a general guide, baby cradle types are suitable

for babies up to 9kgs (20 lbs) and the toddler types are suitable up to around 3 yrs. Other trolley types (baby, double baby, baby and toddler and double toddler etc) are less common, but the larger the store, the greater the range.

While stores usually state that they allow all trolley types out of the store, you may find that, in practice, the combination trolleys are not allowed out of the store boundaries, though if the store owns the car park, this usually makes life easier. Rather than repacking your shopping into another trolley and struggling with a small baby or several children, why not ask for an escort out to your car – make the stores compete for your custom!

Carry Out Service:

Check with at the Customer Services before you start your shop whether this is available. Then, ask at the checkout if you need assistance.

Lost children:

Stores offer a lost child policy, but they tend to differ. The first rule is try not to panic, then contact a member of staff immediately you become aware of the disappearance. Describe what your child was wearing and where you last saw them. Think of anything that might have attracted them on the way round the store. Try to carry some ID that identifies you as the child's carer; a recent photograph is useful. In shopping centres, stores always contact the centre's security. If you can, try to teach your child to approach a member of staff in a shop if they become lost.

We have tried to list those aspects in the following stores which are specific to parents with young children,

Asda Wal-Mart
100 The Jewel
Brunstone EH15 3AR
Tel: 669 9151
also at:
Chesser Avenue
Tel: 444 8425
Baby, double baby, baby and toddler, toddler and double toddler trolleys. Nappies, babyfood. Nappy-changing facilities (M&F). See also Baby and Children's Toys. Toyshops. Range of well-known brands and value-line foods.

Marks and Spencer
Web:www.marksandspencer.com
54 Princes Street
Tel: 225 2301
£5 home delivery of foods Mon-Sat to EH1-EH17 postcodes inclusive, from 54 Princes St. Large selection

of prepared meals for adults, no babyfoods, but do have ready-made novelty birthday cakes.

Gyle Shopping Centre
Has the advantage that the store is all on one floor. Stocks children's, ladies' and men's wear. Also home furnishings, nursery accessories etc.

Morrisons / Safeway
Web: www.morrisons.co.uk

Bughtlin Market, Maybury Drive, East Craigs
Tel: 339 2073
Baby, double baby, baby and toddler, toddler and double toddler trolleys.

38 Comely Bank St
Tel: 332 4469
Baby, toddler and baby, double toddler and toddler trolleys. Car

park entrance on Fettes Ave. 'Parent and Child' parking near lifts. Range of baby foods and accessories. Nappy changing facilities, private breastfeeding area and toilets.

Cramond Road South
Davidson's Mains
Tel: 336 4234
Baby, toddler and baby and toddler trolleys. Baby food, toiletries and nappies. 'Parent and Child' parking near entrance.

Ferry Road
Tel: 315 4970
Large store with coffee shop and petrol station. 'Parent and Child' parking. All combinations of trolleys available. Nappy-changing facilities and toilets.

Gyle Shopping Centre
Tel: 317 1197
Large number of baby, double baby, baby and toddler, toddler and double toddler trolleys. Customer toilets, feeding and changing room to right of entrance within the centre. Post Office within store. Coffee shop with toddler seating areas plus high chairs. Bottle warming. See also Shopping Centres and Markets.

145 Morningside Road
Tel: 447 9955
Car seat, baby, baby and toddler, toddler and double toddler trolleys.

30 New Swanston, Oxgangs
Tel: 445 5647
Baby, baby and toddler, double toddler and toddler trolleys. Free food warming in coffee shop. Free nappies and wipes in changing facilities. Private breastfeeding area.

4 Piersfield Terrace
Tel: 661 5661
Baby, double baby, baby and toddler, double toddler and toddler trolleys. Coffee shop with children's play area. Breastfeeding permitted. Customer toilets and nappy-changing room in front of check-outs.

Sainsbury's
Web: www.sainsbury.co.uk
Web: Sainsburystoyou.com
Internet shopping available: £5 delivery charge.
Sainsbury's have introduced novelty trolleys with toy cars on the front of them, available in some stores. Ideal for older toddlers and children – and parents with good steering capabilities!
185 Craigleith Road
Tel: 332 0704
Full range of trolleys. Store stocks some nursery equipment, baby and toddler food, nappies, wipes etc. Also stocks range of children's clothing and some toys. Customer toilets and feeding and changing room (M&F) behind check-out area. Room is pretty small – and has been unsuitable for use on several occasions; this can be due to previous users, not just the store.
Café:
f-ff, high chairs (3).
Range of snacks and meals. Secure trolley lock-up area at café entrance (on the left) keeps trolleys etc out of the restaurant. Small unsupervised children's play area.

Meadowbank Retail Park
Tel: 656 9377
Large number of baby, double baby, baby and toddler, toddler and trolleys for children with disabilities. Full range of baby and toddler foods and nappies. Limited range of toys. Nappy-changing facilities. Toilets behind checkouts.

Straiton Retail Park
Tel: 448 2181
Full range of trolleys. Large store, with clothing section, toys, large selection of nappies, wipes, creams and some baby equipment. Baby and toddler food. Nappy-changing facilities behind checkouts near foyer. Café, welcomes breastfeeding.

Cameron Toll Shopping Centre, Lady Rd
Tel: 666 5200
Large range of car seat, baby, double baby, baby and toddler, and toddler trolleys. Large store with clothes, toys, lighting and bakery offering personalised cakes. Two aisles

of baby food and toiletries. Wide, easily accessible aisles. Store can provide customer helpers for assistance around store and/or to car park. Nappy-changing room on right, off clothing sales area. Nappies and wipes available at Customer Service desk.

Scotmid Co-operative Society
Many stores throughout the city and outlying areas, ranging from small local shops, to larger stores. Facilities vary from store to store.
37-41 Boswall Parkway
Boswall   EH5 2BR
Tel: 552 2132

132 Bruntsfield Place
Bruntsfield   EH10 4ER
Tel: 228 4015

230 Oxgangs Road North
Colinton Mains   EH13 9BQ
Tel: 441 2915

236-240 Crewe Road North
Crewe Rd   EH15 9LW
Tel: 552 4251

1 Drum Brae Avenue
Drum Brae   EH12 8TE
Tel: 317 7152

Drumbrae - Alldays
40 Duart Crescent   EH4 7JP
Tel: 339 5181

Easter Rd
112 Easter Road   EH7 5RH
Tel: 661 5742

Ferry Road
113 Ferry Rd   EH6 4ET
Tel: 555 1946

Superstore
236 Gorgie Road
Gorgie   EH11 2PL
Tel: 346 7859

21 Gracemount Drive
Gracemount   EH16 6RP
Tel: 664 1663

76 Duke Street
Leith   EH6 8HL
Tel: 555 4000

6 Bath Street
Portobello   EH15 1EY
Tel: 657 1952

283 Calder Road
Sighthill   EH
Tel: 443 6139

56-60 Hamilton Place
Stockbridge   EH3 5AZ
Tel: 220 3657

37-39 Raeburn Place
Stockbridge EH4 1HX
Tel: 332 9791

34 Warrender Park Road
Warrender Park   EH9 1HH
Tel: 229 8195

Somerfield
Web: www.somerfield.co.uk
Baby and toddler trolleys. Range of nappies, food etc.

114 Dalry Road
Tel: 337 6376   EH11 2EZ

36 Cramond Road South
Davidson's Mains
Tel: 336 4234

100 Gorgie Park Road   EH11 2QL
Tel: 337 9451

43 Pennywell Road   EH4 4DR
Tel: 332 9666

49 Shandwick Place EH2 4SD
Tel: 221 5280

Tesco
Web: www.tesco.com.
Internet shopping available: delivery charge, variable dependent on the day you order. Also catalogue shopping – pick up copies in-store.

7 Broughton Road
Tel: 456 8400
Parent and Child parking spaces. Car park monitored to prevent abuse of designated spaces
Baby, single and double toddler trolleys. Some baby and toddler trolleys.
Range of baby food, wipes and nappies. Also carry a decent range of organic food for babies and others, fresh fruit/veg, and frozen foods. Customer toilets and feeding/changing room to rear of checkouts.
14 Colinton Mains Drive
Tel: 470 7400
15 Drumbryden Road, Wester Hailes
Tel: 465 2500
Meadow Place Road
Tel: 470 0700
Baby, baby and toddler, double baby and double toddler trolleys. 'Parent and Child' parking.
Huge choice of nappies, including reusables, plus accessories. Calpol, karvol, teething remedies etc. Large range of baby food plus bowls, spoons, drinking cups. You could buy every party requisite here from the cake, party-bag fillers, present, wrapping paper to the party dress/outfit. Good selection of affordable clothing for babies up to teens. Help with packing and assistance to car. On-line shopping (see web site to check delivery area), for a £3.99-£5.99 fee, has the added bonus of all your purchases delivered not just to your door step but into your kitchen.
Toilets, nappy-changing room and feeding room on right behind checkouts. Café (not 24 hrs) with 5 high chairs, ample space for pushchairs or trolleys, bottles warmed, breastfeeding welcome, baby food available to buy, kids' lunch boxes.

CLOTHING

Most department stores, an increasing number of larger supermarkets, and some chemists stock baby and children's clothes, underwear and socks. Not all are listed here, as we have tried to include those with a good range, exciting stock, competitive prices, or those which have something special to offer.
Apart from the problems of finding the right style, fabric and colour – at the right price – there are two main bugbears when shopping for children's clothes: the lack of a standard sizing system and seasonal availability.
The large department stores and major brand names all have different sizing systems. Most are still based on the now out-of-date British Standard, with manufacturers

adding their own allowances for growth, comfort etc. The age range given to sizes is therefore only a rough guide. Most shops will refund if an item is unsuitable, but always hold on to the receipts.

Some of the smaller shops in this section will make-to-measure, at little or no extra charge for children with specific needs.

Clothes for low birth weight babies (from about 3lbs) are available from some department stores or by post (see Shopping from Home), although more stores are now stocking such ranges. For children's ski wear, see Outdoor and Ski Shops.

This section also includes details of dancewear (although many dance teachers do sell leotards, shoes etc), kilts, schoolwear and shoes.

We have tried to give exact opening hours for these stores, but it's always wise to phone ahead if you are making a special trip, as this information may change.

BABY & CHILDREN'S CLOTHES

Adams Children's Wear

Brightly coloured clothing for girls and boys including outerwear. Also stock baby bodysuits, scratch-mitts (larger sized than most), sleepsuits, padders, hats, gloves etc. Competitively priced.

Unit 11-13
64 St James' Centre   FH1 3SR
Tel: 556 0692
Opening hours: Mon-Wed, Fri-Sat 9.00-17.30; Thu 9.00-19.00; Sun 12.00-16.00.

Unit 26
Cameron Toll Shopping Centre   EH16 5PB
Tel: 664 0776
Opening hours: Mon-Wed, Fri-Sat 9.00-17.30; Thu 9.00-21.00; Sun 11.00-17.00.

Unit 7
Fort Retail Park
Newcraighall   EH15 3HS
Tel: 669 6547
Opening hours: Mon-Tue, Thu-Fri 10.00-20.00; Wed 10.00-17.30; Sat 9.00-17.30; Sun 11.00-17.00.

Ocean Terminal Shopping Centre
Leith   EH6 6JJ
Tel: 555 2728
Opening hours: Mon-Wed, Fri 10.00-21.00; Thu, Sat 10.00-22.00; Sun 10.00-17.00.

Asda Wal-Mart

100 The Jewel
Edinburgh   EH15 3AR
Tel: 669 9151
Opening times: 24 hours
Attractive, reasonably priced babies and children's clothes and footwear. Bibs, padders, underwear, sleepwear, casual clothes, schoolwear and outdoorwear. Also has toys and a café.

Baggins

12 Deanhaugh Street
Stockbridge
Tel: 315 2011
Web: www.bagginsonline.co.uk
Opening times: Tue-Fri 10.00-17.00; Sat 10.00-14.00.
Access: awkward – down a flight of steps to a basement. Personalised clothes for clubs, playgroups, nursery schools etc. Small orders welcomed. A great range of dressing-up clothes and accessories like wands, wings, hats etc. Outfits include: fairies, clowns, spacemen, firemen, tigers, belly dancers, nurses, Indians etc. Toys for all ages. Toys for children to play with while you browse.

BhS

64 Princes St
Tel: 226 2621
Basement: good range of everyday wear for babies and children, at reasonable prices. Casual wear, outdoor wear, underwear, footwear and special occasion clothes. See Department Stores.

Blackadder Gallery

5 Raeburn Place
Stockbridge   EH4 1HU
Tel: 332 4605
Opening times: Mon-Sat 10-17.30.

Stock t-shirts, sleepsuits, tops, hats, mitts etc. Most have quirky logos or are embellished. Stockist of Pesky Kids, Birkenstock and Daisy Roots.

Blessings & Blossoms

132 St Johns Road   EH12 8AX
Tel: 334 8322
Web: www.blessingsandblossoms.co.uk
Opening times: Mon-Sat 09.30-17.00.
This Aladdin's cave in Corstorphine stocks quality traditional and designer clothes and shoes for casual day wear or special events. Everything from flower girl,

bridesmaid, party and communion dresses plus page boy outfits can be made to order by in house designer Pauline Mullanif, or you can choose from the wide range in the shop. There are also christening outfits plus wonderful ideas for baby gifts. Although the shop is small and there are a couple of steps to navigate it is well worth a visit. Breastfeeding and nappy changing, plus toilet available for emergencies. The train in the window is always an attraction plus there are toys to keep the little ones occupied while you browse Online shopping available via website.

Bliss
111A Broughton Street   EH1 3RZ
Tel:556 3311
Opening times: Mon-Sat 10.00-17.30.
Small but lovely range of dresses, tops, t-shirts,sleepsuits etc. Also stock Oriental-style slippers, bags, purses etc. Ranges include Daisy Roots, Pesky Kids, Birkenstock etc.

Boots the Chemist
Web: www.boots.com
Full range of own brand (Mini Mode) baby and children's clothing, up to 6 yrs. Clothes tend to be pretty hardwearing, in bold, bright colours. Many in 100% cotton. Also do baby range for sensitive skins. Boots also stocks a range of clothing for low birth weight babies ('up to 2.3 kg' and 'up to 4.5 kg').

Available from:
101 Princes Street
Tel: 225 8331
Opening times: Mon-Wed, Fri-Sat 8.00-18.30; Thu 8.00-20.00; Sun 10.00-18.00.
Clothing on 1st floor

Craigleith Retail Park
Tel: 332 6114
Opening Times: Mon-Fri 9.00-20.00; Sat 9.00-18.00; Sun 10.00-18.00.

The Fort
Tel: 669 4428
Opening times: Mon-Fri 9.00-20.00; Sat 9.00-18.00; Sun 10.00-18.00.
Clothing also available at other selected stores, but not the Gyle. Osh Kosh stocked in Princes St store.See also Department Stores

Carojacs
4 Howard Street   EH3 5JP
Tel/fax: 556 1242
Email: sales@carojacs.com
Web: www.carojacs.com
Opening Times: Mon-Sat 9.00-17.00.
Small shop near Canonmills which sells a lovely selection of clothing and accessories for babies and children, including blankets, 'buggy bags', pullovers, trousers, hats, mittens, t-shirts etc etc. There's an area to the rear of the shop where fleeces etc are made. Clothes (for both children and adults alike) are made from various fabrics, the patterns of which are just that little bit different.

Debenhams
Wide range of clothing for babies and children (3-14 yrs), including own-brand ranges (Trader, Casual Club and Maine), and designer names. Other names include Babbleboom, Tigerlilly and Jasper Conran for babies. For boys and girls, ranges include Barbie for Girls, JCB, IDX for Girls (7-14 yrs) and Red Herring, as well as those previously listed. See also Department Stores.

Available from:
109-112 Princes Street
Tel: 225 1320
Opening times: Mon-Wed, Fri 9.30-18.00;Thu 9.30-20.00; Sat 9.00-18.00; Sun 11.00-17.00.Times may extend during Festival.
Children's clothing situated on lower ground floor.

Ocean Terminal
Ocean Drive
Tel: 553 8100
Opening hours: Mon-Fri 10.00-20.00; Sat 10.00-19.00; Sun 11.00-18.00.
Slightly smaller range, but carries the same brands as Princes St branch.

The Disney Store
Selection of clothing for under 5s featuring Disney characters, including sleepwear. Also stock Disney character costumes and dressing up wear. See Toys.

Available from:
18 Princes Street
Tel: 557 2772
Opening times: Mon-Wed, Fri-Sat 9.00-19.00; Thu 8.00-20.00; Sun 18.00-18.00.

Gyle Shopping Centre
Tel: 339 4944
Opening times: Mon, Tue, Wed 9.00-20.00; Thu, Fri 9.00-21.00; Sat 9.00-18.00; Sun 10.00-18.00

Gap, Gap Kids & Baby Gap
Offers fashionable babywear 0-4yrs, with extensive newborn collection. Also stock daywear for 2-13 yrs. Range changes regularly.

Fort Kinnaird
Tel: 657 5613
Opening times: Mon-Fri: 10.00-20.00, Sat 9.30-18.00; Sun 10.00-18.00.

Gyle Centre
Tel: 339 5972
Opening times: Mon-Wed, Fri 9.30-20.00; Thu 9.30-21.00; Sat 9.00-18.00; Sun 10.00-18.00.

131-133 Princes Street
Tel: 220 3303
Opening times: Mon-Wed, Fri, Sat 9.00-18.00; Thu 9.00-19.00; Sun 11.00-18.00.
Access: direct access from Princes St. Lift, on left, at rear of shop. Nappy changing facilities.

Ocean Terminal
Tel: 553 6744
Opening times: Mon-Fri 10.00-20.00; Sat 10.00-19.00; Sun 11.00-18.00.

Jenners – Kids at Jenners
48 Princes Street
Tel: 225 2442
Extensive range of quality and designer children's clothing, 0-8 yrs. Ranges include low birth weight baby clothing & beautiful Christening gowns. See Department Stores.

Mackays
www.mackaysstores.co.uk
Good range of affordable baby and children's wear. Lots of co-ordinating outfits, sleepwear, leisure wear, underwear, padders and pram shoes, and clothes for outdoors and school. Staff tend to be friendly and helpful.

Children's wear available from:
Unit 5
Gyle Shopping Centre   EH12 9JT
Tel: 538 8765
Opening times: Mon-Wed, Fri 9.00-20.00; Thu 9.00- 21.00; Sat 9.00-18.00; Sun 10.00-18.00.

Mamas and Papas
Craigleith Retail Park
Tel: 0870 830 7703
Web: www.mamasandpapas.co.uk
Opening times: Mon-Fri, Sat 9.30-18.00; Thu 9.30-19.00; Sun 11.00-17.00.
Stylish baby clothing, up to age 6 mths. Outfits and separates, all in subtle colours. Small range of contemporary designed maternity wear. Also stock prams and ranges of co-ordinating nursery equipment and accessories.

Marks and Spencer
Good range of durable baby and children's clothes, many in 100% cotton. Underwear, sleepwear, leisure wear, and party clothes, as well as clothes for outdoors and school. Also stock dressing up outfits, although these tend to be for over 5s, and link with seasons (such as Hallowe'en) or recent film releases (recent years' outfits have included Narnia and Harry Potter). Range of padders, pram shoes and shoes (up to sizes 39/40). Baby range starts from newborn, with clothing for low birth weight babies.

Available from:
91 Princes Street
Tel: 225 2301
Opening hours: Mon-Wed, Fri 9.00-19.00; Thu 9.00-20.00; Fri 9.00-19.00; Sat 8.30-18.00; Sun 11.00-17.00.

Gyle Shopping Centre
Tel: 317 1333
Opening hours: Mon-Fri 9.00-22.00; Sat 8.00-20.00; Sun 9.00-18.00.

Mothercare
Large selection of own brand clothes for children, from newborn to 10 yrs, including underwear, sleepwear (including sleep gowns), casual and fancy outfits, shoes and outerwear. Also carry a selection of low birth weight clothing. See also Department Stores.

Available from:
The Fort Retail Park
New Craighall Road   EH15 3HH
Tel: 657 4050
Opening hours: Mon-Fri 9.00-21.00; Sat 9.00-18.00; Sun 10.00-18.00.

Hermiston Gait Retail Park
Tel: 453 1383
Opening times: Mon, Wed, Fri 9.00-20.00; Tue, Thu 9.30-20.00; Sat 9.00-18.00 Sun 10.00-1700.

Next

Babies (0-2 yrs), boys' and girls' clothing from 3-10 yrs. Contemporary, hard-wearing separates and casuals in vibrant colours. Underwear, footwear, outdoor wear, many in 100% cotton. Also stock party wear and some dressing up outfits. Schoolwear available via home shopping by catalogue or online. See Shopping from Home for details.

Available from:
107-109 Princes Street
Tel: 225 9290
Opening times: Mon-Wed, Fri, Sat 9.00-18.00; Thu 9.00-19.30; Sun 11.00-18.00.
Children's wear located in basement. Lift access.
Unit 8
Fort Retail Park
Tel: 657 1530
Opening times: Mon-Wed, Fri 9.30-20.00; Thu 9.30-21.00; Sat 9.00-18.00; Sun 10.00-18.00.
Gyle Shopping Centre
Tel: 339 5989
Opening times: Mon-Wed, Fri 9.00-20.00; Thu 9.00-21.00; Sat 9.00-18.00; Sun 9.30-18.00.
St James' Centre
Tel: 558 9590
Opening times: Mon-Wed 9.00-17.30; Thu 9.00-19.30; Fri, Sat 9.00-18.00; Sun 12.00-17.00.

Okaïdï

Unit 31
Ocean Terminal
Ocean Drive EH6 6JJ
Tel: 561 1423
Opening Times: Mon-Fri 10.00-20.00; Sat 10.00-18.00; Sun 11.-18.00.
Range of chic and funky Continental children's clothing. They have 2 brands, Obaïbï (for 0-2yrs) and Okaïdï, for children up to the ages of 14. The sizing is slight, so it's best to try the clothing on before you buy.

Pine and Old Lace

46 Victoria Street
Tel: 225 3287
Opening times: Mon-Sat 10.30-17.00, closed Wed
Phone to check if you are making a special trip, as this is a one-woman shop. Stock always includes antique Christening gowns. Shop not accessible to double pushchairs.

The Royal Edinburgh Repository and Self Aid Society

23a Castle Street
Tel: 220 1187
Opening times: Mon-Thu 9.30-17.00; Fri 9.30-16.30; Sat 9.30-16.30
The Society encourages people, particularly those in low income groups, to work in their own homes, using skills such as knitting, sewing, toy-making etc. The Edinburgh shop sells a unique collection of handmade articles, including beautiful baby and toddler hand-knitted items, handmade smock dresses etc, as well as toys. The shop also sells traditional old-fashioned items such as shawls and sleeping gowns. Special orders can be taken. All the money from the sale of goods is returned to the society members.

DANCEWEAR

Some of Edinburgh's department stores stock dance or keep-fit wear. Some may only have a basic stock, while other may have quite a selection – especially of ballet-related products (John Lewis always has a pretty good range). However, as with all things, it does pay to shop around. Some dance teachers also sell shoes and/or leotards, so it's worth while asking if your child is starting a class.

Dancewear

182 Rose Street
Tel: 226 5457
Email: sales@dancewear-edinburgh.co.uk
Web: www.dancewear-edinburgh.co.uk
Opening times: Mon-Wed, Fri 9.30-17.15; Thu 9.30-18.00; Sat 9.30-17.00; Sun 11.00-16.00

This shop provides a patient and knowledgeable service for children of all ages. Competitive pricdes for ballet shoes (satin and leather), tap, Highland, Irish and jazz. They specialise in pointe toe fitting for all ages.
They also sell leotards, tights, catsuits, salsa wear, flamenco wear, ballet skirts, cross-over cardigans, tu-tus and ballet giftware. Online catalogue - no online ordering though.

KILTS

Edinburgh has several good options when it comes to shopping for kilts. There are specialist shops, although shops such as Aitken and Niven, Jenners, Ortak, and John Lewis stock kilts, tartanwear and/or accessories.

Proper kilt pleats should fold back behind the previous pleat: this is what gives that wonderful swing, but it also makes them rather heavy and very expensive, as so much fabric is used. However, if you do choose to buy a full kilt, you will have a family heirloom, which can be handed down the generations. A reasonable alternative is a 'half kilt', in which not all the pleats are full, but it still swings well and looks good. Many shops also sell kilted skirts off the peg. Small kilts can have straps or a bodice to hold them up, and you can get jabot shirts with elastic around the waist to cover this up.

Shops which sell made-to-measure kilts usually have books of tartan (you may need to choose a tartan with a small set for a small kilt). These stores can usually help you link your surname to a specific sept or clan. They can also give the kilt a good 'wrap around' and a generous hem to let down. Some will change the wrapover side for different sexes.

You can really go overboard with the accompanying regalia, such as: jackets, shirts (with jabot or bow tie), sporran, shoes, socks, flashes – and for teenagers and adults, a sgian dubh. A kilt can also look good with a Fair Isle, Arran or Shetland jumper, or just a plain white shirt and socks. As your children get older, you may find teenagers turn to the trendy alternative look of big boots, pushed-down socks and t-shirts!

What is worn under the kilt is anyone's guess (except toddlers can't resist showing everybody!!). If you only need a kilt for your child (or other family members) for a special occasion, a good alternative is to hire one.

Hector Russell
95 Princes Street
Edinburgh   EH2 2ER
Tel: 225 3315
Fax: 226 3923
E-mail:
HectorRussell@princesstreetstore.freeserve.co.uk

137-141 High Street
Edinburgh
EH1 1SG
Tel: 558 1254

These stores stock boys' kilts and trews and girls' kilted skirts, as well as: kilts, socks, sock flashes, belts, sgian dubh,

shirts, andshoes. Stores also offer a made-to-measure service for children and dancers.

Hector Russel do not currently hire children's outfits, but they do sell a range of off-the-peg outfits, such as kilts, trousers etc. Kilt-hire for adults is available from 95 Princes St. Online mail-order service.

Highland Laddie
6 Hutchison Terrace EH14 1QB
Tel: 455 7505
Complete outfits sold. All accessories available, jackets, shirts, brogues and shoes, sporrans etc.

MAKE YOUR OWN

Edinburgh has an excellent choice of wool and fabric shops, and you always end up with an 'exclusive' outfit. The shops listed below are those which we feel have something special to offer, and those which are more 'out of the way'.

John Lewis and The Cloth Shop probably have the largest choice of pattern books and paper patterns. In these tomes, you'll find everything from maternity wear to pyjamas, dressing gowns and dressing up outfits. 'Teen' dolls can also have an extensive wardrobe to match your own, and there are usually popular soft toy patterns available.

There are many wool shops scattered around the suburbs and most stock baby wools. Pingouin and Rowan have children's knitting patterns in up to the minute designs and Pingouin also has a baby/toddler magazine. Paton's have a wide range of knitting patterns for small babies, starting at 14".

The Cloth Shop - Fabric Warehouse
169 Bonnington Road   EH6 5BQ
Tel: 554 7733
Opening times: Mon-Wed, Fri-Sat 9.30-17.00; Thu 9.30-19.00 Sun 11.00-16.00.

Large warehouse-style shop, with a fantastic selection of dress, curtain and upholstery fabric, and all the haberdashery that goes along with it. Stencil kits and cushion pads available, along with some great tulles and seasonally printed fabrics for dressing up clothes. Small customer toilets near the children's play area. Car parking.

The Embroidery Shop
51 William Street
Tel: 225 8642
Opening times: Mon-Fri 10.00-17.00; Sat 10.00-16.00.
Embroidery supplies, birth sampler kits, lace and tapestry supplies. Also stock patchwork and quilting fabrics, patterns and notions. Specialist shop which also runs classes.

The Finishing Touch
17 St Patrick Square   EH8 9EZ
Tel: 667 0914
Opening times: Mon-Sat 10.00-17.30.
Huge range of buttons in all shapes, sizes and colours. Novelty greetings cards, wrapping paper and ribbons. Every imaginable utensil and ingredient for cake decorating. Lots of helpful hints and advice. See also Birthdays and Celebrations and Hiring.

Jenners
48 Princes Street
Tel: 225 2442
4th floor: extensive range of haberdashery, knitting wools and patterns, and needlework kits. Also have a good range of stencil kits and card-making accessories.. See Department Stores.

John Lewis
St James' Centre
Tel: 556 9121
Fabric & Haberdashery: wide choice of fabrics, from cheap and cheerful prints to sumptuous velvets. Stock sheeting, quilted fabrics, braiding, ribbons, buttons, motifs, lace etc. Craft materials such as beads, felt, fur fabric, tapestry and embroidery yarns, craft and needlework kits including samplers. Dolls' house kits, knitting wools and patterns, sewing and knitting machines and craft books.
Soft furnishings: Some great children's patterns, plus 'blackout' curtain lining, blinds. Also wipe-clean fabric for e.g. tablecovers.

Mandors
131 East Claremont Street EH7 4JA
Tel: 558 3888
Web: www.mandors.co.uk
Opening times: Mon-Sat 9.00-17.30; Sun 12.00-17.00
Stock good range of dressmaking fabrics, for everyday wear through to bridalwear, faux fur etc etc. There's also a good stock of haberdashery, such as ribbons and finishings. Mandors stock patterns.

MATERNITY CLOTHING & GOODS
More and more stores are offering maternity clothing which can reflect your usual dress-sense: no longer are mums-to-be forced to wear white-collared tent dresses. You can have anything from sleek suits to leopard print trousers, and all points in between. Maternity clothes now tend to be comfortable, fashionable and even flattering. See also Make Your Own, Shopping from Home, Hiring and Baby and Children's Clothes.
It's sensible to take time to pamper yourself, especially when pregnant. It keeps your own sense of identity and it's a great excuse for some 'you' time! We've tried to include some ideas of how and where you can get some pampering.
Remember though, don't use essential oils while pregnant, and it's recommended to keep away from nut oil bases, if you're thinking about massage oils etc. This also goes for baby massage/pampering products – you'd be surprised how many have almond oil bases, and how many assistants don't recognise that as a nut!
In general, the only 'safe' essential oils to use with young children are lavender and chammomile; if in doubt, seek professional advice.

The Body Shop
Body Shop range includes all kinds of lotions, gels and pampering items for mums and mums-to-be, including cooling leg gel, massagers, and moisture-rich body creams, which intensify your skin's moisture content (might reduce stretch marks!!) As well as their tried and tested cocoa butter stick, the African Spa range is rich in cocoa butter and has no essential oils in it.
Selection changes throughout the year – there's usually special offers around holiday times.
Gyle Centre
Tel: 538 3333
Opening times: Mon, Tue, Wed 9.30-20.00; Thu, Fri 9.30-21.00; Sat 9.00-18.00; Sun 10.00-18.00.
Ocean Terminal
Tel: 555 4523
Opening times: Mon-Fri 10.00-20.00; Sat 10.00-19.00; Sun 11.00-18.00.
Princes Mall
Tel: 556 2641
Opening hours: Mon-Wed, Fri, Sat 9.00-18.00; Thu 9.00-19.00; Sun 11.00-17.00.
90a Princes St
Tel: 220 6330
Opening times: Mon-Sat 9.00-18.00; Thu 9.00-20.00; Sun 11.00-17.30.

Boots the Chemist
Web: www.boots.com
Stocks a range of maternity accessories, nursing equipment, including washable breast pads. Babitens available to hire.
Craigleith Retail Park
Tel: 332 6114
Opening times: Mon-Fri 9.00-20.00; Sat 9.00-18.00; Sun 10.30-17.30.
The Fort
Tel: 669 4428
Opening times: Mon-Fri 9.00-20.00; Sat 9.00-18.00; Sun 10.00-17.30.
Gyle Shopping Centre
Tel: 317 1288
Opening times: Mon, Tue, Wed 9.30-20.00; Thu, Fri 9.30-21.00; Sat 9.00-18.00; Sun 10.00-18.00.
101 Princes Street
Tel: 225 8331
Opening times: Mon-Sat 9.00-18.00; Thu 9.00-19.30; Sun 12.00-17.00.
Also stocks some maternity bras.

Crabtree and Evelyn (London) Ltd
4 Hanover Street
Tel: 226 2478
Opening times: Mon-Sat 10.00-18.00 (Thu 10.00-19.00 May-Xmas); Sun 12.00-17.00.
Stepping into the shop, you're greeted by the sweet aroma of soaps, shampoos, bath gels and oils for mums in the tub. Creams, lotions, brushes and combs for after. The range includes traditional fragrances as well as more contemporary blends. There's also a range for dads. Small selection of soaps, bubble bath, lotions and creams for children. Also sells room fragrance products.

Dorothy Perkins
Web: www.dorothyperkins.co.uk
Range of co-ordinated maternity separates for both formal and casualwear. Selection of dresses also available. Available from:
Unit 24
Cameron Toll Shopping Centre
Lady Road   EH16 4TG
Tel: 664 7279

Debenhams
109-112 Princes Street
Tel: 718 2274
Concession on 1st floor.

Unit 4a
Fort Retail Park
Newcraighall Road   EH15 3RH
Tel: 657 4351

Unit 17
Gyle Shopping Centre EH12 9JR
Tel: 317 1693

Ocean Terminal
Ocean Drive EH6 6JJ
Tel: 554 6704

30-31 Princes StreetEH2 2BY
Tel: 556 7444

Unit 34-36
St James' Centre EH1 3SL
Tel: 556 5076

Formes
4 Howe Street
Tel : 0131 225 9777
Web: www.formes.com
Opening hours: Mon-Wed, Fri-Sat 10.00-18.00; Thu 10.00-19.00; Sun 12.00-17.00.
The emphasis here is on contemporary styling – so plenty of strong lines. Pricing towards the upper end of high street prices.

Frasers
145 Princes Street
Tel: 225 2472
2nd floor: maternity and nursing bras. Bra fitting service. See Department Stores.

John Lewis
St James' Centre
Tel: 556 9121
Ground floor: maternity tights
1st: casual co-ordinated separates and some more formal suits and dresses. Good range of swimsuits and maternity bras. Helpful, trained staff. See Department Stores.

Mamas and Papas
Craigleith Retail Park
Tel: 0870 830 7703
Web: www.mamasandpapas.co.uk
Opening times: Mon-Wed, Fri 9.30-18.00; Thu 9.30-19.00; Sat 9.00-18.00; Sun 11.00-17.00.
Capsule range of contemporary designed maternity wear. Also nursery accessories and baby clothing up to 6 mths.

Marks and Spencer

Stock maternity underwear and hosiery. Nursing bras also available in the lingerie departments: bra fitting service available. For times, see Department Stores.
Available at:
91 Princes Street
Tel: 225 2301

Gyle Shopping Centre
Tel: 317 1333

Mothercare

Selection of Mothercare branded clothes for both everyday wear and special occasions. Swimwear, nightwear and maternity/nursing bras, plus accessories, such as breast pumps and breast pads. See Department Stores.
Available at:
Fort Retail Park
Tel: 657 4050

Mothercare World
Hermiston Gait Retail Park
Tel: 453 1383

SCHOOL UNIFORMS

Many stores stock skirts, pinafores, shorts, trousers, blazers, shirts and socks in traditional school colours. Their stock is most extensive in May, June and Jul, but most have a reduced stock through the other months. Stores include: Asda-Walmart, BhS, Frasers, John Lewis, Marks & Spencer, Next, Sinsbury's and Woolworths, but there are other outlets.

Aitken and Niven

Web: www.aitken-niven.co.uk
Long-established Edinburgh retailer, which stocks schoolwear, and sportswear, including uniforms for Edinburgh's independent schools.

234 Queensferry Road   EH4 2BP
Tel: 467 8825

6 Falcon Road West
Morningside   EH10 4AQ
Tel: 477 3922
This stores also stocks school shoes, including Start-rite D-H fittings.

Clan House

www.clanhouseofedinburgh.com
Stockists of uniforms, sportswear, equipment etc. Also stocks most Edinburgh school badges to sew on.

117 Grove Street   EH3 8AA
Tel: 229 6857

28-30 Morningside Road   EH10 4DA
Tel: 447 3414

SHOES

Many mothers think that retailers put children's shoe departments in basements or on 1st floors simply to irritate them and to add to the overall hassle of the shoe-buying trip. In fact, it is for safety – to ensure that junior does not take a trip straight out the door into the street when asked to take a few steps to see if the shoes fit!
Many stores now operate a ticketing system: it's best to take a ticket before looking around. Try to avoid Saturdays and school holidays if possible, as these departments tend to be particularly busy.
The shops below with an asterisk mark (*) after their name are listed in the Children's Foot Health Register, whose aims are endorsed by the British Medical Association, and other health, shoes and chiropody associations. The CFHR lists shops which promise to: stock children's shoes in full and half length sizes from infants size 3 to size 51/2 for boys and girls; stock 4 width fittings; employ trained staff to measure both feet and carefully fit shoes at time of sale.

This list is updated annually and is available from:

The Children's Foot Health Register

PO Box 123
Banbury SO
Oxon   OX15 6WB
Tel: 01295 738 726
Email: info@shoe-shop.org.uk
You should enclose a 9"x6" SAE.

Some libraries keep a copy for reference. It also lists the full aims of the register, useful information on foot care and lists footwear retailers throughout Britain, who promise to abide by the register's aims.
Don't be shy where your child's feet are concerned. If you don't think a shoe fits, ask to have it checked by another fitter. Complain to management if you feel standards in a shop have slipped. Several shops which sell nursery equipment also sell soft shoes for babies and toddlers.

The following shops sell good quality 'good brand' names in width fittings.

In the CIty

Aitken and Niven
6 Falcon Street West
Morningside EH10 4AQ
Tel: 225 1461
Start-rite shoes and slippers.

Clarks Shoe Shop*
79 Princes Street
Tel: 220 1261
Opening times: Mon-Wed, Fri 9.30-17.30; Thu 9.30-19.30; Sat 9.00-18.00; Sun 11.00-17.00.
Good selection. A range of pre-walking shoes, available in sizes 3-41/2 and width fittings E-H. As in all Clarks Shops, the Toddler Team Club is available for first shoe customers. A picture is taken of the child in their first 'new shoes', a fitting record is also provided, a competition entry and a booklet outlining general foot care.
Also has an 'odd shoe service'. Once your child's foot has been accurately measured, you select a suitable shoe (most styles are available). This information is then sent to head Office and a pair is sent to the shop in approx 3 weeks. These shoes cost 25% more than a standard pair. For entertainment, there's wall Lego, books and car rides (profits from which go to charity). Children may use staff toilet if accompanied by a parent and a member of staff.
Also at:
Unit 3A
Cameron Toll Shopping Centre   EH16 5BP*
Tel: 664 9111
Opening hours: Mon-Wed, Fri: 9.00-19.00; Thu 9.00-20.00; Sat 9.00-18.00; Sun 10.00-17.00.
Unit 25
Fort Retail Park   EH15 3RD
Tel: 669 1190
Opening times: Mon-Wed 9.00-20.00.
Gyle Shopping Centre   EH12 9EB*
Tel: 317 1456
Opening times: Mon-Wed, Fri: 9.30-20.00; Thu 9.30-21.00; Sat 9.00-18.00; Sun 10.00-18.00.

Harvey Nichols*
30-34 St Andrews Square   EH2 3AD
Tel: 524 8388

Buckle My Shoe stockists

John Lewis
St James' Centre
Tel: 556 9121
Dept on 2nd floor which offers a timed appointment service during peak times. Stocks Start-rite, Clarks, Buckle My Shoe, and various continental and designer brands, such as Elefantin and Timberland. Offers a full range of shoes, slippers, dance shoes, wellies and sandals.

Russell and Bromley Ltd
106 Princes Street   EH2 3AA
Tel: 225 7444
Opening times: Mon-Wed, Fri, Sat 9.30-18.00; Thu 9.30-19.30; Sun 11.00-17.00.
Extensive range of children's shoes. Staff are fully trained in fitting. Children's dept is on the 1st floor. Stock Clark's, Start-rite, Kickers and many more makes of shoe. If required, assistance is given by staff to access it with, for example, a pram. Children may use the staff toilet in an emergency. Accessible by double pushchairs. Also stock wellies and slippers. The colourful carousel horses always attract under 5s attention!
If special help is required when making purchases, the store advises that 'back to school' periods are best avoided, as it's an extremely busy time: otherwise, please phone branch in advance.

Shoos
8 Teviot Place
Tel: 220 4626
Opening times: Mon-Sat 9.30-17.30.
Access: direct from street
Start-rite main stockist with a comprehensive range of shoes and boots in up to 6 width fittings, starting from baby size 2. Also stock slippers, wellies, sandals, canvas shoes and leather trainers in width fittings. Fully trained staff, with a member of the Society of Shoefitters usually present. All on ground level with toilet facilities. Start-rite odd shoe service.

Close to home

Wee Masons*
90 High Street   EH41 3ET
Haddington
Tel: 01620 825600

W L Morrison*
213 High Street
Linlithgow   EH49 7EN
Tel: 01506 842 923
Email: cc@fittingexperience.com

BICYCLES

See Travel & Transport: Cycling for general information on cycling with children.

Child Seats and Equipment
Most shops will fit a child seat for nothing, or for a minimal charge if you have purchased it at their store. Do not lose any of the nuts and bolts, as some are unique and irreplaceable.

The addition of a child seat will obviously affect the handling and stability of your bike, as well as placing a greater strain on it, so keep it well maintained, especially the brakes and the wheels.

Rear Child Seats
The best rear child seats are made from high-impact, rigid moulded plastic, with headrests to support a child who has fallen asleep. They should also have the following items: a safety harness, footguards and straps to prevent feet getting caught in the rear wheel. If you have a sprung saddle, it makes sense to either cover or replace it, so that little fingers do not get caught. Suitable for children from around the age at which they are able to sit unsupported (usually 6/7 mths) until they get too heavy for the seat. This aspect varies with manufacturer recommendation, but it's usually 22kg approx. up to age 3-4.

Front Child Seats
These are not recommended. The child feels colder than would be the case in a rear-mounted seat, shielded by your body. Also, if a child falls asleep in a front mounted seat, you must use one arm to support the child and ride one-handed, which is unsafe.

Child Trailers
These are two wheeled pushchairs that attach to the rear fork of adult bike. The fixing device allows the adult bike to be laid on its side without tipping the trailer up. Most can carry two children from 9 mths- 5/6 yrs, with the limiting factor being the weight of the children – the maximum combined weight is usually 50 kg. A very young child can also be carried when strapped into a child seat, although this will leave no room for a second child. Most trailers also have a luggage space at the back. Trailers usually come with a rain-and-sun cover and a visibility flag. The best also have quick release wheels and can be folded down for easy carriage in trains, buses and cars. They are fairly expensive, but they do tend to have a high resale value. They also make useful luggage or shopping carriers, long after families have grown up. Makes include: Adams, Burley, Bike Trax.

Compared with a child seat, the child misses the view, feels the bumps more and is right at exhaust height on any road. However, a single adult can take two young children at once, the balance of the adult bicycle is less affected and the trailer may stay upright if the adult bicycle falls over.

Trailercycles
These consist of a special frame, without front wheels and with forks, which attach to an adult bike (or tandem), either at the seat post or rear rack. The child can help with the pedalling, but braking and steering are left to the adult. They are excellent for taking children out cycling in situations where either it would not be safe to let a child cycle independently, or where a child wouldn't be able to cope with the distance or hills. It's also a great way for a child to learn about observing traffic, signalling and road positioning while being safely in the control of an experienced adult. Some models have gears so children can learn how to change gear without having to worry about steering at the same time. The great advantage of trailercycles is their versatility. You can buy a 'seconds' tow hitch, which allows the trailercycle to be quickly swapped between adult bikes. A trailercycle can also be carried easily on trains by simply detaching and storing alongside the adult bike in the cycle storage area. Trailer bikes are suitable for children from 3 or 4 yrs up to around age 9 yrs. Makes include: Bike Trax, Adams, Ally Cat.

You can get conversion kits to alter a regular child's bike to a trailercycle. Obviously, they are much cheaper, but they do not really give satisfactory results.

Tandems
There are several options:

'Junior back' style tandem. These have a frame designed for an adult 'pilot' at the front and a child 'stoker' at the back. A potentially good solution if you are to do a lot of cycling, but they're not very versatile. Makes include: Dawes, Orbit, Thorn, Swallow.

Ordinary tandem fitted with 'kiddy cranks' or crank

shorteners. More versatile than a junior back tandem, as it can easily be converted back to an ordinary tandem again.

The advantage of a tandem over a trailercycle is that a few of them can also be fitted with a rear child seat to carry a very young child, in addition to the older child that is pedalling. The disadvantage is that they are not easy to store or to carry on trains.

Tricycles

A tricycle fitted with one or two child seats at the back can also be a good way of getting the family on the move. Suitable for children from 12 mths to 5 yrs.

Helmets

Though not legally compulsory, a helmet should be an essential piece of equipment for all cyclists. It is important to take your child to the shop to have them fitted properly so they don't wobble. Look for one which has a European or American standard, preferably both as these standards have superseded the British one. To make them more acceptable for children, go for the coolest looking one you can afford! Children who are putting a lot of effort into pedalling will also appreciate one with plenty of ventilation. Makes include: Met, Hamax, Cateye, Specialized, Giro, Bell. Helmets are all 'first impact', so after a serious bash, in an accident or in play, they are damaged and should be replaced.

General Safety

Under no circumstances should you cycle with a baby in a backpack or sling.

Keep children's shoelaces short and tucked away. The same applies to scarves and other loose clothing. Dress children in brightly coloured clothing, so that they are visible to motorists. Think twice before carrying a very restless child. Beware of very cold and wet weather. Make sure that the adult bike is kept in good mechanical order. Especially ensure that the brakes are always working well to cope with the additional weight that the bike will be carrying.

A Good Tip!

It's a good idea to try out some of the more expensive items like trailers or trailercycles before you buy, to make sure that you are happy with the handling and that it's the right bit of gear for you. Try and borrow from another family, or consider hiring for a weekend – you could save yourself an expensive mistake!

Go to a bike shop specialising in trailer bikes or tandems for advice on the best and most suitable equipment to buy.

Bicycle Shops

Alpine Bikes
48 Hamilton Places
Tel: 225 3286
Web: www.alpinebikes.co.uk
Opening times: Mon-Wed, Fri, Sat 9.00-18.00; Thu 9.00-19.00; Sun 12.00-17.00
Adult and child bikes, child seats and helmets, trailer bikes and child trailers. Also stock Gore bikewear, Altura clothing and panniers. Bike spares and repair service with 24 hour turn around. Hires out trailer bikes, child trailers and mountain bikes. Also stock demo bikes.

B.G. Cycles and Blades
48 Portobello High Street
Tel: 657 5832
Web: www.bgcycles.co.uk
Opening times: Mon-Fri 9.00-18.30; Sat 9.00-18.00; Sun 10.00-17.00. Appointments also available out of shop hours – please phone for information.
Adult and child bikes, trailer bikes, child seats and helmets. Also in-line skates. Also repairs and spares – can uplift and deliver bikes for repair or service within a 15-mile radius for a small charge. Hires out mountain bikes (adult only) and skates.

The Bicycle Repair Man
111 Newington Road EH9 1QW
Tel: 667 5959
Email: info@edinburghcyclerepairs.co.uk
Web: www.edinburghcyclerepairs.co.uk
Opening times: Mon-Sat 9.00-17.30; Sun 11.00-17.00.
Adult and child bikes, child seats and helmets, trailer bikes and child trailers. Bike spares and same day repair service.

The Bicycleworks
29-30 Argyle Place
Tel: 228 8820
Opening times: Mon-Fri 8.00-20.00; Sat & Sun 10.00-18.00.
A repair and wheel building shop with a wide range of spares and accessories. Also sells child seats. Instant puncture repairs or tyre replacement. Fast turn around on all other repairs/servicing.

Also at:
3 High Street, Peebles
Tel: 01721 723423

Bike Trax
11 Lochrin Place   EH3 9QX
Tel: 228 6633
Email: info@biketrax.co.uk
Web: www.biketrax.co.uk
Opening times: Summer – Mon-Sat 9.30 -18.00; Sun 12.00-17.00. Winter – Mon-Sat 9.30-17.30; Sun 12.00-17.00.
Adult and child bikes, child seats and helmets, trailer bikes, child trailers, tandems and folding bikes. Dawes, Ridgeback, Giant, Brompton etc. Free after sales service. Bike repair shop will repair any make of bike, including children's bikes. 24 hr turn around where possible – miracles take longer. Free estimates. Free advice on cycle matters, local cycle routes, etc. Also hires out bikes and equipment. Hire before you buy, hire charge deducted from purchase price.

Blackhall Cycles
15 Marischal Place   EH4 3NF
Tel: 538 8580
Web: www.blackhallcycles.co.uk
Opening times: Mon-Sat 9.00-18.00 (closed for lunch 13.00-14.00). Closed Sun.
Stocks Ridgeback adult and child bikes, trailer bikes, child trailers, child seats and helmets and bike spares. Free fitting of child seats if seat bought at shop. Same day repairs and servicing.

Dave's Bicycle Store
39 Argyle Place
Tel: 229 8528
Opening times: Mon-Sat 10.00-18.00. Closed Sun.
Used bikes for adults and children. Trade-ins welcome.

Edinburgh Bicycle Co-operative
5-9 Alvanley Terrace
Whitehouse Loan
Tel: 228 3565
Web: www. edinburgh-bicycle.com
Opening times:
Summer hours – April-Sept: Mon-Fri 10.00-19.00; Sat & Sun 10.00-18.00. Winter hours – Oct-March: Mon-Wed, Fri 10.00-18.00; Thu 10.00-19.00; Sat & Sun 10.00-18.00.
Large selection of approved children's helmets. Child seats

from America that can be detachable or permanently fitted to your cycle. Children are welcome and there are toys to keep them amused while you shop. Free customer newsletters and mail order catalogue available. Repair service. Online shopping available.

Edinburgh Cycle Hire & Cycle Safaris
29 Blackfriars Street
Tel: 556 5560
Email: info@cyclescotland.co.uk
Web: www.cyclescotland.co.uk
Opening times: Summer – daily, 9.00-21.00. Winter – usually daily, 10.00-18.00 (but please phone before setting off).
Sells adult and child bikes, child seats, trailer bikes, child trailers, tandems. Repairs and servicing. Also hires out large selection of adult and child bikes, tandem, trailer bikes, child trailer, child seats etc. Also organises cycle tours, holidays and days out.

Freewheelin'
91 Slateford Road
Tel: 337 2351
Opening times: Mon-Fri 9.30-17.30; Sat 9.30-17.00; Sun 11.00-17.00 (Closed on Sun in Jan-Mar).
Adult and children's bikes, child seats and helmets. Can also order trailer bikes, child trailers and tandems. Spares, servicing and repair service with same/next day turn around.

Great Bikes No Bull
276 Leith Walk
Tel: 467 7775
Web: www.greatbikesnobull.com
Opening times: Mon-Wed, Fri, Sat 9.00-17.30; Thu 9.00-17.30. Closed Sun.
Adult and children's bikes. Full range of safety accessories including child seats and helmets. Christmas Club. Hire before you buy, hire charge deducted from purchase price. In basement, Recycling (Tel: 553 1130) offers reconditioned adult and child bikes guaranteed for 3 months. For details of hiring bikes, email: david@greatbikesnobull.com.

Halfords Stores & Superstores
Web: www.halfords.com
Good selection of children's sit-and-ride toys, trikes, pedal cars and bikes - Apollo and Raleigh. Child seats, spare parts and accessories. Christmas club. Free after sales service. Usually repair bikes bought here, but may occasionally do

small outside repairs. Major repairs in-store. Free fitting of child seat if bike bought at Halfords.

Hermiston Gait Retail Park
39 Cultins Road   EH11 4DF
Tel:442 2430
Opening times: Mon-Fri 9.00-20.00; Sat 9.00-18.00; Sun 10.00-17.00.

Seafield Road East
Leith   EH6 7LD
Tel: 554 7639
Opening times: Mon-Fri 9.00-20.00; Sat 9.00-18.00; Sun 10.00-17.00.

11 Straiton Mains
Straiton   EH20 9PW
Tel: 448 2248
Opening times: Mon-Fri 8.00-20.00; Sat 9.00-18.00; Sun 10.00-17.00.

MacDonald Cycles
26-28 Morrison Street   EH3 9 BJ
Tel: 229 8473
Web: www.macdonaldcycles.com
Opening times: Mon-Sat 9.30-18.00; Sun 11.00-17.00.
Good selection of children's trikes and bikes – Raleigh, DiamondBack, Giant and Dawes. Cycle parts (amongst others), child seats, children's helmets, children's cycle capes, spare parts and safety accessories. Christmas club. Free after sales service. Will repair any bike, if parts available. Usually 24-hr turn-around, sometimes quicker for own customers. Will fit child seat free if both bike and seat are bought here, otherwise £8.
Also at:
35 High Street, Musselburgh   EH21 7AD
Tel: 665 1777
Opening times: Mon-Tue & Thu-Sat 9.00-17.30. Closed Wed & Sun.

Sandy Gilchrist Cycles
1 Cadzow Place, Abbeyhill   EH7 5SN
Tel: 652 1760
Opening times: Mon-Wed, Fri 9.30-18.00; Thu 9.30-19.00; Sat 9.00-17.30; Closed Sun.
Children's trikes and bikes – Giant, Peugeot, Universal and Muddy Fox. Wide selection on view. Several types of child seats, both high back and low back. Children's helmets, spares and safety accessories. ACT member. Christmas club. Repairs done on any make of bike, 24-hr turn-around when possible. Free estimates. Small charge to fit child seats. Shimano Centre.

Velo Ecosse
25-27 Bruntsfield Place   EH10 4HJ
Tel: 477 2557
Email: veloecosse@freeuk.com
Web: www.veloecosse.freeuk.com

Opening times: Mon-Wed, Fri 9.30-18.30; Thu 9.30-19.30; Sat/Sun 10.00-18.00.
Children's and adult bikes, child seats and helmets.
Children's and adult bikes, child seats and helmets. Trailercycles and trailers and large range of cycle clothing. Spares and accessories. Repairs and servicing done within 24-48 hours. For serious cyclists, they stock Giant, Pinarello and Shimano amongst others.

BOOKS

Even in these days of Amazon, Sendit and all the other '.coms', there is nothing quite like looking around a real bookshop. No matter whether you are looking for new, second-hand, or trying to track down a title from your childhood, Edinburgh is well-provided.

Admittedly, conditions are not always ideal: small spaces, crammed with bookshelves that seem so appealing when you are childless, suddenly become more of an obstacle course when you are pregnant or have children. However, on the whole, booksellers try to accommodate children – and those shops with trained (or willing!) staff will always be prepared to fetch a title for you, if they know where it is.

Most shops now have some sort of distraction for toddlers and young children, such as boxes of toys, tables and chairs, or reading-books. Better stores have staff who are well-trained, specialise in children's books and can give invaluable advice and recommendations.

If you cannot find the book you require, most bookshops will be happy to order it for you. You may find that the smaller stores can order it in for you just as quickly as the larger chains: In addition to books and audio books, you can also order large print books and books in other than English via bookshops, should you require them.

Despite television and videos, books are still extremely popular with under 5s. Books can be introduced at the baby stage, where the focus is on bold pictures and robust pages. By 9 mths, most babies will be happy to sit on your knee and look at a book, for at least a few moments. The bedtime story for a toddler is an ideal way to wind down after a hectic day, and to spend 10 mins or so talking with the child. Books introduce children to words and language they would not normally hear in normal conversation (or on television!) and greatly increase language development. They can also help introduce children to concepts, ideas and situations out of their normal, everyday life, so helping to stimulate their imagination. There are also titles which can help young children to come to terms with some of the more traumatic aspects of growing up, such as the loss of a grandparent. If you are looking for such titles, ask in your bookshop – the education dept can be helpful if it has one.

There is a tremendous choice for under 5s, superbly illustrated in many different styles, which are entertaining for parent and child alike – though be prepared for the 'favourite' book, you may find yourself reading it at least twice everyday: our family's record is eight times in a row!

We have tried to list the best stocked and most friendly bookshops. Children's books are also sold in supermarkets, department stores, toy shops, some stationers and also via mail order (see Shopping from Home).

New books may seem expensive, but they compare very well with the price of toys and videos, and they offer excellent value for money; well-loved books can be handed down through families as well as toys etc. You could also ask for Book Tokens for gifts for your children at Christmas or birthday time: ask for National Book Tokens, which can be used in most UK bookshops, rather than shop-specific ones. From the age of around 3+, a child will enjoy choosing their very own book!

Look out also for charity shops, church book sales, second-hand and jumble sales. Libraries also host sales, and sometimes you can pick great bargains, such as '10 for the price of 1'!

Library tickets are available for children from birth (see Libraries) and regular library visits help to expand the choice of books available to your child. Some toy libraries also lend books and cassettes. Also, look out for any storytelling or author sessions during holidays in your local library or bookshop.

The Edinburgh Book Festival is an annual event, held in Charlotte Square Gardens, which has storytelling and author events specifically for children, usually from around 3 yrs+. In addition, there is always a children's book marquee, which has a great range of titles, and often has some available in advance of their actual general publication date or at special prices.

A few children's books have an Edinburgh theme. There are many on the subject of Greyfriar's Bobby, and there is also the famous 'Maisie' series. While they have good illustrations, many of them are unfortunately rather too text-heavy for small children. That said, they are often popular choices for gifts: note that some of the 'Maisie' series are also available in Gaelic.

As a child Robert Louis Stevenson lived in Heriot Row, in Edinburgh, and in his 'A Child's Garden of Verse', the poem 'The Lamplighter' is about the man who lit the lamp outside his home – the lamp is still there, though it's electric now. And for older children's interest, JK Rowling wrote the first Harry Potter novel in Edinburgh.

Out of Print Books

Some bookshops offer a free search service for out of print titles. Others may be able to guide you towards companies which specialise in searching and locating out of print titles – it's always worth asking! Alternatively, start trawling the second-hand bookshops, where you can still find hidden jewels.

Blackwell's

53-62 South Bridge,
Edinburgh, EH1 1YS
Tel: 0131 622 8222
Fax: 0131 557 8149
Email: Edinburgh@blackwell.co.uk
Web: www.blackwell.co.uk
Opening times: Mon, Wed-Fri 9:00-20:00; Tue 9:30-20:00; Sat 9:00-18:00; Sun 12:00 to 18:00.

Bright, extensive children's department with playtable, Saturday storytelling and programme of events (ring for details). Scottish Books section, audiobooks, recommendations and reviews. Specialist school department with school texts and revision guides: knowledgeable and friendly staff. All areas pushchair accessible. Lift with room for pushchairs gives easy access to the rest of this large bookshop, where you'll find loads of books for adults and comfy sofas for relaxed browsing. Public toilet with baby-changing facilities in children's department. Instore café with high chairs.

The Book Swop

28 Bruntsfield Place EH10 4HJ
Tel: 229 9451
Opening times: Mon-Sat 10.00-17.00; closed Sun.
Another way to expand on your reading selection. You trade in your unwanted books and, if they are suitable, you receive a credit voucher, valid for 1 year, which can be used to purchase titles from the other pre-owned books. The shop usually has several hundred second-hand children's titles in good condition!

There are also second-hand titles for cash sale only. You

can also return a used book bought from this shop and use it as part exchange for another (a third of the price you pay towards another book).

Also stocks discount and full-price new books, as well as atlases and maps.

Borders
Unit 26
Fort Kinnaird Retail Park   EH15 3RD
Tel: 657 4041
Opening times: Mon-Sat 9.00-22.00; Sun 10.00-20.00.
Car parking: parent & child parking spaces located near to store.
Bright, airy store on one floor. With a good children's area, complete with scatter cushions, towards the rear of the store. Good range of titles, including touchy-feely books, gift boxes with books & related soft toys etc. for younger children. Usually have a range of books with tapes. Store also carries a pretty good range of graphic novels, comics, magazines and journals from around the world. Hosts a storytime every Sat and Sun at noon. During school holidays, there are daily art events (starts at 14.00). Check the events board in store for current details, or phone. Nappy-changing area (M&F).

Ottakar's
57 George St
Tel: 225 4495
Web: www.ottakars.co.uk
Opening hours: Mon-Wed, Fri-Sat 9.00-19.00; Thu 9.00-20.00; Sun 11.30-17.00.
Excellent children's department with a large selection of books and audiobooks, as well as a wide range of games and educational toys, for all ages. Access is via a ramp or steps at the left hand side of the ground floor. Spacious, with plenty of room for pushchairs. Outside of the run-up to Christmas, there's usually a large table with drawing paper and pencils to keep everyone amused if book choosing is taking a long time! There's also a wooden rocking horse for children to have a ride on in the dept: this certainly lengthens our stays! There is also a full-size Dalek. Able to order most UK books if not in stock. Toilet facilities are situated upstairs – there is a lift – beside the café – see Eating Out.

Stockbridge Bookshop
26 North West Circus Place
Tel: 225 5355
Fax: 220 5323
Email: sbridge@flatman.co.uk
Opening times: Mon-Wed, Fri 8.30-20.00; Thu 8.30-21.00; Sat 8.30-20.00; Sun 11.00-19.00.

Colourful, small, children's section up 2 steps at back of shop. Good selection of board books, paperbacks, bargain books and gift books. Some book and tape sets. Range expanded at Christmas. Good general range of hardback, paperback and discounted titles.

Birthday cards and gift wrap paper. Selection of cut-price cds. Table and chairs for browsing.

There is also an extremely well-stocked school's showroom in basement, which has a large selection of non-fiction titles. Happy to donate posters and publicity material to teachers. If you can't find what you're looking for, they are usually happy to check if relevant titles are downstairs, although it's not always possible for them to do so at the weekend. Can produce a computerised list on specific topics requested. Will reserve books, and can also offer a 48 hr order service for general in-print titles: while more obscure titles may take longer, they can often get your order in within 24 hrs. Friendly staff will allow use of the staff toilet for young children, and can find space for breastfeeding.

Waterstone's
www.waterstones.co.uk
13/14 Princes Street EH2 2AN (East End)
Tel: 556 3034
Opening times: Mon-Fri 9.00-20.00; Sat 9.00-19.00; Sun 10.00-19.00.
Well-designed children's section at back of ground floor. Bold colour scheme, lowered ceiling, shelves that children can reach, and seating. Books are classified in age groups. Excellent selection of hardback and paperback titles. Regular activities for children – ask to be put on the children's mailing list. Happy to donate posters and publicity material to teachers. Staff toilet is available in emergencies; it's in the basement, so you have to be escorted by a member of staff. There is a lift which can be used for prams and pushchairs, but again ask for assistance.
Also at:
128 Princes Street EH2 4AD (West End)
Tel: 226 2666
Opening times: Mon-Sat 8.30-20.00; Sun 10.30-19.00.
Lift to children's dept on 1st floor. Good range of books, cushions to sit on. Toilet for the disabled in the basement and a baby room for feeding and changing at front of basement up a few steps. Starbuck's Coffee Shop on 2nd floor.
83 George Street   EH2 3ES
Tel: 225 3436
Opening times: Mon-Fri 9.30-21.00; Sat 9.30-20.00; Sun 11.00-18.00.

A large shop on 2 floors and a mezzanine with a vast range of books for both adults and children. Its emphasis is on 'fun for all the family' with events and long opening hours. The shop is packed with books, but has been made more pushchair friendly. The children's department is on the ground floor. Brightly decorated with unusual kites. Huge selection of titles – and staff are always ready to help. Baby room and public toilet adjacent to the children's section.

Ocean Terminal
98/99 Ocean View   EH6 6JJ
Tel: 554 7732
Opening times: Mon-Fri 10.00-20.00; Sat 10.00-19.00; Sun 11.00-18.00.
Smallish children's section, due toi the compact nature of the store, which stocks a range of well-known authors. Also stock some audio books, activity bokks and so on. While you are less likely to find some of the less well known authors and titles here, Waterstone's do order books, so that's an option. As it's in Ocean Terminal, you have a range of coffee shops to hand, as well as the centre's parent & baby rooms.

The following stores also stock children's books
Bargain Books
100A Princes Street
Tel: 220 1487
Stocks some very cheap picture books and activity books. Some very low cost children's board and picture books – great for party bags etc. Frequent offers include the like of '5 for £5'. Also stocks cut price gift wrap and Christmas paper.

Bookworld
63 Princes Street
Tel: 225 3192

Princes Mall
Tel: 557 1415
Popular children's paperbacks and some very low-priced picture and storybooks, some as low as 30p-50p; great for party prizes and stocking fillers.

Early Learning Centre
St James' Centre   EH1 3SS
Tel 558 1330

Unit 23
Fort Kinnaird   EH15 3RD
Tel: 669 9513

Gyle Shopping Centre
Tel: 538 7172
Small range, but many with film / tv tie-ins.. See Toy Shops for full details.

Jenners
Good selection of popular authors and publishers. Children's books in basement, next to the toy department. See Department Stores.

John Lewis
Stock a range of board, picture and storybooks. Also have musical/noise books. Any book which is in print can be ordered, some within 24 hrs. See Department Stores.

Royal Museum of Scotland Shop
Selection of children's reference books, special emphasis on natural history and activity books.

HAIRCUTS

Having a haircut can be traumatic for a young child. Some love it – enjoying the attention – while others need a little more persuasion.

If you already use a hairdresser regularly, it is worth asking if they would cut your child's hair, and how much they would charge, although what suits you might not be the best for your child: you need someone who is relaxed with children, is patient, and has a calm approach.

Many hairdressers have special seats so that children can sit at the right height, and have books and toys to keep them amused while they are waiting. A few even have videos to show, which is one way of getting your child to keep his or her head still. If your child is shy, it might be worth asking if s/he can sit on your knee while her/his hair is being cut.

Timing of the haircut can be critical, both for your child and the hairdresser. Choose a time when your child is usually on good form, perhaps early in the morning or after a nap. If it's possible, try to choose a quiet period at the hairdressers; there's likely to be a quieter atmosphere, as well as a shorter waiting time.

If it is your child's first visit to a salon, you will probably find it better to make the appointment in person, giving your child the chance to see where s/he is going and what it will be like. It may also help to take your child along if you are having a haircut yourself – though this plan is best put into action only if you have someone who can take your child away for a little while, as an adult cut can change from fascination to boredom pretty quickly!

If you are looking for a new hairdresser for your whole family, why not have a haircut first yourself. It will give you the opportunity to chat to the stylist and find out how keen s/he is to cut your child's hair, or if one of the salon's stylists specialises in children's cuts. Some salons offer reduced rates for children when a parent has a haircut too. Check out local salons – there may be no need to trail across the city with your toddler for a good cut.

Another option if you find it difficult to get out, or you find that your child is intimidated by the surroundings of a salon, would be to have a hairdresser come to your home. Check out Yellow Pages, www.yell.com or local press – or why not ask around at any group you attend. You may find that haircuts at home are a practical solution for your family, and an exciting afternoon for your small child!

While most salons are happy to cut and style children's hair, there is one which specialises in children's haircutting in Edinburgh:

Kids' Stop
36 Morningside Road EH10 4DA
Tel: 446 0123
Opening times: Mon-Fri 9.00-18.00; Sat 09.00-16.00. Closed Sun.

Extremely child-friendly salon, which also welcomes adults! Special children's seat provided (horse, rabbit, bike), video while having a haircut, play area with toys, video and books. Sliding scale of rates, dependent on child's age.
Toilet and nappy changing facilities available. Appointments not always necessary. Make-over parties also available – please call salon for more information.

NURSERY EQUIPMENT & REPAIRS

Many shops in Edinburgh sell well-known brand name equipment. If you decide to buy second-hand or an uncommon make, you must satisfy yourself as to its safety. Second-hand equipment can be in very good condition, but it may not conform to current safety standards. When it comes to cot/Moses basket mattresses, these should always be bought new: never buy a second-hand one. The same applies to car seats: you can't be sure if the seat has been in a traffic accident – there may be stress damage that you can't see, but which could endanger your child. After sales service should be an important consideration

when making your choice of equipment; ask about servicing and repairs before you buy. Most of the outlets that we have listed will do both to the brands they sell, and most will consider lending you a temporary replacement if the repair will take some time. It is a good idea to retain your receipt for a long time, as this is usually required as proof of purchase before repairs will be undertaken. Talk to friends before you buy – you only discover the pros and cons of equipment once you have lived with it for a while.

Shops usually keep one demonstration pram in stock. Ordering your style and colour can usually take from 6 to 20 weeks! No shop will make you buy a pram if you discover you do not need it (if you discover you're having twins, for example) and most will store it until you need it. All other equipment is usually held in stock.

Which? Magazine and Practical Parenting often have reports on nursery equipment and it is worth checking back numbers in the library, even if it's just to see what to look out for. See also 'Hiring', futher on in this chapter.

Argos
Moderate selection of equipment, though individual brand choice may be limited. One year guarantee on pushchairs: catalogue features Graco brand. Superstore in Kinnaird Park has a larger selection than most stores displayed in nursery dept. Argos offers a 16 day money back guarantee – see instore or catalogue for details specific to pushchairs. See Department Stores.

Corstorphine Pram Centre
115-117 St John's Road
Tel: 334 6216
Opening times: phone for current times.
Wide selection of prams, pushchairs, cots, travel cots, backpacks, car seats and other equipment required for baby. Also a large selection of nursery décor ranges and furniture.

The Foam Centre
176 Causewayside, Newington
Tel: 667 1247
Opening times: Mon-Sat 9.30-17.30. Later at Christmas
Different foams cut to any size and shape. Can be made to fit cots, Moses baskets, bumpers, booster seats etc. 'Beans' to top up or to make your own beanbags. Maternity wedges, lumbar supports also supplied.

IKEA
Straiton Mains
Tel: 448 0500
Located on the 1st floor, along with the toys and to the right of the café. Range of cots, changing tables, beds, chairs, tables, highchairs and various storage options etc, the majority of which are flatpacked and reasonably priced. Co-ordinated bedding ranges available. Children's cutlery, crockery and starter packs including training cups also to hand. See Department Stores, Toys and Crèches while Shopping.

John Lewis
St James' Centre   EH1 3SP
Tel: 556 9121
Opening times: Mon-Wed 9.00-18.00, Thu 9.30-20.00; Fri 9.00-20.00; Sat 9.00-18.30; Sun 10.00-18.00.
Good selection of equipment, including pushchairs, prams, highchairs, cots, nursing chairs etc. Ranges include Mamas and Papas, Cossatto, McLaren. Also stocks range of soft furnishings, including own brand options. Larger items of furniture also available.
Free delivery within city boundaries and a little beyond. See Department Stores.

Mamas and Papas
Craigleith Retail Park
Tel: 0870 830 7703
Web: mamasandpapas.co.uk
Opening times: Mon-Wed, Fri 9.30-18.00; Thu 9.30-19.00; Sat 9.00-18.00; Sun 11.00-17.00.
Selection of own-brand prams, travel systems, car seats, cots and other nursery equipment. Also stock ranges of décor and co-ordinating bedding and trims etc.

Musselburgh Pram Centre
35 High Street, Musselburgh EH21 7AD
Tel: 665 2530
Web: www.pramcentre.co.uk
Opening times: Mon-Tue & Thu-Sat 9.00-17.30; Closed Wed & Sun.
Wide selection of nursery equipment including prams, pushchairs, all-terrain strollers, cots, travel systems, backpacks and car seats. Ranges stocked include Mamas & Papas, Silver Cross, Bebecar, Emmaljunga Britax etc. Also wide selection of nursery toys and large selection of nursery décor ranges and furniture. Free parking nearby.

Mothercare
Fort Kinnaird Retail Park
Tel: 657 4050

Mothercare World
Hermiston Gait Retail Park
Tel: 453 1383
Stock large selection of Mothercare, Britax, McLaren, Mamas and Papas, Bébécar, Cossatto etc baby/nursery equipment, including car seats, cots and prams. Baby toiletries, nappies and baby food also available. See Department Stores.

National Childbirth Trust
NCT Centre
University Health Service
5th floor
5 Bristo Square   EH8 9AL
Tel: 668-3257
Web: www.nct.co.uk
Web: nctms.co. (online catalogue)
Please phone centre for current opening times.
The NCT catalogue features baby equipment, as well as books and leaflets on many aspects of pregnancy, birth and parenthood. Phone office for details, or order online. See Health Care.

Tiso
123-125 Rose Street   EH2 3DT
Tel: 225 9486
Email: edinburgh@tiso.com
Web: www.tiso.com
Opening times: Mon, Wed, Fri, Sat 9.30-17.30; Tue 10.00-17.30; Thu 9.30-19.30 Sun 12.00 -17.00
Stocks baby carriers, small toddler- and child-sized rucsacs, nappy bags and pushchairs.

Tiso: Edinburgh Outdoor Experience
41 Commercial Street
Leith   EH6 6JD
Tel: 554 0804
Email: edinburgh_oe@tiso.com
Web: www.tiso.com
Opening times: Mon-Tue, Fri-Sat 9.30-17.30, Wed 9.30-18.00; Thu 9.00-19.30 Sun 11.00-17.00
Stocks Karrimor and Wild Rover baby carriers. Will help to fit. Toddler-sized rucsacs also available. Helpful staff. See also Outdoor and Ski Shops.

Toys'R'Us
Kinnaird Retail Park
Tel: 657 4121

Wide range of pushchairs, car seats, cots and highchairs by McLaren Cindico, Britax and Mamas and Papas. One year guarantee on items, but must retain receipt. Car and home safety equipment also stocked. See Department Stores.

OUTDOOR & SKI SHOPS

For those parents wishing to take their children outdoors in Britain, our weather can always prove problematic. Keeping the small members of the family warm and dry is essential to everyone's enjoyment of an outing. There's a good selection of dedicated outdoor shops in Edinburgh, and many offer clothing and equipment for under 5s.

Babycarriers (or backpacks) allow you to go off the beaten track with your child safely away from mud, wet grass, sheep droppings, and all the other delights a small child can find in the countryside. These carriers can be equally useful in town, allowing negotiation of busy streets without many of the problems associated with pushchairs, such as other people (!), getting through doors and using escalators. The big drawback is the potential strain on your back so the adage 'try before you buy' is essential, as with any piece of outdoor clothing. Remember, you and your partner may be carrying the pack considerable distances. Also, think about your intended use: if you want something for walking in the country, you'll probably want something which is reasonably rugged as well as comfortable. However, if the pack is more for 'urban' use, take this into account.

As with most things, with outdoor equipment and clothing, you get what you pay for. So, keep your primary usage in mind, and keep comfort as a priority.

Blacks Outdoor Leisure Ltd
24 Frederick Street EH2 2JR
Tel: 225 8686

Opening times: Mon-Sat 9.00-17.30; Sun 12.00-17.00. Store stocks Vango babycarriers, plus children's boots and socks. The sales floor is pretty cramped, so some degree of awkward manoeuvring may be called fo.

Nevisport
81 Shandwick Place EH2 4SD
Tel: 229 1197

Opening times: Mon-Wed, Fri-Sat 9.00-17.30; Thu 10.00-18.30; Sun 11.00-16.00.

Stocks Macpac babycarriers for babies from 6mths. Also carries a range of waterproof clothing for toddlers upwards, fleeces and lightweight boots. For skiers there is a range of clothes and equipment for children. Skis from 70cm up, boots from size 16' (mondopoint sizing). Access good, doorway big enough for tandem pushchair, ask for help to basement sales area. Staff toilet available for emergencies.

N.B.: New store in Rose Street, near Jenners.

Snowlines
14/15 Bruntsfield Place
Tel: 229 2402
Web: www.snowlines.co.uk

Opening times: Mon-Fri 9.30-18.00; Sat 9.00-17.30; Sun 11.00-17.00.

Stocks specialist clothing and footwear for running, skiing/snowboarding and outdoor pursuits. Offers a free instore video gait analysis. Operates an instore discount scheme, details of which can be checked out on the website – see cartblanche cards. Skis for hire.

Sports Warehouse
24-26 Coburg Street EH6 6HB
Tel: 553 6003
Web: www.sportswarehouse.co.uk
Opening times: Mon-Sat 9.00-17.00 Sun 11.00-16.00.
This sports and outdoor supplier has the Karrimor and Vango babycarriers. Pentland cagoules and trousers suitable for 3+ yrs. Also stock boots from size 12, junior sleeping bags and swimming aids. Car parking. Staff toilet is available for use in emergencies.

Tiso
123-125 Rose Street EH2 3DT
Tel: 225 9486
Email: edinburgh@tiso.com
Web: www.tiso.com
Opening times: Mon, Wed, Fri, Sat 9.30-17.30;Tue 10.00-17.30; Thu 9.30-19.30 Sun 12.00 -17.00.
This store is located on 4 floors and caters for children from 6 mths to 16 yrs. Clothing includes range of fleeces and waterproof jackets, suits and over trousers, including Wild Rover (own brand), Helly Hansen, Trespass, and Lego. Wellingtons, leather and lightweight boots from size 10. Selection of babycarriers, including Wild Rover and Macpac suitable for 3 mths - 4 yrs as well as pushchairs by Pegasus. Ski goggles, hats and gloves etc are also available in winter months. Customer toilets available.

Tiso: Edinburgh Outdoor Experience
41 Commercial Street
Leith   EH6 6JD
Tel: 554 0804
Email: edinburgh_oe@tiso.com
Web: www.tiso.com
Opening times: Mon-Tue, Fri-Sat 9.30-17.30, Wed 9.30-18.00;Thu 9.00-19.30 Sun 11.00-17.00.
This store – the largest of its kind this side of the country – is situated on one level with a car park available. 'Outdoor Experience' on ground floor is an interactive shop with everything from a 'shower tower' to an ice-wall. – as well as a large range of equipment and clothing. Comfy sofas are available to rest your feet and there's car parking for 60 cars.

PHOTOGRAPHY & ART

Whether it's putting an announcement in the paper, having a family portrait taken for posterity, or taking amould of your child's feet or hands, most families find the idea of recording significant events comes into their lives with the arrival of a baby.
A birth announcement can be placed in the Scotsman or the Evening News (see Help & Information). Unlike death notices, no proof is required to place your announcement and they can be made in person at the Scotsman Offices or by phone with a credit card. Payment is required at time of order.

PHOTOGRAPHY
Department stores such as Boots and Debenhams and shopping centres such as Cameron Toll or The Gyle Centre often have visiting companies which specialise in photographing young children. Look out in the Herald and Post for details of these companies. The Herald and Post also has details of firms which are willing to video or photograph your party or Christening. The following companies have experience in working with under 5s.

Dimple Photos
100 Northfield Crescent
Willowbrae Road EH8 7QB
Tel: 661 5031
Mob: 07946 518 244
Email: Portraits@dimple-photos.co.uk
Established in 1985, servicing maternity hospitals. Photographs of new borns. Specialists in baby portrait packs

David Johnston LMPA
31 Bridgeside Avenue
Whitburn, West Lothian
Tel: 01501 742710
Children's portraits, babies, Christenings, family groups etc. Relaxed, informal photography in studio or on location.

Photo Express
7 Melville Terrace EH9 1ND
Tel: 667 2164
Email: info@photo-express-edinburgh.co.uk
Opening times: Mon-Fri 9.00-17.00; Sat 9.00-12.00
Specialises in children and family groups. Portraits taken in-studio. Toilet facilities available. Roadside metered parking

Genuine European Portraits
Freepost SCO3533
EH10 0BR
Tel: 229 7556
Web: www.portraits.org
Specialises in hand drawn portraits on a sale or return

basis for nurseries, playgroups, toddler groups etc, which receive commission for each portrait, so it's a good fundraiser. Individual drawings from photos can be ordered through the website.

Sarah Elizabeth Photography
Bilston Glen Estate
Loanhead EH20 9LZ
Tel: 448 0111
Email: sarah@sarahelizabeth.co.uk
Web: www.sarahelizabeth.co.uk
Contemporary portraits in the studio. Single portaits or wall montages. Experienced in children's photography.

Venture
Unit 1B
Meadowbank Shopping
Earston Place EH7 5SU
(near Meadowbank Retail Park)
Tel: 652 8130
Web: thisisventure.co.uk
Opening times: 9.00-17.00; Sat-Sun 10.00-17.00; evenings by appointment only.
'New generation photography', which means the poses are not your static, traditional portraiture. Venture frames the resultant photographs. Studios, preview rooms etc.

Imprints
Making a cast or imprint of your child's foot can be a striking way of recording their arrival. Some department stores, such as John Lewis sell plaster imprtin kits. You might also want to consider A tile or plate with your child's hand- or footprint: see Where Shall We Go Today: Ceramic Centres for more details. A more dramatc version is on offer from:

Golden Hands, Silver Feet
Web: goldenhands.co.uk
Babies hands or feet cast in bronze/aluminium as a plaque or a 3D replica; ideal for family presents. Company will travel to your home or even hospital. Gift vouchers available.

Bilston Glen Estate
Loanhead EH20 9LZ
Contact: Jenny
Tel: 448 0151
also:
Contact: Nicky Sommer
Tel: 665 8628

Murals
If you're looking to give your child's room a different look, your could think about having a mural done. One solution is to hire a mural artist to do it for you. If you're artistic, you could attempt it yourself, but bear in mind the time, as well as the scale of the project: otherwise you might end up feeling like Michelangelo painting the Sistine Chapel, with the additional pressure of questions like 'is it finished yet?'

Once Upon a Time
Contact: Tim or Veronica
Tel: 07875 457 585 or 07766 887278
Email: once_upon_a_time_murals@hotmail.com
Based in Peebles, this company provides a range of services, from a full-room extravaganza, to a key feature. Favourtie toys or characters can also be used as an influence or as akey part of the design. Also offer room re-shaping (making best space of the room).

TOYS

Make sure you always satisfy yourself as to the safety of toys – particularly if you are buying from an unorthodox source. When buying for playgroups ctc it is always worth asking whether discounts are available. Many shops and department stores expand their range and extend their opening hours before Christmas.
This section includes doll repair, special gifts and outdoor toys.
See also Department Stores, Supermarkets, the specialist party shops in Birthdays and Celebrations, and Bicycle Shops for full shop details, where limited information is given here.

DRESSING UP
Most children love dressing up. While many department stores keep a range of costumes in their toy departments, there can be some real finds in the smaller shops in and around Edinburgh.

Baggins
12 Deanhaugh Street
Stockbridge
Tel: 315 2011
Web: www.bagginsonline.co.uk
Opening times: Tue-Fri 10.00-17.00; Sat 10.00-14.00.
Access: awkward – down a flight of steps to a basement.

A great range of dressing-up clothes and accessories like wands, wings, hats etc. Outfits include: fairies, clowns, spacemen, firemen, tigers, belly dancers, nurses, Indians etc. Toys for all ages. Toys for children to play with while you browse.

The Magic Wardrobe: Dressing-up Clothes for Kids
Tel 0131 667 4813
Email: cherryledlie@blueyonder.co.uk
Web: www.magicwardrobe.ik.com
The Magic Wardrobe is a local recycling project which turns used and unwanted fabrics into dressing-up clothes for children. All profits go to the NCT in Edinburgh. Costumes can be bought from the Magic Wardrobe stall at various School Fairs, or directly from Cherry any time. Check the website for details of upcoming stalls, or contact Cherry to discuss a commission or private viewing. Ideal Christmas and birthday presents for imaginative kids. Donations of fabric, trimmings, old dress patterns etc always welcome!

TOYSHOPS

Argos
A wide range of popular toys, including up and coming trends. Superstore has most products. See Department Stores.

Arkadia
Edinburgh Zoo
Corstorphine Road
Tel: 334 9171
Opening times: Mon-Sun 9.00-17.30.
Run by the zoo, but with a separate entrance, so you don't have to go into the zoo itself. A real treasure trove, full of animal- and bird-related toys, games, books, clothes, and gifts – including pocket-money toys.

Asda Wal-Mart
Selection of big name toys, including Duplo, Lego, stationery etc. See also Baby and Children's Clothes and Supermarkets.

BhS
Small selection within children's clothes dept, including baby and pre-school toys. Range tends to expand slightly at Christmas. See Department Stores.

Digger
35 West Nicolson Street
Tel: 668 1802
Opening times: Mon-Sat 10.00-18.00.
Small shop up 3 steps. An Aladdin's cave of handmade and traditional wooden toys. Dolls' house furniture, wooden framed mirrors, bookends, clocks decorated with teddies, stocking fillers and party goods.

The Disney Store
18 Princes Street
Tel: 557 2772
Opening times: Mon-Wed, Fri-Sat 9.00-18.00; Thu 9.00-19.00; Sun 11.00-17.00.

Gyle Shopping Centre
Tel: 339 4944
Mon-Wed 9.30-20.00; Thu, Fri 9.30-21.00; Sat 9.00-18.00; Sun 10.00-18.00.
Colourful stores which sell everything in the Disney theme, including collectables and animation art. Both stores have lively laser screen video entertainment for children. Both stores are on one floor, which makes for easy access for pushchairs. Friendly 'cast members'. See also Baby and Children's Clothes.

Early Learning Centre
67-83 Shandwick Place
Tel: 228 3244
Opening times: Mon-Sat 9.00-17.30; Sun in Dec.

Unit 11
Gyle Shopping Centre
Tel: 538 7172
Opening times: Mon-Wed 9.00-19.30; Thu-Fri 9.00-20.00; Sat 9.00-18.00; Sun 10.00-17.00.

61 St James' Centre
Tel: 558 1330
Opening times: Mon-Sat 9.00-17.30; Sun in Dec 12.00-16.00.

Chain which sells toys that are educational, safe and robust, with a focus on younger children. Laid out in the shops under sections such as 'First Years', 'Pretend Play', 'Finding Out', 'Sound and Music' and so on. Also stock a range of outdoor toys including climbing frames, slides, swings, sandpits and trampolines. St James' Centre store is the largest and therefore carries an extended range. Toilet for the disabled and well equipped mother and baby room in St James' Centre store. Sainsbury's also carries a range of the smaller ELC toys. See also Shopping from Home.

Early Learning Playstore
Fort Kinnaird
Tel: 669 9513
Opening times: Mon-Fri 9.00-20.00; Sat 9.00-18.00; Sun 10.00-18.00.
Part of the Early Learning Centre chain, this superstore has a huge play area which allows children to "try before you buy". There are also activities every day, including face painting, messy time, etc at either 10.00 or 14.00 so it's best phone beforehand to find out so that you don't miss out. In the back of the store, there is a baby changing room and a separate baby dining room, which includes bottle warmers, table and chairs, and a chair for breast feeding mothers.

Edinburgh Doll And Teddy Bear Hospital
Geraldine's of Edinburgh
133-135 Canongate   EH8 8BP
Tel: 556 4295
Web: www.dollsandteddies.com
Opening times: Mon-Fri 9.00-17.00; Sat 9.00-13.00, Closed Wed.
Family-run store. Sells teddies, dolls, and toys for any occasion. The unique aspect of this shop is the hospital, where dolls and soft toys can await repair to injuries caused by the ravages of time or over exuberant play. And once your child's (or your) beloved toy is back to full 'health' or complement of limbs etc, this shop also stocks a range of accessories such as dresses, shoes etc to complete the picture – plus other bits and bobs..

Harburn Hobbies Ltd
67 Elm Row, Leith Walk
Tel: 556 3233
Mon-Sat 9.30-18.00
Email: sales@harburnhobbies.com
Web: www.harburnhobbies.com
Please phone for current hours.
Specialises in model railways, Scalextric and stopcks the entire Hornby Thomas the Tank Engine range. Also stocks the Take-a-long Thomas die-cast toys by Racing Champions. They also stock Britain's farm animals and tractors,as well as a range of the French company Papo's forts, knights and fantasy figures. Harburns also have a large stock of colourful wooden dolls' houses and furniture, including the Swedish Lundby dolls house range. As well as this, they have a vast array of die-cast cars, buses and lorries.

IKEA
Straiton Mains
Straiton, Loanhead
Tel: 448 0500
Located on the first floor (lift access) near to the café. Good selection of wooden and soft toys, musical instruments, crafts, and learning games. There are also pocket-money soft toys. There are well-equipped play-houses, so your child can try some of the toys first – and you can work out how noisy they could be!
See Department Stores, Nursery Equipment, Crèches while Shopping.

Jenners
48 Princes Street
Tel: 225 2301
Located in the basement - access by lift from the ground floor. Excellent, enormous and competitively priced toy department. If you can drag yourself away from a walk down memory lane, there is everything from pocket-money toys to rocking horses, train sets, small bikes – they also stock Steiff bears, if you are looking for that extra-special gift.
Other brands stocked include Brio, Duplo, Galt, Lego and Playmobil, although there are many others. There is also a good book, tape and video section. There are TV screens set in the wall at one side to keep young one's attention. Special events held periodically. See also Department Stores.

John Lewis
St James' Centre
Nursery toys such as teddies, rattles, bath toys etc on the first floor (lift access). Wide selection including most big name brands. Also stocks pocket-money toys.
Ordering service for a range of climbing frames, swings, slides, bikes, sandpits and other outdoor toys. These can be delivered, often free of charge (dependent on location). Samples usually on display in the summer months, however, the full range can be viewed via a catalogue.
See Department Stores.

Mothercare
Fort Kinnaird Retail Park
Tel: 657 4050

Mothercare World
Hermiston Gait Retail Park
Tel: 453 1383

Toy department within stores. Includes own-brand toys from small bikes, sit-and-ride cars etc to pencil cases and rattles. Also stock 'famous names' brands. See Department Stores.

The Natural World
Unit U3
Princes Mall
Tel: 556 3659
Email: www.thenaturalworld.com
Toys such as, puppets, educational games, and pocket-money toys. Also stock 'music and sounds of nature' CDs.

The Owl and the Pussycat
166 Bruntsfield Place
Tel: 228 4441
Email: gilliecom@aol.com
Opening times: Mon-Sat 9.30-17.30
Wide selection of teddies and other soft toys, stylish cards and gifts. Local artist Alison has a range of teddy drawings and prints.

Poundstretcher
Budget/value stores. A selection of inexpensive toys, including some educational toys, small bikes and stationery.
42 Shandwick Place
Tel: 225 1611
Opening times: Mon-Wed 9.00-17.30; Thu-Sat 9.00-18.00; Sun 11.00-16.30

10 West Harbour Road
Tel: 552 0213
Opening times: Mon-Fri 10.00-17.30; Sat 9.00-17.30; Sun 12.00-16.30

4/6 Brunswick Place
Tel: 557 0693

Kirkgate Shopping Centre
Tel: 555 5344

100/106 South Bridge
Tel: 225 8540

Fort Kinnard, Newcraighall Road
Tel: 657 4244
Opening times: Mon-Fri 10.00-20.00; Sat 9.00-18.00; Sun 10.00-17.00

Gorgie Road
Tel: 346 7741

Unit 1 Meadowbank Shopping Park
Tel: 652 6005

Unit 36 West Side Plaza, Westerhailes
Tel: 458 4553

Sainsbury's
Cameron Toll Shopping Centre
Craigleith Retail Park
Straiton Retail Park
Small selection of toys, including Duplo, Lego and own brand stationery. Also stocks ELC toy ranges, as well as own-brand 'learning through play' toys. The stores' general ranges expand at Christmas. See Supermarkets for more information.

Seesaw
109 Broughton Street   EH1 3RZ
Tel: 556 9672
Email: info@seesawnappies.co.uk
Web: www.seesawnappies.co.uk
Opening times: Mon-Wed, Fri-Sat 9.00-1800; Thu 9.00-19.30; Sun 12.00-17.00.
Shop stocks a wide range of continental wooden and developmental toys, including wooden rattles, stackers mobiles, pull-alongs, ball-runs etc.

Snapdragon Toys
42 London Street   EH3 6LX
Tel: 556 0222
Email: info@snapdragontoys.co.uk
Opening times: Mon-Sat 9.00-18.00; Sun 11.00-18.00.
A traditionally-styled toy shop, selling a wide range of products, from marbles to rocking horses, children's books and pocket-money toys. Toilet available for use. Premises down a few stairs.

Studio One
10-14 Stafford Street
Tel: 226 5812
Opening times: Mon-Fri 9.30-18.00; Thu 9.30-19.00; Sat 9.30-17.30; Sun 12.00-17.00.
Down steps to basement shop full of pocket-money toys, stocking fillers, novelties, Christmas decorations, wooden toys, colourful rugs, cushions and bedspreads.

Toys Galore
193 Morningside Road   EH10 4QP
Tel: 447 1006
Web: www.
Opening times: Mon-Sat 9.30-17.30, Open Sun in November and December 9.30-17.00.

Good choice of toys for all ages with some to try out while you browse. Most major brands stocked: for example Galt, ERTL. Crayola, Lego, Playmobil. Many others from pocket-money range upwards. 10% discount to playgroups. Difficult to manoeuvre pushchairs, but they can be left supervised at the front of the shop. Goods can only be returned if faulty.

Toys'R'Us
Kinnaird Park
Newcraighall Road
Tel: 657 4121
Opening times: Mon-Sat 9.00-22.00; Sun 10.00-18.00. Operates Bank Holiday hours.
Huge range of pre-school toys, soft toys, dolls, games, Lego, Playmobil, outdoor toys and so on. A store directory points to the different areas and there is a pick-up point for bulky items and electrical toys. Climbing frames, chutes, swings, sandpits and Wendy houses available with samples on display.
There is no play area and as such a vast array of toys may prove tempting, parents may find it easier to shop without their offspring. Toilets. See Department Stores.

Wind Things
11 Cowgatehead / Grassmarket   EH1 1YJ
Tel: 622 7032
Web: www.windthings.co.uk
Opening times: Mon-Sat 10.00-17.30; Sun 12.00-17.00. Scotland's premier kite shop. Sells selection of kites, from stunt kites to pocket-kites.

Wonderland
97-101 Lothian Road   EH3 9ABN
Tel: 229 6428
Email:sales@wonderlandmodel.com
Web: www.wonderlandmodels.com
Opening times: phone for current times.
Specialises in radio controlled cars, boats, planes and helicopters, as well as in model-making kits and railway sets. Stocks Scalextric. Good range of die-cast cars, buses and trucks. Dolls' houses kits or ready assembled, plus accessories. Will order in specific models for customers. Easy access for all pushchairs. Also stock fantasy/graphic novel figures – good for parents/carers too!

Woolworths
Selection of big-name toys, Lego, Duplo etc. Tapes, CDs, videos, stationery. Wide range of pocket-money toys. Range will vary dependent on store size. see also Department Stores.

OUTDOOR TOYS

For bikes and sit-and-ride toys, see Bicycle Shops.

Sand for sand pits is often available from builders' yards and increasingly so from garden centres, but make sure you buy washed or silver sand, as orange sand stains clothes. Washed sand is sometimes sold in bags in the spring and summer by shops selling sand pits. If you are buying or making a sandpit, make sure that you can secure a lid over it: wet sand is no fun – and any sand can prove irresistible to local cats!

Early Learning Centre
Climbing frames, slides, swings, sand pits, sand, trampolines. See above in Toy Shops.

John Lewis
Extensive range of climbing frames, swings, slides, bikes and other outdoor toys. Choose from 'top activity sports' brochure, delivered to your door. Store occasionally has some display samples, especially in the summer months. See Department Stores.

Toys 'R' Us
Climbing frames, slides, swings, sandpits and Wendy houses, with
samples on display. See Department Stores and above in Toys

HIRING

The main thing to remember is to phone in advance to make sure that what you require is available and, particularly when the business is run from home, that someone will be available to help you.

BICYCLES

Alpine Bikes
48 Hamilton Place
Tel: 225 3286
Web: www.alpinebikes.co.uk
Opening times: Mon-Wed, Fri, Sat 9.00-18.00; Thu 9.00-19.00; Sun 12.00-17.00
See Shopping - Bicycles.

Bike Trax
11 Lochrin Place   EH3 9QX
Tel: 228 6633
Email: info@biketrax.co.uk
Web: www.biketrax.co.uk
Opening times: Summer – Mon-Sat 9.30 -18.00; Sun 12.00-17.00. Winter – Mon-Sat 9.30-17.30; Sun 12.00-17.00.

Edinburgh Cycle Hire & Cycle Safaris
29 Blackfriars Street
Tel: 556 5560
Web: www.cyclescotland.co.uk
Opening times: Summer: 9.00-21.00 (7 days/wk); Winter: Usually 10.00-18.00 (but please phone before setting off).
See Shopping - Bicycles.

Great Bikes No Bull
276 Leith Walk
Tel: 467 7775
Opening times: Mon-Wed, Fri-Sat 9.00-17.30; Thu 9.00-17.30. Closed Sun.
See Shopping - Bicycles.

CAKE TINS

The Finishing Touch
17 St Patrick's Square
Tel: 667 0914
Refundable deposit, £1.25/night. Over 40 novelty tins to hire, plus numbers, letters, squares, hexagons etc. Most with instructions and/or pictures.
See Birthdays and Celebrations.

Studio One
71 Morningside Road
Tel: 447 0452
Opening times: Mon-Fri 9.00-18.00 Sat 9.00-17.30 Sun 12.00-16.00
£10 deposit, £2.00/night. Letters, numbers, hearts, squares.

Clothes

Davison Menswear
Dress Hire Shop
31-33 Bruntsfield Place
Tel: 229 0266
Web: www.davison-dresshire.co.uk
Email info@davison-dresshire.co.uk
Opening times: contact shop for current opening hours. Hire of Highland outfits, morning suits(with tails) and top hats from age 2 yrs-adult.

Highland Laddie
6 Hutchison Terrace
Tel: 455 7505
Kilt hire available. See also Kilts

NURSERY EQUIPMENT

National Childbirth Trust
NCT Centre
University Health Service
5th floor
5 Bristo Square   EH8 9AL
Tel: 668 3257
Please phone for current opening times.
Hire of Egnell breast pumps. Person will require package of beakers to fit these pumps. Contact the centre for your local agent.

INFLATABLES

Bennetts Bouncy Castles
9 Meadowplace Road   EH12 7TZ
Tel: 334 4545 (24hrs)
Email: bennettshire@blueyonder.com
Web: www.bennettshire.co.uk
Bouncy castles delivered and set up from £45. All sizes from 10' x 10', suitable for indoor use or in your garden with a shower cover. Specialised designs for under 5s.

Kidbounce
9 Scarlett Park, Musselburgh
East Lothian EH21 8BY
Tel: 0131 653 6243
Operating throughout Edinburgh and the Lothians, we are hirers of bouncy castles and soft play equipment. This company has a number of products specifically designed for children under 5.

Monkey Business
167 Morrison Street
Tel: 228 6636
Web: www.smiffys.com
Opening times: Mon-Wed, Fri-Sat 9.30-17.00; Thu 9.30-18.30; Sun 12.00-16.00.
Castle mini-bouncer and ball pond for hire, suitable for indoor or outdoor use. Full size bouncers also available. Sells a large range of party goods and hires out an automatic helium balloon pump. See also Birthdays and Celebrations.

SKIS

Snowlines
14/15 Bruntsfield Place
Tel: 229 2402
Opening times: Mon-Fri 9.30-18.00; Sat 9.00- 17.30 Sun 11.00-17.00.
Skis for hire. See also Shopping – Outdoor and Ski Shops.

NAPPIES

Modern cloth nappies are not only a la mode, they're easy to use too: no pins, no boiling, no complicated folds and – if you use the local nappy laundry – no washing either. Cloth nappies are effective, comfortable and convenient. They can save you money and they're good for the environment too – did you know that all the disposable nappies used by one baby ion one year would fill 40 black plastic bin bags? Cloth nappies, on the other hand, can be used again and again, and if you have another baby you could even make greater savings.

Edinburgh Real Nappy Network (ERNN)
Tel: 0870 9913 236
Email: info@ernn.org.uk
Web: www.ernn.org.uk
The Network provides unbiased information about cloth nappies. Their website is full of information about why and how to use cloth. You can arrange to see their 'nappy library' or go along to a nappy chat to ask questions and find out more about the different types of cloth nappy.

Edinburgh and Lothians Real Nappy Project Incentive Scheme
LEEP Recycling 36 Newhaven Road
Edinburgh EH6 5PY
Tel: 538 5381
Email: realnappies@leep.org.uk;
Web: www.leep.org.uk/reusablenappies
This project is running an incentive scheme which offers parents the chance to try reusable nappies free of charge. They are offering parents the choice of either a free trial nappy pack (worth £50) or a £30 cash back incentive to help with the initial cost outlay or when signing up with a nappy laundry service. Both incentives have a restricted number and are available on a first come first serve basis.

LOCAL SUPPLIERS

Woolworths
25 Milton Link
Edinburgh
EH15 3QH
Tel: 0131 669 1298
Stock the full range of Cotton Bottoms nappies and accessories.

Earth Matters
67 High Street
North Berwick
East Lothian EH39 5NZ
Tel: 01620 895401
Web: www.earthmatters.co.uk
Stocks a wide range of eco-friendly baby products and clothes. Nappies include Tots Bots, Imse Vimse and Tushies.

John Lewis
See Shopping – Department Stores.
Stock the full range of Cotton Bottoms nappies and accessories. Nappi nippas, own brand terries and nappy buckets.

PurPur Nappies
Edinburgh and West Lothian
Contact: Morag Davidson
Tel: 01506 419083
Email: morag@purpur.co.uk
Web: www.purpur.co.uk

Nappy Consultant with over 10 years experience. Free advice and a no obligation demonstration of the different nappy types and help in choosing what's best for you and your baby. Wide range of nappies, accessories and eco-friendly products available from stock. When ordering via website please enter your consultants name in the comments box.

Musselburgh Pram Centre
See Shopping – Nursery Equipment.
Stock the full range of Bambino Mio nappies and accessories.

Mothercare World
See Shopping – Department Stores.
Stock Kushies nappies and accessories, own brand terries and nappy buckets.

Nippers
131 Bruntsfield Place EH10 4EB
Tel: 228 5086
Email: mail@nippersforkids.com
Web: www.nippersforkids.com
Motherease One-size nappies, Rikki wraps and disposable one-way liners. Range of earth friendly toiletries and Moltex nappies.

Pure Nappies Laundry & Retailer
Unit 7, Block 5
Springkerse Industrial Estate, Munro Road
Stirling FK7 7UU
Tel: 01786 448 599
Email: info@pure-nappies.com
Web: www.pure-nappies.com
A nappy laundry and retailer which covers Edinburgh and East Central Scotland. As well as nappies, Pure Nappies stock a wide range of nappy related accessories including Birth to Potty Kits, and an organic clothes range.
Also provides a laundry service for nurseries.

SeeSaw
109 Broughton Street EH1 3RZ
Tel: 0131 556 9672
Email: info@seesawnappies.co.uk;
Web: www.seesawnappies.co.uk
For nappies, wooden toys, organic potions for mother & baby, fair trade baby clothes, luna and lots more. With a special area for parents to sit and have a nappy demo, play pen for babies, baby changing facilities and toilets.

Simply Nappies
Tel: 343 6544
Email: info@simplynappies.co.uk
Web: www.simplynappies.co.uk
Independent nappy retailer based in Edinburgh, stocking a wide range of cloth nappies and accessories. Unbiased advice on choosing suitable nappies and free local demonstrations.

Supermarkets
Selected branches of Boots, Tesco and Sainsbury's stock a limited range of cloth nappies and accessories.

The Scottish Nappy Company
The Olympic Business Park
Drybridge Road
Dundonald, Ayrshire KA2 9BE
Tel: 0800 0155 570
Email: enquiries@scottishnappy.co.uk
Web: www.scottishnappy.co.uk
A nappy laundry which covers Glasgow, Edinburgh, Ayrshire, Renfrewshire, Lanarkshire and the Lothians.

Tots Bots Ltd
Office 214, Abercromby Business Centre
279 Abercromby Street.
Glasgow G40 2DD
Tel: 0141 550 1514
Email: info@totsbots.com
Web: www.totsbots.com
Tots Bots are a range of shaped towelling nappies made in Scotland. They come in a range of colours and include cotton and bamboo terry. Voted best reusable nappy 2005 by mumsnet.com.

MAIL ORDER NAPPY SUPPLIERS
Listed below is a selection of mail order nappy suppliers. A more extensive list can be found on the ERNN website at www.ernn.org.uk

Eco-Babes
17b Paradise Road
Downham Market
Norfolk PE38 9HS
Tel: 01366 38 7851
Email: nappies@eco-babes.co.uk
Web: www.eco-babes.co.uk
Eco-Babes now also run a separate not for profit organisation:

The Nappy Trial Service
Tel: 01833 640400
Email: www.nappytrialservice.co.uk

Elvika Nappies
36 Kings North Road, Faversham
Kent ME13 8SB
Tel: 08456 443490
Email: nappy@elvika-nappies.co.uk
Web: www.elvika-nappies.co.uk
Independent nappy seller, selling a large selection of cloth nappies.

Greenfibres
See Shopping from Home – Children's Clothes

Little Green Earthlets
See Shopping from Home – Baby Equipment

Schmidt Natural Clothing
See Shopping from Home – Clothes

The Nappy Lady
'Arcady' 16 Hill Brow
Bearsted Maidstone
Kent ME14 4AW
Tel/fax: 0845 456 2441
Email: info@thenappylady.co.uk
Web: www.thenappylady.co.uk

The Natural Collection
See Shopping from Home – Children's Clothes

Twinkle Twinkle
Linpac Building Headley Road East
Woodley, Reading RG5 4HY
Tel: 0118 969 5550
Email: info@twinkleontheweb.co.uk
Web: www.twinkleontheweb.co.uk
Comprehensive selection of washable nappies, potty training, bedwetting aids, natural toiletries, slings. Free advice, downloadable guide on using nappies.

SHOPPING FROM HOME

Shopping from home is much easier than a shopping trip with young children, struggling through crowds with a pushchair: most big-name companies have an internet site these days.

In the last few years there has been a large increase in the number of companies with a presence on the internet, a lot of which are already familiar names, but speciality shops are also reaching a far wider audience by being available on the world wide web. Most sites these days have secure online ordering – and remember it's still more secure to enter credit card details on the web than it is to hand your credit card over to a waiter in a restaurant who takes it out of your sight! Some sites allow you to order a catalogue if you prefer to browse through that and then order. This is a quick, easy and 24-hour way to shop, and now you can also get hold of things that you maybe couldn't get locally.

The Internet is fast becoming the way of researching and buying baby and toddler clothes and equipment. There are a vast number of companies now with a presence on the Internet, and the number is increasing almost every day. The following are just a few of note, but you can find many, many more if you look at one of the Internet search engines, or one of the internet children's directories, such as www.ukchildrensdirectory.com. This section also includes mail order.

Baby Equipment

BabyCentre
Web: www.babycentre.co.uk

This is a UK version of the American sister site (www. babycenter.com) which provides a wealth of information on pregnancy and childcare for babies 0 to 3 (for older children see www.parentcentre.com).
At time of printing, BabyCentre in the UK no longer has an online shop. However, the site produces some great buying guides if you are confused about the range of different baby and toddler paraphernalia available. (www. babycentre.co.uk/buyingguides)

BabyWorld
Web: www.babyworld.co.uk
This site, like BabyCentre, offers information on pregnancy and babies, and also has its own shop for buying equipment and gadgets related to babies. At the time of writing, BabyWorld is part of a bigger site called iCircle, a website aimed specifically at women and women's issues. You can buy various products through it from medicines to clothes to books through their various partners – John Lewis, Boots, Figleaves.com, and Interflora

BickiePegs
Tel: 01224 790626
Web: www.bickiepegs.co.uk
A long-established Scottish firm (trading since 1925). Teething biscuits for babies available from Boots and all leading chemists. Small mail order brochure in pack. 'Doidy' children's training cup, finger toothbrushes. , toothpaste, thermometers and personalised pottery.

The Great Little Trading Company
124 Walcot Street
Bath   BA1 5BG
Tel: 0990 673008
Web: www.gltc.co.uk
Practical products for parents and children. Large catalogue full of helpful and interesting products. Also sells children's clothes. No quibble returns policy.

Little Green Earthlets Ltd
Units 1-3 Stream Farm
Chiddingly
East Sussex   BN8 6HG
Tel: 01825 873301
Web: www.earthlets.co.uk
Amazingly wide range of environmentally friendly baby equipment, products, nappies and clothing. Washable nappies, environmentally friendly baby goods, cotton toys. Also Baby Jogger – the original 3-wheel pushchair, including double, triple, special needs – and bike convertible pushchairs.

Tesco Direct
Tel: 08457 024024
Web: www.tesco.com
Baby and toddler catalogue includes wide range of value-for-money equipment, bedding, clothes, toys etc. You can order all products available through catalogue on their online store, which is also where their online grocery shopping service can be found (see Shopping from Home - Food)

Babies'R'Us
Web: www.babiesrus.co.uk
Babies' equipment section of Toys'R'Us. Babies'R' Us has its own catalogue available instore, and you can order online. Very useful if Toys'R'Us are out of stock in your local store – it can be faster to order online than ask the store to reserve something for you next time it gets into stock.

Mothercare
Web: www.mothercare.com
Familiar big-store site useful for browsing and comparing products. Buying guides available.

John Lewis
Tel: 556 9121
Web: www.johnlewis.com
On-line version of this big department store. All products can also be ordered by calling the store. Excellent customer service. Catalogue and buying guides available.

BABY GIFTS

Brown Paper Packages
PO Box 28764
Edinburgh EH14 7YU
Tel: 0870 240 7659
custserv@brownpaperpackages.co.uk
www.brownpaperpackages.co.uk
Gift Company, specialising in gifts for new babies, new mothers, and also for Christenings. Range includes leather baby shoes, soft toys, luxury toiletries, breakfast sets, photo albums, and hand made cards. Cards can be written for you – and the company offers gift wrapping – in brown paper with organza ribbon and rosebuds.

CARDS & CRAFTS

Joyful Junie Stationery Co.
16 Craig-Na-Gower Avenue
Aviemore   PH22 1RW
Contact: June Armstrong
Tel: 01479 811527
Offers a unique range of hand-made, personalised Birth Announcement & Thank You cards, Christening and Party invitations. The range features delightful ink and wash illustrations.   Speedy service guaranteed. Call for mail order catalogue.

Tryst Crafts
Contact: Lesley Protheroe
Tel: 445 5789
Handmade cards and gifts for any occasion. Can be personalised.

Phoenix Trading Greeting Cards & Giftwrap
Contact: Brenda Cheyne
Tel: 334 1645
This company is the UK's leading direct card selling business. Their aim is to sell cards and giftwrap at sane prices, and so they are much cheaper than most high-street stores. Very wide range of cards for all occasions.

CHILDREN'S BOOKS

Amazon
Web: www.amazon.co.uk
Great for Internet shopping for books – especially if you like following other buyers' recommendations. Estimated delivery times advertised for each book. Wish lists can be set up to allow others to buy what you would prefer. Personalised recommendations based on your past purchases. Also sells large selection of children's toys.

Books For Children
4 Furzeground Way
Stockley Park
Uxbridge   UB11 1DP
Tel: 08701 650299
Web: www.booksforchildren.co.uk
Fifteen catalogues per year. Editor's recommended selection for each of five specific age groups sent automatically. Covers books from 0-12 yrs.

Custom Books Ltd
61 Alpine Street
Reading
Berks   RG1 2PY
Tel 0118 962266601249 812375
Web: www.custombooks.co.uk
Personalised children's books where your child becomes the star of the story. Books can also contain friends' names, home town, pet names, etc. Available in different languages.

The Red House Children's Books Club
Windrush Park
Range Road
Oxfordshire   OX8 5YF
Tel: 0870 1919980 01993 893471
Web: www.redhouse.co.uk
Mail order and online cChildren's book shop.club; no automatic selection/purchase commitment. Monthly magazine and seection of family/practical parenting titles. Hard back and paperback books, audiotapes, CD-Roms, videos, games and activities plus character merchandise.

Usborne Books
Contact: Nicky Sommer
Tel: 665 8628
Local distributor for this publisher. Books, games, puzzles, videos and CD-Roms. Can order direct from Nicky, or she can come to parties or playgroups.

CHILDREN'S CLOTHES

Baby Care by Dollycare
2 Winchester Avenue
Blaby Bypass
Blaby
Leics   LE8 4G2
Tel: 0116 278 3336
Clothes, nappies and soothers made especially for small and premature babies from 1+lbs (500g).

Bishopston Trading Company
193 Gloucester Road
Bishopton
Bristol   BS7 8BG
Tel: 0117 924 5598
Web: www.bishopstontrading.co.uk
Clothes for adults and children from birth-14yrs. Made from natural fabrics, mostly organic cotton. The company is a workers cooperative set up to create employment in a South Indian village. Catalogue and online ordering available. They also sell their stock through One World in St John's Church on the corner of Princes St and Lothian Rd.

Blooming Marvellous, Blooming Kids
PO Box 12F
Chessington
Surrey   KT9 2LS
Tel: 020 8391 0022
Orderline: 0870 751 8944
Web: www.bloomingmarvellous.co.uk
Colourful children's clothes 0-3 yrs. Mix'n'Match range. Maternity clothes, nursery goods, swimwear. See also Mini Marvellous, below

The Children's Warehouse
Unit 4
44 Colville Rd
London   W3 8BL
Tel: 020 8752 1166
Web: www.children's-warehouse.com
Comfortable logo-free clothes in mainly natural fabrics at reasonable prices. Free returns.

Cotton Moon
FREEPOST
PO Box 280
London   SE3 8BR
Tel: 020 8305 0012
Web: www.cottonmoon.co.uk
100% cotton clothing and accessories for boys and girls from 6 months. Free returns.

Dancewear
182 Rose Street EH2 4BA
Tel: 226 5457
Web: www.dancewear-edinburgh.co.uk
Opening times: Mon-Fri 9.30-17.15; Sat 9.00-17.00
This shop can take phone orders, and payment made with credit/chargecard. Website for information only, no online ordering at time of writing.

Freemans
Tel: 0800 900200 for catalogue
Web: www.freemans.com
Branded children's clothing, e.g. Adams, Mothercare, Levis and Kickers amongst others. Interest-free credit subject to status.

Greenfibres
Westbourne House (EF)
Plymouth Road
Totnes
Devon   TQ9 5NB
Tel: 01803 868001
Web: www.greenfibres.com
Organic cotton and wool clothes for babies and children, washable nappies, organic cotton toys.

Hopscotch Dressing Up Clothes
61 Palace Road
London   SW2 3LB
Tel: 0208 674 9853
Web: www.hopscotchmailorder.co.uk
Dressing up outfits 18 mths-9yrs. Cloaks, clowns, princesses, animals, astronauts, etc. Website shows all costumes and you can order online.

La Redoute
PO Box 777
Wakefield
WF2 8XZ
Tel: 0500 777 777
Web: www.laredoute.co.uk
Fashionable children's clothes at reasonable prices, along with teenage and adult ranges. Personal account option. Orders can be taken on website – there are often 'free p&p' options if orders are placed online. Free returns.

Mini Boden
Midland Terrace
Victoria Road
London   NW10 6DB
Tel: 020 8453 1535
Web: www.boden.co.uk
Logo-free, very good quality, reasonably priced and stylish clothes for children up to the age of 12, made mostly of natural fabrics.

NCT (Maternity Sales) Ltd.
239 Shawbridge Street
Glasgow
Tel: 0870 112 1120
Web: www.nctms.co.uk
The catalogue features baby clothes, accessories, gifts, books, leaflets and videos. Also stocks maternity clothing, sleepwear and a good range of MAVA bras. See Maternity, below.

The Natural Collection
Eco House
Monmouth Place
Bath   BA1 2DQ
Tel: 01225 442288
Web: www.naturalcollection.com
Organic cotton clothing, bedding and washable nappies as well as many other eco and/or ethical-friendly products..

Next
Tel: 08456 100 510
Web: www.next.co.uk
All stock available also through their Next for Kids shops. 48 hr 'to your door' courier service. Next also offer service whereby you order your items, but pick them up from your nearest dedicated store; this way you save paying the delivery charge.

Pedlars
The Stables
Glen Dye
by Banchory   AB31 6LT
Tel: 01330 850400
Web: www.pedlars.co.uk
Hard-wearing children's and adults clothes, stylish and colourful in age 2-adult. Cannot order from website, but catalogue available.

Schmidt Natural Clothing
21 Post Horn Close
Forest Row
East Sussex
RH18 5DE
Tel: 01342 822169
Web: www.naturalclothing.co.uk
Organic and natural clothing for babies, children and adults, including fine wool, silk and cotton underwear. Suppliers comply with fair trade guidelines. Small charge for catalogue refundable with first order. 3 months interest-free credit option on larger orders.

Stuck for Words
Tel: 0131 332 1998
Web: www.stuckforwords.co.uk
Hand-painted children's clothes, created in Scotland. Stuck for words is a mail order company offering a range of 100% cotton clothes for children from birth to 10 years. Current products include t-shirts, sleep suits and baby vests, all of which can be decorated with one of their our striking and child-orientated designs. All items are also available tie-dyed in a range of colours.
As you would expect from a company run by the mother of young children, all the clothes are machine washable at 60° (with whites if necessary) and can be tumble-dried. Each item is hand-painted or dyed to order, tied with purple ribbon and despatched in an elegantly simple paper carrier. Call for a brochure.

Tesco
Tel: 08457 024024
Web: www.tesco.com
Good value children's clothes from birth-4yrs, maternity clothes, disposable nappies, baby toys and equipment.

VertBaudet
18 Canal Road
Bradford
PO Box 125
BD99 4XB
Tel: 0500 012345 (freephone)
Web: www.vertbaudet.co.uk
Two hundred-odd page catalogue selling babies', children's and maternity clothes and nursery goods. Also have a range of bedding and children's bedroom accessories. Personal account facility. Free returns. Also stock small range of low birth weight baby clothing.

EbayYahoo Auctions

Web: www.ebay.co.ukuk.auctions.yahoo.com/uk/
(yes – there's no 'www')

Great way of finding cheap children and baby clothes, toys or equipment. You put in your bid, what you're prepared to go up to in case someone else outbids you, and then put your feet up! If you win, you send payment to seller who sends it on to you. Works on trust, but sellers and buyers have ratings to help you. Think of it as car boot sales without the rain or sharp elbows … (or even NCT Nearly New Sales without the queues!)

FOOD

East Coast Organic Boxes (ECOBox)

24 Boggs Holdings, Pencaitland
East Lothian
EH34 5BD
Tel/Fax: 01875 340227
Mobile: 07971 209081
Email: ecobox@eastcoastorganics.freeserve.co.uk
Web: www.eastcoastorganics.co.uk

Organic vegetable boxes as well as organic fruit, eggs and bread. Free delivery service available – phone for details. Collection points throughout Edinburgh or collect direct from farm. Fri 16.00-20.00, Sat 9.00-12.00.

Ian Miller's Organic Meats

Jamesfield Farm
FREEPOST
EH3582
Newburgh
Fife KY14 6BR
Tel: 01738 850498
Fax: 01738 850741

Organic meat, poultry, bacon, fish, haggis, venison, specialty sausages and stuffing.

Iceland

Tel: 0800 328 0800
Web: www.iceland-shop.co.uk

All stock available through website. Min order value £40 on the web, no min order by phone. You can order catalogue by phone no. too. You can place your order up to 4 days in advance and if you order before 15.00 Mon to Fri you can have your shopping delivered the next day. If you order after 15.00, it'll be delivered the day after that. Once you're happy with your order, you'll be offered a choice of available delivery dates and time slots.

Pillars of Hercules Organic Farm

By Falkland
Fife
Tel: 01337 857749
Web: www.pillars.co.uk

Organic vegetable boxes as well as organic fruit and eggs. Free catalogue available. Delivery to Edinburgh and Fife areas.

Sainsbury's

Web: www.sSainsburystoyou.com

Home grocery and delivery service. Shop for your favourites over the Internet, or browse the virtual shelves. It's all delivered to your home for a £5 delivery charge.

Organics Direct:
Simply Organic Food Company Ltd.

Web: www.organicsdirect.co.uksimplyorganic.net

Vast array of organic groceries available to order online. Winner of 2001 Best Organic Home Delivery service. Deliver anywhere on UK mainland by 12 noon on your chosen delivery day, to home or office. They need 36 hrs to put together your order.

Tesco

Web: www.tesco.com

Home grocery shopping and delivery service. You shop on the internet using your usual favourites, browsing, or even choosing recipes and the ingredients are automatically put in your order. You choose the delivery time in 2-hour slots, and off you go. The charge per order varies, dependent on the day you book this service for.

V.W.Quested

Newsagent/Grocery Store
21 Strathearn Road
Tel: 447 1361

Opening times: Mon-Fri 4.00-19.00; Sat 3.30-19.00; Sun 5.00-17.00

As well as daily newspaper delivery also does early morning milk and bread deliveries to Marchmont, Sciennes, Grange and Newington areas. Milk delivery prices compare favourably with supermarket prices. Grocery prices also very competitive and can be delivered.

MATERNITY

We have listed a few home-shopping services, both on-line and catalogues, which stock maternity wear: some have dedicated collections, the other echo the trends of their main lines.

Blooming Marvellous
PO Box 12F
Chessington
Surrey
KT9 2LS
Tel: 020 8391 0022
Orderline: 0870 751 8944
Web: www.bloomingmarvellous.co.uk
Range of contemporary clothing for mothers-to-be. Casual and formal wear, plus hosiery, lingerie, sleepwear and accessories such as breast pads. See also 'Children's Clothing', above.

Formes
Tel: 08689 2288
Email: e-shopping@formes-uk.com
Web: www.formes.com.uk
Browse and buy the clothing available in the boutiques without leaving home. Offers urbanwear, leisurewear and nightwear, along with a range of often funky separates. A pretty website, but it can take ages to load.

JoJo Maman Bébé
Tel: 0870 241 0560
Web: www.jojomamanbebe.co.uk
Online ordering (or mailorder) on a range of modern-styled maternity clothing (incl. workwear, casual and evening collections), and lingerie. Also offer children's wear and home accessories.

NCT (Maternity Sales) Ltd.
239 Shawbridge Street
Glasgow
Tel: 0870 112 1120
Web: www.nctms.co.uk
The catalogue features maternity wear such as swimsuits, bras and nightwear.. Mava bras with zip and drop cups designed by breastfeeding mothers and counsellors. Wide range of sizes from 32A to 46J. Some bras have a high cotton content. Mava bras are recommended by midwives. For the number of your nearest Mava fitting agent contact the NCT Edinburgh Centre on 260 9201.

Next
Tel: 08456 100 510
Web: www.next.co.uk
Catalogue stocks range of maternity wear for casual and formal wear, which echoes the trend styles of main collection. Also stocks maternity swimwear (dependent on season). Next also offer service whereby you order your items, but pick them up from your nearest dedicated store; this way you save paying the delivery charge.

VertBaudet
18 Canal Road
Bradford
PO Box 125
BD99 4XB
Tel: 0500 012345 (freephone)
Web: www.vertbaudet.co.uk
Although primarily a children's wear catalogue, there is a maternity section. Range of mainly casual and daywear, plus some underwear and nightwear. Personal account facility. Free returns. See also 'Children's Clothes', above.

MISCELLANEOUS
Cash's Name Tapes
J&J Cash Ltd
Torrington Ave
Coventry
Tel: 01203 466466
Web: www.jjcash.co.uk
Woven name tapes available online. Also widely available from shops such as John Lewis, Clarks Shoes, Mothercare and Aitken and Niven department stores.

Golden Hands, Silver Feet
Contact: Nicky Sommer
Tel: 665 8628
Web: www.goldenhands.co.uk
Babies' hands or feet cast in bronze/aluminium as a plaque or 3D replica, ideal for family presents. Will travel to your home or even hospital. Gift vouchers available.

Croft Mill
Lowther Lane
Foulridge, Colne
Lancs BB8 7NG
Tel: 01282 869625
Web: www.croftmill.co.uk
Fabric by post. Very reasonable prices. Please note that

none of the fabrics are flame proofed. Website has more information only and brochure ordering service – no online ordering at time of writing.

Nature's Best Health Products Ltd
Freepost PO Box 1
Tunbridge Wells
TN2 3EQ
Tel: 01892 552117
Vitamin and health supplements including children's supplements suitable for age 4+ yrs.

Pharmacy2U
Web: www.pharmacy2u.co.uk
Offers a complete range of high street pharmacy products and services online, including an 'ask our pharmacists' service.

SHOES

If your child has very narrow or broad feet, or he/she has uneven sizes, you may need to have shoes made. This is not as expensive as it sounds, although it does cost slightly more than high street prices. It is also worth investigating these companies if you want a particular style but can't get it in the shops.

Charles MacWatt Handmade Boots and Shoes
7 Christmas Steps
Bristol
BS1 5BS
Tel: 0117 921 4247
Made to measure and to order shoes, boots and sandals for children and adults.

Soled Out
Unit 14,
Forge Lane
Moorlands Industrial Estate
Saltash
Cornwall
PL12 6LX
Tel: 01752 841080
Made to measure shoes and boots for children and adults in bright coloured leather with crepe soles. Shoes made to fit each foot.

TOYS & GIFTS
There are plenty of websites available for children's toys. Below are some names of note. For a fuller list, go to a search engine such as Google.

Bright Minds
Braysdown Yard
Peasedown St John
Bath
BA2 8LL
Tel: 0870 44 22 124
Web: www.brightminds.co.uk
Offer a range of learning educational toys, from ages 2+- adult. For pre-school children, the range include puzzles, games and interactive toys. Products for older children are divided into subject categories, such as maths, music, nature studies, chemistry and so on.

Brown Paper Packages
PO Box 28764
Edinburgh
EH14 7YU
Tel: 0870 240 7659
custserv@brownpaperpackages.co.uk
www.brownpaperpackages.co.uk

Gift Company, specialising in gifts for new babies, new mothers, and also for Christenings. Range includes leather baby shoes, soft toys, luxury toiletries, breakfast sets, photo albums, and hand made cards. Cards can be written for you – and the company offers gift wrapping – in brown paper with organza ribbon and rosebuds.

Colourworld
Regina Thorne
1 Newton Street
Chartham Hatch
Canterbury
CT4 7LT
Tel: 01227 730204
Pretty coloured birch wood toys and gifts, including cookers, coat pegs, etc.

Dawson & Son
Tel: 08700 367 869
Web: www.dawson-and-son.com
Huge selection of wooden toys and games with good search engine – simply type in the age and price range for suitable options.

Early Learning Centre
Tel: 08705 352 352
Web: www.elc.co.uk
Mail order/online ordering of the high street store. Good search facility.

Frog Hollow
PO Box 550
Markyate
Hertfordshire
AL3 8QP
Tel: 01582 842117
Personalised toys and gifts.

Hawkin's Bazaar & Co
St Margaret
Harleston
Norfolk
IP20 0PJ
Tel: 0870 444 646001986 782536
Web: www.hawkin.com

Intriguing catalogue/online shop packed with amusing gifts, toys, novelties and gadgets. Very reasonably priced. Ideal for stocking fillers or difficult to buy for people. Please note that most toys are not suitable for under 3s.

Hopscotch Dressing Up Clothes
See under Shopping from Home – Clothes

Letterbox
PO Box 114
Truro
Cornwall
TR2 5YR
Tel: 0870 600 7878
Web: www.letterbox.co.uk
Collection of games, gifts, wooden farms, arcs, dolls' houses,, dressing up clothes etc. Extensive range of personalised gifts, ranging from name boards, jack-in-the-boxes, to chairs and sleeping bags. Also offer bedroom accessories. Loads of stocking filler/ party bag ideas, many with age recommendations.

Mini Marvellous
www.bloomingmarvellous.co.uk
A range of toys, clothing, accessories etc for children aged 1-5: online shopping available via parent Blooming Marvellous site.

Playsongs Publications
39 Byrne Road
London   SE26 5JT
Tel: 020 8778 0708
Web: www.playsongs.co.uk
Music for the very young. Cassette tapes of all the best songs and nursery rhymes, sung and played by professionals. Action songs, lullabies, lively time and sleepy time songs.

Super Tramp Trampolines
Langlands Business Park
Cullhampton
Devon   EX15 3AA
Tel: 01884 841305
Web: www.supertramp.co.uk
Outdoor garden trampolines and wooden garden play equipment – also available from John Lewis: see Shopping – Dept Stores.

Toys 'R' Us
Web: www.toysrus.co.uk
Online ordering from the familiar toy and game warehouse.

Tridias Creative Toys!
124 Walcot Street
Bath   BA1 5BG
Tel: 0870 2402104
Web: www.tridias.co.uk
Inventive toy and game ideas for children. Catalogue available with over 400 toys and games, or view and order online.

INDEX

INDEX

INDEX

INDEX